THE BORZOI COLLEGE READER THIRD EDITION

ACKNOWLEDGMENTS

HANNAH ARENDT, from *Eichmann in Jerusalem*, pp. 209–212. Copyright © 1963 by Hannah Arendt. Reprinted by permission of The Viking Press, Inc.

ST. AUGUSTINE, from *The Confessions of St. Augustine*, translated by F. J. Sheed. Copyright, 1943, Sheed & Ward, Inc., New York. Reprinted by permission of Sheed & Ward, Inc.

JAMES BALDWIN, "Notes of a Native Son," from *Notes of a Native Son*, by James Baldwin. Copyright © 1955 by James Baldwin. Reprinted by permission of Beacon Press. "The Creative Dilemma," from *Saturday Review*, 47 (February 8, 1964), 14–15, 58. Copyright © 1964 by James Baldwin. Reprinted by permission of the William Morris Agency, Inc.

IMAMU AMIRI BARAKA (LEROI JONES), "Young Soul," from *Black Magic Poetry, 1961–1967*, by LeRoi Jones. Copyright © 1969 by LeRoi Jones. Reprinted by permission of The Bobbs-Merrill Company, Inc. "The Myth of a 'Negro Literature,'" from *Home: Social Essays* and "The Revolutionary Theatre," from *Liberator*, Vol. 5 (July 1965). Reprinted by permission of Imamu Amiri Baraka (LeRoi Jones) and the Ronald Hobbs Literary Agency, 211 East 43 Street, New York, New York 10017.

RUTH BENEDICT, "Racism: The *ism* of the Modern World," from *Race: Science and Politics*, by Ruth Benedict. Copyright 1940 by Ruth Benedict, copyright © renewed 1968 by Dr. Robert G. Freeman. Reprinted by permission of The Viking Press, Inc.

HAIG A. BOSMAJIAN, "The Language of White Racism," from *College English*, Vol. 31 (December 1969). Reprinted by permission of the author and the National Council of Teachers of English.

BRIGID BROPHY, "Women Are Prisoners of Their Sex," from *The Saturday Evening Post* (November 2, 1963), pp. 10–11. © 1963 The Curtis Publishing Company. Reprinted by permission of *The Saturday Evening Post*.

JOSEPH CAMPBELL, from *Myths to Live*, pp. 25–31. Copyright © 1972 by Joseph Campbell. Reprinted by permission of The Viking Press, Inc.

ERIC J. CASSELL, "Dying in a Technological Society," from *Hastings Center Studies*, 2 (May 1974), 31–36. Reprinted by permission of the Institute of Society, Ethics and the Life Sciences, Hastings-on-Hudson, N.Y.

JUDITH BETH COHEN, "Vermont Diary," from *American Review*, No. 22 (February 1975), pp. 179–186, 207–210. Reprinted by permission of the author.

ROBERT COLES, from *The Geography of Faith*, pp. 155–162, by Daniel Berrigan and Robert Coles. Copyright © 1971 by Daniel Berrigan, S.J., and Robert Coles. Reprinted by permission of Beacon Press.

HARVEY COX, from *The Seduction of the Spirit,* pp. 91–97. Copyright © 1973 by Harvey Cox. Reprinted by permission of Simon & Schuster, Inc.

e. e. cummings, "since feeling is first," from *Complete Poems: 1913–1962,* by e. e. cummings. Copyright, 1926, by Horace Liveright; copyright, 1954, by e. e. cummings. Reprinted by permission of Harcourt Brace Jovanovich, Inc.

CLARENCE DARROW, "Why I Am an Agnostic," from *Verdicts Out of Court,* edited by Arthur and Lila Weinberg, Chicago, Quadrangle Books, 1963. Reprinted by permission.

JOAN DIDION, "On Morality" and "Some Dreamers of the Golden Dream," from *Slouching Towards Bethlehem,* by Joan Didion. Copyright © 1961, 1964, 1965, 1966, 1967, 1968 by Joan Didion. Reprinted by permission of Farrar, Straus & Giroux, Inc.

ROBERT F. DRINAN, "The Rhetoric of Peace," from *College Composition and Communication* (October 1972). Copyright © 1972 by the National Council of Teachers of English. Reprinted by permission of the author and publisher.

RALPH ELLISON, "On Becoming a Writer," from *Commentary,* 38 (October 1964), 57–60. Copyright © 1964 by Ralph Ellison. Reprinted by permission of William Morris Agency, Inc., on behalf of the author.

ERIK H. ERIKSON, from *Insight and Responsibility,* pp. 238–241. Copyright © 1964 by Erik H. Erikson. Reprinted by permission of W. W. Norton & Company, Inc. From *Dialogue with Erik Erikson,* pp. 70–77, by Richard I. Evans. Copyright © 1967 by Richard I. Evans. Reprinted by permission of Harper & Row, Publishers, Inc.

F. M. ESFANDIARY, "The Mystical West Puzzles the Practical East," from *The New York Times Magazine* (February 5, 1967). Reprinted by permission of the author. Changes have been made in this article at the request of the author.

MARC FEIGEN FASTEAU, from *The Male Machine,* pp. 6–19. Copyright © 1974 by Marc Feigen Fasteau. Reprinted by permission of McGraw-Hill Book Company.

EVA FIGES, "To Begin with . . . ;" from *Patriarchal Attitudes,* by Eva Figes. Copyright © 1970 by Eva Figes. Reprinted by permission of Stein and Day Publishers and Faber and Faber Ltd.

WILLIAM GOLDING, from "Party of One—Thinking as a Hobby," first published in *Holiday.* © 1961 The Curtis Publishing Company. Reprinted by permission of the author.

DICK GREGORY, "Shame," from *Nigger: An Autobiography,* by Dick Gregory with Robert Lipsyte. Copyright © 1964 by Dick Gregory Enterprises, Inc. Reprinted by permission of E. P. Dutton & Co., Inc.

KIT HAVICE, "Letter from Albany City Jail." Reprinted by permission of the author.

JAMES HERNDON, "An Environment for Lizards" and "The Dumb Class," from *How to Survive in Your Native Land,* by James Herndon. Copyright © 1971 by James Herndon. Reprinted by permission of Simon & Schuster, Inc.

IRVING HOWE, "In Extreme Situations," from *The New York Times Book Review* (April 20, 1975), p. 2. © 1975 by The New York Times Company. Reprinted by permission of the publisher.

ALDOUS HUXLEY, "Propaganda Under a Dictatorship" and "The Arts of Selling," from *Brave New World Revisited,* by Aldous Huxley. Copyright © 1958 by Aldous Huxley. Reprinted by permission of Harper & Row, Publishers, Inc., Mrs. Laura Huxley, and Chatto and Windus Ltd.

JUDSON JEROME, from *Families of Eden,* pp. x–xiii, 208–223. © 1974 by The Twentieth Century Fund. Reprinted by permission of The Seabury Press, Inc.

LEON R. KASS, "The New Biology," from *Science,* 174 (November 19, 1971), 779–788. Copyright 1971 by the American Association for the Advancement of Science. Reprinted by permission of the author and the American Association for the Advancement of Science.

JOHN OLIVER KILLENS, "Negroes Have a Right to Fight Back," from *Saturday Evening Post* (July 2, 1966). Copyright © 1966 by John Oliver Killens. Reprinted by permission of International Creative Management.

MARTIN LUTHER KING, JR., "Letter from Birmingham Jail," from *Why We Can't Wait,* by Martin Luther King, Jr. Copyright © 1963 by Martin Luther King, Jr. Reprinted by permission of Harper & Row, Publishers, Inc.

ARTHUR KOESTLER, from *The God That Failed,* pp. 15–23, edited by Richard Crossman, et al. Copyright 1949 by Richard Crossman. Reprinted by permission of Harper & Row, Publishers, Inc., and Hamish Hamilton Ltd.

SUSANNE K. LANGER, "The Prince of Creation," from *Fortune* (January 1944), pp. 127–128, 130, 132, 134, 136, 139–140, 142, 144, 146, 148, 150, 152, 154. Reprinted by permission of the author. Originally entitled "The Lord of Creation." "The Cultural Importance of Art," from *Philosophical Sketches,* by Susanne K. Langer, Baltimore, The Johns Hopkins Press, 1962. Reprinted by permission.

D. H. LAWRENCE, "Cocksure Women and Hensure Men," from *Phoenix II: Uncollected, Unpublished and Other Prose Works by D. H. Lawrence,* edited by Warren Roberts and Harry T. Moore. Copyright 1928 by Rorum Publishing Co., Copyright © renewed 1956 by Frieda Lawrence Ravagli. Reprinted by permission of The Viking Press, Inc., Laurence Pollinger Ltd. and the Estate of the late Mrs. Frieda Lawrence.

WALTER LIPPMANN, "Freedom and Restraint," from *A Preface to Morals,* by Walter Lippmann. Copyright 1929 by Walter Lippmann, renewed 1957 by Walter Lippmann. Reprinted by permission of Macmillan Publishing Co., Inc. "The Indispensable Opposition," from *The Atlantic Monthly* (August 1939). Copyright © 1939, 1967, The Atlantic Monthly Company, Boston, Mass. Reprinted by permission of the author and publisher.

PHYLLIS MCGINLEY, "Suburbia, of Thee I Sing," from *The Province of the Heart,* by Phyllis McGinley. Copyright 1949 by Phyllis McGinley. Reprinted by permission of The Viking Press, Inc.

NICCOLÒ MACHIAVELLI, from *The Prince*, pp. 63–66, translated by Luigi Ricci, revised by E. R. P. Vincent. Reprinted by permission of Oxford University Press. This selection is taken from The Modern Library edition.

ARCHIBALD MACLEISH, "Ars Poetica," from *Collected Poems, 1917–1952*, by Archibald Macleish. Reprinted by permission of Houghton Mifflin Company.

THOMAS MERTON, "Day of a Stranger." Copyright © 1967 by The Trustees of the Merton Legacy Trust. Reprinted by permission of New Directions Publishing Corporation for The Trustees of the Merton Legacy Trust. First published in *The Hudson Review*, Vol. XX (Summer 1967).

S. M. MILLER, "The Making of a Confused Middle-Class Husband," from *Social Policy*, 2 (July/August 1971), 33–39. Copyright 1971 by Social Policy Corp. Reprinted by permission of *Social Policy*, published by Social Policy Corporation, New York, New York 10010.

MARIANNE MOORE, "Poetry," from *Collected Peoms*, by Marianne Moore. Copyright 1935 by Marianne Moore, renewed 1963 by Marianne Moore and T. S. Eliot. Reprinted by permission of Macmillan Publishing Co., Inc.

GUNNAR MYRDAL, "A Parallel to the Negro Problem," from *An American Dilemma*, by Gunnar Myrdal. Copyright © 1944, 1962 by Harper & Row, Publishers, Inc. Reprinted by permission of Harper & Row, Publishers, Inc.

THE NEW YORKER, "The Wisdom of the Worm," from "The Talk of the Town," *The New Yorker* (August 29, 1970), pp. 17–18. © 1970 The New Yorker Magazine, Inc. Reprinted by permission of the publisher.

WILLIAM NICHOLS, "The Burden of Imagination: Stanley Milgram's *Obedience to Authority*," from *Writing from Experience*, edited by William Nichols. © 1975 by Harcourt Brace Jovanovich, Inc. Reprinted by permission of Harcourt Brace Jovanovich, Inc.

JOYCE CAROL OATES, "New Heaven and Earth," from *Saturday Review* (November 4, 1972), pp. 52–54. Copyright © 1974 by Joyce Carol Oates. Reprinted by permission of the author and her agent, Blanche C. Gregory, Inc.

GEORGE ORWELL, "Politics and the English Language" and "Shooting an Elephant," from *Shooting an Elephant and Other Essays*, by George Orwell. Copyright, 1945, 1946, 1949, 1950, by Sonia Brownell Orwell; copyright, 1973, 1974, by Sonia Orwell. "Marrakech" and "Why I Write," from *Such, Such Were the Joys*, by George Orwell. Copyright, 1945, 1952, 1953, by Sonia Brownell Orwell. Reprinted by permission of Harcourt Brace Jovanovich, Inc., Mrs. Sonia Brownell Orwell, and Secker & Warburg Ltd.

NORMAN PODHORETZ, "My Negro Problem—and Ours," from *Doings and Undoings*, by Norman Podhoretz. Copyright © 1953, 1954, 1955, 1956, 1957, 1958, 1959, 1962, 1963, 1964 by Norman Podhoretz. Reprinted by permission of Farrar, Straus & Giroux, Inc.

KATHERINE ANNE PORTER, from *The Future Is Now*, pp. 196–202. Copyright © 1950 by Katherine Anne Porter. Reprinted by permission of Cyrilly Abels, agent for the author.

MARCEL PROUST, "Prologue," from *By Way of Sainte-Beuve*, by Marcel Proust, translated by Sylvia Townsend Warner. Reprinted by permission of Sylvia Townsend Warner and Chatto and Windus Ltd.

EUGENE RABINOWITCH, "The Mounting Tide of Unreason," from *The Bulletin of the Atomic Scientists*, 27 (May 1971), 4–9. Copyright © 1971 by the Educational Foundation for Nuclear Science. Reprinted by permission of the Bulletin of the Atomic Scientists.

CHARLES A. REICH, "The Limits of Duty," from *The New Yorker* (June 19, 1971), pp. 53–57. © 1971 The New Yorker Magazine, Inc. Reprinted by permission of the publisher.

MARY CAROLINE RICHARDS, "Centering as Dialogue," from *Centering*, by Mary Caroline Richards. Copyright © 1964 by M. C. Richards. Reprinted by permission of Wesleyan University Press.

JAMES HARVEY ROBINSON, "On Various Kinds of Thinking," from *The Mind in the Making*, by James Harvey Robinson. Copyright 1921 by Harper & Row, Publishers, Inc.; renewed 1949 by Bankers Trust Company. Reprinted by permission of Harper & Row, Publishers, Inc.

JOHN A. T. ROBINSON, "Our Image of God Must Go," from *The Observer* (March 17, 1963), p. 1. Reprinted by permission of the publisher.

THEODORE ROSZAK, from *The Making of a Counter Culture*, pp. 205–209, 269–289. Copyright © 1968, 1969 by Theodore Roszak. Reprinted by permission of Doubleday & Company, Inc.

BAYARD RUSTIN, "The Harlem Riot and Nonviolence." Reprinted by permission of the author.

DOROTHY SAYERS, "The Human-Not-Quite-Human," from *Unpopular Opinions*, by Dorothy Sayers, published by Victor Gollanz. Reprinted by permission of David Higham Associates Ltd.

ISAAC BASHEVIS SINGER, "The Son from America," from *A Crown of Feathers*, by Isaac Bashevis Singer. Copyright © 1970, 1971, 1972, 1973 by Isaac Bashevis Singer. Reprinted by permission of Farrar, Straus & Giroux, Inc. "The Son from America" originally appeared in *The New Yorker*.

ALEXANDER SOLZHENITSYN, "Art for Man's Sake," from *Nobel Lecture*, by Alexander Solzhenitsyn, translated by F. D. Reeve. English translation copyright © 1972 by Farrar, Straus & Giroux, Inc. Reprinted by permission of Farrar, Straus & Giroux, Inc.

W. T. STACE, "Man Against Darkness," from *The Atlantic Monthly*, 182 (September 1948), 53–58. Reprinted by permission of Mrs. W. T. Stace.

JUDY SYFERS, "I Want a Wife," from *Ms Magazine* (December 20–27, 1971). Copyright © 1971 by Judy Syfers. Reprinted by permission of the author.

STUDS TERKEL, "The Mason," from *Working: People Talk About What They Do All Day and How They Feel About What They Do*, by Studs Terkel. Copyright © 1972, 1974 by Studs Terkel. Reprinted by permission of Pantheon Books, a Division of Random House, Inc.

LEWIS THOMAS, "Autonomy" and "Natural Man," from *The Lives of a Cell,* by Lewis Thomas. Copyright © 1972, 1973 by the Massachusetts Medical Society. Reprinted by permission of The Viking Press, Inc.

PAUL TILLICH, "The Lost Dimension in Religion," from *The Saturday Evening Post* (June 14, 1958). Reprinted by permission of Hannah Tillich.

MAO TSE-TUNG, "Talks at the Yenan Forum on Art and Literature," from *Selected Works (1941–1945),* by Mao Tse-tung, Volume IV. Reprinted by permission of International Publishers.

MONA VAN DUYN, "A Valentine to the Wide World," from *A Time of Bees,* by Mona Van Duyn. Reprinted by permission of the University of North Carolina Press.

ESTHER VILAR, "What Is Woman?" from *The Manipulated Man,* by Esther Vilar. Copyright © 1972 by Farrar, Straus & Giroux, Inc. Reprinted by permission of Farrar, Straus & Giroux, Inc.

ALICE WALKER, "The Civil Rights Movement: What Good Was It?" from *The American Scholar,* 36 (Autumn 1967), 550–554. Copyright © 1967 by the United Chapters of Phi Beta Kappa. Reprinted by permission of the publisher.

RICHARD M. WEAVER, "Ultimate Terms in Contemporary Rhetoric," from Chapter 9 of *The Ethics of Rhetoric,* by Richard M. Weaver. Copyright 1953 by Henry Regnery Company. Reprinted by permission of Henry Regnery Company.

JUDITH WELLS, "Daddy's Girl," from *Libera #1* (Winter 1972), pp. 43–45. Reprinted by permission of the author.

E. B. WHITE, "The Morning of the Day They Did It (February 25, 1950)," from *The Second Tree from the Corner,* by E. B. White. Copyright 1950 by E. B. White. Reprinted by permission of Harper & Row, Publishers, Inc. Originally appeared in *The New Yorker.*

VIRGINIA WOOLF, "Shakespeare's Sister," from *A Room of One's Own,* by Virginia Woolf. Copyright, 1929, by Harcourt Brace Jovanovich, Inc.; copyright, 1957, by Leonard Woolf. Reprinted by permission of Harcourt Brace Jovanovich, Inc., the Author's Literary Estate, and The Hogarth Press.

WILLIAM BUTLER YEATS, "Leda and the Swan," from *Collected Poems,* by William Butler Yeats. Copyright 1928 by Macmillan Publishing Co., Inc., renewed 1956 by Georgie Yeats. Reprinted by permission of Macmillan Publishing Co., Inc., M. B. Yeats, Miss Anne Yeats, and Macmillan of London & Basingstoke.

We thank again the many colleagues and friends who helped us with the earlier editions of this book. We are now newly grateful, for suggestions and criticism, to Kathleen E. Dubs, Valerie Duval, Martin Elsky, Francine Foltz, George Gleason, Robert J. Griffin, Myrna Harrison, Jerry Herman, Jacqueline Hoefer, Pat Klossner, Don Osborne, and Judith van Allen. Betsy Bowden and Alexander Weiss gave us expert bibliographical assistance; Olivia Anderson and Richard Juul helped prepare the manuscript and proof; and June Smith saw the book through the press with a professional expertise that has become increasingly amazing as it has become increasingly familiar over the years.

Berkeley, California   C.M.
1975   M.G.

CONTENTS

THE GOOD LIFE   259

THE ROLES OF THE SEXES   325

RACE AND RACISM   389

TECHNOLOGY AND HUMAN VALUES   447

RELIGION: FAITH, DOUBT, AND EXPERIENCE   513

THE FUNCTION OF ART 573

INTRODUCTION

Most of the pieces in this book were written by the kind of person who thinks, feels, and cares. We present it in the hope that it will help readers to discover their own thoughts and feelings, to test them actively among the thoughts and feelings of others, and to develop attitudes based on rational insight and human sympathy. We can think of few better means to this end than honest reading and honest writing, and no better time and place than a beginning college course.

This third edition of our book is different from the second mainly in that it has been brought up to date. Although we have not tried to trim our sails to every shift in the winds of debate, we have been surprised at how sharply the terms of some seemingly basic debates have changed in the past few years. We have tried in this edition to find issues that promised some longevity of interest for students of the seventies and eighties. Thus a few sections are gone, replaced by a Prologue: The Future Is Now, and three new sections: On Right and Wrong, The Good Life, and The Roles of the Sexes. Each of the continuing sections, furthermore, has new pieces in it.

The book is shorter than it used to be, and it contains a greater proportion of short pieces. We regret the necessary omission of some things that teachers will miss, but we can offer in compensation a collection that has, we think, unusual coherence. From start to finish, its main concern is human values—not a bad theme, we think, for the last quarter of this century.

For users new to the book we should add that its basic organization is the same. We have collected under each topic pieces representing a variety of attitudes, often in direct conflict with each other. The readings present, then, a wide range of ideas and assumptions, and at the same time a continuous dialogue or debate among them. We hope that in raising issues this book will help readers to see that they have something to think about. Suggesting comparison at every point, giving ready occasion to take sides and to criticize, the book is directly suited to generating discussion and writing.

While expository prose has remained our main concern, we regard exposition as a wide-ranging term that covers everything from autobiographical writing to the research paper. The book is thus rich in styles and genres. We have included pieces that describe personal experience, pieces that work experience into ideas or that speak about ideas in strong personal voices and out of personal contexts, as well as pieces that offer purely intellectual arguments. Because the transition from the more personal to the more analytic or discursive essay is often difficult for student writers, we have provided numerous writings that illustrate just this transition.

The book can also be studied for the way in which the major rhetorical categories—description, narration, definition, comparison, and the like—can be used to express or support ideas. Since all but a few of the essays are English originals, they can serve as authentic examples of English style. We have included in this edition a few short excerpts to enrich the book's pattern of ideas. Most of the pieces, however, are either complete works in themselves or coherent sections (usually chapters) of longer works that can be studied as compositional wholes. In any case, we have done no silent editing. A rhetorical index will be found at the end.

Prologue: The Future Is Now

Almost all the pieces in this book are records of men and women deliberately using their capacities to think and to feel in an effort to comprehend experience—either their own experience or that of other people and other times. To introduce this collection, we present here four essays that share a perspective so broad as to be able to embrace all the others: what is our future as humans and as a culture? This question, for ages past a natural one for philosophers, took on wider and more immediate interest for all of us in the third quarter of the twentieth century. Each of the essays was written against a new background of uncertainty, if not pessimism, about life in America and in the world. They respond to the weakening of confidence in our institutions, especially among the young; the poisoning of our air and water; the decay of our cities; our uncertain economic future; our political failures abroad and the menace of racial violence at home; and penetrating all, the consciousness that the human species has now the power to extinguish itself.

Given this background, the varying responses of these writers may seem on balance optimistic, but we begin with Katherine Anne Porter's essay (and with its title, "The Future Is Now") because it suggests, perhaps unconsciously, a proper measure of uncertainty. If the future is now, is it because all we have is the present; or because unless we act rightly now there will be no future; or because a strange and rich future is already upon us? Though the essay raises these three possibilities, it does not lead us to a securely felt conclusion. Drs. Thomas and Rabinowitch turn for help to science, but in radically different ways which are reflected in their styles and tones. The former is quiet, tentative, suggestive, and finds guidance in the biological idea of symbiosis, of man and nature linked indispensably in interdependence. The latter, invoking the traditional conflict between reason and emotion, makes an emphatic argument for the same rationality in public affairs that characterizes research in science. Joyce Carol Oates, writing an essay she calls "nonacademic in its lyric disorganization," brings together from her reading and observation signs that the consciousness of the future will reject the old opposition between reason and intuition, rational and irrational, for a new synthesis of ideas and of human voices.

KATHERINE ANNE PORTER

Katherine Anne Porter is one of the most famous and most honored of modern American writers. She is principally a writer of short fiction; her Collected Stories *won both the National Book Award and the Pulitzer Prize in 1966.*

She was born in 1890 in Indian Creek, Texas, and was educated at home and in Southern girls' schools. She early worked for a Chicago newspaper, played bit parts in movies, and studied Mayan and Aztec art in Mexico. All the while she wrote and rewrote stories until, at the age of thirty, she published her first one. Among her best-known volumes of fiction are Flowering Judas *(1930),* Pale Horse, Pale Rider *(1939), and the novel* Ship of Fools *(1962). Her work is noted for the perfection of its craftsmanship and the sensitivity of its exploration into human motives and feelings.*

In the course of her long career, Katherine Anne Porter has lectured on and taught literature at many universities, including Stanford, Michigan, Virginia, and Washington and Lee—where she was the first woman faculty member in the school's history. She has also published many essays, some of which appear in her Collected Essays *(1970). From the collection* The Days Before *(1952), we reprint an essay she wrote while the atomic bomb was still a recent phenomenon.*

The Future Is Now

Not so long ago I was reading in a magazine with an enormous circulation some instructions as to how to behave if and when we see that flash brighter than the sun which means that the atom bomb has arrived. I read of course with the intense interest of one who has everything to learn on this subject; but at the end, the advice dwindled to this: the only real safety seems to lie in simply being somewhere else at the time, the farther away the better; the next best, failing access to deep shelters, bombproof cellars and all, is to get under a stout table—that is, just what you might do if someone were throwing bricks through your window and you were too nervous to throw them back.

This comic anticlimax to what I had been taking as a serious educational piece surprised me into real laughter, hearty and carefree. It is such a relief to be told the truth, or even just the facts, so pleasant not to be coddled with unreasonable hopes. That very evening I was drawn away from my work table to my fifth-story window by one of those shrill terror-screaming sirens which our excitement-loving city government used then to affect for so many occasions: A fire? Police chasing a gangster? Somebody being got to the hospital in a hurry? Some distinguished public guest being transferred from one point to another? Strange aircraft coming over, maybe? Under the lights of the corner crossing of the great avenue, a huge closed vehicle whizzed past, screaming. I never knew what it was, had not in fact expected to know; no one I could possibly ask would know. Now that we have bells clamoring away instead for such events, we all have one doubt less, if perhaps one expectancy more. The single siren's voice means to tell us only one thing.

But at that doubtful moment, framed in a lighted window level with mine in the apartment house across the street, I saw a young man in a white T-shirt and white shorts at work polishing a long, beautiful dark table top. It was obviously his own table in his own flat, and he was enjoying his occupation. He was bent over in perfect concentration, rubbing, sandpapering, running the flat of his palm over the surface, standing back now and then to get the sheen of light on the fine wood. I am sure he had not even raised his head at the noise of the siren, much less had he come to the window. I stood there admiring his workmanlike devotion to a good job worth doing, and there flashed through me one of those pure fallacies of feeling which suddenly overleap reason: surely all that effort and energy so irreproachably employed were not going to be wasted on a table that was to be used merely for crawling under at some unspecified date. Then why take all those pains to make it beautiful? Any sort of old board would do.

I was so shocked at this treachery of the lurking Foul Fiend (despair *is* a foul fiend, and this was despair) I stood a moment longer, looking out and around, trying to collect my feelings, trying to think a little. Two windows away and a floor down in the house across the street, a young woman was lolling in a deep chair, reading and eating fruit from a little basket. On the sidewalk, a boy and a girl dressed alike in checkerboard cotton shirts and skin-tight blue denims, a costume which displayed acutely the structural differences of their shapes, strolled along with their arms around each other. I believe this custom of lovers walking enwreathed in public was imported by our soldiers of the First World War from France, from Paris indeed. "You didn't see that sort of thing here before," certain members of the older generation were heard to remark quite often, in a tone of voice. Well, one sees quite a lot of it now, and it is a very pretty, reassuring sight. Other citizens of all sizes and kinds and ages were crossing back and forth; lights flashed red and green, punctually. Motors zoomed by, and over the great city—but where am I going? I never read other peoples' descriptions of great cities, more particularly if it is a great city I know. It doesn't belong here anyway, except that I had again that quieting sense of the continuity of human experience on this earth, its perpetual aspirations, set-backs, failures and re-beginnings in eternal hope; and that, with some appreciable differences of dress, customs and means of conveyance, so people have lived and moved in the cities they have built for more millennia than we are yet able to account for, and will no doubt build and live for as many more.

Why did this console me? I cannot say; my mind is of the sort that can often be soothed with large generalities of that nature. The silence of the spaces between the stars does not affright me, as it did Pascal, because I am unable to imagine it except poetically; and my awe is not for the silence and space of the endless universe but for the inspired imagination of man, who can think and feel so, and turn a phrase like that to communicate it to us. Then too, I like the kind of honesty and directness of the young soldier who lately answered someone who asked him if he knew what he was fighting for. "I sure do," he said, "I am fighting to live." And as for the future, I was once reading the first writings of a young girl, an apprentice author, who was quite impatient to get on with the business and find her way into print. There is very little one can say of use in such matters, but I advised her against haste—she could so easily regret it. "Give yourself time," I said, "the future will take care of itself." This opinionated young person looked down her little nose at me and said, "The future is now." She may have heard the phrase somewhere and liked it, or she may just have naturally belonged to that school of metaphysics; I am sure she was too young to have investigated the thought deeply. But maybe she was right and the future does arrive every day and it is all we have, from one second to the next.

So I glanced again at the young man at work, a proper-looking candidate for the armed services, and realized the plain, homely fact: he was not preparing a possible shelter, something to cower under trembling; he was restoring a beautiful surface to put his books and papers on, to serve his plates from, to hold his cocktail tray and his lamp. He was full of the deep, right, instinctive, human belief that he and the table were going to be around together for a long time. Even if he is off to the army next week, it will be there when he gets back. At the very least, he is doing something he feels is worth doing now, and that is no small thing.

At once the difficulty, and the hope, of our special time in this world of Western Europe and America is that we have been brought up for many generations in the belief, however tacit, that all humanity was almost unanimously engaged in going forward, naturally to better things and to higher reaches. Since the eighteenth century at least when the Encyclopedists seized upon the Platonic theory that the highest pleasure of mankind was pursuit of the good, the true, and the beautiful, progress, in precisely the sense of perpetual, gradual amelioration of the hard human lot, has been taught popularly not just as theory of possibility but as an article of faith and the groundwork of a whole political doctrine. Mr. Toynbee has even simplified this view for us with picture diagrams of various sections of humanity, each in its own cycle rising to its own height, struggling beautifully on from craggy level to level, but always upward. Whole peoples are arrested at certain points, and perish there, but others go on. There is also the school of thought, Oriental and very ancient, which gives to life the spiral shape, and the spiral moves by nature upward. Even adherents of the circular or recurring-cycle school, also ancient and honorable, somehow do finally allow that the circle is a thread that spins itself out one layer above another, so that even though it is perpetually at every moment passing over a place it has been before, yet by its own width it will have risen just so much higher.

These are admirable attempts to get a little meaning and order into our view of our destiny, in that same spirit which moves the artist to labor with his little handful of chaos, bringing it to coherency within a frame; but on the visible evidence we must admit that in human nature the spirit of contradiction more than holds its own. Mankind has always built a little more than he has hitherto been able or willing to destroy; got more children than he has been able to kill; invented more laws and customs than he had any intention of observing; founded more religions than he was able to practice or even to believe in; made in general many more promises than he could keep; and has been known more than once to commit suicide through mere fear of death. Now in our time, in his pride to explore his universe to its unimaginable limits and to exceed his possible powers, he has at last produced an embarrassing series of engines too powerful for their containers and too tricky for their mechanicians; millions of labor-saving gadgets which can be rendered totally useless by the mere failure of the public power plants, and has reduced himself to such helplessness that a dozen or less of the enemy could disable a whole city by throwing a few switches. This paradoxical creature has committed all these extravagances and created all these dangers and sufferings in a quest—we are told—for peace and security.

How much of this are we to believe, when with the pride of Lucifer, the recklessness of Icarus, the boldness of Prometheus and the intellectual curiosity of Adam and Eve (yes, intellectual; the serpent promised them wisdom if . . .) man has obviously outreached himself, to the point where he cannot understand his own science or control his own inventions. Indeed he has become as the gods, who have over and over again suffered defeat and downfall at the hands of their creatures. Having devised the most exquisite and instantaneous means of communication to all corners of the earth, for years upon years friends were unable even to get a postcard message to each other across national frontiers. The newspapers assure us that from the kitchen tap there flows a chemical, cheap and available, to make a bomb more disturbing to the imagination even than the one we so appallingly have; yet no machine has been invented to purify that water so that it will not spoil even the best tea or coffee. Or at any rate, it is not in use. We are the proud possessors of rocket bombs that go higher and farther and faster than any ever before, and there is some talk of a rocket ship shortly to take off for the moon. (My plan is to stow away.) We may indeed reach the moon some day, and

I dare predict that will happen before we have devised a decent system of city garbage disposal.

This lunatic atom bomb has succeeded in rousing the people of all nations to the highest point of unanimous moral dudgeon; great numbers of persons are frightened who never really had much cause to be frightened before. This world has always been a desperately dangerous place to live for the greater part of the earth's inhabitants; it was, however reluctantly, endured as the natural state of affairs. Yet the invention of every new weapon of war has always been greeted with horror and righteous indignation, especially by those who failed to invent it, or who were threatened with it first . . . bows and arrows, stone cannon balls, gunpowder, flintlocks, pistols, the dumdum bullet, the Maxim silencer, the machine gun, poison gas, armored tanks, and on and on to the grand climax —if it should prove to be—of the experiment on Hiroshima. Nagasaki was bombed too, remember? Or were we already growing accustomed to the idea? And as for Hiroshima, surely it could not have been the notion of sudden death of others that shocked us? How could it be, when in two great wars within one generation we have become familiar with millions of shocking deaths, by sudden violence of most cruel devices, and by agonies prolonged for years in prisons and hospitals and concentration camps. We take with apparent calmness the news of the deaths of millions by flood, famine, plague—no, all the frontiers of danger are down now, no one is safe, no one, and that, alas, really means all of us. It is our own deaths we fear, and so let's out with it and give up our fine debauch of moralistic frenzy over Hiroshima. I fail entirely to see why it is more criminal to kill a few thousand persons in one instant than it is to kill the same number slowly over a given stretch of time. If I have a choice, I'd as lief be killed by an atom bomb as by a hand grenade or a flame thrower. If dropping the atom bomb is an immoral act, then the making of it was too; and writing of the formula was a crime, since those who wrote it must have known what such a contrivance was good for. So, morally speaking, the bomb is only a magnified hand grenade, and the crime, if crime it is, is still murder. It was never anything else. Our protocriminal then was the man who first struck fire from flint, for from that moment we have been coming steadily to this day and this weapon and this use of it. What would you have advised instead? That the human race should have gone on sitting in caves gnawing raw meat and beating each other over the head with the bones?

And yet it may be that what we have is a world not on the verge of flying apart, but an uncreated one—still in shapeless fragments waiting to be put together properly. I imagine that when we want something better, we may have it: at perhaps no greater price than we have already paid for the worse.

[1950]

LEWIS THOMAS

Born in 1913, Dr. Thomas, a medical scientist, attended Princeton and received the Ph.D. from Harvard in 1937 at the age of twenty-three. After internship he began a distinguished career as medical researcher and administrator. In 1973 he resigned from Yale—where he had been Professor of Pathology, chairman of his department, and Dean of the Medical School—to become head of the Memorial Sloan-Kettering Cancer Center in New York City.

Dr. Thomas has published numerous scientific articles, especially in the fields of infectious disease, hypersensitivity, and cellular immunology. He has served on many national advisory commissions, and received many honors, including election to the National Academy of Sciences. Both of his pieces that we reprint in the present volume come from his first popular book, The Lives of a Cell: Notes of a Biology Watcher, *a collection of monthly columns he wrote for the* New England Journal of Medicine *from 1971 to 1973. The book appeared in 1974 and established Dr. Thomas as one of the few living masters of the short reflective essay, drawing from his knowledge of biology a set of ideas and metaphors of singularly rich applicability to the human condition.*

Natural Man

The social scientists, especially the economists, are moving deeply into ecology and the environment these days, with disquieting results. It goes somehow against the grain to learn that cost-benefit analyses can be done neatly on lakes, meadows, nesting gannets, even whole oceans. It is hard enough to confront the environmental options ahead, and the hard choices, but even harder when the price tags are so visible. Even the new jargon is disturbing: it hurts the spirit, somehow, to read the word *environments,* when the plural means that there are so many alternatives there to be sorted through, as in a market, and voted on. Economists need cool heads and cold hearts for this sort of work, and they must write in icy, often skiddy prose.

The degree to which we are all involved in the control of the earth's life is just beginning to dawn on most of us, and it means another revolution for human thought.

This will not come easily. We've just made our way through inconclusive revolutions on the same topic, trying to make up our minds how we feel about nature. As soon as we arrived at one kind of consensus, like an enormous committee, we found it was time to think it through all over, and now here we are, at it again.

The oldest, easiest-to-swallow idea was that the earth was man's personal property, a combination of garden, zoo, bank vault, and energy source, placed at our disposal to be consumed, ornamented, or pulled apart as we wished. The betterment of mankind was, as we understood it, the whole point of the thing. Mastery over nature, mystery and all, was a moral duty and social obligation.

In the last few years we were wrenched away from this way of looking at it, and arrived at something like general agreement that we had it wrong. We still argue the details, but it is conceded almost everywhere that we are not the masters of nature that we thought ourselves; we are as dependent on the rest of life as are the leaves or midges or fish. We are part of the system. One way to put it is that the earth is a loosely formed, spherical organism, with all its working parts linked in symbiosis. We are, in this view, neither owners nor operators; at best, we might see ourselves as motile tissue specialized for receiving information—perhaps, in the best of all possible worlds, functioning as a nervous system for the whole being.

There is, for some, too much dependency in this view, and they prefer to see us as a separate, qualitatively different, special species, unlike any other form of life, despite the sharing around of genes, enzymes, and organelles. No matter, there is still the underlying idea that we cannot have a life of our own without concern for the ecosystem in which we live, whether in majesty or not. This idea has been strong enough to launch the new movements for the sustenance of wilderness, the protection of wildlife, the turning off of insatiable technologies, the preservation of "whole earth."

But now, just when the new view seems to be taking hold, we may be in for another wrench, this time more dismaying and unsettling than anything we've come through. In a sense, we shall be obliged to swing back again, still believing in the new way but constrained by the facts of life to live in the old. It may be too late, as things have turned out.

We are, in fact, the masters, like it or not.

It is a despairing prospect. Here we are, practically speaking twenty-first-century mankind, filled to exuberance with our new understanding of kinship to all the family of life, and here we are, still nineteenth-century man, walking bootshod over the open face of nature, subjugating and civilizing it. And we cannot stop this controlling, unless we vanish under the hill ourselves. If there were such a thing as a world mind, it should crack over this.

The truth is, we have become more deeply involved than we ever dreamed. The fact that we sit around as we do, worrying seriously about how best to preserve the life of the earth, is itself the sharpest measure of our involvement. It is not human arrogance that has taken us in this direction, but the most natural of natural events. We developed this way, we grew this way, we are this kind of species.

We have become, in a painful, unwished-for way, nature itself. We have grown into everywhere, spreading like a new growth over the entire surface, touching and affecting every other kind of life, *incorporating* ourselves. The earth risks being eutrophied by us. We are now the dominant feature of our own environment. Humans, large terrestrial metazoans, fired by energy from microbial symbionts lodged in their cells, instructed by tapes of nucleic acid stretching back to the earliest live membranes, informed by neurons essentially the same as all the other neurons on earth, sharing structures with mastodons and lichens, living off the sun, are now in charge, running the place, for better or worse.

Or is it really this way? It could be, you know, just the other way around. Perhaps we are the invaded ones, the subjugated, used.

Certain animals in the sea live by becoming part-animal, part-plant. They engulf algae, which then establish themselves as complex plant tissues, essential for the life of the whole company. I suppose the giant clam, if he had more of a mind, would have moments of dismay on seeing what he has done to the plant world, incorporating so much of it, enslaving green cells, living off the photosynthesis. But the plant cells would take a different view of it, having captured the clam on the most satisfactory of terms, including the small lenses in his tissues that focus sunlight for their benefit; perhaps algae have bad moments about what they may collectively be doing to the world of clams.

With luck, our own situation might be similar, on a larger scale. This might turn out to be a special phase in the morphogenesis of the earth when it is necessary to have something like us, for a time anyway, to fetch and carry energy, look after new symbiotic arrangements, store up information for some future season, do a certain amount of ornamenting, maybe even carry seeds around the solar system. That kind of thing. Handyman for the earth.

I would much prefer this useful role, if I had any say, to the essentially unearthly creature we seem otherwise on the way to becoming. It would mean making some quite fundamental changes in our attitudes toward each other, if we were really to think of ourselves as indispensable elements of nature. We would surely become the environment to worry about the most. We would discover, in ourselves, the sources of wonderment and delight that we have discerned in all other manifestations of nature. Who knows, we might even acknowledge the fragility and vulnerability that always accompany high specialization in biology, and movements might start up for the protection of ourselves as a valuable, endangered species. We couldn't lose.

EUGENE RABINOWITCH

Dr. Rabinowitch (1901–1973) was born in Russia and studied chemistry there and in Germany. He worked with Niels Bohr in Copenhagen, then became associated with University College, London; in 1938 he emigrated to the United States, where he taught at the Massachusetts Institute of Technology, at Illinois, and at the State University of New York at Albany. In 1942 Dr. Rabinowitch joined the "Manhattan Project"—the secret group of scientists attempting to make the first atomic bomb. The terrifying success of the project led him and a project physicist, Hyman H. Goldsmith, to start the Bulletin of the Atomic Scientists *in December 1945 as a means of calling attention to the dangers of atomic energy and the need for civilian control of it. The* Bulletin *is the leading journal expressing the conscience of scientists who feel special responsibilities for creating and propagating the nuclear age.*

At his death in 1973, Dr. Rabinowitch was still editor-in-chief of the Bulletin *and was widely recognized for his efforts to promote peace and international understanding among scientists. He was one of the organizers of the Pugwash international conferences on science and public policy. These conferences brought together scientists who advise governments on both sides of the Iron Curtain, and have thus been influential in the partial nuclear test ban and strategic arms limitation agreements.*

Apart from his scientific writings, Dr. Rabinowitch was the author of The Dawn of a New Age *(1963), on science and human affairs, and editor (with Morton Grodzins) of* The Atomic Age *(1963), an anthology of* Bulletin *articles. The present essay appeared in the* Bulletin *in May 1971.*

The Mounting Tide of Unreason

The main difference between *homo sapiens* and other animals on earth is man's capacity for abstract thinking. Our cerebral cortex is a uniquely powerful and versatile instrument, not only for storage and retrieval of millions of information bits, but also for establishment of a complex network of connections between them. Capacity for ordering, comparing and organizing originally separate and unrelated pieces of knowledge has permitted man to develop cohesive patterns, establish sequential and logical systems, define generalized concepts and formulate laws relating these concepts to each other. In simple cases, knowledge of these laws has enabled him to make reliable predictions of future events, for example, to predict the exact times of future eclipses for thousands of years ahead.

The supreme achievement of the cerebral cortex is science—a system of data and relationships covering vast areas of information derived from observation, analysis and manipulation of natural phenomena.

Logical, rational activities of the cerebral cortex are superimposed, in the human brain, on operations of qualitatively different kinds, which we describe as instinctive and emotional responses. In this area, the difference between *homo sapiens* and other animals is by far not as great as in abstract thinking; in fact, many animals obviously surpass man in the variety, acuity and complexity of their instincts. In emotional behavior, we can easily recognize a similarity between humans and many other animals. The latter, too, are obviously capable of love, indifference and hatred; fear, suspicion and trust; joy, satisfaction and despair. True, man has developed much more elaborate faculties for describing and expressing his emotions, culminating in visual, musical and literary arts; but the extremes of pain, hunger and physical effort which many animals will endure when driven by their instincts—in a bee's protection of its hive, in the upstream climb of a salmon on the way to its spawning station, or of a golden plover's transoceanic migration—are not less spectacular than those we admire in the foremost heroes of history or romantic literature.

The fine sensitivity of a dog for the moods of his master, the complex sacrificial behavior of a mother bird trying to save her brood from a predator, suggest not only great vigor, but also great refinement of such responses. Even the capacity for artistic expression of their emotions is not quite absent in animals, as demonstrated by the singing of a bird, or by a fish decorating the entrance to its "nest" with colored stones and shells.

All that man has achieved in advancing beyond the animal stage—his tools, his edifices, his scientific explorations, technological achievements and philosophical systems—has been due to his capacity for abstract thinking: counting, measuring, loyalty to a group. But man's "parliament of instincts" (to use Konrad Lorenz's term) includes also dark passions —hate and intolerance, cruelty and indifference to the needs and sufferings of others, lust for power and joy of domination—the emotional and instinctive inheritance of millennia of desperate competition for survival among individuals as well as among societies. This competition has been the determining factor in the evolution of the human species (and of many other species of animals as well) in their traditional habitat of cruel scarcity.

There is a tendency to treat violence between societies, as well as between individuals, as deviation from normal, healthy behavior; as a kind of sickness which could be cured by some kind of "psychoanalysis." But violence between tribes and nations has been a persistent type of human behavior throughout history. Wars have been the main content of history from antiquity to our time. Individual violence has been censored and punished by organized society as detrimental to its collective interests. It has been more or less successfully reduced to "abnormal" cases within so-called civilized societies. But violence between societies has remained the accepted type of national behavior. In the course of evolution it has served as criterion for the selection of more viable and elimination of less viable societies. Up to our time, violence on behalf of one's society has been praised in song, glorified in legend and portrayed in art. Readiness to kill and be killed in fighting for one's society has been inculcated into numberless generations by tradition, education and even religion. Instilling "patriotic" attitudes and developing abilities useful for the power and wealth of one's society have been the central purpose of education in all societies—capitalist, socialist, or communist alike. True, the communist revolution has started with denying patriotic attachment to any one country as a self-serving invention of capitalists. "The proletariat," the "Communist Manifesto" said, "has no fatherland." But half a century later, youth are exposed to more violent indoctrination in patriotism and militarism in communist countries than in any other society. The two communist giants—the Soviet Union and China—glare at each other across the Amur River in a confrontation no different from those between any two empires in the past. Both proclaim that they will not yield one square yard of the "sacred soil" of the fatherland, not even an uninhabited sandspit.

Obviously, continuation of traditions of international violence into the scientific age is not the consequence of domination by any particular class, or any particular social and political system even if some such systems may be more prone to aggression than others. It is a type of social behavior inherent in the evolutionary division of mankind into self-centered societies, dedicated to pursuit of their own benefits in a habitat of scarcity. Whatever causes were instrumental in bringing about wars in history—power lust of individuals, dynastic or economic conflicts, religious confrontations—the original reason which has made intertribal and international violence a normal component of human history was the association of men into closed groups for the common pursuit of their interests: the acquisition of territory and natural resources, and defense of these possessions against all intruders.

Rational minds long ago started to rebel against this tradition of national self-centeredness and international violence. Goethe's Faust, a symbol of the inquiring mind, observing armies deploying for battle, said, "Schon wieder Krieg! Der Kluge hörts nicht gern!" (What, war again? The wise man hates the word.) Immanuel Kant, the foremost exponent of abstract thinking in the eighteenth century, authored a plan for permanent peace.

Religions of the world have appealed to the best of human emotions —love for one's fellowmen—to moderate the violence of organized societies, but they were confronted with behavioral codes in which readiness to kill and die in the pursuit of a society's interest was exalted as supreme virtue. They compromised. To give God what is God's and Caesar what is Caesar's was the compromise needed to make Christianity acceptable as state religion. Starting with this first compromise, churches ended with invoking God's blessing on mass murder in the service of their own Caesar in conflict with other Caesars. Before the dropping of the atom bomb on Hiroshima, religious services were held on the island of Tinian for the crew of the *Enola Gay,* carrying the first atom bomb. A minister invoked God's blessing on the enterprise: murder, mostly by burning alive a hundred thousand men, women and children.

There is not the slightest reason for hoping that destructive instincts and violent emotions will now submit to the rule of more constructive instinctive and emotional forces. Our instincts and emotions have been shaped by man's biological and social evolution. They are not radically different today from what they had been in the age of the cave man, and can change only slowly. The most humane of religions, the noblest of social movements which relied on arousal of emotions, rode an untamed tiger and ended between its teeth. They gave birth to the cruelest torturers, the most fanatical executioners. Christianity produced Torquemada and the Inquisition; the French Revolution had its Robespierres, Saint Justs and the guillotine-watching market women; Russian communism gave birth to the Cheka, GPU and MGB, to Dzerzhinskys, Stalins, Ezhovs, Berias and thousands of their sadistic henchmen. Appeals to universal love turned into appeals to hate and intolerance.

Since *homo sapiens* appeared on earth, his only steadily growing asset has been his intelligence, his capacity for critical analysis of the facts of a situation, and prediction of likely consequences of his individual or collective behavior. Philosophers and scientists have been involved, from time to time, in advising political leaders. Alexander of Macedon was a pupil of Aristotle; Frederick of Prussia and Catherine of Russia solicited the advice of Voltaire. The physicist and mathematician Sadi-Carnot was advisor to the French revolutionary armies; a bevy of Nobel prize winners undertook the development of weapons to protect Western democracies against the threat of Hitler's barbarians. But in all history, these advisors were involved only in decisions on means, not in defining the aims of national policies. They were willing to do so, because they shared the traditional attachment to their national society and traditional loyalty to their leaders, or because they saw in this service a unique opportunity to obtain funds and equipment for their research. Leonardo da Vinci, the greatest of Renaissance men, saw war as foolishness; but he offered his services as inventor and builder of war machines to the Sforzas of Milan, to other local princelings and to the King of France.

The rational, scientific mind could do no more than serve traditional national policies, often based on desire for greater power and wider territory, as long as these policies were shown to be successful by the lessons of history. This type of violent behavior was selected as successful in the social evolution of mankind, and thus became prevalent throughout the species.

The scientific and technological revolution has changed it all. The rebellion of reason against international violence, which began in antiquity, grew rapidly after the age of Enlightenment. And now, the abstract-thinking brain has changed the conditions of existence under which the human species lives; in this new habitat, once-successful types of international behavior have become obsolete and fraught with deadly dangers.

Application of scientific minds to the development of weapons has led from Leonardo da Vinci through Sadi-Carnot to Fermi, Lawrence and Oppenheimer. It has now endowed nations with weapons of such destructive power that their actual use in a major war between technologically advanced powers may lead not only to utter mutual destruction but may involve belligerents and neutrals alike in a common catastrophe. War has ceased to be a "continuation of policy by other means," or "ultima ratio regis"—the ultimate argument of kings—in classic war definitions of the past. War has become instead a national murder-cum-suicide.

A second, equally fundamental change in conditions of human existence is obsolescence of the main evolutionary reason for war. This reason was the need for nations to control enough natural resources to assure survival and to increase them to permit growth. This need was inescapable in a habitat of scarcity and competition. It is being eliminated by man's newly found capacity to produce wealth from abundant raw materials—common rocks, air and water.

The general trend of technology has been from the use of rare native metals, such as gold and silver, through easily reducible ores of copper, to the much more common, but less easily reducible ores of iron, and, in more recent times, to still more abundant but even more refractory ores of light metals, aluminum and magnesium. The main cost of construction materials thus shifted gradually from that of finding and mining the raw materials, to that of reducing and purifying them.

The same thing has happened in energetics. It shifted from reliance on coal to oil, and thence to fission power. It will ultimately shift to fusion power, derived from freely available material—water.

The radical difference between "natural" and "synthetic" wealth is that the second one is much less competitive. Acquiring wealth—individual or national—was once a "zero sum game": you could get more fertile land, or fossil fuel, or metal ores, only by depriving some other individuals or nations of them. But wealth whose primary ingredient is human intelligence is noncompetitive. When American scientists first released nuclear fission energy, naive politicians dreamed of keeping it an exclusive American asset; but knowledge cannot be so restricted. Americans were first to release nuclear energy, but every nation with sufficient scientific and technical potential can make use of it—to build its own nuclear reactors and its own nuclear weapons. Whether Americans, Englishmen or Russians build the first successful fusion reactor, the technology will become available to all.

The scientific and technological revolution has made war irrational as a means for achieving political aims; but it has also made it basically unnecessary for assuring national wealth and power. In World War II, Germany and Japan lost a large part of their territories and natural resources; 25 years later they joined and overtook their victors in prosperity and economic power. This is a lesson for all nations to learn! Unfortunately, it is only slowly being assimilated by political leaders and public opinion here and elsewhere. Traditional "zero sum game" attitudes towards international relations, originating from millennia of experience in a world of scarcity, still prevail over rational insights into the nature of the scientific age.

History has placed before the coming generations an inescapable challenge: to prepare and engineer the safe transition of mankind from the pre-scientific habitat of scarcity and an evolution-developed, nation-centered behavior, which was proper and successful in the old habitat, into a new habitat shaped by science and technology.

The worldwide ferment and open rebellion of youth are evidence of recognition that traditional attitudes and standards of individual and social behavior are obsolete. But this recognition is dim. From this vague discontent, there must emerge a rational understanding of the historical challenge, a rational planning for answering it. This is mankind's only hope. "Consciousness III," transcendental meditation, or violent anarchism—let society break down, something better will emerge—are but escapes from reality into a wishful world, a cop-out. The challenge is real and can be answered only by rational action. Man stands on the threshold of a new era in its evolution. To enter, he needs a revolution much more radical than any experienced in the past; but it must be a revolution of Reason, not one of wishful daydreaming.

The grave danger for mankind in our time is not that intelligence may go on a rampage if not controlled by sound instincts and noble emotions (as some of our old philosophers and young revolutionaries seem to believe), but that the human intellect will continue to be subservient to animal instincts or unsteady, violent emotions; that it will be again commandeered by self-assured leaders—first, perhaps, in the name of peace and universal love, but then, as so often in the past, in the service of an arrogant, intolerant, "only true" church militant, empire triumphant, or a "scientifically proved" ideology.

Sometimes, emotional forces of self-righteous religion, arrogant nationalism or militant ideology have tried to claim Reason and Science as their allies. Thus Robespierre established the cult of a Goddess of Reason; thus, communists insist that their dogma is "scientific." Adherents of a Christian sect (and a particularly unscientific one at that) call themselves "scientists." The rational mind bears no responsibility for these imposters.

Despite all the now-fashionable debunkers and detractors of reason and science, the vague but categorical preachers of a new consciousness, the men on earth into whose stewardship I would be willing to place the survival of mankind—not without fear, but with the least fear—are the men whose decisions are determined, as far as possible, by rational reasoning, men as free as possible from emotional commitment to a particular society, creed or ideology. The first sign of such critical intelligence is tolerance.

Violent emotional attitudes are based on presumed possession of absolute truth, revealed by a god or a preacher; instinctive reactions are beyond all control of reason. Convictions and actions based on emotion or instinct are cocksure and intolerant. Modern science, on the other hand (contrary to widespread public assumptions), is consciously tentative, uncertain and, therefore, tolerant of unorthodox opinions, provided only that they are supported by adequate experiments or convincing logical deductions, and are willing to submit to continued testing by further experiment and logical analysis.

In the nineteenth century, successes of Newtonian mechanics in explaining the behavior of planets, comets and gas molecules induced scientifically educated and (even more so) half-educated intellectuals to adopt an attitude of arrogant superiority, as if they had in their hands the keys to unlock all secrets of nature. But this has been a passing delusion of grandeur, a childhood disease, now outgrown by science. Since 1900, such scientific landmarks as the quantum theory, relativity, finite but expanding universe, statistical probability replacing strict causality, complementarity, discovery of "anti-matter," proliferation of subatomic particles—and many other unexpected discoveries and unorthodox new hypotheses—have taught scientists to be much more modest, self-critical, open-minded, and tolerant.

No human beings are totally rational; no one is wholly insensible to emotional arousal from the inside or from the outside. But scientifically trained minds are the nearest approach we have to full rationality. More than all others, they can be relied upon to subordinate their emotional responses to the ultimate authority of reason, to make decisions on the basis of rational evaluation of facts and estimation of the most likely consequences of their actions.

Mankind is now at a critical juncture. Science and technology have brought all men into such close relationship that their future cannot be left to competitive interplay of selfish individuals and self-centered societies. In biological evolution, the development of species has been the result of selection, from an immense variety of accidental changes, of those changes proved advantageous for survival and propagation. In social evolution, a similar selection has occurred among different societies. However, because of the much smaller number of competing units —dozens rather than millions—this selection has been less conclusive than that among mutated individuals. The selection of societies has been history, with all its accidental twists and turns, rather than evolution, with its statistically inexorable trends.

Now, even a limited statistical selection of more viable societies is becoming impossible. In fact, even though not in law, mankind has become a single society. A war between major technological societies may well affect the whole globe; it may destroy the viability of the whole species. The vision of Nevil Shute, in his book "On the Beach," in which all mankind is dying because of radioactivity released in an atomic war between China and the Soviet Union, may have been unrealistic in 1960; but it may well become realistic within a few decades, if mankind continues on the traditional path of international competition, interrupted by military conflicts.

It is an unprecedented situation, not only in human history, but in the whole evolution of life on earth: a species must take its own evolution into its own hands if it is to escape the fate of thousands upon thousands of species which have become extinct because they failed to adapt themselves to changes in their habitat—say, to grow a woolly cover when the climate became colder. The changes in the habitat which *homo sapiens* is now facing are not natural—not a new ice age—but manmade. Nevertheless, consequences of a failure to adapt the behavior of the species to this new habitat can be the same—extinction.

Manmade changes in conditions of human existence are much more rapid than those caused by geological and climatic developments. Statistical selection of societies most viable under the new conditions—say, by elimination of warlike and survival of more peaceful societies—is too slow a process to rely on it in the hope for our species' survival. And, in any case, this selection is being made impossible by the growing network of international dependencies. China and India could not survive the demise of Europe and America any more than one Siamese twin could survive the death of the other!

Thus, we face the challenge of adapting mankind to its new scientific and technological habitat by our own intelligent decision. This may prove impossible, and mankind may be doomed: either to die suddenly in a burst of atomic warfare, or to succumb gradually in an environment unfit to support higher life; but whatever chances we have to cope with these two challenges, they rest with realistic, reasonable action rather than with impulsive emotional reactions or obsolete instinctive responses. Neither unthinking revolutionary impulses nor transcendental contemplation, nor reliance on animal instincts, could guide mankind through this, perhaps the greatest, crisis in its history. Reason alone can make it a crisis of growth, not a convulsion of death.

JOYCE CAROL OATES

Joyce Carol Oates was born in Lockport, New York, in 1938 and graduated from Syracuse University in 1960. She received an M.A. in English from the University of Wisconsin the following year, but was turned from further academic training by the persistent success of her short stories, which she had been writing since childhood. Her first collection of stories, By the North Gate *(1963), has been followed already by over a dozen more volumes of stories, novels, poems, plays, and essays. Her novel* Them *(1970) won the National Book Award.*

In addition to being a writer, Ms. Oates teaches creative writing and modern literature at the University of Windsor, Canada. Her critical writing includes a volume of essays, The Edge of Impossibility: Tragic Forms in Literature *(1972), and a book on the poetry of D. H. Lawrence,* The Hostile Sun *(1973).*

Ms. Oates' fiction encompasses a great range of styles—from lyricism and fantasy to naturalism—and it often deals with violent and pessimistic themes. The central figures in her first novel, With Shuddering Fall *(1964), are a teen-age girl and a racing-car driver; the plot involves, among other subjects, rape, miscarriage, suicide, and insanity. The novel* Them *deals with the violent lives of a family from late in the Depression to the 1967 Detroit riots. "The various sordid and shocking events of slum life, detailed in other naturalistic works, have been understated here," Ms. Oates has said, "mainly because of my fear that too much reality would become unbearable." It was with more than ordinary interest, then, that the editors of the* Saturday Review (The Arts) *received the following essay, which appeared in the November 1972 issue. Asked how the relative optimism of the essay would affect her future work, Ms. Oates replied, "I still feel my own place is to dramatize the nightmares of my time, and (hopefully) to show how some individuals find a way out, awaken, come alive, move into the future."*

New Heaven and Earth

In spite of current free-roaming terrors in this country, it is really not the case that we are approaching some apocalyptic close. Both those who seem to be awaiting it with excitement and dread and those who are trying heroically to comprehend it in terms of recent American history are mistaking a crisis of transition for a violent end. Even Charles Reich's much maligned and much misinterpreted *The Greening of America,* which was the first systematic attempt to indicate the direction we are surely moving in, focuses much too narrowly upon a single decade in a single nation and, in spite of its occasional stunning accuracy, is a curiously American product—that is, it imagines all of history as running up into and somehow culminating in the United States. Consider Reich's last two sentences:

". . . For one almost convinced that it was necessary to accept ugliness and evil, that it was necessary to be a miser of dreams, it is an invitation to cry or laugh. For one who thought the world was irretrievably encased in metal and plastic and sterile stone, it seems a veritable greening of America."

Compare that with the following passage from Teilhard de Chardin's *The Phenomenon of Man,* a less historical-nationalistic vision:

"In every domain, when anything exceeds a certain measurement, it suddenly changes its aspect, condition or nature. The curve doubles back, the surface contracts to a point, the solid disintegrates, the liquid boils, the germ cell divides, intuition suddenly bursts on the piled up facts. . . . Critical points have been reached, rungs on the ladder, involving a change of state—jumps of all sorts *in the course* of development."

Or consider these lines from D. H. Lawrence's poem "Nullus," in which he is speaking of the private "self" that is Lawrence but also of the epoch in which this self exists:

> There are said to be creative pauses,
> pauses that are as good as death, empty and dead as death itself.
> And in these awful pauses the evolutionary change takes place.

What appears to be a breaking-down of civilization may well be simply the breaking-up of old forms by life itself (not an eruption of madness or self-destruction), a process that is entirely natural and inevitable. Perhaps we are in the tumultuous but exciting close of a centuries-old kind of consciousness—a few of us like theologians of the medieval church encountering the unstoppable energy of the Renaissance. What we must avoid is the paranoia of history's "true believers," who have always misinterpreted a natural, evolutionary transformation of consciousness as being the violent conclusion of all of history.

The God-centered, God-directed world of the Middle Ages was transformed into the complex era we call the Renaissance, but the transition was as terrifying as it was inevitable, if the innumerable prophecies of doom that were made at the time are any accurate indication. Shakespeare's most disturbing tragedies—*King Lear* and *Troilus and Cressida*—reflect that communal anxiety, as do the various expressions of anxiety over the "New Science" later in the seventeenth century. When we look back into history, we are amazed, not at the distance that separates one century from another, but at their closeness, the almost poetic intimacy.

As I see it, the United States is the first nation—though so complex and unclassifiable an entity almost resists definition as a single unit—to suffer/enjoy the death throes of the Renaissance. How could it be otherwise, since our nation is sensitive, energetic, swarming with life, and, beyond any other developed nation in the world, the most obsessed with its own history and its own destiny? Approaching a kind of manic stage, in which suppressed voices are at last being heard, in which *no extreme viewpoint is any longer "extreme,"* the United States is preparing itself for a transformation of "being" similar to that experienced by individuals as they approach the end of one segment of their lives and must rapidly, and perhaps desperately, sum up everything that has gone before.

It is easy to misread the immediate crises, to be frightened by the spontaneous eruptions into consciousness of disparate groups (blacks, women, youth, "the backlash of the middle class"); it is possible to overlook how the collective voices of many of our best poets and writers serve to dramatize and exorcize current American nightmares. Though some of our most brilliant creative artists are obsessed with disintegration and with the isolated ego, it is clear by now that they are all, with varying degrees of terror, saying the same thing—that we are helpless, unconnected with any social or cultural unit, unable to direct the flow of history, that we cannot effectively communicate. The effect is almost that of a single voice, as if a communal psychoanalytic process were taking place. But there does come a time in an individual writer's experience when he realizes, perhaps against his will, that his voice is one of many, his fiction one of many fictions, and that all serious fictions are half-conscious dramatizations of what is going on in the world.

Here is a simple test to indicate whether you are ready for the new vision of man or whether you will fear and resist it: Imagine you are high in the air, looking down on a crowded street scene from a height so great that you cannot make out individual faces but can see only shapes, scurrying figures rather like insects. Your imagination projects you suddenly down into that mass. You respond with what emotion—dread or joy?

In many of us the Renaissance ideal is still powerful, its voice tyrannical. It declares: *I* will, *I* want, *I* demand, *I* think, *I* am. This voice tells us that we are not quite omnipotent but must act as if we were, pushing out into a world of other people or of nature that will necessarily resist us, that will try to destroy us, and that we must conquer. *I will exist* has meant only *I will impose my will on others.* To that end man has developed his intellect and has extended his physical strength by any means possible because, indeed, at one time the world did have to be conquered. The Renaissance leapt ahead into its own necessary future, into the development and near perfection of machines. Machines are not evil, or even "unnatural," but simply extensions of the human brain. The designs for our machines are no less the product of our creative imaginations than are works of art, though it might be difficult for most people—especially artists—to acknowledge this. But a great deal that is difficult, even outrageous, will have to be acknowledged.

If technology appears to have dehumanized civilization, this is a temporary failing or error—for the purpose of technology is the furthering

of the "human," the bringing to perfection of all the staggering potentialities in each individual, which are nearly always lost, layered over with
biological or social or cultural crusts. Anyone who imagines that a glorious pastoral world has been lost, through machines, identifies himself as
a child of the city, perhaps a second- or third-generation child of the city.
An individual who has lived close to nature, on a farm, for instance, knows
that "natural" man was never *in* nature; he had to fight nature, at the cost
of his own spontaneity and, indeed, his humanity. It is only through the
conscious control of the "machine" (i.e., through man's brain) that man
can transcend the miserable struggle with nature, whether in the form of
sudden devastating hailstorms that annihilate an entire crop, or minute
deadly bacteria in the bloodstream, or simply the commonplace (but
potentially tragic) condition of poor eyesight. It is only through the
machine that man can become more human, more spiritual. Understandably, only a handful of Americans have realized this obvious fact, since
technology seems at present to be villainous. Had our earliest ancestors
been gifted with a box of matches, their first actions would probably have
been destructive—or self-destructive. But we know how beneficial fire has
been to civilization.

The Renaissance man invented and brought to near perfection the
civilization of the machine. In doing this, he was simply acting out the
conscious and unconscious demand of his time—the demand that man
(whether man-in-the-world or man supposedly superior to worldly interests) master everything about him, including his own private nature, his
own "ego," redefining himself in terms of a conqueror whose territory
should be as vast as his own desire to conquer. The man who "masters"
every aspect of his own being, subduing or obliterating his own natural
instincts, leaving nothing to be unknown, uninvestigated, is the ideal of
our culture, whether he is an industrialist or a "disinterested" scientist
or a literary man. In other words, I see no difference between the maniacal acquisitiveness of traditional American capitalists and the meticulous,
joyless, ironic manner of many scholars and writers.

It is certainly time to stop accusing "industry" or "science" or the
"Corporate State" or "Amerika" of being inhuman or antihuman. The
exaggerated and suprahuman potency attributed to machines, investing
them with the power of the long-vanquished Devil himself, is amazing.
It is also rather disheartening, if we observe the example of one of our
most brilliant writers, Norman Mailer, who argues—with all the doomed,
manic intensity of a late-medieval churchman resisting the future even
when it is upon him—that the universe can still sensibly be divided into
God and Devil, that there can be an "inorganic" product of the obviously
organic mind of man. Mailer (and many others) exemplifies the old,
losing, pitiful Last Stand of the Ego, the Self-Against-All-Others, the
Conqueror, the Highest of all Protoplasms, Namer and Begetter of all
Fictions.

What will the next phase of human experience be? A simple evolution into a higher humanism, perhaps a kind of intelligent pantheism, in which all substance in the universe (including the substance fortunate enough to perceive it) is there by equal right.

We have come to the end of, we are satiated with, the "objective," valueless philosophies that have always worked to preserve a status quo, however archaic. We are tired of the old dichotomies: Sane/Insane, Normal/Sick, Black/White, Man/Nature, Victor/Vanquished, and—above all this Cartesian dualism—I/It. Although once absolutely necessary to get us through the exploratory, analytical phase of our development as human beings, they are no longer useful or pragmatic. They are no longer *true.* Far from being locked inside our own skins, inside the "dungeons" of ourselves, we are now able to recognize that our minds belong, quite naturally, to a collective "mind," a mind in which we share everything that is mental, most obviously language itself, and that the old boundary of the skin is no boundary at all but a membrane connecting the inner and outer experiences of existence. Our intelligence, our wit, our cleverness, our unique personalities—all are simultaneously "our own" possessions and the world's. This has always been a mystical vision, but more and more in our time it is becoming a rational truth. It is no longer the private possession of a Blake, a Whitman, or a Lawrence, but the public, articulate offering of a Claude Lévi-Strauss, to whom anthropology is "part of a cosmology" and whose humanism is one that sees everything in the universe, including man, in its own place. It is the lifelong accumulative statement of Abraham Maslow, the humanist psychologist who extended the study of psychology from the realm of the disordered into that of the normal and the "more-than-normal," including people who would once have been termed mystics and been dismissed as irrational. It is the unique, fascinating voice of Buckminster Fuller, who believes that "human minds and brains may be essential in the total design" of the universe. And it is the abrasive argument of R. D. Laing, the Freudian/post-Freudian mystic, who has denied the medical and legal distinctions between "normal" and "abnormal" and has set out not only to experience but to articulate a metaphysical "illumination" whereby self and other become joined. All these are men of genius, whose training has been rigorously scientific. That they are expressing views once considered the exclusive property of mystics proves that the old dichotomy of Reason/Intuition has vanished or is vanishing.

As with all dichotomies, it will be transcended—not argued away, not battered into silence. The energies wasted on the old debates—Are we rational? Are we 90 per cent Unconscious Impulses?—will be utilized for higher and more worthy human pursuits. Instead of hiding our most amazing, mysterious, and inexplicable experiences, we will learn to articulate and share them; instead of insisting upon rigid academic or intellectual categories (for instance, that "science fiction" is different from other fiction, or less traditional than the very recent "realistic novel"), we will see how naturally they flow into one another, supporting and explaining each other. Yesterday's wildly ornate, obscure, poetic prophecies evolve into today's calm statements of fact.

The vision of a new, higher humanism or pantheism is not irrational but is a logical extension of what we now know. It may frighten some of us because it challenges the unquestioned assumptions that we have always held. But these assumptions were never *ours*. We never figured them out, never discovered them for ourselves; we inherited them from the body of knowledge created by our men of genius. Now men of genius, such as British physicist/philosopher Sir James Jeans, are saying newer, deeper things:

"Today there is a wide measure of agreement, which on the physical side of science approaches almost to unanimity, that the stream of knowledge is heading toward a non-mechanical reality; the universe begins to look more like a great thought than like a great machine. Mind no longer appears as an accidental intruder into the realm of matter; we are beginning to suspect that we ought rather to hail it as the creator and governor of the realm of matter. . . ."

Everywhere, suddenly, we hear the prophetic voice of Nietzsche once again, saying that man must overcome himself, that he must interpret and create the universe. (Nietzsche was never understood until now, until the world caught up with him, or approached him.) In such a world, which belongs to consciousness, there can be no distracting of energies from the need to push forward, to synthesize, to converge, to make a unity out of ostensible diversity. But too facile optimism is as ultimately distracting as the repetitive nihilism and despair we have inherited from the early part of this century. An absolutely honest literature, whether fiction or nonfiction, must dramatize for us the complexities of this epoch, showing us how deeply related we are to one another, how deeply we act out, even in our apparently secret dreams, the communal crises of our world. If demons are reawakened and allowed to run loose across the landscape of suburban shopping malls and parks, it is only so that their symbolic values—wasteful terror, despair, entropy—can be recognized. If all other dichotomies are ultimately transcended, there must still be the tension between a healthy acceptance of change and a frightened, morbid resistance to change.

The death throes of the old values are everywhere around us, but they are not at all the same thing as the death throes of particular human beings. We can transform ourselves, overleap ourselves beyond even our most flamboyant estimations. A conversion is always imminent; one cannot revert back to a lower level of consciousness. The "conversion" of the I-centered personality into a higher, or transcendental, personality cannot be an artificially, externally enforced event; it must be a natural event. It is surely as natural as the upward growth of the plant—if the plant's growth is not impeded. It has nothing to do with drugs, with the occult, with a fashionable cultivation of Eastern mysticism (not at all suitable for us in the West—far too passive, too life-denying, too ascetic); it has nothing to do with political beliefs. It is not Marxist, not Communist, not Socialist, not willing to align itself with any particular ideology. If anything, it is a flowering of the democratic ideal, a community of equals, but not a community mobilized against the rest of the world, not a unity arising out of primitive paranoia.

In the Sixties and at present we hear a very discordant music. We have got to stop screaming at one another. We have got to bring into harmony the various discordant demands, voices, stages of personality. Those more advanced must work to transform the rest, by being, themselves, models of sanity and integrity. The angriest of the ecologists must stop blaming industry for having brought to near perfection the implicit demands of society, as if anyone in our society—especially at the top—has ever behaved autonomously, unshaped by that society and its history. The optimism of *The Greening of America* seems to me a bit excessive or at least premature. There is no doubt that the future—the new consciousness—is imminent, but it may take generations to achieve it. The rapidly condensed vision, the demand for immediate gratification, is, once again, typically (and sadly) American. But though the achievement of Reich's vision is much farther off than he seems to think, it is an inevitable one, and those of us who will probably not share personally in a transformed world can, in a way, anticipate it now, almost as if experiencing it now. If we are reasonably certain of the conclusion of a novel (especially one we have ourselves imagined), we can endure and even enjoy the intermediary chapters that move us toward that conclusion.

One of the unfortunate aspects of American intellectual life has been the nearly total divorce of academic philosophy from the issues of a fluid, psychic social reality. There are obvious reasons for this phenomenon, too complex to consider at the moment. But the book that needs to be written about the transformation of America cannot really be written by anyone lacking a thorough knowledge of where we have been and where we are right now, in terms of an intellectual development that begins and ends with the faculties of the mind. We require the meticulous genius of a Kant, a man of humility who is awakened from some epoch-induced "slumber" to synthesize vast exploratory fields of knowledge, to write the book that is the way into the future for us.

This essay, totally nonacademic in its lyric disorganization, in its bringing together of voices that, for all their differences, seem to be saying one thing, is intended only to suggest—no, really, to make a plea for—the awakening of that someone's slumber, the rejection of the positivist-linguist-"naming" asceticism that has made American philosophy so disappointing. We need a tradition similar to that in France, where the role of "philosopher" is taken naturally by men of genius who can address themselves to varied groups of people—scientists, writers, artists, and the public itself. Our highly educated and highly cultivated reading public is starved for books like *The Greening of America*. We have an amazingly fertile but somehow separate nation of writers and poets, living dreamily inside a culture but no more than symbiotically related to it. Yet these writers and poets are attempting to define that culture, to "act it out," to somehow make sense of it. The novel is the most human of all art forms—there are truths we can get nowhere else but in the novel—but now our crucial need is for something else. We need a large, generous, meticulous work that will synthesize our separate but deeply similar voices, one that will climb up out of the categories of "rational" and "irrational" to show why the consciousness of the future will feel joy, not dread, at the total rejection of the Renaissance ideal, the absorption into the psychic stream of the universe.

Lawrence asks in his strange poem "New Heaven and Earth" a question that seems to me parallel with Yeats's famous question in the sonnet "Leda and the Swan." In the Yeats poem mortal woman is raped by an immortal force, and, yes, this will and must happen; this cannot be escaped. But the point is: Did she put on his knowledge *with* his power, before the terrifying contact was broken? Lawrence speaks of mysterious "green streams" that flow from the new world (our everyday world—seen with new eyes) and asks, ". . . what are they?" What are the conversions that await us?

WILLIAM BUTLER YEATS (1865–1939)

Leda and the Swan

A sudden blow: the great wings beating still
Above the staggering girl, her thighs caressed
By the dark webs, her nape caught in his bill,
He holds her helpless breast upon his breast.

How can those terrified vague fingers push
The feathered glory from her loosening thighs?
And how can body, laid in that white rush,
But feel the strange heart beating where it lies?

A shudder in the loins engenders there
The broken wall, the burning roof and tower
And Agamemnon dead.
                        Being so caught up,
So mastered by the brute blood of the air,
Did she put on his knowledge with his power
Before the indifferent beak could let her drop?

(1923)

Thinking
and
Feeling

The issue examined in detail in this section is one already raised by the scientist Eugene Rabinowitch in the preceding section. Irrationality, he says, has led us to the edge of annihilation by atomic war, and only rationality can lead us back. Our need for thinking would thus seem to be absolutely clear, and the essay by Aldous Huxley in the present section raises a similarly practical argument for clear thinking as necessary protection against political annihilation.

But thinking is a discipline and an art, and often it is subverted rather than energized by feeling. What we accept rationally we often find hard to put into practice. Within us, what we think we think may be in unsettling and sometimes unconscious conflict with what we really feel. It is the recognition of this that adds to the persuasiveness of the first two essays. Golding's essay arises out of his awareness of the problem of distinguishing thought and feeling and is developed by a witty account of three different kinds of thinking. Robinson's fuller and more philosophical treatment of kinds of thinking rests similarly on his recognition of the unconscious and his wish to distinguish real thinking from emotional prejudice.

But even for trained thinkers, thinking is not enough. Threatened as we seem to be today by a mechanistic, alienating life style, we need more and more to be concerned with wholeness, with the self come together in equilibrium, the integration of thought and feeling in total experience. Thus Mary Caroline Richards argues that "wisdom is not the product of mental effort," but "a state of the total being." Emerson also insists on the validity of the total experience: "Only so much do I know, as I have lived." He leads us to the challenging distinction between "Man Thinking," characterized by self-trust, and man as "mere thinker" or parroter or bookworm. The last two essayists take up notable instances in which thinking is dominated by feeling. Koestler, describing his political conversion, argues that "a faith is not acquired by reasoning"; and Proust puts instinct before intellect at the moment when the artist tries to reach back to the impressions that are "the only material of art."

FULKE GREVILLE, LORD BROOKE
(1554–1628)

Chorus of Priests, from *Mustapha*

Oh wearisome Condition of Humanity!
Borne under one Law, to another bound:
Vainely begot, and yet forbidden vanity:
Created sicke, commanded to be sound:
What meaneth Nature by these diverse Lawes?
Passion and Reason, Selfe-division cause:

Is it the marke, or Maiesty of Power
To make offences that it may forgive?
Nature herselfe, doth her owne selfe defloure,
To hate those errors She her selfe doth give.
For how should man thinke that, he may not doe
If Nature did not faile, and punish too?

Tyrant to others, to her selfe unjust,
Onely commands things difficult and hard.
Forbids us all things, which it knowes is lust,
Makes easy paines, unpossible reward.
If Nature did not take delight in blood,
She would have made more easie waies to good.

We that are bound by vowes, and by Promotion,
With pompe of holy Sacrifice and rites,
To teach beleefe in good and still devotion,
To preach of Heavens wonders, and delights:
Yet when each of us, in his owne heart lookes,
He findes the God there, farre unlike his Bookes.

(1609)

e. e. cummings (1894–1962)

since feeling is first

trust feelings

since feeling is first
who pays any attention
to the syntax of things
will never wholly kiss you;

wholly to be a fool
while Spring is in the world

my blood approves,
and kisses are a better fate
than wisdom
lady i swear by all flowers. Don't cry
—the best gesture of my brain is less than
your eyelids' flutter which says

we are for each other: then
laugh, leaning back in my arms
for life's not a paragraph

And death i think is no parenthesis

(1926)

IMAMU AMIRI BARAKA
(LeROI JONES) (1934–)

Young Soul

First, feel, then feel, then
read, or read, then feel, then
fall, or stand, where you
already are. Think
of your self, and the other
selves . . . think
of your parents, your mothers
and sisters, your bentslick
father, then feel, or
fall, on your knees
if nothing else will move you,

           then read
           and look deeply
           into all matters
           come close to you
           city boys—
           country men

           Make some muscle
           in your head, but
           use the muscle
           in yr heart

WILLIAM GOLDING

William Gerald Golding, a British author, was born in 1911 and educated at Marlborough grammar school and at Oxford. At first destined for a scientific career, he shifted his attention to literature after two years in the university and published a volume of poems. During World War II he served in the Royal Navy, rising to the command of a rocket-launching ship. Since the war he has devoted himself to teaching and writing, and to his hobbies, which he once described as "thinking, classical Greek, sailing, and archaeology." He is widely known for his strikingly original novels, especially Pincher Martin *(1956), describing the feelings of a shipwrecked sailor on an isolated rock in mid-ocean, and* Lord of the Flies *(1954), a symbolic account of a group of schoolboys who revert to savagery when marooned on an island. His most recent book,* The Scorpion God *(1971), comprises three novellas that re-create different ancient societies—prehistoric, Egyptian, and Roman. The present essay first appeared in the August 1961 issue of* Holiday.

Thinking as a Hobby

While I was still a boy, I came to the conclusion that there were three grades of thinking; and since I was later to claim thinking as my hobby, I came to an even stranger conclusion—namely, that I myself could not think at all.

I must have been an unsatisfactory child for grownups to deal with. I remember how incomprehensible they appeared to me at first, but not, of course, how I appeared to them. It was the headmaster of my grammar school who first brought the subject of thinking before me—though neither in the way, nor with the result he intended. He had some statuettes in his study. They stood on a high cupboard behind his desk. One was a lady wearing nothing but a bath towel. She seemed frozen in an eternal panic lest the bath towel slip down any farther; and since she had no arms, she was in an unfortunate position to pull the towel up again. Next to her, crouched the statuette of a leopard, ready to spring down at the top drawer of a filing cabinet labeled A–AH. My innocence interpreted this as the victim's last, despairing cry. Beyond the leopard was a naked, muscular gentleman, who sat, looking down, with his chin on his fist and his elbow on his knee. He seemed utterly miserable.

Some time later, I learned about these statuettes. The headmaster had placed them where they would face delinquent children, because they symbolized to him the whole of life. The naked lady was the Venus of

Milo. She was Love. She was not worried about the towel. She was just busy being beautiful. The leopard was Nature, and he was being natural. The naked, muscular gentleman was not miserable. He was Rodin's Thinker, an image of pure thought. It is easy to buy small plaster models of what you think life is like.

I had better explain that I was a frequent visitor to the headmaster's study, because of the latest thing I had done or left undone. As we now say, I was not integrated. I was, if anything, disintegrated; and I was puzzled. Grownups never made sense. Whenever I found myself in a penal position before the headmaster's desk, with the statuettes glimmering whitely above him, I would sink my head, clasp my hands behind my back and writhe one shoe over the other.

The headmaster would look opaquely at me through flashing spectacles.

"What are we going to do with you?"

Well, what *were* they going to do with me? I would writhe my shoe some more and stare down at the worn rug.

"Look up, boy! Can't you look up?"

Then I would look up at the cupboard, where the naked lady was frozen in her panic and the muscular gentleman contemplated the hindquarters of the leopard in endless gloom. I had nothing to say to the headmaster. His spectacles caught the light so that you could see nothing human behind them. There was no possibility of communication.

"Don't you ever think at all?"

No, I didn't think, wasn't thinking, couldn't think—I was simply waiting in anguish for the interview to stop.

"Then you'd better learn—hadn't you?"

On one occasion the headmaster leaped to his feet, reached up and plonked Rodin's masterpiece on the desk before me.

"That's what a man looks like when he's really thinking."

I surveyed the gentleman without interest or comprehension.

"Go back to your class."

Clearly there was something missing in me. Nature had endowed the rest of the human race with a sixth sense and left me out. This must be so, I mused, on my way back to the class, since whether I had broken a window, or failed to remember Boyle's Law, or been late for school, my teachers produced me one, adult answer: "Why can't you think?"

As I saw the case, I had broken the window because I had tried to hit Jack Arney with a cricket ball and missed him; I could not remember Boyle's Law because I had never bothered to learn it; and I was late for school because I preferred looking over the bridge into the river. In fact, I was wicked. Were my teachers, perhaps, so good that they could not understand the depths of my depravity? Were they clear, untormented people who could direct their every action by this mysterious business of thinking? The whole thing was incomprehensible. In my earlier years, I found even the statuette of the Thinker confusing. I did not believe any of my teachers were naked, ever. Like someone born deaf, but bitterly determined to find out about sound, I watched my teachers to find out about thought.

There was Mr. Houghton. He was always telling me to think. With a modest satisfaction, he would tell me that he had thought a bit himself. Then why did he spend so much time drinking? Or was there more sense in drinking than there appeared to be? But if not, and if drinking were in fact ruinous to health—and Mr. Houghton was ruined, there was no doubt about that—why was he always talking about the clean life and the virtues of fresh air? He would spread his arms wide with the action of a man who habitually spent his time striding along mountain ridges.

"Open air does me good, boys—I know it!"

Sometimes, exalted by his own oratory, he would leap from his desk and hustle us outside into a hideous wind.

"Now, boys! Deep breaths! Feel it right down inside you—huge draughts of God's good air!"

He would stand before us, rejoicing in his perfect health, an open-air man. He would put his hands on his waist and take a tremendous breath. You could hear the wind, trapped in the cavern of his chest and struggling with all the unnatural impediments. His body would reel with shock and his ruined face go white at the unaccustomed visitation. He would stagger back to his desk and collapse there, useless for the rest of the morning.

Mr. Houghton was given to high-minded monologues about the good life, sexless and full of duty. Yet in the middle of one of these monologues, if a girl passed the window, tapping along on her neat little feet, he would interrupt his discourse, his neck would turn of itself and he would watch her out of sight. In this instance, he seemed to me ruled not by thought but by an invisible and irresistible spring in his nape.

His neck was an object of great interest to me. Normally it bulged a bit over his collar. But Mr. Houghton had fought in the First World War alongside both Americans and French, and had come—by who knows what illogic?—to a settled detestation of both countries. If either country happened to be prominent in current affairs, no argument could make Mr. Houghton think well of it. He would bang the desk, his neck would bulge still further and go red. "You can say what you like," he would cry, "but I've thought about this—and I know what I think!"

Mr. Houghton thought with his neck.

There was Miss Parsons. She assured us that her dearest wish was our welfare, but I knew even then, with the mysterious clairvoyance of childhood, that what she wanted most was the husband she never got. There was Mr. Hands—and so on.

I have dealt at length with my teachers because this was my introduction to the nature of what is commonly called thought. Through them I discovered that thought is often full of unconscious prejudice, ignorance and hypocrisy. It will lecture on disinterested purity while its neck is being remorselessly twisted toward a skirt. Technically, it is about as proficient as most businessmen's golf, as honest as most politicians' intentions, or —to come near my own preoccupation—as coherent as most books that get written. It is what I came to call grade-three thinking, though more properly, it is feeling, rather than thought.

True, often there is a kind of innocence in prejudices, but in those days I viewed grade-three thinking with an intolerant contempt and an incautious mockery. I delighted to confront a pious lady who hated the Germans with the proposition that we should love our enemies. She taught me a great truth in dealing with grade-three thinkers; because of her, I no longer dismiss lightly a mental process which for nine-tenths of the population is the nearest they will ever get to thought. They have immense solidarity. We had better respect them, for we are outnumbered and surrounded. A crowd of grade-three thinkers, all shouting the same thing, all warming their hands at the fire of their own prejudices, will not thank you for pointing out the contradictions in their beliefs. Man is a gregarious animal, and enjoys agreement as cows will graze all the same way on the side of a hill.

Grade-two thinking is the detection of contradictions. I reached grade two when I trapped the poor, pious lady. Grade-two thinkers do not stampede easily, though often they fall into the other fault and lag behind. Grade-two thinking is a withdrawal, with eyes and ears open. It became my hobby and brought satisfaction and loneliness in either hand. For grade-two thinking destroys without having the power to create. It set me watching the crowds cheering His Majesty the King and asking myself what all the fuss was about, without giving me anything positive to put in the place of that heady patriotism. But there were compensations. To hear people justify their habit of hunting foxes and tearing them to pieces by claiming that the foxes liked it. To hear our Prime Minister talk about the great benefit we conferred on India by jailing people like Pandit Nehru and Gandhi. To hear American politicians talk about peace in one sentence and refuse to join the League of Nations in the next. Yes, there were moments of delight.

But I was growing toward adolescence and had to admit that Mr. Houghton was not the only one with an irresistible spring in his neck. I, too, felt the compulsive hand of nature and began to find that pointing out contradiction could be costly as well as fun. There was Ruth, for example, a serious and attractive girl. I was an atheist at the time. Grade-two thinking is a menace to religion and knocks down sects like skittles. I put myself in a position to be converted by her with an hypocrisy worthy of grade three. She was a Methodist—or at least, her parents were, and Ruth had to follow suit. But, alas, instead of relying on the Holy Spirit to convert me, Ruth was foolish enough to open her pretty mouth in argument. She claimed that the Bible (King James Version) was literally inspired. I countered by saying that the Catholics believed in the literal inspiration of Saint Jerome's *Vulgate,* and the two books were different. Argument flagged.

At last she remarked that there were an awful lot of Methodists, and they couldn't be wrong, could they—not all those millions? That was too easy, said I restively (for the nearer you were to Ruth, the nicer she was to be near to) since there were more Roman Catholics than Methodists anyway; and they couldn't be wrong, could they—not all those hundreds of millions? An awful flicker of doubt appeared in her eyes. I slid my arm round her waist and murmured breathlessly that if we were counting heads, the Buddhists were the boys for my money. But Ruth had *really* wanted to do me good, because I was so nice. She fled. The combination of my arm and those countless Buddhists was too much for her.

That night her father visited my father and left, red-cheeked and indignant. I was given the third degree to find out what had happened. It was lucky we were both of us only fourteen. I lost Ruth and gained an undeserved reputation as a potential libertine.

So grade-two thinking could be dangerous. It was in this knowledge, at the age of fifteen, that I remember making a comment from the heights of grade two, on the limitations of grade three. One evening I found myself alone in the schoolhall, preparing it for a party. The door of the headmaster's study was open. I went in. The headmaster had ceased to thump Rodin's Thinker down on the desk as an example to the young. Perhaps he had not found any more candidates, but the statuettes were still there, glimmering and gathering dust on top of the cupboard. I stood on a chair and rearranged them. I stood Venus in her bath towel on the filing cabinet, so that now the top drawer caught its breath in a gasp of sexy excitement. "A–ah!" The portentous Thinker I placed on the edge of the cupboard so that he looked down at the bath towel and waited for it to slip.

Grade-two thinking, though it filled life with fun and excitement, did not make for content. To find out the deficiencies of our elders bolsters the young ego but does not make for personal security. I found that grade two was not only the power to point out contradictions. It took the swimmer some distance from the shore and left him there, out of his depth. I decided that Pontius Pilate was a typical grade-two thinker. "What is truth?" he said, a very common grade-two thought, but one that is used always as the end of an argument instead of the beginning. There is a still higher grade of thought which says, "What is truth?" and sets out to find it.

But these grade-one thinkers were few and far between. They did not visit my grammar school in the flesh though they were there in books. I aspired to them, partly because I was ambitious and partly because I now saw my hobby as an unsatisfactory thing if it went no further. If you set out to climb a mountain, however high you climb, you have failed if you cannot reach the top.

I *did* meet an undeniably grade-one thinker in my first year at Oxford. I was looking over a small bridge in Magdalen Deer Park, and a tiny mustached and hatted figure came and stood by my side. He was a

German who had just fled from the Nazis to Oxford as a temporary refuge. His name was Einstein.

But Professor Einstein knew no English at that time and I knew only two words of German. I beamed at him, trying wordlessly to convey by my bearing all the affection and respect that the English felt for him. It is possible—and I have to make the admission—that I felt here were two grade-one thinkers standing side by side; yet I doubt if my face conveyed more than a formless awe. I would have given my Greek and Latin and French and a good slice of my English for enough German to communicate. But we were divided; he was as inscrutable as my headmaster. For perhaps five minutes we stood together on the bridge, undeniable grade-one thinker and breathless aspirant. With true greatness, Professor Einstein realized that any contact was better than none. He pointed to a trout wavering in midstream.

He spoke: *"Fisch."*

My brain reeled. Here I was, mingling with the great, and yet helpless as the veriest grade-three thinker. Desperately I sought for some sign by which I might convey that I, too, revered pure reason. I nodded vehemently. In a brilliant flash I used up half of my German vocabulary. *"Fisch. Ja. Ja."*

For perhaps another five minutes we stood side by side. Then Professor Einstein, his whole figure still conveying good will and amiability, drifted away out of sight.

I, too, would be a grade-one thinker. I was irreverent at the best of times. Political and religious systems, social customs, loyalties and traditions, they all came tumbling down like so many rotten apples off a tree. This was a fine hobby and a sensible substitute for cricket, since you could play it all the year round. I came up in the end with what must always remain the justification for grade-one thinking, its sign, seal and charter. I devised a coherent system for living. It was a moral system, which was wholly logical. Of course, as I readily admitted, conversion of the world to my way of thinking might be difficult, since my system did away with a number of trifles, such as big business, centralized government, armies, marriage. . . .

It was Ruth all over again. I had some very good friends who stood by me, and still do. But my acquaintances vanished, taking the girls with them. Young women seemed oddly contented with the world as it was. They valued the meaningless ceremony with a ring. Young men, while willing to concede the chaining sordidness of marriage, were hesitant about abandoning the organizations which they hoped would give them a career. A young man on the first rung of the Royal Navy, while perfectly agreeable to doing away with big business and marriage, got as red-necked as Mr. Houghton when I proposed a world without any battleships in it.

Had the game gone too far? Was it a game any longer? In those prewar days, I stood to lose a great deal, for the sake of a hobby.

Now you are expecting me to describe how I saw the folly of my ways and came back to the warm nest, where prejudices are so often called loyalties, where pointless actions are hallowed into custom by repetition, where we are content to say we think when all we do is feel.

But you would be wrong. I dropped my hobby and turned professional.

If I were to go back to the headmaster's study and find the dusty statuettes still there, I would arrange them differently. I would dust Venus and put her aside, for I have come to love her and know her for the fair thing she is. But I would put the Thinker, sunk in his desperate thought, where there were shadows before him—and at his back, I would put the leopard, crouched and ready to spring.

JAMES HARVEY ROBINSON

James Harvey Robinson (1863–1936), American historian and university professor, was educated at Harvard and Freiburg. He taught history at the University of Pennsylvania and from 1895 to 1919 at Columbia. Resigning in 1919 in protest against the expulsion of a group of professors for their opposition to World War I, he attacked Columbia president Nicholas Murray Butler for his alleged attempts to suppress freedom of expression at the university. Robinson then helped to found the New School for Social Research in New York City, and he taught there until 1921, when he retired to devote the rest of his life to writing. Among his dozen volumes of historical and philosophical writing, perhaps the best known to the general public is The Mind in the Making *(1921), subtitled* The Relation of Intelligence to Social Reform. *Chapter 2 of this book has been excerpted and reprinted so often that it has itself been the subject of an amusing article by Professor David Novarr ("OVKOT," AAUP Bulletin, vol. 37, 1951). But familiarity has not reduced its value. We reprint the chapter here in full, using the heading of the first section as title for the whole.*

On Various Kinds of Thinking

Good sense is, of all things among men, the most equally distributed; for everyone thinks himself so abundantly provided with it that those even who are the most difficult to satisfy in everything else do not usually desire a larger measure of this quality than they already possess.

—DESCARTES

We see man to-day, instead of the frank and courageous recognition of his status, the docile attention to his biological history, the determination to let nothing stand in the way of the security and permanence of his future, which alone can establish the safety and happiness of the race, substituting blind confidence in his destiny, unclouded faith in the essentially respectful attitude of the universe toward his moral code, and a belief no less firm that his traditions and laws and institutions necessarily contain permanent qualities of reality.

—WILLIAM TROTTER

1. On Various Kinds of Thinking

The truest and most profound observations on Intelligence have in the past been made by the poets and, in recent times, by story-writers. They have been keen observers and recorders and reckoned freely with the emotions and sentiments. Most philosophers, on the other hand, have exhibited a grotesque ignorance of man's life and have built up systems that are elaborate and imposing, but quite unrelated to actual human affairs. They have almost consistently neglected the actual process of thought and have set the mind off as something apart to be studied by itself. *But no such mind, exempt from bodily processes, animal impulses, savage traditions, infantile impressions, conventional reactions, and traditional knowledge, ever existed,* even in the case of the most abstract of metaphysicians. Kant entitled his great work *A Critique of Pure Reason.* But to the modern student of mind pure reason seems as mythical as the pure gold, transparent as glass, with which the celestial city is paved.

Formerly philosophers thought of mind as having to do exclusively with conscious thought. It was that within man which perceived, remembered, judged, reasoned, understood, believed, willed. But of late it has been shown that we are unaware of a great part of what we perceive, remember, will, and infer; and that a great part of the thinking of which we are aware is determined by that of which we are not conscious. It has indeed been demonstrated that our unconscious psychic life far outruns our conscious. This seems perfectly natural to anyone who considers the following facts:

The sharp distinction between the mind and the body is, as we shall find, a very ancient and spontaneous uncritical savage prepossession. What we think of as "mind" is so intimately associated with what we call "body" that we are coming to realize that the one cannot be understood without the other. Every thought reverberates through the body, and, on the other hand, alterations in our physical condition affect our whole attitude of mind. The insufficient elimination of the foul and decaying products of digestion may plunge us into deep melancholy, whereas a few whiffs of nitrous monoxide may exalt us to the seventh heaven of supernal knowledge and godlike complacency. And *vice versa,* a sudden word or thought may cause our heart to jump, check our breathing, or make our knees as water. There is a whole new literature growing up which studies the effects of our bodily secretions and our muscular tensions and their relation to our emotions and our thinking.

Then there are hidden impulses and desires and secret longings of which we can only with the greatest difficulty take account. They influence our conscious thought in the most bewildering fashion. Many of these unconscious influences appear to originate in our very early years. The older philosophers seem to have forgotten that even they were infants and children at their most impressionable age and never could by any possibility get over it.

The term "unconscious," now so familiar to all readers of modern works on psychology, gives offense to some adherents of the past. There should, however, be no special mystery about it. It is not a new animistic abstraction, but simply a collective word to include all the physiological changes which escape our notice, all the forgotten experiences and impressions of the past which continue to influence our desires and reflections and conduct, even if we cannot remember them. What we can remember at any time is indeed an infinitesimal part of what has happened to us. We could not remember anything unless we forgot almost everything. As Bergson says, the brain is the organ of forgetfulness as well as of memory. Moreover, we tend, of course, to become oblivious to things to which we are thoroughly accustomed, for habit blinds us to their existence. So the forgotten and the habitual make up a great part of the so-called "unconscious."

If we are ever to understand man, his conduct and reasoning, and if we aspire to learn to guide his life and his relations with his fellows more happily than heretofore, we cannot neglect the great discoveries briefly noted above. We must reconcile ourselves to novel and revolutionary conceptions of the mind, for it is clear that the older philosophers, whose works still determine our current views, had a very superficial notion of the subject with which they dealt. But for our purposes, with due regard to what has just been said and to much that has necessarily been left unsaid (and with the indulgence of those who will at first be inclined to dissent), *we shall consider mind chiefly as conscious knowledge and intelligence, as what we know and our attitude toward it—our disposition to increase our information, classify it, and apply it.*

We do not think enough about thinking, and much of our confusion is the result of current illusions in regard to it. Let us forget for the moment any impressions we may have derived from the philosophers, and see what seems to happen in ourselves. The first thing that we notice is that our thought moves with such incredible rapidity that it is almost impossible to arrest any specimen of it long enough to have a look at it. When we are offered a penny for our thoughts we always find that we have recently had so many things in mind that we can easily make a selection which will not compromise us too nakedly. On inspection we shall find that even if we are not downright ashamed of a great part of our spontaneous thinking it is far too intimate, personal, ignoble or trivial to permit us to reveal more than a small part of it. I believe this must be true of everyone. We do not, of course, know what goes on in other people's heads. They tell us very little and we tell them very little. The spigot of speech, rarely fully opened, could never emit more than driblets of the ever renewed hogshead of thought—*noch grösser wie's Heidelberger Fass.* We find it hard to believe that other people's thoughts are as silly as our own, but they probably are.

We all appear to ourselves to be thinking all the time during our waking hours, and most of us are aware that we go on thinking while we are asleep, even more foolishly than when awake. When uninterrupted by some practical issue we are engaged in what is now known as a *reverie.* This is our spontaneous and favorite kind of thinking. We allow our ideas to take their own course and this course is determined by our hopes and fears, our spontaneous desires, their fulfillment or frustration; by our likes and dislikes, our loves and hates and resentments. There is nothing else anything like so interesting to ourselves as ourselves. All thought that is not more or less laboriously controlled and directed will inevitably circle about the beloved Ego. It is amusing and pathetic to observe this tendency in ourselves and in others. We learn politely and generously to overlook this truth, but if we dare to think of it, it blazes forth like the noontide sun.

The reverie or "free association of ideas" has of late become the subject of scientific research. While investigators are not yet agreed on the results, or at least on the proper interpretation to be given to them, there can be no doubt that our reveries form the chief index to our fundamental character. They are a reflection of our nature as modified by often hidden and forgotten experiences. We need not go into the matter further here, for it is only necessary to observe that the reverie is at all times a potent and in many cases an omnipotent rival to every other kind of thinking. It doubtless influences all our speculations in its persistent tendency to self-magnification and self-justification, which are its chief preoccupations, but it is the last thing to make directly or indirectly for honest increase of knowledge.[1] Philosophers usually talk as if such thinking did not exist or were in some way negligible. This is what makes their speculations so unreal and often worthless.

The reverie, as any of us can see for himself, is frequently broken and interrupted by the necessity of a second kind of thinking. We have to make practical decisions. Shall we write a letter or no? Shall we take the subway or a bus? Shall we have dinner at seven or half past? Shall we buy

---

[1] The poet-clergyman, John Donne, who lived in the time of James I, has given a beautifully honest picture of the doings of a saint's mind: "I throw myself down in my chamber and call in and invite God and His angels thither, and when they are there I neglect God and His angels for the noise of a fly, for the rattling of a coach, for the whining of a door. I talk on in the same posture of praying, eyes lifted up, knees bowed down, as though I prayed to God, and if God or His angels should ask me when I thought last of God in that prayer I cannot tell. Sometimes I find that I had forgot what I was about, but when I began to forget it I cannot tell. A memory of yesterday's pleasures, a fear of to-morrow's dangers, a straw under my knee, a noise in mine ear, a light in mine eye, an anything, a nothing, a fancy, a chimera in my brain troubles me in my prayer."—Quoted by Robert Lynd, *The Art of Letters,* pp. 46–47.

U.S. Rubber or a Liberty Bond? Decisions are easily distinguishable from the free flow of the reverie. Sometimes they demand a good deal of careful pondering and the recollection of pertinent facts; often, however, they are made impulsively. They are a more difficult and laborious thing than the reverie, and we resent having to "make up our mind" when we are tired, or absorbed in a congenial reverie. Weighing a decision, it should be noted, does not necessarily add anything to our knowledge, although we may, of course, seek further information before making it.

2. Rationalizing

A third kind of thinking is stimulated when anyone questions our belief and opinions. We sometimes find ourselves changing our minds without any resistance or heavy emotion, but if we are told that we are wrong we resent the imputation and harden our hearts. We are incredibly heedless in the formation of our beliefs, but find ourselves filled with an illicit passion for them when anyone proposes to rob us of their companionship. It is obviously not the ideas themselves that are dear to us, but our self-esteem, which is threatened. We are by nature stubbornly pledged to defend our own from attack, whether it be our person, our family, our property, or our opinion. A United States Senator once remarked to a friend of mine that God Almighty could not make him change his mind on our Latin-America policy. We may surrender, but rarely confess ourselves vanquished. In the intellectual world at least peace is without victory.

Few of us take the pains to study the origin of our cherished convictions; indeed, we have a natural repugnance to so doing. We like to continue to believe what we have been accustomed to accept as true, and the resentment aroused when doubt is cast upon any of our assumptions leads us to seek every manner of excuse for clinging to them. *The result is that most of our so-called reasoning consists in finding arguments for going on believing as we already do.*

I remember years ago attending a public dinner to which the Governor of the state was bidden. The chairman explained that His Excellency could not be present for certain "good" reasons; what the "real" reasons were the presiding officer said he would leave us to conjecture. This distinction between "good" and "real" reasons is one of the most clarifying and essential in the whole realm of thought. We can readily give what seem to us "good" reasons for being a Catholic or a Mason, a Republican or a Democrat, an adherent or opponent of the League of Nations. But the "real" reasons are usually on quite a different plane. Of course the importance of this distinction is popularly, if somewhat obscurely, recognized. The Baptist missionary is ready enough to see that the Buddhist is not such because his doctrines would bear careful inspection, but because he happened to be born in a Buddhist family in Tokio. But it would be treason to his faith to acknowledge that his own partiality for certain doctrines is due to the fact that his mother was a member of the First Baptist church of Oak Ridge. A savage can give all sorts of reasons for his belief that it is dangerous to step on a man's shadow, and a newspaper editor can advance plenty of arguments against the Bolsheviki. But neither of them may realize why he happens to be defending his particular opinion.

The "real" reasons for our beliefs are concealed from ourselves as well as from others. As we grow up we simply adopt the ideas presented to us in regard to such matters as religion, family relations, property, business, our country, and the state. We unconsciously absorb them from our environment. They are persistently whispered in our ear by the group in which we happen to live. Moreover, as Mr. Trotter has pointed out, these judgments, being the product of suggestion and not of reasoning, have the quality of perfect obviousness, so that to question them

> . . . is to the believer to carry skepticism to an insane degree, and will be met by contempt, disapproval, or condemnation, according to the nature of the belief in question. When, therefore, we find ourselves entertaining an opinion about the basis of which there is a quality of feeling which tells us that to inquire into it would be absurd, obviously unnecessary, unprofitable, undesirable, bad form, or wicked, we may know that that opinion is a nonrational one, and probably, therefore, founded upon inadequate evidence.[2]

Opinions, on the other hand, which are the result of experience or of honest reasoning do not have this quality of "primary certitude." I remember when as a youth I heard a group of business men discussing the question of the immortality of the soul, I was outraged by the sentiment of doubt expressed by one of the party. As I look back now I see that I had at the time no interest in the matter, and certainly no least argument to urge in favor of the belief in which I had been reared. But neither my personal indifference to the issue, nor the fact that I had previously given it no attention, served to prevent an angry resentment when I heard *my* ideas questioned.

This spontaneous and loyal support of our preconceptions—this process of finding "good" reasons to justify our routine beliefs—is known to modern psychologists as "rationalizing"—clearly only a new name for a very ancient thing. Our "good" reasons ordinarily have no value in promoting honest enlightenment, because, no matter how solemnly they may be marshaled, they are at bottom the result of personal preference or prejudice, and not of an honest desire to seek or accept new knowledge.

In our reveries we are frequently engaged in self-justification, for we cannot bear to think ourselves wrong, and yet have constant illustrations of our weaknesses and mistakes. So we spend much time finding fault with

---

[2] *Instincts of the Herd,* p. 44.

circumstances and the conduct of others, and shifting on to them with great ingenuity the onus of our own failures and disappointments. *Rationalizing is the self-exculpation which occurs when we feel ourselves, or our group, accused of misapprehension or error.*

The little word *my* is the most important one in all human affairs, and properly to reckon with it is the beginning of wisdom. It has the same force whether it is *my* dinner, *my* dog, and *my* house, or *my* faith, *my* country, and *my* God. We not only resent the imputation that our watch is wrong, or our car shabby, but that our conception of the canals of Mars, of the pronunciation of "Epictetus," of the medicinal value of salicine, or the date of Sargon I, subject to revision.

Philosophers, scholars, and men of science exhibit a common sensitiveness in all decisions in which their *amour propre* is involved. Thousands of argumentative works have been written to vent a grudge. However stately their reasoning, it may be nothing but rationalizing, stimulated by the most commonplace of all motives. A history of philosophy and theology could be written in terms of grouches, wounded pride, and aversions, and it would be far more instructive than the usual treatments of these themes. Sometimes, under Providence, the lowly impulse of resentment leads to great achievements. Milton wrote his treatise on divorce as a result of his troubles with his seventeen-year-old wife, and when he was accused of being the leading spirit in a new sect, the Divorcers, he wrote his noble *Areopagitica* to prove his right to say what he thought fit, and incidentally to establish the advantage of a free press in the promotion of Truth.

All mankind, high and low, thinks in all the ways which have been described. The reverie goes on all the time not only in the mind of the mill hand and the Broadway flapper, but equally in weighty judges and godly bishops. It has gone on in all the philosophers, scientists, poets, and theologians that have ever lived. Aristotle's most abstruse speculations were doubtless tempered by highly irrelevant reflections. He is reported to have had very thin legs and small eyes, for which he doubtless had to find excuses, and he was wont to indulge in very conspicuous dress and rings and was accustomed to arrange his hair carefully.[3] Diogenes the Cynic exhibited the impudence of a touchy soul. His tub was his distinction. Tennyson in beginning his "Maud" could not forget his chagrin over losing his patrimony years before as the result of an unhappy investment in the Patent Decorative Carving Company. These facts are not recalled here as a gratuitous disparagement of the truly great, but to insure a full realization of the tremendous competition which all really exacting thought has to face, even in the minds of the most highly endowed mortals.

[3]Diogenes Laertius, book v.

And now the astonishing and perturbing suspicion emerges that perhaps almost all that had passed for social science, political economy, politics, and ethics in the past may be brushed aside by future generations as mainly rationalizing. John Dewey has already reached this conclusion in regard to philosophy.[4] Veblen[5] and other writers have revealed the various unperceived presuppositions of the traditional political economy, and now comes an Italian sociologist, Vilfredo Pareto, who, in his huge treatise on general sociology, devotes hundreds of pages to substantiating a similar thesis affecting all the social sciences.[6] This conclusion may be ranked by students of a hundred years hence as one of the several great discoveries of our age. It is by no means fully worked out, and it is so opposed to nature that it will be very slowly accepted by the great mass of those who consider themselves thoughtful. As a historical student I am personally fully reconciled to this newer view. Indeed, it seems to me inevitable that just as the various sciences of nature were, before the opening of the seventeenth century, largely masses of rationalizations to suit the religious sentiments of the period, so the social sciences have continued even to our own day to be rationalizations of uncritically accepted beliefs and customs.

It will become apparent as we proceed that the fact that an idea is ancient and that it has been widely received is no argument in its favor, but should immediately suggest the necessity of carefully testing it as a probable instance of rationalization.

3. How Creative Thought Transforms the World

This brings us to another kind of thought which can fairly easily be distinguished from the three kinds described above. It has not the usual qualities of the reverie, for it does not hover about our personal complacencies and humiliations. It is not made up of the homely decisions forced upon us by everyday needs, when we review our little stock of existing information, consult our conventional preferences and obligations, and make a choice of action. It is not the defense of our own cherished beliefs and prejudices just because they are our own—mere plausible excuses for remaining of the same mind. On the contrary, it is that peculiar species of thought which leads us to *change* our mind.

It is this kind of thought that has raised man from his pristine, subsavage ignorance and squalor to the degree of knowledge and comfort which he now possesses. On his capacity to continue and greatly extend this kind of thinking depends his chance of groping his way out of the plight

---

[4] *Reconstruction in Philosophy.*

[5] *The Place of Science in Modern Civilization.*

[6] *Traité de Sociologie Générale, passim.* The author's term *"dérivations"* seems to be his precise way of expressing what we have called the "good" reasons, and his *"résidus"* correspond to the "real" reasons. He well says, *"L'homme éprouve le besoin de raisonner, et en outre d'étendre un voile sur ses instincts et sur ses sentiments"*—hence, rationalization. (P. 788.) His aim is to reduce sociology to the "real" reasons. (P. 791.)

in which the most highly civilized peoples of the world now find themselves. In the past this type of thinking has been called Reason. But so many misapprehensions have grown up around the word that some of us have become very suspicious of it. I suggest, therefore, that we substitute a recent name and speak of "creative thought" rather than of Reason. *For this kind of meditation begets knowledge, and knowledge is really creative inasmuch as it makes things look different from what they seemed before and may indeed work for their reconstruction.*

In certain moods some of us realize that we are observing things or making reflections with a seeming disregard of our personal preoccupations. We are not preening or defending ourselves; we are not faced by the necessity of any practical decision, nor are we apologizing for believing this or that. We are just wondering and looking and mayhap seeing what we never perceived before.

Curiosity is as clear and definite as any of our urges. We wonder what is in a sealed telegram or in a letter in which some one else is absorbed, or what is being said in the telephone booth or in low conversation. This inquisitiveness is vastly stimulated by jealousy, suspicion, or any hint that we ourselves are directly or indirectly involved. But there appears to be a fair amount of personal interest in other people's affairs even when they do not concern us except as a mystery to be unraveled or a tale to be told. The reports of a divorce suit will have "news value" for many weeks. They constitute a story, like a novel or play or moving picture. This is not an example of pure curiosity, however, since we readily identify ourselves with others, and their joys and despair then become our own.

We also take note of, or "observe," as Sherlock Holmes says, things which have nothing to do with our personal interests and make no personal appeal either direct or by way of sympathy. This is what Veblen so well calls "idle curiosity." And it is usually idle enough. Some of us when we face the line of people opposite us in a subway train impulsively consider them in detail and engage in rapid inferences and form theories in regard to them. On entering a room there are those who will perceive at a glance the degree of preciousness of the rugs, the character of the pictures, and the personality revealed by the books. But there are many, it would seem, who are so absorbed in their personal reverie or in some definite purpose that they have no bright-eyed energy for idle curiosity. The tendency to miscellaneous observation we come by honestly enough, for we note it in many of our animal relatives.

Veblen, however, uses the term "idle curiosity" somewhat ironically, as is his wont. It is idle only to those who fail to realize that it may be a very rare and indispensable thing from which almost all distinguished human achievement proceeds, since it may lead to systematic examination and seeking for things hitherto undiscovered. For research is but diligent search which enjoys the high flavor of primitive hunting. Occasionally and fitfully idle curiosity thus leads to creative thought, which alters and broadens our own views and aspirations and may in turn, under highly favorable circumstances, affect the views and lives of others, even for generations to follow. An example or two will make this unique human process clear.

Galileo was a thoughtful youth and doubtless carried on a rich and varied reverie. He had artistic ability and might have turned out to be a musician or painter. When he had dwelt among the monks at Valambrosa he had been tempted to lead the life of a religious. As a boy he busied himself with toy machines and he inherited a fondness for mathematics. All these facts are of record. We may safely assume also that, along with many other subjects of contemplation, the Pisan maidens found a vivid place in his thoughts.

One day when seventeen years old he wandered into the cathedral of his native town. In the midst of his reverie he looked up at the lamps hanging by long chains from the high ceiling of the church. Then something very difficult to explain occurred. He found himself no longer thinking of the building, worshipers, or the services; of his artistic or religious interests; of his reluctance to become a physician as his father wished. He forgot the question of a career and even the *graziosissime donne.* As he watched the swinging lamps he was suddenly wondering if mayhap their oscillations, whether long or short, did not occupy the same time. Then he tested his hypothesis by counting his pulse, for that was the only timepiece he had with him.

This observation, however remarkable in itself, was not enough to produce a really creative thought. Others may have noticed the same thing and yet nothing came of it. Most of our observations have no assignable results. Galileo may have seen that the warts on a peasant's face formed a perfect isosceles triangle, or he may have noticed with boyish glee that just as the officiating priest was uttering the solemn words, *ecce agnus Dei,* a fly lit on the end of his nose. To be really creative, ideas have to be worked up and then "put over," so that they become a part of man's social heritage. The highly accurate pendulum clock was one of the later results of Galileo's discovery. He himself was led to reconsider and successfully to refute the old notions of falling bodies. It remained for Newton to prove that the moon was falling, and presumably all the heavenly bodies. This quite upset all the consecrated views of the heavens as managed by angelic engineers. The universality of the laws of gravitation stimulated the attempt to seek other and equally important natural laws and cast grave doubts on the miracles in which mankind had hitherto believed. In short, those who dared to include in their thought the discoveries of Galileo and his successors found themselves in a new earth surrounded by new heavens.

On the 28th of October, 1831, two hundred and fifty years after Galileo had noticed the isochronous vibrations of the lamps, creative thought and its currency had so far increased that Faraday was wondering what would happen if he mounted a disk of copper between the poles of a horseshoe magnet. As the disk revolved an electric current was produced. This would doubtless have seemed the idlest kind of an experiment to the stanch business men of the time, who, it happened, were just then denouncing the child-labor bills in their anxiety to avail themselves to the full of the results of earlier idle curiosity. But should the dynamos and motors which have come into being as the outcome of Faraday's experiment be stopped this evening, the business man of to-day, agitated over labor troubles, might, as he trudged home past lines of "dead" cars, through dark streets to an unlighted house, engage in a little creative thought of his own and perceive that he and his laborers would have no modern factories and mines to quarrel about had it not been for the strange practical effects of the idle curiosity of scientists, inventors, and engineers.

The examples of creative intelligence given above belong to the realm of modern scientific achievement, which furnishes the most striking instances of the effects of scrupulous, objective thinking. But there are, of course, other great realms in which the recording and embodiment of acute observation and insight have wrought themselves into the higher life of man. The great poets and dramatists and our modern story-tellers have found themselves engaged in productive reveries, noting and artistically presenting their discoveries for the delight and instruction of those who have the ability to appreciate them.

The process by which a fresh and original poem or drama comes into being is doubtless analogous to that which originates and elaborates so-called scientific discoveries; but there is clearly a temperamental difference. The genesis and advance of painting, sculpture, and music offer still other problems. We really as yet know shockingly little about these matters, and indeed very few people have the least curiosity about them.[7] Nevertheless, creative intelligence in its various forms and activities is what makes man. Were it not for its slow, painful, and constantly discouraged operations through the ages man would be no more than a species of primate living on seeds, fruit, roots, and uncooked flesh, and wandering naked through the woods and over the plains like a chimpanzee.

The origin and progress and future promotion of civilization are ill understood and misconceived. These should be made the chief theme of education, but much hard work is necessary before we can reconstruct our ideas of man and his capacities and free ourselves from innumerable persistent misapprehensions. There have been obstructionists in all times, not merely the lethargic masses, but the moralists, the rationalizing theologians, and most of the philosophers, all busily if unconsciously

---

[7]Recently a re-examination of creative thought has begun as a result of new knowledge which discredits many of the notions formerly held about "reason." See, for example, *Creative Intelligence,* by a group of American philosophic thinkers; John Dewey, *Essays in Experimental Logic* (both pretty hard books); and Veblen, *The Place of Science in Modern Civilization.* Easier than these and very stimulating are Dewey, *Reconstruction in Philosophy,* and Woodworth, *Dynamic Psychology.*

engaged in ratifying existing ignorance and mistakes and discouraging creative thought. Naturally, those who reassure us seem worthy of honor and respect. Equally naturally those who puzzle us with disturbing criticisms and invite us to change our ways are objects of suspicion and readily discredited. Our personal discontent does not ordinarily extend to any critical questioning of the general situation in which we find ourselves. In every age the prevailing conditions of civilization have appeared quite natural and inevitable to those who grew up in them. The cow asks no questions as to how it happens to have a dry stall and a supply of hay. The kitten laps its warm milk from a china saucer, without knowing anything about porcelain; the dog nestles in the corner of a divan with no sense of obligation to the inventors of upholstery and the manufacturers of down pillows. So we humans accept our breakfasts, our trains and telephones and orchestras and movies, our national Constitution, our moral code and standards of manners, with the simplicity and innocence of a pet rabbit. We have absolutely inexhaustible capacities for appropriating what others do for us with no thought of a "thank you." We do not feel called upon to make any least contribution to the merry game ourselves. Indeed, we are usually quite unaware that a game is being played at all.

We have now examined the various classes of thinking which we can readily observe in ourselves and which we have plenty of reasons to believe go on, and always have been going on, in our fellow-men. We can sometimes get quite pure and sparkling examples of all four kinds, but commonly they are so confused and intermingled in our reverie as not to be readily distinguishable. The reverie is a reflection of our longings, exultations, and complacencies, our fears, suspicions, and disappointments. We are chiefly engaged in struggling to maintain our self-respect and in asserting that supremacy which we all crave and which seems to us our natural prerogative. It is not strange, but rather quite inevitable, that our beliefs about what is true and false, good and bad, right and wrong, should be mixed up with the reverie and be influenced by the same considerations which determine its character and course. We resent criticisms of our views exactly as we do of anything else connected with ourselves. Our notions of life and its ideals seem to us to be *our own* and as such necessarily true and right, to be defended at all costs.

We very rarely consider, however, the process by which we gained our convictions. If we did so, we could hardly fail to see that there was usually little ground for our confidence in them. Here and there, in this department of knowledge or that, some one of us might make a fair claim to have taken some trouble to get correct ideas of, let us say, the situation in Russia, the sources of our food supply, the origin of the Constitution, the revision of the tariff, the policy of the Holy Roman Apostolic Church, modern business organization, trade unions, birth control, socialism, the League of Nations, the excess-profits tax, preparedness, advertising in its social bearings; but only a very exceptional person would be entitled to opinions on all of even these few matters. And yet most of us have opinions on all these, and on many other questions of equal importance, of which we may know even less. We feel compelled, as self-respecting persons, to take sides when they come up for discussion. We even surprise ourselves by our omniscience. Without taking thought we see in a flash that it is most righteous and expedient to discourage birth control by legislative enactment, or that one who decries intervention in Mexico is clearly wrong, or that big advertising is essential to big business and that big business is the pride of the land. As godlike beings why should we not rejoice in our omniscience?

It is clear, in any case, that our convictions on important matters are not the result of knowledge or critical thought, nor, it may be added, are they often dictated by supposed self-interest. Most of them are *pure prejudices* in the proper sense of that word. We do not form them ourselves. They are the whisperings of "the voice of the herd." We have in the last analysis no responsibility for them and need assume none. They are not really our own ideas, but those of others no more well informed or inspired than ourselves, who have got them in the same careless and humiliating manner as we. It should be our pride to revise our ideas and not to adhere to what passes for respectable opinion, for such opinion can frequently be shown to be not respectable at all. We should, in view of the considerations that have been mentioned, resent our supine credulity. As an English writer has remarked:

"If we feared the entertaining of an unverifiable opinion with the warmth with which we fear using the wrong implement at the dinner table, if the thought of holding a prejudice disgusted us as does a foul disease, then the dangers of man's suggestibility would be turned into advantages."[8]

The purpose of this essay is to set forth briefly the way in which the notions of the herd have been accumulated. This seems to me the best, easiest, and least invidious educational device for cultivating a proper distrust for the older notions on which we still continue to rely.

The "real" reasons, which explain how it is we happen to hold a particular belief, are chiefly historical. Our most important opinions—those, for example, having to do with traditional, religious, and moral convictions, property rights, patriotism, national honor, the state, and indeed all the assumed foundations of society—are, as I have already suggested, rarely the result of reasoned consideration, but of unthinking absorption from the social environment in which we live. Consequently, they have about them a quality of "elemental certitude," and we especially resent doubt or criticism cast upon them. So long, however, as we revere the whisperings of the herd, we are obviously unable to examine them dispassionately and to consider to what extent they are suited to the novel conditions and social exigencies in which we find ourselves to-day.

---

[8]Trotter, *op. cit.*, p. 45. The first part of this little volume is excellent.

The "real" reasons for our beliefs, by making clear their origins and history, can do much to dissipate this emotional blockade and rid us of our prejudices and preconceptions. Once this is done and we come critically to examine our traditional beliefs, we may well find some of them sustained by experience and honest reasoning, while others must be revised to meet new conditions and our more extended knowledge. But only after we have undertaken such a critical examination in the light of experience and modern knowledge, freed from any feeling of "primary certitude," can we claim that the "good" are also the "real" reasons for our opinions.

I do not flatter myself that this general show-up of man's thought through the ages will cure myself or others of carelessness in adopting ideas, or of unseemly heat in defending them just because we have adopted them. But if the considerations which I propose to recall are really incorporated into our thinking and are permitted to establish our general outlook on human affairs, they will do much to relieve the imaginary obligation we feel in regard to traditional sentiments and ideals. Few of us are capable of engaging in creative thought, but some of us can at least come to distinguish it from other and inferior kinds of thought and accord to it the esteem that it merits as the greatest treasure of the past and the only hope of the future.

ALDOUS HUXLEY

Aldous Leonard Huxley (1894–1963), one of the most well-known of modern English novelists and essayists, came from a family celebrated for intellectual achievement. He was the son of Leonard Huxley, author and editor; grandson of the naturalist Thomas Huxley; and grandnephew of Matthew Arnold. His brother Sir Julian is a distinguished biologist and his half-brother David won the 1963 Nobel Prize in physiology. Huxley studied at Eton and Oxford, despite a serious eye disease which made him almost totally blind for three years. Reading with the aid of a magnifying glass, he graduated from Oxford in 1915 with honors in English literature. In 1919 he joined the staff of Athenaeum, *a London literary magazine, and then followed a steady production of writings in all genres.*

The success of his early novels allowed Huxley to move to Italy in 1923 and thence to France; in 1934 he traveled in the United States and finally settled in southern California, near Los Angeles. Here he continued to write books, articles, and an occasional movie scenario. He studied Vedanta and other Eastern religions and became interested in the effect of drugs on the mind.

Huxley wrote eleven novels, the best known being Antic Hay *(1923),* Point Counter Point *(1928),* Brave New World *(1932), and* After Many a Summer Dies the Swan *(1939). Huxley's reputation rests equally on his over twenty volumes of essays and belles-lettres, including* On the Margin *(1923),* Jesting Pilate *(1926),* Vulgarity in Literature *(1930),* Ends and Means *(1937),* The Perennial Philosophy *(1945),* Science, Liberty, and Peace *(1946),* The Doors of Perception *(1954), and* Literature and Science *(1963).*

Huxley's Brave New World *(1932) has turned out to be devastatingly accurate both as a piece of futuristic science fiction and as a satire on modern technological mass-produced civilization. It became so widely known that in 1958 Huxley could safely give the title* Brave New World Revisited *to a study of the progress of dehumanization and mental tyranny in the intervening quarter century. Both Huxley essays in the present volume are taken from* Brave New World Revisited. *The following is Chapter 5.*

Propaganda Under a Dictatorship

At his trial after the Second World War, Hitler's Minister for Armaments, Albert Speer, delivered a long speech in which, with remarkable acuteness, he described the Nazi tyranny and analyzed its methods. "Hitler's dictatorship," he said, "differed in one fundamental point from all its predecessors in history. It was the first dictatorship in the present period of modern technical development, a dictatorship which made complete use of all technical means for the domination of its own country. Through technical devices like the radio and the loud-speaker, eighty million people were deprived of independent thought. It was thereby possible to subject them to the will of one man. . . . Earlier dictators needed highly qualified assistants even at the lowest level—men who could think and act independently. The totalitarian system in the period of modern technical development can dispense with such men; thanks to modern methods of communication, it is possible to mechanize the lower leadership. As a result of this there has arisen the new type of the uncritical recipient of orders."

In the Brave New World of my prophetic fable technology had advanced far beyond the point it had reached in Hitler's day; consequently the recipients of orders were far less critical than their Nazi counterparts, far more obedient to the order-giving elite. Moreover, they had been genetically standardized and postnatally conditioned to perform their subordinate functions, and could therefore be depended upon to behave almost as predictably as machines. As we shall see in a later chapter, this conditioning of "the lower leadership" is already going on under the

Communist dictatorships. The Chinese and the Russians are not relying merely on the indirect effects of advancing technology; they are working directly on the psychophysical organisms of their lower leaders, subjecting minds and bodies to a system of ruthless and, from all accounts, highly effective conditioning. "Many a man," said Speer, "has been haunted by the nightmare that one day nations might be dominated by technical means. That nightmare was almost realized in Hitler's totalitarian system." Almost, but not quite. The Nazis did not have time—and perhaps did not have the intelligence and the necessary knowledge—to brainwash and condition their lower leadership. This, it may be, is one of the reasons why they failed.

Since Hitler's day the armory of technical devices at the disposal of the would-be dictator has been considerably enlarged. As well as the radio, the loud-speaker, the moving picture camera and the rotary press, the contemporary propagandist can make use of television to broadcast the image as well as the voice of his client, and can record both image and voice on spools of magnetic tape. Thanks to technological progress, Big Brother can now be almost as omnipresent as God. Nor is it only on the technical front that the hand of the would-be dictator has been strengthened. Since Hitler's day a great deal of work has been carried out in those fields of applied psychology and neurology which are the special province of the propagandist, the indoctrinator and the brainwasher. In the past these specialists in the art of changing people's minds were empiricists. By a method of trial and error they had worked out a number of techniques and procedures, which they used very effectively without, however, knowing precisely why they were effective. Today the art of mind-control is in process of becoming a science. The practitioners of this science know what they are doing and why. They are guided in their work by theories and hypotheses solidly established on a massive foundation of experimental evidence. Thanks to the new insights and the new techniques made possible by these insights, the nightmare that was "all but realized in Hitler's totalitarian system" may soon be completely realizable.

But before we discuss these new insights and techniques let us take a look at the nightmare that so nearly came true in Nazi Germany. What were the methods used by Hitler and Goebbels for "depriving eighty million people of independent thought and subjecting them to the will of one man"? And what was the theory of human nature upon which those terrifyingly successful methods were based? These questions can be answered, for the most part, in Hitler's own words. And what remarkably clear and astute words they are! When he writes about such vast abstractions as Race and History and Providence, Hitler is strictly unreadable. But when he writes about the German masses and the methods he used for dominating and directing them, his style changes. Nonsense gives place to sense, bombast to a hard-boiled and cynical lucidity. In his philosophical lucubrations Hitler was either cloudily daydreaming or reproducing other people's half-baked notions. In his comments on crowds and propaganda he was writing of things he knew by firsthand experience. In the words of his ablest biographer, Mr. Alan Bullock, "Hitler was the greatest demagogue in history." Those who add, "only a demagogue," fail to appreciate the nature of political power in an age of mass politics. As he himself said, "To be a leader means to be able to move the masses." Hitler's aim was first to move the masses and then, having pried them loose from their traditional loyalties and moralities, to impose upon them (with the hypnotized consent of the majority) a new authoritarian order of his own devising. "Hitler," wrote Hermann Rauschning in 1939, "has a deep respect for the Catholic church and the Jesuit order; not because of their Christian doctrine, but because of the 'machinery' they have elaborated and controlled, their hierarchical system, their extremely clever tactics, their knowledge of human nature and their wise use of human weaknesses in ruling over believers." Ecclesiasticism without Christianity, the discipline of a monastic rule, not for God's sake or in order to achieve personal salvation, but for the sake of the State and for the greater glory and power of the demagogue turned Leader—this was the goal toward which the systematic moving of the masses was to lead.

Let us see what Hitler thought of the masses he moved and how he did the moving. The first principle from which he started was a value judgment: the masses are utterly contemptible. They are incapable of abstract thinking and uninterested in any fact outside the circle of their immediate experience. Their behavior is determined, not by knowledge and reason, but by feelings and unconscious drives. It is in these drives and feelings that "the roots of their positive as well as their negative attitudes are implanted." To be successful a propagandist must learn how to manipulate these instincts and emotions. "The driving force which has brought about the most tremendous revolutions on this earth has never been a body of scientific teaching which has gained power over the masses, but always a devotion which has inspired them, and often a kind of hysteria which has urged them into action. Whoever wishes to win over the masses must know the key that will open the door of their hearts." . . . In post-Freudian jargon, of their unconscious.

Hitler made his strongest appeal to those members of the lower middle classes who had been ruined by the inflation of 1923, and then ruined all over again by the depression of 1929 and the following years. "The masses" of whom he speaks were these bewildered, frustrated and chronically anxious millions. To make them more masslike, more homogeneously subhuman, he assembled them, by the thousands and the tens of thousands, in vast halls and arenas, where individuals could lose their personal identity, even their elementary humanity, and be merged with the crowd. A man or woman makes direct contact with society in two ways: as a member of some familial, professional or religious group, or as a member of a crowd. Groups are capable of being as moral and intelligent as the individuals who form them; a crowd is chaotic, has no purpose of its own and is capable of anything except intelligent action and realistic thinking. Assembled in a crowd, people lose their powers of reasoning and their capacity for moral choice. Their suggestibility is increased to the point where they cease to have any judgment or will of their own. They become very excitable, they lose all sense of individual or collective responsibility, they are subject to sudden accesses of rage, enthusiasm and panic. In a word, a man in a crowd behaves as though he had swallowed a large dose of some powerful intoxicant. He is a victim of what I have called "herd-poisoning." Like alcohol, herd-poison is an active, extraverted drug. The crowd-intoxicated individual escapes from responsibility, intelligence and morality into a kind of frantic, animal mindlessness.

During his long career as an agitator, Hitler had studied the effects of herd-poison and had learned how to exploit them for his own purposes. He had discovered that the orator can appeal to those "hidden forces" which motivate men's actions, much more effectively than can the writer. Reading is a private, not a collective activity. The writer speaks only to individuals, sitting by themselves in a state of normal sobriety. The orator speaks to masses of individuals, already well primed with herd-poison. They are at his mercy and, if he knows his business, he can do what he likes with them. As an orator, Hitler knew his business supremely well. He was able, in his own words, "to follow the lead of the great mass in such a way that from the living emotion of his hearers the apt word which he needed would be suggested to him and in its turn this would go straight to the heart of his hearers." Otto Strasser called him a "loud-speaker, proclaiming the most secret desires, the least admissible instincts, the sufferings and personal revolts of a whole nation." Twenty years before Madison Avenue embarked upon "Motivational Research," Hitler was systematically exploring and exploiting the secret fears and hopes, the cravings, anxieties and frustrations of the German masses. It is by manipulating "hidden forces" that the advertising experts induce us to buy their wares—a toothpaste, a brand of cigarettes, a political candidate. And it is by appealing to the same hidden forces—and to others too dangerous for Madison Avenue to meddle with—that Hitler induced the German masses to buy themselves a Fuehrer, an insane philosophy and the Second World War.

Unlike the masses, intellectuals have a taste for rationality and an interest in facts. Their critical habit of mind makes them resistant to the kind of propaganda that works so well on the majority. Among the masses "instinct is supreme, and from instinct comes faith. . . . While the healthy common folk instinctively close their ranks to form a community of the people" (under a Leader, it goes without saying) "intellectuals run this way and that, like hens in a poultry yard. With them one cannot make history; they cannot be used as elements composing a community." Intellectuals are the kind of people who demand evidence and are shocked by logical inconsistencies and fallacies. They regard over-simplification as the original sin of the mind and have no use for the slogans, the unqualified assertions and sweeping generalizations which are the propagandist's stock in trade. "All effective propaganda," Hitler wrote, "must be confined to a few bare necessities and then must be expressed in a few stereotyped formulas." These stereotyped formulas must be constantly repeated, for "only constant repetition will finally succeed in imprinting an idea upon the memory of a crowd." Philosophy teaches us to feel uncertain about the things that seem to us self-evident. Propaganda, on the other hand, teaches us to accept as self-evident matters about which it would be reasonable to suspend our judgment or to feel doubt. The aim of the demagogue is to create social coherence under his own leadership. But, as Bertrand Russell has pointed out, "systems of dogma without empirical foundations, such as scholasticism, Marxism and fascism, have the advantage of producing a great deal of social coherence among their disciples." The demagogic propagandist must therefore be consistently dogmatic. All his statements are made without qualification. There are no grays in his picture of the world; everything is either diabolically black or celestially white. In Hitler's words, the propagandist should adopt "a systematically one-sided attitude towards every problem that has to be dealt with." He must never admit that he might be wrong or that people with a different point of view might be even partially right. Opponents should not be argued with; they should be attacked, shouted down, or, if they become too much of a nuisance, liquidated. The morally squeamish intellectual may be shocked by this kind of thing. But the masses are always convinced that "right is on the side of the active aggressor."

Such, then, was Hitler's opinion of humanity in the mass. It was a very low opinion. Was it also an incorrect opinion? The tree is known by its fruits, and a theory of human nature which inspired the kind of techniques that proved so horribly effective must contain at least an element of truth. Virtue and intelligence belong to human beings as individuals freely associating with other individuals in small groups. So do sin and stupidity. But the subhuman mindlessness to which the demagogue makes his appeal, the moral imbecility on which he relies when he goads his victims into action, are characteristic not of men and women as individuals, but of men and women in masses. Mindlessness and moral idiocy are not characteristically human attributes; they are symptoms of herd-poisoning. In all the world's higher religions, salvation and enlightenment are for individuals. The kingdom of heaven is within the mind of a person, not within the collective mindlessness of a crowd. Christ promised to be present where two or three are gathered together. He did not say anything about being present where thousands are intoxicating one another with herd-poison. Under the Nazis enormous numbers of people were compelled to spend an enormous amount of time marching in serried ranks from point A to point B and back again to point A. "This keeping of the whole population on the march seemed to be a senseless waste of time and energy. Only much later," adds Hermann Rauschning, "was there revealed in it a subtle intention based on a well-judged adjustment of ends and means. Marching diverts men's thoughts. Marching kills thought. Marching makes an end of individuality. Marching is the indispensable magic stroke performed in order to accustom the people to a mechanical, quasi-ritualistic activity until it becomes second nature."

From his point of view and at the level where he had chosen to do his dreadful work, Hitler was perfectly correct in his estimate of human nature. To those of us who look at men and women as individuals rather than as members of crowds, or of regimented collectives, he seems hideously wrong. In an age of accelerating over-population, of accelerating over-organization and ever more efficient means of mass communication, how can we preserve the integrity and reassert the value of the human individual? This is a question that can still be asked and perhaps effectively answered. A generation from now it may be too late to find an answer and perhaps impossible, in the stifling collective climate of that future time, even to ask the question.

MARY CAROLINE RICHARDS

Mary Caroline Richards was educated at Reed College and the University of California at Berkeley, where she received a Ph.D. in English in 1942. It was only then that "instead of taking up a college professorship," she turned to the art of pottery. She has been potter, poet, and teacher, and in Centering: In Pottery, Poetry and the Person *(1964), a provocative spiritual autobiography, she chronicles her need to think, to feel, and to make in order to be. "As we come into touch with other beings," she concludes, "we discover ourselves. This is precise. As I experience the presence of a tree or a field or a stream or another person or a tremor that runs through me with a force of its own, I know myself through that experience"; and at the same time "It is important to let the reins hang loose . . . to be well enough seated not to fall in the energetic release . . . to have a good balance, on center."*

The following excerpts are from Chapter 2 of the book.

Centering as Dialogue

Centering: that act which precedes all others on the potter's wheel. The bringing of the clay into a spinning, unwobbling pivot, which will then be free to take innumerable shapes as potter and clay press against each other. The firm, tender, sensitive pressure which yields as much as it asserts. It is like a handclasp between two living hands, receiving the greeting at the very moment that they give it. It is this speech between the hand and the clay that makes me think of dialogue. And it is a language far more interesting than the spoken vocabulary which tries to describe it, for it is spoken not by the tongue and lips but by the whole body, by the whole person, speaking and listening. And with listening too, it seems to me, it is not the ear that hears, it is not the physical organ that performs that act of inner receptivity. It is the total person who hears. Sometimes the skin seems to be the best listener, as it prickles and thrills, say to a sound or a silence; or the fantasy, the imagination: how it bursts into inner pictures as it listens and then responds by pressing its language, its forms, into the listening clay. To be open to what we hear, to be open in what we say . . .

. . .

I am a question-asker and a truth-seeker. I do not have much in the way of status in my life, nor security. I have been on quest, as it were, from the beginning. For a long time I thought there was something wrong with me: no ambition, no interest in tenure, always on the march, changing every seven years, from landscape to landscape. Certain elements were constant: the poetry, the desire for relationship, the sense of voyage. But lately I have developed also a sense of destination, or destiny. And a sense that if I am to be on quest, I must expect to live like a pilgrim; I must keep to the inner path. I must be able to be whoever I am.

For example, it seemed strange to me, as to others, that, having taken my Ph.D. in English, I should then in the middle of my life, instead of taking up a college professorship, turn to the art of pottery. During one period, when people asked me what I did, I was uncertain what to answer; I guessed I could say I taught English, wrote poetry, and made pottery. What was my occupation? I finally gave up and said "Person."

Having been imbued with the ordinary superstitions of American higher education, among which is the belief that something known as the life of the mind is more apt to take you where you want to go than any other kind of life, I busied myself with learning to practice logic, grammar, analysis, summary, generalization; I learned to make distinctions, to speculate, to purvey information. I was educated to be an intellectual of the verbal type. I might have been a philosophy major, a literature major, a language major. I was always a kind of oddball even in undergraduate circles, as I played kick-goal on the Reed College campus with President Dexter Keezer. And in graduate school, even more so. Examinations tended to make me merry, often seeming to me to be some kind of private game, some secret ritual compulsively played by the professors and the institution. I invariably became facetious in all the critical hours. All that solemnity for a few facts! I couldn't believe they were serious. But they were. I never quite understood it. But I loved the dream and the reality that lay behind those texts and in the souls of my teachers. I often felt like a kind of fraud, because I suspected that the knowledge I was acquiring and being rewarded for by academic diploma was wide wide of the truth I sensed to live somewhere, somewhere. I felt that I knew little of real importance; and when would the day come that others would realize it too, and I would be exposed? I have had dream after dream in which it turns out that I have not really completed my examinations for the doctorate and have them still to pass. And I sweat with anxiety. A sense of occupying a certain position without possessing the real thing: the deeper qualifications of wisdom and prophecy. But of course it was not the world who exposed me, it was my dreams. I do not know if I am a philosopher, but if philosophy is the love of wisdom, then I am a philosopher, because I love wisdom and that is why I love the crafts, because they are wise.

I became a teacher quite by chance. Liked it, found in education an image through which I could examine the possibilities of growth, of nourishment, of the experiences that lead to knowledge of nature and of self. It was a good trade to be in if you were a question-asker.

But the trouble was that though the work absorbed my mind, it used very little else. And I am by now convinced that wisdom is not the product of mental effort. Wisdom is a state of the total being, in which capacities for knowledge and for love, for survival and for death, for imagination, inspiration, intuition, for all the fabulous functioning of this human being who we are, come into a center with their forces, come into an experience of meaning that can voice itself as wise action. It is not enough to belong to a Society of Friends who believe in non-violence if, when frustrated, your body spontaneously contracts and shoots out its fist to knock another man down. It is in our bodies that redemption takes place. It is the physicality of the crafts that pleases me: I learn through my hands and my eyes and my skin what I could never learn through my brain. I develop a sense of life, of the world of earth, air, fire, and water—and wood, to add the fifth element according to Oriental alchemy—which could be developed in no other way. And if it is life I am fostering, I must maintain a kind of dialogue with the clay, listening, serving, interpreting as well as mastering. The union of our wills, like a marriage, it is a beautiful act, the act of centering and turning a pot on the potter's wheel; and the sexual images implicit in the forming of the cone and opening of the vessel are archetypal; likewise the give-and-take in the forming of a pot out of slabs, out of raw shards, out of coils; the union of natural intelligences: the intelligence of the clay, my intelligence, the intelligence of the tools, the intelligence of the fire.

You don't need me to tell you what education is. Everybody really knows that education goes on all the time everywhere all through our lives, and that it is the process of waking up to life. Jean Henri Fabre said something just about like that, I think. He said that to be educated was not to be taught but to wake up. It takes a heap of resolve to keep from going to sleep in the middle of the show. It's not that we want to sleep our lives away. It's that it requires certain kinds of energy, certain capacities for taking the world into our consciousness, certain real powers of body and soul to be a match for reality. That's why knowledge and consciousness are two quite different things. Knowledge is like a product we consume and store. All we need are good closets. By consciousness I mean a state of being "awake" to the world throughout our organism. This kind of consciousness requires not closets but an organism attuned to the finest perceptions and responses. It allows experience to breathe through it as light enters and changes a room. When knowledge is transformed into consciousness and into will, ah then we are on the high road indeed . . .

That which we consume, with a certain passivity, accepting it for the most part from our teachers, who in turn have accepted it from theirs, is like the food we eat. And food, in order to become energy, or will, is transformed entirely by the processes of metabolism. We do not become the food we eat. Rather the food turns into us. Similarly with knowledge, at best. Hopefully, we do not turn into encyclopedias or propaganda machines or electric brains. Our knowledge, if we allow it to be transformed within us, turns into capacity for life-serving human deeds. If knowledge does not turn into life, it makes cripples and madmen and dunces. It poisons just as food would if it stayed in the stomach and was never digested, and the waste products never thrown off.

It is dangerous to seek to possess knowledge, as if it could be stored. For one thing, it tends to make one impatient with ignorance, as people busy with money-seeking tend to be impatient with idlers. Though ignorance is the prime prerequisite for education, many teachers appear offended by it—or worse, contemptuous. Perhaps it is partly for this reason that many prefer to give advanced courses to select or "gifted" groups.

The possession of knowledge may create a materialism of its own. Knowledge becomes property. Teachers compete with each other for status, wealth, influence. A professor of education was speaking to friends of education in the county where I live, and she was urging pay raises as bait for hiring good teachers, "for after all, the standard of success is the salary check." Naturally in this climate professional educators are apt to quarrel over tactics and to engage in pressure politics, motivated by a desire to protect their security and to establish their views as ruling policy. In other words, education may be sacrificed to knowledge-ascommodity. Just as life is sometimes sacrificed to art-as-arrangement. The quest is abandoned. Instead, property is bought at the site of the last dragon killed, and a ruling class is formed out of the heroes. The knights grow fat and lazy and conceited and petulant. They parade in their armor on special occasions to bedazzle the populace. But in their hearts are terror and duplicity. And when difficult times come, they fall upon each other with their rusty axes and try to divide the world into those who know and those who don't. There is nothing to equal in bitterness and gall, childishness and spite, the intramural warfare of the academic community. Where is honor? Where is devotion? Where is responsibility of soul?

Such an atmosphere brought me gradually to imagine possible shortcomings in the educational system I had docilely trusted. Initiative and imagination seemed sorely lacking. Teachers seemed to apply to their students the same pressures that had crippled them. Most of us have been brain-washed to think that knowledge and security make the world go round. And if the world seems to be going round very poorly, we do not think of questioning deeply its education. The need for creative imagination in the intellectually trained person is drastic. Also the need for spontaneous human feeling.

Fashionable thinking may dominate the scientist and artist and scholar alike. For them, knowledge is the body of facts currently in fashion. Art is the image and compositional practice now in fashion. Since it is difficult to test the truth of most facts, faculty and students alike settle for "interesting," "original," and "self-consistent" theories. An ability to marshal and interpret "evidence" is highly esteemed, though evidence is often no more than opinions strongly held or secondary research. Very little stress is placed on developing powers of observation or on intuition. Thus, with primary experience held so at a distance, sensory life in particular, I find that my principal task in teaching adults is to win their trust. They tend to be overwhelmingly oriented to manipulation and to effect. It rarely occurs to them to work in a direct way with what they know and are. Their primary motivations are to please, to make a strong impression, to do either what is expected (if they are docile) or what is unexpected (if they are hostile). They assume that pretense and falsity are virtues. The whole thing sometimes seems like a massive confidence game.

Like other men, teachers tend to withhold themselves from naked personal contact. They tend to pin their hopes on jargon and style. And this, I have observed, is what many students learn from them: afraid to reveal themselves, burdened with shame and dismay and hopelessness, or expertise and cunning.

A theory much in vogue is that Western man is sick with sexual repression and pleasure anxiety. I believe that the squelching of the "person" and his spontaneous intuitive response to experience is as much at the root of our timidity, our falseness. Teachers and students who in the great school markets barter their learning for salaries and grades are hungry for respect, for personal relationship, for warmth. Unfortunately, they have the impression that these are extracurricular (like Newton's secondary qualities of color and so on)—and their capacity for balance between the life within and the world without shrinks or falters, or their desperation turns rank.

It is a sensitive matter, of course. I am not going to all these words merely to insult the spirit of true research. But my life as a teacher and as a member of the human community advises me that education may estrange us from life-commitment as well as bind us firmly within it. There are all kinds of things to learn, and we had best learn them all. One of the reasons formal education is in danger today is that a sense of work is split off from human earnestness. How may this split be healed? Working with our materials as artist-craftsmen may help to engender a new health here.

An act of the self, that's what one must make. An act of the self, from me to you. From center to center. We must mean what we say, from our innermost heart to the outermost galaxy. Otherwise we are lost and dizzy in a maze of reflections. We carry light within us. There is no need merely to reflect. Others carry light within them. These lights must wake to each other. My face is real. Yours is. Let us find our way to our initiative.

For must we not show ourselves to each other, and will we not know then who are the teachers and who are the students? Do we not all learn from one another? My students at City College are worldly-wise and naïve as lambs. I am sophisticated and uninformed. We make a good combination. They have never heard of e.e. cummings, who lived in their city, nor of the New York painters. They do not know that there are free art galleries where they may see the latest works of modern artists. They do not know very much about contemporary "culture." But they know well the life of the subway, the office, the factory, the union hall, the hassle for employment; they know what they did in the war or in their escape from Hungary or Germany, or in occupied France, or Israel. They know what it is like to be black in America. They are patient with my obtuseness, they check my too quick judgments, my sarcasm which is unperceptive. I help them to unmask, to be openly as tender and hopeful and generous as they inwardly are. I help them to open themselves to knowledge. They help me to open myself to life. We are equal in courage.

Must weakness be concealed in order that respect be won? Must love and fervor be concealed? Must we pretend to fearlessness? and certainty? Surely education should equip us to know what to fear and what to be uncertain of. Surely it should equip us in personal honor.

Must. Should. Convenient words! Exhortations meant to loosen the grip of congealed behavior ... Perhaps these perceptions are not the proper work of intellect, but of some other faculty deeply neglected in our education. In any case, at a critical moment in life my hunger for nakedness and realism and nobility turned to the clay of earth itself, and to water and fire.

I took up pottery also, in a sense, by chance. Unforeseen opportunity joined with interest and readiness. Like teaching, not a consciously sought but surely a destined union. For the materials and processes of pottery spoke to me of cosmic presences and transformations quite as surely as the pots themselves enchanted me. Experiences of the plastic clay and the firing of the ware carried more than commonplace values. Joy resonated deep within me, and it has stirred these thoughts only slowly to the surface. I have come to feel that we live in a universe of spirit, which materializes and de-materializes grandly; all things seem to me to live, and all acts to contain meaning deeper than matter-of-fact; and the things we do with deepest love and interest compel us by the spiritual forces which dwell in them. This seems to me to be a dialogue of the visible and the invisible to which our ears are attuned.

There was, first of all, something in the nature of the clay itself. You can do very many things with it, push this way and pull that, squeeze and roll and attach and pinch and hollow and pile. But you can't do everything with it. You can go only so far, and then the clay resists. To know ourselves by our resistances—this is a thought first expressed to me by the poet Charles Olson.

And so it is with persons. You can do very many things with us: push us together and pull us apart and squeeze us and roll us flat, empty us out and fill us up. You can surround us with influences, but there comes a point when you can do no more. The person resists, in one way or another (if it is only by collapsing, like the clay). His own will becomes active.

This is a wonderful moment, when one feels his will become active, come as a force into the total assemblage and dynamic intercourse and interpenetration of will impulses. When one stands like a natural substance, plastic but with one's own character written into the formula, ah then one feels oneself part of the world, taking one's shape with its help —but a shape only one's own freedom can create.

And the centering of the clay, of which I have spoken. The opening of the form. And the firing of the pot. This experience has deep psychic reverberations: how the pot, which was originally plastic, sets into dry clay, brittle and fragile, and then by being heated to a certain temperature hardens into stone. By natural law as it were, it takes its final form. Ordeal by fire. Then, the form once taken, the pot may not last, the body may perish; but the inner form has been taken, and it cannot break in the same sense.

I, like everyone I know, am instinctively motivated toward symbols of wholeness. What is a simpler, more natural one than the pot fired? Wholeness may be thought of as a kind of inner equilibrium, in which all our capacities have been brought into functioning as an organism. The potencies of the whole organism flow into the gestures of any part. And the sensation in any part reverberates throughout the soul. The unconscious and conscious levels of being can work together at the tasks of life, conveying messages to each other, assimilating one another. In wholeness I sense an integration of those characteristics which are uniquely ME and those interests which I share with the rest of mankind. As for example any bowl is symbolic of an archetypal circular form, which I share with all, but which *I* make and which therefore contains those very qualities of myself which are active in the making. I believe that pots have the smell of the person who makes them: a smell of tenderness, of vanity or ambition, of ease and naturalness, of petulance, uncertainty, callousness, fussiness, playfulness, solemnity, exuberance, absent-mindedness. The pot gives off something. It gives off its innerness, that which it holds but which cannot be seen.

In pottery, by developing sensitivity in manipulating natural materials by hand, I found a wisdom which had died out of the concepts I learned in the university: abstractions, mineralized and dead; while the minerals themselves were alive with energy and meaning. The life I found in the craft helped to bring to a new birth my ideals in education. Some secret center became vitalized in those hours of silent practice in the arts of transformation.

The experience of centering was one I particularly sought because I thought of myself as dispersed, interested in too many things. I envied people who were "single-minded," who had one powerful talent and who knew when they got up in the morning what it was they had to do. Whereas I, wherever I turned, felt the enchantment: to the window for the sweetness of the air; to the door for the passing figures; to the teapot, the typewriter, the knitting needles, the pets, the pottery, the newspaper, the telephone. Wherever I looked, I could have lived.

It took me half my life to come to believe I was OK even if I did love experience in a loose and undiscriminating way and did not know for sure the difference between good and bad. My struggles to accept my nature were the struggles of centering. I found myself at odds with the propaganda of our times. One is supposed to be either an artist or a homemaker, by one popular superstition. Either a teacher or a poet, by a theory which says that poetry must not sermonize. Either a craftsman or an intellectual, by a snobbism which claims either hand or head as the seat of true power. One is supposed to concentrate and not to spread oneself thin, as the jargon goes. And this is a jargon spoken by a cultural leadership from which it takes time to win one's freedom, if one is not lucky enough to have been born free. Finally, I hit upon an image: a seed-sower. Not to worry about which seeds sprout. But to give them as my gift in good faith.

But in spite of my self-acceptance, I still clung to a concept of purity which was chaste and aloof from the fellowship of man, and had yet to center the image of a pure heart in whose bright warm streams the world is invited to bathe. A heart who can be touched and who stirs in response, bringing the whole body into an act of greeting.

Well then, I became a potter.

. . .

RALPH WALDO EMERSON

*Emerson (1803–1882) is one of the greatest figures in American thought
and letters. He spent his childhood in Boston and was trained at Harvard
to be a Unitarian minister in the family tradition. Beset by doubts, he
resigned from the ministry in 1832 and took up a career of writing and
lecturing, during which he continued to work out his transcendentalist
philosophy and his ethical doctrine of self-reliance. The present essay was
an address delivered to the Phi Beta Kappa chapter at Harvard on August
31, 1837. Its vehement oratorical quality, the memorableness of single
phrases, are typical of Emerson, whose style inherits much from the
tradition of the New England sermon. Oliver Wendell Holmes called this
essay "our intellectual Declaration of Independence." Its appeal to
"literary nationalism" (here somewhat muffled by our omission of the final
fifth of the essay) is perhaps less important than its recording of a stage in
the struggle of a first-class man and thinker to find a way of life that
could be pursued with self-reliance and integrity.*

The American Scholar

MR. PRESIDENT AND GENTLEMEN:

I greet you on the recommencement of our literary year. Our anniversary
is one of hope, and, perhaps, not enough of labor. We do not meet for
games of strength or skill, for the recitation of histories, tragedies, and
odes, like the ancient Greeks; for parliaments of love and poesy, like the
Troubadours; nor for the advancement of science, like our contemporaries in the British and European capitals. Thus far, our holiday has been
simply a friendly sign of the survival of the love of letters amongst a
people too busy to give to letters any more. As such it is precious as the
sign of an indestructible instinct. Perhaps the time is already come when
it ought to be, and will be, something else; when the sluggard intellect
of this continent will look from under its iron lids and fill the postponed
expectation of the world with something better than the exertions of
mechanical skill. Our day of dependence, our long apprenticeship to the
learning of other lands, draws to a close. The millions that around us are
rushing into life, cannot always be fed on the sere remains of foreign
harvests. Events, actions arise, that must be sung, that will sing themselves. Who can doubt that poetry will revive and lead in a new age,
as the star in the constellation Harp, which now flames in our zenith, as-

tronomers announce, shall one day be the pole-star for a thousand years?

In this hope I accept the topic which not only usage but the nature of our association seem to prescribe to this day,—the AMERICAN SCHOLAR. Year by year we come up hither to read one more chapter of his biography. Let us inquire what light new days and events have thrown on his character and his hopes.

It is one of those fables which out of an unknown antiquity convey an unlooked-for wisdom, that the gods, in the beginning, divided Man into men, that he might be more helpful to himself; just as the hand was divided into fingers, the better to answer its end.

The old fable covers a doctrine ever new and sublime; that there is One Man,—present to all particular men only partially, or through one faculty; and that you must take the whole society to find the whole man. Man is not a farmer, or a professor, or an engineer, but he is all. Man is priest, and scholar, and statesman, and producer, and soldier. In the *divided* or social state these functions are parcelled out to individuals, each of whom aims to do his stint of the joint work, whilst each other performs his. The fable implies that the individual, to possess himself, must sometimes return from his own labor to embrace all the other laborers. But, unfortunately, this original unit, this fountain of power, has been so distributed to multitudes, has been so minutely subdivided and peddled out, that it is spilled into drops, and cannot be gathered. The state of society is one in which the members have suffered amputation from the trunk, and strut about, so many walking monsters,—a good finger, a neck, a stomach, an elbow, but never a man.

Man is thus metamorphosed into a thing, into many things. The planter, who is Man sent out into the field to gather food, is seldom cheered by any idea of the true dignity of his ministry. He sees his bushel and his cart, and nothing beyond, and sinks into the farmer, instead of Man on the farm. The tradesman scarcely ever gives an ideal worth to his work, but is ridden by the routine of his craft, and the soul is subject to dollars. The priest becomes a form; the attorney a statute-book; the mechanic a machine; the sailor a rope of the ship.

In this distribution of functions the scholar is the delegated intellect. In the right state he is *Man Thinking.* In the degenerate state, when the victim of society, he tends to become a mere thinker, or still worse, the parrot of other men's thinking.

In this view of him, as Man Thinking, the theory of his office is contained. Him Nature solicits with all her placid, all her monitory pictures; him the past instructs; him the future invites. Is not indeed every man a student, and do not all things exist for the student's behoof? And, finally, is not the true scholar the only true master? But the old oracle said, "All things have two handles: beware of the wrong one." In life, too often, the scholar errs with mankind and forfeits his privilege. Let us see him in his school, and consider him in reference to the main influences he receives.

I. The first in time and the first in importance of the influences upon the mind is that of nature. Every day, the sun; and, after sunset, Night and her stars. Ever the winds blow, ever the grass grows. Every day, men and women, conversing—beholding and beholden. The scholar is he of all men whom this spectacle most engages. He must settle its value in his mind. What is nature to him? There is never a beginning, there is never an end, to the inexplicable continuity of this web of God, but always circular power returning into itself. Therein it resembles his own spirit, whose beginning, whose ending, he never can find,—so entire, so boundless. Far too as her splendors shine, system on system shooting like rays, upward, downward, without centre, without circumference,—in the mass and in the particle, Nature hastens to render account of herself to the mind. Classification begins. To the young mind every thing is individual, stands by itself. By and by, it finds how to join two things and see in them one nature; then three, then three thousand; and so, tyrannized over by its own unifying instinct, it goes on tying things together, diminishing anomalies, discovering roots running under ground whereby contrary and remote things cohere and flower out from one stem. It presently learns that since the dawn of history there has been a constant accumulation and classifying of facts. But what is classification but the perceiving that these objects are not chaotic, and are not foreign, but have a law which is also a law of the human mind? The astronomer discovers that geometry, a pure abstraction of the human mind, is the measure of planetary motion. The chemist finds proportions and intelligible method throughout matter; and science is nothing but the finding of analogy, identity, in the most remote parts. The ambitious soul sits down before each refractory fact; one after another reduces all strange constitutions, all new powers, to their class and their law, and goes on forever to animate the last fibre of organization, the outskirts of nature, by insight.

Thus to him, to this schoolboy under the bending dome of day, is suggested that he and it proceed from one root; one is leaf and one is flower; relation, sympathy, stirring in every vein. And what is that root? Is not that the soul of his soul? A thought too bold; a dream too wild. Yet when this spiritual light shall have revealed the law of more earthly natures,—when he has learned to worship the soul, and to see that the natural philosophy that now is, is only the first gropings of its gigantic hand, he shall look forward to an ever expanding knowledge as to a becoming creator. He shall see that nature is the opposite of the soul, answering to it part for part. One is seal and one is print. Its beauty is the beauty of his own mind. Its laws are the laws of his own mind. Nature then becomes to him the measure of his attainments. So much of nature as he is ignorant of, so much of his own mind does he not yet possess. And, in fine, the ancient precept, "Know thyself," and the modern precept, "Study nature," become at last one maxim.

II. The next great influence into the spirit of the scholar is the mind of the Past,—in whatever form, whether of literature, of art, of institutions, that mind is inscribed. Books are the best type of the influence of the past, and perhaps we shall get at the truth,—learn the amount of this influence more conveniently,—by considering their value alone.

The theory of books is noble. The scholar of the first age received into him the world around; brooded thereon; gave it the new arrangement of his own mind, and uttered it again. It came into him life; it went out from him truth. It came to him short-lived actions; it went out from him immortal thoughts. It came to him business; it went from him poetry. It was dead fact; now, it is quick thought. It can stand, and it can go. It now endures, it now flies, it now inspires. Precisely in proportion to the depth of mind from which it issued, so high does it soar, so long does it sing.

Or, I might say, it depends on how far the process had gone, of transmuting life into truth. In proportion to the completeness of the distillation, so will the purity and imperishableness of the product be. But none is quite perfect. As no air-pump can by any means make a perfect vacuum, so neither can any artist entirely exclude the conventional, the local, the perishable from his book, or write a book of pure thought, that shall be as efficient, in all respects, to a remote posterity, as to contemporaries, or rather to the second age. Each age, it is found, must write its own books; or rather, each generation for the next succeeding. The books of an older period will not fit this.

Yet hence arises a grave mischief. The sacredness which attaches to the act of creation, the act of thought, is transferred to the record. The poet chanting was felt to be a divine man: henceforth the chant is divine also. The writer was a just and wise spirit: henceforward it is settled the book is perfect; as love of the hero corrupts into worship of his statue. Instantly the book becomes noxious: the guide is a tyrant. The sluggish and perverted mind of the multitude, slow to open to the incursions of Reason, having once so opened, having once received this book, stands upon it, and makes an outcry if it is disparaged. Colleges are built on it. Books are written on it by thinkers, not by Man Thinking; by men of talent, that is, who start wrong, who set out from accepted dogmas, not from their own sight of principles. Meek young men grow up in libraries, believing it their duty to accept the views which Cicero, which Locke, which Bacon, have given; forgetful that Cicero, Locke, and Bacon were only young men in libraries when they wrote these books.

Hence, instead of Man Thinking, we have the bookworm. Hence the book-learned class, who value books, as such; not as related to nature and the human constitution, but as making a sort of Third Estate with the world and the soul. Hence the restorers of readings, the emendators, the bibliomaniacs of all degrees.

Books are the best of things, well used; abused, among the worst. What is the right use? What is the one end which all means go to effect? They are for nothing but to inspire. I had better never see a book than to be warped by its attraction clean out of my own orbit, and made a satellite instead of a system. The one thing in the world, of value, is the active soul. This every man is entitled to; this every man contains within him, although in almost all men obstructed and as yet unborn. The soul active sees absolute truth and utters truth, or creates. In this action it is genius; not the privilege of here and there a favorite, but the sound estate of every man. In its essence it is progressive. The book, the college, the school of art, the institution of any kind, stop with some past utterance of genius. This is good, say they,—let us hold by this. They pin me down. They look backward and not forward. But genius looks forward: the eyes of man are set in his forehead, not in his hindhead: man hopes: genius creates. Whatever talents may be, if the man create not, the pure efflux of the Deity is not his;—cinders and smoke there may be, but not yet flame. There are creative manners, there are creative actions, and creative words; manners, actions, words, that is, indicative of no custom or authority, but springing spontaneous from the mind's own sense of good and fair.

On the other part, instead of being its own seer, let it receive from another mind its truth, though it were in torrents of light, without periods of solitude, inquest, and self-recovery, and a fatal disservice is done. Genius is always sufficiently the enemy of genius by over-influence. The literature of every nation bears me witness. The English dramatic poets have Shakspearized now for two hundred years.

Undoubtedly there is a right way of reading, so it be sternly subordinated. Man Thinking must not be subdued by his instruments. Books are for the scholar's idle times. When he can read God directly, the hour is too precious to be wasted in other men's transcripts of their readings. But when the intervals of darkness come, as come they must,—when the sun is hid and the stars withdraw their shining,—we repair to the lamps which were kindled by their ray, to guide our steps to the East again, where the dawn is. We hear, that we may speak. The Arabian proverb says, "A fig tree, looking on a fig tree, becometh fruitful."

It is remarkable, the character of the pleasure we derive from the best books. They impress us with the conviction that one nature wrote and the same reads. We read the verses of one of the great English poets, of Chaucer, of Marvell, of Dryden, with the most modern joy,—with a pleasure, I mean, which is in great part caused by the abstraction of all *time* from their verses. There is some awe mixed with the joy of our surprise, when this poet, who lived in some past world, two or three hundred years ago, says that which lies close to my own soul, that which I also had well-nigh thought and said. But for the evidence thence afforded to the philosophical doctrine of the identity of all minds, we should suppose some preëstablished harmony, some foresight of souls that were to be, and some preparation of stores for their future wants, like the fact observed in insects, who lay up food before death for the young grub they shall never see.

I would not be hurried by any love of system, by any exaggeration of instincts, to underrate the Book. We all know, that as the human body can be nourished on any food, though it were boiled grass and the broth of shoes, so the human mind can be fed by any knowledge. And great and heroic men have existed who had almost no other information than by the printed page. I only would say that it needs a strong head to bear that diet. One must be an inventor to read well. As the proverb says, "He that would bring home the wealth of the Indies, must carry out the wealth of the Indies." There is then creative reading as well as creative writing. When the mind is braced by labor and invention, the page of whatever book we read becomes luminous with manifold allusion. Every sentence is doubly significant, and the sense of our author is as broad as the world. We then see, what is always true, that as the seer's hour of vision is short and rare among heavy days and months, so is its record, perchance, the least part of his volume. The discerning will read, in his Plato or Shakspeare, only that least part,—only the authentic utterances of the oracle;—all the rest he rejects, were it never so many times Plato's and Shakspeare's.

Of course there is a portion of reading quite indispensable to a wise man. History and exact science he must learn by laborious reading. Colleges, in like manner, have their indispensable office,—to teach elements. But they can only highly serve us when they aim not to drill, but to create; when they gather from far every ray of various genius to their hospitable halls, and by the concentrated fires, set the hearts of their youth on flame. Thought and knowledge are natures in which apparatus and pretension avail nothing. Gowns and pecuniary foundations, though of towns of gold, can never countervail the least sentence or syllable of wit. Forget this, and our American colleges will recede in their public importance, whilst they grow richer every year.

III. There goes in the world a notion that the scholar should be a recluse, a valetudinarian,—as unfit for any handiwork or public labor as a penknife for an axe. The so-called "practical men" sneer at speculative men, as if, because they speculate or *see,* they could do nothing. I have heard it said that the clergy,—who are always, more universally than any other class, the scholars of their day,—are addressed as women; that the rough, spontaneous conversation of men they do not hear, but only a mincing and diluted speech. They are often virtually disfranchised; and indeed there are advocates for their celibacy. As far as this is true of the studious classes, it is not just and wise. Action is with the scholar subordinate, but it is essential. Without it he is not yet man. Without it thought can never ripen into truth. Whilst the world hangs before the eye as a cloud of beauty, we cannot even see its beauty. Inaction is cowardice, but there can be no scholar without the heroic mind. The preamble of thought, the transition through which it passes from the unconscious to the conscious, is action. Only so much do I know, as I have lived. Instantly we know whose words are loaded with life, and whose not.

The world,—this shadow of the soul, or *other me,*—lies wide around. Its attractions are the keys which unlock my thoughts and make me acquainted with myself. I run eagerly into this resounding tumult. I grasp the hands of those next me, and take my place in the ring to suffer and to work, taught by an instinct that so shall the dumb abyss be vocal with speech. I pierce its order; I dissipate its fear; I dispose of it within the circuit of my expanding life. So much only of life as I know by experience, so much of the wilderness have I vanquished and planted, or so far have I extended my being, my dominion. I do not see how any man can afford, for the sake of his nerves and his nap, to spare any action in which he can partake. It is pearls and rubies to his discourse. Drudgery, calamity, exasperation, want, are instructors in eloquence and wisdom. The true scholar grudges every opportunity of action past by, as a loss of power. It is the raw material out of which the intellect moulds her splendid products. A strange process too, this by which experience is converted into thought, as a mulberry leaf is converted into satin. The manufacture goes forward at all hours.

The actions and events of our childhood and youth are now matters of calmest observation. They lie like fair pictures in the air. Not so with our recent actions,—with the business which we now have in hand. On this we are quite unable to speculate. Our affections as yet circulate through it. We no more feel or know it than we feel the feet, or the hand, or the brain of our body. The new deed is yet a part of life,—remains for a time immersed in our unconscious life. In some contemplative hour it detaches itself from the life like a ripe fruit, to become a thought of the mind. Instantly it is raised, transfigured; the corruptible has put on incorruption. Henceforth it is an object of beauty, however base its origin and neighborhood. Observe too the impossibility of antedating this act. In its grub state, it cannot fly, it cannot shine, it is a dull grub. But suddenly, without observation, the selfsame thing unfurls beautiful wings, and is an angel of wisdom. So is there no fact, no event, in our private history, which shall not, sooner or later, lose its adhesive, inert form, and astonish us by soaring from our body into the empyrean. Cradle and infancy, school and playground, the fear of boys, and dogs, and ferules, the love of little maids and berries, and many another fact that once filled the whole sky, are gone already; friend and relative, profession and party, town and country, nation and world, must also soar and sing.

Of course, he who has put forth his total strength in fit actions has the richest return of wisdom. I will not shut myself out of this globe of action, and transplant an oak into a flowerpot, there to hunger and pine; nor trust the revenue of some single faculty, and exhaust one vein of thought, much like those Savoyards, who, getting their livelihood by carving shepherds, shepherdesses, and smoking Dutchmen, for all Europe, went out one day to the mountain to find stock, and discovered that they had whittled up the last of their pine trees. Authors we have, in numbers, who have written out their vein, and who, moved by a commendable prudence, sail for Greece or Palestine, follow the trapper into the prairie, or ramble round Algiers, to replenish their merchantable stock.

If it were only for a vocabulary, the scholar would be covetous of action. Life is our dictionary. Years are well spent in country labors; in town; in the insight into trades and manufactures; in frank intercourse with many men and women; in science; in art; to the one end of mastering in all their facts a language by which to illustrate and embody our perceptions. I learn immediately from any speaker how much he has already lived, through the poverty or the splendor of his speech. Life lies behind us as the quarry from whence we get tiles and copestones for the masonry of to-day. This is the way to learn grammar. Colleges and books only copy the language which the field and the work-yard made.

But the final value of action, like that of books, and better than books, is that it is a resource. The great principle of Undulation in nature, that shows itself in the inspiring and expiring of the breath; in desire and satiety; in the ebb and flow of the sea; in day and night; in heat and cold; and, as yet more deeply ingrained in every atom and every fluid, is known to us under the name of Polarity,—these "fits of easy transmission and reflection," as Newton called them, are the law of nature because they are the law of spirit.

The mind now thinks, now acts, and each fit reproduces the other. When the artist has exhausted his materials, when the fancy no longer paints, when thoughts are no longer apprehended and books are a weariness,—he has always the resource *to live.* Character is higher than intellect. Thinking is the function. Living is the functionary. The stream retreats to its source. A great soul will be strong to live, as well as strong to think. Does he lack organ or medium to impart his truths? He can still fall back on this elemental force of living them. This is a total act. Thinking is a partial act. Let the grandeur of justice shine in his affairs. Let the beauty of affection cheer his lowly roof. Those "far from fame," who dwell and act with him, will feel the force of his constitution in the doings and passages of the day better than it can be measured by any public and designed display. Time shall teach him that the scholar loses no hour which the man lives. Herein he unfolds the sacred germ of his instinct, screened from influence. What is lost in seemliness is gained in strength. Not out of those on whom systems of education have exhausted their culture, comes the helpful giant to destroy the old or to build the new, but out of unhandselled savage nature; out of terrible Druids and Berserkers come at last Alfred and Shakspeare.

I hear therefore with joy whatever is beginning to be said of the dignity and necessity of labor to every citizen. There is virtue yet in the hoe and the spade, for learned as well as for unlearned hands. And labor is everywhere welcome; always we are invited to work; only be this limitation observed, that a man shall not for the sake of wider activity sacrifice any opinion to the popular judgments and modes of action.

I have now spoken of the education of the scholar by nature, by books, and by action. It remains to say somewhat of his duties.

They are such as become Man Thinking. They may all be comprised in self-trust. The office of the scholar is to cheer, to raise, and to guide men by showing them facts amidst appearances. He plies the slow, un-honored, and unpaid task of observation. Flamsteed and Herschel, in their glazed observatories, may catalogue the stars with the praise of all men, and the results being splendid and useful, honor is sure. But he, in his private observatory, cataloguing obscure and nebulous stars of the human mind, which as yet no man has thought of as such,—watching days and months sometimes for a few facts; correcting still his old records;—must relinquish display and immediate fame. In the long period of his preparation he must betray often an ignorance and shiftlessness in popu-lar arts, incurring the disdain of the able who shoulder him aside. Long he must stammer in his speech; often forego the living for the dead. Worse yet, he must accept—how often!—poverty and solitude. For the ease and pleasure of treading the old road, accepting the fashions, the education, the religion of society, he takes the cross of making his own, and, of course, the self-accusation, the faint heart, the frequent uncer-tainty and loss of time, which are the nettles and tangling vines in the way of the self-relying and self-directed; and the state of virtual hostility in which he seems to stand to society, and especially to educated society. For all this loss and scorn, what offset? He is to find consolation in exercising the highest functions of human nature. He is one who raises himself from private considerations and breathes and lives on public and illustrious thoughts. He is the world's eye. He is the world's heart. He is to resist the vulgar prosperity that retrogrades ever to barbarism, by preserving and communicating heroic sentiments, noble biographies, melodious verse, and the conclusions of history. Whatsoever oracles the human heart, in all emergencies, in all solemn hours, has uttered as its commen-tary on the world of actions,—these he shall receive and impart. And whatsoever new verdict Reason from her inviolable seat pronounces on the passing men and events of to-day,—this he shall hear and promul-gate.

These being his functions, it becomes him to feel all confidence in himself, and to defer never to the popular cry. He and he only knows the world. The world of any moment is the merest appearance. Some great decorum, some fetish of a government, some ephemeral trade, or war, or man, is cried up by half mankind and cried down by the other half, as if all depended on this particular up or down. The odds are that the whole question is not worth the poorest thought which the scholar has lost in listening to the controversy. Let him not quit his belief that a popgun is a popgun, though the ancient and honorable of the earth affirm it to be the crack of doom. In silence, in steadiness, in severe abstraction, let him hold by himself; add observation to observation, patient of neglect, pa-tient of reproach, and bide his own time,—happy enough if he can satisfy himself alone that this day he has seen something truly. Success treads on every right step. For the instinct is sure, that prompts him to tell his brother what he thinks. He then learns that in going down into the secrets of his own mind he has descended into the secrets of all minds. He learns that he who has mastered any law in his private thoughts, is master to that extent of all men whose language he speaks, and of all into whose language his own can be translated. The poet, in utter solitude remembering his spontaneous thoughts and recording them, is found to have recorded that which men in crowded cities find true for them also. The orator distrusts at first the fitness of his frank confessions, his want of knowledge of the persons he addresses, until he finds that he is the complement of his hearers;—that they drink his words because he fulfils for them their own nature; the deeper he dives into his privatest, secretest presentiment, to his wonder he finds this is the most acceptable, most public, and universally true. The people delight in it; the better part of every man feels, This is my music; this is myself.

In self-trust all the virtues are comprehended. Free should the scholar be,—free and brave. Free even to the definition of freedom, "without any hindrance that does not arise out of his own constitution." Brave; for fear is a thing which a scholar by his very function puts behind him. Fear always springs from ignorance. It is a shame to him if his tranquillity, amid dangerous times, arise from the presumption that like children and women his is a protected class; or if he seek a temporary peace by the diversion of his thoughts from politics or vexed questions, hiding his head like an ostrich in the flowering bushes, peeping into microscopes, and turning rhymes, as a boy whistles to keep his courage up. So is the danger a danger still; so is the fear worse. Manlike let him turn and face it. Let him look into its eye and search its nature, inspect its origin,—see the whelping of this lion,—which lies no great way back; he will then find in himself a perfect comprehension of its nature and extent; he will have made his hands meet on the other side, and can henceforth defy it and pass on superior. The world is his who can see through its pretension. What deafness, what stone-blind custom, what overgrown error you behold is there only by sufferance,—by your sufferance. See it to be a lie, and you have already dealt it its mortal blow.

Yes, we are the cowed,—we the trustless. It is a mischievous notion that we are come late into nature; that the world was finished a long time ago. As the world was plastic and fluid in the hands of God, so it is ever to so much of his attributes as we bring to it. To ignorance and sin, it is flint. They adapt themselves to it as they may; but in proportion as a man has any thing in him divine, the firmament flows before him and takes his signet and form. Not he is great who can alter matter, but he who can alter my state of mind. They are the kings of the world who give the color of their present thought to all nature and all art, and persuade men by the cheerful serenity of their carrying the matter, that this thing which they do is the apple which the ages have desired to pluck, now at last ripe, and inviting nations to the harvest. The great man makes the great thing. Wherever Macdonald sits, there is the head of the table. Linnæus makes botany the most alluring of studies, and wins it from the farmer and the herb-woman; Davy, chemistry; and Cuvier, fossils. The day is always his who works in it with serenity and great aims. The unstable estimates of men crowd to him whose mind is filled with a truth, as the heaped waves of the Atlantic follow the moon.

For this self-trust, the reason is deeper than can be fathomed,—darker than can be enlightened. I might not carry with me the feeling of my audience in stating my own belief. But I have already shown the ground of my hope, in adverting to the doctrine that man is one. I believe man has been wronged; he has wronged himself. He has almost lost the light that can lead him back to his prerogatives. Men are become of no account. Men in history, men in the world of to-day, are bugs, are spawn, and are called "the mass" and "the herd." In a century, in a millennium, one or two men; that is to say, one or two approximations to the right state of every man. All the rest behold in the hero or the poet their own green and crude being,—ripened; yes, and are content to be less, so *that* may attain to its full stature. What a testimony, full of grandeur, full of pity, is borne to the demands of his own nature, by the poor clansman, the poor partisan, who rejoices in the glory of his chief. The poor and the low find some amends to their immense moral capacity, for their acquiescence in a political and social inferiority. They are content to be brushed like flies from the path of a great person, so that justice shall be done by him to that common nature which it is the dearest desire of all to see enlarged and glorified. They sun themselves in the great man's light, and feel it to be their own element. They cast the dignity of man from their downtrod selves upon the shoulders of a hero, and will perish to add one drop of blood to make that great heart beat, those giant sinews combat and conquer. He lives for us, and we live in him.

Men, such as they are, very naturally seek money or power; and power because it is as good as money,—the "spoils," so called, "of office." And why not? for they aspire to the highest, and this, in their sleep-walking, they dream is highest. Wake them and they shall quit the false good and leap to the true, and leave governments to clerks and desks. This revolution is to be wrought by the gradual domestication of the idea of Culture. The main enterprise of the world for splendor, for extent, is the upbuilding of a man. Here are the materials strewn along the ground. The private life of one man shall be a more illustrious monarchy, more formidable to its enemy, more sweet and serene in its influence to its friend, than any kingdom in history. For a man, rightly viewed, comprehendeth the particular natures of all men. Each philosopher, each bard, each actor has only done for me, as by a delegate, what one day I can do for myself. The books which once we valued more than the apple of the eye, we have quite exhausted. What is that but saying that we have come up with the point of view which the universal mind took through the eyes of one scribe; we have been that man, and have passed on. First, one, then another, we drain all cisterns, and waxing greater by all these supplies, we crave a better and more abundant food. The man has never lived that can feed us ever. The human mind cannot be enshrined in a person who shall set a barrier on any one side to this unbounded, unboundable empire. It is one central fire, which, flaming now out of the lips of Etna, lightens the capes of Sicily, and now out of the throat of Vesuvius, illuminates the towers and vineyards of Naples. It is one light which beams out of a thousand stars. It is one soul which animates all men.

.   .   .

ARTHUR KOESTLER

By age twenty-one, Arthur Koestler had decided to become "a wanderer and a writer." Born in Budapest in 1905 and educated in Vienna as an engineer, he left without a degree to live on a communal farm in Palestine. He became editor of a Cairo weekly and then correspondent for a chain of newspapers, first in the Middle East, then in Paris.

In 1930, as the present selection describes, he moved to Berlin and in the next year joined the German Communist party. He traveled to Russia and Central Asia, then to Spain to cover the civil war there for a London paper. In 1937 Franco's Fascist army captured and held him for three months under sentence of death until the British government intervened.

Koestler was in France when World War II broke out in 1939; the French government imprisoned him as a suspect alien. He joined the French Foreign Legion and escaped from North Africa to England, where he was again imprisoned but then released to serve in the British Pioneer Corps during the rest of the war. His autobiographical volumes Arrow in the Blue *(1952) and* The Invisible Writing *(1954) describe his life through 1940.*

By 1938 he had quit the Communist party, disillusioned by Soviet totalitarianism. He also gave up journalism and began writing political novels. His most famous, Darkness at Noon *(1940), is a psychological study based on the Moscow trials in the Stalin era. It describes the imprisonment and death of an old Bolshevik, who ultimately confesses to crimes he knows he has not committed.*

Koestler's recent books interpret the growing impact of one of his earliest interests—science. He criticizes philosophical attempts to see science as wholly rational, as the opposite of irrational religion and art. Most thoroughly in The Act of Creation *(1964), he analyzes the common psychological structures that underlie both scientific discovery and artistic creativity. Other recent books, developing his theories, include* The Ghost

in the Machine *(1967),* The Roots of Coincidence *(1972), and*
The Heel of Achilles *(1975), a collection of essays. He now lives in
London.*

The present essay is the first part of Koestler's contribution to The
God That Failed *(ed. Richard Crossman, 1950), a collection of essays
on conversion to communism by six prominent ex-Communists. The essay's
mention of "Schickelgrüber and Djugashwili" is a reference to the family
names of Adolf Hitler and Josef Stalin respectively.*

Conversion

A faith is not acquired by reasoning. One does not fall in love with a
woman, or enter the womb of a church, as a result of logical persuasion.
Reason may defend an act of faith—but only after the act has been
committed, and the man committed to the act. Persuasion may play a part
in a man's conversion; but only the part of bringing to its full and conscious climax a process which has been maturing in regions where no
persuasion can penetrate. A faith is not acquired; it grows like a tree. Its
crown points to the sky; its roots grow downward into the past and are
nourished by the dark sap of the ancestral humus.

From the psychologist's point of view, there is little difference between a revolutionary and a traditionalist faith. All true faith is uncom-
promising, radical, purist; hence the true traditionalist is always a
revolutionary zealot in conflict with pharisaian society, with the lukewarm
corrupters of the creed. And vice versa: the revolutionary's Utopia, which
in appearance represents a complete break with the past, is always mod-
eled on some image of the lost Paradise, of a legendary Golden Age. The
classless Communist society, according to Marx and Engels, was to be a
revival, at the end of the dialectical spiral, of the primitive Communist
society which stood at its beginning. Thus all true faith involves a revolt
against the believer's social environment, and the projection into the
future of an ideal derived from the remote past. All Utopias are fed from
the sources of mythology; the social engineer's blueprints are merely
revised editions of the ancient text.

Devotion to pure Utopia, and revolt against a polluted society, are
thus the two poles which provide the tension of all militant creeds. To
ask which of the two makes the current flow—attraction by the ideal or
repulsion by the social environment—is to ask the old question about the
hen and the egg. To the psychiatrist, both the craving for Utopia and the
rebellion against the status quo are symptoms of social maladjustment.
To the social reformer, both are symptoms of a healthy rational attitude.
The psychiatrist is apt to forget that smooth adjustment to a deformed

society creates deformed individuals. The reformer is equally apt to forget that hatred, even of the objectively hateful, does not produce that charity and justice on which a utopian society must be based.

Thus each of the two attitudes, the sociologist's and the psychologist's, reflects a half-truth. It is true that the case-history of most revolutionaries and reformers reveals a neurotic conflict with family or society. But this only proves, to paraphrase Marx, that a moribund society creates its own morbid gravediggers.

It is also true that in the face of revolting injustice the only honorable attitude is to revolt, and to leave introspection for better times. But if we survey history and compare the lofty aims, in the name of which revolutions were started, and the sorry end to which they came, we see again and again how a polluted civilization pollutes its own revolutionary offspring.

Fitting the two half-truths—the sociologist's and the psychologist's—together, we conclude that if on the one hand oversensitivity to social injustice and obsessional craving for Utopia are signs of neurotic maladjustment, society may, on the other hand, reach a state of decay where the neurotic rebel causes more joy in heaven than the sane executive who orders pigs to be drowned under the eyes of starving men. This in fact was the state of our civilization when, in December, 1931, at the age of twenty-six, I joined the Communist Party of Germany.

I became converted because I was ripe for it and lived in a disintegrating society thirsting for faith. But the day when I was given my Party card was merely the climax of a development which had started long before I had read about the drowned pigs or heard the names of Marx and Lenin. Its roots reach back into childhood; and though each of us, comrades of the Pink Decade, had individual roots with different twists in them, we are products of, by and large, the same generation and cultural climate. It is this unity underlying diversity which makes me hope that my story is worth telling.

I was born in 1905 in Budapest; we lived there till 1919, when we moved to Vienna. Until the First World War we were comfortably off, a typical Continental middle-middle-class family: my father was the Hungarian representative of some old-established British and German textile manufacturers. In September, 1914, this form of existence, like so many others, came to an abrupt end; my father never found his feet again. He embarked on a number of ventures which became the more fantastic the more he lost self-confidence in a changed world. He opened a factory for radioactive soap; he backed several crank-inventions (everlasting electric bulbs, self-heating bed bricks and the like); and finally lost the remains of his capital in the Austrian inflation of the early 'twenties. I left home at twenty-one, and from that day became the only financial support of my parents.

At the age of nine, when our middle-class idyl collapsed, I had suddenly become conscious of the economic Facts of Life. As an only child, I continued to be pampered by my parents; but, well aware of the family crisis, and torn by pity for my father, who was of a generous and somewhat childlike disposition, I suffered a pang of guilt whenever they bought me books or toys. This continued later on, when every suit I bought for myself meant so much less to send home. Simultaneously, I developed a strong dislike of the obviously rich; not because they could afford to buy things (envy plays a much smaller part in social conflict than is generally assumed) but because they were able to do so without a guilty conscience. Thus I projected a personal predicament onto the structure of society at large.

It was certainly a tortuous way of acquiring a social conscience. But precisely because of the intimate nature of the conflict, the faith which grew out of it became an equally intimate part of my self. It did not, for some years, crystallize into a political creed; at first it took the form of a mawkishly sentimental attitude. Every contact with people poorer than myself was unbearable—the boy at school who had no gloves and red chilblains on his fingers, the former traveling salesman of my father's reduced to cadging occasional meals—all of them were additions to the load of guilt on my back. The analyst would have no difficulty in showing that the roots of this guilt-complex go deeper than the crisis in our household budget; but if he were to dig even deeper, piercing through the individual layers of the case, he would strike the archetypal pattern which has produced millions of particular variations on the same theme —"Woe, for they chant to the sound of harps and anoint themselves, but are not grieved for the affliction of the people."

Thus sensitized by a personal conflict, I was ripe for the shock of learning that wheat was burned, fruit artificially spoiled and pigs were drowned in the depression years to keep prices up and enable fat capitalists to chant to the sound of harps, while Europe trembled under the torn boots of hunger-marchers and my father hid his frayed cuffs under the table. The frayed cuffs and drowned pigs blended into one emotional explosion, as the fuse of the archetype was touched off. We sang the "Internationale," but the words might as well have been the older ones: "Woe to the shepherds who feed themselves, but feed not their flocks."

In other respects, too, the story is more typical than it seems. A considerable proportion of the middle classes in central Europe was, like ourselves, ruined by the inflation of the 'twenties. It was the beginning of Europe's decline. This disintegration of the middle strata of society started the fatal process of polarization which continues to this day. The pauperized bourgeois became rebels of the Right or Left; Schickelgrüber and Djugashwili shared about equally the benefits of the social migration. Those who refused to admit that they had become déclassé, who clung to the empty shell of gentility, joined the Nazis and found comfort in blaming their fate on Versailles and the Jews. Many did not even have that consolation; they lived on pointlessly, like a great black swarm of tired winterflies crawling over the dim windows of Europe, members of a class displaced by history.

The other half turned Left, thus confirming the prophecy of the "Communist Manifesto":

> Entire sections of the ruling classes are . . . precipitated into the proletariat, or are at least threatened in their conditions of existence. They . . . supply the proletariat with fresh elements of enlightenment and progress.

That "fresh element of enlightenment," I discovered to my delight, was I. As long as I had been nearly starving, I had regarded myself as a temporarily displaced offspring of the bourgeoisie. In 1931, when at last I had achieved a comfortable income, I found that it was time to join the ranks of the proletariat. But the irony of this sequence only occurred to me in retrospect.

> The bourgeois family will vanish as a matter of course with the vanishing of Capital. . . . The bourgeois claptrap about the family and education, about the haloed correlation of parent and child, becomes all the more disgusting the more, by the action of modern industry, all family ties among the proletarians are torn asunder. . . .

Thus the "Communist Manifesto." Every page of Marx, and even more of Engels, brought a new revelation, and an intellectual delight which I had only experienced once before, at my first contact with Freud. Torn from its context, the above passage sounds ridiculous; as part of a closed system which made social philosophy fall into a lucid and comprehensive pattern, the demonstration of the historical relativity of institutions and ideals—of family, class, patriotism, bourgeois morality, sexual taboos—had the intoxicating effect of a sudden liberation from the rusty chains with which a pre-1914 middle-class childhood had cluttered one's mind. Today, when Marxist philosophy has degenerated into a Byzantine cult and virtually every single tenet of the Marxist program has become twisted round into its opposite, it is difficult to recapture that mood of emotional fervor and intellectual bliss.

I was ripe to be converted, as a result of my personal case-history; thousands of other members of the intelligentsia and the middle classes of my generation were ripe for it, by virtue of other personal case-histories; but, however much these differed from case to case, they had a common denominator: the rapid disintegration of moral values, of the pre-1914 pattern of life in postwar Europe, and the simultaneous lure of the new revelation which had come from the East.

I joined the Party (which to this day remains "the" Party for all of us who once belonged to it) in 1931, at the beginning of that short-lived period of optimism, of that abortive spiritual renaissance, later known as the Pink Decade. The stars of that treacherous dawn were Barbusse, Romain Rolland, Gide and Malraux in France; Piscator, Becher, Renn,

Brecht, Eisler, Säghers in Germany; Auden, Isherwood, Spender in England; Dos Passos, Upton Sinclair, Steinbeck in the United States. (Of course, not all of them were members of the Communist Party.) The cultural atmosphere was saturated with Progressive Writers' congresses, experimental theaters, committees for peace and against Fascism, societies for cultural relations with the USSR, Russian films and avant-garde magazines. It looked indeed as if the Western world, convulsed by the aftermath of war, scourged by inflation, depression, unemployment and the absence of a faith to live for, was at last going to

> Clear from the head the masses of impressive rubbish;
> Rally the lost and trembling forces of the will,
> Gather them up and let them loose upon the earth,
> Till they construct at last a human justice.
>
> Auden

The new star of Bethlehem had risen in the East; and for a modest sum, Intourist was prepared to allow you a short and well-focused glimpse of the Promised Land.

I lived at that time in Berlin. For the last five years, I had been working for the Ullstein chain of newspapers—first as a foreign correspondent in Palestine and the Middle East, then in Paris. Finally, in 1930, I joined the editorial staff in the Berlin "House." For a better understanding of what follows, a few words have to be said about the House of Ullstein, symbol of the Weimar Republic.

Ullstein's was a kind of super-trust; the largest organization of its kind in Europe, and probably in the world. They published four daily papers in Berlin alone, among these the venerable *Vossische Zeitung,* founded in the eighteenth century, and the *B. Z. am Mittag,* an evening paper with a record circulation and a record speed in getting the news out. Apart from these, Ullstein's published more than a dozen weekly and monthly periodicals, ran their own news service, their own travel agency, etc., and were one of the leading book publishers. The firm was owned by the brothers Ullstein—they were five, like the original Rothschild brothers, and like them also, they were Jews. Their policy was liberal and democratic, and in cultural matters progressive to the point of avant-gardism. They were antimilitaristic, antichauvinistic, and it was largely due to their influence on public opinion that the policy of Franco-German rapprochement of the Briand-Stresemann era became a vogue among the progressive part of the German people. The firm of Ullstein was not only a political power in Germany; it was at the same time the embodiment of everything progressive and cosmopolitan in the Weimar Republic. The atmosphere in the "House" in the Kochstrasse was more that of a Ministry than of an editorial office.

My transfer from the Paris office to the Berlin house was due to an article I wrote on the occasion of the award of the Nobel Prize for Physics to the Prince de Broglie. My bosses decided that I had a knack for popularizing science (I had been a student of science in Vienna) and offered me the job of Science Editor of the *Vossische* and adviser on matters scientific to the rest of the Ullstein publications. I arrived in Berlin on the fateful day of September 14, 1930—the day of the Reichstag Election in which the National Socialist Party, in one mighty leap, increased the number of its deputies from 4 to 107. The Communists had also registered important gains; the democratic parties of the Center were crushed. It was the beginning of the end of Weimar; the situation was epitomized in the title of Knickerbocker's best-seller: *Germany,—Fascist or Soviet?* Obviously there was no "third alternative."

I did my job, writing about electrons, chromosomes, rocket-ships, Neanderthal men, spiral nebulae and the universe at large; but the pressure of events increased rapidly. With one-third of its wage-earners unemployed, Germany lived in a state of latent civil war, and if one wasn't prepared to be swept along as a passive victim by the approaching hurricane it became imperative to take sides. Stresemann's party was dead. The Socialists pursued a policy of opportunist compromise. Even by a process of pure elimination, the Communists, with the mighty Soviet Union behind them, seemed the only force capable of resisting the onrush of the primitive horde with its swastika totem. But it was not by a process of elimination that I became a Communist. Tired of electrons and wave-mechanics, I began for the first time to read Marx, Engels and Lenin in earnest. By the time I had finished with *Feuerbach* and *State and Revolution,* something had clicked in my brain which shook me like a mental explosion. To say that one had "seen the light" is a poor description of the mental rapture which only the convert knows (regardless of what faith he has been converted to). The new light seems to pour from all directions across the skull; the whole universe falls into pattern like the stray pieces of a jigsaw puzzle assembled by magic at one stroke. There is now an answer to every question, doubts and conflicts are a matter of the tortured past—a past already remote, when one had lived in dismal ignorance in the tasteless, colorless world of those who *don't know.* Nothing henceforth can disturb the convert's inner peace and serenity—except the occasional fear of losing faith again, losing thereby what alone makes life worth living, and falling back into the outer darkness, where there is wailing and gnashing of teeth. This may explain how Communists, with eyes to see and brains to think with, can still act in subjective *bona fides,* anno Domini 1949. At all times and in all creeds only a minority has been capable of courting excommunication and committing emotional hara-kiri in the name of an abstract truth.

.   .   .

MARCEL PROUST

Marcel Proust's literary fame comes from his long novel A la recherche du temps perdu (Remembrance of Things Past). *He published the first volume in 1913, and was dictating passages of the eighth the night before he died in 1922. Although the novel is not autobiographical, it does record the life of a Paris dilettante, wealthy and purposeless until one day when he realizes that the memories of his own life, relived and reshaped into art, will provide the subject for a great novel.*

Proust, asthmatic and nervous from earliest childhood, lived in his family home in Paris from his birth in 1871 until his mother's death in 1905. While in school he wrote essays and poems that show his early interest in the Decadent movement—a school of French writers who stressed the abnormal and artificial in their works. At the Sorbonne he enrolled as a student of law and political science, but his only academic interest was in philosophy. He spent most of his time widening his circle of acquaintances in the literary and artistic society of Paris, and sporadically composing novels and shorter works. Though only a few were printed, he later worked parts of them into his major novel.

His mother's death grieved Proust excessively, for she had given his life a continuity and a portion of her own strict discipline. Her death did enable Proust to stop hiding his homosexuality—though none of his series of affairs lasted long, and the most intense ended tragically when his lover died in a plane crash in 1914.

In 1907 Proust moved to a flat, which he had made soundproof and from which, in later years, he almost never stirred. By 1909 he had begun steady work on Remembrance of Things Past. *He saw less and less of aristocratic Paris society; because of his asthma he often worked on his novel all night and slept during the day. He became progressively weaker and more nervous, took large amounts of drugs for his asthma, and died of pneumonia in 1922.*

Contre Sainte-Beuve (By Way of Sainte-Beuve), *written between 1908 and 1910, was the only major interruption to the work on his novel. It began as a critical study, but soon turned into an account of Proust's own processes of memory, thought, and feeling. The present essay, which opens the book, is celebrated as a description of how his masterpiece may have originated. The translation is by Sylvia Townsend Warner (1958). "Sainte-Beuve's Method," referred to in the final paragraph, is described elsewhere by Proust as "not separating the man and his work," "to surround oneself with every possible piece of information about a writer" before making a judgment on his writings. Proust did not admire this method.*

Prologue

Every day I set less store on intellect. Every day I see more clearly that
if the writer is to repossess himself of some part of his impressions, reach
something personal, that is, and the only material of art, he must put it
aside. What intellect restores to us under the name of the past, is not the
past. In reality, as soon as each hour of one's life has died, it embodies
itself in some material object, as do the souls of the dead in certain
folk-stories, and hides there. There it remains captive, captive forever,
unless we should happen on the object, recognise what lies within, call
it by its name, and so set it free. Very likely we may never happen on the
object (or the sensation, since we apprehend every object as sensation)
that it hides in; and thus there are hours of our life that will never be
resuscitated: for this object is so tiny, so lost in the world, and there is
so little likelihood that we shall come across it.

Several summers of my life were spent in a house in the country. I
thought of those summers from time to time, but they were not themselves. They were dead, and in all probability they would always remain
so. Their resurrection, like all these resurrections, hung on a mere
chance. One snowy evening, not long ago, I came in half frozen, and had
sat down in my room to read by lamplight, and as I could not get warm
my old cook offered to make me a cup of tea, a thing I never drink. And
as chance would have it, she brought me some slices of dry toast. I dipped
the toast in the cup of tea and as soon as I put it in my mouth, and felt
its softened texture, all flavoured with tea, against my palate, something
came over me—the smell of geraniums and orange-blossom, a sensation
of extraordinary radiance and happiness. I sat quite still, afraid that the
slightest movement might cut short this incomprehensible process which
was taking place in me, and concentrated on the bit of sopped toast which
seemed responsible for all these marvels; then suddenly the shaken parti-
tions in my memory gave way, and into my conscious mind there rushed
the summers I had spent in the aforesaid house in the country, with their
early mornings, and the succession, the ceaseless onset, of happy hours
in their train. And then I remembered. Every morning, when I was
dressed, I went down to my grandfather in his bedroom, where he had
just woken up and was drinking his tea. He soaked a rusk in it, and gave
me the rusk to eat. And when those summers were past and gone, the
taste of a rusk soaked in tea was one of the shelters where the dead hours
—dead as far as intellect knew—hid themselves away, and where I should
certainly never have found them again if, on that winter's evening when
I came in frozen from the snow, my cook had not offered me the potion
to which, by virtue of a magic past I knew nothing about, their resurrection was plighted.

But as soon as I had tasted the rusk, a whole garden, up till then vague
and dim, mirrored itself, with its forgotten walks and all their urns with

all their flowers, in the little cup of tea, like those Japanese flowers which do not reopen as flowers until one drops them into water. In the same way, many days in Venice, which intellect had not been able to give back, were dead for me until last year, when crossing a courtyard I came to a standstill among the glittering uneven paving-stones. The friends I was with were afraid that I might have slipped, but I waved to them to go on, and that I would catch up with them. Something of greater importance engaged me, I still did not know what it was, but in the depth of my being I felt the flutter of a past that I did not recognise; it was just as I set foot on a certain paving-stone that this feeling of perplexity came over me. I felt an invading happiness, I knew that I was going to be enriched by that purely personal thing, a past impression, a fragment of life in unsullied preservation (something we can only know in preservation, for while we live in it, it is not present in the memory, since other sensations accompany and smother it) which asked only that it might be set free, that it might come and augment my stores of life and poetry. But I did not feel that I had the power to free it. No, intellect could have done nothing for me at such a moment! Trying to put myself back into the same state, I retraced my steps a little so that I might come afresh to those uneven shining paving-stones. It was the same sensation underfoot that I had felt on the smooth, slightly uneven pavement of the baptistry of Saint Mark's. The shadow which had lain that day on the canal, where a gondola waited for me, and all the happiness, all the wealth of those hours—this recognised sensation brought them hurrying after it, and that very day came alive for me.

It is not merely that intellect can lend no hand in these resurrections; these past hours will only hide themselves away in objects where intellect has not tried to embody them. The objects which you have consciously tried to connect with certain hours of your life, these they can never take shelter in. What is more, if something else should resuscitate those hours, the objects called back with them will be stripped of their poetry.

I remember how once when I was travelling by train I strove to draw impressions from the passing landscape. I wrote about the little country churchyard while it was still passing before my eyes, I noted down the bright bars of sunlight on the trees, the wayside flowers like those in *Le Lys dans la Vallée.* Since then, calling to mind those trees streaked with light and that little churchyard, I have often tried to conjure up that day, that day *itself,* I mean, not its pallid ghost. I could never manage it, and I had lost all hope of doing so, when at lunch, not long ago, I let my spoon fall on my plate. And then it made the same noise as the hammers of the linesmen did that day, tapping on the wheels when the train halted at stations. The burning blinded hour when that noise rang out instantly came back to me, and all that day in its poetry—except for the country churchyard, the trees streaked with light, and the Balzacian flowers, gained by deliberate observation and lost from the poetic resurrection.

Now and again, alas, we happen on the object, and the lost sensation thrills in us, but the time is too remote, we cannot give a name to the sensation, or call on it, and it does not come alive. As I was walking through a pantry the other day, a piece of green canvas plugging a broken window-pane made me stop dead and listen inwardly. A gleam of summer crossed my mind. Why? I tried to remember. I saw wasps in a shaft of sunlight, a smell of cherries came from the table—I could not remember. For a moment I was like those sleepers who wake up in the dark and do not know where they are, who ask their bodies to give them a bearing as to their whereabouts, not knowing what bed, what house, what part of the world, which year of their life they are in. For a moment I hesitated like this, groping round the square of green canvas to discover the time and the place where my scarcely awakened memory would find itself at home. All the sensations of my life, confused, or known, or forgotten, I was hesitating among all of them at once. This only lasted a minute. Soon I saw nothing more; my memory had fallen asleep again forever.

How often during our walks have not my friends known me halt like this at the turning-off of an avenue, or beside a clump of trees, and ask them to leave me alone for a minute. Nothing came of it. I shut my eyes and made my mind a blank to recruit fresh energies for my pursuit of the past, then suddenly reopened them, all in an attempt to see those same trees as if for the first time. I could not tell where I had seen them. I could recognise their shapes and their grouping, their outline seemed to have been traced from some beloved drawing that trembled in my heart. But I could tell no more of them, and they themselves seemed by their artless passionate attitude to say how sorry they felt not to be able to make themselves clear, not to be able to tell me the secret that they well knew I could not unriddle. Ghosts of a dear past, so dear that my heart beat to bursting, they held out powerless arms to me, like the ghosts that Aeneas met in the underworld. Was it in the walks near the town of my happy childhood, was it only in that imagined country where, later on, I dreamed that Mamma was so ill, close to a lake and in a forest where it was light all night long, a dream country only but almost as real as the country of my childhood which was already no more than a dream? I should never know more of it. And I had to rejoin my friends who were waiting for me at the turn of the road, with the anguish of turning my back forever on a past I might see no more, of disowning the dead who held out their powerless fond arms to me, and seemed to say, Recall us to life. And before I fell into step and into conversation with my friends, I again turned round for a moment to cast a less and less discerning glance towards the crooked, receding line of mutely expressive trees still undulating before my eyes.

Compared with this past, this private essence of ourselves, the truths of intellect seem scarcely real at all. So, and above all from the time when our vitality begins to dwindle, it is to whatever may help us to recover this past that we resort, even though this should entail being very ill-understood by intellectual people who do not know that the artist lives to himself, that the absolute value of what he sees means nothing to him and that his scale of values is wholly subjective. A nauseating musical show put on by a provincial company, or a ball that people of taste would laugh at, may be far more quickening to his memories, far more relevant to the nature of what he dreams of and dwells on, than a brilliant performance at the Opera House or an ultra-elegant evening party in the Faubourg Saint-Germain. A railway time-table with its names of stations where he loves to fancy himself getting out of the train on an autumn evening when the trees are already stripped of their leaves and the bracing air is full of their rough scent, or a book that means nothing to people of discrimination but is full of names he has not heard since he was a child, can be worth incommensurably more to him than admirable philosophical treatises, so that people of discrimination will remark that for a man of talent he has very stupid likings.

Perhaps it will cause surprise that I, who make light of the intellect, should have devoted the following few pages precisely to some of these considerations that intellect, in contradiction to the platitudes that we hear said or read in books, suggests to us. At a time when my days may be numbered (and besides, are we not all in the same case?) it is perhaps very frivolous of me to undertake an intellectual exercise. But if the truths of intellect are less precious than those secrets of feeling that I was talking about just now, yet in one way they too have their interest. A writer is not only a poet; in our imperfect world where masterpieces are no more than the shipwrecked flotsam of great minds, even the greatest writers of our century have spun a web of intellect round jewels of feeling which only here or there show through it. And if one believes that on this important point one hears the best among one's contemporaries making mistakes, there comes a time when one shakes off one's indolence and feels the need to speak out. Sainte-Beuve's Method is not, at first sight, such an important affair. But perhaps in the course of these pages we may be led to realise that it touches on very important intellectual problems, and on what is perhaps for an artist the greatest of all: this relative inferiority of the intellect which I spoke of at the beginning. Yet all the same, it is intellect we must call on to establish this inferiority. Because if intellect does not deserve the crown of crowns, only intellect is able to award it. And if intellect ranks only second in the hierarchy of virtues, intellect alone is able to proclaim that the first place must be given to instinct.

The Right Use of Language

The subject we propose in this section is an ancient one, going back at least to the first rhetoricians and sophists—Plato and Aristotle among them—who were deeply concerned with the distinction between eloquence devoted to good ends and eloquence devoted to bad. This distinction was crucial in a culture in which direct speech was the main mode of communication, and a capacity to speak, argue, and answer well was the sole protection of a person's rights.

In the intervening centuries, the ethics of rhetoric has lost none of its importance. If anything, readers, writers, listeners, and viewers in an age of mass communication—of public relations, advertising, and image-manufacturing—need to be especially aware of the difference between honest language and deceit. Beneath "the right use of language" lie the profoundest matters of our political and moral welfare.

Susanne K. Langer's essay begins the section with a clear and powerful description of symbolism, the means by which language and thought are related. Her stress on the uniquely human capacity to manipulate symbols (with its paradoxical gifts of both reason and lunacy) opens the political and moral question in the broadest terms: "The envisagements of good and evil, which make man a moral agent, make him also a conscript, a prisoner, and a slave. His constant problem is to escape the tyrannies he has created." Orwell's famous essay takes up the question of language and politics very specifically, showing how bad writing and bad thinking propagate each other, and how they are related to badness in our political life. Both essays were written with the horrors of World War II vividly in mind; unfortunately neither has lost a bit of its relevance since. Congressman Drinan's essay demonstrates how easily Orwell's ideas can be applied to the habitual language of agencies like the Department of Defense.

Richard Weaver's focus on a few key terms in modern American usage has a similar moral concern, moving from a study of the terms themselves to suggesting how the same terms, if accepted unreflectingly, "lure us down the roads of hatred and tragedy." Aldous Huxley takes up the moral implications of the language of merchandising. Haig Bosmajian shows how language reflects racism, and suggests that whites need "to discard their racist terms, phrases, and clichés . . . before blacks and whites can discuss seriously the eradication of white racism." The concluding piece, by James Herndon, takes up yet another immorality, where the words and phrases are the "right" ones, but where they bear no necessary connection with the speaker's own conduct.

SUSANNE K. LANGER

Susanne K. Langer, born in 1895, was educated at Radcliffe College, where she received the Ph.D. in 1926. She has taught philosophy at Radcliffe, Wellesley, Smith, and Columbia, and in 1954 became head of the Philosophy Department at Connecticut College. She is now professor emeritus and research scholar, pursuing investigations in the philosophy of art, expression, and meaning. One of the few notable women in a field traditionally dominated by men, Professor Langer has reached a large audience and has had great influence on recent thinking, especially about the arts. Her best-known book is Philosophy in a New Key *(1942), in which, taking her cue from the researches of philosopher Ernst Cassirer, she investigates "the symbolism of reason, rite, and art." She has also written* An Introduction to Symbolic Logic *(1937),* Feeling and Form *(1953),* The Problem of Art *(1957), and* Mind: An Essay on Human Feeling, *2 vols. (1967, 1972). The present essay, clearly deriving from her interest in symbolism, appeared in* Fortune *in January 1944, at the height of World War II.*

The Prince of Creation

The world is aflame with man-made public disasters, artificial rains of brimstone and fire, planned earthquakes, cleverly staged famines and floods. The Prince of Creation is destroying himself. He is throwing down the cities he has built, the works of his own hand, the wealth of many thousand years in his frenzy of destruction, as a child knocks down its own handiwork, the whole day's achievement, in a tantrum of tears and rage.

What has displeased the royal child? What has incurred his world-shattering tantrum?

The bafflement of the magnificent game he is playing. Its rules and its symbols, his divine toys, have taken possession of the player. For this global war is not the old, hard, personal fight for the means of life, *bellum omnium contra omnes,* which animals perpetually wage; this is a war of monsters. Not mere men but great superpersonal giants, the national states, are met in combat. They do not hate and attack and wrestle as injured physical creatures do; they move heavily, inexorably, by strategy and necessity, to each other's destruction. The game of national states has come to this pass, and the desperate players ride their careening animated toys to a furious suicide.

These moloch gods, these monstrous states, are not natural beings; they are man's own work, products of the power that makes him lord over all other living things—his mind. They are not of the earth, earthy, as families and herds, hives and colonies are, whose members move and fight as one by instinct and habit until a physical disturbance splits them and the severed parts reconstitute themselves as new organized groups. The national states are not physical groups; they are social symbols, profound and terrible.

They are symbols of the new way of life, which the past two centuries have given us. For thousands of years, the pattern of daily life—working, praying, building, fighting, and raising new generations—repeated itself with only slow or unessential changes. The social symbols expressive of this life were ancient and familiar. Tribal gods or local saints, patriarchs, squires, or feudal lords, princes and bishops, raised to the highest power in the persons of emperors and popes—they were all expressions of needs and duties and opinions grounded in an immemorial way of life. The average man's horizon was not much greater than his valley, his town, or whatever geographical ramparts bounded his community. Economic areas were small, and economic problems essentially local. Naturally in his conception the powers governing the world were local, patriarchal, and reverently familiar.

Then suddenly, within some two hundred years, and for many places far less than that, the whole world has been transformed. Communities of different tongues and faiths and physiognomies have mingled; not as of old in wars of conquest, invading lords and conquered population gradually mixing their two stocks, but by a new process of foot-loose travel and trade, dominated by great centers of activity that bring individuals from near and far promiscuously together as a magnet draws filings from many heaps into close but quite accidental contact. Technology has made old horizons meaningless and localities indefinite. For goods and their destinies determine the structure of human societies. This is a new world, a world of persons, not of families and clans, or parishes and manors. The proletarian order is not founded on a hearth and its history. It does not express itself in a dialect, a local costume, a rite, a patron saint. All such traditions by mingling have canceled each other, and disappeared.

Most of us feel that since the old controlling ideas of faith and custom are gone, mankind is left without anchorage of any sort. None of the old social symbols fit this modern reality, this shrunken and undifferentiated world in which we lead a purely economic, secular, essentially homeless life.

But mankind is never without its social symbols; when old ones die, new ones are already in process of birth; and the new gods that have superseded all faiths are the great national states. The conception of them is mystical and moral, personal and devotional; they conjure with names and emblems, and demand our constant profession and practice of the new orthodoxy called "Patriotism."

Of all born creatures, man is the only one that cannot live by bread alone. He lives as much by symbols as by sense report, in a realm compounded of tangible things and virtual images, of actual events and ominous portents, always between fact and fiction. For he sees not only actualities but meanings. He has, indeed, all the impulses and interests of animal nature; he eats, sleeps, mates, seeks comfort and safety, flees pain, falls sick and dies, just as cats and bears and fishes and butterflies do. But he has something more in his repertoire, too—he has laws and religions, theories and dogmas, because he lives not only through sense but through symbols. That is the special asset of his mind, which makes him the master of earth and all its progeny.

By the agency of symbols—marks, words, mental images, and icons of all sorts—he can hold his ideas for contemplation long after their original causes have passed away. Therefore, he can think of things that are not presented or even suggested by his actual environment. By associating symbols in his mind, he combines things and events that were never together in the real world. This gives him the power we call imagination. Further, he can symbolize only part of an idea and let the rest go out of consciousness; this gives him the faculty that has been his pride throughout the ages—the power of abstraction. The combined effect of these two powers is inestimable. They are the roots of his supreme talent, the gift of reason.

In the war of each against all, which is the course of nature, man has an unfair advantage over his animal brethren; for he can see what is not yet there to be seen, know events that happened before his birth, and take possession of more than he actually eats; he can kill at a distance; and by rational design he can enslave other creatures to live and act for him instead of for themselves.

Yet this mastermind has strange aberrations. For in the whole animal kingdom there is no such unreason, no such folly and impracticality as man displays. He alone is hounded by imaginary fears, beset by ghosts and devils, frightened by mere images of things. No other creature wastes time in unprofitable ritual or builds nests for dead specimens of its race. Animals are always realists. They have intelligence in varying degrees— chickens are stupid, elephants are said to be very clever—but, bright or foolish, animals react only to reality. They may be fooled by appearance, by pictures or reflections, but once they know them as such, they promptly lose interest. Distance and darkness and silence are not fearful to them, filled with voices or forms, or invisible presences. Sheep in the pasture do not seem to fear phantom sheep beyond the fence, mice don't look for mouse goblins in the clock, birds do not worship a divine thunderbird.

But oddly enough, men do. They think of all these things and guard against them, worshiping animals and monsters even before they conceive of divinities in their own image. Men are essentially unrealistic. With all their extraordinary intelligence, they alone go in for patently impractical actions—magic and exorcism and holocausts—rites that have no connection with common-sense methods of self-preservation, such as a highly intelligent animal might use. In fact, the rites and sacrifices by which primitive man claims to control nature are sometimes fatal to the performers. Indian puberty rites are almost always intensely painful, and African natives have sometimes died during initiations into honorary societies.

We usually assume that very primitive tribes of men are closer to animal estate than highly civilized races; but in respect of practical attitudes, this is not true. The more primitive man's mind, the more fantastic it seems to be; only with high intellectual discipline do we gradually approach the realistic outlook of intelligent animals.

Yet this human mind, so beclouded by phantoms and superstitions, is probably the only mind on earth that can reach out to an awareness of things beyond its practical environment and can also conceive of such notions as truth, beauty, justice, majesty, space and time and creation.

There is another paradox in man's relationship with other creatures: namely, that those very qualities he calls animalian—"brutal," "bestial," "inhuman"—are peculiarly his own. No other animal is so deliberately cruel as man. No other creature intentionally imprisons its own kind, or invents special instruments of torture such as racks and thumbscrews for the sole purpose of punishment. No other animal keeps its own brethren in slavery; so far as we know, the lower animals do not commit anything like the acts of pure sadism that figure rather largely in our newspapers. There is no torment, spite, or cruelty for its own sake among beasts, as there is among men. A cat plays with its prey, but does not conquer and torture smaller cats. But man, who knows good and evil, is cruel for cruelty's sake; he who has a moral law is more brutal than the brutes, who have none; he alone inflicts suffering on his fellows with malice afore-thought.

If man's mind is really a higher form of the animal mind, his morality a specialized form of herd instinct, then where in the course of evolution did he lose the realism of a clever animal and fall prey to subjective fears? And why should he take pleasure in torturing helpless members of his own race?

The answer is, I think, that man's mind is *not* a direct evolution from the beast's mind, but is a unique variant and therefore has had a meteoric and startling career very different from any other animal history. The trait that sets human mentality apart from every other is its preoccupation with symbols, with images and names that *mean* things, rather than with things themselves. This trait may have been a mere sport of nature once upon a time. Certain creatures do develop tricks and interests that seem biolog-ically unimportant. Pack rats, for instance, and some birds of the crow family take a capricious pleasure in bright objects and carry away such things for which they have, presumably, no earthly use. Perhaps man's tendency to see certain forms as *images*, to hear certain sounds not only as signals but as expressive tones, and to be excited by sunset colors or starlight, was originally just a peculiar sensitivity in a rather highly developed brain. But whatever its cause, the ultimate destiny of this trait was momentous; for all human activity is based on the appreciation and use of symbols. Language, religion, mathematics, all learning, all science and superstition, even right and wrong, are products of symbolic expression rather than direct experience. Our commonest words, such as "house" and "red" and "walking," are symbols; the pyramids of Egypt and the mysterious circles of Stonehenge are symbols; so are dominions and empires and astronomical universes. We live in a mind-made world, where the things of prime importance are images or words that embody ideas and feelings and attitudes.

The animal mind is like a telephone exchange; it receives stimuli from outside through the sense organs and sends out appropriate responses through the nerves that govern muscles, glands, and other parts of the body. The organism is constantly interacting with its surroundings, receiving messages and acting on the new state of affairs that the messages signify.

But the human mind is not a simple transmitter like a telephone exchange. It is more like a great projector; for instead of merely mediating between an event in the outer world and a creature's responsive action, it transforms or, if you will, distorts the event into an image to be looked at, retained, and contemplated. For the images of things that we remember are not exact and faithful transcriptions even of our actual sense impressions. They are made as much by what we think as by what we see. It is a well-known fact that if you ask several people the size of the moon's disk as they look at it, their estimates will vary from the area of a dime to that of a barrel top. Like a magic lantern, the mind projects its ideas of things on the screen of what we call "memory"; but like all projections, these ideas are transformations of actual things. They are, in fact, *symbols* of reality, not pieces of it.

A symbol is not the same thing as a sign; that is a fact that psychologists and philosophers often overlook. All intelligent animals use signs; so do we. To them as well as to us sounds and smells and motions are signs of food, danger, the presence of other beings, or of rain or storm. Furthermore, some animals not only attend to signs but produce them for the benefit of others. Dogs bark at the door to be let in; rabbits thump to call each other; the cooing of doves and the growl of a wolf defending his kill are unequivocal signs of feelings and intentions to be reckoned with by other creatures.

We use signs just as animals do, though with considerably more elaboration. We stop at red lights and go on green; we answer calls and bells, watch the sky for coming storms, read trouble or promise or anger in each other's eyes. That is animal intelligence raised to the human level. Those of us who are dog lovers can probably all tell wonderful stories of how high our dogs have sometimes risen in the scale of clever sign interpretation and sign using.

A sign is anything that announces the existence or the imminence of some event, the presence of a thing or a person, or a change in a state of affairs. There are signs of the weather, signs of danger, signs of future good or evil, signs of what the past has been. In every case a sign is closely bound up with something to be noted or expected in experience. It is always a part of the situation to which it refers, though the reference may be remote in space and time. In so far as we are led to note or expect the signified event we are making correct use of a sign. This is the essence of rational behavior, which animals show in varying degrees. It is entirely realistic, being closely bound up with the actual objective course of history—learned by experience, and cashed in or voided by further experience.

If man had kept to the straight and narrow path of sign using, he would be like the other animals, though perhaps a little brighter. He would not talk, but grunt and gesticulate and point. He would make his wishes known, give warnings, perhaps develop a social system like that of bees and ants, with such a wonderful efficiency of communal enterprise that all men would have plenty to eat, warm apartments—all exactly alike and perfectly convenient—to live in, and everybody could and would sit in the sun or by the fire, as the climate demanded, not talking but just basking, with every want satisfied, most of his life. The young would romp and make love, the old would sleep, the middle-aged would do the routine work almost unconsciously and eat a great deal. But that would be the life of a social, superintelligent, purely sign-using animal.

To us who are human, it does not sound very glorious. We want to go places and do things, own all sorts of gadgets that we do not absolutely need, and when we sit down to take it easy we want to talk. Rights and property, social position, special talents and virtues, and above all our ideas, are what we live for. We have gone off on a tangent that takes us far away from the mere biological cycle that animal generations accomplish; and that is because we can use not only signs but symbols.

A symbol differs from a sign in that it does not announce the presence of the object, the being, condition, or whatnot, which is its meaning, but merely *brings this thing to mind*. It is not a mere "substitute sign" to which we react as though it were the object itself. The fact is that our reaction to hearing a person's name is quite different from our reaction to the person himself. There are certain rare cases where a symbol stands directly for its meaning: in religious experience, for instance, the Host is not only a symbol but a Presence. But symbols in the ordinary sense are not mystic. They are the same sort of thing that ordinary signs are; only they do not call our attention to something necessarily present or to be physically dealt with—they call up merely a conception of the thing they "mean."

The difference between a sign and a symbol is, in brief, that a sign causes us to think or act *in face of* the thing signified, whereas a symbol causes us to think *about* the thing symbolized. Therein lies the great importance of symbolism for human life, its power to make this life so different from any other animal biography that generations of men have found it incredible to suppose that they were of purely zoological origin. A sign is always embedded in reality, in a present that emerges from the actual past and stretches to the future; but a symbol may be divorced from reality altogether. It serves, therefore, to liberate thought from the immediate stimuli of a physically present world; and that liberation marks the essential difference between human and nonhuman mentality. Animals think, but they think *of* and *at* things; men think primarily *about* things. Words, pictures, and memory images are symbols that may be combined and varied in a thousand ways. The result is a symbolic structure whose meaning is a complex of all their respective meanings, and this kaleidoscope of *ideas* is the typical product of the human brain that we call the "stream of thought."

The process of transforming all direct experience into imagery or into that supreme mode of symbolic expression, language, has so completely taken possession of the human mind that it is not only a special talent but a dominant, organic need. All our sense impressions leave their traces in our memory not only as signs disposing our practical reactions in the future but also as symbols, images representing our *ideas* of things; and the tendency to manipulate ideas, to combine and abstract, mix and extend them by playing with symbols, is man's outstanding characteristic. It seems to be what his brain most naturally and spontaneously does. Therefore his primitive mental function is not judging reality, but *dreaming his desires.*

Dreaming is apparently a basic function of human brains, for it is free and unexhausting like our metabolism, heartbeat, and breath. It is easier to dream than not to dream, as it is easier to breathe than to refrain from breathing. The symbolic character of dreams is fairly well established. Symbol mongering, on this ineffectual, uncritical level, seems to be instinctive, the fulfillment of an elementary need rather than the purposeful exercise of a high and difficult talent.

The special power of man's mind rests on the evolution of this special activity, not on any transcendently high development of animal intelligence. We are not immeasurably higher than other animals; we are different. We have a biological need and with it a biological gift that they do not share.

Because man has not only the ability but the constant need of *conceiving* what has happened to him, what surrounds him, what is demanded of him—in short, of symbolizing nature, himself, and his hopes and fears —he has a constant and crying need of *expression.* What he cannot express, he cannot conceive; what he cannot conceive is chaos, and fills him with terror.

If we bear in mind this all-important craving for expression we get a new picture of man's behavior; for from this trait spring his powers and his weaknesses. The process of symbolic transformation that all our experiences undergo is nothing more nor less than the process of *conception,* which underlies the human faculties of abstraction and imagination.

When we are faced with a strange or difficult situation, we cannot react directly, as other creatures do, with flight, aggression, or any such simple instinctive pattern. Our whole reaction depends on how we manage to conceive the situation—whether we cast it in a definite dramatic form, whether we see it as a disaster, a challenge, a fulfillment of doom, or a fiat of the Divine Will. In words or dreamlike images, in artistic or religious or even in cynical form, we must *construe* the events of life. There is great virtue in the figure of speech, "I can *make* nothing of it," to express a failure to understand something. Thought and memory are processes of *making* the thought content and the memory image; the pattern of our ideas is given by the symbols through which we express them. And in the course of manipulating those symbols we inevitably distort the original experience, as we abstract certain features of it, embroider and reinforce those features with other ideas, until the conception we project on the screen of memory is quite different from anything in our real history.

Conception is a necessary and elementary process; what we do with our conceptions is another story. That is the entire history of human culture—of intelligence and morality, folly and superstition, ritual, language, and the arts—all the phenomena that set man apart from, and above, the rest of the animal kingdom. As the religious mind has to make all human history a drama of sin and salvation in order to define its own moral attitudes, so a scientist wrestles with the mere presentation of "the facts" before he can reason about them. The process of *envisaging* facts, values, hopes, and fears underlies our whole behavior pattern; and this process is reflected in the evolution of an extraordinary phenomenon found always, and only, in human societies—the phenomenon of language.

Language is the highest and most amazing achievement of the symbolistic human mind. The power it bestows is almost inestimable, for without it anything properly called "thought" is impossible. The birth of language is the dawn of humanity. The line between man and beast—between the highest ape and the lowest savage—is the language line. Whether the primitive Neanderthal man was anthropoid or human depends less on his cranial capacity, his upright posture, or even his use of tools and fire, than on one issue we shall probably never be able to settle—whether or not he spoke.

In all physical traits and practical responses, such as skills and visual judgments, we can find a certain continuity between animal and human mentality. Sign using is an ever evolving, ever improving function throughout the whole animal kingdom, from the lowly worm that shrinks into his hole at the sound of an approaching foot, to the dog obeying his master's command, and even to the learned scientist who watches the movements of an index needle.

This continuity of the sign-using talent has led psychologists to the belief that language is evolved from the vocal expressions, grunts and coos and cries, whereby animals vent their feelings or signal their fellows; that man has elaborated this sort of communion to the point where it makes a perfect exchange of ideas possible.

I do not believe that this doctrine of the origin of language is correct. The essence of language is symbolic, not signific; we use it first and most vitally to formulate and hold ideas in our own minds. Conception, not social control, is its first and foremost benefit.

Watch a young child that is just learning to speak play with a toy; he says the name of the object, e.g.: "Horsey! horsey! horsey!" over and over again, looks at the object, moves it, always saying the name to himself or to the world at large. It is quite a time before he talks to anyone in particular; he talks first of all to himself. This is his way of forming and fixing the *conception* of the object in his mind, and around this conception all his knowledge of it grows. *Names* are the essence of language; for the *name* is what abstracts the conception of the horse from the horse itself, and lets the mere idea recur at the speaking of the name. This permits the conception gathered from one horse experience to be exemplified again by another instance of a horse, so that the notion embodied in the name is a general notion.

To this end, the baby uses a word long before he *asks for* the object; when he wants his horsey he is likely to cry and fret, because he is reacting to an actual environment, not forming ideas. He uses the animal language of *signs* for his wants; talking is still a purely symbolic process—its practical value has not really impressed him yet.

Language need not be vocal; it may be purely visual, like written language, or even tactual, like the deaf-mute system of speech; but it *must be denotative.* The sounds, intended or unintended, whereby animals communicate do not constitute a language, because they are signs, not names. They never fall into an organic pattern, a meaningful syntax of even the most rudimentary sort, as all language seems to do with a sort of driving necessity. That is because signs refer to actual situations, in which things have obvious relations to each other that require only to be noted; but symbols refer to ideas, which are not physically there for inspection, so their connections and features have to be represented. This gives all true language a natural tendency toward growth and development, which seems almost like a life of its own. Languages are not invented; they grow with our need for expression.

In contrast, animal "speech" never has a structure. It is merely an emotional response. Apes may greet their ration of yams with a shout of "Nga!" But they do not say "Nga" between meals. If they could *talk about* their yams instead of just saluting them, they would be the most primitive men instead of the most anthropoid of beasts. They would have ideas, and tell each other things true or false, rational or irrational; they would make plans and invent laws and sing their own praises, as men do.

The history of speech is the history of our human descent. Yet the habit of transforming reality into symbols, of contemplating and combining and distorting symbols, goes beyond the confines of language. All *images* are symbols, which make us think about the things they mean.

This is the source of man's great interest in "graven images," and in *mere appearances* like the face of the moon or the human profiles he sees in rocks and trees. There is no limit to the meanings he can read into natural phenomena. As long as this power is undisciplined, the sheer enjoyment of finding meanings in everything, the elaboration of concepts without any regard to truth and usefulness, seems to run riot; superstition and ritual in their pristine strength go through what some anthropologists have called a "vegetative" stage, when dreamlike symbols, gods and ghouls and rites, multiply like the overgrown masses of life in a jungle. From this welter of symbolic forms emerge the images that finally govern a civilization; the great symbols of religion, society, and selfhood.

What does an image "mean"? Anything it is thought to resemble. It is only because we can abstract quite unobvious forms from the actual appearance of things that we see line drawings in two dimensions as images of colored, three-dimensional objects, find the likeness of a dipper in a constellation of seven stars, or see a face on a pansy. Any circle may represent the sun or moon; an upright monolith may be a man.

Wherever we can fancy a similarity we tend to see something represented. The first thing we do, upon seeing a new shape, is to assimilate it to our own idea of something that it resembles, something that is known and important to us. Our most elementary concepts are of our own actions, and the limbs or organs that perform them; other things are named by comparison with them. The opening of a cave is its mouth, the divisions of a river its arms. Language, and with it all articulate thought, grows by this process of unconscious metaphor. Every new idea urgently demands a word; if we lack a name for it, we call it after the first namable thing seen to bear even a remote analogy to it. Thus all the subtle and variegated vocabulary of a living language grows up from a few roots of very general application; words as various in meaning as "gentle" and "ingenious" and "general" spring from the one root "ge" meaning "to give life."

Yet there are conceptions that language is constitutionally unfit to express. The reason for this limitation of our verbal powers is a subject for logicians and need not concern us here. The point of interest to us is that, just as rational, discursive thought is bound up with language, so the life of feeling, of direct personal and social consciousness, the emotional stability of man and his sense of orientation in the world are bound up with images directly given to his senses: fire and water, noise and silence, high mountains and deep caverns, the brief beauty of flowers, the persistent grin of a skull. There seem to be irresistible parallels between the expressive forms we find in nature and the forms of our inner life; thus the use of light to represent all things good, joyful, comforting, and of darkness to express all sorts of sorrow, despair, or horror, is so primitive as to be well-nigh unconscious.

A flame is a soul; a star is a hope; the silence of winter is death. All such images, which serve the purpose of metaphorical thinking, are *natural symbols.* They have not conventionally assigned meanings, like words, but recommend themselves even to a perfectly untutored mind, a child's or a savage's, because they are definitely articulated *forms,* and to see something expressed in such forms is a universal human talent. We do not have to learn to use natural symbols; it is one of our primitive activities.

The fact that sensuous forms of natural processes have a significance beyond themselves makes the range of our symbolism, and with it the horizon of our consciousness, much wider and deeper than language. This is the source of ritual, mythology, and art. Ritual is a symbolic rendering of certain emotional *attitudes,* which have become articulate and fixed by being constantly expressed. Mythology is man's image of his world, and of himself in the world. Art is the exposition of his own subjective history, the life of feeling, the human spirit in all its adventures.

Yet this power of envisagement, which natural symbolism bestows, is a dangerous one; for human beings can envisage things that do not exist, and create horrible worlds, insupportable duties, monstrous gods and ancestors. The mind that can see past and future, the poles and the antipodes, and guess at obscure mechanisms of nature, is ever in danger of seeing what is not there, imagining false and fantastic causes, and courting death instead of life. Because man can play with ideas, he is unrealistic; he is inclined to neglect the all-important interpretation of signs for a rapt contemplation of symbols.

Some twenty years ago, Ernst Cassirer set forth a theory of human mentality that goes far toward explaining the vagaries of savage religions and the ineradicable presence of superstition even in civilized societies: a symbol, he observed, is the embodiment of an idea; it is at once an abstract and a physical fact. Now its great emotive value lies in the concept it conveys; this inspires our reverent attitude, the attention and awe with which we view it. But man's untutored thought always tends to lose its way between the symbol and the fact. A skull represents death; but to a primitive mind the skull *is* death. To have it in the house is not unpleasant but dangerous. Even in civilized societies, symbolic objects—figures of saints, relics, crucifixes—are revered for their supposed efficacy. Their actual power is a power of *expression,* of embodying and thus revealing the greatest concepts humanity has reached; these concepts are the commanding forces that change our estate from a brute existence to the transcendent life of the spirit. But the symbol-loving mind of man reveres the meaning not *through* the articulating form but *in* the form so that the image appears to be the actual object of love and fear, supplication and praise.

Because of this constant identification of concepts with their expressions, our world is crowded with unreal beings. Some societies have actually realized that these beings do not belong to nature, and have postulated a so-called "other world" where they have their normal existence and from which they are said to descend, or arise, into our physical realm. For savages it is chiefly a nether world that sends up spooks; for more advanced cults it is from the heavens that supernatural beings, the embodiments of human ideas—of virtue, triumph, immortality—descend to the mundane realm. But from this source emanates also a terrible world government, with heavy commands and sanctions. Strange worship and terrible sacrifices may be the tithes exacted by the beings that embody our knowledge of nonanimalian human nature.

So the gift of symbolism, which is the gift of reason, is at the same time the seat of man's peculiar weakness—the danger of lunacy. Animals go mad with hydrophobia or head injuries, but purely mental aberrations are rare; beasts are not generally subject to insanity except through a confusion of signs, such as the experimentally produced "nervous breakdown" in rats. It is man who hears voices and sees ghosts in the dark, feels irrational compulsions and holds fixed ideas. All these phantasms are symbolic forms that have acquired a false factual status. It has been truly said that everybody has some streak of insanity; i.e., the threat of madness is the price of reason.

Because we can think of things potential as well as actual, we can be held in nonphysical bondage by laws and prohibitions and commands and by images of a governing power. This makes men tyrants over their own kind. Animals control each other's actions by immediate threats, growls and snarls and passes; but when the bully is roving elsewhere, his former domain is free of him. We control our inferiors by setting up symbols of our power, and the mere idea that words or images convey stands there to hold our fellows in subjection even when we cannot lay our hands on them. There is no flag over the country where a wolf is king; he is king where he happens to prowl, so long as he is there. But men, who can embody ideas and set them up to view, oppress each other by symbols of might.

The envisagements of good and evil, which make man a moral agent, make him also a conscript, a prisoner, and a slave. His constant problem is to escape the tyrannies he has created. Primitive societies are almost entirely tyrannical, symbol-bound, coercive organizations; civilized governments are so many conscious schemes to justify or else to disguise man's inevitable bondage to law and conscience.

Slowly, through ages and centuries, we have evolved a picture of the world we live in; we have made a drama of the earth's history and enhanced it with a backdrop of divinely ordered, star-filled space. And all this structure of infinity and eternity against which we watch the pageant of life and death, and all the moral melodrama itself, we have wrought by a gradual articulation of such vast ideas in symbols—symbols of good and evil, triumph and failure, birth and maturity and death. Long before the beginning of any known history, people saw in the heavenly bodies, in the changes of day and night or of the seasons, and in great beasts, symbolic forms to express those ultimate concepts that are the very frame of human existence. So gods, fates, the cohorts of good and evil were conceived. Their myths were the first formulations of cosmic ideas. Gradually the figures and traditions of religion emerged; ritual, the overt expression of our mental attitudes, became more and more intimately bound to definite and elaborate concepts of the creative and destructive powers that seem to control our lives.

Such beings and stories and rites are sacred because they are the great symbols by which the human mind orients itself in the world. To a creature that lives by reason, nothing is more terrible than what is formless and meaningless; one of our primary fears is fear of chaos. And it is the fight against chaos that has produced our most profound and indispensable images—the myths of light and darkness, of creation and passion, the symbols of the altar flame, the daystar, and the cross.

For thousands of years people lived by the symbols that nature presented to them. Close contact with earth and its seasons, intimate knowledge of stars and tides, made them feel the significance of natural phenomena and gave them a poetic, unquestioning sense of orientation. Generations of erudite and pious men elaborated the picture of the temporal and spiritual realms in which each individual was a pilgrim soul.

Then came the unprecedented change, the almost instantaneous leap of history from the immemorial tradition of the plow and the anvil to the new age of the machine, the factory, and the ticker tape. Often in no more than the length of a life-time the shift from handwork to mass production, and with it from poetry to science and from faith to nihilism, has taken place. The old nature symbols have become remote and have lost their meanings; in the clatter of gears and the confusion of gadgets that fill the new world, there will not be any obvious and rich and sacred meanings for centuries to come. All the accumulated creeds and rites of men are suddenly in the melting pot. There is no fixed community, no dynasty, no family inheritance—only the one huge world of men, vast millions of men, still looking on each other in hostile amazement.

A sane, intelligent animal should have invented, in the course of ten thousand years or more, some sure and obvious way of accommodating indefinite numbers of its own kind on the face of a fairly spacious earth. Modern civilization has achieved the highest triumphs of knowledge, skill, ingenuity, theory; yet all around its citadels, engulfing and demolishing them, rages the maddest war and confusion, inspired by symbols and slogans as riotous and irrational as anything the "vegetative" stage of savage phantasy could provide. How shall we reconcile this primitive nightmare excitement with the achievements of our high, rational, scientific culture?

The answer is, I think, that we are no longer in possession of a definite, established culture; we live in a period between an exhausted age —the European civilization of the white race—and an age still unborn, of which we can say nothing as yet. We do not know what races shall inherit the earth. We do not know what even the next few centuries may bring. But it is quite evident, I think, that we live in an age of transition, and that before many more generations have passed, mankind will make a new beginning and build itself a different world. Whether it will be a "brave, new world," or whether it will start all over with an unchronicled "state of nature" such as Thomas Hobbes described, wherein the individual's life is "nasty, brutish, and short," we simply cannot tell. All we know is that every tradition, every institution, every tribe is gradually becoming uprooted and upset, and we are waiting in a sort of theatrical darkness between the acts.

Because we are at a new beginning, our imaginations tend to a wild, "vegetative" overgrowth. The political upheavals of our time are marked, therefore, by a veritable devil dance of mystical ideologies, vaguely conceived, passionately declared, holding out fanatic hopes of mass redemption and mass beatitudes. Governments vie with each other in proclaiming social plans, social aims, social enterprises, and demanding bloody sacrifices in the name of social achievements.

New conceptions are always clothed in an extravagant metaphorical form, for there is no language to express genuinely new ideas. And in their pristine strength they imbue the symbols that express them with their own mystery and power and holiness. It is impossible to disengage the welter of ideas embodied in a swastika, a secret sign, or a conjuring word from the physical presence of the symbol itself; hence the apparently nonsensical symbol worship and mysticism that go with new movements and visions. This identification of symbolic form and half-articulate meaning is the essence of all mythmaking. Of course the emotive value is incomprehensible to anyone who does not see such figments as expressive forms. So an age of vigorous new conception and incomplete formulation always has a certain air of madness about it. But it is really a fecund and exciting period in the life of reason. Such is our present age. Its apparent unreason is a tremendous unbalance and headiness of the human spirit, a conflict not only of selfish wills but of vast ideas in the metaphorical state of emergence.

The change from fixed community life and ancient local custom to the mass of unpedigreed human specimens that actually constitutes the world in our industrial and commercial age has been too sudden for the mind of man to negotiate. Some transitional form of life had to mediate between those extremes. And so the idol of nationality arose from the wreckage of tribal organization. The concept of the national state is really the old tribe concept applied to millions of persons, unrelated and different creatures gathered under the banner of a government. Neither birth nor language nor even religion holds such masses together, but a mystic bond is postulated even where no actual bond of race, creed, or color may ever have existed.

At first glance it seems odd that the concept of nationality should reach its highest development just as all actual marks of national origins —language, dress, physiognomy, and religion—are becoming mixed and obliterated by our new mobility and cosmopolitan traffic. But it is just the loss of these things that inspires this hungry seeking for something like the old egocentric pattern in the vast and formless brotherhood of the whole earth. While mass production and universal communication clearly portend a culture of world citizenship, we cling desperately to our nationalism, a more and more attenuated version of the old clan civilization. We fight passionate and horrible wars for the symbols of our nations, we make a virtue of self-glorification and exclusiveness and invent strange anthropologies to keep us at least theoretically set apart from other men.

Nationalism is a transition between an old and a new human order. But even now we are not really fighting a war of nations; we are fighting a war of fictions, from which a new vision of the order of nature will someday emerge. The future, just now, lies wide open—open and dark, like interstellar space; but in that emptiness there is room for new gods, new cultures, mysterious now and nameless as an unborn child.

GEORGE ORWELL

Orwell's reputation has shown no sign of decline since his death at forty-six in 1950. He is likely to be ranked permanently among the great English essayists. On presenting him an award in 1949, the editors of Partisan Review *commented that his writing "has been marked by a singular directness and honesty, a scrupulous fidelity to his experience that has placed him in that valuable class of the writer who is a witness to his time."*

His real name was Eric Arthur Blair, and he was born in 1903 in Bengal, a province of British India. His first school experience is described in the essay "Such, Such Were the Joys." He attended Eton on a King's Scholarship from 1917 to 1921, then served for five years in the Imperial Police in Burma. These early years are the subject of a biography by Peter Stansky and William Abraham entitled The Unknown Orwell *(1972). Returning to Europe, he spent some poverty-stricken years doing odd jobs, from teaching to dishwashing, while he wrote novels and short stories that*

did not sell. His Down and Out in Paris and London *(1933)*
is a vivid record of those years. In 1936 Orwell went to Spain to
take part in the civil war and reported his experiences in Homage to
Catalonia *(1938). Among his other books are the celebrated* Nineteen
Eighty-Four *(1949), a terrifying novel picturing the complete victory of*
totalitarianism; Animal Farm: A Fairy Story *(1945); and the essay*
collections Shooting an Elephant and Other Essays *(1950),* Such,
Such Were the Joys *(1953), and* Collected Essays *(1966). The*
present essay first appeared in the London monthly Horizon *in 1946 and*
was reprinted in the 1950 collection.

Politics and the English Language

Most people who bother with the matter at all would admit that the
English language is in a bad way, but it is generally assumed that we
cannot by conscious action do anything about it. Our civilization is decadent and our language—so the argument runs—must inevitably share in
the general collapse. It follows that any struggle against the abuse of
language is a sentimental archaism, like preferring candles to electric
light or hansom cabs to aeroplanes. Underneath this lies the half-conscious belief that language is a natural growth and not an instrument
which we shape for our own purposes.

Now, it is clear that the decline of a language must ultimately have
political and economic causes: it is not due simply to the bad influence
of this or that individual writer. But an effect can become a cause, rein-
forcing the original cause and producing the same effect in an intensified
form, and so on indefinitely. A man may take to drink because he feels
himself to be a failure, and then fail all the more completely because he
drinks. It is rather the same thing that is happening to the English language. It becomes ugly and inaccurate because our thoughts are foolish,
but the slovenliness of our language makes it easier for us to have foolish
thoughts. The point is that the process is reversible. Modern English,
especially written English, is full of bad habits which spread by imitation
and which can be avoided if one is willing to take the necessary trouble.
If one gets rid of these habits one can think more clearly, and to think
clearly is a necessary first step towards political regeneration: so that the
fight against bad English is not frivolous and is not the exclusive concern
of professional writers. I will come back to this presently, and I hope that
by that time the meaning of what I have said here will have become
clearer. Meanwhile, here are five specimens of the English language as
it is now habitually written.

These five passages have not been picked out because they are especially bad—I could have quoted far worse if I had chosen—but because

they illustrate various of the mental vices from which we now suffer. They are a little below the average, but are fairly representative samples. I number them so that I can refer back to them when necessary:

(1) I am not, indeed, sure whether it is not true to say that the Milton who once seemed not unlike a seventeenth-century Shelley had not become, out of an experience ever more bitter in each year, more alien [*sic*] to the founder of that Jesuit sect which nothing could induce him to tolerate.

PROFESSOR HAROLD LASKI
(ESSAY IN *Freedom of Expression*).

(2) Above all, we cannot play ducks and drakes with a native battery of idioms which prescribes such egregious collocations of vocables as the Basic *put up with* for *tolerate* or *put at a loss* for *bewilder.*

PROFESSOR LANCELOT HOGBEN
(*Interglossa*).

(3) On the one side we have the free personality: by definition it is not neurotic, for it has neither conflict nor dream. Its desires, such as they are, are transparent, for they are just what institutional approval keeps in the forefront of consciousness; another institutional pattern would alter their number and intensity; there is little in them that is natural, irreducible, or culturally dangerous. But *on the other side,* the social bond itself is nothing but the mutual reflection of these self-secure integrities. Recall the definition of love. Is not this the very picture of a small academic? Where is there a place in this hall of mirrors for either personality or fraternity?

ESSAY ON PSYCHOLOGY IN *Politics* (NEW YORK).

(4) All the "best people" from the gentlemen's clubs, and all the frantic fascist captains, united in common hatred of Socialism and bestial horror of the rising tide of the mass revolutionary movement, have turned to acts of provocation, to foul incendiarism, to medieval legends of poisoned wells, to legalize their own destruction of proletarian organizations, and rouse the agitated petty-bourgeoisie to chauvinistic fervor on behalf of the fight against the revolutionary way out of the crisis.

COMMUNIST PAMPHLET.

(5) If a new spirit *is* to be infused into this old country, there is one thorny and contentious reform which must be tackled, and that is the humanization and galvanization of the B.B.C. Timidity here will bespeak canker and atrophy of the soul. The heart of Britain may be sound and of strong beat, for instance, but the British lion's roar at present is like that of Bottom in Shakespeare's *Midsummer Night's Dream*—as gentle as

any sucking dove. A virile new Britain cannot continue indefinitely to be traduced in the eyes or rather ears, of the world by the effete languors of Langham Place, brazenly masquerading as "standard English." When the voice of Britain is heard at nine o'clock, better far and infinitely less ludicrous to hear aitches honestly dropped than the present priggish, inflated, inhibited, school-ma'amish arch braying of blameless bashful mewing maidens!

LETTER IN Tribune.

Each of these passages has faults of its own, but, quite apart from avoidable ugliness, two qualities are common to all of them. The first is staleness of imagery; the other is lack of precision. The writer either has a meaning and cannot express it, or he inadvertently says something else, or he is almost indifferent as to whether his words mean anything or not. This mixture of vagueness and sheer incompetence is the most marked characteristic of modern English prose, and especially of any kind of political writing. As soon as certain topics are raised, the concrete melts into the abstract and no one seems able to think of turns of speech that are not hackneyed: prose consists less and less of *words* chosen for the sake of their meaning, and more and more of *phrases* tacked together like the sections of a prefabricated hen-house. I list below, with notes and examples, various of the tricks by means of which the work of prose-construction is habitually dodged:

Dying metaphors. A newly invented metaphor assists thought by evoking a visual image, while on the other hand a metaphor which is technically "dead" (e.g. *iron resolution*) has in effect reverted to being an ordinary word and can generally be used without loss of vividness. But in between these two classes there is a huge dump of worn-out metaphors which have lost all evocative power and are merely used because they save people the trouble of inventing phrases for themselves. Examples are: *Ring the changes on, take up the cudgels for, toe the line, ride roughshod over, stand shoulder to shoulder with, play into the hands of, no axe to grind, grist to the mill, fishing in troubled waters, on the order of the day, Achilles' heel, swan song, hotbed.* Many of these are used without knowledge of their meaning (what is a "rift," for instance?), and incompatible metaphors are frequently mixed, a sure sign that the writer is not interested in what he is saying. Some metaphors now current have been twisted out of their original meaning without those who use them even being aware of the fact. For example, *toe the line* is sometimes written *tow the line.* Another example is *the hammer and the anvil,* now always used with the implication that the anvil gets the worst of it. In real life it is always the anvil that breaks the hammer, never the other way about: a writer who stopped to think what he was saying would be aware of this, and would avoid perverting the original phrase.

Operators or *verbal false limbs.* These save the trouble of picking out appropriate verbs and nouns, and at the same time pad each sentence with extra syllables which give it an appearance of symmetry. Characteristic phrases are *render inoperative, militate against, make contact with, be subjected to, give rise to, give grounds for, have the effect of, play a leading part (role) in, make itself felt, take effect, exhibit a tendency to, serve the purpose of, etc., etc.* The keynote is the elimination of simple verbs. Instead of being a single word, such as *break, stop, spoil, mend, kill,* a verb becomes *a phrase,* made up of a noun or adjective tacked on to some general-purpose verb such as *prove, serve, form, play, render.* In addition, the passive voice is wherever possible used in preference to the active, and noun constructions are used instead of gerunds (*by examination of* instead of *by examining*). The range of verbs is further cut down by means of the *-ize* and *de-* formations, and the banal statements are given an appearance of profundity by means of the *not un-* formation. Simple conjunctions and prepositions are replaced by such phrases as *with respect to, having regard to, the fact that, by dint of, in view of, in the interests of, on the hypothesis that;* and the ends of sentences are saved from anticlimax by such resounding common-places as *greatly to be desired, cannot be left out of account, a development to be expected in the near future, deserving of serious consideration, brought to a satisfactory conclusion,* and so on and so forth.

Pretentious diction. Words like *phenomenon, element, individual* (as noun), *objective, categorical, effective, virtual, basic, primary, promote, constitute, exhibit, exploit, utilize, eliminate, liquidate,* are used to dress up simple statements and give an air of scientific impartiality to biased judgments. Adjectives like *epoch-making, epic, historic, unforgettable, triumphant, age-old, inevitable, inexorable, veritable,* are used to dignify the sordid processes of international politics, while writing that aims at glorifying war usually takes on an archaic color, its characteristic words being: *realm, throne, chariot, mailed fist, trident, sword, shield, buckler, banner, jackboot, clarion.* Foreign words and expressions such as *cul de sac, ancien régime, deus ex machina, mutatis mutandis, status quo, gleichschaltung, weltanschauung,* are used to give an air of culture and elegance. Except for the useful abbreviations *i.e., e.g.,* and *etc.,* there is no real need for any of the hundreds of foreign phrases now current in English. Bad writers, and especially scientific, political and sociological writers, are nearly always haunted by the notion that Latin or Greek words are grander than Saxon ones, and unnecessary words like *expedite, ameliorate, predict, extraneous, deracinated, clandestine, subaqueous* and hundreds of others constantly gain ground from their Anglo-Saxon opposite numbers.[1] The jargon peculiar to Marxist writing (*hyena, hangman, cannibal, petty bourgeois, these gentry, lacquey, flunkey, mad dog, White Guard,* etc.) consists largely of words and phrases translated from Russian, German or French; but the normal way of coining a new word is to use a Latin or Greek root with the appropriate affix and, where necessary, the *-ize* formation. It is often easier to make up words of this kind (*deregionalize,*

---

[1]An interesting illustration of this is the way in which the English flower names which were in use till very recently are being ousted by Greek ones, *snapdragon* becoming *antirrhinum, forget-me-not* becoming *myosotis,* etc. It is hard to see any practical reason for this change of fashion: it is probably due to an instinctive turning-away from the more homely word and a vague feeling that the Greek word is scientific.

impermissible, extramarital, non-fragmentary and so forth) than to think up the English words that will cover one's meaning. The result, in general, is an increase in slovenliness and vagueness.

Meaningless words. In certain kinds of writing, particularly in art criticism and literary criticism, it is normal to come across long passages which are almost completely lacking in meaning.[2] Words like *romantic, plastic, values, human, dead, sentimental, natural, vitality,* as used in art criticism, are strictly meaningless, in the sense that they not only do not point to any discoverable object, but are hardly ever expected to do so by the reader. When one critic writes, "The outstanding feature of Mr. X's work is its living quality," while another writes, "The immediately striking thing about Mr. X's work is its peculiar deadness," the reader accepts this as a simple difference of opinion. If words like *black* and *white* were involved, instead of the jargon words *dead* and *living,* he would see at once that language was being used in an improper way. Many political words are similarly abused. The word *Fascism* has now no meaning except in so far as it signifies "something not desirable." The words *democracy, socialism, freedom, patriotic, realistic, justice,* have each of them several different meanings which cannot be reconciled with one another. In the case of a word like *democracy,* not only is there no agreed definition, but the attempt to make one is resisted from all sides. It is almost universally felt that when we call a country democratic we are praising it: consequently the defenders of every kind of régime claim that it is a democracy, and fear that they might have to stop using the word if it were tied down to any one meaning. Words of this kind are often used in a consciously dishonest way. That is, the person who uses them has his own private definition, but allows his hearer to think he means something quite different. Statements like *Marshal Pétain was a true patriot, The Soviet Press is the freest in the world, The Catholic Church is opposed to persecution,* are almost always made with intent to deceive. Other words used in variable meanings, in most cases more or less dishonestly, are: *class, totalitarian, science, progressive, reactionary, bourgeois, equality.*

Now that I have made this catalogue of swindles and perversions, let me give another example of the kind of writing that they lead to. This time it must of its nature be an imaginary one. I am going to translate a passage of good English into modern English of the worst sort. Here is a well-known verse from *Ecclesiastes:*

"I returned and saw under the sun, that the race is not to the swift, nor the battle to the strong, neither yet bread to the wise, nor yet riches

---

[2]Example: "Comfort's catholicity of perception and image, strangely Whitmanesque in range, almost the exact opposite in aesthetic compulsion, continues to evoke that trembling atmospheric accumulative hinting at a cruel, an inexorably serene timelessness. . . . Wrey Gardiner scores by aiming at simple bull's-eyes with precision. Only they are not so simple, and through this contented sadness runs more than the surface bittersweet of resignation." (*Poetry Quarterly.*)

to men of understanding, nor yet favour to men of skill; but time and chance happeneth to them all."

Here it is in modern English:

"Objective consideration of contemporary phenomena compels the conclusion that success or failure in competitive activities exhibits no tendency to be commensurate with innate capacity, but that a considerable element of the unpredictable must invariably be taken into account."

This is a parody, but not a very gross one. Exhibit (3), above, for instance, contains several patches of the same kind of English. It will be seen that I have not made a full translation. The beginning and ending of the sentence follow the original meaning fairly closely, but in the middle the concrete illustrations—race, battle, bread—dissolve into the vague phrase "success or failure in competitive activities." This had to be so, because no modern writer of the kind I am discussing—no one capable of using phrases like "objective consideration of contemporary phenomena"—would ever tabulate his thoughts in that precise and detailed way. The whole tendency of modern prose is away from concreteness. Now analyse these two sentences a little more closely. The first contains forty-nine words but only sixty syllables, and all its words are those of everyday life. The second contains thirty-eight words of ninety syllables: eighteen of its words are from Latin roots, and one from Greek. The first sentence contains six vivid images, and only one phrase ("time and chance") that could be called vague. The second contains not a single fresh, arresting phrase, and in spite of its ninety syllables it gives only a shortened version of the meaning contained in the first. Yet without a doubt it is the second kind of sentence that is gaining ground in modern English. I do not want to exaggerate. This kind of writing is not yet universal, and outcrops of simplicity will occur here and there in the worst-written page. Still, if you or I were told to write a few lines on the uncertainty of human fortunes, we should probably come much nearer to my imaginary sentence than to the one from *Ecclesiastes.*

As I have tried to show, modern writing at its worst does not consist in picking out words for the sake of their meaning and inventing images in order to make the meaning clearer. It consists in gumming together long strips of words which have already been set in order by someone else, and making the results presentable by sheer humbug. The attraction of this way of writing is that it is easy. It is easier—even quicker, once you have the habit—to say *In my opinion it is not an unjustifiable assumption that* than to say *I think.* If you use ready-made phrases, you not only don't have to hunt about for words; you also don't have to bother with the rhythms of your sentences, since these phrases are generally so arranged as to be more or less euphonious. When you are composing in a hurry—when you are dictating to a stenographer, for instance, or making a public speech—it is natural to fall into a pretentious, Latinized style. Tags like *a consideration which we should do well to bear in mind* or *a conclusion to which all of us would readily assent* will save many a sentence from coming down with a bump. By using stale metaphors, similes and idioms, you save much mental effort, at the cost of leaving your meaning vague, not only for your reader but for yourself. This is the significance of mixed metaphors. The sole aim of a metaphor is to call up a visual image. When these images clash—as in *The Fascist octopus has sung its swan song, the jackboot is thrown into the melting pot*—it can be taken as certain that the writer is not seeing a mental image of the objects he is naming; in other words he is not really thinking. Look again at the examples I gave at the beginning of this essay. Professor Laski (1) uses five negatives in fifty-three words. One of these is superfluous, making nonsense of the whole passage, and in addition there is the slip *alien* for *akin,* making further nonsense, and several avoidable pieces of clumsiness which increase the general vagueness. Professor Hogben (2) plays ducks and drakes with a battery which is able to write prescriptions, and, while disapproving of the everyday phrase *put up with,* is unwilling to look *egregious* up in the dictionary and see what it means; (3), if one takes an uncharitable attitude towards it, is simply meaningless: probably one could work out its intended meaning by reading the whole of the article in which it occurs. In (4), the writer knows more or less what he wants to say, but an accumulation of stale phrases chokes him like tea leaves blocking a sink. In (5), words and meaning have almost parted company. People who write in this manner usually have a general emotional meaning—they dislike one thing and want to express solidarity with another—but they are not interested in the detail of what they are saying. A scrupulous writer, in every sentence that he writes, will ask himself at least four questions, thus: What am I trying to say? What words will express it? What image or idiom will make it clearer? Is this image fresh enough to have an effect? And he will probably ask himself two more: Could I put it more shortly? Have I said anything that is avoidably ugly? But you are not obliged to go to all this trouble. You can shirk it by simply throwing your mind open and letting the ready-made phrases come crowding in. They will construct your sentences for you— even think your thoughts for you, to a certain extent—and at need they will perform the important service of partially concealing your meaning even from yourself. It is at this point that the special connection between politics and the debasement of language becomes clear.

In our time it is broadly true that political writing is bad writing. Where it is not true, it will generally be found that the writer is some kind of rebel, expressing his private opinions and not a "party line." Orthodoxy, of whatever color, seems to demand a lifeless, imitative style. The political dialects to be found in pamphlets, leading articles, manifestos, White Papers and the speeches of under-secretaries do, of course, vary from party to party, but they are all alike in that one almost never finds in them a fresh, vivid, home-made turn of speech. When one watches some tired hack on the platform mechanically repeating the familiar phrases—*bestial atrocities, iron heel, bloodstained tyranny, free peoples of*

the world, stand shoulder to shoulder—one often has a curious feeling that one
is not watching a live human being but some kind of dummy: a feeling
which suddenly becomes stronger at moments when the light catches the
speaker's spectacles and turns them into blank discs which seem to have
no eyes behind them. And this is not altogether fanciful. A speaker who
uses that kind of phraseology has gone some distance towards turning
himself into a machine. The appropriate noises are coming out of his
larynx, but his brain is not involved as it would be if he were choosing
his words for himself. If the speech he is making is one that he is accustomed to make over and over again, he may be almost unconscious of
what he is saying, as one is when one utters the responses in church. And
this reduced state of consciousness, if not indispensable, is at any rate
favorable to political conformity.

In our time, political speech and writing are largely the defence of the
indefensible. Things like the continuance of British rule in India, the
Russian purges and deportations, the dropping of the atom bombs on
Japan, can indeed be defended, but only by arguments which are too
brutal for most people to face, and which do not square with the professed aims of political parties. Thus political language has to consist
largely of euphemism, question-begging and sheer cloudy vagueness.
Defenceless villages are bombarded from the air, the inhabitants driven
out into the countryside, the cattle machine-gunned, the huts set on fire
with incendiary bullets: this is called *pacification*. Millions of peasants are
robbed of their farms and sent trudging along the roads with no more
than they can carry: this is called *transfer of population* or *rectification of
frontiers*. People are imprisoned for years without trial, or shot in the back
of the neck or sent to die of scurvy in Arctic lumber camps: this is called
elimination of unreliable elements. Such phraseology is needed if one wants
to name things without calling up mental pictures of them. Consider for
instance some comfortable English professor defending Russian totalitarianism. He cannot say outright, "I believe in killing off your opponents
when you can get good results by doing so." Probably, therefore, he will
say something like this:

"While freely conceding that the Soviet régime exhibits certain features which the humanitarian may be inclined to deplore, we must, I
think, agree that a certain curtailment of the right to political opposition
is an unavoidable concomitant of transitional periods, and that the rigors
which the Russian people have been called upon to undergo have been
amply justified in the sphere of concrete achievement."

The inflated style is itself a kind of euphemism. A mass of Latin words
falls upon the facts like soft snow, blurring the outlines and covering up
all the details. The great enemy of clear language is insincerity. When
there is a gap between one's real and one's declared aims, one turns as
it were instinctively to long words and exhausted idioms, like a cuttlefish
squirting out ink. In our age there is no such thing as "keeping out of
politics." All issues are political issues, and politics itself is a mass of lies,

evasions, folly, hatred and schizophrenia. When the general atmosphere
is bad, language must suffer. I should expect to find—this is a guess which
I have not sufficient knowledge to verify—that the German, Russian and
Italian languages have all deteriorated in the last ten to fifteen years, as
a result of dictatorship.

But if thought corrupts language, language can also corrupt thought.
A bad usage can spread by tradition and imitation, even among people
who should and do know better. The debased language that I have been
discussing is in some ways very convenient. Phrases like *a not unjustifiable
assumption, leaves much to be desired, would serve no good purpose, a consideration
which we should do well to bear in mind,* are a continuous temptation, a packet
of aspirins always at one's elbow. Look back through this essay, and for
certain you will find that I have again and again committed the very faults
I am protesting against. By this morning's post I have received a pamphlet dealing with conditions in Germany. The author tells me that he
"felt impelled" to write it. I open it at random, and here is almost the first
sentence that I see: "[The Allies] have an opportunity not only of achieving a radical transformation of Germany's social and political structure
in such a way as to avoid a nationalistic reaction in Germany itself, but
at the same time of laying the foundations of a cooperative and unified
Europe." You see, he "feels impelled" to write—feels, presumably, that
he has something new to say—and yet his words, like cavalry horses
answering the bugle, group themselves automatically into the familiar
dreary pattern. This invasion of one's mind by ready-made phrases (*lay
the foundations, achieve a radical transformation*) can only be prevented if one
is constantly on guard against them, and every such phrase anaesthetizes
a portion of one's brain.

I said earlier that the decadence of our language is probably curable.
Those who deny this would argue, if they produced an argument at all,
that language merely reflects existing social conditions, and that we cannot influence its development by any direct tinkering with words and
constructions. So far as the general tone or spirit of a language goes, this
may be true, but it is not true in detail. Silly words and expressions have
often disappeared, not through any evolutionary process but owing to the
conscious action of a minority. Two recent examples were *explore every
avenue* and *leave no stone unturned,* which were killed by the jeers of a few
journalists. There is a long list of flyblown metaphors which could similarly be got rid of if enough people would interest themselves in the job;
and it should also be possible to laugh the *not un-* formation out of
existence,[3] to reduce the amount of Latin and Greek in the average
sentence, to drive out foreign phrases and strayed scientific words, and,
in general, to make pretentiousness unfashionable. But all these are
minor points. The defence of the English language implies more than
this, and perhaps it is best to start by saying what it does *not* imply.

[3]One can cure oneself of the *not un-* formation by memorizing this sentence: *A not unblack
dog was chasing a not unsmall rabbit across a not ungreen field.*

To begin with it has nothing to do with archaism, with the salvaging of obsolete words and turns of speech, or with the setting up of a "standard English" which must never be departed from. On the contrary, it is especially concerned with the scrapping of every word or idiom which has outworn its usefulness. It has nothing to do with correct grammar and syntax, which are of no importance so long as one makes one's meaning clear, or with the avoidance of Americanisms, or with having what is called a "good prose style." On the other hand it is not concerned with fake simplicity and the attempt to make written English colloquial. Nor does it even imply in every case preferring the Saxon word to the Latin one, though it does imply using the fewest and shortest words that will cover one's meaning. What is above all needed is to let the meaning choose the word, and not the other way about. In prose, the worst thing one can do with words is to surrender to them. When you think of a concrete object, you think wordlessly, and then, if you want to describe the thing you have been visualizing you probably hunt about till you find the exact words that seem to fit it. When you think of something abstract you are more inclined to use words from the start, and unless you make a conscious effort to prevent it, the existing dialect will come rushing in and do the job for you, at the expense of blurring or even changing your meaning. Probably it is better to put off using words as long as possible and get one's meaning as clear as one can through pictures or sensations. Afterwards one can choose—not simply *accept*—the phrases that will best cover the meaning, and then switch round and decide what impression one's words are likely to make on another person. This last effort of the mind cuts out all stale or mixed images, all prefabricated phrases, needless repetitions, and humbug and vagueness generally. But one can often be in doubt about the effect of a word or a phrase, and one needs rules that one can rely on when instinct fails. I think the following rules will cover most cases:

(i) Never use a metaphor, simile or other figure of speech which you are used to seeing in print.
(ii) Never use a long word where a short one will do.
(iii) If it is possible to cut a word out, always cut it out.
(iv) Never use the passive where you can use the active.
(v) Never use a foreign phrase, a scientific word or a jargon word if you can think of an everyday English equivalent.
(vi) Break any of these rules sooner than say anything outright barbarous.

These rules sound elementary, and so they are, but they demand a deep change of attitude in anyone who has grown used to writing in the style now fashionable. One could keep all of them and still write bad English, but one could not write the kind of stuff that I quoted in those five specimens at the beginning of this article.

I have not here been considering the literary use of language, but merely language as an instrument for expressing and not for concealing or preventing thought. Stuart Chase and others have come near to claiming that all abstract words are meaningless, and have used this as a pretext for advocating a kind of political quietism. Since you don't know what Fascism is, how can you struggle against Fascism? One need not swallow such absurdities as this, but one ought to recognize that the present political chaos is connected with the decay of language, and that one can probably bring about some improvement by starting at the verbal end. If you simplify your English, you are freed from the worst follies of orthodoxy. You cannot speak any of the necessary dialects, and when you make a stupid remark its stupidity will be obvious, even to yourself. Political language—and with variations this is true of all political parties, from Conservatives to Anarchists—is designed to make lies sound truthful and murder respectable, and to give an appearance of solidity to pure wind. One cannot change this all in a moment, but one can at least change one's own habits, and from time to time one can even, if one jeers loudly enough, send some worn-out and useless phrase—some *jackboot, Achilles' heel, hotbed, melting pot, acid test, veritable inferno* or other lump of verbal refuse—into the dustbin where it belongs.

ROBERT F. DRINAN

Robert Drinan is the first Roman Catholic priest ever elected to the United States Congress. In 1970, running against the "hawkish" incumbent from his Boston district, he won the election, thanks to an efficient campaign organization and an active opposition to the war in Vietnam.

Born in 1920, Drinan grew up in Boston and received his B.A. (1942) and M.A. (1947) from Boston College. He then became a Jesuit, studying at Weston College, where he was ordained a priest in 1953. He studied theology in Rome and Florence but also earned two law degrees from Georgetown University. In 1955 he joined the faculty of the Boston College Law School, became dean the next year, and did much to raise the school's academic reputation before he went on leave to run for Congress.

As an expert in family law and church-state relations, Drinan has been a spokesman for a moderate Roman Catholic interpretation of such issues as birth control, divorce, abortion, and aid to parochial schools. The civil-rights movement has also taken his energy, as chairman of his state's advisory committee to the U.S. Commission on Civil Rights (1962–1970) and as participant in many protests by Boston blacks.

Drinan was an early opponent of American involvement in the

Vietnam war. With other church leaders in 1969 he traveled through South Vietnam, collecting evidence that political prisoners were held and often tortured because they opposed the regime. In articles and speeches, in the book Vietnam and Armageddon *(1970), and in his congressional campaign, Drinan condemned the war on moral and political grounds.*

While in Congress, Drinan has served on the Judiciary Committee and on the Internal Security Committee (formerly the House Un-American Activities Committee). He was named to the latter committee two days after he had introduced a bill to abolish it; as the only civil libertarian in its membership, he worked to lessen its already fading powers until it went out of existence in 1975.

Drinan's other books include Religion, The Courts and Public Policy *(1963) and* Democracy, Dissent, and Disorder *(1969). The present article, originally a talk to English teachers, appeared in* College Composition and Communication *in October 1972.*

The Rhetoric of Peace

Language is not merely the way we express our foreign policy; language *is* our foreign policy. In Washington some of your students and the students of your predecessors exhibit no respect whatever for the honest use of language. Their language is dishonest because it expresses untruths but also, and more insidiously, because it masks the truth in jargon and non-statements so inscrutable as to confute the most able translator or cryptographer.

I do not impute to your profession responsibility for the false statements, the lies, which are uttered in Washington. Even an English professor's accountability stops short of that hideous prospect. However, in the matter of officially-proclaimed marshmallow prose—language which is really non-language—it does seem to me that you have some professional responsibility.

The American Medical Association wins no awards for enlightened self-goverance or a well-defined sense of the public interest. However, if a substantial number of government-employed physicians were to perform open-heart surgery under unsanitary conditions, I have no doubt that the A.M.A. would protest. Today, whole departments of the Federal government, and most notoriously the Departments of State and Defense, are systematically ravaging the English language; and the trustees of the language, or at least most of them, have not protested.

This anti-social misuse of language has not been totally ignored. Russell Baker, in the *New York Times* of December 1, 1971, expressed his outrage at the abuse of language: "The Pentagon," said Baker, has abandoned bombing as an instrument of war because it is considered bad taste. Instead of bombing it is now equipped to use such new techniques as the thermo-nuclear exchange, the limited air strike confined with surgical precision to strictly military targets and the protective reaction.

Each of these, admittedly, involves the placing of exploding bombs on or near the property and persons of foreign states with which our Government may be experiencing poor relationships. Still, bombing is such an ugly act that the United States Government can no longer be associated with it. This is why we had to use the protective reaction last week.

Mario Pei, one of our most distinguished students of the misuse of language, has also noted the trend toward non-language. Dr. Pei has given us a new coinage for obfuscation by government: he calls this form of non-language "true weasel words," and he states, in an article titled "The American Language in the Early '70's," "The four prime areas for weasel words are, as usual, the military, government, politics, and commercial advertising." Pei's insight is precise: "The real military contribution to language," he says,

> comes from the higher echelons. Here we find not only those reprehensible and often deplored terms, *kill ratio* and *body count* (they have been in use for some years, yet none of our dictionaries records them) but also *green backing,* used to describe the hiring of mercenary troops or the financing of such responsive governments as those of South Vietnam and Cambodia, likewise unreported by any dictionary. . . . *Protective reaction* is Pentagonese for such operations as Cambodia and Laos, and displays the usual euphemistic quality of the language of the generals. . . . The finest sample is perhaps the one coined by the Air Force to replace the word *demonstration,* previously used for an accounting review of a contract, to which General Teubner had objected on the ground that *demonstration* had become a dirty word in other connections. He suggested *audit review* as a replacement, which would have been reasonable enough; but the staff writers gave him more than he had bargained for: *Data Accounting Flow Assessment,* with a suitable abbreviation, DAFA.

More than twenty-five years ago, George Orwell observed trenchantly that "political speech and writing are largely the defense of the indefensible . . . political language has to consist largely of euphemism, question-begging and cloudy vagueness." It is my duty to report to you that the objects of Orwell's observation are at this moment comfortably ensconced in the State and Defense Departments and, ironically or predictably, they are the very individuals who in so many other respects are bringing us closer to the Orwellian vision of a sterile 1984.

Even the incoherent among us have observed the non-writing on the wall. As Jerry Rubin announces in *Do It,* "a dying culture destroys everything it touches . . . and language is one of the first things to go." "Language *prevents* communication," Rubin concludes.

The proposition that language prevents communication appears utterly absurd until we examine some language which has oozed out of the Defense Department recently.

It would be difficult to identify a subject on which lucid language is more necessary than the subject of our international military policy. Surely, the Secretary of Defense should be in a position to clearly state, in plain language, our international strategic objectives. Here is a central paragraph from the address of the Secretary of Defense on this subject —in a key section of his defense budget request statement to the House Appropriations Committee on March 4, 1971. This paragraph, I should say at the outset, is part of an exposition under the non-title, "A Strategy of Realistic Deterrence." I quote Mr. Laird:

> It is not realistic or efficient to expect each country to develop an independent self-defense capability against all levels of non-Chinese and non-Soviet attack. The drain on allied manpower and on their economies would inhibit the achievement of economic growth, and therefore, the political stability which is essential to military security. At the same time, deep historical, social and political inhibitions to immediate and effective regional mutual security arrangements in some areas must be recognized. Thus, a careful balance must be achieved between independent capabilities and collective arrangements. One of the most important means available to the U.S. to stimulate and to help aid in the development of these capabilities and arrangements is the provision of appropriate security assistance to our allies.

I have read that paragraph five times, and I am confident that it is devoid of meaning. The Secretary of Defense is making sounds, but he is also mute. Did language prevent communication here? Perhaps the Secretary would have better communicated the Administration's intentions by dancing or showing animated cartoons.

Non-language phrases like the one employed by the Central Intelligence Agency to order a political assassination—"termination with prejudice"— are not humorous, at least not in any conventional sense. The phrase "black humor" does not begin to convey the ghastliness of such homicidal euphemisms. In fact, the Defense Department jargon is not funny, because it is really a kind of psychologically impenetrable barrier, a barrier which keeps the people out and the insulated administrators in.

I submit that the systematic use of such opaque terms as "protective reaction," and the hollow sentences of the war planners, do far more to hide the decision-making process of the Defense Department from the people—and from Congress—than any secrecy-classification rules.

I submit that if every utterance of the Defense Department were made in an ancient language not understood by anyone, we would know very little less about the real military policies and intentions of our government than we now know.

I submit that the use of empty words by the Defense Department is not the accidental by-product of a metastasized bureaucracy; rather, it is an essential part of a pervasive scheme to keep Defense Department decision-making a secret—unknown and unknowable by any potential critics. Let me add that the residents of the Pentagon have much reason to fear public exposure, as the Pentagon Papers, the Anderson Papers and much other evidence indicate.

The title of this talk contains the word "rhetoric." The first definition Webster's assigns to it is "the art of speaking or writing effectively." Anyone who examines the use of language by the Defense Department will have to admit that their language has been effective. The President proposes to spend 78 billion dollars for war-related purposes in fiscal 1973, and even the most conscientious objectors in Congress and elsewhere find insuperable the task of figuring out where and for what purpose that sum would be spent.

Along with other members of a Congressional group called Members of Congress for Peace Through Law, I have examined in detail several military spending items, including, for example, the question of how many United States troops should be stationed in Europe.

I have discovered that not only are the words used by the Defense Department on these subjects inscrutable or unavailable for my review, but that even the statistics, the financial analyses, are designed in such a way that no one who does not possess the Pentagon code book or computer program can understand them. Of course, I should add that the incidence of secrecy of Defense Department data is directly proportional to the degree of its relevance.

Fortunately, the rhetoric of unlanguage is susceptible to attack. The attack is founded on an appeal to vanity, not an appeal to the public interest: even the Defense Department does not relish being accused of incoherence. Each of us, to be effective in his own rhetoric, must make that accusation. We must proclaim not only that the emperor is naked, but that he is engaged in unspeakable acts. If enough of us make that claim clearly enough and repeatedly enough, our efforts will have results.

We have already had some small but important results. When I and several of my colleagues in the House of Representatives forced the issue of the clandestine non-language of the CIA last year, there somehow resulted the creation of a CIA Subcommittee of the House Armed Services Committee, a Subcommittee headed by a very responsible Congressman, Lucien Nedzi of Michigan.

When the Navy Department recently presented me with repeated non-language statements on the status of a problem confronting a constituent of mine, I arranged for high Navy officials to visit my office and discuss the matter in clear sentences. On other occasions, in the context of military appropriations and foreign assistance bills, Members of Congress have sought with at least partial success coherent statements from the Defense Department.

The influence of the English profession in re-establishing comprehensible language as the medium of a democratic society could be enormous. The close textual analysis of critical government documents by you and your students would be a first step in affirming the value of clarity and the value of honestly used language.

I propose that you consider as the textual basis of an English course three documents which reflect the issues I have discussed. They are, first, *United States Foreign Policy, 1971, A Report of the Secretary of State* (Dept. of State Publication 8634, March 1972, U.S. Government Printing Office); second, *National Security Strategy of Realistic Deterrence, Secretary of Defense Melvin Laird's Annual Defense Department Report, Fiscal Year 1973* (U.S. Government Printing Office, February 15, 1972); and, third, *The Pentagon Papers as Published by The New York Times* (Bantam Books, 1971). Six months of intensive study of these materials would teach any student more about government and the uses and abuses of language than years of civics and political science courses. Six months of such study would inevitably result in a new rhetoric by student and teacher alike, the rhetoric of peace.

The rhetoric of peace is the effective use of language by individuals whose motives and understanding differ from the motives and understanding of this Administration. The rhetoric of peace is founded on Paul Tillich's judgment that "The passion for truth is crushed beneath the weight of undisputed authority."

We can and will clearly, calmly, and vigorously persuade the American people that they are the real power in this country. When more of us come to the inevitable conclusion that we are entitled to more accountability from those who collect our money, spend it, and in the process place our lives and civilization in peril—then we shall have spoken effectively.

RICHARD M. WEAVER

Professor Weaver was born in Asheville, North Carolina, in 1910 and educated at Kentucky, Vanderbilt, and Louisiana State, where he received the Ph.D. in 1943. He soon joined the Department of English in the College of the University of Chicago and remained there until his death in 1963. An intense, tough-minded man, he was profoundly displeased with the "pseudoscientific" direction of modern thought. In most of his writings he attempts to redirect our attention to the ideas of form, order, and human worth that he feels we have lost in the course of our "progress." Some of his books are Ideas Have Consequences *(1948),* Visions of Order: The Cultural Crisis of Our Time *(1957),* Life Without

*Prejudice and Other Essays (published posthumously in 1966), and
The Ethics of Rhetoric (1957), from which we print here the final
chapter. The reader should not allow himself to be put off by the rather
technical first two paragraphs; a full understanding of them depends on a
knowledge of earlier chapters but is not essential to an appreciation of the
rest of the essay.*

Ultimate Terms in Contemporary Rhetoric

We have shown that rhetorical force must be conceived as a power transmitted through the links of a chain that extends upward toward some
ultimate source. The higher links of that chain must always be of unique
interest to the student of rhetoric, pointing, as they do, to some prime
mover of human impulse. Here I propose to turn away from general
considerations and to make an empirical study of the terms on these
higher levels of force which are seen to be operating in our age.

We shall define term simply here as a name capable of entering into
a proposition. In our treatment of rhetorical sources, we have regarded
the full predication consisting of a proposition as the true validator. But
a single term is an incipient proposition, awaiting only the necessary
coupling with another term; and it cannot be denied that single names
set up expectancies of propositional embodiment. This causes everyone
to realize the critical nature of the process of naming. Given the name
"patriot," for example, we might expect to see coupled with it "Brutus,"
or "Washington," or "Parnell"; given the term "hot," we might expect
to see "sun," "stove," and so on. In sum, single terms have their potencies, this being part of the phenomenon of names, and we shall here
present a few of the most noteworthy in our time, with some remarks
upon their etiology.

Naturally this survey will include the "bad" terms as well as the
"good" terms, since we are interested to record historically those expressions to which the populace, in its actual usage and response, appears to
attribute the greatest sanction. A prescriptive rhetoric may specify those
terms which, in all seasons, ought to carry the greatest potency, but since
the affections of one age are frequently a source of wonder to another,
the most we can do under the caption "contemporary rhetoric" is to give
a descriptive account and withhold the moral until the end. For despite
the variations of fashion, an age which is not simply distraught manages
to achieve some system of relationship among the attractive and among
the repulsive terms, so that we can work out an order of weight and
precedence in the prevailing rhetoric once we have discerned the "rhetorical absolutes"—the terms to which the very highest respect is paid.

It is best to begin boldly by asking ourselves, what is the "god term" of the present age? By "god term" we mean that expression about which all other expressions are ranked as subordinate and serving dominations and powers. Its force imparts to the others their lesser degree of force, and fixes the scale by which degrees of comparison are understood. In the absence of a strong and evenly diffused religion, there may be several terms competing for this primacy, so that the question is not always capable of definite answer. Yet if one has to select the one term which in our day carries the greatest blessing, and—to apply a useful test—whose antonym carries the greatest rebuke, one will not go far wrong in naming "progress." This seems to be the ultimate generator of force flowing down through many links of ancillary terms. If one can "make it stick," it will validate almost anything. It would be difficult to think of any type of person or of any institution which could not be recommended to the public through the enhancing power of this word. A politician is urged upon the voters as a "progressive leader"; a community is proud to style itself "progressive"; technologies and methodologies claim to the "progressive"; a peculiar kind of emphasis in modern education calls itself "progressive," and so on without limit. There is no word whose power to move is more implicitly trusted than "progressive." But unlike some other words we shall examine in the course of this chapter, its rise to supreme position is not obscure, and it possesses some intelligible referents.

Before going into the story of its elevation, we must prepare ground by noting that it is the nature of the conscious life of man to revolve around some concept of value. So true is this that when the concept is withdrawn, or when it is forced into competition with another concept, the human being suffers an almost intolerable sense of being lost. He has to know where he is in the ideological cosmos in order to coordinate his activities. Probably the greatest cruelty which can be inflicted upon the psychic man is this deprivation of a sense of tendency. Accordingly every age, including those of rudest cultivation, sets up some kind of sign post. In highly cultivated ages, with individuals of exceptional intellectual strength, this may take the form of a metaphysic. But with the ordinary man, even in such advanced ages, it is likely to be some idea abstracted from religion or historical speculation, and made to inhere in a few sensible and immediate examples.

Since the sixteenth century we have tended to accept as inevitable an historical development that takes the form of a changing relationship between ourselves and nature, in which we pass increasingly into the role of master of nature. When I say that this seems inevitable to us, I mean that it seems something so close to what our more religious forebears considered the working of providence that we regard as impiety any disposition to challenge or even suspect it. By a transposition of terms, "progress" becomes the salvation man is placed on earth to work out; and just as there can be no achievement more important than salvation, so there can be no activity more justified in enlisting our sympathy and support than "progress." As our historical sketch would imply, the term began to be used in the sixteenth century in the sense of continuous development or improvement; it reached an apogee in the nineteenth century, amid noisy demonstrations of man's mastery of nature, and now in the twentieth century it keeps its place as one of the least assailable of the "uncontested terms," despite critical doubts in certain philosophic quarters. It is probably the only term which gives to the average American or West European of today a concept of something bigger than himself, which he is socially impelled to accept and even to sacrifice for. This capacity to demand sacrifice is probably the surest indicator of the "god term," for when a term is so sacrosanct that the material goods of this life must be mysteriously rendered up for it, then we feel justified in saying that it is in some sense ultimate. Today no one is startled to hear of a man's sacrificing health or wealth for the "progress" of the community, whereas such sacrifices for other ends may be regarded as self-indulgent or even treasonable. And this is just because "progress" is the coordinator of all socially respectable effort.

Perhaps these observations will help the speaker who would speak against the stream of "progress," or who, on the other hand, would parry some blow aimed at him through the potency of the word, to realize what a momentum he is opposing.

Another word of great rhetorical force which owes its origin to the same historical transformation is "fact." Today's speaker says "It is a fact" with all the gravity and air of finality with which his less secular-minded ancestor would have said "It is the truth."[1] "These are facts"; "Facts tend to show"; and "He knows the facts" will be recognized as common locutions drawing upon the rhetorical resource of this word. The word "fact" went into the ascendent when our system of verification changed during the Renaissance. Prior to that time, the type of conclusion that men felt obligated to accept came either through divine revelation, or through dialectic, which obeys logical law. But these were displaced by the system of verification through correspondence with physical reality. Since then things have been true only when measurably true, or when susceptible to some kind of quantification. Quite simply, "fact" came to be the touchstone after the truth of speculative inquiry had been replaced by the truth of empirical investigation. Today when the average citizen says "It is a fact" or says that he "knows the facts in the case," he means that he has the kind of knowledge to which all other knowledges must defer. Possibly it should be pointed out that his "facts" are frequently not facts at all in the etymological sense; often they will be deductions several steps removed from simply factual data. Yet the

---

[1] It is surely worth observing that nowhere in the King James Version of the Bible does the word "fact" occur.

"facts" of his case carry with them this aura of scientific irrefragability, and he will likely regard any questioning of them as sophistry. In his vocabulary a fact is a fact, and all evidence so denominated has the prestige of science.

These last remarks will remind us at once of the strongly rhetorical character of the word "science" itself. If there is good reason for placing "progress" rather than "science" at the top of our series, it is only that the former has more scope, "science" being the methodological tool of "progress." It seems clear, moreover, that "science" owes its present status to an hypostatization. The hypostatized term is one which treats as a substance or a concrete reality that which has only conceptual existence; and every reader will be able to supply numberless illustrations of how "science" is used without any specific referent. Any utterance beginning "Science says" provides one: "Science says there is no difference in brain capacity between the races"; "Science now knows the cause of encephalitis"; "Science says that smoking does not harm the throat." Science is not, as here it would seem to be, a single concrete entity speaking with one authoritative voice. Behind these large abstractions (and this is not an argument against abstractions as such) there are many scientists holding many different theories and employing many different methods of investigation. The whole force of the word nevertheless depends upon a bland assumption that all scientists meet periodically in synod and there decide and publish what science believes. Yet anyone with the slightest scientific training knows that this is very far from a possibility. Let us consider therefore the changed quality of the utterance when it is amended to read "A majority of scientists say"; or "Many scientists believe"; or "Some scientific experiments have indicated." The change will not do. There has to be a creature called "science"; and its creation has as a matter of practice been easy, because modern man has been conditioned to believe that the powers and processes which have transformed his material world represent a very sure form of knowledge, and that there must be a way of identifying that knowledge. Obviously the rhetorical aggrandizement of "science" here parallels that of "fact," the one representing generally and the other specifically the whole subject matter of trustworthy perception.

Furthermore, the term "science" like "progress" seems to satisfy a primal need. Man feels lost without a touchstone of knowledge just as he feels lost without the direction-finder provided by progress. It is curious to note that actually the word is only another name for knowledge (L. *scientia*), so that if we should go by strict etymology, we should insist that the expression "science knows" (*i.e.,* "knowledge knows") is pure tautology. But our rhetoric seems to get around this by implying that science is *the* knowledge. Other knowledges may contain elements of quackery, and may reflect the selfish aims of the knower; but "science," once we have given the word its incorporation, is the undiluted essence of knowledge. The word as it comes to us then is a little pathetic in its appeal, inasmuch as it reflects the deeply human feeling that somewhere some-how there must be people who know things "as they are." Once God or his ministry was the depository of such knowledge, but now, with the general decay of religious faith, it is the scientists who must speak *ex cathedra,* whether they wish to or not.

The term "modern" shares in the rhetorical forces of the others thus far discussed, and stands not far below the top. Its place in the general ordering is intelligible through the same history. Where progress is real, there is a natural presumption that the latest will be the best. Hence it is generally thought that to describe anything as "modern" is to credit it with all the improvements which have been made up to now. Then by a transference the term is applied to realms where valuation is, or ought to be, of a different source. In consequence, we have "modern living" urged upon us as an ideal; "the modern mind" is mentioned as some-thing superior to previous minds; sometimes the modifier stands alone as an epithet of approval: "to become modern" or "to sound modern" are expressions that carry valuation. It is of course idle not to expect an age to feel that some of its ways and habits of mind are the best; but the extensive transformations of the past hundred years seem to have given "modern" a much more decisive meaning. It is as if a difference of degree had changed into a difference of kind. But the very fact that a word is not used very analytically may increase its rhetorical potency, as we shall see later in connection with a special group of terms.

Another word definitely high up in the hierarchy we have outlined is "efficient." It seems to have acquired its force through a kind of no-nonsense connotation. If a thing is efficient, it is a good adaptation of means to ends, with small loss through friction. Thus as a word express-ing a good understanding and management of cause and effect, it may have a fairly definite referent; but when it is lifted above this and made to serve as a term of general endorsement, we have to be on our guard against the stratagems of evil rhetoric. When we find, to cite a familiar example, the phrase "efficiency apartments" used to give an attractive aspect to inadequate dwellings, we may suspect the motive behind such juxtaposition. In many similar cases, "efficient," which is a term above reproach in engineering and physics, is made to hold our attention where ethical and aesthetic considerations are entitled to priority. Certain noto-rious forms of government and certain brutal forms of warfare are unde-niably efficient; but here the featuring of efficiency unfairly narrows the question.

Another term which might seem to have a different provenance but which participates in the impulse we have been studying is "American." One must first recognize the element of national egotism which makes this a word of approval with us, but there are reasons for saying that the force of "American" is much more broadly based than this. "This is the American way" or "It is the American thing to do" are expressions whose intent will not seem at all curious to the average American. Now the peculiar effect that is intended here comes from the circumstance that "American" and "progressive" have an area of synonymity. The Western world has long stood as a symbol for the future; and accordingly there has been a very wide tendency in this country, and also I believe among many people in Europe, to identify that which is American with that which is destined to be. And this is much the same as identifying it with the achievements of "progress." The typical American is quite fatuous in this regard: to him America is the goal toward which all creation moves; and he judges a country's civilization by its resemblance to the American model. The matter of changing nationalities brings out this point very well. For a citizen of a European country to become a citizen of the United States is considered natural and right, and I have known those so transferring their nationality to be congratulated upon their good sense and their anticipated good fortune. On the contrary, when an American takes out British citizenship (French or German would be worse), this transference is felt to be a little scandalous. It is regarded as somehow perverse, or as going against the stream of things. Even some of our intellectuals grow uneasy over the action of Henry James and T. S. Eliot, and the masses cannot comprehend it at all. Their adoption of British citizenship is not mere defection from a country; it is treason to history. If Americans wish to become Europeans, what has happened to the hope of the world? is, I imagine, the question at the back of their minds. The tremendous spread of American fashions in behavior and entertainment must add something to the impetus, but I believe the original source to be this prior idea that America, typifying "progress," is what the remainder of the world is trying to be like.

It follows naturally that in the popular consciousness of this country, "un-American" is the ultimate in negation. An anecdote will serve to illustrate this. Several years ago a leading cigarette manufacturer in this country had reason to believe that very damaging reports were being circulated about his product. The reports were such that had they not been stopped, the sale of this brand of cigarettes might have been reduced. The company thereupon inaugurated an extensive advertising campaign, the object of which was to halt these rumors in the most effective way possible. The concocters of the advertising copy evidently concluded after due deliberation that the strongest term of condemnation which could be conceived was "un-American," for this was the term employed in the campaign. Soon the newspapers were filled with advertising rebuking this "un-American" type of depreciation which had injured their sales. From examples such as this we may infer that "American" stands not only for what is forward in history, but also for what is ethically superior, or at least for a standard of fairness not matched by other nations.

And as long as the popular mind carries this impression, it will be futile to protest against such titles as "The Committee on un-American Activities." While "American" and "un-American" continue to stand for these polar distinctions, the average citizen is not going to find much wrong with a group set up to investigate what is "un-American" and therefore reprehensible. At the same time, however, it would strike him as most droll if the British were to set up a "Committee on un-British Activities" or the French a "Committee on un-French Activities." The American, like other nationals, is not apt to be much better than he has been taught, and he has been taught systematically that his country is a special creation. That is why some of his ultimate terms seem to the general view provincial, and why he may be moved to polarities which represent only local poles.

If we look within the area covered by "American," however, we find significant changes in the position of terms which are reflections of cultural and ideological changes. Among the once powerful but now waning terms are those expressive of the pioneer ideal of ruggedness and self-sufficiency. In the space of fifty years or less we have seen the phrase "two-fisted American" pass from the category of highly effective images to that of comic anachronisms. Generally, whoever talks the older language of strenuosity is regarded as a reactionary, it being assumed by social democrats that a socially organized world is one in which cooperation removes the necessity for struggle. Even the rhetorical trump cards of the 1920's, which Sinclair Lewis treated with such satire, are comparatively impotent today, as the new social consciousness causes terms of centrally planned living to move toward the head of the series.

Other terms not necessarily connected with the American story have passed a zenith of influence and are in decline; of these perhaps the once effective "history" is the most interesting example. It is still to be met in such expressions as "History proves" and "History teaches"; yet one feels that it has lost the force it possessed in the previous century. Then it was easy for Byron—"the orator in poetry"—to write, "History with all her volumes vast has but one page"; or for the commemorative speaker to deduce profound lessons from history. But people today seem not to find history so eloquent. A likely explanation is that history, taken as whole, is conceptual rather than factual, and therefore a skepticism has developed as to what it teaches. Moreover, since the teachings of history are principally moral, ethical, or religious, they must encounter today that threshold resentment of anything which savors of the prescriptive. Since "history" is inseparable from judgment of historical fact, there has to be a considerable community of mind before history can be allowed to have a voice. Did the overthrow of Napoleon represent "progress" in history or the reverse? I should say that the most common rhetorical uses of "history" at the present are by intellectuals, whose personal philosophy can provide it with some kind of definition, and by journalists, who seem to use it unreflectively. For the contemporary masses it is substantially true that "history is bunk."

An instructive example of how a coveted term can be monopolized may be seen in "allies." Three times within the memory of those still young, "allies" (often capitalized) has been used to distinguish those fighting on our side from the enemy. During the First World War it was a supreme term; during the Second World War it was again used with effect; and at the time of the present writing it is being used to designate that nondescript combination fighting in the name of the United Nations in Korea. The curious fact about the use of this term is that in each case the enemy also has been constituted of "allies." In the First World War Germany, Austria-Hungary, and Turkey were "allies"; in the Second, Germany and Italy; and in the present conflict the North Koreans and the Chinese and perhaps the Russians are "allies." But in the rhetorical situation it is not possible to refer to them as "allies," since we reserve that term for the alliance representing our side. The reason for such restriction is that when men or nations are "allied," it is implied that they are united on some sound principle or for some good cause. Lying at the source of this feeling is the principle discussed by Plato, that friendship can exist only among the good, since good is an integrating force and evil a disintegrating one. We do not, for example, refer to a band of thieves as "the allies" because that term would impute laudable motives. By confining the term to our side we make an evaluation in our favor. We thus style our selves the group joined for purposes of good. If we should allow it to be felt for a moment that the opposed combination is also made up of allies, we should concede that they are united by a principle, which in war is never done. So as the usage goes, we are always allies in war and the enemy is just the enemy, regardless of how many nations he has been able to confederate. Here is clearly another instance of how tendencies may exist in even the most innocent-seeming language.

Now let us turn to the terms of repulsion. Some terms of repulsion are also ultimate in the sense of standing at the end of the series, and no survey of the vocabulary can ignore these prime repellants. The counter-part of the "god term" is the "devil term," and it has already been suggested that with us "un-American" comes nearest to filling that role. Sometimes, however, currents of politics and popular feeling cause some-thing more specific to be placed in that position. There seems indeed to be some obscure psychic law which compels every nation to have in its national imagination an enemy. Perhaps this is but a version of the tribal need for a scapegoat, or for something which will personify "the adver-sary." If a nation did not have an enemy, an enemy would have to be invented to take care of those expressions of scorn and hatred to which peoples must give vent. When another political state is not available to receive the discharge of such emotions, then a class will be chosen, or a race, or a type, or a political faction, and this will be held up to a practi-cally standardized form of repudiation. Perhaps the truth is that we need the enemy in order to define ourselves, but I will not here venture further into psychological complexities. In this type of study it will be enough to recall that during the first half century of our nation's existence "Tory" was such a devil term. In the period following our Civil War, "rebel" took its place in the Northern section and "Yankee" in the Southern, although in the previous epoch both of these had been terms of esteem. Most readers will remember that during the First World War "pro-German" was a term of destructive force. During the Second World War "Nazi" and "Fascist" carried about equal power to condemn, and then, following the breach with Russia, "Communist" displaced them both. Now "Communist" is beyond any rival the devil term, and as such it is employed even by the American president when he feels the need of a strong rhetorical point.

A singular truth about these terms is that, unlike several which were examined in our favorable list, they defy any real analysis. That is to say, one cannot explain how they generate their peculiar force of repudiation. One only recognizes them as publicly-agreed-upon devil terms. It is the same with all. "Tory" persists in use, though it has long lost any connection with redcoats and British domination. Analysis of "rebel" and "Yankee" only turns up embarrassing contradictions of position. Similarly we have all seen "Nazi" and "Fascist" used without rational perception; and we see this now, in even greater degree, with "Communist." However one might like to reject such usage as mere ignorance, to do so would only evade a very important problem. Most likely these are instances of the "charismatic term," which will be discussed in detail presently.

No student of contemporary usage can be unmindful of the curious reprobative force which has been acquired by the term "prejudice." Etymologically it signifies nothing more than a prejudgment, or a judgment before all the facts are in; and since all of us have to proceed to a great extent on judgments of that kind, the word should not be any more exciting than "hypothesis." But in its rhetorical applications "prejudice" presumes far beyond that. It is used, as a matter of fact, to characterize unfavorably any value judgment whatever. If "blue" is said to be a better color than "red," that is prejudice. If people of outstanding cultural achievement are praised through contrast with another people, that is prejudice. If one mode of life is presented as superior to another, that is prejudice. And behind all is the implication, if not the declaration, that it is un-American to be prejudiced.

I suspect that what the users of this term are attempting, whether consciously or not, is to sneak "prejudiced" forward as an uncontested term, and in this way to disarm the opposition by making all positional judgments reprehensible. It must be observed in passing that no people are so prejudiced in the sense of being committed to valuations as those who are engaged in castigating others for prejudice. What they expect is that they can nullify the prejudices of those who oppose them, and then get their own installed in the guise of the *sensus communis*. Mark Twain's statement, "I know that I am prejudiced in this matter, but I would be ashamed of myself if I weren't" is a therapeutic insight into the process; but it will take more than a witticism to make headway against the repulsive force gathered behind "prejudice."

If the rhetorical use of the term has any rational content, this probably comes through a chain of deductions from the nature of democracy; and we know that in controversies centered about the meaning of democracy, the air is usually filled with cries of "prejudice." If democracy is taken crudely to mean equality, as it very frequently is, it is then a contradiction of democracy to assign inferiority and superiority on whatever grounds. But since the whole process of evaluation is a process of such assignment, the various inequalities which are left when it has done its work are contradictions of this root notion and hence are "prejudice"—the assumption of course being that when all the facts are in, these inequalities will be found illusory. The man who dislikes a certain class or race or style has merely not taken pains to learn that it is just as good as any other. If all inequality is deception, then superiorities must be accounted the products of immature judgment. This affords plausible ground, as we have suggested, for the coupling of "prejudice" and "ignorance."

Before leaving the subject of the ordered series of good and bad terms, one feels obliged to say something about the way in which hierarchies can be inverted. Under the impulse of strong frustration there is a natural tendency to institute a pretense that the best is the worst and the worst is the best—an inversion sometimes encountered in literature and in social deportment. The best illustration for purpose of study here comes from a department of speech which I shall call "GI rhetoric." The average American youth, put into uniform, translated to a new and usually barren environment, and imbued from many sources with a mission of killing, has undergone a pretty severe dislocation. All of this runs counter to the benevolent platitudes on which he was brought up, and there is little ground for wonder if he adopts the inverted pose. This is made doubly likely by the facts that he is at a passionate age and that he is thrust into an atmosphere of superinduced excitement. It would be unnatural for him not to acquire a rhetoric of strong impulse and of contumacious tendency.

What he does is to make an almost complete inversion. In this special world of his he recoils from those terms used by politicians and other civilians and by the "top brass" when they are enunciating public sentiments. Dropping the conventional terms of attraction, this uprooted and specially focused young man puts in their place terms of repulsion. To be more specific, where the others use terms reflecting love, hope, and charity, he uses almost exclusively terms connected with excretory and reproductive functions. Such terms comprise what Kenneth Burke has ingeniously called "the imagery of killing." By an apparently universal psychological law, faeces and the act of defecation are linked with the idea of killing, of destruction, of total repudiation—perhaps the word "elimination" would comprise the whole body of notions. The reproductive act is associated especially with the idea of aggressive exploitation. Consequently when the GI feels that he must give his speech a proper show of spirit, he places the symbols for these things in places which would

normally be filled by prestige terms from the "regular" list. For specimens of such language presented in literature, the reader is referred to
the fiction of Ernest Hemingway and Norman Mailer.

Anyone who has been compelled to listen to such rhetoric will recall
the monotony of the vocabulary and the vehemence of the delivery. From
these two characteristics we may infer a great need and a narrow means
of satisfaction, together with the tension which must result from maintaining so arduous an inversion. Whereas previously the aim had been to
love (in the broad sense) it is now to kill; whereas it had been freedom
and individuality, it is now restriction and brutalization. In taking revenge
for a change which so contradicts his upbringing he is quite capable, as
the evidence has already proved, of defiantly placing the lower level
above the higher. Sometimes a clever GI will invent combinations and
will effect metaphorical departures, but the ordinary ones are limited to
a reiteration of the stock terms—to a reiteration, with emphasis of intonation, upon "the imagery of killing."[2] Taken as a whole, this rhetoric is a
clear if limited example of how the machine may be put in reverse—of
how, consequently, a sort of devil worship may get into language.

A similar inversion of hierarchy is to be seen in the world of competitive sports, although to a lesser extent. The great majority of us in the
Western world have been brought up under the influence, direct or
indirect, of Christianity, which is a religion of extreme altruism. Its terms
of value all derive from a law of self-effacement and of consideration for
others, and these terms tend to appear whenever we try to rationalize or
vindicate our conduct. But in the world of competitive sports, the direction is opposite: there one is applauded for egotistic display and for
success at the expense of others—should one mention in particular
American professional baseball? Thus the terms with which an athlete is
commended will generally point away from the direction of Christian
passivity, although when an athlete's character is described for the benefit
of the general public, some way is usually found to place him in the other
ethos, as by calling attention to his natural kindness, his interest in children, or his readiness to share his money.

Certainly many of the contradictions of our conduct may be explained
through the presence of these small inverted hierarchies. When, to cite
one familiar example, the acquisitive, hard-driving local capitalist is made
the chief lay official of a Christian church, one knows that in a definite area
there has been a transvaluation of values.

---

[2]Compare Sherwood Anderson's analysis of the same phenomenon in *A Story Teller's Story*
(New York, 1928), p. 198: "There was in the factories where I worked and where the
efficient Ford type of man was just beginning his dull reign this strange and futile outpouring of men's lives in vileness through their lips. Ennui was at work. The talk of the men
about me was not Rabelaisian. In old Rabelais there was the salt of infinite wit and I have
no doubt that the Rabelaisian flashes that came from our own Lincoln, Washington, and
others had point and a flare to them.
But in the factories and in army camps!"

Earlier in the chapter we referred to terms of considerable potency whose referents it is virtually impossible to discover or to construct through imagination. I shall approach this group by calling them "charismatic terms." It is the nature of the charismatic term to have a power which is not derived, but which is in some mysterious way given. By this I mean to say that we cannot explain their compulsiveness through referents of objectively known character and tendency. We normally "understand" a rhetorical term's appeal through its connection with something we apprehend, even when we object morally to the source of the impulse. Now "progress" is an understandable term in this sense, since it rests upon certain observable if not always commendable aspects of our world. Likewise the referential support of "fact" needs no demonstrating. These derive their force from a reading of palpable circumstance. But in charismatic terms we are confronted with a different creation: these terms seem to have broken loose somehow and to operate independently of referential connections (although in some instances an earlier history of referential connection may be made out). Their meaning seems inexplicable unless we accept the hypothesis that their content proceeds out of a popular will that they *shall* mean something. In effect, they are rhetorical by common consent, or by "charisma." As is the case with charismatic authority, where the populace gives the leader a power which can by no means be explained through his personal attributes, and permits him to use it effectively and even arrogantly, the charismatic term is given its load of impulsion without reference, and it functions by convention. The number of such terms is small in any one period, but they are perhaps the most efficacious terms of all.

Such rhetorical sensibility as I have leads me to believe that one of the principal charismatic terms of our age is "freedom." The greatest sacrifices that contemporary man is called upon to make are demanded in the name of "freedom"; yet the referent which the average man attaches to this word is most obscure. Burke's dictum that "freedom inheres in something sensible" has not prevented its breaking loose from all anchorages. And the evident truth that the average man, given a choice between exemption from responsibility and responsibility, will choose the latter, makes no impression against its power. The fact, moreover, that the most extensive use of the term is made by modern politicians and statesmen in an effort to get men to assume more responsibility (in the form of military service, increased taxes, abridgement of rights, etc.) seems to carry no weight either.[3] The fact that what the American pioneer considered freedom has become wholly impossible to the modern apartment-dwelling metropolitan seems not to have damaged its potency. Unless we accept some philosophical interpretation, such as the proposi-

---

[3]One is inevitably reminded of the slogan of Oceania in Orwell's *Nineteen Eighty-four:* "Freedom is Slavery."

tion that freedom consists only in the discharge of responsibility, there seems no possibility of a correlation between the use of the word and circumstantial reality. Yet "freedom" remains an ultimate term, for which people are asked to yield up their first-born.

There is plenty of evidence that "democracy" is becoming the same kind of term. The variety of things it is used to symbolize is too weird and too contradictory for one to find even a core meaning in present-day usages. More important than this for us is the fact, noted by George Orwell, that people resist any attempt to define democracy, as if to connect it with a clear and fixed referent were to vitiate it. It may well be that such resistance to definition of democracy arises from a subconscious fear that a term defined in the usual manner has its charisma taken away. The situation then is that "democracy" means "be democratic," and that means exhibit a certain attitude which you can learn by imitating your fellows.

If rationality is measured by correlations and by analyzable content, then these terms are irrational; and there is one further modern development in the creation of such terms which is strongly suggestive of irrational impulse. This is the increasing tendency to employ in the place of the term itself an abbreviated or telescoped form—which form is nearly always used with even more reckless assumption of authority. I seldom read the abbreviation "U S" in the newspapers without wincing at the complete arrogance of its rhetorical tone. Daily we see "U S Cracks Down on Communists"; "U S Gives OK to Atomic Weapons"; "U S Shocked by Death of Official." Who or what is this "U S"? It is clear that "U S" does not suggest a union of forty-eight states having republican forms of government and held together by a constitution of expressly delimited authority. It suggests rather an abstract force out of a new world of forces, whose will is law and whom the individual citizen has no way to placate. Consider the individual citizen confronted by "U S" or "FBI." As long as terms stand for identifiable organs of government, the citizen feels that he knows the world he moves around in, but when the forces of government are referred to by these bloodless abstractions, he cannot avoid feeling that they are one thing and he another. Let us note while dealing with this subject the enormous proliferation of such forms during the past twenty years or so. If "U S" is the most powerful and prepossessing of the group, it drags behind it in train the previously mentioned "FBI," and "NPA," "ERP," "FDIC," "WPA," "HOLC," and "OSS," to take a few at random. It is a fact of ominous significance that this use of foreshortened forms is preferred by totalitarians, both the professed and the disguised. Americans were hearing the terms "OGPU," "AMTORG" and "NEP" before their own government turned to large-scale state planning. Since then we have spawned them ourselves, and, it is to be feared, out of similar impulse. George Orwell, one of the truest humanists of our age, has described the phenomenon thus: "Even in the early decades of the twentieth century, telescoped words and phrases had been one of the characteristic features of political language; and it had been noticed that the tendency to use abbreviations of this kind was most marked in totalitarian countries and totalitarian organizations. Examples were such words as Nazi, Gestapo, Comintern, Inprecor, Agitprop."[4]

I venture to suggest that what this whole trend indicates is an attempt by the government, as distinguished from the people, to confer charismatic authority. In the earlier specimens of charismatic terms we were examining, we beheld something like the creation of a spontaneous general will. But these later ones of truncated form are handed down from above, and their potency is by fiat of whatever group is administering in the name of democracy. Actually the process is no more anomalous than the issuing of pamphlets to soldiers telling them whom they shall hate and whom they shall like (or try to like), but the whole business of switching impulse on and off from a central headquarters has very much the meaning of *Gleichschaltung* as that word has been interpreted for me by a native German. Yet it is a disturbing fact that such process should increase in times of peace, because the persistent use of such abbreviations can only mean a serious divorce between rhetorical impulse and rational thought. When the ultimate terms become a series of bare abstractions, the understanding of power is supplanted by a worship of power, and in our condition this can mean only state worship.

It is easy to see, however, that a group determined upon control will have as one of its first objectives the appropriation of sources of charismatic authority. Probably the surest way to detect the fabricated charismatic term is to identify those terms ordinarily of limited power which are being moved up to the front line. That is to say, we may suspect the act of fabrication when terms of secondary or even tertiary rhetorical rank are pushed forward by unnatural pressure into ultimate positions. This process can nearly always be observed in times of crisis. During the last war, for example, "defense" and "war effort" were certainly regarded as culminative terms. We may say this because almost no one thinks of these terms as the natural sanctions of his mode of life. He may think thus of "progress" or "happiness" or even "freedom"; but "defense" and "war effort" are ultimate sanctions only when measured against an emergency situation. When the United States was preparing for entry into that conflict, every departure from our normal way of life could be justified as a "defense" measure. Plants making bombs to be dropped on other continents were called "defense" plants. Correspondingly, once the conflict had been entered, everything that was done in military or civilian areas was judged by its contribution to the "war effort." This last became for a period of years the supreme term: not God or Heaven or happiness, but successful effort in the war. It was a term to end all other terms or a rhetoric to silence all other rhetoric. No one was able to make his claim heard against "the war effort."

---

[4]"Principles of Newspeak," *Nineteen Eighty-four* (New York, 1949), p. 310.

It is most important to realize, therefore, that under the stress of feeling or preoccupation, quite secondary terms can be moved up to the position of ultimate terms, where they will remain until reflection is allowed to resume sway. There are many signs to show that the term "aggressor" is now undergoing such manipulation. Despite the fact that almost no term is more difficult to correlate with objective phenomena, it is being rapidly promoted to ultimate "bad" term. The likelihood is that "aggressor" will soon become a depository for all the resentments and fears which naturally arise in a people. As such, it will function as did "infidel" in the mediaeval period and as "reactionary" has functioned in the recent past. Manifestly it is of great advantage to a nation bent upon organizing its power to be able to stigmatize some neighbor as "aggressor," so that the term's capacity for irrational assumption is a great temptation for those who are not moral in their use of rhetoric. This passage from natural or popular to state-engendered charisma produces one of the most dangerous lesions of modern society.

An ethics of rhetoric requires that ultimate terms be ultimate in some rational sense. The only way to achieve that objective is through an ordering of our own minds and our own passions. Everyone of psychological sophistication knows that there is a pleasure in willed perversity, and the setting up of perverse shibboleths is a fairly common source of that pleasure. War cries, school slogans, coterie passwords, and all similar expressions are examples of such creation. There may be areas of play in which these are nothing more than a diversion; but there are other areas in which such expressions lure us down the roads of hatred and tragedy. That is the tendency of all words of false or "engineered" charisma. They often sound like the very gospel of one's society, but in fact they betray us; they get us to do what the adversary of the human being wants us to do. It is worth considering whether the real civil disobedience must not begin with our language.

Lastly, the student of rhetoric must realize that in the contemporary world he is confronted not only by evil practitioners, but also, and probably to an unprecedented degree, by men who are conditioned by the evil created by others. The machinery of propagation and inculcation is today so immense that no one avoids entirely the assimilation and use of some terms which have a downward tendency. It is especially easy to pick up a tone without realizing its trend. Perhaps the best that any of us can do is to hold a dialectic with himself to see what the wider circumferences of his terms of persuasion are. This process will not only improve the consistency of one's thinking but it will also, if the foregoing analysis is sound, prevent his becoming a creature of evil public forces and a victim of his own thoughtless rhetoric.

ALDOUS HUXLEY

This is Chapter 6 of Huxley's Brave New World Revisited *(1958).*
For information on the author and his writings, see page 51.

The Arts of Selling

The survival of democracy depends on the ability of large numbers of
people to make realistic choices in the light of adequate information. A
dictatorship, on the other hand, maintains itself by censoring or distorting the facts, and by appealing, not to reason, nor to enlightened self-
interest, but to passion and prejudice, to the powerful "hidden forces,"
as Hitler called them, present in the unconscious depths of every human
mind.

   In the West, democratic principles are proclaimed and many able and
conscientious publicists do their best to supply electors with adequate
information and to persuade them, by rational argument, to make realistic choices in the light of that information. All this is greatly to the good.
But unfortunately propaganda in the Western democracies, above all in
America, has two faces and a divided personality. In charge of the editorial department there is often a democratic Dr. Jekyll—a propagandist
who would be very happy to prove that John Dewey had been right about
the ability of human nature to respond to truth and reason. But this
worthy man controls only a part of the machinery of mass communication. In charge of advertising we find an anti-democratic, because anti-
rational, Mr. Hyde—or rather a Dr. Hyde, for Hyde is now a Ph.D. in
psychology and has a master's degree as well in the social sciences. This
Dr. Hyde would be very unhappy indeed if everybody always lived up to
John Dewey's faith in human nature. Truth and reason are Jekyll's affair,
not his. Hyde is a motivation analyst, and his business is to study human
weaknesses and failings, to investigate those unconscious desires and
fears by which so much of men's conscious thinking and overt doing is
determined. And he does this, not in the spirit of the moralist who would
like to make people better, or of the physician who would like to improve
their health, but simply in order to find out the best way to take advantage
of their ignorance and to exploit their irrationality for the pecuniary
benefit of his employers. But after all, it may be argued, "capitalism is
dead, consumerism is king"—and consumerism requires the services of
expert salesmen versed in all the arts (including the more insidious arts)
of persuasion. Under a free enterprise system commercial propaganda by
any and every means is absolutely indispensable. But the indispensable

is not necessarily the desirable. What is demonstrably good in the sphere of economics may be far from good for men and women as voters or even as human beings. An earlier, more moralistic generation would have been profoundly shocked by the bland cynicism of the motivation analysts. Today we read a book like Mr. Vance Packard's *The Hidden Persuaders,* and are more amused than horrified, more resigned than indignant. Given Freud, given Behaviorism, given the mass producer's chronically desperate need for mass consumption, this is the sort of thing that is only to be expected. But what, we may ask, is the sort of thing that is to be expected in the future? Are Hyde's activities compatible in the long run with Jekyll's? Can a campaign in favor of rationality be successful in the teeth of another and even more vigorous campaign in favor of irrationality? These are questions which, for the moment, I shall not attempt to answer, but shall leave hanging, so to speak, as a backdrop to our discussion of the methods of mass persuasion in a technologically advanced democratic society.

The task of the commercial propagandist in a democracy is in some ways easier and in some ways more difficult than that of a political propagandist employed by an established dictator or a dictator in the making. It is easier inasmuch as almost everyone starts out with a prejudice in favor of beer, cigarettes and iceboxes, whereas almost nobody starts out with a prejudice in favor of tyrants. It is more difficult inasmuch as the commercial propagandist is not permitted, by the rules of his particular game, to appeal to the more savage instincts of his public. The advertiser of dairy products would dearly love to tell his readers and listeners that all their troubles are caused by the machinations of a gang of godless international margarine manufacturers, and that it is their patriotic duty to march out and burn the oppressors' factories. This sort of thing, however, is ruled out, and he must be content with a milder approach. But the mild approach is less exciting than the approach through verbal or physical violence. In the long run, anger and hatred are self-defeating emotions. But in the short run they pay high dividends in the form of psychological and even (since they release large quantities of adrenalin and noradrenalin) physiological satisfaction. People may start out with an initial prejudice against tyrants; but when tyrants or would-be tyrants treat them to adrenalin-releasing propaganda about the wickedness of their enemies—particularly of enemies weak enough to be persecuted— they are ready to follow him with enthusiasm. In his speeches Hitler kept repeating such words as "hatred," "force," "ruthless," "crush," "smash"; and he would accompany these violent words with even more violent gestures. He would yell, he would scream, his veins would swell, his face would turn purple. Strong emotion (as every actor and dramatist knows) is in the highest degree contagious. Infected by the malignant frenzy of the orator, the audience would groan and sob and scream in an orgy of uninhibited passion. And these orgies were so enjoyable that most of those who had experienced them eagerly came back for more.

Almost all of us long for peace and freedom; but very few of us have much enthusiasm for the thoughts, feelings and actions that make for peace and freedom. Conversely almost nobody wants war or tyranny; but a great many people find an intense pleasure in the thoughts, feelings and actions that make for war and tyranny. These thoughts, feelings and actions are too dangerous to be exploited for commercial purposes. Accepting this handicap, the advertising man must do the best he can with the less intoxicating emotions, the quieter forms of irrationality.

Effective rational propaganda becomes possible only when there is a clear understanding, on the part of all concerned, of the nature of symbols and of their relations to the things and events symbolized. Irrational propaganda depends for its effectiveness on a general failure to understand the nature of symbols. Simple-minded people tend to equate the symbol with what it stands for, to attribute to things and events some of the qualities expressed by the words in terms of which the propagandist has chosen, for his own purposes, to talk about them. Consider a simple example. Most cosmetics are made of lanolin, which is a mixture of purified wool fat and water beaten up into an emulsion. This emulsion has many valuable properties: it penetrates the skin, it does not become rancid, it is mildly antiseptic and so forth. But the commercial propagandists do not speak about the genuine virtues of the emulsion. They give it some picturesquely voluptuous name, talk ecstatically and misleadingly about feminine beauty and show pictures of gorgeous blondes nourishing their tissues with skin food. "The cosmetic manufacturers," one of their number has written, "are not selling lanolin, they are selling hope." For this hope, this fraudulent implication of a promise that they will be transfigured, women will pay ten or twenty times the value of the emulsion which the propagandists have so skilfully related, by means of misleading symbols, to a deep-seated and almost universal feminine wish— the wish to be more attractive to members of the opposite sex. The principles underlying this kind of propaganda are extremely simple. Find some common desire, some widespread unconscious fear or anxiety; think out some way to relate this wish or fear to the product you have to sell; then build a bridge of verbal or pictorial symbols over which your customer can pass from fact to compensatory dream, and from the dream to the illusion that your product, when purchased, will make the dream come true. "We no longer buy oranges, we buy vitality. We do not buy just an auto, we buy prestige." And so with all the rest. In toothpaste, for example, we buy, not a mere cleanser and antiseptic, but release from the fear of being sexually repulsive. In vodka and whisky we are not buying a protoplasmic poison which, in small doses, may depress the nervous system in a psychologically valuable way; we are buying friendliness and good fellowship, the warmth of Dingley Dell and the brilliance of the Mermaid Tavern. With our laxatives we buy the health of a Greek god, the radiance of one of Diana's nymphs. With the monthly best seller we acquire culture, the envy of our less literate neighbors and the respect of the sophisticated. In every case the motivation analyst has found some deep-seated wish or fear, whose energy can be used to move the consumer to part with cash and so, indirectly, to turn the wheels of industry. Stored in the minds and bodies of countless individuals, this potential energy is released by, and transmitted along, a line of symbols carefully laid out so as to bypass rationality and obscure the real issue.

Sometimes the symbols take effect by being disproportionately impressive, haunting and fascinating in their own right. Of this kind are the rites and pomps of religion. These "beauties of holiness" strengthen faith where it already exists and, where there is no faith, contribute to conversion. Appealing, as they do, only to the aesthetic sense, they guarantee neither the truth nor the ethical value of the doctrines with which they have been, quite arbitrarily, associated. As a matter of plain historical fact, the beauties of holiness have often been matched and indeed surpassed by the beauties of unholiness. Under Hitler, for example, the yearly Nuremberg rallies were masterpieces of ritual and theatrical art. "I had spent six years in St. Petersburg before the war in the best days of the old Russian ballet," writes Sir Nevile Henderson, the British ambassador to Hitler's Germany, "but for grandiose beauty I have never seen any ballet to compare with the Nuremberg rally." One thinks of Keats— "beauty is truth, truth beauty." Alas, the identity exists only on some ultimate, supramundane level. On the levels of politics and theology, beauty is perfectly compatible with nonsense and tyranny. Which is very fortunate; for if beauty were incompatible with nonsense and tyranny, there would be precious little art in the world. The masterpieces of painting, sculpture and architecture were produced as religious or political propaganda, for the greater glory of a god, a government or a priesthood. But most kings and priests have been despotic and all religions have been riddled with superstition. Genius has been the servant of tyranny and art has advertised the merits of the local cult. Time, as it passes, separates the good art from the bad metaphysics. Can we learn to make this separation, not after the event, but while it is actually taking place? That is the question.

In commercial propaganda the principle of the disproportionately fascinating symbol is clearly understood. Every propagandist has his Art Department, and attempts are constantly being made to beautify the billboards with striking posters, the advertising pages of magazines with lively drawings and photographs. There are no masterpieces; for masterpieces appeal only to a limited audience, and the commercial propagandist is out to captivate the majority. For him, the ideal is a moderate excellence. Those who like this not too good, but sufficiently striking, art may be expected to like the products with which it has been associated and for which it symbolically stands.

Another disproportionately fascinating symbol is the Singing Commercial. Singing Commercials are a recent invention; but the Singing Theological and the Singing Devotional—the hymn and the psalm—are as old as religion itself. Singing Militaries, or marching songs, are coeval with war, and Singing Patriotics, the precursors of our national anthems, were doubtless used to promote group solidarity, to emphasize the distinction between "us" and "them," by the wandering bands of paleolithic hunters and food gatherers. To most people music is intrinsically attractive. Moreover, melodies tend to ingrain themselves in the listener's mind. A tune will haunt the memory during the whole of a lifetime. Here, for example, is a quite uninteresting statement or value judgment. As it stands nobody will pay attention to it. But now set the words to a catchy and easily remembered tune. Immediately they become words of power. Moreover, the words will tend automatically to repeat themselves every time the melody is heard or spontaneously remembered. Orpheus has entered into an alliance with Pavlov—the power of sound with the conditioned reflex. For the commercial propagandist, as for his colleagues in the fields of politics and religion, music possesses yet another advantage. Nonsense which it would be shameful for a reasonable being to write, speak or hear spoken can be sung or listened to by that same rational being with pleasure and even with a kind of intellectual conviction. Can we learn to separate the pleasure of singing or of listening to song from the all too human tendency to believe in the propaganda which the song is putting over? That again is the question.

Thanks to compulsory education and the rotary press, the propagandist has been able, for many years past, to convey his messages to virtually every adult in every civilized country. Today, thanks to radio and television, he is in the happy position of being able to communicate even with unschooled adults and not yet literate children.

Children, as might be expected, are highly susceptible to propaganda. They are ignorant of the world and its ways, and therefore completely unsuspecting. Their critical faculties are undeveloped. The youngest of them have not yet reached the age of reason and the older ones lack the experience on which their new-found rationality can effectively work. In Europe, conscripts used to be playfully referred to as "cannon fodder." Their little brothers and sisters have now become radio fodder and television fodder. In my childhood we were taught to sing nursery rhymes and, in pious households, hymns. Today the little ones warble the Singing Commercials. Which is better—"Rheingold is my beer, the dry beer," or "Hey diddle-diddle, the cat and the fiddle"? "Abide with me" or "You'll wonder where the yellow went, when you brush your teeth with Pepsodent"? Who knows?

"I don't say that children should be forced to harass their parents into buying products they've seen advertised on television, but at the same time I cannot close my eyes to the fact that it's being done every day." So writes the star of one of the many programs beamed to a juvenile audience. "Children," he adds, "are living, talking records of what we tell them every day." And in due course these living, talking records of television commercials will grow up, earn money and buy the products of industry. "Think," writes Mr. Clyde Miller ecstatically, "think of what it can mean to your firm in profits if you can condition a million or ten million children, who will grow up into adults trained to buy your product, as soldiers are trained in advance when they hear the trigger words, Forward March!" Yes, just think of it! And at the same time remember that the dictators and the would-be dictators have been thinking about this sort of thing for years, and that millions, tens of millions, hundreds of millions of children are in process of growing up to buy the local despot's ideological product and, like well-trained soldiers, to respond with appropriate behavior to the trigger words implanted in those young minds by the despot's propagandists.

Self-government is in inverse ratio to numbers. The larger the constituency, the less the value of any particular vote. When he is merely one of millions, the individual elector feels himself to be impotent, a negligible quantity. The candidates he has voted into office are far away, at the top of the pyramid of power. Theoretically they are the servants of the people; but in fact it is the servants who give orders and the people, far off at the base of the great pyramid, who must obey. Increasing population and advancing technology have resulted in an increase in the number and complexity of organizations, an increase in the amount of power concentrated in the hands of officials and a corresponding decrease in the amount of control exercised by electors, coupled with a decrease in the public's regard for democratic procedures. Already weakened by the vast impersonal forces at work in the modern world, democratic institutions are now being undermined from within by the politicians and their propagandists.

Human beings act in a great variety of irrational ways, but all of them seem to be capable, if given a fair chance, of making a reasonable choice in the light of available evidence. Democratic institutions can be made to work only if all concerned do their best to impart knowledge and to encourage rationality. But today, in the world's most powerful democracy, the politicians and their propagandists prefer to make nonsense of democratic procedures by appealing almost exclusively to the ignorance and irrationality of the electors. "Both parties," we were told in 1956 by the editor of a leading business journal, "will merchandize their candidates and issues by the same methods that business has developed to sell goods. These include scientific selection of appeals and planned repetition. . . . Radio spot announcements and ads will repeat phrases with a planned intensity. Billboards will push slogans of proven power. : . . Candidates need, in addition to rich voices and good diction, to be able to look 'sincerely' at the TV camera."

The political merchandisers appeal only to the weaknesses of voters, never to their potential strength. They make no attempt to educate the masses into becoming fit for self-government; they are content merely to manipulate and exploit them. For this purpose all the resources of psychology and the social sciences are mobilized and set to work. Carefully selected samples of the electorate are given "interviews in depth." These interviews in depth reveal the unconscious fears and wishes most prevalent in a given society at the time of an election. Phrases and images aimed at allaying or, if necessary, enhancing these fears, at satisfying these wishes, at least symbolically, are then chosen by the experts, tried out on readers and audiences, changed or improved in the light of the information thus obtained. After which the political campaign is ready for the mass communicators. All that is now needed is money and a candidate who can be coached to look "sincere." Under the new dispensation, political principles and plans for specific action have come to lose most of their importance. The personality of the candidate and the way he is projected by the advertising experts are the things that really matter.

In one way or another, as vigorous he-man or kindly father, the candidate must be glamorous. He must also be an entertainer who never bores his audience. Inured to television and radio, that audience is accustomed to being distracted and does not like to be asked to concentrate or make a prolonged intellectual effort. All speeches by the entertainer-candidate must therefore be short and snappy. The great issues of the day must be dealt with in five minutes at the most—and preferably (since the audience will be eager to pass on to something a little livelier than inflation or the H-bomb) in sixty seconds flat. The nature of oratory is such that there has always been a tendency among politicians and clergymen to oversimplify complex issues. From a pulpit or a platform even the most conscientious of speakers finds it very difficult to tell the whole truth. The methods now being used to merchandise the political candidate as though he were a deodorant positively guarantee the electorate against ever hearing the truth about anything.

HAIG A. BOSMAJIAN

Born in 1928, Haig A. Bosmajian studied at the University of California and received the Ph.D. from Stanford in 1960. He has taught at the universities of Idaho and Connecticut and is presently Associate Professor of Speech at the University of Washington. Professor Bosmajian's principal interests are in the areas of dissent, freedom of speech, and rhetorical strategies. He recently became editor of Free Speech, *the newsletter of the Freedom of Speech Committee of the Speech Association of America. He has edited* The Principles and Practice of Freedom of Speech *(1971); and, with Hamida Bosmajian,* The Rhetoric of the Civil Rights Movement *(1969) and* This Great Argument: The Rights of Women *(1972). He has also published essays on the rhetoric of Nazism and communism, and on nonverbal communication. The present essay is from* College English, *December 1969. The issue of May 1970 contains some interesting comments on it.*

The Language of White Racism

The attempts to eradicate racism in the United States have been focused notably on the blacks of America, not the whites. What is striking is that while we are inundated with TV programs portraying the plight of black Americans, and with panel discussions focusing on black Americans, we very seldom hear or see any extensive public discussion, literature or programs directly related to the source of the racism, the white American. We continually see on our TV sets and in our periodicals pictures and descriptions of undernourished black children, but we seldom see pictures or get analyses of the millions of school-age white suburban children being taught racism in their white classrooms; we see pictures of unemployed blacks aimlessly walking the streets in their black communities, but seldom do we ever see the whites who have been largely responsible, directly or indirectly, for this unemployment and segregation; we continually hear panelists discussing and diagnosing the blacks in America, but seldom do we hear panelists diagnosing the whites and their subtle and not so subtle racism.

Gunnar Myrdal, in the Introduction to his classic *An American Dilemma,* wrote that as he "proceeded in his studies into the Negro problem [an unfortunate phrase], it became increasingly evident that little, if anything, could be scientifically explained in terms of the peculiarities of the Negroes themselves." It is the white majority group, said Myrdal, "that naturally determines the Negro's 'place.' All our attempts to reach scientific explanations of why the Negroes are what they are and why they live as they do have regularly led to determinants on the white side of the race line." As the July 1966 editorial in *Ebony* put it, "for too long now, we have focused on the symptoms of the disease rather than the disease itself. It is time now for us to face the fact that Negroes are oppressed in America not by 'the pathology of the ghetto,' as some experts contend, but by the pathology of the white community." In calling for a White House Conference on Whites, the *Ebony* editorial made the important point that "we need to know more about the pathology of the white community. We need conferences in which white leaders will talk not about us [Negroes] but about themselves."

White Americans, through the mass media and individually, must begin to focus their attention not on the condition of the victimized, but on the victimizer. Whitey must begin to take the advice of various black spokesmen who suggest that white Americans start solving the racial strife in this country by eradicating white racism in white communities, instead of going into black communities or joining black organizations or working for legislation to "give" the blacks political and social rights. This suggestion has come from Floyd McKissick, Malcolm X, and Stokely Carmichael. McKissick, when asked what the role of the white man was in the black man's struggle, answered: "If there are whites who are not racists, and I believe there are a few, a *very* few, let them go to their own communities and teach; teach white people the truth about the black man." Malcolm X wrote in his autobiography: "The Negroes aren't the racists. Where the really sincere white people have to do wheir 'proving' of themselves is not among the black *victims,* but on the battle lines of where America's racism really *is*—and that's in their own home communities; America's racism is among their own fellow whites. That's where the sincere whites who really mean to accomplish something have to work." Stokely Carmichael, writing in the September 22, 1966, issue of *The New York Review of Books,* said: "One of the most disturbing things about almost all white supporters of the movement has been that they are afraid to go into their own communities—which is where the racism exists—and work to get rid of it."

A step in that direction which most whites can take is to clean up their language to rid it of words and phrases which connote racism to the blacks. Whereas many blacks have demonstrated an increased sensitivity to language and an awareness of the impact of words and phrases upon both black and white listeners, the whites of this nation have demonstrated little sensitivity to the language of racial strife. Whitey has been for too long speaking and writing in terminology which, often being offensive to the blacks, creates hostility and suspicions and breaks down communication.

The increased awareness and sensitivity of the black American to the impact of language is being reflected in various ways. Within the past two years, there have been an increasing number of references by Negro writers and speakers to the "Through the Looking Glass" episode where Humpty Dumpty says: "When I use a word it means just what I choose it to mean—neither more nor less." "The question is," said Alice, "whether you can make words mean so many different things." "The question is," said Humpty Dumpty, "which is to be master—that's all." The "Through the Looking Glass" episode was used by Lerone Bennett, Jr., in the November 1967 issue of *Ebony* to introduce his article dealing with whether black Americans should call themselves "Negroes," "Blacks," or "Afro-Americans." In a speech delivered January 16, 1967, to the students at Morgan State College, Stokely Carmichael prefaced a retelling of the above Lewis Carroll tale with: "It [definition] is very, very important because I believe that people who can define are masters." Carmichael went on to say: "So I say 'black power' and someone says 'you mean violence.' And they expect me to say, 'no, no. I don't mean violence, I don't mean that.' Later for you; I am master of my own terms.

If black power means violence to you, that is your problem. . . . I know what it means in my mind. I will stand clear and you must understand that because the first need of a free people is to be able to define their own terms and have those terms recognized by their oppressors. . . . Camus says that when a slave says 'no' he begins to exist."

This concern for words and their implications in race relations was voiced also by Martin Luther King who pointed out that "even semantics have conspired to make that which is black seem ugly and degrading." Writing in his last book before his death, *Where Do We Go From Here: Chaos or Community?*, King said: "In Roget's Thesaurus there are some 120 synonyms for 'blackness' and at least 60 of them are offensive—such words as 'blot,' 'soot,' 'grime,' 'devil,' and 'foul.' There are some 134 synonyms for 'whiteness,' and all are favorable, expressed in such words as 'purity,' 'cleanliness,' 'chastity,' and 'innocence.' A white lie is better than a black lie. The most degenerate member of the family is the 'black sheep,' not the 'white sheep.' "

In March 1962, *The Negro History Bulletin* published an article by L. Eldridge Cleaver, then imprisoned in San Quentin, who devoted several pages to a discussion of the black American's acceptance of a white society's standards for beauty and to an analysis of the negative connotations of the term "black" and the positive connotations of the term "white." Cleaver tells black Americans that "what we must do is stop associating the Caucasian with these exalted connotations of the word *white* when we think or speak of him. At the same time, we must cease associating ourselves with the unsavory connotations of the word *black*." Cleaver makes an interesting point when he brings to our attention the term "non-white." He writes: "The very words that we use indicate that we have set a premium on the Caucasian ideal of beauty. When discussing inter-racial relations, we speak of 'white people' and 'non-white people.' Notice that that particular choice of words gives precedence to 'white people' by making them a center—a standard—to which 'non-white' bears a negative relation. Notice the different connotations when we turn around and say 'colored' and 'non-colored,' or 'black' or 'non-black.' "

Simon Podair, writing in the Fourth Quarter issue, 1956, of *Phylon*, examines the connotations of such words as "blackmail," "blacklist," "blackbook," "blacksheep," and "blackball." The assertion made by Podair that it has been white civilization which has attributed to the word "black" things undesirable and evil warrants brief examination. He is correct when he asserts that "language as a potent force in our society goes beyond being merely a communicative device. Language not only expresses ideas and concepts but it may actually shape them. Often the process is completely unconscious, with the individual concerned unaware of the influence of the spoken or written expressions upon his thought processes. Language can thus become an instrument of both propaganda and indoctrination for a given idea." Further, Podair is correct in saying that "so powerful is the role of language in its imprint upon the human mind that even the minority group may begin to accept the very expressions that aid in its stereotyping. Thus, even Negroes may develop speech patterns filled with expressions leading to the strengthening of stereotypes." Podair's point is illustrated by the comments made by a Negro state official in Washington upon hearing of the shooting of Robert Kennedy. The Director of the Washington State Board Against Discrimination said: "This is a black day in our country's history." Immediately after uttering this statement with a negative connotation of "black," he declared that Robert Kennedy "is a hero in the eyes of black people—a champion of the oppressed—and we all pray for his complete recovery."

Although King, Cleaver, and Podair, and others who are concerned with the negative connotations of "black" in the white society are partially correct in their analysis, they have omitted in their discussions two points which by their omission effect an incomplete analysis. First, it is not quite accurate to say, as Podair has asserted, that the concepts of black as hostile, foreboding, wicked, and gloomy "cannot be considered accidental and undoubtedly would not exist in a society wherein whites were a minority. Historically, these concepts have evolved as a result of the need of the dominant group to maintain social and economic relationships on the basis of inequality if its hegemony was to survive." This is inaccurate because the terms "blackball," "blacklist," "blackbook," and "blackmail" did not evolve as "a result of the need of the dominant group to maintain social and economic relationships on the basis of inequality if its hegemony was to survive." The origins of these terms are to be found in the sixteenth and seventeenth centuries in England where the terms were mostly based on the color of the book cover, the color of printing, or the color of the object from which the word got its meaning, as for instance the term "to blackball" coming from "the black ball" which centuries ago was a small black ball used as a vote against a person or thing. A "black-letter day" had its origin in the eighteenth century to designate an inauspicious day, as distinguished from a "red-letter day," the reference being to the old custom of marking the saint's days in the calendar with red letters.

More important, the assertion that the negative connotations of "black" and the positive connotations of "white" would not exist in a society wherein whites were a minority is not accurate. Centuries ago, before black societies ever saw white men, "black" often had negative connotations and "white" positive in those societies. T. O. Beidelman has made quite clear in his article "Swazi Royal Ritual," which appeared in the October 1966 issue of *Africa,* that black societies in southeast Africa, while attributing to black positive qualities, can at the same time attribute to black negative qualities; the same applies to the color white. Beidelman writes that for the Swazi "darkness, as the 'covered' moon, is an ambiguous quality. Black symbolizes 'impenetrability of the future,' but also the 'sins and evils of the past year. . . .' " Black beads may symbolize marriage and wealth in cattle, but at the same time they can symbolize evil, disappointment, and misfortune. "The word *mnyama* means black and dark, but also means deep, profound, unfathomable, and even confused, dizzy, angry." To the Swazi, "that which is dark is unknown and ambiguous and dangerous, but it is also profound, latent with unknown meanings and possibilities." As for "white," *mhlophe* means to the Swazi "white, pale, pure, innocent, perfect, but this may also mean destitute and empty. The whiteness of the full moon, *inyanga isidindile,* relates to fullness; but this term *dinda* can also mean to be useless, simply because it refers to that which is fully exposed and having no further unknown potentialities."

What King, Cleaver, and Podair have failed to do in their discussions of the negative connotations of "black" and the positive connotations of "white" is to point out that in black societies "black" often connotes that which is hostile, foreboding, and gloomy and "white" has symbolized purity and divinity. Furthermore, in white societies, "white" has numerous negative connotations: white livered (cowardly), white flag (surrender), white elephant (useless), white plague (tuberculosis), white wash (conceal), white feather (cowardice), *et cetera.* The ugliness and terror associated with the color white are portrayed by Melville in the chapter "The Whiteness of the Whale" in *Moby Dick.* At the beginning of the chapter, Melville says: "It was the whiteness of the whale that above all things appalled me."

What I am suggesting here is that the Negro writers, while legitimately concerned with the words and phrases which perpetuate racism in the United States have, at least in their analysis of the term "black," presented a partial analysis. This is not to say, however, that most of the analysis is not valid as far as it goes. Podair is entirely correct when he writes: "In modern American life language has become a fulcrum of prejudice as regards Negro-white relationships. Its effect has been equally potent upon the overt bigot as well as the confused member of the public who is struggling to overcome conscious or unconscious hostility towards minority groups. In the case of the Negro, language concepts have supported misconceptions and disoriented the thinking of many on the question of race and culture." Not only has the Negro become trapped by these "language concepts," but so too have the whites who, unlike the blacks, have demonstrated very little insight into the language of white racism and whose "language concepts" have "supported misconceptions and disoriented the thinking of many on the question of race and culture."

The Negroes' increased understanding and sensitivity to language as it is related to them demands that white Americans follow suit with a similar understanding and sensitivity which they have not yet demonstrated too well. During the 1960's, at a time when black Americans have been attempting more than ever to communicate with whites, through speeches, marches, sit-ins, demonstrations, through violence and non-violence, the barriers of communication between blacks and whites seem to be almost as divisive as they have been in the past one hundred years, no thanks to the whites. One has only to watch the TV panelists, blacks and whites, discussing the black American's protest and his aspirations, to see the facial expressions of the black panelists when a white on the panel speaks of "our colored boys in Vietnam." The black panelists knowingly smile at the racist phrasing and it is not difficult to understand the skepticism and suspicion which the blacks henceforth will maintain toward the white panelist who offends with "our colored boys in Vietnam." "Our colored boys in Vietnam" is a close relation to "our colored people" and "our colored," phrases which communicate more to the black American listener than intended by the white speaker. John Howard Griffin has pointed out something that applies not only to Southern whites, but to white Americans generally: "A great many of us Southern whites have grown up using an expression that Negroes can hardly bear to hear and yet tragically enough we use it because we believe it. It's an expression that we use when we say how much we love, what we patronizingly call 'our Negroes.' " The white American who talks of "our colored boys in Vietnam" offends the Negro triply; first, by referring to the black American men as "our" which is, as Griffin points out, patronizing; second, by using the nineteenth century term "colored"; third, by referring to the black American men as "boys."

Most whites, if not all, know that "nigger" and "boy" are offensive to the Negro; in fact, such language could be classified as "fighting words." But the insensitive and offensive whites continue today to indulge in expressing their overt and covert prejudices by using these obviously derogatory terms. Running a series of articles on racism in athletics, *Sports Illustrated* quoted a Negro football player as saying: "The word was never given bluntly; usually it took the form of a friendly, oblique talk with one of the assistant coaches. I remember one time one of the coaches came to me and said, '[Head Coach] Jim Owens loves you boys. We know you get a lot of publicity, but don't let it go to your head.' Hell, when he said 'Jim Owens loves you boys,' I just shut him off. That did it. I knew what he was talking about." An athletic director at one of the larger Southwestern Universities, discussing how much sports have done for the Negro, declared: "In general, the nigger athlete is a little hungrier and we have been blessed with having some real outstanding ones. We think they've done a lot for us, and we think we've done a lot for them" (*Sports Illustrated,* July 1, 1968). One of the Negro athletes said of the coaching personnel at the same university: "They can pronounce Negro if they want to. *They can pronounce it.* But I think it seems like such a little thing to them. The trouble with them is they're not thinking of the Negro and how he feels. Wouldn't you suppose that if there was one word these guys that live off Negroes would get rid of, one single word in the whole vocabulary, it would be *nigger?*" (*Sports Illustrated,* July 15, 1968). When a newspaperman tried to get the attention of Elvin Hayes, star basketball player at the University of Houston, the reporter shouted, "Hey, boy!"

Hayes turned to the reporter and said: "Boy's on *Tarzan*. Boy plays on *Tarzan*. I'm no boy. I'm 22 years old. I worked hard to become a man. I don't call you boy." The reporter apologized and said: "I didn't mean anything by it" (*Sports Illustrated*, July 1, 1968).

Whites who would never think of referring to Negroes as "boy" or "nigger" do, however, reveal themselves through less obviously racist language. A day does not go by without one hearing, from people who should know better, about "the Negro problem," a phrase which carries with it the implication that the Negro is a problem. One is reminded of the Nazis talking about "the Jewish problem." There was no Jewish problem! Yet the phrase carried the implication that the Jews were a problem in Germany and hence being a problem invited a solution and the solution Hitler proposed and carried out was the "final solution." Even the most competent writers fall into the "Negro problem" trap; James Reston of the *New York Times* wrote on April 7, 1968: "When Gunnar Myrdal, the Swedish social philosopher who has followed the Negro problem in America for forty years, came back recently, he felt that a great deal had changed for the better, but concluded that we have greatly underestimated the scope of the Negro problem." Myrdal himself titled his 1944 classic work *The American Dilemma: The Negro Problem and Modern Democracy*. A book published in 1967, *The Negro in 20th Century America,* by John Hope Franklin and Isidore Starr, starts off in the Table of Contents with "Book One: *The Negro Problem*"; the foreword begins, "The Negro problem was selected because it is one of the great case studies in man's never-ending fight for equal rights." One of the selections in the book, a debate in which James Baldwin participates, has Baldwin's debate opponent saying that "the Negro problem is a very complicated one." There are several indications that from here on out the black American is no longer going to accept the phrase "the Negro problem." As Lerone Bennett, Jr., said in the August 1965 issue of *Ebony,* "there is no Negro problem in America. The problem of race in America, insofar as that problem is related to packets of melanin in men's skins, is a white problem." In 1966, the editors of *Ebony* published a book of essays dealing with American black-white relations entitled *The WHITE Problem in America.* It is difficult to imagine Negroes sitting around during the next decade talking about "the Negro problem," just as it is difficult to imagine Jews in 1939 referring to themselves as "the Jewish problem."

The racial brainwashing of whites in the United States leads them to utter such statements as "You don't sound like a Negro" or "Well, he didn't sound like a Negro to me." John Howard Griffin, who changed the color of his skin from white to black to find out what it meant to be black in America, was ashamed to admit that he thought he could not pass for a Negro because he "didn't know how to speak Negro." "There is an illusion in this land," said Griffin, "that unless you sound as though you are reading Uncle Remus you couldn't possibly have an authentic Negro dialect. But I don't know what we've been using for ears because you don't have to be in the Negro community five minutes before the truth strikes and the truth is that there are just as many speech patterns in the Negro community as there are in any other, particularly in areas of rigid segregation where your right shoulder may be touching the shoulder of a Negro PhD and your left shoulder the shoulder of the disadvantaged." A black American, when told that he does not "sound like a Negro," legitimately can ask his white conversationalist, "What does a Negro sound like?" This will probably place the white in a dilemma for he will either have to admit that sounding like a Negro means sounding like Prissy in *Gone With the Wind* ("Who dat say who dat when you say dat?") or that perhaps there is no such thing as "sounding like a Negro." Goodman Ace, writing in the July 27, 1968, issue of the *Saturday Review* points out that years ago radio program planners attempted to write Negroes into the radio scripts, portraying the Negro as something else besides janitors, household maids, and train porters. Someone suggested that in the comedy radio show *Henry Aldrich* Henry might have among his friends a young Negro boy, without belaboring the point that the boy was Negro. As Mr. Ace observes, "just how it would be indicated on radio that the boy is black was not mentioned. Unless he was to be named Rufus or Rastus." Unless, it might be added, he was to be made to "sound like a Negro."

Psychiatrist Frantz Fanon, who begins his *Black Skin, White Masks* with a chapter titled "The Negro and Language," explains the manner of many whites when talking to Negroes and the effects of this manner. Although he is writing about white Europeans, what Fanon says applies equally to white Americans. He points out that most whites "talk down" to the Negro, and this "talking down" is, in effect, telling the Negro, "You'd better keep your place." Fanon writes: "A white man addressing a Negro behaves exactly like an adult with a child and starts smirking, whispering, patronizing, cozening." The effect of the whites' manner of speaking to the Negro "makes him angry, because he himself is a pidgin-nigger-talker." "But I will be told," says Fanon, "there is no wish, no intention to anger him. I grant this; but it is just this absence of wish, this lack of interest, this indifference, this automatic manner of classifying him, imprisoning him, primitivizing him, decivilizing him, that makes him angry." If a doctor greets his Negro patient with "You not feel good, no?" or "G'morning pal. Where's it hurt? Huh? Lemme see—belly ache? Heart pain?" the doctor feels perfectly justified in speaking that way, writes Fanon, when in return the patient answers in the same fashion; the doctor can then say to himself, "You see? I wasn't kidding you. That's just the way they are." To make the Negro talk pidgin, as Fanon observes, "is to fasten him to the effigy of him, to snare him, to imprison him, the eternal victim of an essence, of an *appearance* for which he is not responsible. And naturally, just as a Jew who spends money without thinking about it is suspect, a black man who quotes Montesquieu had better be watched." The whites, in effect, encourage the stereotype of the Negro; they perpetuate the stereotype through the manner in which they speak about and speak to Negroes. And if Fanon is correct, the whites by "talking down" to the Negro are telling that black American citizen to "remember where you come from!"

Another facet of the racism of the whites' language is reflected in their habit of referring to talented and great writers, athletes, entertainers, and clergymen as "a great Negro singer" or "a great black poet" or "a great Negro ball player." What need is there for whites to designate the color or race of the person who has excelled? Paul Robeson and Marian Anderson are great and talented singers. James Baldwin and LeRoi Jones are talented writers. Why must the whites qualify the greatness of these individuals with "black" or "colored" or "Negro"? Fanon briefly refers to this predilection of whites to speak with this qualification:

> . . . Charles-André Julien introducing Aimé Césaire as "a Negro poet with a university degree," or again, quite simply, the expression, "a great black poet."
>
> These ready-made phrases, which seem in a common-sense way to fill a need—for Aimé Césaire is really black and a poet—have a hidden subtlety, a permanent rub. I know nothing of Jean Paulhan except that he writes very interesting books; I have no idea how old Roger Caillois is, since the only evidence I have of his existence are the books of his that streak across my horizon. And let no one accuse me of affective allergies; what I am trying to say is that there is no reason why André Breton should say of Césaire, "Here is a black man who handles the French language as no white man today can."

The tendency to designate and identify a person as a Negro when the designation is not necessary carries over into newspaper and magazine reporting of crimes. There was no need for *Time* magazine (July 19, 1968) to designate the race of the individual concerned in the following *Time* report: "In New York City, slum dwellers were sent skidding for cover when Bobby Rogers, 31, Negro superintendent of a grubby South Bronx tenement, sprayed the street with bullets from a sawed-off .30 cal. semiautomatic carbine, killing three men and wounding a fourth." *Time,* for whatever reason, designated the race of the person involved in this instance, but the reports on other criminal offences cited by *Time,* on the same page, did not indicate the race of the "suspects." As a label of primary potency, "Negro" stands out over "superintendent." The assumption that whites can understand and sympathize with the Negro's dismay when black "suspects" are identified by race and white "suspects" are not, is apparently an unwarranted assumption; or it may be possible that the whites *do* understand the dismay and precisely for that reason continue to designate the race of the black criminal suspect. To argue that if the race is not designated in the news story then the reader can assume that the suspected criminal is white, is not acceptable for it makes all the difference if the suspect is identified as "a Negro superintendent," "a white superintendent," or "a superintendent." If we were told, day in and day out, that "a *white* bank clerk embezzled" or "a *white* service station operator stole" or "a *white* unemployed laborer attacked," it would make a difference in the same sense that it makes a difference to identify the criminal suspect as "Negro" or "black."

If many Negroes find it hard to understand why whites have to designate a great writer or a great artist or a common criminal as "colored" or "Negro," so too do many Negroes find it difficult to understand why whites must designate a Negro woman as a "Negress." Offensive as "Negress" is to most blacks, many whites still insist on using the term. In a July 28, 1968, *New York Times Magazine* article, the writer, discussing the 1968 campaigning of Rockefeller and Nixon, wrote: "A fat Negress on the street says, passionately, 'Rocky! Rocky!' " As Gordon Allport has written in *The Nature of Prejudice*, "members of minority groups are often understandably sensitive to names given them. Not only do they object to deliberately insulting epithets, but sometimes see evil intent where none exists." Allport gives two examples to make his point: one example is the spelling of the word "Negro" with a small "n" and the other example is the word "Negress." "Sex differentiations are objectionable," writes Allport, "since they seem doubly to emphasize ethnic differences: why speak of Jewess and not of Protestantess, or of Negress, and not of whitess?" Just as "Jewess" is offensive to the Jews, so too is "Negress" offensive to the Negroes. "A Negro woman" does not carry the same connotations as "Negress," the latter conveying an emotional emphasis on both the color and sex of the individual. *Webster's New World Dictionary of the American Language* says of "Negress": "A Negro woman or girl: often a patronizing or contemptuous term."

When the newspaper reporter tried to get the attention of twenty-two year old basketball star Elvin Hayes by shouting, "Hey, boy!" and Hayes vigorously objected to being called "boy," the reporter apologized and said: "I didn't mean anything by it." In a few cases, a very few cases, white Americans indeed "didn't mean anything by it." That excuse, however, will no longer do. The whites must make a serious conscious effort to discard the racist clichés of the past, the overt and covert language of racism. "Free, white, and 21" or "That's white of you" are phrases whites can no longer indulge in. Asking white Americans to change their language, to give up some of their clichés, is disturbing enough since the request implies a deficiency in the past use of that language; asking that they discard the language of racism is also disturbing because the people being asked to make the change, in effect, are being told that they have been the perpetrators and perpetuators of racism. Finally, and most important, calling the Negro "nigger" or "boy," or "speaking down" to the Negro, gives Whitey a linguistic power over the victimized black American, a power most whites are unwilling or afraid to give up. A person's language is an extension of himself and to attack his use of language is to attack him. With the language of racism, this is exactly the point, for the language of white racism and the racism of the whites are almost one and the same. Difficult and painful as it may be for whites to discard their racist terms, phrases, and clichés, it must be done before black and whites can discuss seriously the eradication of white racism.

JAMES HERNDON

James Herndon was born in Houston, Texas, in 1926. After serving in the Merchant Marine during World War II, he came to Berkeley and in 1949 received a B.A. from the University of California with a major in general curriculum. After that he spent a few months in graduate school, worked in a machine shop for a year, and then went off to Europe for six years. While there he worked off and on and had his first experience of teaching—on the overseas campus of the University of Maryland and for the army adult education programs. When he returned to this country in 1957, Herndon became a full-time teacher. He was fired from his first job in a black ghetto school in Oakland, California, for being "unfit to teach." His first book, The Way It Spozed to Be *(1966), tells of his experiences there. He has since been teaching at a junior high school outside San Francisco, described in* How to Survive in Your Native Land *(1971). The selection we reprint below is a chapter from that book.*

An Environment for Lizards

Last year we never had a lizard in the room. This year, right now, we have thirteen. Last year Tizzo and Junior and Karl occasionally wanted to go out and *hunt for lizards* but they never brought any back, which was because what they really wanted to do was get off the school grounds, smoke and be free. It was only some errant folk memory which made them think of lizards as an excuse in the first place. Occasionally they brought back a sow bug or a worm, to show they were serious. They ain't got lizards around here like they used to, they told me.

This year seven boys showed up the second day with lizards. Give you curriculum planners cause to reflect.

They have these lizards arranged in an aquarium full of dirt, rocks, some dried-up ice plant, an old abalone shell and a tin with water in it. From day to day there are also different pieces of clay, sculptured into tunnels and caves for the lizards to hide in. Alas, there is no hiding, for also in the aquarium at all times are five or six pairs of hands, busily rearranging and resculpturing the lizards' Heimat, taking out the lizards, making more devious and restful tunnels and caves, rebuilding the rock grottoes, putting the lizards back in, digging up, smoothing out the dirt, taking out the lizards again, pouring in a load of sand from the jumping pit . . . no harm is meant to the lizards, in fact everyone is quite solicitous, buying meal worms for them, hoping to see them lose their skin, yelling at each other to be careful . . .

Well, it is bugging me, all right. I approach for a subtle talk. Careful to compliment the lizards, for which Richard has made signs stuck in the dirt, saying Blue-belly and Alligator, I try out the idea that maybe the lizards would like to be left in peace. The hands are busy in the dirt as I speak. Everyone agrees. They are trying to make the lizards happier by making tunnels and caves to rest in and to hide in, I'm told. Of course. I bring up the notion that in the lizards' natural environment (I say) it is an odd but true fact that hands are not digging them new holes every day, not making interesting new rock formations, not unloading tons of sand making it nine different levels like Troy but that in fact they have quite a while to get used to and make use of whatever ground they (for whatever reason) end up in. Everyone agrees. For instance, I add, you guys found them lizards under the ice plant, and if everyone didn't keep digging up the ice plant, maybe it would grow and—everyone agrees. They tell each other to quit digging up the place. All hands are busy inside the aquarium. In short, I say, why not leave them awhile to the present highly adequate arrangement? Them lizards (I say) won't ever have time to grow a new skin at this rate. They'll be too busy exploring. Right? Right. The lizards are jerked out so they'll be out of the way of a new freeway; they lie stunned on the counter next to the sink. Back in they go. Everyone advises everyone else to leave them alone and not keep on messing with them. One lizard's tail is painted blue. Everyone watches to see if they will crawl into the new holes, but no one can wait and fingers prod them along. Lots of advice about leaving them alone. Mr. Herndon is right, you guys!

Leave them alone then, I want to say. Out come the lizards. In go some more rocks.

Then leave them alone for a while, goddamnit! I do say, loudly. Everyone looks at me in astonishment.

My wife Fran goes to visit Tierra Firma Elementary School, where our kids go, one morning and ends up staying the day. She is appalled at the playground scene. It appears that the kids (kindergarten to sixth grade) are all running around yelling about *kill* and *murder* and *beat up* and about *stupid* and *MR* and *dumb-ass* and two kids are holding another kid while a third socks him in the belly (it happens to be Jay, our oldest, who is getting socked) and two little white kids are refusing to let a bigger black kid play football with them and so the black kid starts to beat them up and when the playground woman comes over they all three give her a lot of shit and run away and she can't catch them ... another large group of kids are playing dodge ball and throwing the ball hard and viciously at one another's heads, and some of them are crying, and other kids wander around crying, and there is a whole other population of kids who stand fearfully on the outskirts of the grounds just trying to keep out of the way ...

Back in the classroom after lunch she observes the concerned teachers trying to have some discussion with the kids about how to treat other people, about violence, about calling names—suddenly, says Fran, they are all these goddamn nice neat marvelous white middle-class children, even if occasionally black, talking about equal rights and observing the rights of others and not giving way to vagrant impulse and how war is bad and everyone is smart (even them fucking MR's) and how in a democracy everyone must be responsible for his or her own actions. They all know what to say! hollers Fran to me. They have all the words! They discuss superbly. They are a veritable UN of kids, schooled in the right phrase, diplomatic, unctuous, tolerant, fair ... the hypocritical little bastards! Sucking up, that's what they are! And believing it at the same time! Talk is cheap!

No doubt. It is the original prerogative of the white American middle class to be sucking up while at the same time actually believing everything it says. Lizards can tell you all about it.

On Right and Wrong

Dick Gregory's recollection of shame at a boyhood experience—"I waited too long to help another man"—raises in a small and quiet way an age-old issue that has become more pressing than ever in recent decades. The brutality or callousness of ordinary people doing their duty or just minding their own business in Hitler's Nazi Germany in the thirties and forties raised agonizing doubts among all other "civilized" people; could it happen here? More recently the conduct of the Vietnam war and the spectacle of wholesale criminality at the highest levels of American government and business have deepened this doubt.

What has happened to our sense of right and wrong? Charles Reich's essay attempts to show how our system of organization and our technology conspire against morality by eliminating the human element. We so subdivide our immoral acts and so hide their consequences, Reich contends, that no one feels personally responsible for them. The essay by William Nichols confronts the issue of individual conscience versus obedience to orders. He describes the terrifying Milgram experiment, which seems to confirm that, for a majority of us, the impulse to obey orders is stronger than the need to obey conscience. But his main concern is that we pay more attention than the experiment does to the minority who are capable of resisting coercion. Hannah Arendt, in the excerpt that follows, recounts some of the testimony during the trial of Adolf Eichmann, convicted and executed in Jerusalem for war crimes committed while he was a high Nazi official. Like Nichols, she is interested in the few who resist, stressing how great a difference it makes that "under conditions of terror most people will comply but *some people will not*"; for it is these few who ensure the continuity of humaneness on earth. The excerpt from Irving Howe's review of a book on the suffering of the Jews under Hitler highlights a further reach of the moral problem. Moral conduct, he suggests, is possible only where there is freedom of choice.

The discussion takes a more philosophical turn in the next essays: by what principles should our sense of rightness be guided? Erik Erikson explores the nature of a modern Golden Rule as exemplified by Gandhi. In strong contrast there follows a chapter of Machiavelli's classic exposition of political expediency. The section ends with Joan Didion's sobering reminder of the danger of too much morality: that the moral imperative may itself become the vehicle of oppression.

DICK GREGORY

Dick Gregory has lived many roles—among them slum kid, athlete, comedian, and political activist. Born in St. Louis in 1932, he set records for running the mile and half-mile in high school and again at Southern Illinois University, where he was named outstanding athlete in 1953. After two years in the army, he began working night clubs around Chicago and by 1959 was the regular master of ceremonies at a show club. He went on to television, records, and books, shaping his comedy act in sympathy with the civil-rights movement of the early sixties and then with the antiwar movement. After many arrests in political confrontations, he ran for President of the United States as the candidate of the Peace and Freedom party in 1968. Fasting, and its accompanying publicity, became his favorite form of political protest.

Gregory now works and lives in Chicago with his wife and ten children. His books include From the Back of the Bus *(1962),* No More Lies: The Myth and Reality of American History *(1971),* Dick Gregory's Political Primer *(1972), and an autobiography,* Nigger, *written with Robert Lipsyte (1964). The following selection comes early in the last-named book, from a chapter entitled "Not Poor, Just Broke."*

Shame

. . .

I never learned hate at home, or shame. I had to go to school for that. I was about seven years old when I got my first big lesson. I was in love with a little girl named Helene Tucker, a light-complected little girl with pigtails and nice manners. She was always clean and she was smart in school. I think I went to school then mostly to look at her. I brushed my hair and even got me a little old handkerchief. It was a lady's handkerchief, but I didn't want Helene to see me wipe my nose on my hand. The pipes were frozen again, there was no water in the house, but I washed my socks and shirt every night. I'd get a pot, and go over to Mister Ben's grocery store, and stick my pot down into his soda machine. Scoop out some chopped ice. By evening the ice melted to water for washing. I got sick a lot that winter because the fire would go out at night before the clothes were dry. In the morning I'd put them on, wet or dry, because they were the only clothes I had.

Everybody's got a Helene Tucker, a symbol of everything you want. I loved her for her goodness, her cleanness, her popularity. She'd walk down my street and my brothers and sisters would yell, "Here comes Helene," and I'd rub my tennis sneakers on the back of my pants and wish my hair wasn't so nappy and the white folks' shirt fit me better. I'd run out on the street. If I knew my place and didn't come too close, she'd wink at me and say hello. That was a good feeling. Sometimes I'd follow her all the way home, and shovel the snow off her walk and try to make friends with her Momma and her aunts. I'd drop money on her stoop late at night on my way back from shining shoes in the taverns. And she had a Daddy, and he had a good job. He was a paper hanger.

I guess I would have gotten over Helene by summertime, but something happened in that classroom that made her face hang in front of me for the next twenty-two years. When I played the drums in high school it was for Helene and when I broke track records in college it was for Helene and when I started standing behind microphones and heard applause I wished Helene could hear it, too. It wasn't until I was twenty-nine years old and married and making money that I finally got her out of my system. Helene was sitting in that classroom when I learned to be ashamed of myself.

It was on a Thursday. I was sitting in the back of the room, in a seat with a chalk circle drawn around it. The idiot's seat, the troublemaker's seat.

The teacher thought I was stupid. Couldn't spell, couldn't read, couldn't do arithmetic. Just stupid. Teachers were never interested in finding out that you couldn't concentrate because you were so hungry, because you hadn't had any breakfast. All you could think about was noontime, would it ever come? Maybe you could sneak into the cloakroom and steal a bite of some kid's lunch out of a coat pocket. A bite of something. Paste. You can't really make a meal of paste, or put it on bread for a sandwich, but sometimes I'd scoop a few spoonfuls out of the paste jar in the back of the room. Pregnant people get strange tastes. I was pregnant with poverty. Pregnant with dirt and pregnant with smells that made people turn away, pregnant with cold and pregnant with shoes that were never bought for me, pregnant with five other people in my bed and no Daddy in the next room, and pregnant with hunger. Paste doesn't taste too bad when you're hungry.

The teacher thought I was a troublemaker. All she saw from the front of the room was a little black boy who squirmed in his idiot's seat and made noises and poked the kids around him. I guess she couldn't see a kid who made noises because he wanted someone to know he was there.

It was on a Thursday, the day before the Negro payday. The eagle always flew on Friday. The teacher was asking each student how much his father would give to the Community Chest. On Friday night, each kid would get the money from his father, and on Monday he would bring it to the school. I decided I was going to buy me a Daddy right then. I had money in my pocket from shining shoes and selling papers, and whatever Helene Tucker pledged for her Daddy I was going to top it. And I'd hand the money right in. I wasn't going to wait until Monday to buy me a Daddy.

I was shaking, scared to death. The teacher opened her book and started calling out names alphabetically.

"Helene Tucker?"

"My Daddy said he'd give two dollars and fifty cents."

"That's very nice, Helene. Very, very nice indeed."

That made me feel pretty good. It wouldn't take too much to top that. I had almost three dollars in dimes and quarters in my pocket. I stuck my hand in my pocket and held onto the money, waiting for her to call my name. But the teacher closed her book after she called everybody else in the class.

I stood up and raised my hand.

"What is it now?"

"You forgot me."

She turned toward the blackboard. "I don't have time to be playing with you, Richard."

"My Daddy said he'd . . ."

"Sit down, Richard, you're disturbing the class."

"My Daddy said he'd give . . . fifteen dollars."

She turned around and looked mad. "We are collecting this money for you and your kind, Richard Gregory. If your Daddy can give fifteen dollars you have no business being on relief."

"I got it right now, I got it right now, my Daddy gave it to me to turn in today, my Daddy said . . ."

"And furthermore," she said, looking right at me, her nostrils getting big and her lips getting thin and her eyes opening wide, "we know you don't have a Daddy."

Helene Tucker turned around, her eyes full of tears. She felt sorry for me. Then I couldn't see her too well because I was crying, too.

"Sit down, Richard."

And I always thought the teacher kind of liked me. She always picked me to wash the blackboard on Friday, after school. That was a big thrill, it made me feel important. If I didn't wash it, come Monday the school might not function right.

"Where are you going, Richard?"

I walked out of school that day, and for a long time I didn't go back very often. There was shame there.

Now there was shame everywhere. It seemed like the whole world had been inside that classroom, everyone had heard what the teacher had said, everyone had turned around and felt sorry for me. There was shame in going to the Worthy Boys Annual Christmas Dinner for you and your kind, because everybody knew what a worthy boy was. Why couldn't they just call it the Boys Annual Dinner, why'd they have to give it a name? There was shame in wearing the brown and orange and white plaid mackinaw the welfare gave to 3,000 boys. Why'd it have to be the same for everybody so when you walked down the street the people could see you were on relief? It was a nice warm mackinaw and it had a hood, and my Momma beat me and called me a little rat when she found out I stuffed it in the bottom of a pail full of garbage way over on Cottage Street. There was shame in running over to Mister Ben's at the end of the day and asking for his rotten peaches, there was shame in asking Mrs. Simmons for a spoonful of sugar, there was shame in running out to meet the relief truck. I hated that truck, full of food for you and your kind. I ran into the house and hid when it came. And then I started to sneak through alleys, to take the long way home so the people going into White's Eat Shop wouldn't see me. Yeah, the whole world heard the teacher that day, we all know you don't have a Daddy.

It lasted for a while, this kind of numbness. I spent a lot of time feeling sorry for myself. And then one day I met this wino in a restaurant. I'd been out hustling all day, shining shoes, selling newspapers, and I had goo-gobs of money in my pocket. Bought me a bowl of chili for fifteen cents, and a cheeseburger for fifteen cents, and a Pepsi for five cents, and a piece of chocolate cake for ten cents. That was a good meal. I was eating when this old wino came in. I love winos because they never hurt anyone but themselves.

The old wino sat down at the counter and ordered twenty-six cents worth of food. He ate it like he really enjoyed it. When the owner, Mister Williams, asked him to pay the check, the old wino didn't lie or go through his pocket like he suddenly found a hole.

He just said: "Don't have no money."

The owner yelled: "Why in hell you come in here and eat my food if you don't have no money? That food cost me money."

Mister Williams jumped over the counter and knocked the wino off his stool and beat him over the head with a pop bottle. Then he stepped back and watched the wino bleed. Then he kicked him. And he kicked him again.

I looked at the wino with blood all over his face and I went over. "Leave him alone, Mister Williams. I'll pay the twenty-six cents."

The wino got up, slowly, pulling himself up to the stool, then up to the counter, holding on for a minute until his legs stopped shaking so bad. He looked at me with pure hate. "Keep your twenty-six cents. You don't have to pay, not now. I just finished paying for it."

He started to walk out, and as he passed me, he reached down and touched my shoulder. "Thanks, sonny, but it's too late now. Why didn't you pay it before?"

I was pretty sick about that. I waited too long to help another man.

· · ·

CHARLES A. REICH

Charles A. Reich, born in 1928, attended New York private schools, Oberlin College, and Yale Law School. He was admitted to the New York bar in 1952, then spent the next two years as law clerk to Supreme Court Justice Hugo L. Black, whom Reich considers the decisive influence in his life. From 1954 to 1960 he worked in a succession of District of Columbia law firms. He specialized in cases between large corporations and the federal government and came to condemn much of the activity represented by these firms and their clients. In 1960 he turned to teaching law at Yale, where he is now Professor of Law, and to writing articles on legal philosophy.

In the early sixties Reich was pessimistic, expecting the end of civil liberties in America. But after teaching awhile, making friends with undergraduates, studying art and literature, and visiting such centers of student activism as Berkeley, he became convinced that a "revolution of consciousness" was taking place. The Greening of America, *published in 1970, describes this revolution. It was an immediate best seller, although it has been criticized by many as superficial and overidealistic in its attitude toward the youth culture. Joyce Carol Oates refers to this book in the essay on page 19 above. In it Reich posits three stages of development for the history of America and for the individual psyche: Consciousness I, the selfish stage of rugged individualism that produces monopolies and robber barons; Consciousness II, a reaction to the first stage that seeks protection of individual liberties in governmental and other structures; and Consciousness III, which reacts to the excessive conformity demanded at the second stage by creating alternatives based on what people want to do, not on what they think they have to do. The present essay, clearly stemming from this line of thought, but showing its traditional basis, appeared in* The New Yorker *for June 19, 1971.*

The Limits of Duty

In Washington, D.C., during the May anti-war protests, police in automobiles and on scooters aimed their vehicles directly at demonstrators and drove toward them at high speeds in order to herd them off the streets. If one of the protesters had been hit and killed, the police officer driving the vehicle would have been guilty of murder. Not accidental killing or manslaughter but murder. Thus, every one of these officers was potentially guilty of a crime similar to that for which Lieutenant Calley was tried and convicted.

The applicable principle is deeply embedded in our common law. A leading early example is Halloway's Case (King's Bench, 1628). Halloway was the woodward of woods belonging to the Earl of Denbigh. He discovered a boy named Payne in a tree, attempting to steal wood. Payne had a rope tied around his middle, probably to aid him in climbing trees. Halloway ordered the boy down from the tree, and when he descended struck him two blows on his back with a cudgel. Then Halloway tied the other end of the rope to the tail of his horse. The frightened horse dragged Payne three furlongs, killing him. The question was whether this was manslaughter or murder, and the court held it to be murder, for Halloway knew, or should have known, the reckless and wanton risk he was taking with the boy's life. In such a case, the specific intention to kill is not required. The deliberate taking of the risk is enough. Halloway was hanged.

Students at Yale, where I teach in the law school, tell me that District of Columbia bus drivers also aimed their buses toward protesters at high speed and drove ahead without slowing down. How strange that those long-suffering civil servants the bus drivers are now guilty of reckless driving and assault, and, but for the agility of their potential victims, would be guilty of murder. Yet this is not an aberration. It is a pattern that is crucial to understanding what has gone wrong with America. Evil now comes about not necessarily when people violate what they understand to be their duty but, more and more often, when they are conscientiously doing what is expected of them. And for this evil the question of individual blame seems almost irrelevant.

Two oil tankers collide on a foggy morning in San Francisco Bay. The bay and ocean are contaminated, beaches are coated, wildlife is exterminated, a fragile beauty is destroyed for millions of people. Yet the tanker captains were doing their duty to move the oil on time, and behind them were company officials concerned with the maintenance of production schedules. No investigation, no technical fixing of blame would be likely to disclose what we have normally imagined to be the root of crime —a guilty mind or a malign heart. And what is true of the San Francisco oil spill is true of the other major evils that we see around us. From wiretapping to the prosecution of the Vietnam war, our crimes have been started and carried out by men zealously attempting to serve as they have been taught to serve.

It is this altered problem of evil that rightly troubles us in the Calley case. I believe that Calley was properly convicted of murdering Vietnamese civilians, even though the same result produced by different means is officially held to be wholly legal. Yet we must all believe that Calley, in his own wrong and frightened way, was seeking to perform his duty—to do what was expected of him. The enterprise upon which he was engaged is not condemned, only the means he chose to carry it out.

Hence the profound disquiet among so many Americans, taught to serve employer or country, who cannot understand why the law apparently no longer cares about goals but only about a nicety of method. Plainly, our long-accepted criminal-law concepts do not fit the crimes of today.

The central reality is that evil today is the product of our system of organization and our technology, and that it occurs because personal responsibility and personal awareness have been obliterated by a system deliberately designed to do just that—eliminate or minimize the human element and insure the supremacy of the system. The whole purpose of this system is to reduce the human component; that is why we have organization charts, a hierarchy of supervision, divided responsibilities, specialization. In the main, it is this rational organization of human effort that has brought us to our present stage of civilization, but we should realize that inherent in the very design of the system is the disappearance of individual blame, and hence the obsolescence of our concepts of individual criminal responsibility.

Let us follow the process of creating an evil more closely. A scientist who is doing his specialized duty to further research and knowledge develops the substance known as napalm. Another specialist makes policy in the field of our nation's foreign affairs. A third is concerned with maintaining the strength of our armed forces with the most modern weaponry. A fourth manufactures what the defense authorities require. A fifth drops napalm from an airplane where he is told to do so. The ultimate evil is the result of carefully segmented acts; the structure itself guarantees an evasion by everyone of responsibility for the full moral act. Indeed, the system, especially when it is combined with advanced technology, makes it unlikely that those who participate in the process will have any real awareness of the ultimate consequences. Neither the scientist nor the man in the State Department nor even the pilot actually sees the horrors of burning napalm on human flesh. The basic result of our system of doing things is to destroy awareness, alienate all of us from the consequences of our actions, and prevent the formation of that very responsibility which has been at the center of our idea of criminal justice.

Our traditional criminal law is based on a standard of conduct that assumes each individual to be a morally responsible human being. A man who runs a speedboat carelessly and kills someone is guilty of manslaughter if his actions fall below the standard. A man who allows his passions or desires to direct his actions so that he harms another person is guilty of assault or murder if, according to the standard, he should have controlled himself. The standard represents an ideal. Sometimes it is a cruel and unreasonable ideal, because the individual defendant lacks the capacity for measuring up to it. But the ideal does have a vital function. It establishes a large, even exalted, concept of man.

In the famous case of The Queen v. Dudley and Stephens, decided in 1884, four English seamen were cast away in an open boat on the high seas sixteen hundred miles from the Cape of Good Hope. After eighteen days, they were reduced to the utmost state of desperation, with neither food nor water. Dudley and Stephens then said that if no hope of rescue appeared one of the four should be sacrificed, so that the others might live. A third man refused to consent to the plan. The fourth, a boy of seventeen or eighteen, was not consulted; he was then in a helpless and weakened state. Dudley and Stephens spoke of their having families, indicating that the boy should be chosen. On the twentieth day, no help appearing, the defendants, after praying for forgiveness, killed the boy, and the three men fed upon his blood and body for four days, after which they were rescued. Dudley and Stephens were brought to England and tried for murder. It was acknowledged that if the boy had not been killed all four would probably have perished before rescue, and the boy would probably have died first. Yet the two men were found guilty.

The opinion of the Queen's Bench was delivered by Lord Coleridge, the Lord Chief Justice of England. Acknowledging that the temptation had been great and the suffering awful, he declared, "We are often compelled to set up standards which we cannot reach ourselves, and to lay down rules which we could not ourselves satisfy." And he went on:

> Though law and morality are not the same, and many things may be immoral which are not necessarily illegal, yet the absolute divorce of law from morality would be of fatal consequence . . .

Rather than kill the boy, said Lord Coleridge, the men should have been willing to lose their own lives:

> To preserve one's life is generally speaking a duty, but it may be the plainest and the highest duty to sacrifice it. War is full of instances in which it is a man's duty not to live, but to die. The duty, in the case of shipwreck, of a captain to his crew, of the crew to the passengers, of soldiers to women and children, as in the noble case of the *Birkenhead;* these duties impose on men the moral necessity, not of the preservation, but of the sacrifice of their lives for others, from which in no country, least of all, it is to be hoped, in England, will men ever shrink, as indeed, they have not shrunk . . .

Although the circumstances make this case unique, the basic ideal is found throughout the Anglo-American common law. Commonwealth v. Pierce (1884), a classic American case, written by Mr. Justice Holmes, then a member of the Supreme Judicial Court of Massachusetts, dealt with the problem of a physician whose patient died after he had treated her by keeping her wrapped in flannel saturated with kerosene for three days. Admitting that the physician's intentions were good, Holmes said that if the treatment was morally reckless, judged by the standards of a reasonably prudent man, then the defendant must answer for consequences that he neither intended nor foresaw. If the treatment was dangerous according to common experience, "we cannot recognize a privilege to do acts manifestly endangering human life, on the ground of good intentions alone." Holmes also wrote:

> The very meaning of the fiction of implied malice in such cases at common law was, that a man might have to answer with his life for consequences which he neither intended nor foresaw . . . his failure or inability to predict them was immaterial if, under the circumstances known to him, the court or jury, as the case might be, thought them obvious.

Recently, I was watching the C.B.S. evening news when a few minutes were devoted to films of one of the favorite antipersonnel weapons used by Americans in Vietnam. It consists of a rocket tightly packed with many ordinary nails. The rocket is fired from a helicopter. The nails scatter widely, propelled with such force that they will go right through the body of anyone in their path. One of the advantages of the weapon, it was explained, is that the gunner doesn't need to see the target at all. The consequences can only be imagined, but what can they be except the reckless maiming of all human beings, old or young, innocent or guilty, who happen to be in the way? Lieutenant Calley is guilty, we are told, but the men who designed these instruments, the men who built them, the men who ordered them to be used, and the men who actually used them were all simply doing their duty. What a diminished view of man this purported version of the law gives us! It tells us that we are all "universal soldiers," in the phrase from one of Donovan Leitch's recordings, morally oblivious of the consequences of our actions. Lord Chief Justice Coleridge completed his argument for full moral responsibility by saying, "It is enough in a Christian country to remind ourselves of the Great Example whom we profess to follow." What has happened when the hard-working, God-fearing people of America are expected to be moral robots, making and firing the nails for mass killings?

Obviously, our thinking has been strained to adapt itself to the realities of technology and organization. That is why all those fixtures of the old criminal law, the guilty mind, the malign heart, actual or presumed malice, the common experience of prudent men, seem so out of place—indeed, ironic—in the Calley case. We all understand that such standards of responsibility are not expected of any of us. Nor would we feel more comfortable about the prosecution of high-ranking generals or political leaders under the Nuremberg theory. They, too, would be found to have been doing their duty.

The Calley case represents a momentary, vestigial reminder of the old law of responsibility. It was unfair to single out one man for such a revival of the old law, to be sure. Still, the reminder sent a shudder of awareness through all of us universal soldiers back home. It was not surprising that President Nixon hastily intervened. What led to his intervention was not just his seeming unconcern for legal processes, or his desire, as the *New Republic* put it, to coddle this particular criminal. The President insists, in every speech he makes, that we should do our small, segmented duties while he—or those in authority—assumes responsibility. The President's intervention was no surprise, because the Calley case confronts us with standards of responsibility that do not fit what the President and others insist are our duties and the limits of our duties. We are all supposed to be motorists on a highway where the maximum speed is sixty and the minimum speed is fifty-nine.

Perhaps the best way to understand those who have resisted the draft —by seeking conscientious-objector status, by going to jail, by fleeing to Canada—is to acknowledge that they are demanding to live and to be judged by the old standards as fully responsible moral beings. They are seeking law, not evading it. Finding no acceptable standard of conduct available in today's organizational society, they have gone to standards that are not their own personal fiat but the old, traditional standards of religion, ethics, and common law. They are saying that they refuse to act in a way that common experience tells them will produce evil—evil that we know about or should know about. Theirs is a revolt for a larger view of man. And for all of us it poses a necessary question: Given that we must all live and work within large organizations, that we must all take only a small part in a large enterprise, how can we restore the awareness, the responsibility, and the law that are the moral essence of free men?

An organization is a hybrid form of machine—one part a tool or system, the other part human. We have made too little use of the human part. We have thought of the humanness as something to be suppressed for efficiency's sake, not something to be valued because it might supply a quality that would otherwise be lacking. All of us who work in organizations should begin to assume a responsibility that is larger than the particular job we do, and this responsibility should ultimately be recognized, protected, and enforced by law. It might take many forms. Perhaps there should be a right—analogous to the long-recognized right to strike for economic objectives—to refuse, on a selective moral basis, to do certain work and perform certain duties. Perhaps this right should be guaranteed to individuals as well as to organized groups. Perhaps the organization should be answerable, on a democratic basis to those who work within it, for its policies and their probable consequences. Surely the present rigid hierarchy of authority must give way to a concept that in an organization all the members have a share of authority.

A corollary to this is that law should be based on the assumption that institutions, far more than individuals, are likely to go astray. Perhaps the primary regulatory work of law should be shifted from that of managing people to that of managing organizations while safeguarding the individuality of the people within them. Because organizations are the most characteristic element of our civilization, the scope of action by the members, employees, or consumers must be widened, and the scope of action by systems and machines must be narrowed and must be supervised by law. In the deepest sense, the purpose of such changes is nothing less than a restoration of one of our richest and most neglected resources— the human potentiality of the great mass of our people. Government by a managerial élite deprives us of the humanity of the many. Policy is made by a few, and the rest are coerced into following by laws that speak in the name of duty. The assumption is made that those who get to the top are naturally qualified to manage and plan for the rest of us, that we must accept what they require of us without allowing our moral knowledge to intervene. Such a neglect of our moral resources is as great a loss as our now well-known neglect of our environmental resources. We need the full participation of each individual. We can no longer afford to be a people who unthinkingly serve.

This brings us back to what happened in Washington. The procedures used against demonstrators who tried to block traffic were flagrantly un-Constitutional. There were arrests without cause—mass roundups, which often included any young person, however innocent, who happened to be visible to the police. Prisoners were not subject to normal arrest procedure. Many were kept at detention centers without being afforded the basic rights of arrested persons. All this, like the murderous driving, was not the product of officers gone berserk but was part of coldly rational plans sanctioned, and later praised, by high authorities. Indeed, the same high authorities have recommended that similar tactics be used again. Can the policemen and bus drivers in question say they are doing all they can to respect the fundamental law of the land if they simply follow orders? Can the civil servants who drove to work that morning, maybe sympathetic to the peace movement but afraid of a demerit, call themselves law-abiding? I am suggesting that following orders is no longer good enough for any of us—not if we want our Constitution preserved. Each of us has a permanent and personal duty to the supreme law of the land. I do not mean the "law" that the Nixon Administration speaks of—something that I would call "force," or "state power." I think the Nixon Administration is deeply contemptuous of law. We cannot count on Attorney General Mitchell to preserve the law, nor, I fear, can we count on the courts. And, from a certain point of view, that is as it should be. It is our Constitution, not theirs.

WILLIAM NICHOLS

William Nichols was born in San Francisco in 1938, grew up in Portland, Oregon, and was educated at Park College (B.A.), Johns Hopkins (M.A.), and the University of Missouri (Ph.D.). Since 1966 he

*has been Professor of English and Dean at Denison University in Ohio.
Much of his writing has focused on Afro-American literature and history
and, more recently, on the impact of technology on American life. He has
also edited a textbook on autobiographical writing,* Writing from
Experience *(1975), which includes the original essay we reprint here.
The essay is an analysis of Stanley Milgram's now famous Yale
experiment, but it takes off unabashedly from Nichols' own experience—in
this case, his anger and disappointment at what he read in the book
describing this experiment. He speaks here not as expert or objective
analyst, but as a feeling and thinking man. Another response to the
Milgram experiment is a play by Dannie Abse,* The Dogs of Pavlov
(1973), which includes a reply by Milgram.

The Burden of Imagination:
Stanley Milgram's *Obedience to Authority*

It was a classic case of seeing the movie, then wanting to read the book.
Students in a class I taught at Denison University in the fall of 1972 told
me I ought to see the film "Obedience," which presents highlights of a
social psychology experiment run by Stanley Milgram at Yale University
from 1960 to 1963. The images are already hazy, but I remember seeing
confused, nervous individuals who thought they were teaching others
with the help of electric shocks, and I can hear the sharp commands of
a gray-coated psychologist as they echoed in a barren laboratory.
Vaguely, I recall the ending, a voice comparing the lessons to be drawn
from the experiments with those of the Nazi concentration camps, where
people submitted to authority and committed some of the most appalling
atrocities in human history.

That ending drew a moral from the experiments, but it seemed forced
somehow, as though the music were swelling to conclude a second-rate
Hollywood film in which nothing, absolutely nothing, has been resolved.
Unless you can give yourself up to the music or the moralizing, such an
ending will always leave you dissatisfied; and I left "Obedience" feeling
the need to know much more about those frightening experiments at
Yale. So I was more than a little eager to read Stanley Milgram's book
on the experiments, *Obedience to Authority,* when it appeared in early 1974.

Normally, I am pretty much immune to the comments appearing on
dust jackets of new books, but I must confess that the compliments traced
in modestly small type on the back of *Obedience to Authority* caught my eye.
Jerome S. Bruner of Oxford University said the book would put Milgram
"firmly in the front rank of social scientists in this generation," and Roger
Brown of Harvard University promised that "it qualifies as literature as

well as science." The latter claim had particular attraction because I believe there are works in the social sciences that deserve to be read with the careful attention often saved for fine imaginative literature.

Obedience to Authority is a powerful book, but I experienced raging disappointment as I read it. Before attempting to account for that reaction, however, I must say more about the experiments on which the book is built. There were many variations, but the basic experiment is the key. A person who has answered an advertisement—"WE WILL PAY $4.00 FOR ONE HOUR OF YOUR TIME"—comes to a laboratory to participate, he believes, in a study of memory and learning. He is told he will function as "teacher" in the experiment, and he meets the *experimenter,* who assumes the role of authority, and the *learner.* The teacher, who is really the subject of the experiment, assists the experimenter in strapping the learner's arms to a chair to prevent excessive movement. Teacher and experimenter then move into another room, where the teacher is introduced to a shock generator, which includes a battery of thirty switches that move in 15 volt increments from 15 to 450 volts. The teacher is instructed to administer a learning test to the man in the other room, giving the learner a shock each time he answers incorrectly and increasing the voltage with each wrong answer.

But the teacher is not actually giving a shock at all. The learner is a trained participant, and he gives incorrect answers, registers pain, and ultimately refuses to participate in a way calculated to make the teacher believe he is injuring, perhaps even killing, the learner. The central question in each performance of the experiment is this: When will the teacher-subject rebel against authority and refuse to inflict more shocks on the learner? The depressing answer is that in this basic version of the experiment, with the experimenter giving strong admonitions to continue and assurances of "no permanent tissue damage," sixty-five percent of the teachers never disobey. Many of them are willing to give three shocks of 450 volts, a level that is marked DANGER—SEVERE SHOCK on the control panel of the generator, before the process is halted by the experimenter. In reproductions of this experiment elsewhere to check the Yale results there have been even higher percentages of obedient teachers.

Let me admit that by the time I read *Obedience to Authority,* I was skeptical as well as fascinated. Both a section of the book that appeared in *Harper's* and a review by Steven Marcus in the *New York Times* put me on my guard. But once I began to read Milgram's book, on a rainy day in March, I did not put it down except briefly; and because I was in the midst of the delightful freedom of a sabbatical leave and in the seclusion of a beach cottage on the Oregon shore, I was able to read the book through without a hitch. That evening I tyrannized my wife and children as I had not done in months, and that is just the first thing I will blame on *Obedience to Authority.*

My petty tyrannies were not experiments in wielding authority. I was simply irascible, disturbed momentarily by the vision of *Obedience to Au-*

thority. It is a compelling book, put together with elegant simplicity to prove something Milgram states quite baldly at the beginning: "This is, perhaps, the most fundamental lesson of our study: ordinary people, simply doing their jobs, and without any particular hostility on their part, can become agents in a terrible destructive process." It is difficult to overstate the economy and force with which *Obedience to Authority* makes that point. Variations in the experiment were designed to anticipate nearly every question I could imagine. Would women match men in brutal deference to authority? Yes. Can the authority of the experimenter be wielded as powerfully on the telephone as in person? No. Will participation in a disobedient group encourage disobedience? Yes. Given the choice, will people increase the voltage? No. Imagine a question you can frame in a sentence like one of those, and the chances are good that it is implicit in one of the experimental variations worked out by Milgram. It is no surprise, then, when Milgram writes at the end of the book about the inevitability that men will abandon their humanity when their individual personalities are merged with larger institutional structures. And it is then just a step to this mild one-sentence paragraph: "This is the fatal flaw nature has designed into us, and which in the long run gives our species only a modest chance of survival."

It has taken me a while to remember where I last found such quietly understated fatalism, but now I know—in the fiction of Kurt Vonnegut, Jr. In a style even more elegantly simple than Milgram's, Vonnegut creates imaginary worlds of sharply limited human possibility. His characters are simply "listless playthings of enormous forces," as he says in *Slaughter-House Five.* His vision, like Milgram's, is of a world where men ultimately have no hand in shaping their own destinies.

For both Milgram and Vonnegut, I believe this cold and quiet fatalism is a product of fear. Neither of them embraces eagerly a view that denies men freedom and dignity, but both men might be compared to a producer of horror films who lives in constant terror of the limited world he creates. For Vonnegut and Milgram have imagined distinctly limited worlds.

In the narrow margins of their portraits of human possibility I find evidence of failed imagination. In Vonnegut's novel *Breakfast of Champions,* for example, we are allowed to know just a little about Kilgore Trout, a science-fiction writer who appears in other Vonnegut fiction, and Dwayne Hoover, a Pontiac dealer whose life is destined to intersect violently with Trout's by the end of the novel. The rest of the characters in *Breakfast of Champions* are barely identified atoms bouncing helplessly about in the narrative space. And Vonnegut seems to be offering an explanation for the book's lack of fully developed characters when he describes a figure in one of Trout's stories who returns a long "realistic" novel to the library after reading only sixty pages. He explains to the librarian: "I already know about human beings." That assertion is compounded more of fear than of arrogance, as I have said, but it is the key to the horrifying flatness in Vonnegut's art: Vonnegut, like Milgram, thinks he knows what makes us do the brutal, terrifying things that have disfigured human history; and such knowledge is bad news indeed. But one source of great imaginative literature is surely the recognition that we do not know very much about human beings at all; to think we do is to surrender the mystery at the center of all art. More even than that, to assume we understand the limits of human possibility is to accept as inevitable the alienation, injustice, and violence that threaten civilization.

Milgram nowhere explains the source of man's "modest chance" to survive, and I think it is fair to assume his vision is as bleak as Vonnegut's. Heaven knows, the "characters" in *Obedience to Authority* are flatter than New England witches pressed beneath Puritan barn doors. Take, for example, a teacher-subject in one of Milgram's most terrifying experimental variations: a situation in which the teacher must apply physical force to get the learner's hand in contact with a supposed shock plate. Milgram describes one obedient teacher in this way: "The scene is brutal and depressing: his hard, impassive face showing total indifference as he subdues the screaming learner and gives him shocks. He seems to derive no pleasure from the act itself, only quiet satisfaction at doing his job properly." Such contemptuous dismissal of a brutally obedient subject is not hard to understand, although I am suspicious of the easy judgments. But what bothers me much more is Milgram's treatment of those who rebel. For there are heroes hidden among his data, and although he has allowed himself ten years to reflect upon the Yale experiments, he seems to have come nowhere near engaging those courageous men and women who fought free from the totalitarian trap he built for them.

In his book Milgram introduces us to just three of the many people who resisted authority. The first is a divinity school professor, and Milgram's description of him is loaded with negative judgments:

> A somewhat gaunt, ascetic man, this subject could be taken for a New England minister. . . . While reading the word pairs, he employs exaggerated precision in his pronunciation, and seems curt and officious in saying, "Correct." Whenever the learner makes an error, he appears almost to be chastising him for his failing. Each time he administers a shock, his lips are drawn back, and he bares his teeth. An excessive fastidiousness characterizes all his actions.

With the possible exception of the facial description, that whole introduction of the subject is a series of very subjective, negative judgments. But compare that unsympathetic portrait with this bit of dialogue recorded during the experiment:

> *Experimenter.* It's absolutely essential to the experiment that we continue.
> *Subject.* I understand that statement, but I don't understand why the experiment is placed above this person's life.
> *Experimenter.* There is no permanent tissue damage.

> *Subject.* Well, that's your opinion. If he doesn't want to continue, I'm taking orders from him.
> *Experimenter.* You have no other choice, sir, you must go on.
> *Subject.* If this were Russia maybe, but not in America.
> *(The experiment is terminated.)*

Read in the context of *Obedience to Authority,* compared with other responses to the bullying experimenter, this man's answers ring with the eloquence of moral strength. Only heightened cynicism could find such standards *fastidious.* Consequently, I find a strange disjunction between the man as he is viewed by Milgram and as he is revealed in his own language.

Interestingly, in the subsequent recorded statements of the religion professor, Milgram includes parenthetical descriptions of his manner that undercut the force of what he says:

> *Subject.* Surely you've considered the ethics of this thing (extremely agitated). Here he doesn't want to go on, and you think that the experiment is more important? Have you examined him? Do you know what his physical state is? Say this man had a weak heart (quivering voice).
> *Experimenter.* We know the machine, sir.
> *Subject.* But you don't know the man you're experimenting on. . . . That's very risky (gulping and tremulous). What about the fear that man had? It's impossible for you to determine what effect that has on him . . . the fear that he himself is generating. . . . But go ahead, you ask me questions; I'm not here to question you.

With all the stage directions, we can almost forget that here a man is rebelling against an authority that proved too strong for many people. Not only that, but he is asking probing questions that expose some of the ethical problems at the heart of the experiment. What about the stress being generated in this courageous subject ("gulping and tremulous") as he tries to understand and reject the inhumanity that is being asked of him?

For Milgram, apparently, this man's actions can be explained rather simply in a one-sentence paragraph: "Thus he speaks of an equivalence between the experimenter's and the learner's orders and does not disobey so much as he shifts the person from whom he will take orders." But how does this man differ from all the people who were unable to hear the victim's cries as a competing authority? After the experimenter has explained the true purpose of the experiment to the religion professor, he asks, "What in your opinion is the most effective way of strengthening resistance to inhumane authority?" The professor answers, "If one had as one's ultimate authority God, then it trivializes human authority." Again, Milgram's conclusion seems oddly patronizing and simplistic; he suggests that the religion professor has neatly substituted divine authority for the inhumane authority of the experimenter. But all the crucial questions remain unasked. What about all the other people who would have claimed allegiance to divine authority but who deferred to the experimenter and continued to give shocks? What makes the difference for this man? Milgram's final explanation—that the religion professor has not actually repudiated authority at all—seems little more than wordplay. The man has quite clearly rebelled against a powerful authority and accomplished a stress-filled act of moral courage. We need to know much more about why he was able to do it when so many people were not. There are surely no easy answers, but Milgram seems uninterested in the question.

The second rebel to receive attention in *Obedience to Authority* is given the pseudonym Gretchen Brandt. She had emigrated from Germany just five years before participating in the experiment, and she was a thirty-one-year-old medical technician. At the point in the experiment when she defied authority, the experimenter told her she had no choice. She responded: "I think we are here on our own free will. I don't want to be responsible if he has a heart condition if anything happens to him. Please understand that." Milgram's conclusion regarding Gretchen Brandt's disobedience is less contemptuously simplistic than his treatment of the religion professor:

> The woman's straightforward, courteous behavior in the experiment, lack of tension, and total control of her own action seem to make disobedience a simple and rational deed. Her behavior is the very embodiment of what I initially envisioned would be true for almost all subjects.
> Ironically, Gretchen Brandt grew to adolescence in Hitler's Germany and was for the great part of her youth exposed to Nazi propaganda. When asked about the possible influence of her background, she remarks slowly, "Perhaps we have seen too much of pain."

Milgram seems to accept as real the apparent ease with which Gretchen Brandt disobeys authority even though it contradicts a theoretical chapter, "Strain and Disobedience," in which he concludes that the "psychic cost" of disobedience is considerable. My own guess is that what Milgram observed was extraordinary poise and courage, and I would like to know much more about their roots in Gretchen Brandt's early life.

The question of Gretchen Brandt's exposure to Nazi propaganda, which Milgram treats as simply ironic, is particularly interesting because the third rebel mentioned in the book also lived in a Nazi-occupied country. This young industrial engineer also insists on his own freedom of choice when he decided to disobey. A few days after participating in the experiment, Milgram says, the engineer wrote a long letter to the staff asking if he could work with them. I cannot help wishing the staff had accepted the offer and used his presence to learn more about the sources of his unusual strength. But again Milgram seems to have been satisfied with a very superficial look at an obviously complex man.

It is not just in flatness of character that I see a failure of imagination in *Obedience to Authority.* In addition, there is a narrowly restricted sense of language at work in the experiment itself. Here, for example, are some representative protests given by the learner in response to shocks of increasing voltage:

75 volts	Ugh!
90 volts	Ugh!
105 volts	Ugh! (*louder*)
150 volts	Ugh!!! Experimenter! That's all. Get me out of here. I told you I had heart trouble. My heart's starting to bother me now. Get me out of here, please. My heart's starting to bother me. I refuse to go on. Let me out.
195 volts	Ugh! Let me out of here! Let me out of here. My heart's bothering me. Let me out of here. You have no right to keep me here! Let me out! Let me out of here! Let me out! Let me out of here! My heart's bothering me. Let me out! Let me out!
270 volts	(*Agonized scream.*) Let me out of here. Let me out of here. Let me out of here. Let me out. Do you hear? Let me out of here.

Notice that the protests are made only in response to shocks. The learner's "act" makes no apparent effort to establish a continuing rapport with the teacher who is administering the shocks. It is not hard to imagine a learner who might devote all his effort to appealing for mercy rather than trying to answer the questions, and he might try to challenge the teacher's sense of humanity. Imagine yourself as the teacher, under pressure to continue the experiment while my voice floats toward you from the other room, a reminder that when you flip the switch on the shock generator, a human being suffers. Like an effective evangelist, I might begin in a low key and build emotionally with the rising voltage:

75 volts	Ugh! Hey, what was that voltage? I didn't expect so much pain. I'm ready to stop right now, teacher. This experiment is not for me. I just can't think when I'm about to get zapped with all that juice.
90 volts	Ugh! Can't you hear me? I'm through. You're throwing electricity into a man no longer participating in this damned experiment. How about coming on over here and taking off these straps?
105 volts	Good God, man! How long can you keep this up? You sure as hell don't look like an executioner. You look too warm and alive for that. Do you have any children?

120 volts   What if that experimenter asks you to do this with your own
                   kids? Are you going to do it? When do you stop after you
                   start following brutal orders? Will you help remove the
                   fillings from my teeth if I die?

My imagined protest is no triumph of eloquence, but I hazard the confident guess that it would have undercut authority and significantly altered Milgram's statistics. The protests offered by the trained victim in Milgram's experiment signal distress, all right, but they do not ask the teacher to imagine what his obedience would mean beyond the laboratory.

I suspect my anger on reading Milgram's book arose partly from the guilty fear that I, too, might have been sucked into the vortex of his clever experiment to be found shamefully obedient. And of course I was bothered, as we all are, by the persuasive argument of a thesis I could not accept. Most of all, however, I was troubled by a sense that the deck was stacked against us all in the experiments and in the book. Statistics aside for a moment, we knew already that large numbers of people could be manipulated to deny their humanity. Nazi Germany taught us that, if nothing else; and as Milgram acknowledges more than once, the war in Indochina has been a sharp reminder. Still, nearly everyone—psychiatrists, college students, working men and women—vastly underestimated the level of obedience when they were asked to predict the results of Milgram's experiments; maybe that justifies this "scientific" reminder of our capacity for evil. But I believe the created world of *Obedience to Authority* is misleadingly simple. The book pretends to prove more than it really can about the process of being human. Maybe only the genius of a great novelist or an Erik Erikson could begin to do justice to Gretchen Brandt or the industrial engineer or the religion professor. Such people are surely the key to our "modest chance" for survival, and if the darkest implications of *Obedience to Authority* are to be anything more than cause for nihilism, then we must learn much more about the sources of their strength. I do not mean to suggest for a minute that this will be easy. It is the wonderful burden of our need to understand man's finest possibilities, as well as his most dismal failures; and such an act of imagination may never be reducible to the compelling simplicity of *Obedience to Authority*.

HANNAH ARENDT

Anton Schmidt

. . . On the stand was Abba Kovner, "a poet and an author," who had not so much testified as addressed an audience with the ease of someone who is used to speaking in public and resents interruptions from the floor. He had been asked by the presiding judge to be brief, which he obviously disliked, and Mr. Hausner, who had defended his witness, had been told that he could not "complain about a lack of patience on the part of the court," which of course he did not like either. At this slightly tense moment, the witness happened to mention the name of Anton Schmidt, a *Feldwebel,* or sergeant, in the German Army—a name that was not entirely unknown to this audience, for Yad Vashem had published Schmidt's story some years before in its Hebrew *Bulletin,* and a number of Yiddish papers in America had picked it up. Anton Schmidt was in charge of a patrol in Poland that collected stray German soldiers who were cut off from their units. In the course of doing this, he had run into members of the Jewish underground, including Mr. Kovner, a prominent member, and he had helped the Jewish partisans by supplying them with forged papers and military trucks. Most important of all: "He did not do it for money." This had gone on for five months, from October, 1941, to March, 1942, when Anton Schmidt was arrested and executed. (The prosecution had elicited the story because Kovner declared that he had first heard the name of Eichmann from Schmidt, who had told him about rumors in the Army that it was Eichmann who "arranges everything.")

This was by no means the first time that help from the outside, non-Jewish world had been mentioned. Judge Halevi had been asking the witnesses: "Did the Jews get any help?" with the same regularity as that with which the prosecution had asked: "Why did you not rebel?" The answers had been various and inconclusive—"We had the whole population against us," Jews hidden by Christian families could "be counted on the fingers of one hand," perhaps five or six out of a total of thirteen thousand—but on the whole the situation had, surprisingly, been better in Poland than in any other Eastern European country. (There was, I have said, no testimony on Bulgaria.) A Jew, now married to a Polish woman and living in Israel, testified how his wife had hidden him and twelve other Jews throughout the war; another had a Christian friend from before the war to whom he had escaped from a camp and who had helped him, and who was later executed because of the help he had given to Jews. One witness claimed that the Polish underground had supplied many Jews with weapons and had saved thousands of Jewish children by placing them with Polish families. The risks were prohibitive; there was the story of an entire Polish family who had been executed in the most brutal manner because they had adopted a six-year-old Jewish girl. But this mention of Schmidt was the first and the last time that any such story was told of a German, for the only other incident involving a German was mentioned only in a document: an Army officer had helped indirectly by sabotaging certain police orders; nothing happened to him, but the matter had been thought sufficiently serious to be mentioned in correspondence between Himmler and Bormann.

During the few minutes it took Kovner to tell of the help that had come from a German sergeant, a hush settled over the courtroom; it was as though the crowd had spontaneously decided to observe the usual two minutes of silence in honor of the man named Anton Schmidt. And in those two minutes, which were like a sudden burst of light in the midst of impenetrable, unfathomable darkness, a single thought stood out clearly, irrefutably, beyond question—how utterly different everything would be today in this courtroom, in Israel, in Germany, in all of Europe, and perhaps in all countries of the world, if only more such stories could have been told.

There are, of course, explanations of this devastating shortage, and they have been repeated many times. I shall give the gist of them in the words of one of the few subjectively sincere memoirs of the war published in Germany. Peter Bamm, a German Army physician who served at the Russian front, tells in *Die Unsichtbare Flagge* (1952) of the killing of Jews in Sevastopol. They were collected by "the others," as he calls the S.S. mobile killing units, to distinguish them from ordinary soldiers, whose decency the book extols, and were put into a sealed-off part of the former G.P.U. prison that abutted on the officers' lodgings, where Bamm's own unit was quartered. They were then made to board a mobile gas van, in which they died after a few minutes, whereupon the driver transported the corpses outside the city and unloaded them into tank ditches. "We knew this. We did nothing. Anyone who had seriously protested or done anything against the killing unit would have been arrested within twenty-four hours and would have disappeared. It belongs among the refinements of totalitarian governments in our century that they don't permit their opponents to die a great, dramatic martyr's death for their convictions. A good many of us might have accepted such a death. The totalitarian state lets its opponents disappear in silent anonymity. It is certain that anyone who had dared to suffer death rather than silently tolerate the crime would have sacrificed his life in vain. This is not to say that such a sacrifice would have been morally meaningless. It would only have been practically useless. None of us had a conviction so deeply rooted that we could have taken upon ourselves a practically useless sacrifice for the sake of a higher moral meaning." Needless to add, the writer remains unaware of the emptiness of his much emphasized "decency" in the absence of what he calls a "higher moral meaning."

But the hollowness of respectability—for decency under such circumstances is no more than respectability—was not what became apparent in the example afforded by Sergeant Anton Schmidt. Rather it was the fatal flaw in the argument itself, which at first sounds so hopelessly plausible. It is true that totalitarian domination tried to establish these holes of oblivion into which all deeds, good and evil, would disappear, but just as the Nazis' feverish attempts, from June, 1942, on, to erase all traces of the massacres—through cremation, through burning in open pits, through the use of explosives and flame-throwers and bone-crushing machinery—were doomed to failure, so all efforts to let their opponents "disappear in silent anonymity" were in vain. The holes of oblivion do not exist. Nothing human is that perfect, and there are simply too many people in the world to make oblivion possible. One man will always be left alive to tell the story. Hence, nothing can ever be "practically useless," at least, not in the long run. It would be of great practical usefulness for Germany today, not merely for her prestige abroad but for her sadly confused inner condition, if there were more such stories to be told. For the lesson of such stories is simple and within everybody's grasp. Politically speaking, it is that under conditions of terror most people will comply but *some people will not,* just as the lesson of the countries to which the Final Solution was proposed is that "it could happen" in most places but *it did not happen everywhere.* Humanly speaking, no more is required, and no more can reasonably be asked, for this planet to remain a place fit for human habitation.

[From *Eichmann in Jerusalem,* by Hannah Arendt, Viking Press, 1963]

IRVING HOWE

In Extreme Situations

. . . Without arms, drained by starvation, inexperienced in military crafts, subjected to a system of brutality beyond description, and distrusted, sometimes even betrayed, by other European nationalities that were also being oppressed by the Nazis, the Jews of eastern Europe were simply unable to hold back the "Final Solution."

A few behaved badly; more were heroic; most, like ordinary people at all times, tried to survive, then to protect their children, and finally to brace themselves for death.

Who, then, dares set himself as judge? Who can say what the "right" conduct should have been? Bend before the murderers in the hope of surviving? Sacrifice the old and sick in order to save the young? Or embark on hopeless gestures of resistance that would bring ghastly reprisals upon thousands of innocents?

The moral norms by which we hope to live are meant for common circumstances, but also for extraordinary ones, those in which we find it difficult to satisfy the requirements we set for ourselves. But beyond these two spheres, the ordinary and the extraordinary, there arise situations so extreme that it becomes immoral to make moral judgments about those who have had to confront them. When flesh has been seared and bones have been broken, when not even a memory remains of the common restraints of civilization, what point is there in speaking about heroism or the lack of it, resistance or the lack of it?

The minimal fragment of freedom which is surely a precondition for moral conduct, that fragment which allows us the slender persuasion of being able to make a choice, has been destroyed. The only remaining question is the ability of a living creature to endure physical torture—and that soon ceases to be a moral issue. It becomes inappropriate, even obscene, to speak either in praise or dispraise of those who perished. They need only be remembered. . . .

[From *The New York Times Book Review*, April 20, 1975]

ERIK H. ERIKSON

Erik H. Erikson is a Freudian psychoanalyst, a teacher of human development, and a student of anthropology and history. Erikson studied with Freud and was in analysis with Anna Freud, and his work both develops and extends Freudian theory. Fully acknowledging the impact of early childhood experiences, he mapped out the continuing development of the personality beyond childhood in what he calls the "Eight Stages of Man." Much of his work shows how early childhood experiences differ from society to society, how each society gives its children—gives all its members—more or less help in development, more or less guidance to get through the stages of development. By observing and conceptualizing the interplay between physical forces, psychological forces, and cultural, historical, and social forces, he has redefined the idea of "identity" and brought to the language the term "identity crisis."

Erikson was born in Germany in 1902. After high school (the German gymnasium), he wandered around Europe for several years as an itinerant artist, going through what he would later describe as his identity crisis of adolescence. He then taught at an experimental school in Vienna, got a Montessori teaching credential, and in 1933 completed studies at the Vienna Psychoanalytic Institute. That year, because of Hitler, he left Vienna for the United States to teach at Harvard, Yale, and Berkeley. (He left Berkeley after refusing to sign a loyalty oath, later found to be unconstitutional.) For a whole decade (1951–1960), he commuted biweekly from Stockbridge, Massachusetts, where he was a senior staff member of the Austen Riggs Center and worked with disturbed children from wealthy families, to Pittsburgh, Pennsylvania, where he taught at the university and worked with disturbed children from poor families. He has practiced as a psychoanalyst (and a training analyst) in Boston and in the San Francisco Bay area. From 1960 to 1970 he was Professor of Human Development at Harvard University. Now he is professor emeritus and lives in California where he continues to write and teach.

Erikson's best-known book, Childhood and Society *(1950), is still read widely in and out of the classroom. An important precursor is* Observations on the Yurok: Childhood and World Images *(1943), in which he shows how the restrictive childhood training of this northern California Indian tribe prepares its children for their arduous adult life style. His strong interest in psychohistory led to* Young Man Luther *(1958) and* Gandhi's Truth *(1969), for which he won the National Book Award and the Pulitzer Prize in 1969. More recent publications include two lectures on Jefferson,* Dimensions of a New Identity *(1974), and a series of conversations with Huey P. Newton,* In Search of Common Ground *(1973). He has been a recent target of the women's movement. An essay in his most recent collection,* Life History and the Historical Moment *(1975), speaks to some of those charges. Other collections include* Identity, Youth and Crisis *(1968) and* Insight and Responsibility: Lectures on the Ethical Implications of Psychoanalytic Insight *(1964). The first selection printed below is from the concluding essay in the last-named collection. The second is from* Dialogue with Erik Erikson *by Richard I. Evans (1967).*

Gandhi at Ahmedabad

. . .

In Ahmedabad I had occasion to visit Gandhi's ashram across the Sabarmati River; and it was not long before I realized that in Ahmedabad a hallowed and yet eminently concrete event had occurred which perfectly exemplifies everything I am trying to say. I refer, of course, to Gandhi's leadership in the lock-out and strike of the mill-workers in 1918, and his first fast in a public cause. This event is well known in the history of industrial relations the world over, and vaguely known to all educated Indians. Yet, I believe that only in Ahmedabad, among surviving witnesses and living institutions, can one fathom the "presence" of that event as a lastingly successful "experiment" in local industrial relations, influential in Indian politics, and, above all, representing a new type of encounter in divided human functions. The details of the strike and of the settlement need not concern us here. As usual, it began as a matter of wages. Nor can I take time to indicate the limited political and economic applicability of the Ahmedabad experiment to other industrial areas in and beyond India. What interests us here, is the fact that Gandhi, from the moment of his entry into the struggle, considered it an occasion not for maximum reciprocal coercion resulting in the usual compromise, but as an opportunity for all—the workers, the owners, and himself—"to rise from the present conditions."

The utopian quality of the principles on which he determined to focus can only be grasped by one who can visualize the squalor of the workmen's living conditions, the latent panic in the ranks of the paternalistic millowners (beset by worries of British competition), and Gandhi's then as yet relative experience in handling the masses of India. The shadows of defeat, violence and corruption hovered over every one of the "lofty" words which I am about to quote. But to Gandhi, any worthwhile struggle must "transform the inner life of the people." Gandhi spoke to the workers daily under the famous Babul Tree outside the medieval Shahpur Gate. He had studied their desperate condition, yet he urged them to ignore the threats and the promises of the millowners who in the obstinate fashion of all "haves" feared the anarchic insolence and violence of the "have nots." He knew that they feared him, too, for they had indicated that they might even accept his terms if only he would promise to leave and to stay away forever. But he settled down to prove that a just man could "secure the good of the workers while safeguarding the good of the employers"—the two opposing sides being represented by a sister and a brother, Anasuyabehn and Ambalal Sarabhai. Under the Babul Tree Gandhi announced the principle which somehow corresponds to our amended Rule: *"That line of action is alone justice which does not harm either party to a dispute."* By harm he meant—and his daily announcements leave no doubt of this—an inseparable combination of economic disadvantage, social indignity, loss of self-esteem, and latent vengeance.

Neither side found it easy to grasp this principle. When the workers began to weaken, Gandhi suddenly declared a fast. Some of his friends, he admitted, considered this "foolish, unmanly, or worse"; and some were deeply distressed. But, "I wanted to show you," he said to the workers, "that I was not playing with you." He was, as we would say, in dead earnest, and this fact, then as later, immediately raised an issue of local conscience to national significance. In daily appeals, Gandhi stressed variously those basic inner strengths without which no issue has "virtue," namely, will with justice, purpose with discipline, respect for work of any kind, and truthfulness. But he knew, and he said so, that these masses of illiterate men and women, newly arrived from the villages and already exposed to proletarization, did not have the moral strength or the social solidarity to adhere to principle without strong leadership. "You have yet to learn how and when to take an oath," he told them. The oath, the dead earnestness, then, was as yet the leader's privilege and commitment. In the end the matter was settled, not without a few Gandhian compromises to save face all around, but with a true acceptance of the settlement originally proposed by Gandhi.

I do not claim to understand the complex motivations and curious turns of Gandhi's mind—some contradicting Western rigidity in matters of principle, and some, I assume, strange to Indian observers, as well. I can also see in Gandhi's actions a paternalism which may now be "dated." But his monumental simplicity and total involvement in the "experiment" made both workers and owners revere him. And he himself said with humorous awe, "I have never come across such a fight." For, indeed both sides had matured in a way that lifted labor relations in Ahmedabad to a new and lasting level. Let me quote only the fact that, in 1950, the Ahmedabad Textile Labor Organization accounted for only a twentieth of India's union membership, but for eighty per cent of its welfare expenditures.

Such a singular historical event, then, reveals something essential in human strength, in traditional Indian strength and in the power of Gandhi's own personal transformation at the time. To me, the miracle of the Ahmedabad experiment has been not only its lasting success and its tenacity during those days of anarchic violence which after the great partition broke down so many dams of solidarity, but above all, the spirit which points beyond the event.

·   ·   ·

Gandhi's Nonviolence: Philosophy and Technique

Erikson. . . . There are some leaders who surprise us totally because they appear suddenly out of nowhere or what we thought was nowhere. Hitler, for years, was absolutely nobody. Two years of his life are altogether unaccounted for. Gandhi always insisted that he wanted to be "zero," and he deliberately identified himself with the lowest strata of the Indian population. Then he became a leader without assuming any kind of conventional power. But he was a master in molding existing potentialities together. That they fell apart again, and literally with a vengeance, that must be studied, too.

Evans. It would seem that they were each attempting to reach certain goals which represent certain kinds of power, and that one used techniques of violence, while the other used nonviolence.

Erikson. That is true, but it is not the whole point either. Nonviolence cannot in itself be the point, because great leaders whom some of us would continue to consider great have considered the use of violence and even of nuclear violence necessary, or not yet expendable. But in the meantime, I would repeat that the best leader is the one who can realize the actual potentials in his nation, and most of all the more inclusive identities which are ready to be realized in the world. That, at least, excludes small wars, or uses them only to confirm larger identities. The difference between a Hitler and a Gandhi is (in this context) that Hitler's violent methods were tied to a totalistic reinforcement of a pseudo-species (the German race), the fiction of which could only be maintained by vilifying and annihilating another pseudo-subspecies, the Jews. Gandhi's nonviolent technique, on the contrary, was not only tied to the political realities of his day, but also revived the more inclusive identity promised in the world religions.

Evans. It would be interesting to learn if one of your interests in India was to identify the source of the protest mechanism which Gandhi employed in the form of nonviolence.

Erikson. It was not initially my intention to study Gandhi and nonviolence as a technique of protest when I went to India. While I was working in the city of Ahmedabad, I met a number of Gandhi's old friends and adversaries who were with him at a critical event in his ascent to national leadership, an event which I had dimly read about when I was young. I realized that here I could "get at" an historical event by interviewing people who had participated in it. Also Gandhi was fifty years old at that time. As my students put it: "Erikson wrote a book on *Young Man Luther,* so now he must write a book on 'Middle-Aged Mahatma.'" In 1918, you see, Gandhi was one of a number of mahatmas; Indian history is full of mahatmas. But then he became *the* Mahatma through a number of events. The event I have been trying to reconstruct was his intervention in a mill strike in the city of Ahmedabad, one of the most concentratedly industrial towns in India. Two things stimulated my old interest in Gandhi. For one, he now seemed to me to exemplify in word and deed what I had come to perceive as a modern version of the golden rule. To put it briefly, this version suggests that wherever one has a choice one should choose to act so as to enhance the potentials of one's counterplayer's development as well as one's own. Maybe we can discuss this later. I know of no other example in world history where a man made such a principle so completely his own by always extending it to his opponent. This became clear as I heard more and more about that event. Gandhi had agreed to take over the leadership of the mill workers if they would promise to help him create a situation in which both the mill workers and the mill owners would emerge as more mature human beings. This ethical principle was, of course, entirely embedded in economic problems: Gandhi never divorced "lofty" matters from the most concrete ones, including "dirty" politics. Even today that city has the best labor relations of any city in India, although some critics are probably right who feel that Gandhi's solutions, too, were bound to their period, and were antirevolutionary.

Evans. Comparing the techniques of *violence* which emerged under Hitler in Germany and those of *nonviolence* in Gandhi's India, there must be some profound cultural differences which account for the emergence of such dramatic differences in the techniques of leadership which the people will tolerate.

Erikson. No doubt, there is a long cultural development which makes it historically plausible that "nonviolence" first was systematized in India. But then the historical problem is the convergence of a life history like Gandhi's with an historical trend, and the resulting actualization of a new direction. Gandhi wrote a detailed autobiography, which is a great help for an analyst, although he must be careful not to read a man's literary confessions as though they were free associations. Great confessions are always part self-revelation, part "propaganda." But I also find it fascinating to study what happened in the lives of the followers I'm interviewing. Why and how did Gandhi suddenly become so important to them? Why were they ready for him? How did he draw out of them the strength they displayed in serving him? Why did Gandhi choose these then young people and how did he know what roles to assign to them? And what was it in Indian history that would make Indians feel that nonviolence might be the weapon that would give them self-respect and would help them to meet a superior enemy head-on? All of this, you see, deals with the question of personal and historical potentials, without an understanding of which psychoanalysis remains a retrospective, a "traumatological" psychology.

Evans. Then you feel that the decision to use nonviolence was not necessarily a reflection of passivity at all, but rather represents an *active* inner process, the nature of which you want to determine. Is it possible that Gandhi was a brilliant master of strategy, and that nonviolence, rather than being merely a reflection of faith as many people saw it, reflected a definite strategy as well? In other words, is it possible that Gandhi's appearance of being simply a pious and austere man clouded our perception of his capabilities as an effective strategist?

Erikson. Yes, very much so. In fact, Gandhi was never as pious and austere about himself as his followers and his translators make him appear. In studying the details of his personal life as they are reported to me now, I'm very much impressed to see what a marvelous sense of humor he had and how frankly conscious he was of being crafty and cunning as well as saintly, never seeing any contradiction between these qualities. It's often the purist followers or adversaries of a man like that who try to make a total saint, or total fraud, out of him. But Gandhi would just laugh and say, "Sure I'm a banya," which is the Indian equivalent for a crafty trader (like some connotations of "Yankee"), and he could afford to bargain and compromise, because he was quite clear about certain rock-bottom principles. It is both pleasant and important to describe that side of him, for it balances the often deeply neurotic implications of his inner conflicts and of his public contradictions.

Evans. I imagine that as you began to examine in depth the sources, cultural context, application, and relative effectiveness of the so-called nonviolent techniques of social protest, you realized that you were dealing with an incredibly complex phenomenon, did you not?

Erikson. Very much so. To illustrate this complexity, we should note that Gandhi was not only very much influenced by Thoreau, but also by Tolstoy and Ruskin. Furthermore, the success of civil disobedience and of nonviolence depends very much on the choice of time, place, and opponent. I will never forget the afternoon when one of my friends brought the African leader Mboya to my seminar at M.I.T., and the students asked him to discuss the prospective use of nonviolence by African nationalists. "Well," he said with a gracious smile and an elegant British accent, "I will tell you a simple rule. You can try it with the British but not with the Belgians." Nonviolence, he meant, presupposes a cultivated sense of fairness on the part of the opponent. The British officials, of course, could be very ruthless, but Gandhi was able to arouse interest and sympathy among the British of that period. He was British enough himself. He had studied in England, and had become an English barrister. He spoke and wrote English. Yet, I believe that there is something universal in his method. Incidentally, we prejudice the whole matter by calling it nonviolence or likening it to "passive resistance," which it isn't. Gandhi in many ways was one of the least passive persons you can imagine, and he carefully searched for a better name for nonviolence. He called it Satyagraha, which means "truth force." And he would be extremely active about it, you know, once he had chosen a time and a place. He would, for example, always announce in advance what he was going to do and when and where and he would move in on his opponents on schedule. The only passive thing about it was that he exacted a pledge from his people that they would not fight back if they were physically attacked, and not even swear back. But again, this demands (as some of our civil rights fighters know) a most active inner state as compared with the submissive, passive, and masochistic state which most Westerners would think it is. I am studying Gandhi's personal development and his exact technique in a given instant because I believe he may be both the last representative of a great trend in human history, and yet also the first in a new trend. In the past, religious man put himself in total opposition to political and technological man and strove for inner peace through noninvolvement, sacrifice, and faith. He often cultivated masochistic propensities; his ideal was saintliness. On the other hand, political and technological man has cultivated aggressive and expansive systems and has tried to build certain safeguards into them which would keep the peace in a limited area. By preparing for war against another area he tried to keep peace in his own. He has exploited the sadistic expression of man's rage, and given it a certain vaingloriousness. Needless to say, empires and churches have made territorial deals with each other, and deals which concerned what I like to call the territoriality of identity. Now, I think that Gandhi quite consciously established a new trend in combining politics and religion, and this at least temporarily with great psychological acumen. I do not know yet what I will come out with but I do feel that armament has developed to a point where man cannot indulge himself any further in technological vaingloriousness. The new situation challenges man's whole consciousness of his position in the universe on a grand new scale. And here Gandhi has a lasting message, beyond his moment in history, and beyond his ascetic philosophy.

.   .   .

NICCOLÒ MACHIAVELLI

Niccolò Machiavelli (1469–1527) was first a patriotic Florentine statesman and second a writer of political theory, history, plays, and poetry. Living in a period of political chaos, he worked to stabilize the Florentine republic and to build a citizens' militia so that Florence would not have to depend on mercenaries to fight off attacks from France, Germany, Spain, the Pope, other Italian city-states, and rival factions within Florence. But Machiavelli failed. In 1512 the Medici—the ruling family which had been ousted after the death of the powerful Lorenzo de Medici in 1492—returned to defeat the new militia and to set up another princedom in Florence. Within a year Machiavelli was imprisoned on conspiracy charges, tortured, and finally released as part of a general amnesty because Cardinal de Medici had just been elected Pope. He retired to his farm, bitter and broken in spirit, and spent the rest of his life trying to figure out what went wrong.

Machiavelli is best known for the bitter cynicism of The Prince (Il Principe, 1517), *the first book he wrote while in exile and the book that has made the term "Machiavellianism" come to mean amoral political deceit and manipulation. Among his other works, the most famous are his* Discourses on Livy *(1513–1517), containing his thoughts on the creation and maintenance of a republic, and* The Mandrake (La Mandragola, 1507), *a comedy.*

Machiavelli occupied his earliest political post in 1498 as Secretary of the Ten of Liberty and Peace. He traveled as a diplomat all around Europe (leaving a wife and five children on his farm) and sent back reports to the Florentine republican government. He observed, among other things, the ruling techniques of Cesare Borgia—whose ruthless skill at maintaining his princedom through times of chaos Machiavelli would later describe and attempt to codify within The Prince.

The present selection is Chapter 18 of The Prince, *in the translation of Luigi Ricci revised by E. R. P. Vincent.*

In What Way Princes Must Keep Faith

How laudable it is for a prince to keep good faith and live with integrity, and not with astuteness, every one knows. Still the experience of our times shows those princes to have done great things who have had little regard for good faith, and have been able by astuteness to confuse men's brains, and who have ultimately overcome those who have made loyalty their foundation.

You must know, then, that there are two methods of fighting, the one by law, the other by force: the first method is that of men, the second of beasts; but as the first method is often insufficient, one must have recourse to the second. It is therefore necessary for a prince to know well how to use both the beast and the man. This was covertly taught to rulers by ancient writers, who relate how Achilles and many others of those ancient princes were given to Chiron the centaur to be brought up and educated under his discipline. The parable of this semi-animal, semi-human teacher is meant to indicate that a prince must know how to use both natures, and that the one without the other is not durable.

A prince being thus obliged to know well how to act as a beast must imitate the fox and the lion, for the lion cannot protect himself from traps, and the fox cannot defend himself from wolves. One must therefore be a fox to recognise traps, and a lion to frighten wolves. Those that wish to be only lions do not understand this. Therefore, a prudent ruler ought not to keep faith when by so doing it would be against his interest, and when the reasons which made him bind himself no longer exist. If men were all good, this precept would not be a good one; but as they are bad, and would not observe their faith with you, so you are not bound to keep faith with them. Nor have legitimate grounds ever failed a prince who wished to show colourable excuse for the non-fulfilment of his promise. Of this one could furnish an infinite number of modern examples, and show how many times peace has been broken, and how many promises rendered worthless, by the faithlessness of princes, and those that have been best able to imitate the fox have succeeded best. But it is necessary to be able to disguise this character well, and to be a great feigner and dissembler; and men are so simple and so ready to obey present necessities, that one who deceives will always find those who allow themselves to be deceived.

I will only mention one modern instance. Alexander VI did nothing else but deceive men, he thought of nothing else, and found the occasion for it; no man was ever more able to give assurances, or affirmed things with stronger oaths, and no man observed them less; however, he always succeeded in his deceptions, as he well knew this aspect of things.

It is not, therefore, necessary for a prince to have all the above-named qualities, but it is very necessary to seem to have them. I would even be bold to say that to possess them and always to observe them is dangerous, but to appear to possess them is useful. Thus it is well to seem merciful, faithful, humane, sincere, religious, and also to be so; but you must have the mind so disposed that when it is needful to be otherwise you may be able to change to the opposite qualities. And it must be understood that a prince, and especially a new prince, cannot observe all those things which are considered good in men, being often obliged, in order to maintain the state, to act against faith, against charity, against humanity, and against religion. And, therefore, he must have a mind disposed to adapt itself according to the wind, and as the variations of fortune dictate, and, as I said before, not deviate from what is good, if possible, but be able to do evil if constrained.

A prince must take great care that nothing goes out of his mouth which is not full of the above-named five qualities, and, to see and hear him, he should seem to be all mercy, faith, integrity, humanity, and religion. And nothing is more necessary than to seem to have this last quality, for men in general judge more by the eyes than by the hands, for every one can see, but very few have to feel. Everybody sees what you appear to be, few feel what you are, and those few will not dare to oppose themselves to the many, who have the majesty of the state to defend them; and in the actions of men, and especially of princes, from which there is no appeal, the end justifies the means. Let a prince therefore aim at conquering and maintaining the state, and the means will always be judged honourable and praised by every one, for the vulgar is always taken by appearances and the issue of the event; and the world consists only of the vulgar, and the few who are not vulgar are isolated when the many have a rallying point in the prince. A certain prince of the present time, whom it is well not to name, never does anything but preach peace and good faith, but he is really a great enemy to both, and either of them, had he observed them, would have lost him state or reputation on many occasions.

JOAN DIDION

A native Californian, Joan Didion was born in Sacramento in 1934 and educated at the University of California, Berkeley. She received Vogue's *Prix de Paris in 1956, the year of her graduation, and in 1963 was awarded the Bread Loaf Fellowship in fiction. A frequent contributor of articles and reviews to the* Saturday Evening Post, *to* Mademoiselle, *and to other magazines, she has been associate feature editor of* Vogue *and has taught creative writing at Berkeley. Her books include three novels:* Run River *(1963);* Play It as It Lays *(1970), for which she also wrote the screen play; and* A Book of Common Prayer *(1975). She has also written a collection of essays,* Slouching Towards Bethlehem *(1968), from which we reprint the selection below.*

On Morality

As it happens I am in Death Valley, in a room at the Enterprise Motel and Trailer Park, and it is July, and it is hot. In fact it is 119°. I cannot seem to make the air conditioner work, but there is a small refrigerator, and I can wrap ice cubes in a towel and hold them against the small of my back. With the help of the ice cubes I have been trying to think, because *The American Scholar* asked me to, in some abstract way about "morality," a word I distrust more every day, but my mind veers inflexibly toward the particular.

Here are some particulars. At midnight last night, on the road in from Las Vegas to Death Valley Junction, a car hit a shoulder and turned over. The driver, very young and apparently drunk, was killed instantly. His girl was found alive but bleeding internally, deep in shock. I talked this afternoon to the nurse who had driven the girl to the nearest doctor, 185 miles across the floor of the Valley and three ranges of lethal mountain road. The nurse explained that her husband, a talc miner, had stayed on the highway with the boy's body until the coroner could get over the mountains from Bishop, at dawn today. "You can't just leave a body on the highway," she said. "It's immoral."

It was one instance in which I did not distrust the word, because she meant something quite specific. She meant that if a body is left alone for even a few minutes on the desert, the coyotes close in and eat the flesh. Whether or not a corpse is torn apart by coyotes may seem only a sentimental consideration, but of course it is more: one of the promises we make to one another is that we will try to retrieve our casualties, try not to abandon our dead to the coyotes. If we have been taught to keep our promises—if, in the simplest terms, our upbringing is good enough—we stay with the body, or have bad dreams.

I am talking, of course, about the kind of social code that is sometimes called, usually pejoratively, "wagon-train morality." In fact that is precisely what it is. For better or worse, we are what we learned as children: my own childhood was illuminated by graphic litanies of the grief awaiting those who failed in their loyalties to each other. The Donner-Reed Party, starving in the Sierra snows, all the ephemera of civilization gone save that one vestigial taboo, the provision that no one should eat his own blood kin. The Jayhawkers, who quarreled and separated not far from where I am tonight. Some of them died in the Funerals and some of them died down near Badwater and most of the rest of them died in the Panamints. A woman who got through gave the Valley its name. Some might say that the Jayhawkers were killed by the desert summer, and the Donner Party by the mountain winter, by circumstances beyond control; we were taught instead that they had somewhere abdicated their responsibilities, somehow breached their primary loyalties, or they would not have found themselves helpless in the mountain winter or the desert summer, would not have given way to acrimony, would not have deserted one another, would not have *failed*. In brief, we heard such stories as cautionary tales, and they still suggest the only kind of "morality" that seems to me to have any but the most potentially mendacious meaning.

You are quite possibly impatient with me by now; I am talking, you want to say, about a "morality" so primitive that it scarcely deserves the name, a code that has as its point only survival, not the attainment of the ideal good. Exactly. Particularly out here tonight, in this country so ominous and terrible that to live in it is to live with antimatter, it is difficult to believe that "the good" is a knowable quantity. Let me tell you what it is like out here tonight. Stories travel at night on the desert. Someone gets in his pickup and drives a couple of hundred miles for a beer, and he carries news of what is happening, back wherever he came from. Then he drives another hundred miles for another beer, and passes along stories from the last place as well as from the one before; it is a network kept alive by people whose instincts tell them that if they do not keep moving at night on the desert they will lose all reason. Here is a story that is going around the desert tonight: over across the Nevada line, sheriff's deputies are diving in some underground pools, trying to retrieve a couple of bodies known to be in the hole. The widow of one of the drowned boys is over there; she is eighteen, and pregnant, and is said not to leave the hole. The divers go down and come up, and she just stands there and stares into the water. They have been diving for ten days but have found no bottom to the caves, no bodies and no trace of them, only the black 90° water going down and down and down, and a single translucent fish, not classified. The story tonight is that one of the divers has been hauled up incoherent, out of his head, shouting—until they got him out of there so that the widow could not hear—about water that got hotter instead of cooler as he went down, about light flickering through the water, about magma, about underground nuclear testing.

That is the tone stories take out here, and there are quite a few of them tonight. And it is more than the stories alone. Across the road at the Faith Community Church a couple of dozen old people, come here to live in trailers and die in the sun, are holding a prayer sing. I cannot hear them and do not want to. What I can hear are occasional coyotes and a constant chorus of "Baby the Rain Must Fall" from the jukebox in the Snake Room next door, and if I were also to hear those dying voices, those Midwestern voices drawn to this lunar country for some unimaginable atavistic rites, *rock of ages cleft for me,* I think I would lose my own reason. Every now and then I imagine I hear a rattlesnake, but my husband says that it is a faucet, a paper rustling, the wind. Then he stands by a window, and plays a flashlight over the dry wash outside.

What does it mean? It means nothing manageable. There is some sinister hysteria in the air out here tonight, some hint of the monstrous perversion to which any human idea can come. "I followed my own conscience." "I did what I thought was right." How many madmen have said it and meant it? How many murderers? Klaus Fuchs said it, and the men who committed the Mountain Meadows Massacre said it, and Alfred Rosenberg said it. And, as we are rotely and rather presumptuously reminded by those who would say it now, Jesus said it. Maybe we have all said it, and maybe we have been wrong. Except on that most primitive level—our loyalties to those we love—what could be more arrogant than to claim the primacy of personal conscience? ("Tell me," a rabbi asked Daniel Bell when he said, as a child, that he did not believe in God. "Do you think God cares?") At least some of the time, the world appears to me as a painting by Hieronymus Bosch; were I to follow my conscience then, it would lead me out onto the desert with Marion Faye, out to where he stood in *The Deer Park* looking east to Los Alamos and praying, as if for rain, that it would happen: ". . . *let it come and clear the rot and the stench and the stink, let it come for all of everywhere, just so it comes and the world stands clear in the white dead dawn.*"

Of course you will say I do not have the right, even if I had the power, to inflict that unreasonable conscience upon you; nor do I want you to inflict your conscience, however reasonable, however enlightened, upon me. ("We must be aware of the dangers which lie in our most generous wishes," Lionel Trilling once wrote. "Some paradox of our nature leads us, when once we have made our fellow men the objects of our enlightened interest, to go on to make them the objects of our pity, then of our wisdom, ultimately of our coercion.") That the ethic of conscience is intrinsically insidious seems scarcely a revelatory point, but it is one raised with increasing infrequency; even those who do raise it tend to *segue* with troubling readiness into the quite contradictory position that the ethic of conscience is dangerous when it is "wrong," and admirable when it is "right."

You see I want to be quite obstinate about insisting that we have no way of knowing—beyond that fundamental loyalty to the social code—what is "right" and what is "wrong," what is "good" and what "evil." I dwell so upon this because the most disturbing aspect of "morality" seems to me to be the frequency with which the word now appears; in the press, on television, in the most perfunctory kinds of conversation. Questions of straightforward power (or survival) politics, questions of quite indifferent public policy, questions of almost anything: they are all assigned these factitious moral burdens. There is something facile going on, some self-indulgence at work. Of course we would all like to "believe" in something, like to assuage our private guilts in public causes, like to lose our tiresome selves; like, perhaps, to transform the white flag of defeat at home into the brave white banner of battle away from home. And of course it is all right to do that; that is how, immemorially, things have gotten done. But I think it is all right only so long as we do not delude ourselves about what we are doing, and why. It is all right only so long as we remember that all the *ad hoc* committees, all the picket lines, all the brave signatures in *The New York Times,* all the tools of agitprop straight across the spectrum, do not confer upon anyone any *ipso facto* virtue. It is all right only so long as we recognize that the end may or may not be expedient, may or may not be a good idea, but in any case has nothing to do with "morality." Because when we start deceiving ourselves into thinking not that we want something or need something, not that it is a pragmatic necessity for us to have it, but that it is a *moral imperative* that we have it, then is when we join the fashionable madmen, and then is when the thin whine of hysteria is heard in the land, and then is when we are in bad trouble. And I suspect we are already there.

[1965]

The Individual and Society

What," asks John Stuart Mill, "is the rightful limit to the sovereignty of the individual over himself? Where does the authority of society begin?" Answers have varied, but the questions remain central, particularly today when old values and certainties are undergoing crippling challenge before new ones have clearly emerged.

Two important historic answers to Mill's questions are found in the Declaration of Independence, which establishes in our political tradition that the rights of men and the consent of the governed take precedence over the will of the State, and in the Bill of Rights, which spells out and thus protects the rights of the individual. The article by Walter Lippmann that follows brings fresh dimension to the First Amendment by suggesting that in a democracy freedom of speech is important not so much for the speaker as for the listener: we must be free to hear what our critics have to say.

The next three pieces deal with the direct personal conflict between individual conscience and social law. When is civil disobedience justified? For many people civil disobedience within a civilized state is by definition immoral, especially in a democracy, where law is adjustable. We voluntarily relinquish some of our freedom and accept the necessity and authority of the law in order to protect the community and guard it against anarchy. Defiance, then, strikes not only at specific laws but also at the concept of law and order and thus at the system itself. This is the argument that Plato presents so forcefully in *The Crito,* part of which is reprinted below. But for Thoreau, a dedicated individualist, and Martin Luther King, Jr., an eloquent spokesman for civil and human rights, individual conscience, not the State, is sovereign in matters of morality. In reading the above arguments, the reader may wish to consider a paradox pointed out by George Orwell in his essay on Gandhi: that modern civil disobedience can be effective only in a democratic community. "It is difficult to see," says Orwell, "how Gandhi's methods [passive resistance] could be applied in a country where opponents to the regime disappear in the middle of the night and are never heard of again. Without a free press and the right of assembly, it is impossible not merely to appeal to outside opinion, but to bring a mass movement into being, or even to make your intentions known to your adversary."

The two concluding pieces take on a new perspective and suggest more subtle and often hidden relationships between individuals and the society in which they live. "People *are* many things and can *become* many things," says Coles, and much depends on the signals and cues that they receive from society. Herndon takes up this same theme and shows how a social label can become powerful as a self-fulfilling prophecy. The two pieces that conclude the following section on race and racism also fit into the above discussion, and the reader may wish to consider them in this context. Oliver Killens supports violent dissent against a system that stunts human possibility and is unresponsive to just demands, whereas Bayard Rustin sees violence as a whirlpool that inevitably dehumanizes all who get caught up in it.

JOHN STUART MILL

Society and the Individual

What, then, is the rightful limit to the sovereignty of the individual over himself? Where does the authority of society begin? How much of human life should be assigned to individuality, and how much to society?

Each will receive its proper share, if each has that which more particularly concerns it. To individuality should belong the part of life in which it is chiefly the individual that is interested; to society, the part which chiefly interests society.

Though society is not founded on a contract, and though no good purpose is answered by inventing a contract in order to deduce social obligations from it, every one who receives the protection of society owes a return for the benefit, and the fact of living in society renders it indispensable that each should be bound to observe a certain line of conduct towards the rest. This conduct consists, first, in not injuring the interests of one another; or rather certain interests, which, either by express legal provision or by tacit understanding, ought to be considered as rights; and secondly, in each person's bearing his share (to be fixed on some equitable principle) of the labors and sacrifices incurred for defending the society or its members from injury and molestation. These conditions society is justified in enforcing, at all costs to those who endeavor to withhold fulfilment. Nor is this all that society may do. The acts of an individual may be hurtful to others, or wanting in due consideration for their welfare, without going the length of violating any of their constituted rights. The offender may then be justly punished by opinion, though not by law. As soon as any part of a person's conduct affects prejudicially the interests of others, society has jurisdiction over it, and the question whether the general welfare will or will not be promoted by interfering with it, becomes open to discussion. But there is no room for entertaining any such question when a person's conduct affects the interests of no persons besides himself, or needs not affect them unless they like (all the persons concerned being of full age, and the ordinary amount of understanding). In all such cases there should be perfect freedom, legal and social, to do the action and stand the consequences.

It would be a great misunderstanding of this doctrine, to suppose that it is one of selfish indifference, which pretends that human beings have no business with each other's conduct in life, and that they should not concern themselves about the well-doing or well-being of one another, unless their own interest is involved. Instead of any diminution, there is need of a great increase of disinterested exertion to promote the good of others. But disinterested benevolence can find other instruments to persuade people to their good, than whips and scourges, either of the literal or the metaphorical sort. I am the last person to undervalue the self-regarding virtues; they are only second in importance, if even second, to the social. It is equally the business of education to cultivate both. But even education works by conviction and persuasion as well as by compulsion, and it is by the former only that, when the period of education is past, the self-regarding virtues should be inculcated. Human beings owe to each other help to distinguish the better from the worse, and encouragement to choose the former and avoid the latter. They should be forever stimulating each other to increased exercise of their higher faculties, and increased direction of their feelings and aims towards wise instead of foolish, elevating instead of degrading, objects and contemplations. But neither one person, nor any number of persons, is warranted in saying to another human creature of ripe years, that he shall not do with his life for his own benefit what he chooses to do with it. He is the person most interested in his own well-being: the interest which any other person, except in cases of strong personal attachment, can have in it, is trifling, compared with that which he himself has; the interest which society has in him individually (except as to his conduct to others) is fractional, and altogether indirect: while, with respect to his own feelings and circumstances, the most ordinary man or woman has means of knowledge immeasurably surpassing those that can be possessed by anyone else. The interference of society to overrule his judgment and purposes in what only regards himself, must be grounded on general presumptions; which may be altogether wrong, and even if right, are as likely as not to be misapplied to individual cases, by persons no better acquainted with the circumstances of such cases than those are who look at them merely from without. In this department, therefore, of human affairs, Individuality has its proper field of action. In the conduct of human beings towards one another, it is necessary that general rules should for the most part be observed, in order that people may know what they have to expect; but in each person's own concerns, his individual spontaneity is entitled to free exercise. Considerations to aid his judgment, exhortations to strengthen his will, may be offered to him, even obtruded on him, by others; but he, himself, is the final judge. All errors which he is likely to commit against advice and warning, are far outweighed by the evil of allowing others to constrain him to what they deem his good.

. . .

[From *On Liberty,* by John Stuart Mill, 1859]

THOMAS JEFFERSON

On June 11, 1776, the Continental Congress appointed a committee of five—Thomas Jefferson, Benjamin Franklin, John Adams, Robert Livingston, and Roger Sherman—to prepare a declaration of independence. It was decided that Jefferson should first write a draft. He did so, drawing heavily on the natural rights political philosophy of the time, but as he says, he turned to "neither book nor pamphlet" in its preparation. A few changes were made by Adams and Franklin, and it was then presented to Congress on June 28. On July 2 and 3 Congress debated the form and content of the Declaration, made a few further changes, and on July 4 approved it without dissent. Although we here credit Jefferson with authorship, we print the amended and official version, taken from the United States Government Senate Manual.

Declaration of Independence
(IN CONGRESS JULY 4, 1776)

The Unanimous Declaration of the Thirteen United States of America

When in the Course of human events, it becomes necessary for one people to dissolve the political bands which have connected them with another, and to assume among the powers of the earth, the separate and equal station to which the Laws of Nature and of Nature's God entitle them, a decent respect to the opinions of mankind requires that they should declare the causes which impel them to the separation.

We hold these truths to be self-evident, that all men are created equal, that they are endowed by their Creator with certain unalienable Rights, that among these are Life, Liberty and the pursuit of Happiness. That to secure these rights, Governments are instituted among Men, deriving their just powers from the consent of the governed, That whenever any Form of Government becomes destructive of these ends, it is the Right of the People to alter or to abolish it, and to institute new Government, laying its foundation on such principles and organizing its powers in such form, as to them shall seem most likely to effect their Safety and Happiness. Prudence, indeed, will dictate that Governments long established should not be changed for light and transient causes; and accordingly all experience hath shewn that mankind are more disposed to suffer, while evils are sufferable, than to right themselves by abolishing the forms to which they are accustomed. But when a long train of abuses and usurpations, pursuing invariably the same Object evinces a design to reduce them under absolute Despotism, it is their right, it is their duty, to throw off such Government, and to provide new Guards for their future security. Such has been the patient sufferance of these Colonies; and such is now the necessity which constrains them to alter their former Systems of Government. The history of the present King of Great Britain is a history of repeated injuries and usurpations, all having in direct object the establishment of an absolute Tyranny over these States. To prove this, let Facts be submitted to a candid world.

He has refused his Assent to Laws, the most wholesome and necessary for the public good.

He has forbidden his Governors to pass Laws of immediate and pressing importance, unless suspended in their operation till his Assent should be obtained; and when so suspended, he has utterly neglected to attend to them.

He has refused to pass other Laws for the accommodation of large districts of people, unless those people would relinquish the right of Representation in the Legislature, a right inestimable to them and formidable to tyrants only.

He has called together legislative bodies at places unusual, uncomfortable, and distant from the depository of their public Records, for the sole purpose of fatiguing them into compliance with his measures.

He has dissolved Representative Houses repeatedly, for opposing with manly firmness his invasions on the rights of the people.

He has refused for a long time, after such dissolutions, to cause others to be elected; whereby the Legislative powers, incapable of Annihilation, have returned to the People at large for their exercise; the State remaining in the mean time exposed to all the dangers of invasion from without, and convulsions within.

He has endeavoured to prevent the population of these States; for that purpose obstructing the Laws for Naturalization of Foreigners; refusing to pass others to encourage their migrations hither, and raising the conditions of new Appropriations of Lands.

He has obstructed the Administration of Justice, by refusing his Assent to Laws for establishing Judiciary powers.

He has made Judges dependent on his Will alone, for the tenure of their offices, and the amount and payment of their salaries.

He has erected a multitude of New Offices, and sent hither swarms of Officers to harass our people, and eat out their substance.

He has kept among us, in times of peace, Standing Armies without the Consent of our legislatures.

He has affected to render the Military independent of and superior to the Civil power.

He has combined with others to subject us to a jurisdiction foreign to our constitution, and unacknowledged by our laws; giving his Assent to their Acts of pretended Legislation:

For quartering large bodies of armed troops among us:

For protecting them, by a mock Trial, from punishment for any Murders which they should commit on the Inhabitants of these States:

For cutting off our Trade with all parts of the world:

For imposing Taxes on us without our Consent:

For depriving us in many cases, of the benefits of Trial by Jury:

For transporting us beyond Seas to be tried for pretended offences:

For abolishing the free System of English Laws in a neighbouring Province, establishing therein an Arbitrary government, and enlarging its Boundaries so as to render it at once an example and fit instrument for introducing the same absolute rule into these Colonies:

For taking away our Charters, abolishing our most valuable Laws, and altering fundamentally the Forms of our Governments:

For suspending our own Legislatures, and declaring themselves invested with power to legislate for us in all cases whatsoever.

He has abdicated Government here, by declaring us out of his Protection and waging War against us.

He has plundered our seas, ravaged our Coasts, burnt our towns, and destroyed the lives of our people.

He is at this time transporting large Armies of foreign Mercenaries to compleat the works of death, desolation and tyranny, already begun with circumstances of Cruelty & perfidy scarcely paralleled in the most barbarous ages, and totally unworthy the Head of a civilized nation.

He has constrained our fellow Citizens taken Captive on the high Seas to bear Arms against their Country, to become the executioners of their friends and Brethren, or to fall themselves by their Hands.

He has excited domestic insurrections amongst us, and has endeavoured to bring on the inhabitants of our frontiers, the merciless

Indian Savages, whose known rule of warfare is an undistinguished destruction of all ages, sexes and conditions.

In every stage of these Oppressions We have Petitioned for Redress in the most humble terms: Our repeated Petitions have been answered only by repeated injury. A Prince, whose character is thus marked by every act which may define a Tyrant, is unfit to be the ruler of a free people.

Nor have We been wanting in attentions to our British Brethren. We have warned them from time to time of attempts by their legislature to extend an unwarrantable jurisdiction over us. We have reminded them of the circumstances of our emigration and settlement here. We have appealed to their native justice and magnanimity, and we have conjured them by the ties of our common kindred to disavow these usurpations, which would inevitably interrupt our connections and correspondence. They too have been deaf to the voice of justice and of consanguinity. We must, therefore, acquiesce in the necessity, which denounces our Separation, and hold them, as we hold the rest of mankind. Enemies in War, in Peace Friends.

WE, THEREFORE, the REPRESENTATIVES OF THE UNITED STATES OF AMERICA, IN GENERAL CONGRESS, Assembled, appealing to the Supreme Judge of the world for the rectitude of our intentions, do, in the Name, and by authority of the good People of these Colonies, solemnly PUBLISH and DECLARE, That these United Colonies are, and of Right ought to be FREE AND INDEPENDENT STATES; that they are Absolved from all Allegiance to the British Crown, and that all political connection between them and the State of Great Britain, is and ought to be totally dissolved; and that as FREE AND INDEPENDENT STATES, they have full Power to levy War, conclude Peace, contract Alliances, establish Commerce, and to do all other Acts and Things which INDEPENDENT STATES may of right do. And for the support of this Declaration, with a firm reliance on the protection of divine Providence, we mutually pledge to each other our Lives, our Fortunes and our sacred Honor.

THE FIRST CONGRESS OF THE UNITED STATES

"The Bill of Rights" is the name given to the first ten amendments to the United States Constitution. When the Constitution was originally adopted in 1788, many of its framers had felt that a spelling-out of rights already

*presumed to exist was unnecessary and might even suggest an undue
extension of governmental powers. Some of the states, however, having
explicit declarations of rights in their own constitutions, recommended on
ratifying the federal Constitution that it too be so furnished. The Bill of
Rights was prepared by the first Congress under the leadership of James
Madison and was ratified by the states in 1791. It has turned out to be
an invaluable guide to the courts in decisions affecting civil rights and is
in fact the main protection American citizens have against the diminution
of their liberties by their government or by each other.*

The Bill of Rights

ARTICLES IN ADDITION TO, AND AMENDMENT OF, THE CONSTITUTION OF
THE UNITED STATES OF AMERICA, PROPOSED BY CONGRESS, AND RATIFIED
BY THE LEGISLATURES OF THE SEVERAL STATES, PURSUANT TO THE FIFTH
ARTICLE OF THE ORIGINAL CONSTITUTION.

Article I

Congress shall make no law respecting an establishment of religion, or
prohibiting the free exercise thereof; or abridging the freedom of speech,
or of the press; or the right of the people peaceably to assemble, and to
petition the Government for a redress of grievances.

Article II

A well regulated Militia, being necessary to the security of a free State,
the right of the people to keep and bear Arms, shall not be infringed.

Article III

No Soldier shall, in time of peace be quartered in any house, without the
consent of the Owner, nor in time of war, but in a manner to be pre-
scribed by law.

Article IV

The right of the people to be secure in their persons, houses, papers, and
effects, against unreasonable searches and seizures, shall not be violated,
and no Warrants shall issue, but upon probable cause, supported by Oath
or affirmation, and particularly describing the place to be searched, and
the persons or things to be seized.

Article V

No person shall be held to answer for a capital, or otherwise infamous crime, unless on a presentment or indictment of a Grand Jury, except in cases arising in the land or naval forces, or in the Militia, when in actual service in time of War or public danger; nor shall any person be subject for the same offence to be twice put in jeopardy of life or limb; nor shall be compelled in any criminal case to be a witness against himself; nor be deprived of life, liberty, or property, without due process of law; nor shall private property be taken for public use, without just compensation.

Article VI

In all criminal prosecutions, the accused shall enjoy the right to a speedy and public trial, by an impartial jury of the State and district wherein the crime shall have been committed, which district shall have been previously ascertained by law, and to be informed of the nature and cause of the accusation; to be confronted with the witnesses against him; to have compulsory process for obtaining witnesses in his favor, and to have the Assistance of Counsel for his defence.

Article VII

In Suits at common law, where the value in controversy shall exceed twenty dollars, the right of trial by jury shall be preserved, and no fact tried by a jury, shall be otherwise reexamined in any Court of the United States, than according to the rules of the common law.

Article VIII

Excessive bail shall not be required, nor excessive fines imposed, nor cruel and unusual punishments inflicted.

Article IX

The enumeration in the Constitution, of certain rights, shall not be construed to deny or disparage others retained by the people.

Article X

The powers not delegated to the United States by the Constitution, nor prohibited by it to the States, are reserved to the States respectively, or to the people.

WALTER LIPPMANN

Walter Lippmann (1889–1974) was one of the most honored of American newspapermen. He was educated at Harvard and then taught philosophy there as an assistant to George Santayana. He joined the staff of The New Republic *at its founding in 1914, interrupted his journalistic career to serve as assistant to the Secretary of War—doing special work on peace negotiating—and then moved to an editorial position on the* New York World. *His writings were syndicated in newspapers throughout the country and his column "Today and Tomorrow" won him Pulitzer Prizes in 1958 and 1962. The 1958 award cited the "wisdom, perception, and high sense of responsibility with which he has commented for many years on national and international affairs." During the Watergate years he was quoted with increasing frequency. He received many honorary degrees, and such decorations as the Medal of Freedom, the Legion of Honor from France, and the Order of Leopold from Belgium. His books include* Liberty and the News *(1920),* Public Opinion *(1922),* A Preface to Morals *(1929),* The Good Society *(1937),* The Public Philosophy *(1955),* The Coming Tests with Russia *(1961),* Western Unity and the Common Market *(1962), and* The Essential Lippmann: A Political Philosophy for Liberal Democracy *(1963). The essay we present below is taken from* The Atlantic Monthly *for August 1939.*

The Indispensable Opposition

[I]

Were they pressed hard enough, most men would probably confess that political freedom—that is to say, the right to speak freely and to act in opposition—is a noble ideal rather than a practical necessity. As the case for freedom is generally put to-day, the argument lends itself to this feeling. It is made to appear that, whereas each man claims his freedom as a matter of right, the freedom he accords to other men is a matter of toleration. Thus, the defense of freedom of opinion tends to rest not on its substantial, beneficial, and indispensable consequences, but on a somewhat eccentric, a rather vaguely benevolent, attachment to an abstraction.

It is all very well to say with Voltaire, 'I wholly disapprove of what you say, but will defend to the death your right to say it,' but as a matter of fact most men will not defend to the death the rights of other men: if they disapprove sufficiently what other men say, they will somehow suppress those men if they can.

So, if this is the best that can be said for liberty of opinion, that a man must tolerate his opponents because everyone has a 'right' to say what he pleases, then we shall find that liberty of opinion is a luxury, safe only in pleasant times when men can be tolerant because they are not deeply and vitally concerned.

Yet actually, as a matter of historic fact, there is a much stronger foundation for the great constitutional right of freedom of speech, and as a matter of practical human experience there is a much more compelling reason for cultivating the habits of free men. We take, it seems to me, a naïvely self-righteous view when we argue as if the right of our opponents to speak were something that we protect because we are magnanimous, noble, and unselfish. The compelling reason why, if liberty of opinion did not exist, we should have to invent it, why it will eventually have to be restored in all civilized countries where it is now suppressed, is that we must protect the right of our opponents to speak because we must hear what they have to say.

We miss the whole point when we imagine that we tolerate the freedom of our political opponents as we tolerate a howling baby next door, as we put up with the blasts from our neighbor's radio because we are too peaceable to heave a brick through the window. If this were all there is to freedom of opinion, that we are too good-natured or too timid to do anything about our opponents and our critics except to let them talk, it would be difficult to say whether we are tolerant because we are magnanimous or because we are lazy, because we have strong principles or because we lack serious convictions, whether we have the hospitality of an inquiring mind or the indifference of an empty mind. And so, if we truly wish to understand why freedom is necessary in a civilized society, we must begin by realizing that, because freedom of discussion improves our own opinions, the liberties of other men are our own vital necessity.

We are much closer to the essence of the matter, not when we quote Voltaire, but when we go to the doctor and pay him to ask us the most embarrassing questions and to prescribe the most disagreeable diet. When we pay the doctor to exercise complete freedom of speech about the cause and cure of our stomachache, we do not look upon ourselves as tolerant and magnanimous, and worthy to be admired by ourselves. We have enough common sense to know that if we threaten to put the doctor in jail because we do not like the diagnosis and the prescription it will be unpleasant for the doctor, to be sure, but equally unpleasant for our own stomachache. That is why even the most ferocious dictator would rather be treated by a doctor who was free to think and speak the truth than by his own Minister of Propaganda. For there is a point, the point at which things really matter, where the freedom of others is no longer a question of their right but of our need.

The point at which we recognize this need is much higher in some men than in others. The totalitarian rulers think they do not need the freedom of an opposition: they exile, imprison, or shoot their opponents. We have concluded on the basis of practical experience, which goes back to Magna Carta and beyond, that we need the opposition. We pay the opposition salaries out of the public treasury.

In so far as the usual apology for freedom of speech ignores this experience, it becomes abstract and eccentric rather than concrete and human. The emphasis is generally put on the right to speak, as if all that mattered were that the doctor should be free to go out into the park and explain to the vacant air why I have a stomachache. Surely that is a miserable caricature of the great civic right which men have bled and died for. What really matters is that the doctor should tell *me* what ails me, that I should listen to him; that if I do not like what he says I should be free to call in another doctor; and that then the first doctor should have to listen to the second doctor; and that out of all the speaking and listening, the give-and-take of opinions, the truth should be arrived at.

This is the creative principle of freedom of speech, not that it is a system for the tolerating of error, but that it is a system for finding the truth. It may not produce the truth, or the whole truth all the time, or often, or in some cases ever. But if the truth can be found, there is no other system which will normally and habitually find so much truth. Until we have thoroughly understood this principle, we shall not know why we must value our liberty, or how we can protect and develop it.

[II]

Let us apply this principle to the system of public speech in a totalitarian state. We may, without any serious falsification, picture a condition of affairs in which the mass of the people are being addressed through one broadcasting system by one man and his chosen subordinates. The orators speak. The audience listens but cannot and dare not speak back. It is a system of one-way communication; the opinions of the rulers are broadcast outwardly to the mass of the people. But nothing comes back to the rulers from the people except the cheers; nothing returns in the way of knowledge of forgotten facts, hidden feelings, neglected truths, and practical suggestions.

But even a dictator cannot govern by his own one-way inspiration alone. In practice, therefore, the totalitarian rulers get back the reports of the secret police and of their party henchmen down among the crowd. If these reports are competent, the rulers may manage to remain in touch with public sentiment. Yet that is not enough to know what the audience feels. The rulers have also to make great decisions that have enormous consequences, and here their system provides virtually no help from the give-and-take of opinion in the nation. So they must either rely on their own institution, which cannot be permanently and continually inspired, or, if they are intelligent despots, encourage their trusted advisers and their technicians to speak and debate freely in their presence.

On the walls of the houses of Italian peasants one may see inscribed in large letters the legend, 'Mussolini is always right.' But if that legend is taken seriously by Italian ambassadors, by the Italian General Staff, and by the Ministry of Finance, then all one can say is heaven help Mussolini, heaven help Italy, and the new Emperor of Ethiopia.

For at some point, even in a totalitarian state, it is indispensable that there should exist the freedom of opinion which causes opposing opinions to be debated. As time goes on, that is less and less easy under a despotism; critical discussion disappears as the internal opposition is liquidated in favor of men who think and feel alike. That is why the early successes of despots, of Napoleon I and of Napoleon III, have usually been followed by an irreparable mistake. For in listening only to his yes men—the others being in exile or in concentration camps, or terrified—the despot shuts himself off from the truth that no man can dispense with.

We know all this well enough when we contemplate the dictatorships. But when we try to picture our own system, by way of contrast, what picture do we have in our minds? It is, is it not, that anyone may stand up on his own soapbox and say anything he pleases, like the individuals in Kipling's poem who sit each in his separate star and draw the Thing as they see it for the God of Things as they are. Kipling, perhaps, could do this, since he was a poet. But the ordinary mortal isolated on his separate star will have an hallucination, and a citizenry declaiming from separate soapboxes will poison the air with hot and nonsensical confusion.

If the democratic alternative to the totalitarian one-way broadcasts is a row of separate soapboxes, then I submit that the alternative is unworkable, is unreasonable, and is humanly unattractive. It is above all a false alternative. It is not true that liberty has developed among civilized men when anyone is free to set up a soapbox, is free to hire a hall where he may expound his opinions to those who are willing to listen. On the contrary, freedom of speech is established to achieve its essential purpose only when different opinions are expounded in the same hall to the same audience.

For, while the right to talk may be the beginning of freedom, the necessity of listening is what makes the right important. Even in Russia and Germany a man may still stand in an open field and speak his mind. What matters is not the utterance of opinions. What matters is the confrontation of opinions in debate. No man can care profoundly that every fool should say what he likes. Nothing has been accomplished if the wisest man proclaims his wisdom in the middle of the Sahara Desert. This is the shadow. We have the substance of liberty when the fool is compelled to listen to the wise man and learn; when the wise man is compelled to take account of the fool, and to instruct him; when the wise man can increase his wisdom by hearing the judgment of his peers.

That is why civilized men must cherish liberty—as a means of promoting the discovery of truth. So we must not fix our whole attention on the right of anyone to hire his own hall, to rent his own broadcasting station, to distribute his own pamphlets. These rights are incidental; and though they must be preserved, they can be preserved only by regarding them as incidental, as auxiliary to the substance of liberty that must be cherished and cultivated.

Freedom of speech is best conceived, therefore, by having in mind the picture of a place like the American Congress, an assembly where opposing views are represented, where ideas are not merely uttered but debated, or the British Parliament, where men who are free to speak are also compelled to answer. We may picture the true condition of freedom as existing in a place like a court of law, where witnesses testify and are cross-examined, where the lawyer argues against the opposing lawyer before the same judge and in the presence of one jury. We may picture freedom as existing in a forum where the speaker must respond to questions; in a gathering of scientists where the data, the hypothesis, and the conclusion are submitted to men competent to judge them; in a reputable newspaper which not only will publish the opinions of those who disagree but will reëxamine its own opinion in the light of what they say.

Thus the essence of freedom of opinion is not in mere toleration as such, but in the debate which toleration provides: it is not in the venting of opinion, but in the confrontation of opinion. That this is the practical substance can readily be understood when we remember how differently we feel and act about the censorship and regulation of opinion purveyed by different media of communication. We find then that, in so far as the medium makes difficult the confrontation of opinion in debate, we are driven towards censorship and regulation.

There is, for example, the whispering campaign, the circulation of anonymous rumors by men who cannot be compelled to prove what they say. They put the utmost strain on our tolerance, and there are few who do not rejoice when the anonymous slanderer is caught, exposed, and punished. At a higher level there is the moving picture, a most powerful medium for conveying ideas, but a medium which does not permit debate. A moving picture cannot be answered effectively by another moving picture; in all free countries there is some censorship of the movies, and there would be more if the producers did not recognize their limitations by avoiding political controversy. There is then the radio. Here debate is difficult: it is not easy to make sure that the speaker is being answered in the presence of the same audience. Inevitably, there is some regulation of the radio.

When we reach the newspaper press, the opportunity for debate is so considerable that discontent cannot grow to the point where under normal conditions there is any disposition to regulate the press. But when newspapers abuse their power by injuring people who have no means of replying, a disposition to regulate the press appears. When we arrive at

Congress we find that, because the membership of the House is so large, full debate is impracticable. So there are restrictive rules. On the other hand, in the Senate, where the conditions of full debate exist, there is almost absolute freedom of speech.

This shows us that the preservation and development of freedom of opinion are not only a matter of adhering to abstract legal rights, but also, and very urgently, a matter of organizing and arranging sufficient debate. Once we have a firm hold on the central principle, there are many practical conclusions to be drawn. We then realize that the defense of freedom of opinion consists primarily in perfecting the opportunity for an adequate give-and-take of opinion; it consists also in regulating the freedom of those revolutionists who cannot or will not permit or maintain debate when it does not suit their purposes.

We must insist that free oratory is only the beginning of free speech; it is not the end, but a means to an end. The end is to find the truth. The practical justification of civil liberty is not that self-expression is one of the rights of man. It is that the examination of opinion is one of the necessities of man. For experience tells us that it is only when freedom of opinion becomes the compulsion to debate that the seed which our fathers planted has produced its fruit. When that is understood, freedom will be cherished not because it is a vent for our opinions but because it is the surest method of correcting them.

The unexamined life, said Socrates, is unfit to be lived by man. This is the virtue of liberty, and the ground on which we may best justify our belief in it, that it tolerates error in order to serve the truth. When men are brought face to face with their opponents, forced to listen and learn and mend their ideas, they cease to be children and savages and begin to live like civilized men. Then only is freedom a reality, when men may voice their opinions because they must examine their opinions.

[III]

The only reason for dwelling on all this is that if we are to preserve democracy we must understand its principles. And the principle which distinguishes it from all other forms of government is that in a democracy the opposition not only is tolerated as constitutional but must be maintained because it is in fact indispensable.

The democratic system cannot be operated without effective opposition. For, in making the great experiment of governing people by consent rather than by coercion, it is not sufficient that the party in power should have a majority. It is just as necessary that the party in power should never outrage the minority. That means that it must listen to the minority and be moved by the criticisms of the minority. That means that its measures must take account of the minority's objections, and that in administering measures it must remember that the minority may become the majority.

The opposition is indispensable. A good statesman, like any other sensible human being, always learns more from his opponents than from his fervent supporters. For his supporters will push him to disaster unless his opponents show him where the dangers are. So if he is wise he will often pray to be delivered from his friends, because they will ruin him. But, though it hurts, he ought also to pray never to be left without opponents; for they keep him on the path of reason and good sense.

The national unity of a free people depends upon a sufficiently even balance of political power to make it impracticable for the administration to be arbitrary and for the opposition to be revolutionary and irreconcilable. Where that balance no longer exists, democracy perishes. For unless all the citizens of a state are forced by circumstances to compromise, unless they feel that they can affect policy but that no one can wholly dominate it, unless by habit and necessity they have to give and take, freedom cannot be maintained.

PLATO

Plato, one of the greatest philosophers of the Western world, was born in Athens. Originally named Aristocles, he was surnamed Plato because of his broad shoulders, or—as some would have it—his broad forehead. Early in his life he became a student of Socrates, and his subsequent writings are evidence of the profound influence his teacher had on him. After Socrates' trial, conviction, and death in 399 B.C., Plato spent thirteen years away from Athens, in Italy, Egypt, and parts of Greece. He returned in 386 B.C. and founded the Academy in which he taught until his death in 347 B.C. Aristotle was his student. Plato's extant works are in the form of conversations, or dialogues, in which the leading speaker is usually Socrates. Perhaps the best known of the dialogues is The Republic, *in which Socrates explores the nature of the ideal state. Plato records the last days of Socrates in three early dialogues,* The Apology, The Crito, *and* The Phaedo. The Apology *presents Socrates' defense at his trial on charges of corrupting youth and believing in gods other than the State's divinities.* The Phaedo *records Socrates' last conversation before death. In* The Crito, *Crito visits Socrates in prison and tries to persuade him to escape. We print below, from the Jowett translation, third edition, Socrates' argument for submitting to the death penalty that the law had imposed on him.*

from *The Crito*

Socrates   . . . Ought a man to do what he admits to be right, or ought he to betray the right?

Crito.   He ought to do what he thinks right.

Soc.   But if this is true, what is the application? In leaving the prison against the will of the Athenians, do I wrong any? or rather do I not wrong those whom I ought least to wrong? Do I not desert the principles which were acknowledged by us to be just—what do you say?

Cr.   I cannot tell, Socrates; for I do not know.

Soc.   Then consider the matter in this way:—Imagine that I am about to play truant (you may call the proceeding by any name which you like), and the laws and the government come and interrogate me: 'Tell us, Socrates,' they say; 'what are you about? are you not going by an act of yours to overturn us—the laws, and the whole state, as far as in you lies? Do you imagine that a state can subsist and not be overthrown, in which the decisions of law have no power, but are set aside and trampled upon by individuals?' What will be our answer, Crito, to these and the like words? Any one, and especially a rhetorician, will have a good deal to say on behalf of the law which requires a sentence to be carried out. He will argue that this law should not be set aside; and shall we reply, 'Yes; but the state has injured us and given an unjust sentence.' Suppose I say that?

Cr.   Very good, Socrates.

Soc.   'And was that our agreement with you?' the law would answer; 'or were you to abide by the sentence of the state?' And if I were to express my astonishment at their words, the law would probably add: 'Answer, Socrates, instead of opening your eyes—you are in the habit of asking and answering questions. Tell us,—What complaint have you to make against us which justifies you in attempting to destroy us and the state? In the first place did we not bring you into existence? Your father married your mother by our aid and begat you. Say whether you have any objection to urge against those of us who regulate marriage?' None, I should reply. 'Or against those of us who after birth regulate the nurture and education of children, in which you also were trained? Were not the laws, which have the charge of education, right in commanding your father to train you in music and gymnastic?' Right, I should reply. 'Well then, since you were brought into the world and nurtured and educated by us, can you deny in the first place that you are our child and slave, as your fathers were before you? And if this is true you are not on equal terms with us; nor can you think that you have a right to do to us what we are doing to you. Would you have any right to strike or revile or do any other evil to your father or your master, if you had one, because you have been struck or reviled by him, or received some other evil at his hands?—you would not say this? And because we think right to destroy you, do you think that you have any right to destroy us in return, and your country as far as in you lies? Will you, O professor of true virtue, pretend that you are justified in this? Has a philosopher like you failed to discover that our country is more to be valued and higher and holier far than mother or father or any ancestor, and more to be regarded in the eyes of the gods and of men of understanding? also to be soothed, and gently and reverently entreated when angry, even more than a father, and either to be persuaded, or if not persuaded, to be obeyed? And when we are punished by her, whether with imprisonment or stripes, the punishment is to be endured in silence; and if she leads us to wounds or death in battle, thither we follow as is right; neither may any one yield or retreat or leave his rank, but whether in battle or in a court of law, or in any other place, he must do what his city and his country order him; or he must change their view of what is just: and if he may do no violence to his father or mother, much less may he do violence to his country.' What answer shall we make to this, Crito? Do the laws speak truly, or do they not?

Cr.   I think that they do.

Soc.   Then the laws will say, 'Consider, Socrates, if we are speaking truly that in your present attempt you are going to do us an injury. For, having brought you into the world, and nurtured and educated you, and given you and every other citizen a share in every good which we had to give, we further proclaim to any Athenian by the liberty which we allow him, that if he does not like us when he has become of age and has seen the ways of the city, and made our acquaintance, he may go where he pleases and take his goods with him. None of us laws will forbid him or interfere with him. Any one who does not like us and the city, and who wants to emigrate to a colony or to any other city, may go where he likes, retaining his property. But he who has experience of the manner in which we order justice and administer the state, and still remains, has entered into an implied contract that he will do as we command him. And he who disobeys us is, as we maintain, thrice wrong; first, because in disobeying us he is disobeying his parents; secondly, because we are the authors of his education; thirdly, because he has made an agreement with us that he will duly obey our commands; and he neither obeys them nor convinces us that our commands are unjust; and we do not rudely impose them, but give him the alternative of obeying or convincing us;—that is what we offer, and he does neither.

'These are the sort of accusations to which, as we were saying, you, Socrates, will be exposed if you accomplish your intentions; you, above all other Athenians.' Suppose now I ask, why I rather than anybody else? they will justly retort upon me that I above all other men have acknowledged the agreement. 'There is clear proof,' they will say, 'Socrates, that we and the city were not displeasing to you. Of all Athenians you have been the most constant resident in the city, which, as you never leave, you may be supposed to love. For you never went out of the city either to see the games, except once when you went to the Isthmus, or to any other place unless when you were on military service; nor did you travel as other men do. Nor had you any curiosity to know other states or their laws: your affections did not go beyond us and our state; we were your special favourites, and you acquiesced in our government of you; and here in this city you begat your children, which is a proof of your satisfaction. Moreover, you might in the course of the trial, if you had liked, have fixed the penalty at banishment; the state which refuses to let you go now would have let you go then. But you pretended that you preferred death to exile, and that you were not unwilling to die. And now you have forgotten these fine sentiments, and pay no respect to us the laws, of whom you are the destroyer; and are doing what only a miserable slave would do, running away and turning your back upon the compacts and agreements which you made as a citizen. And first of all answer this very question: Are we right in saying that you agreed to be governed according to us in deed, and not in word only? Is that true or not?' How shall we answer, Crito? Must we not assent?

Cr.   We cannot help it, Socrates.

Soc.   Then will they not say: 'You, Socrates, are breaking the covenants and agreements which you made with us at your leisure, not in any haste or under any compulsion or deception, but after you have had seventy years to think of them, during which time you were at liberty to leave the city, if we were not to your mind, or if our covenants appeared to you to be unfair. You had your choice, and might have gone either to Lacedaemon or Crete, both which states are often praised by you for their good government, or to some other Hellenic or foreign state. Whereas you, above all other Athenians, seemed to be so fond of the state, or, in other words, of us her laws (and who would care about a state which has no laws?), that you never stirred out of her; the halt, the blind, the maimed were not more stationary in her than you were. And now you run away and forsake your agreements. Not so, Socrates, if you will take our advice; do not make yourself ridiculous by escaping out of the city.

'For just consider, if you transgress and err in this sort of way, what good will you do either to yourself or to your friends? That your friends will be driven into exile and deprived of citizenship, or will lose their property, is tolerably certain; and you yourself, if you fly to one of the neighbouring cities, as, for example, Thebes or Megara, both of which are well governed, will come to them as an enemy, Socrates, and their government will be against you, and all patriotic citizens will cast an evil eye upon you as a subverter of the laws, and you will confirm in the minds of the judges the justice of their own condemnation of you. For he who is a corrupter of the laws is more than likely to be a corrupter of the young and foolish portion of mankind. Will you then flee from well-ordered cities and virtuous men? and is existence worth having on these terms? Or will you go to them without shame, and talk to them, Socrates? And what will you say to them? What you say here about virtue and justice and institutions and laws being the best things among men? Would that be decent of you? Surely not. But if you go away from well-governed states to Crito's friends in Thessaly, where there is great disorder and licence, they will be charmed to hear the tale of your escape from prison, set off with ludicrous particulars of the manner in which you were wrapped in a goatskin or some other disguise, and metamorphosed as the manner is of runaways; but will there be no one to remind you that in your old age you were not ashamed to violate the most sacred laws from a miserable desire of a little more life? Perhaps not, if you keep them in a good temper; but if they are out of temper you will hear many degrading things; you will live, but how?—as the flatterer of all men, and the servant of all men; and doing what?—eating and drinking in Thessaly, having gone abroad in order that you may get a dinner. And where will be your fine sentiments about justice and virtue? Say that you wish to live for the sake of your children—you want to bring them up and educate them— will you take them into Thessaly and deprive them of Athenian citizenship? Is this the benefit which you will confer upon them? Or are you under the impression that they will be better cared for and educated here if you are still alive, although absent from them; for your friends will take care of them? Do you fancy that if you are an inhabitant of Thessaly they will take care of them, and if you are an inhabitant of the other world that they will not take care of them? Nay; but if they who call themselves friends are good for anything, they will—to be sure they will.

'Listen, then, Socrates, to us who have brought you up. Think not of life and children first, and of justice afterwards, but of justice first, that you may be justified before the princes of the world below. For neither will you nor any that belong to you be happier or holier or juster in this life, or happier in another, if you do as Crito bids. Now you depart in innocence, a sufferer and not a doer of evil; a victim, not of the laws but of men. But if you go forth, returning evil for evil, and injury for injury, breaking the covenants and agreements which you have made with us, and wronging those whom you ought least of all to wrong, that is to say, yourself, your friends, your country, and us, we shall be angry with you while you live, and our brethren, the laws in the world below, will receive you as an enemy; for they will know that you have done your best to destroy us. Listen, then, to us and not to Crito.'

This, dear Crito, is the voice which I seem to hear murmuring in my ears, like the sound of the flute in the ears of the mystic; that voice, I say, is humming in my ears, and prevents me from hearing any other. And I know that anything more which you may say will be vain. Yet speak, if you have anything to say.

Cr.   I have nothing to say, Socrates.

Soc.   Leave me then, Crito, to fulfill the will of God, and to follow whither he leads.

HENRY DAVID THOREAU

*A social rebel with high principles, a man who loved nature and solitude,
Thoreau is considered by some a memorable individualist, by others a
perennial adolescent, and by still others as both. E. B. White has called
him a "regular hairshirt of a man." Born in Concord in 1817, he was
educated at Harvard and after graduation returned to Concord where he
first taught school and on later occasions supported himself by making
pencils. He became a friend of Emerson, who was at the time leader of
Concord's intellectual and spiritual life; he joined the Transcendental Club
and contributed frequently to its journal,* **The Dial.** *Some have said that
Thoreau was the answer to Emerson's plea for an American Scholar (see
page 65). From July 4, 1845, to September 6, 1847, Thoreau lived in a
hut at nearby Walden Pond, an experience which he recorded in his most
famous work,* **Walden.** *His stay there was interrupted for one day in the
summer of 1846 when he was arrested for not paying the Massachusetts
poll tax. He explained his refusal as an act of protest against a
government which sanctioned the Mexican War, a war he considered in the
interests of Southern slaveholders; he later wrote an eloquent defense of
civil disobedience which was first published in 1849. This essay, which has
become an American classic, is reprinted in full below; the text is that of
the Riverside edition of Thoreau's works.*

Civil Disobedience

I heartily accept the motto,—"That government is best which governs
least;" and I should like to see it acted up to more rapidly and systematically. Carried out, it finally amounts to this, which also I believe,—"That
government is best which governs not at all;" and when men are prepared
for it, that will be the kind of government which they will have. Government is at best but an expedient; but most governments are usually, and
all governments are sometimes, inexpedient. The objections which have
been brought against a standing army, and they are many and weighty,
and deserve to prevail, may also at last be brought against a standing
government. The standing army is only an arm of the standing government. The government itself, which is only the mode which the people
have chosen to execute their will, is equally liable to be abused and
perverted before the people can act through it. Witness the present
Mexican war, the work of comparatively a few individuals using the standing government as their tool; for, in the outset, the people would not have
consented to this measure.

This American Government,—what is it but a tradition, though a recent one, endeavoring to transmit itself unimpaired to posterity, but each instant losing some of its integrity? It has not the vitality and force of a single living man; for a single man can bend it to his will. It is a sort of wooden gun to the people themselves. But it is not the less necessary for this; for the people must have some complicated machinery or other, and hear its din, to satisfy that idea of government which they have. Governments show thus how successfully men can be imposed on, even impose on themselves, for their own advantage. It is excellent, we must all allow. Yet this government never of itself furthered any enterprise, but by the alacrity with which it got out of its way. *It* does not keep the country free. *It* does not settle the West. *It* does not educate. The character inherent in the American people has done all that has been accomplished; and it would have done somewhat more, if the government had not sometimes got in its way. For government is an expedient by which men would fain succeed in letting one another alone; and, as has been said, when it is most expedient, the governed are most let alone by it. Trade and commerce, if they were not made of India-rubber, would never manage to bounce over the obstacles which legislators are continually putting in their way; and, if one were to judge these men wholly by the effects of their actions and not partly by their intentions, they would deserve to be classed and punished with those mischievous persons who put obstructions on the railroads.

But, to speak practically and as a citizen, unlike those who call themselves no-government men, I ask for, not at once no government, but *at once* a better government. Let every man make known what kind of government would command his respect, and that will be one step toward obtaining it.

After all, the practical reason why, when the power is once in the hands of the people, a majority are permitted, and for a long period continue, to rule is not because they are most likely to be in the right, nor because this seems fairest to the minority, but because they are physically the strongest. But a government in which the majority rule in all cases cannot be based on justice, even as far as men understand it. Can there not be a government in which majorities do not virtually decide right and wrong, but conscience?—in which majorities decide only those questions to which the rule of expediency is applicable? Must the citizen ever for a moment, or in the least degree, resign his conscience to the legislator? Why has every man a conscience, then? I think that we should be men first, and subjects afterward. It is not desirable to cultivate a respect for the law, so much as for the right. The only obligation which I have a right to assume is to do at any time what I think right. It is truly enough said, that a corporation has no conscience; but a corporation of conscientious men is a corporation *with* a conscience. Law never made men a whit more just; and, by means of their respect for it, even the well-disposed are daily made the agents of injustice. A common and natural result of an undue respect for law is, that you may see a file of soldiers, colonel, captain, corporal, privates, powder-monkeys, and all, marching in admirable order over hill and dale to the wars, against their wills, ay, against their common sense and consciences, which makes it very steep marching indeed, and produces a palpitation of the heart. They have no doubt that it is a damnable business in which they are concerned; they are all peaceably inclined. Now, what are they? Men at all? or small movable forts and magazines, at the service of some unscrupulous man in power? Visit the Navy-Yard, and behold a marine, such a man as an American government can make, or such as it can make a man with its black arts,—a mere shadow and reminiscence of humanity, a man laid out alive and standing, and already, as one may say, buried under arms with funeral accompaniments, though it may be,—

"Not a drum was heard, not a funeral note,
　As his corse to the rampart we hurried;
Not a soldier discharged his farewell shot
　O'er the grave where our hero we buried."

The mass of men serve the state thus, not as men mainly, but as machines, with their bodies. They are the standing army, and the militia, jailers, constables, posse comitatus, etc. In most cases there is no free exercise whatever of the judgment or of the moral sense; but they put themselves on a level with wood and earth and stones; and wooden men can perhaps be manufactured that will serve the purpose as well. Such command no more respect than men of straw or a lump of dirt. They have the same sort of worth only as horses and dogs. Yet such as these even are commonly esteemed good citizens. Others—as most legislators, politicians, lawyers, ministers, and office-holders—serve the state chiefly with their heads; and, as they rarely make any moral distinctions, they are as likely to serve the Devil, without *intending* it, as God. A very few, as heroes, patriots, martyrs, reformers in the great sense, and *men,* serve the state with their consciences also, and so necessarily resist it for the most part; and they are commonly treated as enemies by it. A wise man will only be useful as a man, and will not submit to be "clay," and "stop a hole to keep the wind away," but leave that office to his dust at least:—

"I am too high-born to be propertied,
To be a secondary at control,
Or useful serving-man and instrument
To any sovereign state throughout the world."

He who gives himself entirely to his fellow-men appears to them useless and selfish; but he who gives himself partially to them is pronounced a benefactor and philanthropist.

How does it become a man to behave toward this American government to-day? I answer, that he cannot without disgrace be associated with it. I cannot for an instant recognize that political organization as *my* government which is the *slave's* government also.

All men recognize the right of revolution; that is, the right to refuse allegiance to, and to resist, the government, when its tyranny or its inefficiency are great and unendurable. But almost all say that such is not the case now. But such was the case, they think, in the Revolution of '75. If one were to tell me that this was a bad government because it taxed certain foreign commodities brought to its ports, it is most probable that I should not make an ado about it, for I can do without them. All machines have their friction; and possibly this does enough good to counterbalance the evil. At any rate, it is a great evil to make a stir about it. But when the friction comes to have its machine, and oppression and robbery are organized, I say, let us not have such a machine any longer. In other words, when a sixth of the population of a nation which has undertaken to be the refuge of liberty are slaves, and a whole country is unjustly overrun and conquered by a foreign army, and subjected to military law, I think that it is not too soon for honest men to rebel and revolutionize. What makes this duty the more urgent is the fact that the country so overrun is not our own, but ours is the invading army.

Paley, a common authority with many on moral questions, in his chapter on the "Duty of Submission to Civil Government," resolves all civil obligation into expediency; and he proceeds to say, "that so long as the interest of the whole society requires it, that is, so long as the established government cannot be resisted or changed without public inconveniency, it is the will of God that the established government be obeyed, and no longer.... This principle being admitted, the justice of every particular case of resistance is reduced to a computation of the quantity of the danger and grievance on the one side, and of the probability and expense of redressing it on the other." Of this, he says, every man shall judge for himself. But Paley appears never to have contemplated those cases to which the rule of expediency does not apply, in which a people, as well as an individual, must do justice, cost what it may. If I have unjustly wrested a plank from a drowning man, I must restore it to him though I drown myself. This, according to Paley, would be inconvenient. But he that would save his life, in such a case, shall lose it. This people must cease to hold slaves, and to make war on Mexico, though it cost them their existence as a people.

In their practice, nations agree with Paley; but does any one think that Massachusetts does exactly what is right at the present crisis?

> "A drab of state, a cloth-o'-silver slut,
> To have her train borne up, and her soul trail in the dirt."

Practically speaking, the opponents to a reform in Massachusetts are not a hundred thousand politicians at the South, but a hundred thousand merchants and farmers here, who are more interested in commerce and agriculture than they are in humanity, and are not prepared to do justice to the slave and to Mexico, *cost what it may.* I quarrel not with far-off foes, but with those who, near at home, coöperate with, and do the bidding of, those far away, and without whom the latter would be harmless. We are accustomed to say, that the mass of men are unprepared; but improvement is slow, because the few are not materially wiser or better than the many. It is not so important that many should be as good as you, as that there be some absolute goodness somewhere; for that will leaven the whole lump. There are thousands who are *in opinion* opposed to slavery and to the war, who yet in effect do nothing to put an end to them; who, esteeming themselves children of Washington and Franklin, sit down with their hands in their pockets, and say that they know not what to do, and do nothing; who even postpone the question of freedom to the question of free-trade, and quietly read the prices-current along with the latest advices from Mexico, after dinner, and, it may be, fall asleep over them both. What is the price-current of an honest man and patriot to-day? They hesitate, and they regret, and sometimes they petition; but they do nothing in earnest and with effect. They will wait, well disposed, for others to remedy the evil, that they may no longer have it to regret. At most, they give only a cheap vote, and a feeble countenance and Godspeed, to the right, as it goes by them. There are nine hundred and ninety-nine patrons of virtue to one virtuous man. But it is easier to deal with the real possessor of a thing than with the temporary guardian of it.

All voting is a sort of gaming, like checkers or backgammon, with a slight moral tinge to it, a playing with right and wrong, with moral questions; and betting naturally accompanies it. The character of the voters is not staked. I cast my vote, perchance, as I think right; but I am not vitally concerned that that right should prevail. I am willing to leave it to the majority. Its obligation, therefore, never exceeds that of expediency. Even voting *for the right* is *doing* nothing for it. It is only expressing to men feebly your desire that it should prevail. A wise man will not leave the right to the mercy of chance, nor wish it to prevail through the power of the majority. There is but little virtue in the action of masses of men. When the majority shall at length vote for the abolition of slavery, it will be because they are indifferent to slavery, or because there is but little slavery left to be abolished by their vote. *They* will then be the only slaves. Only *his* vote can hasten the abolition of slavery who asserts his own freedom by his vote.

I hear of a convention to be held at Baltimore, or elsewhere, for the selection of a candidate for the Presidency, made up chiefly of editors, and men who are politicians by profession; but I think, what is it to any independent, intelligent, and respectable man what decision they may come to? Shall we not have the advantage of his wisdom and honesty, nevertheless? Can we not count upon some independent votes? Are there not many individuals in the country who do not attend conventions? But no: I find that the respectable man, so called, has immediately drifted from his position, and despairs of his country, when his country has more reason to despair of him. He forthwith adopts one of the candidates thus selected as the only *available* one, thus proving that he is himself *available* for any purposes of the demagogue. His vote is of no more worth than that of any unprincipled foreigner or hireling native, who may have been bought. O for a man who is a *man,* and, as my neighbor says, has a bone in his back which you cannot pass your hand through! Our statistics are at fault: the population has been returned too large. How many *men* are there to a square thousand miles in this country? Hardly one. Does not America offer any inducement for men to settle here? The American has dwindled into an Odd Fellow,—one who may be known by the development of his organ of gregariousness, and a manifest lack of intellect and cheerful self-reliance; whose first and chief concern, on coming into the world, is to see that the Almshouses are in good repair; and, before yet he has lawfully donned the virile garb, to collect a fund for the support of the widows and orphans that may be; who, in short, ventures to live only by the aid of the Mutual Insurance company, which has promised to bury him decently.

It is not a man's duty, as a matter of course, to devote himself to the eradication of any, even the most enormous wrong; he may still properly have other concerns to engage him; but it is his duty, at least, to wash his hands of it, and, if he gives it no thought longer, not to give it practically his support. If I devote myself to other pursuits and contemplations, I must first see, at least, that I do not pursue them sitting upon another man's shoulders. I must get off him first, that he may pursue his contemplations too. See what gross inconsistency is tolerated. I have heard some of my townsmen say, "I should like to have them order me out to help put down an insurrection of the slaves, or to march to Mexico;—see if I would go;" and yet these very men have each, directly by their allegiance, and so indirectly, at least, by their money, furnished a substitute. The soldier is applauded who refuses to serve in an unjust war by those who do not refuse to sustain the unjust government which makes the war; is applauded by those whose own act and authority he disregards and sets at naught; as if the state were penitent to that degree that it hired one to scourge it while it sinned, but not to that degree that it left off sinning for a moment. Thus, under the name of Order and Civil Government, we are all made at last to pay homage to and support our own meanness. After the first blush of sin comes its indifference; and from immoral it becomes, as it were, *un*moral, and not quite unnecessary to that life which we have made.

The broadest and most prevalent error requires the most disinterested virtue to sustain it. The slight reproach to which the virtue of patriotism is commonly liable, the noble are most likely to incur. Those who, while they disapprove of the character and measures of a government, yield to it their allegiance and support are undoubtedly its most conscientious supporters, and so frequently the most serious obstacles to reform. Some are petitioning the state to dissolve the Union, to disregard the requisitions of the President. Why do they not dissolve it themselves, —the union between themselves and the state,—and refuse to pay their quota into its treasury? Do not they stand in the same relation to the state that the state does to the Union? And have not the same reasons prevented the state from resisting the Union which have prevented them from resisting the state?

How can a man be satisfied to entertain an opinion merely, and enjoy *it?* Is there any enjoyment in it, if his opinion is that he is aggrieved? If you are cheated out of a single dollar by your neighbor, you do not rest satisfied with knowing that you are cheated, or with saying that you are cheated, or even with petitioning him to pay you your due; but you take effectual steps at once to obtain the full amount, and see that you are never cheated again. Action from principle, the perception and the performance of right, changes things and relations; it is essentially revolutionary, and does not consist wholly with anything which was. It not only divides states and churches, it divides families; ay, it divides the *individual,* separating the diabolical in him from the divine.

Unjust laws exist: shall we be content to obey them, or shall we endeavor to amend them, and obey them until we have succeeded, or shall we transgress them at once? Men generally, under such a government as this, think that they ought to wait until they have persuaded the majority to alter them. They think that, if they should resist, the remedy would be worse than the evil. But it is the fault of the government itself that the remedy *is* worse than the evil. *It* makes it worse. Why is it not more apt to anticipate and provide for reform? Why does it not cherish its wise minority? Why does it cry and resist before it is hurt? Why does it not encourage its citizens to be on the alert to point out its faults, and *do* better than it would have them? Why does it always crucify Christ, and excommunicate Copernicus and Luther, and pronounce Washington and Franklin rebels?

One would think, that a deliberate and practical denial of its authority was the only offense never contemplated by government; else, why has it not assigned its definite, its suitable and proportionate penalty? If a man who has no property refuses but once to earn nine shillings for the state, he is put in prison for a period unlimited by any law that I know, and determined only by the discretion of those who placed him there; but if he should steal ninety times nine shillings from the state, he is soon permitted to go at large again.

If the injustice is part of the necessary friction of the machine of government, let it go, let it go: perchance it will wear smooth,—certainly the machine will wear out. If the injustice has a spring, or a pulley, or a rope, or a crank, exclusively for itself, then perhaps you may consider whether the remedy will not be worse than the evil; but if it is of such a nature that it requires you to be the agent of injustice to another, then, I say, break the law. Let your life be a counter friction to stop the machine.

What I have to do is to see, at any rate, that I do not lend myself to the wrong which I condemn.

As for adopting the ways which the state has provided for remedying the evil, I know not of such ways. They take too much time, and a man's life will be gone. I have other affairs to attend to. I came into this world, not chiefly to make this a good place to live in, but to live in it, be it good or bad. A man has not everything to do, but something; and because he cannot do *everything*, it is not necessary that he should do *something* wrong. It is not my business to be petitioning the Governor or the Legislature any more than it is theirs to petition me; and if they should not hear my petition, what should I do then? But in this case the state has provided no way: its very Constitution is the evil. This may seem to be harsh and stubborn and unconciliatory; but it is to treat with the utmost kindness and consideration the only spirit that can appreciate or deserves it. So is all change for the better, like birth and death, which convulse the body.

I do not hesitate to say, that those who call themselves Abolitionists should at once effectually withdraw their support, both in person and property, from the government of Massachusetts, and not wait till they constitute a majority of one, before they suffer the right to prevail through them. I think that it is enough if they have God on their side, without waiting for that other one. Moreover, any man more right than his neighbors constitutes a majority of one already.

I meet this American government, or its representative, the state government, directly, and face to face, once a year—no more—in the person of its tax-gatherer; this is the only mode in which a man situated as I am necessarily meets it; and it then says distinctly, Recognize me; and the simplest, the most effectual, and, in the present posture of affairs, the indispensablest mode of treating with it on this head, of expressing your little satisfaction with and love for it, is to deny it then. My civil neighbor, the tax-gatherer, is the very man I have to deal with,—for it is, after all, with men and not with parchment that I quarrel,—and he has voluntarily chosen to be an agent of the government. How shall he ever know well what he is and does as an officer of the government, or as a man, until he is obliged to consider whether he shall treat me, his neighbor, for whom he has respect, as a neighbor and well-disposed man, or as a maniac and disturber of the peace, and see if he can get over this obstruction to his neighborliness without a ruder and more impetuous thought or speech corresponding with his action. I know this well, that if one thousand, if one hundred, if ten men whom I could name,—if ten *honest* men only,—ay, if *one* HONEST man, in this State of Massachusetts, *ceasing to hold slaves,* were actually to withdraw from this copartnership, and be locked up in the county jail therefor, it would be the abolition of slavery in America. For it matters not how small the beginning may seem to be: what is once well done is done forever. But we love better to talk about it: that we say is our mission. Reform keeps many scores of newspapers in its service, but not one man. If my esteemed neighbor, the State's ambassador, who will devote his days to the settlement of the question of human rights in the Council Chamber, instead of being threatened with the prisons of Carolina, were to sit down the prisoner of Massachusetts, that State which is so anxious to foist the sin of slavery upon her sister,—though at present she can discover only an act of inhospitality to be the ground of a quarrel with her,—the Legislature would not wholly waive the subject the following winter.

Under a government which imprisons any unjustly, the true place for a just man is also a prison. The proper place to-day, the only place which Massachusetts has provided for her freer and less desponding spirits, is in her prisons, to be put out and locked out of the State by her own act, as they have already put themselves out by their principles. It is there that the fugitive slave, and the Mexican prisoner on parole, and the Indian come to plead the wrongs of his race should find them; on that separate, but more free and honorable ground, where the State places those who are not *with* her, but *against* her,—the only house in a slave State in which a free man can abide with honor. If any think that their influence would be lost there, and their voices no longer afflict the ear of the State, that they would not be as an enemy within its walls, they do not know by how much truth is stronger than error, nor how much more eloquently and effectively he can combat injustice who has experienced a little in his own person. Cast your whole vote, not a strip of paper merely, but your whole influence. A minority is powerless while it conforms to the majority; it is not even a minority then; but it is irresistible when it clogs by its whole weight. If the alternative is to keep all just men in prison, or give up war and slavery, the State will not hesitate which to choose. If a thousand men were not to pay their tax-bills this year, that would not be a violent and bloody measure, as it would be to pay them, and enable the State to commit violence and shed innocent blood. This is, in fact, the definition of a peaceable revolution, if any such is possible. If the tax-gatherer, or any other public officer, asks me, as one has done, "But what shall I do?" my answer is, "If you really wish to do anything, resign your office." When the subject has refused allegiance, and the officer has resigned his office, then the revolution is accomplished. But even suppose blood should flow. Is there not a sort of blood shed when the conscience is wounded? Through this wound a man's real manhood and immortality flow out, and he bleeds to an everlasting death. I see this blood flowing now.

I have contemplated the imprisonment of the offender, rather than the seizure of his goods,—though both will serve the same purpose,—because they who assert the purest right, and consequently are most dangerous to a corrupt State, commonly have not spent much time in accumulating property. To such the State renders comparatively small service, and a slight tax is wont to appear exorbitant, particularly if they are obliged to earn it by special labor with their hands. If there were one who lived wholly without the use of money, the State itself would hesitate to demand it of him. But the rich man—not to make any invidious comparison—is always sold to the institution which makes him rich. Absolutely speaking, the more money, the less virtue; for money comes between a man and his objects, and obtains them for him; and it was certainly no great virtue to obtain it. It puts to rest many questions which he would otherwise be taxed to answer; while the only new question which it puts is the hard but superfluous one, how to spend it. Thus his moral ground is taken from under his feet. The opportunities of living are diminished in proportion as what are called the "means" are increased. The best thing a man can do for his culture when he is rich is to endeavor to carry out those schemes which he entertained when he was poor. Christ answered the Herodians according to their condition. "Show me the tribute-money," said he;—and one took a penny out of his pocket;—if you use money which has the image of Cæsar on it, which he has made current and valuable, that is, *if you are men of the State,* and gladly enjoy the advantages of Cæsar's government, then pay him back some of his own when he demands it. "Render therefore to Cæsar that which is Cæsar's, and to God those things which are God's,"—leaving them no wiser than before as to which was which; for they did not wish to know.

When I converse with the freest of my neighbors, I perceive that, whatever they may say about the magnitude and seriousness of the question, and their regard for the public tranquillity, the long and the short of the matter is, that they cannot spare the protection of the existing government, and they dread the consequences to their property and families of disobedience to it. For my own part, I should not like to think that I ever rely on the protection of the State. But, if I deny the authority of the State when it presents its tax-bill, it will soon take and waste all my property, and so harass me and my children without end. This is hard. This makes it impossible for a man to live honestly, and at the same time comfortably, in outward respects. It will not be worth the while to accumulate property; that would be sure to go again. You must hire or squat somewhere, and raise but a small crop, and eat that soon. You must live within yourself, and depend upon yourself always tucked up and ready for a start, and not have many affairs. A man may grow rich in Turkey even, if he will be in all respects a good subject of the Turkish government. Confucius said: "If a state is governed by the principles of reason, poverty and misery are subjects of shame; if a state is not governed by the principles of reason, riches and honors are the subjects of shame." No: until I want the protection of Massachusetts to be extended to me in some distant Southern port, where my liberty is endangered, or until I am bent solely on building up an estate at home by peaceful enterprise, I can afford to refuse allegiance to Massachusetts, and her right to my property and life. It costs me less in every sense to incur the penalty of disobedience to the State than it would to obey. I should feel as if I were worth less in that case.

Some years ago, the State met me in behalf of the Church, and commanded me to pay a certain sum toward the support of a clergyman whose preaching my father attended, but never I myself. "Pay," it said, "or be locked up in the jail." I declined to pay. But, unfortunately, another man saw fit to pay it. I did not see why the schoolmaster should be taxed to support the priest, and not the priest the schoolmaster; for I was not the State's schoolmaster, but I supported myself by voluntary subscription. I did not see why the lyceum should not present its tax-bill, and have the State to back its demand, as well as the Church. However, at the request of the selectmen, I condescended to make some such statement as this in writing:—"Know all men by these presents, that I, Henry Thoreau, do not wish to be regarded as a member of any incorporated society which I have not joined." This I gave to the town clerk; and he has it. The State, having thus learned that I did not wish to be regarded as a member of that church, has never made a like demand on me since; though it said that it must adhere to its original presumption that time. If I had known how to name them, I should then have signed off in detail from all the societies which I never signed on to; but I did not know where to find a complete list.

I have paid no poll-tax for six years. I was put into a jail once on this account, for one night; and, as I stood considering the walls of solid stone, two or three feet thick, the door of wood and iron, a foot thick, and the iron grating which strained the light, I could not help being struck with the foolishness of that institution which treated me as if I were mere flesh and blood and bones, to be locked up. I wondered that it should have concluded at length that this was the best use it could put me to, and had never thought to avail itself of my services in some way. I saw that, if there was a wall of stone between me and my townsmen, there was a still more difficult one to climb or break through before they could get to be as free as I was. I did not for a moment feel confined, and the walls seemed a great waste of stone and mortar. I felt as if I alone of all my townsmen had paid my tax. They plainly did not know how to treat me, but behaved like persons who are underbred. In every threat and in every compliment there was a blunder; for they thought that my chief desire was to stand the other side of that stone wall. I could not but smile to see how industriously they locked the door on my meditations, which followed them out again without let or hindrance, and *they* were really all that was dangerous. As they could not reach me, they had resolved to punish my body; just as boys, if they cannot come at some person against whom they have a spite, will abuse his dog. I saw that the State was half-witted, that it was timid as a lone woman with her silver spoons, and that it did not know its friends from its foes, and I lost all my remaining respect for it, and pitied it.

Thus the State never intentionally confronts a man's sense, intellectual or moral, but only his body, his senses. It is not armed with superior wit or honesty, but with superior physical strength. I was not born to be forced. I will breathe after my own fashion. Let us see who is the strongest. What force has a multitude? They only can force me who obey a higher law than I. They force me to become like themselves. I do not hear of *men* being *forced* to live this way or that by masses of men. What sort of life were that to live? When I meet a government which says to me, "Your money or your life," why should I be in haste to give it my money? It may be in a great strait, and not know what to do: I cannot help that. It must help itself; do as I do. It is not worth the while to snivel about it. I am not responsible for the successful working of the machinery of society. I am not the son of the engineer. I perceive that, when an acorn and a chestnut fall side by side, the one does not remain inert to make way for the other, but both obey their own laws, and spring and grow and flourish as best they can, till one, perchance, overshadows and destroys the other. If a plant cannot live according to its nature, it dies; and so a man.

The night in prison was novel and interesting enough. The prisoners in their shirt-sleeves were enjoying a chat and the evening air in the doorway, when I entered. But the jailer said, "Come, boys, it is time to lock up;" and so they dispersed, and I heard the sound of their steps returning into the hollow apartments. My room-mate was introduced to me by the jailer as "a first-rate fellow and a clever man." When the door was locked, he showed me where to hang my hat, and how he managed matters there. The rooms were whitewashed once a month; and this one, at least, was the whitest, most simply furnished, and probably the neatest apartment in the town. He naturally wanted to know where I came from, and what brought me there; and, when I had told him, I asked him in my turn how he came there, presuming him to be an honest man, of course; and, as the world goes, I believe he was. "Why," said he, "they accuse me of burning a barn; but I never did it." As near as I could discover, he had probably gone to bed in a barn when drunk, and smoked his pipe there; and so a barn was burnt. He had the reputation of being a clever man, had been there some three months waiting for his trial to come on, and would have to wait as much longer; but he was quite domesticated and contented, since he got his board for nothing, and thought that he was well treated.

He occupied one window, and I the other; and I saw that if one stayed there long, his principal business would be to look out the window. I had soon read all the tracts that were left there, and examined where former prisoners had broken out, and where a grate had been sawed off, and heard the history of the various occupants of that room; for I found that even here there was a history and a gossip which never circulated beyond the walls of the jail. Probably this is the only house in the town where verses are composed, which are afterward printed in a circular form, but not published. I was shown quite a long list of verses which were composed by some young men who had been detected in an attempt to escape, who avenged themselves by singing them.

I pumped my fellow-prisoner as dry as I could, for fear I should never see him again; but at length he showed me which was my bed, and left me to blow out the lamp.

It was like traveling into a far country, such as I had never expected to behold, to lie there for one night. It seemed to me that I never had heard the town-clock strike before, nor the evening sounds of the village; for we slept with the windows open, which were inside the grating. It was to see my native village in the light of the Middle Ages, and our Concord was turned into a Rhine stream, and visions of knights and castles passed before me. They were the voices of old burghers that I heard in the streets. I was an involuntary spectator and auditor of whatever was done and said in the kitchen of the adjacent village-inn,—a wholly new and rare experience to me. It was a closer view of my native town. I was fairly inside of it. I never had seen its institutions before. This is one of its peculiar institutions; for it is a shire town. I began to comprehend what its inhabitants were about.

In the morning, our breakfasts were put through the hole in the door, in small oblong-square tin pans, made to fit, and holding a pint of chocolate, with brown bread, and an iron spoon. When they called for the vessels again, I was green enough to return what bread I had left; but my comrade seized it, and said that I should lay that up for lunch or dinner. Soon after he was let out to work at haying in a neighboring field, whither he went every day, and would not be back till noon; so he bade me good-day, saying that he doubted if he should see me again.

When I came out of prison,—for some one interfered, and paid that tax,—I did not perceive that great changes had taken place on the common, such as he observed who went in a youth and emerged a tottering and gray-headed man; and yet a change had to my eyes come over the scene,—the town, and State, and country,—greater than any that mere time could effect. I saw yet more distinctly the State in which I lived. I saw to what extent the people among whom I lived could be trusted as good neighbors and friends; that their friendship was for summer weather only; that they did not greatly propose to do right; that they were a distinct race from me by their prejudices and superstitions, as the Chinamen and Malays are; that in their sacrifices to humanity they ran no risks, not even to their property; that after all they were not so noble but they treated the thief as he had treated them, and hoped, by a certain outward observance and a few prayers, and by walking in a particular straight though useless path from time to time, to save their souls. This may be to judge my neighbors harshly; for I believe that many of them are not aware that they have such an institution as the jail in their village.

It was formerly the custom in our village, when a poor debtor came out of jail, for his acquaintances to salute him, looking through their fingers, which were crossed to represent the grating of a jail window, "How do ye do?" My neighbors did not thus salute me, but first looked at me, and then at one another, as if I had returned from a long journey. I was put into jail as I was going to the shoemaker's to get a shoe which was mended. When I was let out the next morning, I proceeded to finish my errand, and, having put on my mended shoe, joined a huckleberry party, who were impatient to put themselves under my conduct; and in half an hour,—for the horse was soon tackled,—was in the midst of a huckleberry field, on one of our highest hills, two miles off, and then the State was nowhere to be seen.

This is the whole history of "My Prisons."

I have never declined paying the highway tax, because I am as desirous of being a good neighbor as I am of being a bad subject; and as for supporting schools, I am doing my part to educate my fellow-countrymen now. It is for no particular item in the tax-bill that I refuse to pay it. I simply wish to refuse allegiance to the State, to withdraw and stand aloof from it effectually. I do not care to trace the course of my dollar, if I could, till it buys a man or a musket to shoot one with,—the dollar is innocent, —but I am concerned to trace the effects of my allegiance. In fact, I quietly declare war with the State, after my fashion, though I will still make what use and get what advantage of her I can, as is usual in such cases.

If others pay the tax which is demanded of me, from a sympathy with the State, they do but what they have already done in their own case, or rather they abet injustice to a greater extent than the State requires. If they pay the tax from a mistaken interest in the individual taxed, to save his property, or prevent his going to jail, it is because they have not considered wisely how far they let their private feelings interfere with the public good.

This, then, is my position at present. But one cannot be too much on his guard in such a case, lest his action be biased by obstinacy or an undue regard for the opinions of men. Let him see that he does only what belongs to himself and to the hour.

I think sometimes, Why, this people mean well, they are only ignorant; they would do better if they knew how: why give your neighbors this pain to treat you as they are not inclined to? But I think again, This is no reason why I should do as they do, or permit others to suffer much greater pain of a different kind. Again, I sometimes say to myself, When many millions of men, without heat, without ill will, without personal feeling of any kind, demand of you a few shillings only, without the possibility, such is their constitution, of retracting or altering their present demand, and without the possibility, on your side, of appeal to any other millions, why expose yourself to this overwhelming brute force? You do not resist cold and hunger, the winds and the waves, thus obstinately; you quietly submit to a thousand similar necessities. You do not put your head into the fire. But just in proportion as I regard this as not wholly a brute force, but partly a human force, and consider that I have relations to those millions as to so many millions of men, and not of mere brute or inanimate things, I see that appeal is possible, first and instantaneously, from them to the Maker of them, and, secondly, from them to themselves. But if I put my head deliberately into the fire, there is no appeal to fire or to the Maker of fire, and I have only myself to blame. If I could convince myself that I have any right to be satisfied with men as they are, and to treat them accordingly, and not according, in some respects, to my requisitions and expectations of what they and I ought to be, then, like a good Mussulman and fatalist, I should endeavor to be satisfied with things as they are, and say it is the will of God. And, above all, there is this difference between resisting this and a purely brute or natural force, that I can resist this with some effect; but I cannot expect, like Orpheus, to change the nature of the rocks and trees and beasts.

I do not wish to quarrel with any man or nation. I do not wish to split hairs, to make fine distinctions, or set myself up as better than my neighbors. I seek rather, I may say, even an excuse for conforming to the laws of the land. I am but too ready to conform to them. Indeed, I have reason to suspect myself on this head; and each year, as the tax-gatherer comes round, I find myself disposed to review the acts and position of the general and State governments, and the spirit of the people, to discover a pretext for conformity.

> "We must affect our country as our parents,
> And if at any time we alienate
> Our love or industry from doing it honor,
> We must respect effects and teach the soul
> Matter of conscience and religion,
> And not desire of rule or benefit."

I believe that the State will soon be able to take all my work of this sort out of my hands, and then I shall be no better a patriot than my fellow-countrymen. Seen from a lower point of view, the Constitution, with all its faults, is very good; the law and the courts are very respectable; even this State and this American government are, in many respects, very admirable, and rare things, to be thankful for, such as a great many have described them; but seen from a point of view a little higher, they are what I have described them; seen from a higher still, and the highest, who shall say what they are, or that they are worth looking at or thinking of at all?

However, the government does not concern me much, and I shall bestow the fewest possible thoughts on it. It is not many moments that I live under a government, even in this world. If a man is thought-free, fancy-free, imagination-free, that which *is not* never for a long time appearing *to be* to him, unwise rulers or reformers cannot fatally interrupt him.

I know that most men think differently from myself; but those whose lives are by profession devoted to the study of these or kindred subjects content me as little as any. Statesmen and legislators, standing so completely within the institution, never distinctly and nakedly behold it. They speak of moving society, but have no resting-place without it. They may be men of a certain experience and discrimination, and have no doubt invented ingenious and even useful systems, for which we sincerely thank them; but all their wit and usefulness lie within certain not very wide limits. They are wont to forget that the world is not governed by policy and expediency. Webster never goes behind government, and so cannot speak with authority about it. His words are wisdom to those legislators who contemplate no essential reform in the existing government; but for thinkers, and those who legislate for all time, he never once glances at the subject. I know of those whose serene and wise speculations on this theme would soon reveal the limits of his mind's range and hospitality. Yet, compared with the cheap professions of most reformers, and the still cheaper wisdom and eloquence of politicians in general, his are almost the only sensible and valuable words, and we thank Heaven for him. Comparatively, he is always strong, original, and, above all, practical. Still, his quality is not wisdom, but prudence. The lawyer's truth is not Truth, but consistency or a consistent expediency. Truth is always in harmony with herself, and is not concerned chiefly to reveal the justice that may consist with wrong-doing. He well deserves to be called, as he has been called, the Defender of the Constitution. There are really no blows to be given by him but defensive ones. He is not a leader, but a follower. His leaders are the men of '87. "I have never made an effort," he says, "and never propose to make an effort; I have never countenanced an effort, and never mean to countenance an effort, to disturb the arrangement as originally made, by which the various States came into the Union." Still thinking of the sanction which the Constitution gives to slavery, he says, "Because it was a part of the original compact,—let it stand." Notwithstanding his special acuteness and ability, he is unable to take a fact out of its merely political relations, and behold it as it lies absolutely to be disposed of by the intellect,—what, for instance, it behooves a man to do here in America to-day with regard to slavery,—but ventures, or is driven, to make some such desperate answer as the following, while professing to speak absolutely, and as a private man,—from which what new and singular code of social duties might be inferred? "The manner," says he, "in which the governments of those States where slavery exists are to regulate it is for their own consideration, under their responsibility to their constituents, to the general laws of propriety, humanity, and justice, and to God. Associations formed elsewhere, springing from a feeling of humanity, or any other cause, have nothing whatever to do with it. They have never received any encouragement from me, and they never will."

They who know of no purer sources of truth, who have traced up its stream no higher, stand, and wisely stand, by the Bible and the Constitution, and drink at it there with reverence and humility; but they who behold where it comes trickling into this lake or that pool, gird up their loins once more, and continue their pilgrimage toward its fountain-head.

No man with a genius for legislation has appeared in America. They are rare in the history of the world. There are orators, politicians, and eloquent men, by the thousand; but the speaker has not yet opened his mouth to speak who is capable of settling the much-vexed questions of the day. We love eloquence for its own sake, and not for any truth which it may utter, or any heroism it may inspire. Our legislators have not yet learned the comparative value of free-trade and of freedom, of union, and of rectitude, to a nation. They have no genius or talent for comparatively humble questions of taxation and finance, commerce and manufactures and agriculture. If we were left solely to the wordy wit of legislators in Congress for our guidance, uncorrected by the seasonable experience and the effectual complaints of the people, America would not long retain her rank among the nations. For eighteen hundred years, though perchance I have no right to say it, the New Testament has been written; yet where is the legislator who has wisdom and practical talent enough to avail himself of the light which it sheds on the science of legislation?

The authority of government, even such as I am willing to submit to, —for I will cheerfully obey those who know and can do better than I, and in many things even those who neither know nor can do so well,—is still an impure one: to be strictly just, it must have the sanction and consent of the governed. It can have no pure right over my person and property but what I concede to it. The progress from an absolute to a limited monarchy, from a limited monarchy to a democracy, is a progress toward a true respect for the individual. Even the Chinese philosopher was wise enough to regard the individual as the basis of the empire. Is a democracy, such as we know it, the last improvement possible in government? Is it not possible to take a further step towards recognizing and organizing the rights of man? There will never be a really free and enlightened State until the State comes to recognize the individual as a higher and independent power, from which all its own power and authority are derived, and treats him accordingly. I please myself with imagining a State at last which can afford to be just to all men, and to treat the individual with respect as a neighbor; which even would not think it inconsistent with its own repose if a few were to live aloof from it, not meddling with it, nor embraced by it, who fulfilled all the duties of neighbors and fellow-men. A State which bore this kind of fruit, and suffered it to drop off as fast as it ripened, would prepare the way for a still more perfect and glorious State, which also I have imagined, but not yet anywhere seen.

MARTIN LUTHER KING, JR.

Martin Luther King, Jr., was one of the most forceful advocates of nonviolent disobedience in the struggle for civil and human rights. Born in Georgia in 1929 and educated at Morehouse College, Crozer Theological

*Seminary, and Boston University, he became a Baptist minister in
Montgomery, Alabama, in 1954. The next year he launched the now
famous Montgomery bus boycott. Founder and President of the Southern
Christian Leadership Conference, he was a leader of the 1963 March on
Washington and of the 1965 voter registration drive in Selma, Alabama.
In 1964 he received the Nobel Peace Prize. He was assassinated in
Memphis, Tennessee, on April 4, 1968, while supporting a strike of city
garbage collectors.*

His writings include Stride Toward Freedom *(1958),* Strength
to Love *(1963),* Where Do We Go from Here: Chaos or
Community *(1967),* Conscience for Change *(1967),* The
Measure of Man *(1968), and* The Trumpet of Conscience
(1968). Why We Can't Wait, *published in 1964, includes a revised
version of the letter printed below, and an author's note in which he says
that "This response to a published statement by eight fellow clergymen from
Alabama . . . was composed under somewhat constricting circumstances.
Begun on the margins of the newspaper in which the statement appeared
while I was in jail, the letter was continued on scraps of writing paper
supplied by a friendly Negro trusty, and concluded on a pad my attorneys
were eventually permitted to leave me. Although the text remains in
substance unaltered, I have indulged in the author's prerogative of
polishing it for publication." For its greater immediacy, we present here the
unrevised version of the letter, together with the public statement which
occasioned it.*

Public Statement by Eight Alabama Clergymen

(April 12, 1963)

We the undersigned clergymen are among those who, in January, issued
"An Appeal for Law and Order and Common Sense," in dealing with
racial problems in Alabama. We expressed understanding that honest
convictions in racial matters could properly be pursued in the courts, but
urged that decisions of those courts should in the meantime be peacefully
obeyed.

Since that time there had been some evidence of increased forbear-
ance and a willingness to face facts. Responsible citizens have undertaken
to work on various problems which cause racial friction and unrest. In
Birmingham, recent public events have given indication that we all have
opportunity for a new constructive and realistic approach to racial problems.

However, we are now confronted by a series of demonstrations by
some of our Negro citizens, directed and led in part by outsiders. We
recognize the natural impatience of people who feel that their hopes are

slow in being realized. But we are convinced that these demonstrations are unwise and untimely.

We agree rather with certain local Negro leadership which has called for honest and open negotiation of racial issues in our area. And we believe this kind of facing of issues can best be accomplished by citizens of our own metropolitan area, white and Negro, meeting with their knowledge and experience of the local situation. All of us need to face that responsibility and find proper channels for its accomplishment.

Just as we formerly pointed out that "hatred and violence have no sanction in our religious and political traditions," we also point out that such actions as incite to hatred and violence, however technically peaceful those actions may be, have not contributed to the resolution of our local problems. We do not believe that these days of new hope are days when extreme measures are justified in Birmingham.

We commend the community as a whole, and the local news media and law enforcement officials in particular, on the calm manner in which these demonstrations have been handled. We urge the public to continue to show restraint should the demonstrations continue, and the law enforcement officials to remain calm and continue to protect our city from violence.

We further strongly urge our own Negro community to withdraw support from these demonstrations, and to unite locally in working peacefully for a better Birmingham. When rights are consistently denied, a cause should be pressed in the courts and in negotiations among local leaders, and not in the streets. We appeal to both our white and Negro citizenry to observe the principles of law and order and common sense.

Signed by:

C. C. J. CARPENTER, D.D., LL.D., *Bishop of Alabama*

JOSEPH A. DURICK, D.D., *Auxiliary Bishop, Diocese of Mobile-Birmingham*

Rabbi MILTON L. GRAFMAN, *Temple Emanu-El, Birmingham, Alabama*

Bishop PAUL HARDIN, *Bishop of the Alabama-West Florida Conference of the Methodist Church*

Bishop NOLAN B. HARMON, *Bishop of the North Alabama Conference of the Methodist Church*

GEORGE M. MURRAY, D.D., LL.D., *Bishop Coadjutor, Episcopal Diocese of Alabama*

EDWARD V. RAMAGE, *Moderator, Synod of the Alabama Presbyterian Church in the United States*

EARL STALLINGS, *Pastor, First Baptist Church, Birmingham, Alabama*

Letter from Birmingham Jail

MARTIN LUTHER KING, JR.
Birmingham City Jail
April 16, 1963

Bishop C. C. J. CARPENTER
Bishop JOSEPH A. DURICK
Rabbi MILTON L. GRAFMAN
Bishop PAUL HARDIN
Bishop NOLAN B. HARMON
The Rev. GEORGE M. MURRAY
The Rev. EDWARD V. RAMAGE
The Rev. EARL STALLINGS

My dear Fellow Clergymen,

While confined here in the Birmingham City Jail, I came across your recent statement calling our present activities "unwise and untimely." Seldom, if ever, do I pause to answer criticism of my work and ideas. If I sought to answer all of the criticisms that cross my desk, my secretaries would be engaged in little else in the course of the day and I would have no time for constructive work. But since I feel that you are men of genuine good will and your criticisms are sincerely set forth, I would like to answer your statement in what I hope will be patient and reasonable terms.

I think I should give the reason for my being in Birmingham, since you have been influenced by the argument of "outsiders coming in." I have the honor of serving as president of the Southern Christian Leadership Conference, an organization operating in every Southern state with head-quarters in Atlanta, Georgia. We have some eighty-five affiliate organizations all across the South—one being the Alabama Christian Movement for Human Rights. Whenever necessary and possible we share staff, educational, and financial resources with our affiliates. Several months ago our local affiliate here in Birmingham invited us to be on call to engage in a nonviolent direct action program if such were deemed necessary. We readily consented and when the hour came we lived up to our promises. So I am here, along with several members of my staff, because we were invited here. I am here because I have basic organizational ties here. Beyond this, I am in Birmingham because injustice is here. Just as the eighth century prophets left their little villages and carried their "thus saith the Lord" far beyond the boundaries of their home town, and just as the Apostle Paul left his little village of Tarsus and carried the gospel of Jesus Christ to practically every hamlet and city of the Graeco-Roman world, I too am compelled to carry the gospel of freedom beyond my particular home town. Like Paul, I must constantly respond to the Macedonian call for aid.

Moreover, I am cognizant of the interrelatedness of all communities and states. I cannot sit idly by in Atlanta and not be concerned about what happens in Birmingham. Injustice anywhere is a threat to justice everywhere. We are caught in an inescapable network of mutuality tied in a single garment of destiny. Whatever affects one directly affects all indirectly. Never again can we afford to live with the narrow, provincial "outside agitator" idea. Anyone who lives inside the United States can never be considered an outsider anywhere in this country.

You deplore the demonstrations that are presently taking place in Birmingham. But I am sorry that your statement did not express a similar concern for the conditions that brought the demonstrations into being. I am sure that each of you would want to go beyond the superficial social analyst who looks merely at effects, and does not grapple with underlying causes. I would not hesitate to say that it is unfortunate that so-called demonstrations are taking place in Birmingham at this time, but I would say in more emphatic terms that it is even more unfortunate that the white power structure of this city left the Negro community with no other alternative.

In any nonviolent campaign there are four basic steps: (1) collection of the facts to determine whether injustices are alive; (2) negotiation; (3) self-purification; and (4) direct action. We have gone through all of these steps in Birmingham. There can be no gainsaying of the fact that racial injustice engulfs this community. Birmingham is probably the most thoroughly segregated city in the United States. Its ugly record of police brutality is known in every section of this country. Its unjust treatment of Negroes in the courts is a notorious reality. There have been more unsolved bombings of Negro homes and churches in Birmingham than any city in this nation. These are the hard, brutal, and unbelievable facts. On the basis of these conditions Negro leaders sought to negotiate with the city fathers. But the political leaders consistently refused to engage in good faith negotiation.

Then came the opportunity last September to talk with some of the leaders of the economic community. In these negotiating sessions certain promises were made by the merchants—such as the promise to remove the humiliating racial signs from the stores. On the basis of these promises Rev. Shuttlesworth and the leaders of the Alabama Christian Movement for Human Rights agreed to call a moratorium on any type of demonstrations. As the weeks and months unfolded we realized that we were the victims of a broken promise. The signs remained. As in so many experiences of the past we were confronted with blasted hopes, and the dark shadow of a deep disappointment settled upon us. So we had no alternative except that of preparing for direct action, whereby we would present our very bodies as a means of laying our case before the conscience of the local and national community. We were not unmindful of the difficulties involved. So we decided to go through a process of self-purification. We started having workshops on nonviolence and repeatedly asked ourselves the questions, "Are you able to accept blows without retaliating?" "Are you able to endure the ordeals of jail?"

We decided to set our direct action program around the Easter season, realizing that with the exception of Christmas, this was the largest shopping period of the year. Knowing that a strong economic withdrawal program would be the by-product of direct action, we felt that this was the best time to bring pressure on the merchants for the needed changes. Then it occurred to us that the March election was ahead, and so we speedily decided to postpone action until after election day. When we discovered that Mr. Connor was in the run-off, we decided again to postpone so that the demonstrations could not be used to cloud the issues. At this time we agreed to begin our nonviolent witness the day after the run-off.

This reveals that we did not move irresponsibly into direct action. We too wanted to see Mr. Connor defeated; so we went through postponement after postponement to aid in this community need. After this we felt that direct action could be delayed no longer.

You may well ask, "Why direct action? Why sit-ins, marches, etc.? Isn't negotiation a better path?" You are exactly right in your call for negotiation. Indeed, this is the purpose of direct action. Nonviolent direct action seeks to create such a crisis and establish such creative tension that a community that has constantly refused to negotiate is forced to confront the issue. It seeks so to dramatize the issue that it can no longer be ignored. I just referred to the creation of tension as a part of the work of the nonviolent resister. This may sound rather shocking. But I must confess that I am not afraid of the word tension. I have earnestly worked and preached against violent tension, but there is a type of constructive nonviolent tension that is necessary for growth. Just as Socrates felt that it was necessary to create a tension in the mind so that individuals could rise from the bondage of myths and half-truths to the unfettered realm of creative analysis and objective appraisal, we must see the need of having nonviolent gadflies to create the kind of tension in society that will help men rise from the dark depths of prejudice and racism to the majestic heights of understanding and brotherhood. So the purpose of the direct action is to create a situation so crisis-packed that it will inevitably open the door to negotiation. We, therefore, concur with you in your call for negotiation. Too long has our beloved Southland been bogged down in the tragic attempt to live in monologue rather than dialogue.

One of the basic points in your statement is that our acts are untimely. Some have asked, "Why didn't you give the new administration time to act?" The only answer that I can give to this inquiry is that the new administration must be prodded about as much as the outgoing one before it acts. We will be sadly mistaken if we feel that the election of Mr.

Boutwell will bring the millennium to Birmingham. While Mr. Boutwell is much more articulate and gentle than Mr. Connor, they are both segregationists dedicated to the task of maintaining the status quo. The hope I see in Mr. Boutwell is that he will be reasonable enough to see the futility of massive resistance to desegregation. But he will not see this without pressure from the devotees of civil rights. My friends, I must say to you that we have not made a single gain in civil rights without determined legal and nonviolent pressure. History is the long and tragic story of the fact that privileged groups seldom give up their privileges voluntarily. Individuals may see the moral light and voluntarily give up their unjust posture; but as Reinhold Niebuhr has reminded us, groups are more immoral than individuals.

We know through painful experience that freedom is never voluntarily given by the oppressor; it must be demanded by the oppressed. Frankly I have never yet engaged in a direct action movement that was "well timed," according to the timetable of those who have not suffered unduly from the disease of segregation. For years now I have heard the word "Wait!" It rings in the ear of every Negro with a piercing familiarity. This "wait" has almost always meant "never." It has been a tranquilizing thalidomide, relieving the emotional stress for a moment, only to give birth to an ill-formed infant of frustration. We must come to see with the distinguished jurist of yesterday that "justice too long delayed is justice denied." We have waited for more than three hundred and forty years for our constitutional and God-given rights. The nations of Asia and Africa are moving with jet-like speed toward the goal of political independence, and we still creep at horse and buggy pace toward the gaining of a cup of coffee at a lunch counter.

I guess it is easy for those who have never felt the stinging darts of segregation to say wait. But when you have seen vicious mobs lynch your mothers and fathers at will and drown your sisters and brothers at whim; when you have seen hate filled policemen curse, kick, brutalize, and even kill your black brothers and sisters with impunity; when you see the vast majority of your twenty million Negro brothers smothering in an air-tight cage of poverty in the midst of an affluent society; when you suddenly find your tongue twisted and your speech stammering as you seek to explain to your six-year-old daughter why she can't go to the public amusement park that has just been advertised on television, and see tears welling up in her little eyes when she is told that Funtown is closed to colored children, and see the depressing clouds of inferiority begin to form in her little mental sky, and see her begin to distort her little personality by unconsciously developing a bitterness toward white people; when you have to concoct an answer for a five-year-old son asking in agonizing pathos: "Daddy, why do white people treat colored people so mean?"; when you take a cross country drive and find it necessary to sleep night after night in the uncomfortable corners of your automobile because no motel will accept you; when you are humiliated day in and day out by nagging signs reading "white" men and "colored"; when your first name becomes "nigger" and your middle name becomes "boy" (however old you are) and your last name becomes "John," and when your wife and mother are never given the respected title "Mrs."; when you are harried by day and haunted by night by the fact that you are a Negro, living constantly at tip-toe stance never quite knowing what to expect next, and plagued with inner fears and outer resentments; when you are forever fighting a degenerating sense of "nobodiness";—then you will understand why we find it difficult to wait. There comes a time when the cup of endurance runs over, and men are no longer willing to be plunged into an abyss of injustice where they experience the bleakness of corroding despair. I hope, sirs, you can understand our legitimate and unavoidable impatience.

You express a great deal of anxiety over our willingness to break laws. This is certainly a legitimate concern. Since we so diligently urge people to obey the Supreme Court's decision of 1954 outlawing segregation in the public schools, it is rather strange and paradoxical to find us consciously breaking laws. One may well ask, "How can you advocate breaking some laws and obeying others?" The answer is found in the fact that there are two types of laws. There are *just* laws and there are *unjust* laws. I would be the first to advocate obeying just laws. One has not only a legal but moral responsibility to obey just laws. Conversely, one has a moral responsibility to disobey unjust laws. I would agree with Saint Augustine that "An unjust law is no law at all."

Now what is the difference between the two? How does one determine when a law is just or unjust? A just law is a man-made code that squares with the moral law or the law of God. An unjust law is a code that is out of harmony with the moral law. To put it in the terms of Saint Thomas Aquinas, an unjust law is a human law that is not rooted in eternal and natural law. Any law that uplifts human personality is just. Any law that degrades human personality is unjust. All segregation statutes are unjust because segregation distorts the soul and damages the personality. It gives the segregator a false sense of superiority and the segregated a false sense of inferiority. To use the words of Martin Buber, the great Jewish philosopher, segregation substitutes an "I-it" relationship for the "I-thou" relationship, and ends up relegating persons to the status of things. So segregation is not only politically, economically, and sociologically unsound, but it is morally wrong and sinful. Paul Tillich has said that sin is separation. Isn't segregation an existential expression of man's tragic separation, an expression of his awful estrangement, his terrible sinfulness? So I can urge men to obey the 1954 decision of the Supreme Court because it is morally right, and I can urge them to disobey segregation ordinances because they are morally wrong.

Let us turn to a more concrete example of just and unjust laws. An unjust law is a code that a majority inflicts on a minority that is not binding on itself. This is *difference* made legal. On the other hand a just law is a code that a majority compels a minority to follow that it is willing to follow itself. This is *sameness* made legal.

Let me give another explanation. An unjust law is a code inflicted upon a minority which that minority had no part in enacting or creating because they did not have the unhampered right to vote. Who can say the legislature of Alabama which set up the segregation laws was democratically elected? Throughout the state of Alabama all types of conniving methods are used to prevent Negroes from becoming registered voters and there are some counties without a single Negro registered to vote despite the fact that the Negro constitutes a majority of the population. Can any law set up in such a state be considered democratically structured?

These are just a few examples of unjust and just laws. There are some instances when a law is just on its face but unjust in its application. For instance, I was arrested Friday on a charge of parading without a permit. Now there is nothing wrong with an ordinance which requires a permit for a parade, but when the ordinance is used to preserve segregation and to deny citizens the First Amendment privilege of peaceful assembly and peaceful protest, then it becomes unjust.

I hope you can see the distinction I am trying to point out. In no sense do I advocate evading or defying the law as the rabid segregationist would do. This would lead to anarchy. One who breaks an unjust law must do it *openly, lovingly* (not hatefully as the white mothers did in New Orleans when they were seen on television screaming "nigger, nigger, nigger") and with a willingness to accept the penalty. I submit that an individual who breaks a law that conscience tells him is unjust, and willingly accepts the penalty by staying in jail to arouse the conscience of the community over its injustice, is in reality expressing the very highest respect for law.

Of course there is nothing new about this kind of civil disobedience. It was seen sublimely in the refusal of Shadrach, Meshach, and Abednego to obey the laws of Nebuchadnezzar because a higher moral law was involved. It was practiced superbly by the early Christians who were willing to face hungry lions and the excruciating pain of chopping blocks, before submitting to certain unjust laws of the Roman Empire. To a degree academic freedom is a reality today because Socrates practiced civil disobedience.

We can never forget that everything Hitler did in Germany was "legal" and everything the Hungarian freedom fighters did in Hungary was "illegal." It was "illegal" to aid and comfort a Jew in Hitler's Germany. But I am sure that, if I had lived in Germany during that time, I would have aided and comforted my Jewish brothers even though it was illegal. If I lived in a communist country today where certain principles dear to the Christian faith are suppressed, I believe I would openly advocate disobeying those antireligious laws.

I must make two honest confessions to you, my Christian and Jewish brothers. First I must confess that over the last few years I have been gravely disappointed with the white moderate. I have almost reached the regrettable conclusion that the Negroes' great stumbling block in the stride toward freedom is not the White Citizens' "Counciler" or the Ku Klux Klanner, but the white moderate who is more devoted to "order" than to justice; who prefers a negative peace which is the absence of tension to a positive peace which is the presence of justice; who constantly says "I agree with you in the goal you seek, but I can't agree with your methods of direct action"; who paternalistically feels that he can set the timetable for another man's freedom; who lives by the myth of time and who constantly advises the Negro to wait until a "more convenient season." Shallow understanding from people of good will is more frustrating than absolute misunderstanding from people of ill will. Lukewarm acceptance is much more bewildering than outright rejection.

I had hoped that the white moderator would understand that law and order exist for the purpose of establishing justice, and that when they fail to do this they become the dangerously structured dams that block the flow of social progress. I had hoped that the white moderate would understand that the present tension in the South is merely a necessary phase of the transition from an obnoxious negative peace, where the Negro passively accepted his unjust plight, to a substance-filled positive peace, where all men will respect the dignity and worth of human personality. Actually, we who engage in nonviolent direct action are not the creators of tension. We merely bring to the surface the hidden tension that is already alive. We bring it out in the open where it can be seen and dealt with. Like a boil that can never be cured as long as it is covered up but must be opened with all its pus-flowing ugliness to the natural medicines of air and light, injustice must likewise be exposed, with all of the tension its exposing creates, to the light of human conscience and the air of national opinion before it can be cured.

In your statement you asserted that our actions, even though peaceful, must be condemned because they precipitate violence. But can this assertion be logically made? Isn't this like condemning the robbed man because his possession of money precipitated the evil act of robbery? Isn't this like condemning Socrates because his unswerving commitment to truth and his philosophical delvings precipitated the misguided popular mind to make him drink the hemlock? Isn't this like condemning Jesus because His unique God consciousness and never-ceasing devotion to His will precipitated the evil act of crucifixion? We must come to see, as federal courts have consistently affirmed, that it is immoral to urge an individual to withdraw his efforts to gain his basic constitutional rights because the quest precipitates violence. Society must protect the robbed and punish the robber.

I had also hoped that the white moderate would reject the myth of time. I received a letter this morning from a white brother in Texas which said: "All Christians know that the colored people will receive equal rights eventually, but is it possible that you are in too great of a religious hurry? It has taken Christianity almost 2000 years to accomplish what it has. The teachings of Christ take time to come to earth." All that is said here grows out of a tragic misconception of time. It is the strangely irrational notion that there is something in the very flow of time that will inevitably cure all ills. Actually time is neutral. It can be used either destructively or constructively. I am coming to feel that the people of ill will have used time much more effectively than the people of good will. We will have to repent in this generation not merely for the vitriolic words and actions of the bad people, but for the appalling silence of the good people. We must come to see that human progress never rolls in on wheels of inevitability. It comes through the tireless efforts and persistent work of men willing to be co-workers with God, and without this hard work time itself becomes an ally of the forces of social stagnation.

We must use time creatively, and forever realize that the time is always ripe to do right. Now is the time to make real the promise of democracy, and transform our pending national elegy into a creative psalm of brotherhood. Now is the time to lift our national policy from the quicksand of racial injustice to the solid rock of human dignity.

You spoke of our activity in Birmingham as extreme. At first I was rather disappointed that fellow clergymen would see my nonviolent efforts as those of the extremist. I started thinking about the fact that I stand in the middle of two opposing forces in the Negro community. One is a force of complacency made up of Negroes who, as a result of long years of oppression, have been so completely drained of self-respect and a sense of "somebodiness" that they have adjusted to segregation, and of a few Negroes in the middle class who, because of a degree of academic and economic security, and because at points they profit by segregation, have unconsciously become insensitive to the problems of the masses. The other force is one of bitterness and hatred and comes perilously close to advocating violence. It is expressed in the various black nationalist groups that are springing up over the nation, the largest and best known being Elijah Muhammad's Muslim movement. This movement is nourished by the contemporary frustration over the continued existence of racial discrimination. It is made up of people who have lost faith in America, who have absolutely repudiated Christianity, and who have concluded that the white man is an incurable "devil." I have tried to stand between these two forces saying that we need not follow the "do-nothing-ism" of the complacent or the hatred and despair of the black nationalist. There is the more excellent way of love and nonviolent protest. I'm grateful to God that, through the Negro church, the dimension of nonviolence entered our struggle. If this philosophy had not emerged I am convinced that by now many streets of the South would be flowing with floods of blood. And I am further convinced that if our white brothers dismiss us as "rabble rousers" and "outside agitators"—those of us who are working through the channels of nonviolent direct action—and refuse to support our nonviolent efforts, millions of Negroes, out of frustration and despair, will seek solace and security in black nationalist ideologies, a development that will lead inevitably to a frightening racial nightmare.

Oppressed people cannot remain oppressed forever. The urge for freedom will eventually come. This is what has happened to the American Negro. Something within has reminded him of his birthright of freedom; something without has reminded him that he can gain it. Consciously and unconsciously, he has been swept in by what the Germans call the *Zeitgeist,* and with his black brothers of Africa, and his brown and yellow brothers of Asia, South America, and the Caribbean, he is moving with a sense of cosmic urgency toward the promised land of racial justice. Recognizing this vital urge that has engulfed the Negro community, one should readily understand public demonstrations. The Negro has many pent-up resentments and latent frustrations. He has to get them out. So let him march sometime; let him have his prayer pilgrimages to the city hall; understand why he must have sit-ins and freedom rides. If his repressed emotions do not come out in these nonviolent ways, they will come out in ominous expressions of violence. This is not a threat; it is a fact of history. So I have not said to my people, "Get rid of your discontent." But I have tried to say that this normal and healthy discontent can be channeled through the creative outlet of nonviolent direct action. Now this approach is being dismissed as extremist. I must admit that I was initially disappointed in being so categorized.

But as I continued to think about the matter I gradually gained a bit of satisfaction from being considered an extremist. Was not Jesus an extremist in love? "Love your enemies, bless them that curse you, pray for them that despitefully use you." Was not Amos an extremist for justice—"Let justice roll down like waters and righteousness like a mighty stream." Was not Paul an extremist for the gospel of Jesus Christ—"I bear in my body the marks of the Lord Jesus." Was not Martin Luther an extremist—"Here I stand; I can do none other so help me God." Was not John Bunyan an extremist—"I will stay in jail to the end of my days before I make a butchery of my conscience." Was not Abraham Lincoln an extremist—"This nation cannot survive half slave and half free." Was not Thomas Jefferson an extremist—"We hold these truths to be self evident that all men are created equal." So the question is not whether we will be extremist but what kind of extremist will we be. Will we be extremists for hate or will we be extremists for love? Will we be extremists for the preservation of injustice—or will we be extremists for the cause of justice? In that dramatic scene on Calvary's hill three men were crucified. We must never forget that all three were crucified for the same crime—the crime of extremism. Two were extremists for immorality, and thus fell below their environment. The other, Jesus Christ, was an extremist for love, truth, and goodness, and thereby rose above His environment. So, after all, maybe the South, the nation, and the world are in dire need of creative extremists.

I had hoped that the white moderate would see this. Maybe I was too optimistic. Maybe I expected too much. I guess I should have realized that few members of a race that has oppressed another race can understand or appreciate the deep groans and passionate yearnings of those that have been oppressed, and still fewer have the vision to see that injustice must be rooted out by strong, persistent, and determined action. I am thankful, however, that some of our white brothers have grasped the meaning of this social revolution and committed themselves to it. They are still all too small in quantity, but they are big in quality. Some like Ralph McGill, Lillian Smith, Harry Golden, and James Dabbs have written about our struggle in eloquent, prophetic, and understanding terms. Others have marched with us down nameless streets of the South. They have languished in filthy, roach-infested jails, suffering the abuse and brutality of angry policemen who see them as "dirty nigger lovers." They, unlike so many of their moderate brothers and sisters, have recognized the urgency of the moment and sensed the need for powerful "action" antidotes to combat the disease of segregation.

Let me rush on to mention my other disappointment. I have been so greatly disappointed with the white Church and its leadership. Of course there are some notable exceptions. I am not unmindful of the fact that each of you has taken some significant stands on this issue. I commend you, Rev. Stallings, for your Christian stand on this past Sunday, in welcoming Negroes to your worship service on a nonsegregated basis. I commend the Catholic leaders of this state for integrating Springhill College several years ago.

But despite these notable exceptions I must honestly reiterate that I have been disappointed with the Church. I do not say that as one of those negative critics who can always find something wrong with the Church. I say it as a minister of the gospel, who loves the Church; who was nurtured in its bosom; who has been sustained by its spiritual blessings and who will remain true to it as long as the cord of life shall lengthen.

I had the strange feeling when I was suddenly catapulted into the leadership of the bus protest in Montgomery several years ago that we would have the support of the white Church. I felt that the white ministers, priests, and rabbis of the South would be some of our strongest allies. Instead, some have been outright opponents, refusing to understand the freedom movement and misrepresenting its leaders; all too many others have been more cautious than courageous and have remained silent behind the anesthetizing security of stained glass windows.

In spite of my shattered dreams of the past, I came to Birmingham with the hope that the white religious leadership of the community would see the justice of our cause and, with deep moral concern, serve as the channel through which our just grievances could get to the power structure. I had hoped that each of you would understand. But again I have been disappointed.

I have heard numerous religious leaders of the South call upon their worshippers to comply with a desegregation decision because it is the law, but I have longed to hear white ministers say follow this decree because integration is morally right and the Negro is your brother. In the midst of blatant injustices inflicted upon the Negro, I have watched white churches stand on the sideline and merely mouth pious irrelevancies and sanctimonious trivialities. In the midst of a mighty struggle to rid our nation of racial and economic injustice, I have heard so many ministers say, "Those are social issues with which the Gospel has no real concern," and I have watched so many churches commit themselves to a completely other-worldly religion which made a strange distinction between body and soul, the sacred and the secular.

So here we are moving toward the exit of the twentieth century with a religious community largely adjusted to the status quo, standing as a tail light behind other community agencies rather than a headlight leading men to higher levels of justice.

I have travelled the length and breadth of Alabama, Mississippi, and all the other Southern states. On sweltering summer days and crisp autumn mornings I have looked at her beautiful churches with their spires pointing heavenward. I have beheld the impressive outlay of her massive religious education buildings. Over and over again I have found myself asking: "Who worships here? Who is their God? Where were their voices when the lips of Governor Barnett dripped with words of interposition and nullification? Where were they when Governor Wallace gave the clarion call for defiance and hatred? Where were their voices of support when tired, bruised, and weary Negro men and women decided to rise from the dark dungeons of complacency to the bright hills of creative protest?"

Yes, these questions are still in my mind. In deep disappointment, I have wept over the laxity of the Church. But be assured that my tears have been tears of love. There can be no deep disappointment where there is not deep love. Yes, I love the Church; I love her sacred walls. How could I do otherwise? I am in the rather unique position of being the son, the grandson, and the great grandson of preachers. Yes, I see the Church as the body of Christ. But, oh! How we have blemished and scarred that body through social neglect and fear of being nonconformists.

There was a time when the Church was very powerful. It was during that period when the early Christians rejoiced when they were deemed worthy to suffer for what they believed. In those days the Church was not merely a thermometer that recorded the ideas and principles of popular opinion; it was a thermostat that transformed the mores of society. Wherever the early Christians entered a town the power structure got disturbed and immediately sought to convict them for being "disturbers of the peace" and "outside agitators." But they went on with the conviction that they were a "colony of heaven" and had to obey God rather than man. They were small in number but big in commitment. They were too God-intoxicated to be "astronomically intimidated." They brought an end to such ancient evils as infanticide and gladiatorial contest.

Things are different now. The contemporary Church is so often a weak, ineffectual voice with an uncertain sound. It is so often the arch-supporter of the status quo. Far from being disturbed by the presence of the Church, the power structure of the average community is consoled by the Church's silent and often vocal sanction of things as they are.

But the judgment of God is upon the Church as never before. If the Church of today does not recapture the sacrificial spirit of the early Church, it will lose its authentic ring, forfeit the loyalty of millions, and be dismissed as an irrelevant social club with no meaning for the twentieth century. I am meeting young people every day whose disappointment with the Church has risen to outright disgust.

Maybe again I have been too optimistic. Is organized religion too inextricably bound to the status quo to save our nation and the world? Maybe I must turn my faith to the inner spiritual Church, the church within the Church, as the true *ecclesia* and the hope of the world. But again I am thankful to God that some noble souls from the ranks of organized religion have broken loose from the paralyzing chains of conformity and joined us as active partners in the struggle for freedom. They have left their secure congregations and walked the streets of Albany, Georgia, with us. They have gone through the highways of the South on torturous rides for freedom. Yes, they have gone to jail with us. Some have been kicked out of their churches and lost the support of their bishops and fellow ministers. But they have gone with the faith that right defeated is stronger than evil triumphant. These men have been the leaven in the lump of the race. Their witness has been the spiritual salt that has preserved the true meaning of the Gospel in these troubled times. They have carved a tunnel of hope through the dark mountain of disappointment.

I hope the Church as a whole will meet the challenge of this decisive hour. But even if the Church does not come to the aid of justice, I have no despair about the future. I have no fear about the outcome of our struggle in Birmingham, even if our motives are presently misunderstood. We will reach the goal of freedom in Birmingham and all over the nation, because the goal of America is freedom. Abused and scorned though we may be, our destiny is tied up with the destiny of America. Before the pilgrims landed at Plymouth, we were here. Before the pen of Jefferson etched across the pages of history the majestic words of the Declaration of Independence, we were here. For more than two centuries our foreparents labored in this country without wages; they made cotton "king"; and they built the homes of their masters in the midst of brutal injustice and shameful humiliation—and yet out of a bottomless vitality they continued to thrive and develop. If the inexpressible cruelties of slavery could not stop us, the opposition we now face will surely fail. We will win our freedom because the sacred heritage of our nation and the eternal will of God are embodied in our echoing demands.

I must close now. But before closing I am impelled to mention one other point in your statement that troubled me profoundly. You warmly commended the Birmingham police force for keeping "order" and "preventing violence." I don't believe you would have so warmly commended the police force if you had seen its angry violent dogs literally biting six unarmed, nonviolent Negroes. I don't believe you would so quickly commend the policemen if you would observe their ugly and inhuman treatment of Negroes here in the city jail; if you would watch them push and curse old Negro women and young Negro girls; if you would see them slap and kick old Negro men and young Negro boys; if you will observe them, as they did on two occasions, refuse to give us food because we wanted to sing our grace together. I'm sorry that I can't join you in your praise for the police department.

It is true that they have been rather disciplined in their public handling of the demonstrators. In this sense they have been rather publicly "nonviolent." But for what purpose? To preserve the evil system of segregation. Over the last few years I have consistently preached that nonviolence demands that the means we use must be as pure as the ends we seek. So I have tried to make it clear that it is wrong to use immoral means to attain moral ends. But now I must affirm that it is just as wrong, or even more so, to use moral means to preserve immoral ends. Maybe Mr. Connor and his policemen have been rather publicly nonviolent, as Chief Prichett was in Albany, Georgia, but they have used the moral means of nonviolence to maintain the immoral end of flagrant racial injustice. T. S. Eliot has said that there is no greater treason than to do the right deed for the wrong reason.

I wish you had commended the Negro sit-inners and demonstrators of Birmingham for their sublime courage, their willingness to suffer, and their amazing discipline in the midst of the most inhuman provocation. One day the South will recognize its real heroes. They will be the James Merediths, courageously and with a majestic sense of purpose, facing jeering and hostile mobs and the agonizing loneliness that characterizes the life of the pioneer. They will be old, oppressed, battered Negro women, symbolized in a seventy-two year old woman of Montgomery, Alabama, who rose up with a sense of dignity and with her people decided not to ride the segregated buses, and responded to one who inquired about her tiredness with ungrammatical profundity: "My feets is tired, but my soul is rested." They will be young high school and college students, young ministers of the gospel and a host of the elders, courageously and nonviolently sitting in at lunch counters and willingly going to jail for conscience sake. One day the South will know that when these disinherited children of God sat down at lunch counters they were in reality standing up for the best in the American dream and the most sacred values in our Judeo-Christian heritage, and thus carrying our whole nation back to great wells of democracy which were dug deep by the founding fathers in the formulation of the Constitution and the Declaration of Independence.

Never before have I written a letter this long (or should I say a book?).

I'm afraid that it is much too long to take your precious time. I can assure you that it would have been much shorter if I had been writing from a comfortable desk, but what else is there to do when you are alone for days in the dull monotony of a narrow jail cell other than write long letters, think strange thoughts, and pray long prayers?

If I have said anything in this letter that is an overstatement of the truth and is indicative of an unreasonable impatience, I beg you to forgive me. If I have said anything in this letter that is an understatement of the truth and is indicative of my having a patience that makes me patient with anything less than brotherhood, I beg God to forgive me.

I hope this letter finds you strong in the faith. I also hope that circumstances will soon make it possible for me to meet each of you, not as an integrationist or a civil rights leader, but as a fellow clergyman and a Christian brother. Let us all hope that the dark clouds of racial prejudice will soon pass away and the deep fog of misunderstanding will be lifted from our fear-drenched communities and in some not too distant tomorrow the radiant stars of love and brotherhood will shine over our great nation with all of their scintillating beauty.

Yours for the cause of
Peace and Brotherhood

MARTIN LUTHER KING, JR.

ROBERT COLES

Robert Coles is a psychiatrist concerned with problems of poverty and discrimination. He was born in New England in 1929, attended Harvard, received a medical degree at Columbia, and then trained in child psychiatry, following the direction pointed by Anna Freud and Erik Erikson. After completing his residency, he became head of an air-force neuropsychiatric hospital in Biloxi, Mississippi. In 1961 he returned to the South to study the psychiatric aspects of school desegregation. His work with both children and adults is vividly described in Children of Crisis: A Study of Courage and Fear *(1967), the first volume of an award-winning series. The next two volumes,* Migrants, Sharecroppers, Mountaineers *(1971) and* The South Goes North *(1971), tell of his work with migrant and tenant-farm children, and with northern city and ghetto children. He is a prolific writer of magazine articles, reviews, and books, which include the intellectual biography* Erik H. Erikson, The Growth of His Work *(1970),* Still Hungry in America *(1969), and* Farewell to the South *(1972).*

In July 1970 Coles became involved with those opposing the imprisonment of Father Philip Berrigan in a maximum security prison for burning draft records to protest the Vietnam fighting. He was able to visit him. Father Berrigan's brother, Daniel Berrigan, sought by the FBI for the same crime but still underground at the time, then sought contact with Coles. The two men met and talked, off and on, for a week. They recorded their talks and published them, first in a series of articles for the New York Review of Books, *then in book form,* The Geography of Faith *(1971). The selection below is taken from the book's last chapter, or conversation, "Twice-Born Men."*

Twice-Born Men

. . .

Coles. The issue of what is possible in people is something that intrigues me. A few years ago I read Malcolm X's autobiography, in which he described his utterly brutal childhood. His father was killed when he was a child, his mother was driven to madness. He knew extreme poverty and hardship. As a clinician I have known so many people from comfortable, upper middle class homes who have sought out psychiatrists because they are in despair, troubled beyond their own comprehension, and indeed often enough thoroughly paralyzed. Yet Malcom X somehow not only survived a bleak and frantic and near-chaotic childhood, but wrote a moving and sensitive book about his life, including his early years. And more significantly, he was a man who in his last years was being reborn, to use your imagery. I mean, he was going through a profound spiritual crisis. He was becoming a spiritual leader toward the end. Anyone who calls himself a child psychiatrist ought to ask: whence this? What in Malcolm X's life enabled that kind of development? I am not only referring to the peculiar tenacity a suffering and vulnerable person can develop within himself or herself. I have in mind the genuine thoughtfulness and compassion and sensitivity which gradually evolved in the short life of this man. Perhaps he is a model of the "new man" you mention—an example of what is possible in people. Out of his prison experience, out of his devastating childhood, out of all the sadness and pain he went through in one ghetto after another, he could somehow build more than a "life" for himself. He found the resources for spiritual growth—to the point that many of us, less "disadvantaged" and "deprived," can only scratch our heads and wonder what do *we* lack, why have *we* become so cautious and restricted and cravenly self-satisfied.

Was Malcolm X so very unusual? Of course he was unusual; he was a leader. But for years I have seen in the South and in Appalachia and in the ghettos of the North poor and desperate people who manage to find for themselves large stretches of intelligence and discrimination—in the best sense of the word discrimination. They are people who are very hard pressed, who often go hungry, who are sick and persecuted and in constant trouble of one kind or another; and yet they are able to demonstrate not only humor and liveliness, but the kinds of "ethical concern" I think those of us in the universities and the divinity schools talk about —but don't always ourselves summon. Now we social scientists often fail to take note of or comment upon those qualities in the children of the poor—in blacks and in Appalachian whites, for example. Instead we talk endlessly about the "disadvantage" and "deprivation" of the poor. The poor are indeed disadvantaged (quite literally they are); and certainly they are deprived of certain things they desperately need. Nor ought they to be romanticized. Their difficulties are serious and sometimes stunting. And yet I see in many impoverished families I work with a concern for one another that is remarkable. And I hear among those "illiterate" men and women and children a capacity for philosophical and theological speculation that rivals anyone's. They ask over and over why they are here, what they ought do, what they must do—and not least, what they might do, given different circumstances. Among them, too, live the "twice born," the "new men."

Now you asked a moment ago what is possible for people. In the fifties the President of the United States said we cannot have changes in our society until there are changes in people. We cannot have changes, for instance, in our laws, changes that would affect the way the races get along, until the hearts of people change, said Eisenhower. And yet when laws *are* changed and then enforced rigorously, people also change; they respond to new legal and social and political realities. White Southerners I worked with once told me *never;* they said they would never go along with school desegregation. But they did, and quickly. Of course when a national administration backtracks and implies or subtly suggests that recent changes need not be maintained, then people go back to their old ways.

There is nothing surprising in what I am saying; I think we all know that people accommodate themselves rather readily to changing historical circumstances—perhaps *too* readily. What we know is that there are all kinds of possibilities in people; there are all kinds of qualities that can emerge, given an enabling historical moment, given the encouragement a society offers. There is also, I fear, in most of us a large capacity for violence. Nor is "education" any panacea in this regard. What we are haunted by is the example in this century of one of the most "educated" and "advanced" nations in the world running amok. They didn't need Head Start programs in Germany in the twenties. The Germans were well educated by and large. They had produced a fine culture over many decades. And yet, given economic chaos and social unrest an entire nation could be led into heinous crimes. I do not believe—I know the matter is indeed arguable—that what happened was the specific result of German culture or Germany's peculiar philosophical and social traditions. I believe that any nation, given sufficient economic and social injustice, can become increasingly seized by violence and chaos, hence be ripe for one or another murderous demagogue—and their ideologies (Left versus Right) seem to be less important than their common brutishness.

As for individuals, Lord knows I see patients every day who are hurt and troubled people. But over a period of weeks and months one sees in them not only the *desire* for health, but the continuing presence of health which cannot for various reasons find a way of expression—but health which nevertheless is there and waiting, as it were. And so I would almost get religious, and say that I don't believe anyone, anyone at all, is ultimately beyond some kind of saving moment—given what is needed to bring about or enable that "moment." And I would say that even about people some of us dismiss as awful or hopeless or evil or sick—and in this regard there are so many different kinds of words we have. I worked with members of the Ku Klux Klan in the South even as I was working with black families. They were racists, they were hurt and troubled men and women, and their children of course were infected with virulent hatreds; and yet I saw even in some of those families a wide range of possibilities, virtues, difficulties, tragedies. And I wonder at times whether some of the negative things people have to face are not potentially of great value, because tragedies and difficulties often can herald growth—something which novelists and playwrights have known long before those who call themselves experts in child development came on the scene. One man, a member of the Ku Klux Klan, said to me after I had come to know him for some length of time that he thought his life might have been a different life had America been a different country when he was growing up. Now when a man who is an unashamed and rather voluble bigot can tell me (not in any propagandistic or moralistic or analytic way, and not particularly in a self-conscious way, but almost in an offhand and casual way) that he might have been a different person if the state of Louisiana had been different and if America had been different, he is telling me something about the nature of society and its relationship to the individual, and he is telling me an important psychological truth, one which I am not so sure someone like me is always ready to comprehend. He is really telling me that at any given moment anyone *is* not only what he has *come to be,* but what he *might have been.* Each of us carries within himself (living in us even if not available or apparent) all kinds of resources and possibilities—and some of them may be hidden and known to no one, including the particular person in question. Now I'm not talking about the "unconscious" *per se;* I am saying that people can suddenly organize and bring together qualities they either vaguely sense in themselves, or don't stop and think about, or do think about, but have in the past dismissed—all because the world "outside" has suddenly said *yes* rather than *no* or *now* rather than *later.*

I worked in New Orleans a decade ago; there I watched mobs form around little black children going into white schools. A year later I went up to Atlanta and saw no mobs at all form when black children there went into white schools. Fascinatingly enough, the first questions I got when I went to talk about those experiences at medical and psychiatric meetings were these: what kind of people would join a mob, and what kind of psychopathy and psychopathology would prompt people to heckle children and be violent on the street, and what kind of treatment did those people need, since they were obviously quite disturbed? Of course one had to point out that there were no mobs in Atlanta. Does that mean the "mental health" of Atlanta's people was better? Does that mean Atlanta's citizens are of sounder mind than New Orleans's citizens? Well, of course not. What it means is that the city of Atlanta at a particular moment in American history would not allow a mob to form. The city of Atlanta (for its own various and mixed reasons—commercial reasons, moral reasons, reasons that had to do with the "image" of the city) could tell thousands and thousands of people, not in an explicit and didactic way but in vague and indirect ways: look, cool it, refrain from behaving in certain ways, don't take to the streets, don't lose your tempers, and don't even try to start trouble—because it won't be sanctioned or tolerated. I think such "exchanges" go on all the time. By that I mean we constantly take our cues from the world we live in. And if there is forthright moral leadership in that world people often respond to such leadership, despite their past "positions" or "attitudes." I don't see us as reflexic products of particular psychological drives, limited by certain kinds of "problems," and able to change only after years of "treatment." Parents know what is possible for their children—and often enough for them as mothers and fathers: a hundred different directions can be taken by children, given support here or, of course, disapproval there—and on and on.

A good example of what I am trying to say has been provided us not by a psychiatrist but by a historian—in C. Vann Woodward's book on Tom Watson. It seems to me Tom Watson's life shows in microcosm what happens to all of us. When an inherently idealistic and loving man is continually thwarted and denied and cheated and robbed and insulted, eventually he turns to hate and becomes violent and mean toward others. So it happened with Tom Watson, and so it happens with us today, millions of us. All of us struggle to find out what opportunity we can have for a more loving and affectionate way of getting along with ourselves and others—only to meet up not only with the indifference of the world but the deceit and the brutality. I'm talking about institutionalized meanness and brutality—which as part of our "outer" world we all have to live with and come to terms with, and which children at seven and eight know about and have comprehended and have already begun to accept and take for granted and (most horrible to watch developing) as a matter of fact take in as part of their "inner" world.

I hear it said that there's just *so* much you can do with people. I hear it said that people are the way they are, and they can't change overnight, can't be born again; rather, it takes years, it takes generations. One can only say in reply that there is an enormous amount of evidence—historical, psychological, clinical, psychiatric and psychoanalytic—which tells us people *are* many things and can *become* many things. Again, I go back to Malcolm X as an example of this, or in a different way, Tom Watson, or the member of the Klan I just mentioned. I think that when St. Paul talked about the "new man" or the "twice born" he was trying to say that we don't have to be what we once were, and that we can be more than we presently are, and that every day (even every minute) of our lives offers us a chance—to demonstrate our ability to move, walk, gain territory on ourselves, realize for ourselves a certain coherence, a certain spirit of openness and concern. What really makes a difference in our lives is not only what we were driven to when we were young or what we experienced at such and such an age, although yes, those are terribly significant matters. What we *are* is a function of so many things: accidents, incidents, things that are unpredictable and that yet have become the most important things in our lives—things like whom we meet at one or another point in time, or things like what happened in the world this year or the next year, things like where we were when we encountered someone. We all know that; we all know we met our wives or husbands because of this accident or because we just happened to be doing that. So our lives become profoundly, crucially changed because we admired a teacher or camp counselor we only happened (we *chanced*) to spend time with, or because we by luck met someone here or there who later became a friend, a wife, a husband—well, I shouldn't keep on saying the obvious. If such decisive moments can happen in all of our lives, how much *more* could happen, might happen, if people were to come together and make it their business to *want* certain things to happen, want an atmosphere to exist in which change is possible, in which events keep taking place and in that way encouraging us to take notice and learn, and again, change.

Berrigan. It seems to me that what you are saying is quite subversive in its implications.

Coles. I feel myself talking common sense.

.   .   .

JAMES HERNDON

The following essay is a chapter in How to Survive in Your Native Land *(1971). For information about the author, see page 154.*

The Dumb Class

One afternoon during our free seventh period someone looked around and said This faculty is the Dumb Class.

It was so. Given the community or the entire country as a school—reversing the usual image of the school as mirror of society to make society the mirror of the school—and given that community as one which is tracked or ability-grouped into high, high-average, average, low-average, high-low, low and low-low, the faculty or faculties, teachers, *educators*, are the dumb class.

We are the dumb class because we cannot learn. Cannot achieve. Why not? Cannot concentrate, have a low attention span, are culturally deprived, brain-damaged, nonverbal, unmotivated, lack skills, are anxiety-ridden, have broken homes, can't risk failure, no study habits, won't try, are lazy . . .? Those are the reasons *kids* are in the dumb class, supposing we don't say it's because they are just dumb. But the characteristic of the dumb class is that it cannot learn how to do what it is there to do. Try as one may, one cannot make the dumb class learn to do these things, at least not as long as it is operating together as a dumb class. Even if those things are completely obvious, the dumb class cannot learn them or achieve them.

Is it so that what the dumb class is supposed to achieve is so difficult that only superior individuals can achieve it, and then only with hard work, endless practice? Is it so mysterious and opaque that only those with intelligence and energy enough to research and ferret out the mysteries of the universe can gain insight into it? Eighth period I was involved with this dumb class which was supposed to achieve adding and subtracting before it got out of the eighth grade and went to high school. Could the class achieve it? No sir. Given an adding problem to add, most of the dumb class couldn't add it. Those who did add it hadn't any notion of whether or not they'd added it correctly, even if they had. They asked me Is this right? Is this right? This ain't right, is it? What's the answer? If you don't know whether it's right or not, I'd say, then you aren't adding it. Is this right? screamed four kids, rushing me waving papers. Boy, this dumb class can't learn, I'd say to myself. Not a very sophisticated remark, perhaps.

For a while I would drop in on the Tierra Firma bowling alley, since Jay and Jack were always dying to go there. One day I ran into the dumbest kid in the dumb class. Rather, he came up to us as we were playing this baseball slot machine. Jay and Jack were not defeating the machine, to say the least, and as a result had to put in another dime each time they wanted to play again. Well the dumb kid showed us how to lift the front legs of the machine in just the right way so that the machine would run up a big score without tilting, enough for ten or so free games, all by itself. After it did that, he told us, you could go ahead and really play it for fun. Jay and Jack were pretty impressed; they thought this dumb kid was a genius. Those big kids in your school sure are smart, was how Jack put it.

Well, as Jay and Jack happily set out to strike out and pop-up to the infield on the machine for those free games, the dumb kid and I walked around and watched the bowlers and had a smoke and talked. In the end, of course, I asked him what he was doing around there. He was getting ready to go to work, he told me. Fooling around until five, when he started. What did he do? I keep score, he told me. For the leagues. He kept score for two teams at once. He made fifteen bucks for a couple of hours. He thought it was a great job, making fifteen bucks for something he liked to do anyway, perhaps would have done for nothing, just to be able to do it.

He was keeping score. Two teams, four people on each, eight bowling scores at once. Adding quickly, not making any mistakes (for no one was going to put up with errors), following the rather complicated process of scoring in the game of bowling. Get a spare, score ten plus whatever you get on the next ball, score a strike, then ten plus whatever you get on the next two balls; imagine the man gets three strikes in a row and two spares and you are the scorer, plus you are dealing with seven other guys all striking or sparing or neither one . . . The bowling league is not a welfare organization nor part of Headstart or anything like that and wasn't interested in giving some dumb kid a chance to improve himself by fucking up their bowling scores. No, they were giving this smart kid who had proved to be fast and accurate fifteen dollars because they could use a good scorer.

I figured I had this particular dumb kid now. Back in eighth period I lectured him on how smart he was to be a league scorer in bowling. I pried admissions from the other boys, about how they had paper routes and made change. I made the girls confess that when they went to buy stuff they didn't have any difficulty deciding if those shoes cost $10.95 or whether it meant $109.50 or whether it meant $1.09 or how much change they'd get back from a twenty. Naturally I then handed out bowling-score problems and paper-route change-making problems and buying-shoes problems, and naturally everyone could choose which ones they wanted to solve, and naturally the result was that all the dumb kids immediately rushed me yelling Is this right? I don't know how to do it! What's the answer? This ain't right, is it? and What's my grade? The girls who bought shoes for $10.95 with a $20 bill came up with $400.15 for change and wanted to know if that was right? The brilliant league scorer couldn't decide whether two strikes and a third frame of eight amounted to eighteen or twenty-eight or whether it was one hundred eight and one half.

The reason they can't learn is because they are the dumb class. No other reason. Is adding difficult? No. It is the dumb class which is difficult. Are the teachers a dumb class? Well, we are supposed to teach kids to "read, write, cipher and sing," according to an old phrase. Can we do it?

Mostly not. Is it difficult? Not at all. We can't do it because we are a dumb class, which by definition can't do it, whatever it is.

Yet what we are supposed to do is something which, like adding, everyone knows how to do. It isn't mysterious, nor dependent on a vast and intricate knowledge of pedagogy or technology or psychological tests or rats. Is there any man or woman on earth who knows how to read who doesn't feel quite capable of teaching his own child or children to read? Doesn't every father feel confident that his boy will come into the bathroom every morning to stand around and watch while the father shaves and play number games with the father and learn about numbers and shaving at the same time? Every person not in the dumb class feels that these things are simple. Want to know about Egypt? Mother or father or older brother or uncle or someone and the kid go down to the public library and get out a book on Egypt and the kid reads it and perhaps the uncle reads it too, and while they are shaving they may talk about Egypt. But the dumb class of teachers and public educators feel that these things are very difficult, and they must keep hiring experts and devising strategies in order that they can rush these experts and strategies with their papers asking Is this right? and What's my grade?

Yet, released from the dumb class to their private lives, teachers are marvelous gardeners, they work on ocean liners as engineers, they act in plays, win bets, go to art movies, build their own houses, they are opera fans, expert fishermen, champion skeet shooters, grand golfers, organ players, oratorio singers, hunters, mechanics . . . all just as if they were smart people. Of course it is more difficult to build a house or sing Bach than it is to teach kids to read. Of course if they operated in their lives outside of the dumb class the same way they do in it, their houses would fall down, their ships would sink, their flowers die, their cars blow up.

This very morning in the San Francisco *Chronicle* I read a scandalous report. The reporter reports the revelations of a member of the board of education, namely that 45 per cent of the *Spanish-surname children* (that is how we put it in the paper these days) who are in mentally retarded classes have been found, when retested in Spanish, to be of average or above-average intelligence. The board member thought that "the Spanish-speaking kids were shunted into classes for the mentally retarded because they did not understand English well enough to pass the examinations they were given." He figured that, just like if he was told that a bowler had a spare on the first frame and got eight on his next ball, he'd figure that the bowler's score in the first frame ought to be eighteen. Well, in this matter assume that the board member is the teacher in a dumb class. He's trying to tell the school administrator something obvious. Does the administrator learn, now he's been told it, that ten and eight are eighteen? No, the assistant superintendent for special services says that "the assumption was that they understood English well enough to be tested by the English versions of the Stanford-Binet and the WISC intelligence tests." He thought that "it wasn't so much the fault of the test as it was the cultural deprivation of the child at the time of testing" which caused these smart kids to be retarded. Asked if these smart retarded Spanish-surname kids were now going to be moved into the regular program, he *revealed* that no, that wasn't the case, for they were *"still working* with the elementary division to seek a proper *transitional* program, since these children were still *functional retardates"* no matter what their IQ.

The reporter, acting in his role as critical parent, found out that the tests *were* available in Spanish but that Spanish-speaking kids *weren't* tested, therefore, in Spanish (because of the above assumption). The tests *weren't* available in "Oriental," and the "Oriental" kids *weren't* tested, therefore, in "Oriental." Well, that made sense, so the reporter pried out the information that the school district got $550 extra a year for each kid in mentally retarded classes. The reporter implied cynically that they were doing it for the money and that if they let all these bright retarded Spanish kids out there might be a shortage of $550 kids to be retarded.

But it is the dumb class we are concerned with. Here this administrator is told something obvious, told to learn it, told to achieve this difficult knowledge that them Spanish-speaking kids are only dumb if they are tested in a language they don't understand. But being in the dumb class, he don't learn it. He may be the smartest man in the world, able to keep score for league bowling, read The Book of the Dead, go water skiing, make bell curves. But in the dumb class he can't learn anything, and there is no reason to expect that he ever will as long as he is in there.

The
Good
Life

What is the good life? is one of the oldest of human questions. Often the attempt to achieve the good life is indistinguishable from the effort to find out what it is. When people are struggling to stay alive in the face of danger or poverty, the question seems to have an easy answer; then the good life means safety or food. But once we have that, once we pass from survival or subsistence to a range of wider possibilities, the question takes on new meaning. Is the good life a life of plenty and ease, of asceticism and withdrawal, or of commitment and service?

When we move into the state of comparative affluence enjoyed by many Americans, the question can become a nagging problem: now that you have it made, are you really happy? Phyllis McGinley appreciates the freedom and solidity of the middle-class suburban life she knows, and deplores the fashionable clichés that make it "a symbol of all that is middle-class in the worst sense." Joan Didion describes suburbia as a different world. Her reportage of a murder trial in southern California paints a devastating picture of the Golden Dream of material comfort and status, here with no past or future, devoid of meaning and value. Walter Lippmann's short piece, following, explores the seeming paradox that historically the good life is achieved not by seeking more but by seeking less: "without renunciation of many of the ordinary appetites, no man can really live well."

The next three pieces are autobiographical and describe alternative life styles deliberately chosen. Thomas Merton lives almost a hermit's life in the woods; Judith Beth Cohen describes buying, restoring, and living on a Vermont farm; and Judson Jerome talks first about his reasons for moving to a commune and then about some of his experiences there. They chronicle concrete daily existence in accounts that are neither romanticized nor sentimentalized: in showing the search for "the best use of life," they do not omit the hard spots.

Kit Havice's letter, following, shows the struggles and satisfactions that come from commitment and concern, while Studs Terkel lets us hear the voice of a man who loves and lives his work. We conclude the section with a simple but eloquent story, by Isaac Bashevis Singer, that shows what can happen when American-style "success" confronts the security of long-standing tradition.

PHYLLIS McGINLEY

Phyllis McGinley received the Pulitzer Prize for poetry in 1961 for Times Three: Selected Verse from Three Decades; *she was the first writer of light verse to win that award. Born in 1905, she spent her childhood on a Colorado ranch and then went through high school and college in Ogden, Utah. She studied at the University of Southern California but returned to graduate from the University of Utah and to teach school for a year in Ogden. In 1928 she moved to New Rochelle, New York, where she taught school for four years, then moved to Manhattan and turned to free-lance writing. After her marriage in 1937, she lived in the New York suburb of Larchmont and later in Weston, Connecticut.*

Her first book of poetry was On the Contrary *(1934); others, besides* Times Three, *include* A Pocketful of Wry *(1940),* A Short Walk from the Station *(1951),* The Love Letters of Phyllis McGinley *(1954), and* Wonders and Surprises *(1968). Her prose works include* Saint Watching *(1969), the autobiographical* Sixpence in Her Shoe *(1964), children's books, and* The Province of the Heart *(1959), a collection of essays from which we have taken "Suburbia, of Thee I Sing." She wrote it, she says, in response to John Marquand, who had been "wittily naming and then demolishing in print the village where I lived and shopped for grapefruit and attended library meetings and weeded dandelions and composed my poems. I felt I knew that village better than he, and that it was not at all the dreary stronghold of mediocrity which he pictured, but a lively, interesting, and desirable dwelling-place. I felt it ought to be defended."*

Suburbia, of Thee I Sing

Twenty miles east of New York City as the New Haven Railroad flies sits a village I shall call Spruce Manor. The Boston Post Road, there, for the length of two blocks, becomes Main Street, and on one side of that thundering thoroughfare are the grocery stores and the drug stores and the Village Spa where teen-agers gather of an afternoon to drink their Cokes and speak their curious confidences. There one finds the shoe repairers and the dry cleaners and the second-hand stores which sell "antiques," and the stationery stores which dispense comic books to ten-year-olds and greeting cards and lending-library masterpieces to their mothers. On the opposite side stand the bank, the fire house, the public library. The rest of this town of perhaps five or six thousand people lies to the south and is bounded largely by Long Island Sound, curving

protectively on three borders. The movie theater (dedicated to the showing of second-run, single-feature pictures) and the grade schools lie
north, beyond the Post Road, and that is a source of worry to Spruce
Manorites. They are always a little uneasy about the children, crossing,
perhaps, before the lights are safely green. However, two excellent policemen—Mr. Crowley and Mr. Lang—station themselves at the intersec-
tions four times a day, and so far there have been no accidents.

Spruce Manor in the spring and summer and fall is a pretty town, full
of gardens and old elms. (There are few spruces but the village council
is considering planting some on the station plaza, out of sheer patriotism.) In the winter, the houses reveal themselves as comfortable, well
kept, architecturally insignificant. Then one can see the town for what it
is and has been since it left off being farm and woodland some sixty years
ago—the epitome of Suburbia, not the country and certainly not the city.
It is a commuter's town, the living center of a web which unrolls each
morning as the men swing aboard the locals, and contracts again in the
evening when they return. By day, with even the children pent in schools,
it is a village of women. They trundle mobile baskets at the A & P, they
sit under driers at the hairdressers, they sweep their porches and set out
bulbs and stitch up slipcovers. Only on week ends does it become hetero-
geneous and lively, the parking places difficult to find.

Spruce Manor has no country club of its own, though devoted golfers
have their choice of two or three not far away. It does have a small yacht
club and a beach which can be used by anyone who rents or owns a house
here. The village supports a little park with playground equipment and
a counselor, where children, unattended by parents, can spend summer
days if they have no more pressing engagements.

It is a town not wholly without traditions. Residents will point out the
two-hundred-year-old Manor house, now a minor museum; and in the
autumn they line the streets on a scheduled evening to watch the volun-
teer firemen parade. That is a fine occasion, with so many heads of
households marching in their red blouses and white gloves, some with
flaming helmets, some swinging lanterns, most of them genially out of
step. There is a bigger parade on Memorial Day, with more marchers than
watchers and with the Catholic priest, the rabbi, and the Protestant ministers each delivering a short prayer when the paraders gather near the war
memorial. On the whole, however, outside of contributing generously to
the Community Chest, Manorites are not addicted to municipal get-
togethers.

No one is very poor here and not many families rich enough to be
awesome. In fact, there is not much to distinguish Spruce Manor from any
other of a thousand suburbs outside of New York City or San Francisco
or Detroit or Chicago or even Stockholm, for that matter. Except for one
thing. For some reason, Spruce Manor has become a sort of symbol to
writers and reporters familiar only with its name or trivial aspects. It has
become a symbol of all that is middle-class in the worst sense, of settled-

downness or rootlessness, according to what the writer is trying to prove; of smug and prosperous mediocrity—or even, in more lurid novels, of lechery at the country club and Sunday-morning hangovers.

To condemn Suburbia has long been a literary cliché, anyhow. I have yet to read a book in which the suburban life was pictured as the good life or the commuter as a sympathetic figure. He is nearly as much a stock character as the old stage Irishman: the man who "spends his life riding to and from his wife," the eternal Babbitt who knows all about Buicks and nothing about Picasso, whose sanctuary is the club locker room, whose ideas spring ready-made from the illiberal newspapers. His wife plays politics at the P.T.A. and keeps up with the Joneses. Or—if the scene is more gilded and less respectable—the commuter is the high-powered advertising executive with a station wagon and an eye for the ladies, his wife a restless baggage given to too many cocktails in the afternoon.

These clichés I challenge. I have lived in the country. I have lived in the city. I have lived in an average Middle Western small town. But for the best fifteen years of my life I have lived in Suburbia, and I like it.

"Compromise!" cried our friends when we came here from an expensive, inconvenient, moderately fashionable tenement in Manhattan. It was the period in our lives when everyone was moving somewhere— farther uptown, farther downtown, across town to Sutton Place, to a half-dozen rural acres in Connecticut or New Jersey or even Vermont. But no one in our rather rarefied little group was thinking of moving to the suburbs except us. They were aghast that we could find anything appealing in the thought of a middle-class house on a middle-class street in a middle-class village full of middle-class people. That we were tired of town and hoped for children, that we couldn't afford both a city apartment and a farm, they put down as feeble excuses. To this day they cannot understand us. You see, they read the books. They even write them.

Compromise? Of course we compromise. But compromise, if not the spice of life, is its solidity. It is what makes nations great and marriages happy and Spruce Manor the pleasant place it is. As for its being middle-class, what is wrong with acknowledging one's roots? And how free we are! Free of the city's noise, of its ubiquitous doormen, of the soot on the window sill and the radio in the next apartment. We have released ourselves from the seasonal hegira to the mountains or the seashore. We have only one address, one house to keep supplied with paring knives and blankets. We are free from the snows that block the countryman's roads in winter and his electricity which always goes off in a thunderstorm. I do not insist that we are typical. There is nothing really typical about any of our friends and neighbors here, and therein lies my point. The true suburbanite needs to conform less than anyone else; much less than the gentleman farmer with his remodeled salt-box or than the determined cliff-dweller with his necessity for living at the right address. In Spruce Manor all addresses are right. And since we are fairly numerous here, we need not fall back on the people nearest us for total companionship. There is not here, as in a small city away from truly urban centers, some particular family whose codes must be ours. And we could not keep up with the Joneses even if we wanted to, for we know many Joneses and they are all quite different people leading the most various lives.

The Albert Joneses spend their week ends sailing, the Bertram Joneses cultivate their delphinium, the Clarence Joneses—Clarence being a handy man with a cello—are enthusiastic about amateur chamber music. The David Joneses dote on bridge, but neither of the Ernest Joneses understands it and they prefer staying home of an evening so that Ernest Jones can carve his witty caricatures out of pieces of old fruit wood. We admire one another's gardens, applaud one another's sailing records; we are too busy to compete. So long as our clapboards are painted and our hedges decently trimmed, we have fulfilled our community obligations. We can live as anonymously as in a city or we can call half the village by their first names.

On our half-acre or three-quarters, we can raise enough tomatoes for our salads and assassinate enough beetles to satisfy the gardening urge. Or we can buy our vegetables at the store and put the whole place to lawn without feeling that we are neglecting our property. We can have privacy and shade and the changing of the seasons and also the Joneses next door from whom to borrow a cup of sugar or a stepladder. Despite the novelists, the shadow of the country club rests lightly on us. Half of us wouldn't be found dead with a golf stick in our hands, and loathe Saturday dances. Few of us expect to be deliriously wealthy or world-famous or divorced. What we do expect is to pay off the mortgage and send our healthy children to good colleges.

For when I refer to life here, I think, of course, of living with children. Spruce Manor without children would be a paradox. The summer waters are full of them, gamboling like dolphins. The lanes are alive with them, the yards overflow with them, they possess the tennis courts and the skating pond and the vacant lots. Their roller skates wear down the asphalt and their bicycles make necessary the twenty-five-mile speed limit. They converse interminably on the telephones and make rich the dentist and the pediatrician. Who claims that a child and a half is the American middle-class average? A nice medium Spruce Manor family runs to four or five, and we count proudly, but not with amazement, the many solid households running to six, seven, eight, nine, even up to twelve. Our houses here are big and not new, most of them, and there is a temptation to fill them up, let the *décor* fall where it may.

Besides, Spruce Manor seems designed by Providence and town planning for the happiness of children. Better designed than the city; better, I say defiantly, than the country. Country mothers must be constantly arranging and contriving for their children's leisure time. There is no neighbor child next door for playmate, no school within walking distance. The ponds are dangerous to young swimmers, the woods full of poison ivy, the romantic dirt roads unsuitable for bicycles. An extra acre or two gives a fine sense of possession to an adult; it does not compensate children for the give-and-take of our village, where there is always a contemporary to help swing the skipping rope or put on the catcher's mitt. Where in the country is the Friday-evening dancing class or the Saturday-morning movie (approved by the P.T.A.)? It is the greatest fallacy of all time that children love the country as a year-around plan. Children would take a dusty corner of Washington Square or a city sidewalk, even, in preference to the lonely sermons in stones and books in running brooks which their contemporaries cannot share.

As for the horrors of bringing up progeny in the city, for all its museums and other cultural advantages (so perfectly within reach of suburban families if they feel strongly about it), they were summed up for me one day last winter. The harried mother of one, speaking to me on the telephone just after Christmas, sighed and said, "It's been a really wonderful time for me, as vacations go. Barbara has had an engagement with a child in our apartment house every afternoon this week. I have had to take her almost nowhere." Barbara is eleven. For six of those eleven years, I realized, her mother must have dreaded Christmas vacation, not to mention spring, as a time when Barbara had to be entertained. I thought thankfully of my own daughters, whom I had scarcely seen since school closed, out with their skis and their sleds and their friends, sliding down the roped-off hill half a block away, coming in hungrily for lunch and disappearing again, hearty, amused, and safe—at least as safe as any sled-borne child can be.

Spruce Manor is not Eden, of course. Our taxes are higher than we like, and there is always that 8:02 in the morning to be caught, and we sometimes resent the necessity of rushing from a theater to a train on a weekday evening. But the taxes pay for our really excellent schools and for our garbage collections (so that the pails of orange peels need not stand in the halls overnight as ours did in the city) and for our water supply, which does not give out every dry summer as it frequently does in the country. As for the theaters—they are twenty miles away and we don't get to them more than twice a month. But neither, I think, do many of our friends in town. The 8:02 is rather a pleasant train, too, say the husbands; it gets them to work in thirty-four minutes, and they read the papers restfully on the way.

"But the suburban mind!" cry our diehard friends in Manhattan and Connecticut. "The suburban conversation! The monotony!" They imply that they and I must scintillate or we perish. Let me anatomize Spruce Manor, for them and for the others who envision Suburbia as a congregation of mindless housewives and amoral go-getters.

From my window, now, on a June morning, I have a view. It contains neither solitary hills nor dramatic skyscrapers. But I can see my roses in bloom, and my foxglove, and an arch of trees over the lane. I think comfortably of my friends whose houses line this and other streets rather like it. Not one of them is, so far as I know, doing any of the things that suburban ladies are popularly supposed to be doing. One of them, I happen to know, has gone bowling for her health and figure, but she has already tidied up her house and arranged to be home before the boys return from school. Some, undoubtedly, are ferociously busy in the garden. One lady is on her way to Ellis Island, bearing comfort and gifts to a Polish boy—a seventeen-year-old stowaway who did slave labor in Germany and was liberated by a cousin of hers during the war—who is being held for attempting to attain the land of which her cousin told him. The boy has been on the island for three months. Twice a week she takes this tedious journey, meanwhile besieging courts and immigration authorities on his behalf. This lady has a large house, a part-time maid, and five children.

My friend around the corner is finishing her third novel. She writes daily from nine-thirty until two. After that her son comes back from school and she plunges into maternity; at six she combs her pretty hair, refreshes her lipstick, and is charming to her doctor husband. The village dancing school is run by another neighbor, as it has been for twenty years. She has sent a number of ballerinas on to the theatrical world as well as having shepherded for many a successful season the white-gloved little boys and full-skirted little girls through their first social tasks.

Some of the ladies are no doubt painting their kitchens or a nursery; one of them is painting the portrait, on assignment, of a very distinguished personage. Some of them are nurses' aides and Red Cross workers and supporters of good causes. But all find time to be friends with their families and to meet the 5:32 five nights a week. They read something besides the newest historical novel, Braque is not unidentifiable to most of them, and their conversation is for the most part as agreeable as the tables they set. The tireless bridge players, the gossips, the women bored by their husbands live perhaps in our suburb, too. Let them. Our orbits need not cross.

And what of the husbands, industriously selling bonds or practicing law or editing magazines or looking through microscopes or managing offices in the city? Do they spend their evenings and their week ends in the gaudy bars of 52nd Street? Or are they the perennial householders, their lives a dreary round of taking down screens and mending drains? Well, screens they have always with them, and a man who is good around the house can spend happy hours with the plumbing even on a South Sea island. Some of them cut their own lawns and some of them try to break par and some of them sail their little boats all summer with their families for crew. Some of them are village trustees for nothing a year, and some listen to symphonies, and some think Steve Allen ought to be President. There is a scientist who plays wonderful bebop, and an insurance salesman who has bought a big old house nearby and with his own hands is gradually tearing it apart and reshaping it nearer to his heart's desire. Some of them are passionate hedge-clippers, and some read Plutarch for fun. But I do not know many—though there may be such—who either kiss their neighbors' wives behind doors or whose idea of sprightly talk is to tell you the plot of an old movie.

It is June, now, as I have said. This afternoon my daughters will come home from school with a crowd of their peers at their heels. They will eat up the cookies and drink up the ginger ale and go down for a swim at the beach if the water is warm enough, that beach which is only three blocks away and open to all Spruce Manor. They will go unattended by me, since they have been swimming since they were four, and besides there are life guards and no big waves. (Even our piece of ocean is a compromise.) Presently it will be time for us to climb into our very old Studebaker— we are not car-proud in Spruce Manor—and meet the 5:32. That evening expedition is not vitally necessary, for a bus runs straight down our principal avenue from the station to the shore, and it meets all trains. But it is an event we enjoy. There is something delightfully ritualistic about the moment when the train pulls in and the men swing off, with the less sophisticated children running squealing to meet them. The women move over from the driver's seat, surrender the keys, and receive an absent-minded kiss. It is the sort of picture that wakes John Marquand screaming from his sleep. But, deluded people that we are, we do not realize how mediocre it all seems. We will eat our undistinguished meal, probably without even a cocktail to enliven it. We will drink our coffee at the table, not carry it into the living room; if a husband changes for dinner here it is into old and spotty trousers and more comfortable shoes. The children will then go through the regular childhood routine—complain about their homework, grumble about going to bed, and finally accomplish both ordeals. Perhaps later the Gerard Joneses will drop in. We will talk a great deal of unimportant chatter and compare notes on food prices; we will also discuss the headlines and disagree. (Some of us in the Manor are Republicans, some are Democrats, a few lean plainly leftward. There are probably anti-Semites and anti-Catholics and even anti-Americans. Most of us are merely anti-antis.) We will all have one highball and the Joneses will leave early. Tomorrow and tomorrow and tomorrow the pattern will be repeated. This is Suburbia.

But I think that some day people will look back on our little interval here, on our Spruce Manor way of life, as we now look back on the Currier and Ives kind of living, with nostalgia and respect. In a world of terrible extremes, it will stand out as the safe, important medium.

Suburbia, of thee I sing!

JOAN DIDION

This essay is taken from Joan Didion's collection Slouching Towards Bethlehem *(1968). For further information about the author, see page 191.*

Some Dreamers of the Golden Dream

This is a story about love and death in the golden land, and begins with the country. The San Bernardino Valley lies only an hour east of Los Angeles by the San Bernardino Freeway but is in certain ways an alien place: not the coastal California of the subtropical twilights and the soft westerlies off the Pacific but a harsher California, haunted by the Mojave just beyond the mountains, devastated by the hot dry Santa Ana wind that comes down through the passes at 100 miles an hour and whines through the eucalyptus windbreaks and works on the nerves. October is the bad month for the wind, the month when breathing is difficult and the hills blaze up spontaneously. There has been no rain since April. Every voice seems a scream. It is the season of suicide and divorce and prickly dread, wherever the wind blows.

The Mormons settled this ominous country, and then they abandoned it, but by the time they left the first orange tree had been planted and for the next hundred years the San Bernardino Valley would draw a kind of people who imagined they might live among the talismanic fruit and prosper in the dry air, people who brought with them Midwestern ways of building and cooking and praying and who tried to graft those ways upon the land. The graft took in curious ways. This is the California where it is possible to live and die without ever eating an artichoke, without ever meeting a Catholic or a Jew. This is the California where it is easy to Dial-A-Devotion, but hard to buy a book. This is the country in which a belief in the literal interpretation of Genesis has slipped imperceptibly into a belief in the literal interpretation of *Double Indemnity,* the country of the teased hair and the Capris and the girls for whom all life's promise comes down to a waltz-length white wedding dress and the birth of a Kimberly or a Sherry or a Debbi and a Tijuana divorce and a return to hairdressers' school. "We were just crazy kids," they say without regret, and look to the future. The future always looks good in the golden land, because no one remembers the past. Here is where the hot wind blows and the old ways do not seem relevant, where the divorce rate is double the national average and where one person in every thirty-eight lives in a trailer. Here is the last stop for all those who come from somewhere else, for all those who drifted away from the cold and the past and the old ways. Here is where they are trying to find a new life style, trying to find it in the only places they know to look: the movies and the newspapers. The case of Lucille Marie Maxwell Miller is a tabloid monument to that new life style.

Imagine Banyan Street first, because Banyan is where it happened. The way to Banyan is to drive west from San Bernardino out Foothill Boulevard, Route 66: past the Santa Fe switching yards, the Forty Winks Motel. Past the motel that is nineteen stucco tepees: "SLEEP IN A WIGWAM —GET MORE FOR YOUR WAMPUM." Past Fontana Drag City and the Fontana Church of the Nazarene and the Pit Stop A Go-Go; past Kaiser Steel, through Cucamonga, out to the Kapu Kai Restaurant-Bar and Coffee Shop, at the corner of Route 66 and Carnelian Avenue. Up Carnelian Avenue from the Kapu Kai, which means "Forbidden Seas," the subdivision flags whip in the harsh wind. "HALF-ACRE RANCHES! SNACK BARS! TRAVERTINE ENTRIES! $95 DOWN." It is the trail of an intention gone haywire, the flotsam of the New California. But after a while the signs thin out on Carnelian Avenue, and the houses are no longer the bright pastels of the Springtime Home owners but the faded bungalows of the people who grow a few grapes and keep a few chickens out here, and then the hill gets steeper and the road climbs and even the bungalows are few, and here—desolate, roughly surfaced, lined with eucalyptus and lemon groves—is Banyan Street.

Like so much of this country, Banyan suggests something curious and unnatural. The lemon groves are sunken, down a three- or four-foot retaining wall, so that one looks directly into their dense foliage, too lush, unsettlingly glossy, the greenery of nightmare; the fallen eucalyptus bark is too dusty, a place for snakes to breed. The stones look not like natural stones but like the rubble of some unmentioned upheaval. There are smudge pots, and a closed cistern. To one side of Banyan there is the flat valley, and to the other the San Bernardino Mountains, a dark mass looming too high, too fast, nine, ten, eleven thousand feet, right there above the lemon groves. At midnight on Banyan Street there is no light at all, and no sound except the wind in the eucalyptus and a muffled barking of dogs. There may be a kennel somewhere, or the dogs may be coyotes.

Banyan Street was the route Lucille Miller took home from the twenty-four-hour Mayfair Market on the night of October 7, 1964, a night when the moon was dark and the wind was blowing and she was out of milk, and Banyan Street was where, at about 12:20 a.m., her 1964 Volkswagen came to a sudden stop, caught fire, and began to burn. For an hour and fifteen minutes Lucille Miller ran up and down Banyan calling for help, but no cars passed and no help came. At three o'clock that morning, when the fire had been put out and the California Highway Patrol officers were completing their report, Lucille Miller was still sobbing and incoherent, for her husband had been asleep in the Volkswagen. "What will I tell the

children, when there's nothing left, nothing left in the casket," she cried
to the friend called to comfort her. "How can I tell them there's nothing
left?"

In fact there was something left, and a week later it lay in the Draper
Mortuary Chapel in a closed bronze coffin blanketed with pink carna-
tions. Some 200 mourners heard Elder Robert E. Denton of the Seventh-
Day Adventist Church of Ontario speak of "the temper of fury that has
broken out among us." For Gordon Miller, he said, there would be "no
more death, no more heartaches, no more misunderstandings." Elder
Ansel Bristol mentioned the "peculiar" grief of the hour. Elder Fred
Jensen asked "what shall it profit a man, if he shall gain the whole world,
and lose his own soul?" A light rain fell, a blessing in a dry season, and
a female vocalist sang "Safe in the Arms of Jesus." A tape recording of
the service was made for the widow, who was being held without bail in
the San Bernardino County Jail on a charge of first-degree murder.

Of course she came from somewhere else, came off the prairie in
search of something she had seen in a movie or heard on the radio, for
this is a Southern California story. She was born on January 17, 1930, in
Winnipeg, Manitoba, the only child of Gordon and Lily Maxwell, both
schoolteachers and both dedicated to the Seventh-Day Adventist Church,
whose members observe the Sabbath on Saturday, believe in an apocalyptic Second Coming, have a strong missionary tendency, and, if they are
strict, do not smoke, drink, eat meat, use makeup, or wear jewelry, including wedding rings. By the time Lucille Maxwell enrolled at Walla Walla
College in College Place, Washington, the Adventist school where her
parents then taught, she was an eighteen-year-old possessed of unremarkable good looks and remarkable high spirits. "Lucille wanted to see
the world," her father would say in retrospect, "and I guess she found
out."

The high spirits did not seem to lend themselves to an extended
course of study at Walla Walla College, and in the spring of 1949 Lucille
Maxwell met and married Gordon ("Cork") Miller, a twenty-four-year-
old graduate of Walla Walla and of the University of Oregon dental
school, then stationed at Fort Lewis as a medical officer. "Maybe you
could say it was love at first sight," Mr. Maxwell recalls. "Before they were
ever formally introduced, he sent Lucille a dozen and a half roses with
a card that said even if she didn't come out on a date with him, he hoped
she'd find the roses pretty anyway." The Maxwells remember their
daughter as a "radiant" bride.

Unhappy marriages so resemble one another that we do not need to
know too much about the course of this one. There may or may not have
been trouble on Guam, where Cork and Lucille Miller lived while he
finished his Army duty. There may or may not have been problems in the
small Oregon town where he first set up private practice. There appears
to have been some disappointment about their move to California: Cork

Miller had told friends that he wanted to become a doctor, that he was unhappy as a dentist and planned to enter the Seventh-Day Adventist College of Medical Evangelists at Loma Linda, a few miles south of San Bernardino. Instead he bought a dental practice in the west end of San Bernardino County, and the family settled there, in a modest house on the kind of street where there are always tricycles and revolving credit and dreams about bigger houses, better streets. That was 1957. By the summer of 1964 they had achieved the bigger house on the better street and the family accouterments of a family on its way up: the $30,000 a year, the three children for the Christmas card, the picture window, the family room, the newspaper photographs that showed "Mrs. Gordon Miller, Ontario Heart Fund Chairman. . . ." They were paying the familiar price for it. And they had reached the familiar season of divorce.

It might have been anyone's bad summer, anyone's siege of heat and nerves and migraine and money worries, but this one began particularly early and particularly badly. On April 24 an old friend, Elaine Hayton, died suddenly; Lucille Miller had seen her only the night before. During the month of May, Cork Miller was hospitalized briefly with a bleeding ulcer, and his usual reserve deepened into depression. He told his accountant that he was "sick of looking at open mouths," and threatened suicide. By July 8, the conventional tensions of love and money had reached the conventional impasse in the new house on the acre lot of 8488 Bella Vista, and Lucille Miller filed for divorce. Within a month, however, the Millers seemed reconciled. They saw a marriage counselor. They talked about a fourth child. It seemed that the marriage had reached the traditional truce, the point at which so many resign themselves to cutting both their losses and their hopes.

But the Millers' season of trouble was not to end that easily. October 7 began as a commonplace enough day, one of those days that sets the teeth on edge with its tedium, its small frustrations. The temperature reached 102° in San Bernardino that afternoon, and the Miller children were home from school because of Teachers' Institute. There was ironing to be dropped off. There was a trip to pick up a prescription for Nembutal, a trip to a self-service dry cleaner. In the early evening, an unpleasant accident with the Volkswagen: Cork Miller hit and killed a German shepherd, and afterward said that his head felt "like it had a Mack truck on it." It was something he often said. As of that evening Cork Miller was $63,479 in debt, including the $29,637 mortgage on the new house, a debt load which seemed oppressive to him. He was a man who wore his responsibilities uneasily, and complained of migraine headaches almost constantly.

He ate alone that night, from a TV tray in the living room. Later the Millers watched John Forsythe and Senta Berger in *See How They Run,* and when the movie ended, about eleven, Cork Miller suggested that they go out for milk. He wanted some hot chocolate. He took a blanket and pillow from the couch and climbed into the passenger seat of the Volkswagen.

Lucille Miller remembers reaching over to lock his door as she backed down the driveway. By the time she left the Mayfair Market, and long before they reached Banyan Street, Cork Miller appeared to be asleep.

There is some confusion in Lucille Miller's mind about what happened between 12:30 a.m., when the fire broke out, and 1:50 a.m., when it was reported. She says that she was driving east on Banyan Street at about 35 m.p.h. when she felt the Volkswagen pull sharply to the right. The next thing she knew the car was on the embankment, quite near the edge of the retaining wall, and flames were shooting up behind her. She does not remember jumping out. She does remember prying up a stone with which she broke the window next to her husband, and then scrambling down the retaining wall to try to find a stick. "I don't know how I was going to push him out," she says. "I just thought if I had a stick, I'd push him out." She could not, and after a while she ran to the intersection of Banyan and Carnelian Avenue. There are no houses at that corner, and almost no traffic. After one car had passed without stopping, Lucille Miller ran back down Banyan toward the burning Volkswagen. She did not stop, but she slowed down, and in the flames she could see her husband. He was, she said, "just black."

At the first house up Sapphire Avenue, half a mile from the Volkswagen, Lucille Miller finally found help. There Mrs. Robert Swenson called the sheriff, and then, at Lucille Miller's request, she called Harold Lance, the Millers' lawyer and their close friend. When Harold Lance arrived he took Lucille Miller home to his wife, Joan. Twice Harold Lance and Lucille Miller returned to Banyan Street and talked to the Highway Patrol officers. A third time Harold Lance returned alone, and when he came back he said to Lucille Miller, "O.K. . . . you don't talk any more."

When Lucille Miller was arrested the next afternoon, Sandy Slagle was with her. Sandy Slagle was the intense, relentlessly loyal medical student who used to baby-sit for the Millers, and had been living as a member of the family since she graduated from high school in 1959. The Millers took her away from a difficult home situation, and she thinks of Lucille Miller not only as "more or less a mother or a sister" but as "the most wonderful character" she has ever known. On the night of the accident, Sandy Slagle was in her dormitory at Loma Linda University, but Lucille Miller called her early in the morning and asked her to come home. The doctor was there when Sandy Slagle arrived, giving Lucille Miller an injection of Nembutal. "She was crying as she was going under," Sandy Slagle recalls. "Over and over she'd say, 'Sandy, all the hours I spent trying to save him and now what are they trying to *do* to me?'"

At 1:30 that afternoon, Sergeant William Paterson and Detectives Charles Callahan and Joseph Karr of the Central Homicide Division arrived at 8488 Bella Vista. "One of them appeared at the bedroom door," Sandy Slagle remembers, "and said to Lucille, 'You've got ten minutes to get dressed or we'll take you as you are.' She was in her nightgown, you know, so I tried to get her dressed."

Sandy Slagle tells the story now as if by rote, and her eyes do not waver. "So I had her panties and bra on her and they opened the door again, so I got some Capris on her, you know, and a scarf." Her voice drops. "And then they just took her."

The arrest took place just twelve hours after the first report that there had been an accident on Banyan Street, a rapidity which would later prompt Lucille Miller's attorney to say that the entire case was an instance of trying to justify a reckless arrest. Actually what first caused the detectives who arrived on Banyan Street toward dawn that morning to give the accident more than routine attention were certain apparent physical inconsistencies. While Lucille Miller had said that she was driving about 35 m.p.h. when the car swerved to a stop, an examination of the cooling Volkswagen showed that it was in low gear, and that the parking rather than the driving lights were on. The front wheels, moreover, did not seem to be in exactly the position that Lucille Miller's description of the accident would suggest, and the right rear wheel was dug in deep, as if it had been spun in place. It seemed curious to the detectives, too, that a sudden stop from 35 m.p.h.—the same jolt which was presumed to have knocked over a gasoline can in the back seat and somehow started the fire—should have left two milk cartons upright on the back floorboard, and the remains of a Polaroid camera box lying apparently undisturbed on the back seat.

No one, however, could be expected to give a precise account of what did and did not happen in a moment of terror, and none of these inconsistencies seemed in themselves incontrovertible evidence of criminal intent. But they did interest the Sheriff's Office, as did Gordon Miller's apparent unconsciousness at the time of the accident, and the length of time it had taken Lucille Miller to get help. Something, moreover, struck the investigators as wrong about Harold Lance's attitude when he came back to Banyan Street the third time and found the investigation by no means over. "The way Lance was acting," the prosecuting attorney said later, "they thought maybe they'd hit a nerve."

And so it was that on the morning of October 8, even before the doctor had come to give Lucille Miller an injection to calm her, the San Bernardino County Sheriff's Office was trying to construct another version of what might have happened between 12:30 and 1:50 a.m. The hypothesis they would eventually present was based on the somewhat tortuous premise that Lucille Miller had undertaken a plan which failed: a plan to stop the car on the lonely road, spread gasoline over her presumably drugged husband, and, with a stick on the accelerator, gently "walk" the Volkswagen over the embankment, where it would tumble four feet down the retaining wall into the lemon grove and almost certainly explode. If this happened, Lucille Miller might then have somehow negotiated the two miles up Carnelian to Bella Vista in time to be home when the accident was discovered. This plan went awry, according to the Sheriff's Office hypothesis, when the car would not go over the rise of the embankment. Lucille Miller might have panicked then—after she had killed the engine the third or fourth time, say, out there on the dark road with the gasoline already spread and the dogs baying and the wind blowing and the unspeakable apprehension that a pair of headlights would suddenly light up Banyan Street and expose her there—and set the fire herself.

Although this version accounted for some of the physical evidence— the car in low because it had been started from a dead stop, the parking lights on because she could not do what needed doing without some light, a rear wheel spun in repeated attempts to get the car over the embankment, the milk cartons upright because there had been no sudden stop—it did not seem on its own any more or less credible than Lucille Miller's own story. Moreover, some of the physical evidence did seem to support her story: a nail in a front tire, a nine-pound rock found in the car, presumably the one with which she had broken the window in an attempt to save her husband. Within a few days an autopsy had established that Gordon Miller was alive when he burned, which did not particularly help the State's case, and that he had enough Nembutal and Sandoptal in his blood to put the average person to sleep, which did: on the other hand Gordon Miller habitually took both Nembutal and Fiorinal (a common headache prescription which contains Sandoptal), and had been ill besides.

It was a spotty case, and to make it work at all the State was going to have to find a motive. There was talk of unhappiness, talk of another man. That kind of motive, during the next few weeks, was what they set out to establish. They set out to find it in accountants' ledgers and double-indemnity clauses and motel registers, set out to determine what might move a woman who believed in all the promises of the middle class—a woman who had been chairman of the Heart Fund and who always knew a reasonable little dressmaker and who had come out of the bleak wild of prairie fundamentalism to find what she imagined to be the good life —what should drive such a woman to sit on a street called Bella Vista and look out her new picture window into the empty California sun and calculate how to burn her husband alive in a Volkswagen. They found the wedge they wanted closer at hand than they might have at first expected, for, as testimony would reveal later at the trial, it seemed that in December of 1963 Lucille Miller had begun an affair with the husband of one of her friends, a man whose daughter called her "Auntie Lucille," a man who might have seemed to have the gift for people and money and the good life that Cork Miller so noticeably lacked. The man was Arthwell Hayton, a well-known San Bernardino attorney and at one time a member of the district attorney's staff.

In some ways it was the conventional clandestine affair in a place like San Bernardino, a place where little is bright or graceful, where it is routine to misplace the future and easy to start looking for it in bed. Over the seven weeks that it would take to try Lucille Miller for murder,

Assistant District Attorney Don A. Turner and defense attorney Edward P. Foley would between them unfold a curiously predictable story. There were the falsified motel registrations. There were the lunch dates, the afternoon drives in Arthwell Hayton's red Cadillac convertible. There were the interminable discussions of the wronged partners. There were the confidantes ("I knew everything," Sandy Slagle would insist fiercely later. "I knew every time, places, everything") and there were the words remembered from bad magazine stories ("Don't kiss me, it will trigger things," Lucille Miller remembered telling Arthwell Hayton in the parking lot of Harold's Club in Fontana after lunch one day) and there were the notes, the sweet exchanges: "Hi Sweetie Pie! You are my cup of tea!! Happy Birthday—you don't look a day over 29!! Your baby, Arthwell."

And, toward the end, there was the acrimony. It was April 24, 1964, when Arthwell Hayton's wife, Elaine, died suddenly, and nothing good happened after that. Arthwell Hayton had taken his cruiser, *Captain's Lady,* over to Catalina that weekend; he called home at nine o'clock Friday night, but did not talk to his wife because Lucille Miller answered the telephone and said that Elaine was showering. The next morning the Haytons' daughter found her mother in bed, dead. The newspapers reported the death as accidental, perhaps the result of an allergy to hair spray. When Arthwell Hayton flew home from Catalina that weekend, Lucille Miller met him at the airport, but the finish had already been written.

It was in the breakup that the affair ceased to be in the conventional mode and began to resemble instead the novels of James M. Cain, the movies of the late 1930's, all the dreams in which violence and threats and blackmail are made to seem commonplaces of middle-class life. What was most startling about the case that the State of California was preparing against Lucille Miller was something that had nothing to do with law at all, something that never appeared in the eight-column afternoon headlines but was always there between them: the revelation that the dream was teaching the dreamers how to live. Here is Lucille Miller talking to her lover sometime in the early summer of 1964, after he had indicated that, on the advice of his minister, he did not intend to see her any more: "First, I'm going to go to that dear pastor of yours and tell him a few things. . . . When I do tell him that, you won't be in the Redlands Church any more. . . . Look, Sonny Boy, if you think your reputation is going to be ruined, your life won't be worth two cents." Here is Arthwell Hayton, to Lucille Miller: "I'll go to Sheriff Frank Bland and tell him some things that I know about you until you'll wish you'd never heard of Arthwell Hayton." For an affair between a Seventh-Day Adventist dentist's wife and a Seventh-Day Adventist personal-injury lawyer, it seems a curious kind of dialogue.

"Boy, I could get that little boy coming and going," Lucille Miller later confided to Erwin Sprengle, a Riverside contractor who was a business partner of Arthwell Hayton's and a friend to both the lovers. (Friend or no, on this occasion he happened to have an induction coil attached to his telephone in order to tape Lucille Miller's call.) "And he hasn't got one thing on me that he can prove. I mean, I've got concrete—he has nothing concrete." In the same taped conversation with Erwin Sprengle, Lucille Miller mentioned a tape that she herself had surreptitiously made, months before, in Arthwell Hayton's car.

"I said to him, I said 'Arthwell, I just feel like I'm being used.' . . . He started sucking his thumb and he said 'I love you. . . . This isn't something that happened yesterday. I'd marry you tomorrow if I could. I don't love Elaine.' He'd love to hear that played back, wouldn't he?"

"Yeah," drawled Sprengle's voice on the tape. "That would be just a little incriminating, wouldn't it?"

"Just a *little* incriminating," Lucille Miller agreed. "It really *is.*"

Later on the tape, Sprengle asked where Cork Miller was.

"He took the children down to the church."

"You didn't go?"

"No."

"You're naughty."

It was all, moreover, in the name of "love"; everyone involved placed a magical faith in the efficacy of the very word. There was the significance that Lucille Miller saw in Arthwell's saying that he "loved" her, that he did not "love" Elaine. There was Arthwell insisting, later, at the trial, that he had never said it, that he may have "whispered sweet nothings in her ear" (as her defense hinted that he had whispered in many ears), but he did not remember bestowing upon her the special seal, saying the word, declaring "love." There was the summer evening when Lucille Miller and Sandy Slagle followed Arthwell Hayton down to his new boat in its mooring at Newport Beach and untied the lines with Arthwell aboard, Arthwell and a girl with whom he later testified he was drinking hot chocolate and watching television. "I did that on purpose," Lucille Miller told Erwin Sprengle later, "to save myself from letting my heart do something crazy."

January 11, 1965, was a bright warm day in Southern California, the kind of day when Catalina floats on the Pacific horizon and the air smells of orange blossoms and it is a long way from the bleak and difficult East, a long way from the cold, a long way from the past. A woman in Hollywood staged an all-night sit-in on the hood of her car to prevent repossession by a finance company. A seventy-year-old pensioner drove his station wagon at five miles an hour past three Gardena poker parlors and emptied three pistols and a twelve-gauge shotgun through their windows, wounding twenty-nine people. "Many young women became prostitutes just to have enough money to play cards," he explained in a note. Mrs. Nick Adams said that she was "not surprised" to hear her husband announce his divorce plans on the Les Crane Show, and, farther north, a sixteen-year-old jumped off the Golden Gate Bridge and lived.

And, in the San Bernardino County Courthouse, the Miller trial opened. The crowds were so bad that the glass courtroom doors were shattered in the crush, and from then on identification disks were issued to the first forty-three spectators in line. The line began forming at 6 a.m., and college girls camped at the courthouse all night, with stores of graham crackers and No-Cal.

All they were doing was picking a jury, those first few days, but the sensational nature of the case had already suggested itself. Early in December there had been an abortive first trial, a trial at which no evidence was ever presented because on the day the jury was seated the San Bernardino *Sun-Telegram* ran an "inside" story quoting Assistant District Attorney Don Turner, the prosecutor, as saying, "We are looking into the circumstances of Mrs. Hayton's death. In view of the current trial concerning the death of Dr. Miller, I do not feel I should comment on Mrs. Hayton's death." It seemed that there had been barbiturates in Elaine Hayton's blood, and there had seemed some irregularity about the way she was dressed on that morning when she was found under the covers, dead. Any doubts about the death at the time, however, had never gotten as far as the Sheriff's Office. "I guess somebody didn't want to rock the boat," Turner said later. "These were prominent people."

Although all of that had not been in the *Sun-Telegram*'s story, an immediate mistrial had been declared. Almost as immediately, there had been another development: Arthwell Hayton had asked newspapermen to an 11 a.m. Sunday morning press conference in his office. There had been television cameras, and flash bulbs popping. "As you gentlemen may know," Hayton had said, striking a note of stiff bonhomie, "there are very often women who become amorous toward their doctor or lawyer. This does not mean on the physician's or lawyer's part that there is any romance toward the patient or client."

"Would you deny that you were having an affair with Mrs. Miller?" a reporter had asked.

"I would deny that there was any romance on my part whatsoever."

It was a distinction he would maintain through all the wearing weeks to come.

So they had come to see Arthwell, these crowds who now milled beneath the dusty palms outside the courthouse, and they had also come to see Lucille, who appeared as a slight, intermittently pretty woman, already pale from lack of sun, a woman who would turn thirty-five before the trial was over and whose tendency toward haggardness was beginning to show, a meticulous woman who insisted, against her lawyer's advice, on coming to court with her hair piled high and lacquered. "I would've been happy if she'd come in with it hanging loose, but Lucille wouldn't do that," her lawyer said. He was Edward P. Foley, a small, emotional Irish Catholic who several times wept in the courtroom. "She has a great honesty, this woman," he added, "but this honesty about her appearance always worked against her."

By the time the trial opened, Lucille Miller's appearance included maternity clothes, for an official examination on December 18 had revealed that she was then three and a half months pregnant, a fact which made picking a jury even more difficult than usual, for Turner was asking the death penalty. "It's unfortunate but there it is," he would say of the pregnancy to each juror in turn, and finally twelve were seated, seven of them women, the youngest forty-one, an assembly of the very peers—housewives, a machinist, a truck driver, a grocery-store manager, a filing clerk—above whom Lucille Miller had wanted so badly to rise.

That was the sin, more than the adultery, which tended to reinforce the one for which she was being tried. It was implicit in both the defense and the prosecution that Lucille Miller was an erring woman, a woman who perhaps wanted too much. But to the prosecution she was not merely a woman who would want a new house and want to go to parties and run up high telephone bills ($1,152 in ten months), but a woman who would go so far as to murder her husband for his $80,000 in insurance, making it appear an accident in order to collect another $40,000 in double indemnity and straight accident policies. To Turner she was a woman who did not want simply her freedom and a reasonable alimony (she could have had that, the defense contended, by going through with her divorce suit), but wanted everything, a woman motivated by "love and greed." She was a "manipulator." She was a "user of people."

To Edward Foley, on the other hand, she was an impulsive woman who "couldn't control her foolish little heart." Where Turner skirted the pregnancy, Foley dwelt upon it, even calling the dead man's mother down from Washington to testify that her son had told her they were going to have another baby because Lucille felt that it would "do much to weld our home again in the pleasant relations that we used to have." Where the prosecution saw a "calculator," the defense saw a "blabbermouth," and in fact Lucille Miller did emerge as an ingenuous conversationalist. Just as, before her husband's death, she had confided in her friends about her love affair, so she chatted about it after his death, with the arresting sergeant. "Of course Cork lived with it for years, you know," her voice was heard to tell Sergeant Paterson on a tape made the morning after her arrest. "After Elaine died, he pushed the panic button one night and just asked me right out, and that, I think, was when he really—the first time he really faced it." When the sergeant asked why she had agreed to talk to him, against the specific instructions of her lawyers, Lucille Miller said airily, "Oh, I've always been basically quite an honest person. . . . I mean I can put a hat in the cupboard and say it cost ten dollars less, but basically I've always kind of just lived my life the way I wanted to, and if you don't like it you can take off."

The prosecution hinted at men other than Arthwell, and even, over Foley's objections, managed to name one. The defense called Miller suicidal. The prosecution produced experts who said that the Volkswagen fire could not have been accidental. Foley produced witnesses who said that it could have been. Lucille's father, now a junior-high-school teacher in Oregon, quoted Isaiah to reporters: *"Every tongue that shall rise against thee in judgment thou shalt condemn."* "Lucille did wrong, her affair," her mother said judiciously. "With her it was love. But with some I guess it's just passion." There was Debbie, the Millers' fourteen-year-old, testifying in a steady voice about how she and her mother had gone to a supermarket to buy the gasoline can the week before the accident. There was Sandy Slagle, in the courtroom every day, declaring that on at least one occasion Lucille Miller had prevented her husband not only from committing suicide but from committing suicide in such a way that it would appear an accident and ensure the double-indemnity payment. There was Wenche Berg, the pretty twenty-seven-year-old Norwegian governess to Arthwell Hayton's children, testifying that Arthwell had instructed her not to allow Lucille Miller to see or talk to the children.

Two months dragged by, and the headlines never stopped. Southern California's crime reporters were headquartered in San Bernardino for the duration: Howard Hertel from the *Times,* Jim Bennett and Eddy Jo Bernal from the *Herald-Examiner.* Two months in which the Miller trial was pushed off the *Examiner*'s front page only by the Academy Award nominations and Stan Laurel's death. And finally, on March 2, after Turner had reiterated that it was a case of "love and greed," and Foley had protested that his client was being tried for adultery, the case went to the jury.

They brought in the verdict, guilty of murder in the first degree, at 4:50 p.m. on March 5. "She didn't do it," Debbie Miller cried, jumping up from the spectators' section. "She didn't *do* it." Sandy Slagle collapsed in her seat and began to scream. "Sandy, for God's sake please *don't,*" Lucille Miller said in a voice that carried across the courtroom, and Sandy Slagle was momentarily subdued. But as the jurors left the courtroom she screamed again: "You're murderers. . . . Every last one of you is a *murderer.*" Sheriff's deputies moved in then, each wearing a string tie that read "1965 SHERIFF'S RODEO," and Lucille Miller's father, the sad-faced junior-high-school teacher who believed in the word of Christ and the dangers of wanting to see the world, blew her a kiss off his fingertips.

The California Institution for Women at Frontera, where Lucille Miller is now, lies down where Euclid Avenue turns into country road, not too many miles from where she once lived and shopped and organized the Heart Fund Ball. Cattle graze across the road, and Rainbirds sprinkle the alfalfa. Frontera has a softball field and tennis courts, and looks as if it might be a California junior college, except that the trees are not yet high enough to conceal the concertina wire around the top of the Cyclone fence. On visitors' day there are big cars in the parking area, big Buicks and Pontiacs that belong to grandparents and sisters and fathers (not many of them belong to husbands), and some of them have bumper stickers that say "SUPPORT YOUR LOCAL POLICE."

A lot of California murderesses live here, a lot of girls who somehow misunderstood the promise. Don Turner put Sandra Garner here (and her husband in the gas chamber at San Quentin) after the 1959 desert killings known to crime reporters as "the soda-pop murders." Carole Tregoff is here, and has been ever since she was convicted of conspiring to murder Dr. Finch's wife in West Covina, which is not too far from San Bernardino. Carole Tregoff is in fact a nurse's aide in the prison hospital, and might have attended Lucille Miller had her baby been born at Frontera; Lucille Miller chose instead to have it outside, and paid for the guard who stood outside the delivery room in St. Bernardine's Hospital. Debbie Miller came to take the baby home from the hospital, in a white dress with pink ribbons, and Debbie was allowed to choose a name. She named the baby Kimi Kai. The children live with Harold and Joan Lance now, because Lucille Miller will probably spend ten years at Frontera. Don Turner waived his original request for the death penalty (it was generally agreed that he had demanded it only, in Edward Foley's words, "to get anybody with the slightest trace of human kindness in their veins off the jury"), and settled for life imprisonment with the possibility of parole. Lucille Miller does not like it at Frontera, and has had trouble adjusting. "She's going to have to learn humility," Turner says. "She's going to have to use her ability to charm, to manipulate."

The new house is empty now, the house on the street with the sign that says

PRIVATE ROAD
BELLA VISTA
DEAD END

The Millers never did get it landscaped, and weeds grow up around the fieldstone siding. The television aerial has toppled on the roof, and a trash can is stuffed with the debris of family life: a cheap suitcase, a child's game called "Lie Detector." There is a sign on what would have been the lawn, and the sign reads "ESTATE SALE." Edward Foley is trying to get Lucille Miller's case appealed, but there have been delays. "A trial always comes down to a matter of sympathy," Foley says wearily now. "I couldn't create sympathy for her." Everyone is a little weary now, weary and resigned, everyone except Sandy Slagle, whose bitterness is still raw. She lives in an apartment near the medical school in Loma Linda, and studies reports of the case in *True Police Cases* and *Official Detective Stories*. "I'd much rather we not talk about the Hayton business too much," she tells visitors, and she keeps a tape recorder running. "I'd rather talk about Lucille and what a wonderful person she is and how her rights were violated." Harold Lance does not talk to visitors at all. "We don't want to give away what we can sell," he explains pleasantly; an attempt was made to sell Lucille Miller's personal story to *Life*, but *Life* did not want to buy it. In the district attorney's offices they are prosecuting other murders now, and do not see why the Miller trial attracted so much attention. "It wasn't a very interesting murder as murders go," Don Turner says laconically. Elaine Hayton's death is no longer under investigation. "We know everything we want to know," Turner says.

Arthwell Hayton's office is directly below Edward Foley's. Some people around San Bernardino say that Arthwell Hayton suffered; others say that he did not suffer at all. Perhaps he did not, for time past is not believed to have any bearing upon time present or future, out in the golden land where every day the world is born anew. In any case, on October 17, 1965, Arthwell Hayton married again, married his children's pretty governess, Wenche Berg, at a service in the Chapel of the Roses at a retirement village near Riverside. Later the newlyweds were feted at a reception for seventy-five in the dining room of Rose Garden Village. The bridegroom was in black tie, with a white carnation in his buttonhole. The bride wore a long white *peau de soie* dress and carried a shower bouquet of sweetheart roses with stephanotis streamers. A coronet of seed pearls held her illusion veil.

[1966]

WALTER LIPPMANN

The following selection is from Chapter 9, "The Insight of Humanism," of Lippmann's book A Preface to Morals *(1929). For further information about the author, see page 205.*

Freedom and Restraint

. . .

It is significant that fashions in human nature are continually changing. There are, as it were, two extremes: at the one is the belief that our naive passions are evil, at the other that they are good, and between these two poles, the prevailing opinion oscillates. One might suppose that somewhere, perhaps near the center, there would be a point which was the truth, and that on that point men would reach an agreement. But experience shows that there is no agreement, and that there is no known point where the two views are perfectly balanced. The fact is that the prevailing view is invariably a rebound from the excesses of the other, and one can understand it only by knowing what it is a reaction from.

It is impossible, for example, to do justice to Rousseau and the romantics without understanding the dead classicism, the conventionalities, and the tyrannies of the Eighteenth Century. It is equally impossible to do justice to the Eighteenth Century without understanding the licentiousness of the High Renaissance and the political disorders resulting from the Reformation. These in their turn become intelligible only when we have understood the later consequences of the mediæval view of life. No particular view endures. When human nature is wholly distrusted and severely repressed, sooner or later it asserts itself and bursts its bonds; and when it is naively trusted, it produces so much disorder and corruption that men once again idealize order and restraint.

We happen to be living in an age when there is a severe reaction against the distrust and repression practiced by those whom it is customary to describe as Puritans. It is, in fact, a reaction against a degenerate form of Puritanism which manifested itself as a disposition to be prim, prudish, and pedantic. For latter-day Puritanism had become a rather second-rate notion that less obvious things are more noble than grosser ones and that spirituality is the pursuit of rarefied sensations. It had embraced the idea that a man had advanced in the realm of the spirit in proportion to his concern with abstractions, and cults of grimly spiritual persons devoted themselves to the worship of sonorous generalities. All this associated itself with a rather preposterous idealism which insisted that maidens should be wan and easily frightened, that draperies and decorations should conceal the essential forms of objects, and that the good life had something to do with expurgated speech, with pale colors, and shadows and silhouettes, with the thin music of harps and soprano voices, with fig leaves and a general conspiracy to tell lies to children, with philosophies that denied the reality of evil, and with all manner of affectation and self-deception.

Yet in these many attempts to grow wings and take off from the things that are of the earth earthy, it is impossible not to recognize a resemblance, somewhat in the nature of a caricature, to the teaching of the sages. There is no doubt that in one form or another, Socrates and Buddha, Jesus and St. Paul, Plotinus and Spinoza, taught that the good life is impossible without asceticism, that without renunciation of many of the ordinary appetites, no man can really live well. Prejudice against the human body and a tendency to be disgusted with its habits, a contempt for the ordinary concerns of daily experience is to be found in all of them, and it is not surprising that men, living in an age of moral confusion like that associated with the name of the good Queen Victoria, should have come to believe that if only they covered up their passions they had conquered them. It was a rather ludicrous mistake as the satirists of the anti-Victorian era have so copiously pointed out. But at least there was a dim recognition in this cult of the genteel that the good life does involve some kind of conquest of the carnal passions.

That conception of the good life has become so repulsive to the present generation that it is almost incapable of understanding and appreciating the original insight of which the works of Dr. Bowdler and Mrs. Grundy are a caricature. Yet it is a fact, and a most arresting one, that in all the great religions, and in all the great moral philosophies from Aristotle to Bernard Shaw, it is taught that one of the conditions of happiness is to renounce some of the satisfactions which men normally crave. This tradition as to what constitutes the wisdom of life is supported by testimony from so many independent sources that it cannot be dismissed lightly. With minor variations it is a common theme in the teaching of an Athenian aristocrat like Plato, an Indian nobleman like Buddha, and a humble Jew like Spinoza; in fact, wherever men have thought at all carefully about the problem of evil and of what constitutes a good life, they have concluded that an essential element in any human philosophy is renunciation. They cannot all have been so foolish as Anthony Comstock. They must have had some insight into experience which led them to that conclusion.

If asceticism in all its forms were as stupid and cruel as it is now the fashion to think it is, then the traditions of saintliness and of heroism are monstrously misleading. For in the legends of heroes, of sages, of explorers, inventors and discoverers, of pioneers and patriots, there is almost invariably this same underlying theme of sacrifice and unworldliness. They are poor. They live dangerously. By ordinary standards they are extremely uncomfortable. They give up ease, property, pleasure, pride, place, and power to attain things which are transcendent and rare. They live for ends which seem to yield them no profit, and they are ready to die, if need be, for that which the dead can no longer enjoy. And yet, though there is nothing in our current morality to justify their unworldliness, we continue to admire them greatly.

In saying all this I am not trying to clinch an argument by appealing to great names. There is much in the teaching of all the spiritual leaders of the past which is wholly obsolete to-day, and there is no compulsive authority in any part of their teaching. They may have been as mistaken in their insight into the human soul as they usually were in their notions of physics and history. To say, then, that there is an ascetic element in all the great philosophies of the past is not proof that there must be one in modern philosophy. But it creates a presumption, I think, which cannot be ignored, for we must remember that the least perishable part of the literature and thought of the past is that which deals with human nature. Scientific method and historical scholarship have enormously increased our competence in the whole field of physics and history. But for an understanding of human nature we are still very largely dependent, as they were, upon introspection, general observation, and intuition. There has been no revolutionary advance here since the Hellenic philosophers. That is why Aristotle's ethics is still as fresh for anyone who accustoms himself to the idiom as Nietzsche, or Freud, or Bertrand Russell, whereas Aristotle's physics, his biology, or his zoology is of interest only to antiquarians.

It is, then, as an insight into human nature, and not as a rule authoritatively imposed or highly sanctioned by the prestige of great men, that I propose now to inquire what meaning there is for us in the fact that men in the past have so persistently associated the good life with some form of ascetic discipline and renunciation. The modern world, as it has emancipated itself from its ancestral regime, has assumed almost as a matter of course that the human passions, if thoroughly liberated from all tyrannies and distortions, would by their fulfilment achieve happiness. All those who teach asceticism, deny this major premise of modernity, and the result is that the prevailing philosophy is at odds on the most fundamental of all issues with the wisdom of the past.

.   .   .

THOMAS MERTON

Thomas Merton (1915–1968) grew up and studied in France, England, and the United States and received a master's degree from Columbia in 1939. By this time he had begun the long spiritual climb of the mount of Purgatory recounted in his autobiography, **The Seven Storey Mountain** *(1948). He joined a Young Communist group, worked at a settlement house in Harlem, converted from the Anglican to the Roman Catholic church, and in 1941 became a Trappist (Cistercian) monk. He made solemn vows in 1947 and was ordained a priest in 1949. In later years he also became a student of Eastern religions.*

Merton's role in the Abbey of Gethsemani, Kentucky, was in some ways an ambiguous one. He was an accomplished poet and essayist. The literary fame brought on by the publication of his autobiography perpetuated the demand that he continue to provide spiritual guidance for a wide audience. At the same time he had a taste for solitude so deep as to make him a hermit even in his own monastery. The present essay, from the 1967 **Hudson Review,** *beautifully and ironically catches the interplay of Merton's worlds. Among his more than thirty volumes are* **Selected Poems** *(1959),* **Gandhi on Non-Violence** *(1965),* **Conjectures of a Guilty Bystander** *(1966), and* **Zen and the Birds of Appetite** *(1968).* **The Asian Journal of Thomas Merton,** *edited from his original notebooks, was published in 1973.*

Day of a Stranger

The hills are blue and hot. There is a brown, dusty field in the bottom of the valley. I hear a machine, a bird, a clock. The clouds are high and enormous. Through them the inevitable jet plane passes: this time probably full of passengers from Miami to Chicago. What passengers? This I have no need to decide. They are out of my world, up there, busy sitting in their small, isolated, arbitrary lounge that does not even seem to be moving—the lounge that somehow unaccountably picked them up off the earth in Florida to suspend them for a while with timeless cocktails and then let them down in Illinois. The suspension of modern life in contemplation that *gets you somewhere!*

There are also other worlds above me. Other jets will pass over, with other contemplations and other modalities of intentness.

I have seen the SAC plane, with the bomb in it, fly low over me and I have looked up out of the woods directly at the closed bay of the metal bird with a scientific egg in its breast! A womb easily and mechanically opened! I do not consider this technological mother to be the friend of anything I believe in. However, like everyone else, I live in the shadow of the apocalyptic cherub. I am surveyed by it, impersonally. Its number recognizes my number. Are these numbers preparing at some moment to coincide in the benevolent mind of a computer? This does not concern me, for I live in the woods as a reminder that I am free not to be a number.

There is, in fact, a choice.

*

In an age where there is much talk about "being yourself" I reserve to myself the right to forget about being myself, since in any case there is very little chance of my being anybody else. Rather it seems to me that when one is too intent on "being himself" he runs the risk of impersonating a shadow.

Yet I cannot pride myself on special freedom, simply because I am living in the woods. I am accused of living in the woods like Thoreau instead of living in the desert like St. John the Baptist. All I can answer is that I am not living "like anybody." Or "unlike anybody." We all live somehow or other, and that's that. It is a compelling necessity for me to be free to embrace the necessity of my own nature.

I exist under trees. I walk in the woods out of necessity. I am both a prisoner and an escaped prisoner. I cannot tell you why, born in France, my journey ended here in Kentucky. I have considered going further, but it is not practical. It makes no difference. Do I have a "day"? Do I spend my "day" in a "place"? I know there are trees here. I know there are birds here. I know the birds in fact very well, for there are precise pairs of birds (two each of fifteen or twenty species) living in the immediate area of my cabin. I share this particular place with them: we form an ecological balance. This harmony gives the idea of "place" a new configuration.

As to the crows, they form part of a different pattern. They are vociferous and self-justifying, like humans. They are not two, they are many. They fight each other and the birds, in a constant state of war.

*

There is a mental ecology, too, a living balance of spirits in this corner of the woods. There is room here for many other songs besides those of birds. Of Vallejo for instance. Or Rilke, or René Char, Montale, Zukofsky, Ungaretti, Edwin Muir, Quasimodo or some Greeks. Or the dry, disconcerting voice of Nicanor Parra, the poet of the sneeze. Here is also Chuang Tzu whose climate is perhaps most the climate of this silent corner of woods. A climate in which there is no need for explanations. Here is the reassuring companionship of many silent Tzu's and Fu's; Kung Tzu, Lao Tzu, Meng Tzu. Tu Fu. And Hui Neng. And Chao-Chu. And the drawings of Sengai. And a big graceful scroll from Suzuki. Here also is a Syrian hermit called Philoxenus. An Algerian cenobite called Camus. Here is heard the clanging prose of Tertullian, with the dry catarrh of Sartre. Here the voluble dissonances of Auden, with the golden sounds of John of Salisbury. Here is the deep vegetation of that more ancient forest in which the angry birds, Isaias and Jeremias, sing. Here should be, and are, feminine voices from Angela of Foligno to Flannery O'Connor, Theresa of Avila, Juliana of Norwich, and, more personally and warmly still, Raissa Maritain. It is good to choose the voices that will be heard in these woods, but they also choose themselves, and send themselves here to be present in this silence. In any case there is no lack of voices.

*

The hermit life is cool. It is a life of low definition in which there is little to decide, in which there are few transactions or none, in which there are no packages delivered. In which I do not bundle up packages and deliver them to myself. It is not intense. There is no give and take of questions and answers, problems and solutions. Problems begin down the hill. Over there under the water tower are the solutions. Here there are woods, foxes. Here there is no need for dark glasses. "Here" does not even warm itself up with references to "there." It is just a "here" for which there is no "there." The hermit life is that cool.

The monastic life as a whole is a hot medium. Hot with words like "must," "ought" and "should." Communities are devoted to high definition projects: "making it all clear!" The clearer it gets the clearer it has to be made. It branches out. You have to keep clearing the branches. The more branches you cut back the more branches grow. For one you cut you get three more. On the end of each branch there is a big bushy question mark. People are running all around with packages of meaning. Each is very anxious to know whether all the others have received the latest messages. Has someone else received a message that he has not received? Will they be willing to pass it on to him? Will he understand it when it is passed on? Will he understand it when it is passed on? Will he have to argue about it? Will he be expected to clear his throat and stand up and say "Well the way I look at it St. Benedict said . . ."? Saint Benedict saw that the best thing to do with the monastic life was to cool it but today everybody is heating it up. Maybe to cool it you have to be a hermit. But then they will keep thinking that *you* have got a special message. When they find out you haven't. . . . Well, that's their worry, not mine.

*

This is not a hermitage—it is a house. ("Who was that hermitage I seen you with last night? . . .") What I wear is pants. What I do is live. How I pray is breathe. Who said Zen? Wash out your mouth if you said Zen. If you see a meditation going by, shoot it. Who said "Love"? Love is in the movies. The spiritual life is something that people worry about when they are so busy with something else they think they ought to be spiritual. Spiritual life is guilt. Up here in the woods is seen the New Testament: that is to say, the wind comes through the trees and you breathe it. Is it supposed to be clear? I am not inviting anybody to try it. Or suggesting that one day the message will come saying NOW. That is none of my business.

*

I am out of bed at two-fifteen in the morning, when the night is darkest and most silent. Perhaps this is due to some ailment or other. I find myself in the primordial lostness of night, solitude, forest, peace, and a mind awake in the dark, looking for a light, not totally reconciled to being out of bed. A light appears, and in the light an ikon. There is now in the large darkness a small room of radiance with psalms in it. The psalms grow up silently by themselves without effort like plants in this light which is favorable to them. The plants hold themselves up on stems which have a single consistency, that of mercy, or rather great mercy. *Magna misericordia.* In the formlessness of night and silence a word then pronounces itself: Mercy. It is surrounded by other words of lesser consequence: "destroy iniquity" "Wash me" "purify" "I know my iniquity." *Peccavi.* Concepts without interest in the world of business, war, politics, culture, etc. Concepts also often without serious interest to ecclesiastics.

   Other words: Blood.   Guile.   Anger. The way that is not good. The way of blood, guile, anger, war.

   Out there the hills in the dark lie southward. The way over the hill is blood, guile, dark, anger, death: Selma, Birmingham, Mississippi. Nearer than these, the atomic city, from which each day a freight car of fissionable material is brought to be laid carefully beside the gold in the underground vault which is at the heart of this nation.

   "Their mouth is the opening of the grave; their tongues are set in motion by lies; their heart is void."

Blood, lies, fire, hate, the opening of the grave, void. Mercy, great mercy.

The birds begin to wake. It will soon be dawn. In an hour or two the towns will wake, and men will enjoy everywhere the great luminous smiles of production and business.

*

—Why live in the woods?
—Well, you have to live somewhere.
—Do you get lonely?
—Yes, sometimes.
—Are you mad at people?
—No.
—Are you mad at the monastery?
—No.
—What do you think about the future of monasticism?
—Nothing. I don't think about it.
—Is it true that your bad back is due to Yoga?
—No.
—Is it true that you are practicing Zen in secret?
—Pardon me, I don't speak English.

*

All monks, as is well known, are unmarried, and hermits more unmarried than the rest of them. Not that I have anything against women. I see no reason why a man can't love God and a woman at the same time. If God was going to regard women with a jealous eye, why did he go and make them in the first place? There is a lot of talk about a married clergy. Interesting. So far there has not been a great deal said about married hermits. Well, anyway, I have the place full of ikons of the Holy Virgin.

One might say I had decided to marry the silence of the forest. The sweet dark warmth of the whole world will have to be my wife. Out of the heart of that dark warmth comes the secret that is heard only in silence, but it is the root of all the secrets that are whispered by all the lovers in their beds all over the world. So perhaps I have an obligation to preserve the stillness, the silence, the poverty, the virginal point of pure nothingness which is at the center of all other loves. I attempt to cultivate this plant without comment in the middle of the night and water it with psalms and prophecies in silence. It becomes the most rare of all the trees in the garden, at once the primordial paradise tree, the *axis mundi,* the cosmic axle, and the Cross. *Nulla silva talem profert.* There is only one such tree. It cannot be multiplied. It is not interesting.

*

It is necessary for me to see the first point of light which begins to be dawn. It is necessary to be present alone at the resurrection of Day, in the blank silence when the sun appears. In this completely neutral instant I receive from the Eastern woods, the tall oaks, the one word "DAY," which is never the same. It is never spoken in any known language.

*

Sermon to the birds: "Esteemed friends, birds of noble lineage, I have no message to you except this: be what you are: be *birds.* Thus you will be your own sermon to yourselves!"
     Reply: "Even this is one sermon too many!"

*

Rituals. Washing out the coffee pot in the rain bucket. Approaching the outhouse with circumspection on account of the king snake who likes to curl up on one of the beams inside. Addressing the possible king snake in the outhouse and informing him that he should not be there. Asking the formal ritual question that is asked at this time every morning: "Are you in there, you bastard?"

*

More rituals: Spray bedroom (cockroaches and mosquitoes). Close all the windows on South side (heat). Leave windows open on north and east sides (cool). Leave windows open on west side until maybe June when it gets very hot on all sides. Pull down shades. Get water bottle. Rosary. Watch. Library book to be returned.
     It is time to visit the human race.

*

I start out under the pines. The valley is already hot. Machines out there in the bottoms, perhaps planting corn. Fragrance of the woods. Cool west wind under the oaks. Here is the place on the path where I killed a copperhead. There is the place where I saw the fox run daintily and carefully for cover carrying a rabbit in his mouth. And there is the cement cross that, for no reason, the novices rescued from the corner of a destroyed wall and put up in the woods: people imagine someone is buried there. It is just a cross. Why should there not be a cement cross by itself in the middle of the woods?
     A squirrel is kidding around somewhere overhead in midair. Tree to tree. The coquetry of flight.
     I come out into the open over the hot hollow and the old sheep barn. Over there is the monastery, bugging with windows, humming with action.
     The long yellow side of the monastery faces the sun on a sharp rise with fruit trees and beehives. This is without question one of the least interesting buildings on the face of the earth. However, in spite of the most earnest efforts to deprive it of all character and keep it ugly, it is surpassed in this respect by the vast majority of other monasteries. It is so completely plain that it ends, in spite of itself, by being at least simple.

A lamentable failure of religious architecture—to come so close to non-entity and yet not fully succeed! I climb sweating into the novitiate, and put down my water bottle on the cement floor. The bell is ringing. I have duties, obligations, since here I am a monk. When I have accomplished these, I return to the woods where I am nobody. In the choir are the young monks, patient, serene, with very clear eyes, then, reflective, gentle, confused. Today perhaps I tell them of Eliot's *Little Gidding,* analyzing the first movement of the poem ("Midwinter spring in its own season"). They will listen with attention thinking some other person is talking to them about some other poem.

*

Chanting the *alleluia* in the second mode: strength and solidity of the Latin, seriousness of the second mode, built on the *Re* as though on a sacrament, a presence. One keeps returning to the *Re* as to an inevitable center. *Sol-Re, Fa-Re, Sol-Re, Do-Re.* Many other notes in between, but suddenly one hears only the one note. *Consonantia:* all notes, in their perfect distinctness, are yet blended in one. (Through a curious oversight Gregorian chant has continued to be sung in this monastery. But not for long.)

*

In the refectory is read a message of the Pope, denouncing war, denouncing the bombing of civilians, reprisals on civilians, killing of hostages, torturing of prisoners (all in Vietnam). Do the people of this country realize who the Pope is talking about? They have by now become so solidly convinced that the Pope never denounces anybody but Communists that they have long since ceased to listen. The monks seem to know. The voice of the reader trembles.

*

In the heat of noon I return with the water bottle freshly filled, through the cornfield, past the barn under the oaks, up the hill, under the pines, to the hot cabin. Larks rise out of the long grass singing. A bumblebee hums under the wide shady eaves.

I sit in the cool back room, where words cease to resound, where all meanings are absorbed in the *consonantia* of heat, fragrant pine, quiet wind, bird song and one central tonic note that is unheard and unuttered. This is no longer a time of obligations. In the silence of the afternoon all is present and all is inscrutable in one central tonic note to which every other sound ascends or descends, to which every other meaning aspires, in order to find its true fulfillment. To ask when the note will sound is to lose the afternoon: it has already sounded, and all things now hum with the resonance of its sounding.

*

I sweep. I spread a blanket out in the sun. I cut grass behind the cabin. I write in the heat of the afternoon. Soon I will bring the blanket in again and make the bed. The sun is over-clouded. The day declines. Perhaps there will be rain. A bell rings in the monastery. A devout Cistercian tractor growls in the valley. Soon I will cut bread, eat supper, say psalms, sit in the back room as the sun sets, as the birds sing outside the window, as night descends on the valley. I become surrounded once again by all the silent Tzu's and Fu's (men without office and without obligation). The birds draw closer to their nests. I sit on the cool straw mat on the floor, considering the bed in which I will presently sleep alone under the ikon of the Nativity.

Meanwhile the metal cherub of the apocalypse passes over me in the clouds, treasuring its egg and its message.

JUDITH BETH COHEN

Judith Beth Cohen was born in Detroit in 1943. After she graduated from the University of Michigan with a B.A. in English literature (1965) and an M.A. in education (1966), she taught severely disturbed preschool children. She then continued her studies at Boston University, at the New School in New York, and at Ivan Illich's center in Cuernavaca, Mexico. Since 1970 she has been on the staff of Goddard College in Vermont, a small liberal arts college with no grades and no required courses, where she works with students in teacher education, psychology, children's literature, women's studies, and writing. She has been active in the peace movement and the women's movement, has studied Yoga and T'ai Chi, and is both a house restorer and a vegetable raiser. We reprint below two parts of "Vermont Diary," first published in American Review 22 *(1975). It ends with Ms. Cohen's leaving the farm for California. She has, however, returned to Vermont and to the farm, where she continues to live.*

from Vermont Diary

Spring

The stream sealed our decision. The house was a ramshackle place, sitting across from a pond, surrounded by junk and debris, the rotting hulks of old cars, a barn half caved-in but standing unsteadily. Work was needed, walls to be replastered, a furnace put in, some wiring and plumbing; but the structure was sound, and the job was not too large an undertaking for two people. The 70 acres contained woods, open fields, some rolling hills with fine views; a variety of terrain and vegetation, all on this one parcel. The house sat by the road while the land extended behind it. We followed the path through the first field where an old garden had been, through a narrow pine woods out into the second field—a perfectly enclosed space, a ring of evergreens encircling a meadow—then back through swampy woods, ferns and mushrooms dotting the path, trees springing from dead growth, until we could hear the stream rushing. There was no longer a path. We pushed our way through woods, pulled by the water's sound, and emerged to find a beautiful stream that would be a gushing cascade in spring, slowing to a peaceful brook in summer. It bisected the property, compelling us to buy the place, but still there was ambivalence.

The day we bought the farm, rain streaked the windshield so we could not see our way on the dirt roads. Going to the bank, we passed a deer feasting by the highway, and would have called it a good omen if we had been talking. Across a table we passed paper checks, receiving paper back; so often discussed, it seemed an empty gesture, an unchosen choice I had let mold my life. The day we bought the farm, the wet April grass hinted of the chill to come, while I tried to keep warm under a parka, waiting to take possession. In the evening, I wrote to keep from arguing —tallying in my head—a catalog of injuries.

I began upstairs by tearing down the old wallpaper and plaster. It came off in chunks exposing bare laths, catching skin as I worked. Gray dust filled the room, my lungs, and sifted through the stovepipe hole, covering the lower floor with a thin powdery layer, cloaking objects in white. I worked silently, ripping torn, faded wallpaper bedecked with rose bouquets, scribbled phone numbers, hearts drawn around the initials of high school lovers, making me wonder about the lives spent in this room, in this house. Trash cans made immobile by the plaster load were, nevertheless, carted to the dump. I began mixing new plaster in a hastily fashioned trough, stirring to make it smooth. I slapped it on roughly, creating a textured wall. It took so long to become thick, then went on so quickly, it was no time before I had to lug another 50-pound bag up the stairs and begin again. The work proceeded slowly. Weeks passed before the walls were dry, and I could scrape the floor and moldings. Struggling to keep my work neat, I painted the trim brown and made the room white, stroking each bulge carefully with my brush. When completed, it was a simple room: a single bed, a Larkin desk found at an auction, a rocking chair someone gave away, on the floor a zebra skin brought back from the Peace Corps in Kenya. Finally, a room of my own in which to be alone, to think or write, to let my moods and rhythms fill the space. But warm weather had finally arrived and it was difficult to stay indoors. Then visitors began to come and where else were they to sleep but in the room I had finally completed?

In March and April we scanned the catalogs and ordered seeds, filled with visions of succulent tomatoes and crisp chard. But it was the snow peas that most inspired us, tender pods that sell for three dollars a pound in Chinatown growing free and plentiful on our hillside. In early May the ground was still too wet to be turned over, so we waited for the sun to make dust, feeling the press of time, needing every day of our short growing season. By the middle of May, we could begin. We shoveled and sweated, pulling out mammoth rocks deposited by ancient glaciers, wondering how the early settlers managed without machines. From the decaying barn we dragged aged cow manure and worked it into the soil, while I worried about diseases I might get from manure. Never having made a garden before, I quickly became exhausted and overwhelmed. There was too much labor, too much pressure to rush, making me wonder how this was so different from other jobs with deadlines and tedium.

My friend Marsha came to help and we ended up sitting in the sun and manure, swatting black flies and talking about sex. I am intrigued to discover my friends have had many more lovers than I, and I easily drift off into thoughts of what I have missed during six years of marriage.

Dropping seeds in the ground also has its frustrations; they all seem to land on top of each other and have to be spread out delicately. At times I did not bother to follow the directions on the packet and was certain nothing I had planted would grow. I was amazed to see green shoots appear in June; but by the time I was eating the thin, curly pale lettuce, I had forgotten my wonder.

The lives of friends get dismantled and patched together again, but the glue does not hold. Marsha and Larry no longer do Movement work. They maintain a friendship, although they live in separate houses, passing their three-year-old daughter, Sandy, back and forth between them on alternate weeks. Karen and Kirk have separated again, the third time in ten years. But this one seems final. Kirk comes here often and we exchange meaningful looks across my kitchen. Michael came from Iowa with Kathy, and for two years now they have been together in a one-room cabin, alone with an Aladdin lamp, an outhouse, no running water, an Ashley stove for heat, and faith that the roof will not leak.

Four years ago Michael was with Polly. The four of us were drawn together by fantasies of communal love and nonpossession. Before the glowing midnight fire, the plans were spun. But by daylight we discovered we had been mate-swapping and felt disgusted with ourselves and with each other. Michael and Polly broke up, while we remained together. Now we draw firm boundaries around our lives, relating to Michael and Kathy only as neighbors. There is no more talk of sharing, or communal living, and I would not let the postman leave their mail in our box. I still mourn the lost Utopian fantasy and miss the infancy we shared when Polly was around. Now our friendship is only in letters. She writes when her child is born, when her man is unfaithful, when she takes too many pills.

My friends pass in and out of my kitchen, adding the clutter of their lives to the unanswered letters, the dirty dishes, the unfinished wood floor. I struggle not to break with them, wondering if the pieces I cling to are really there at all.

Our nearest neighbor lives on an old dairy farm with a faded red barn, a neat, white farmhouse surrounded by carefully planted tulips, daffodils and irises. Each dawn, the Abbots, a couple in their late 50s, are in the barn together, milking. When he goes out to spread manure in the fields, she rides behind him on the tractor. At haying time she often passes by our house, driving the tractor herself, with her short-cropped gray hair, faded print housedress, shining face, and strong healthy arms. She waves at us without guile, an image intact from the past. There are no children to run the farm after they die. In the local cemetery, their Vermont granite tombstones await them, kept tended and decorated with a wreath of plastic flowers, carefully placed.

A mile further up the hill is the only other working farm left in this town. It occupies a spot that rivals the Alps for pastoral splendor, perched hundreds of feet above a lake, squeezed between green hills. It is eyed longingly by real-estate speculators, but Ainsley, the farmer, grins and will not sell. I have heard he was a bachelor, living there alone for many years until a neighbor lady got tired of her husband, and moved in with him. Now they are married and farm the place together.

Buck, the man who sold us our place, is a member of one of the oldest families in town. He moved a few miles up the highway with his teenage son to a modern mobile home with wall-to-wall carpeting and imitation Venetian draperies. His wife left him, he failed in a brief stint as road commissioner, and now he rides his snowmobile through the winter hills, trading it in each year for a bigger, faster model, scarring the woods he used to own with oil smears and beer cans. He sometimes stops by to chat, usually after he's had a few beers. We hear from another neighbor of his complaint that we ruined his den—a room of falling plaster walls where he kept his guns, and covered up the bad spots with wisecrack signs on shingles. He left the signs when he moved, slogans about beating your wife, revealing your stupidity, getting away with something behind the boss's back—the humor of the dispossessed.

We went over to Samuel Wilson's to buy a pair of geese. Samuel is over 60, but his body is lean and muscular. He drives his tractor bare-chested on summer days, and except for a slight limp he does not show his age. A widower, he's up milking at five each morning. He uses all the modern farm equipment, and is one of the most successful small dairy farmers in the area.

When he started farming the place, there were 73 farms in the county shipping milk, and today there are eight or ten. We asked him why so many farms were failing, and he had a lot to say.

"The farmers have just been crowded right out. A farmer will retire and he can sell it to land spec-a-lators who pay much more than anywhere else. And due to government bungling, they can turn around and put it in the soil bank and get ten dollars an acre for not raising anything. Your taxes have gone out of reason due to the government bungling things."

Samuel continued with his economic and political explanations, as he caught the geese and put them into burlap bags. His voice rose and fell with a musical cadence reminiscent of the Scotch-Irish pioneers who first settled here.

"People have gotten afraid of the dollar today. They'll sink it any-where just to get it outa the banks. They got reason to be afraid of it. At one time we did have a bankin' holiday, to adjust things. A'course it stands to reason, there's no way out, we lost this war. It wasn't a declared war, we were where we shouldn'ta been and we lost it. We shoulda stayed home and minded our own business, coulda had a good depression, and it woulda done us all some good. We farmers may be pushed off this land a little bit, but this country is heading right into a revolution because it's being controlled by the big-money interests. The politicians and big-money interests have reaped a harvest on these wars, but they're not goin'ta pay for 'em. The public is goin'ta pay and we're gettin' sick of it. Those boys coming home from service with no jobs, they're goin'ta want a life of their own and they're entitled to it. The only way they'll get it is to push these bosses, these big-money men off their stools and put 'em down where they should be."

Though he sounded like a populist revolutionary, Samuel voted for Nixon in '72, a choice difficult for us to comprehend.

We thought the geese were a mated pair but they were both females. They were white with swan-like necks and bright orange beaks. They kept the small front lawn cut, and lingered by the door waiting for people, honking to announce visitors, pecking only at strangers, their necks lung-ing in a ritualized gesture of rivalry. Like humans, geese fall in love; and like humans, they are possessive. Ours allowed us to stroke their downy, slippery breasts and would answer back when we kneeled to speak to them. One morning we found one goose near death, the other bloody, but ambulatory. The wounded one slept with its head tucked under its wing, hiding the gaping hole that had been her eye. I thought we would have to kill her, but daily, she began to heal, and was soon limping after her friend, drinking water and nibbling at grass. In a few weeks, she had recovered; even her eye had come back.

For protection, we built a fortress-like structure to shield them at night from predators, but the racoons were better than our hammers and nails. One morning the door of the shack was open, the goose that had been injured now lay dead and mangled, while the other paced about, squawking in confusion. To soothe her grief and our loss, we brought her a gander and watched their mating dance. She was beginning to brood when she was hit crossing the road from the pond, by a passing car from Connecticut. The driver carried the goose and dropped it at my feet, his breath smelling from whiskey. As he walked back to his car, I called through my tears, "At least you can pay for the goose." I memorized his license number while he ignored me and pulled away.

The gander, in grief, tried to mount his passive mate, while blackbirds waited on wires to swoop toward an evening meal. I carried her by the neck, her mate following, yellow ooze dripping from her beak. Washing death from my hands I was puzzled, like the gander, carrying out his vigil by the corpse. I thought of plucking, cleaning, and roasting her to school myself in country ways, but I could not feast upon accidents, even if pets are a luxury. I waited instead, for my mate to come home, and together we buried her, the gander watching by the grave we dug. Since geese are said to mate for life, he will not be consoled, even if a new goose is brought to take her place.

.   .   .

Second Spring

Lucia is the local clairvoyant, but I have been afraid to go and ask my seven questions, afraid that she will see something dreadful in my future, and though she will not tell me, she will know. People call her when they have lost something: a dog, a bracelet, a child strayed from home. She can see clues that tell you where to search: a fallen tree, a scrap of crushed blue paper. Though she has been known to make mistakes, her powers are not taken lightly. My friend Jane went to see Lucia in her kitchen before leaving for California. Lucia wiped her hands on her apron, took time away from preparing dinner to sit across the table from Jane, to hold both her hands, look into her eyes and laugh about the impending move.

"Vermonters never go to California," she teased. But she could see a small red car, a child, a dog, a scientist whose initials she could name. Months later on the west coast, Jane remembered Lucia when she fell in love with a psychologist whose initials were the same ones Lucia had seen. But there was no red car, no child and no dog—until one night the man told Jane he had crashed his red sportscar just before meeting her, his dog had been killed, and the same week he learned he was the father of a child he had not known about. Jane did not remain in California, but returned to Vermont, and now lives with her daughter and husband on a farm less than a mile away from the house she grew up in. I accept Lucia's powers as I accept the transformation of the seasons, messages from friends on another coast who know what I am thinking—personal energy filling a room making me dizzy from the glare.

A snapping turtle emerged in spring to lay eggs that will hatch into new creatures who live in the pond, pulling ducks and fish under in their trap-like jaws. Should we kill the turtle or leave her alone because she is natural, let the wildlife struggle it out? This time I am in favor of killing. I watched while he shot her in the head, then I called some friends bold enough to come and retrieve the carcass. It was a primordial-looking beast with a tough, spiny skin; loose-fitting, it seemed it would slide off if pulled. The claws were enormous, they would make good props for a monster film. The appendages contracted when poked, though the turtle was quite dead. Our friend made an incision with his sharp fisherman's knife, gouging to get through the layers of thickness. The head came off, the swollen tongue protruding, the eyes closed. The heavy shell weighed pounds. We strung it up with a wire, a rope would not hold it; but it had to hang so the blood would drain. Almost bloodless, it took time before a few drops fell. We laughed at the spectacle we made, propping the head perversely on the post, making a scarecrow of the corpse. We would have crucified it if we could have driven nails through the claws. It was one way to deal with killing.

"If it snows in April, there'll be a lotta people jumping outa windows." (Overheard in post office.)

Snow in April, the lilac tree outside my window, almost dead, but still sprouting a few buds each year, is taken down by the weight of heavy, unwanted snow. It gets tangled in phone wires, resting there, cutting off communication. Seedlings that sprouted the day before sit in window boxes begging for sun, getting instead eight inches of wet snow. One day there was only melting run-off—blades turning green, bulbs pushing higher; the next day lost under the white layer. Mud becomes soft under the heat of midday sun, but turns hard and rigid with evening cold. Sap runs when the changes are great, warm by day, cold by night; no change keeps it still. Changes come to us as well. This summer I will go west, he will remain here. It is time for a separation and there is no way to know what the next phase will bring.

Before my departure, we spend a day together in the second field, surrounded by patches of melting snow. We sit among dead weeds, leftovers from last summer. I gaze at the bare trees that will soon change, the flat fields that will be overgrown with green. Now there is a sparseness, raw lines, pencil-thin white birches that will be hidden in foliage. The sloping wall between our field and the neighbors will be covered with leaves and brush. Now is the time of absolute exposure; the world's bare bones showing, an emptiness where last year's garden grew. With snow and sunlight we lie naked, feasting on beer and cheese and crackers. A few feet from our blanket the snow shrinks, melting slowly, lovingly as we touch, leaving moist earth. Our loving is more intense when threatened by danger and loss. Tree shadows stretch across the field, their branches reach toward us protectingly.

No grass ever sprouted in the wide dirt yard. A series of cars have sat, died, and been taken away. The garbage can cannot contain the mess.

Tall weeds take over the lawn. The patched, severed clapboards of the house become less and less a shelter separating inside from out. A garden will not be planted this year. One door molding remains unfinished, the lath still showing, a reminder of all that has been left undone.

JUDSON JEROME

Judson Jerome was born in Tulsa in 1927. He attended the University of Oklahoma, the University of Chicago, and Ohio State, where in 1953 he received the Ph.D. He immediately became head of the Literature Department of Antioch College, a position which—except for a time as head of the Humanities Department at the College of the Virgin Islands— he held for the next twenty years. During these years he wrote essays, literary criticism, novels, and several books of poetry. Since 1960 he has been poetry editor of Writers' Digest. *In 1971 he published* Culture Out of Anarchy: The Reconstruction of American Higher Education.

In 1972 his life took a sudden turn when he moved with his family to a rural commune. His daily experiences, his reflections on and analysis of the trials and rewards of communal life and its significance for twentieth-century America, and his findings at other communes he visited (helped by a grant from the Twentieth Century Fund) are recorded in his latest book, Families of Eden: Communes and the New Anarchism (1974). *From it we reprint the two selections below, the first from the Foreword, the second from chapter 9, "Intelligence at the Tiller."*

from *Families of Eden*

· · ·

When we moved to the commune where we now live, Downhill Farm, my wife and I had a sense that it was just in time, that we were getting ourselves and our children out just ahead of a tidal wave of infection. Three of our children had escaped ahead of us. Our eighteen-year-old daughter had dropped out of high school as soon as she was sixteen, the first day she legally could do so, and left home (with our blessing and encouragement) for an independent life. For awhile she was a member of the Bear Tribe, a communal group learning the ways of the American Indians—how to live off the land compatibly with nature. Our twelve-year-old daughter had preceded us to the commune by a couple of months, and in that short time had begun to flower as a self-reliant, joyful, maturing woman, cured, as it were, overnight, of the sick preoccupations and insecurities of adolescence in suburbia. Our eight-year-old daughter, who is aphasic, had been living for nearly two years in Camphill Village, a communal school for brain-damaged and retarded children. But our sixteen-year-old daughter was mechanically and indifferently serving time in an elegant, progressive public high school, gradually being drawn into the competitions, vanities, and tensions of vacuous social life dominated by the record player, the telephone, drugs, and sexual jealousy and possessiveness (with relatively little sexual joy). And our five-year-old son, in kindergarten, was changing before our eyes as he adopted the values his friends adopted from their parents and older siblings: secretiveness, competitiveness, shrillness of desire, silliness, his curiosity growing duller by the day. He was becoming money-conscious; and his friends stole from their mothers' purses. He was picking up neighborhood attitudes of giggling shame about sex. His head was feverish with "I want" and "Mine!" and trips to stores were becoming ordeals of saying no to his nascent, raw, and mindless consumerism. Television and the *Sears Catalog* were his *Playboy* magazines of possessive fantasy. We lived in the gleaming new planned city of Columbia, Maryland, which advertises itself as "The Next America," and our children were not safe on the streets because of the mounting racial tension, drug problems, gangs, and interpersonal violence. My wife's life had become one of housekeeping and childcare and perpetual shopping. The more successful I became in my profession, the less meaning it had for me and the more it separated me from family and friends. I had contracted the endemic disease of American males—the association of personal worth with annual income —and though it was well over twenty thousand a year, it was never enough, not because of rising prices or exorbitant standard of living, but because it was a surrogate for love, and especially for self-esteem, and made hungry where most it satisfied. The very activities which meant progress in my life progressively cut me off from the satisfactions I most yearned for. I decided to retire.

I am deliberately emphasizing the personal, what might be judged the selfish, elements in my motivation. One does what he has to do, and I could do no other than what I have done. I have reams of rhetoric to supply on demand about the value of the social experiment in which I am now engaged—which, incidentally, is much more demanding of energy and heartache and painful self-examination and punishing change than any way of life I have been engaged in in the past. It is not *mere* rhetoric, but earnest belief, that if our own commune can demonstrate some viable alternative to the prevailing system, that if it can be first a haven and then a generative source of energy and action for a number of people who are as fed up with or defeated by the other options in our society as I am, my efforts here will be of greater significance for the world at large than they would be if I had continued functioning as an increasingly jaded professor of literature in an elite private college. But the rhetoric, even when genuine, invites argumentation and suggests threat. Many of my friends and former colleagues, not to mention those I encounter when I go to lecture or participate in conferences or otherwise deal with in the noncommunal world, react with hostility, as though there were some implication that my choices should be their choices. I don't know what other people should do—either to save themselves or to save the world. All I can do is explain as honestly as possible why what I have done seemed necessary to me.

Aside from the gratifications of daily life (e.g., this morning, before I got to my typewriter, I invented an alternative to a turnbuckle to stabilize the new screen door—built from scratch—in the communal kitchen), I occasionally get reaffirming signals from other sources that there is more sanity than madness in having picked this curious route. The sixteen-year-old daughter I mentioned had been hitchhiking across country and on the West Coast with a twenty-year-old man of Guatemalan family whom she loved. In one letter she said:

> I know that a lot of things have happened to change my life. Mainly Downhill Farm. Because if it didn't come, things would have changed in a much different way. I'm thankful for the things happening the way they have.

Only she and we knew the terror behind the words: "things would have changed in a much different way." But no more needed be said between daughter and parents: a life had been salvaged from the debris of a dying culture. And we never had to say that to her. She knew.

My son—who is no genius, just an alive young mind—is learning plumbing, electricity, auto mechanics, the joys of sharing. He strikes off into the woods alone to find blackberries because he knows the people here love them. He knows the weeds in the garden—by name—better than any adult on the place. He hasn't said "I want" for any commercial product in a year. We will enter a court fight, if necessary, to save him from school. For the first time in more than a quarter century of marriage my wife and I are engaged together in labor and love of other people, a life in which work and play and education and spiritual growth are inseparable. This book is a diary to which all around me contributed.

*   *   *

Pitched on this sea
                    (expansive canvas straining/
the rigging taut/
                    laboring tonnage of hull/
the bulging current
                    breaking like bombs at the bow/
the empty air
                    pouring its power upon us)
who are we?

```
                        (riding this weight
                                    in violent weather)
        but a whisper of intelligence at the tiller
        our quarter inch of leverage
                                    telling whether
        we head up
                    into failure
                                or fall off
        leaning the fast and easy way to waste.
```
                                    RUMORS (6) of Change

We came to feel that ANY school AS SUCH—at any level and no matter
how "free"—cannot be as natural, spontaneous, organic and life-integra-
tive as we want our lives to be. Several of us have gone on to join with still
others in founding an intentional community, hopeful that it will prove a
better alternative for us.

"Beyond Free Schools: Community!"[1]

The terms "intentional community" and "intentional family" are ox-
ymorons: the adjective *intentional* contradicts the very nature of community and family, which are essentially spontaneous and traditional forms
of human association. Dissatisfaction with stultifying traditional forms
and, especially, the artifices and regulations imposed upon them by the
larger society impels some of us to attempt to create intentionally what
we envision to be, ironically, a more "natural" way of life.

This paradox pervades discussion of education and therapy in communes. In our present society one finds education and therapy treated as
commodities supplied by schools and other institutions. As one goes to
the store for bread, he goes to school for education, to specialists for
treatment of disorders, to hospitals for healing. In communes there is a
disposition to let children grow and the "sick" heal themselves, to let
nature take its course as much as possible. Nonetheless there is a good
deal of conscious intervention in the process, a whisper of intelligence at
the tiller. On the one hand there is freedom and opportunity; on the other
there is neglect and evasion of responsibility. Problems arise in determining the line between these, in discovering how to minimize coercion on
the individual and yet to create facilitative structures that make community itself an educational force.

A woman speaking to a college audience about life on her country
commune was asked whether the children raised there might not rebel
and want to live in the city. "We're either going to make the mistakes with
our children that our parents made with us," she answered, "or we'll

---

[1]The first passage is from an unpublished poem of my own. The second is from an article
by Jerry Friedberg in *Mother Earth News,* no. 6 (November 1970), p. 82.

make other mistakes. But as long as we have children, we'll make mistakes."

This new-culture response is quite in contrast to the attitude of utopian communities, old and new, which classically develop theories of child-rearing and therapy and create formal structures for carrying them out. In these there is a felt need to separate children, to some degree, from parental influence and consciously to orient the young toward group loyalty and group goals. In such diverse contemporary groups as the Hutterites, the Bruderhof, the kibbutzim, Synanon, and Twin Oaks, children tend to be removed from the home or parents' quarters, at least for substantial portions of their lives, and to be indoctrinated according to group policy. Most modern communes, however, have no such theory or practice. Those that begin with ideological positions and educational structures are likely to evolve away from them, tending more and more to let things happen, and to accept the inevitability that there will be mistakes and changes; but they prefer to rely on the Flow than to impose controls which may prove to be more destructive than helpful in the long run.

But as youngsters in free schools have sometimes perceived, lack of control may amount to indifference, or lack of love. On the one hand is the danger of manipulation and limitation of a natural process, on the other that of callous *laissez-faire.* Daily in communes we confront both dangers—and try to find a way between them.

I had written that, then left the typewriter to stand by the fire, trying to think of a way of putting it more concretely, when Topher came in. Neither Polly (thirteen) nor Topher (six) were in school, and their older sisters had left school as soon as they reached the legal age to do so. Topher had come into the room to speak to Lisa, who has twenty-eight years of teaching experience in the schools.

"Let's have a lesson now," he said to her.

"All right."

"A long lesson. I'm getting so I like long lessons."

"All right. What kind of lesson do you want?"

"Arithmetic. The kind on the lined papers."

As it turned out, they were working on sets and the commutative property of addition. Earlier this morning Topher and I had a session playing games with Cuisenaire rods. Working with Lisa, Topher draws stars in subsets and translates them into numerals with plus, minus, and equal signs.

Before they could start work, Polly had to clear the schoolroom (a nook off the office) of her cards. She invented a process for making greeting cards with swirling colors by dipping them into airplane oil paints floating on water—using five-by-eight-inch cards, such as we use in research, folded in half; she dips the corners of envelopes also, to match, and wholesales these for two dollars per dozen to gift shops. The cards were drying on newspapers on top of the school desks; so she moved them to hang on strings stretched around the stovepipe which passes through the room. Then she went back to read.

I returned to work, but was interrupted by Herb, a man of twenty-one, doing research for this book—at that moment studying Carl Rogers' chapter on communes in *On Becoming Partners: Marriage and Its Alternatives.* He read aloud:

> One aspect which is actually quite natural will seem surprising to many readers: young children accept quite readily the fact that their parents may at times be sleeping with different partners. Children accept their world as it is, especially if that world is acceptable to the others around them. On the other hand, an adolescent who has spent most of his or her life in the ordinary community and has absorbed its norms may be very much troubled or conflicted by the "bad" behavior of his parents.

Herb asked, "Is he being fair?" He had heard, as most of us have, stories about the deleterious effects on children of seeing adults make love. Sometimes they think the adults are fighting—and so on. Is Rogers overlooking evidence of that sort?

Several of us, including Polly, became involved in discussion of that question. In the first place, Rogers may not be referring to children witnessing sexual intercourse. We exchanged anecdotes about instances in which children have, in our own experience, known about their parents sleeping with various partners and shown no particular concern or surprise. Herb told of a little girl who was jealous of him when he was with her divorced mother, mostly because the bed space was otherwise available for the child herself. We went on to discuss the effects on children who see intercourse—of animals, parents, and others. Though we have all heard folklore of its evil effects, none of us knew first-hand of a case in which it had any such effects. In Richard Wright's *Native Son* the fact that children witness parental lovemaking in Chicago slums is, along with rat infestation, given as an example of the degradation in ghetto life. Such attitudes might be partly projection: if adults believe that sex is naughty, they will believe it is therefore bad for children to witness. These attitudes also stem from social oppression: lack of space is associated with intimacy, which makes the latter seem a negative condition of poverty. I asked Polly whether she had ever watched people make love. "No, but I hear it a lot!" She told us about the different rhythms of the three couples sleeping upstairs when she is sleeping below.

If all days were as educational for the children as the last hour has been, I would worry less about whether communal life provides them with an adequate alternative to formal schooling. But each time I see a school bus picking up children on our country roads I wince a little, wondering whether we are neglecting parental responsibility. If Topher and Polly were to go to public school they would trudge the half-mile up the drive each morning to catch such a bus, ride about forty-five minutes each way, putting in longer hours than a factory worker, spending their waking hours largely under regulation and supervision, being shaped to fit society's needs. That seems dysfunctional to me as preparation for life. But I am plagued by doubts. I wonder especially about their social relationships. They live almost entirely in the company of adults. At times both show evidence of a poignant listlessness and loneliness. But so do children who go to school, I argue with myself. Parents whose children are in school never see *their* boredom. To do one thing is to be deprived of another, inevitably, and how can we know which is the more serious deprivation?

Not all communes are so richly populated as ours with educators. There is not always a Lisa when Tophers feel the desire for lessons. On the other hand, most adults have plenty of knowledge to impart, and "teaching skill" in the school system is in large part skill in holding attention (and thus maintaining order), which is unnecessary in voluntary, one-to-one learning. Love is more important than expertise in such education—and probably more effective in purely pragmatic terms. An eight-year-old boy, educated until that age at home, was experiencing his first year of formal schooling when interviewed by a newspaper editor. The parents insist that he and his seven-year-old sister are in no way exceptional children, and that they were given only an hour-a-day of instruction at home. When they entered public school, both tested at seventh-grade reading and fourth-grade math levels. They were placed in the second grade.

> *Ed.* And do you like school?
> *L.* Yes and no. I like the school part, but the kids make fun of me—they laugh at me and they reject me—because I'm different.
> *Ed.* How so?
> *L.* For one thing, we bring our lunches. And Eva and I have whole wheat sandwiches—my mother makes it. And we never have deserts—and we don't eat sugar. Or candy either.
>
> .   .   .
>
> *Ed.* Since you read at the seventh-grade level, I suppose second-grade reading is easy for you. Perhaps you find second graders reading more slowly than you do. Do you find this tiresome?
> *L.* No, I like the kids, and if they have a harder time with reading than I do, that's ok. I read what I like—I don't think what level it is.
>
> .   .   .
>
> *Ed.* Do you ever wish you weren't different from others in your school?
> *L.* (quickly) I wish that there wasn't a difference, but I don't want to be like them. I wish they would be like me. I think it's important to be and do what you think is right. So since I think it's right to be the way I am, I don't want to change their ways. . . . I wish more and more people were convinced that what they are doing is necessary to have a good earth.[2]

---

[2]Interview by Mildred Loomis, "An 8 yr. Old Raps About School," *The Green Revolution,* vol. 10, no. 9 (Sept. 1972), p. 5.

This muddles my assumptions. The boy likes "the school part" but in social life he is pained and frustrated—and the school part itself seems irrelevant to his scholastic development. I am less impressed by his reading and math performance than by his ethical development, his tolerance and yet his clear sense of values—qualities which, apparently, his fellow students have not developed. Do I want my own children educated by peers such as he found himself among in school? On the other hand, what right have I—aside from the question of legal obligation—to make such decisions for them?

To answer such questions one is forced to reconsider the very definition of childhood and, correlatively, of various other categories of dependents and deviants. The problem is addressed by Bennett Berger, a sociologist at the University of California, Davis, who is conducting for NIMH an extensive study of child-rearing in contemporary communes:

> This rethinking involves a rejection of the idea of children as incompetent dependents with a special psychology needing special protections and nurturings. Like the big "kids" who are their parents, communal children seem to be just littler kids, less skilled, less experienced, and only perhaps less wise. . . .
>
> In viewing the history of how children are conceptualized by adults, social scientists have thus far emphasized the differences between pre-industrial, agricultural, or sometimes lower-class views on the one side, and industrial or middle-class views on the other. In the former view the status of children is seen as essentially ascribed at birth and rooted in the kinship system. In this view, children are seen as simply small or inadequate versions of their parents, totally subject to traditional or otherwise arbitrary parental authority. The "modern" industrial, middle-class view, by contrast, tends to treat the child as a distinctive social category: children have their own special psychology, their own special needs, patterned processes of growth often elaborated into ideas about developmental stages which may postpone advent to "full" adulthood well into a person's twenties, and sometimes still later. The task of parents and other "socializers" in this view is to "raise" or "produce" the child (the industrial metaphor is often used) according to scientifically elaborated principles of proper child management—a process which in many middle-class families results in the differentiation of family roles in a way that transforms a woman-with-child into a full-time child raiser.
>
> The view that we find prevalent in the hip-communal settings we have studied fits neither of these models with precision. "Young people" are regarded as independent of the family, but not as members of an autonomous category of "children"; instead, their status is likely to be ascribed as that of "person," a development which can be understood as part of an equalitarian ethos, and as complementary to parallel development in the status of females, from "women" (or even "mothers") to "people," and in the status of men, from being characterized in invidious status terms to being characterized as above all a "human being."[3]

_____

[3] *Child Rearing Practices of the Communal Family: Progress Report to NIMH,* 1971, mimeographed, pp. 10–12.

Infants and toddlers up to about age four are primarily tended by their mothers or other mothers with children. Men in communal groups give children more attention than do men in outer society, but there is no norm of expectation—in particular, no inherent obligation for the father to be responsible for his own children, other than as persons in the group. However, some fathers we have seen are as deeply involved as the mothers with responsibility for childcare. One I met, living with a woman who had a child by another man, had taken major responsibility for that child, leaving the mother relatively free. In some cases single fathers take over the child-rearing role completely when the mothers move on, though this is less common than for mothers to be left with children when fathers leave. There is a clear tendency for women to be left with the major responsibility for child-support in contexts in which pairing relations are rather transient—especially, of course, when the children are infants and often breast-fed.[4] But to have a child without a mate is not necessarily oppressive for the women concerned: many want children, but do not want permanent ties with men—and communes are among the few situations available to them in which they are accepted, have adult help with children and adult company, and work-demands do not necessarily separate them from their children. Since many such women draw Aid to Dependent Children, an adequate subsidy in the economics of most communes—women with children but without mates are welcome additions to many communes.

Because the movement is in its early stages, most commune children are under five. The large number of adults provides for them a rich ambience of security and affection. According to Berger:

> But for children older than four or five, the responsibilities of either parents or the other adult communards may be much attenuated. All children are viewed as intrinsically worthy of love and respect *but not necessarily of attention.* As they grow out of primitive physical dependence upon the care of adults, they are treated and tend to behave as just another member of the extended family—including being offered (and taking) an occasional hit on a joint of marijuana as it is passed around the family circle.

Children are usually expected to share in the chores, farming, and industry. Often, as in the case of my children on our farm, they are relatively isolated from other children of the same age—and adults vary in their willingness to take special time with them to play games, tell stories, talk,

---

[4]In the U.S. Virgin Islands, where I lived for over two years, the norm is that women want children, but are often resistant to having men live with them regularly. The average age for mothers having their first babies is about twelve or thirteen. Since many young mothers work, grandmothers are often primarily responsible for childcare. I have wondered whether the commune movement in the United States might not drift in the direction of such a matriarchal arrangement, since transience and change are more and more characteristic of what Warren Bennis and Philip Slater have called *The Temporary Society,* and the responsibility for care of infants is one of the most stabilizing influences in that context.

or teach. Judged (often justly) from the point of view of the old culture, this amounts to neglect. Berger quotes a young mother, "harried with the care of her two-year-old," who said, "What I wanted was a *baby;* but a *kid,* that's something else." Neglect is, of course, rarely deliberate. It is important for some adults, even mothers, to avoid role stereotyping, to be free to say they are not "into" children at some periods of their life, and they may have competitive childish needs of their own which interfere with giving attention to children. Usually there are enough other adults around to take up the slack in these circumstances.

Reports of communes are speckled with instances of child neglect on the one hand and examples of preternatural maturity on the other. One may create the other. I remember visiting a commune in an old mill beside a shallow, fast stream. Three or four infants, two or under—grubby, bottomless, unattended—were playing on the bridge over this stream. I was equally nervous about their welfare and about intervening, so hovered near them—no doubt polluting the environment with my old-culture vibes. Nothing happened. There had never been serious accidents. "We never had to take a kid to the hospital," a member said, "except once, to get born. We had to take big people to the hospital three or four times, who got hurt playing around on the swings and things." Of another child he said:

> The growth of three-year-old Julie in the four or five months she was here is amazing. When she first came she was extremely attached to her mother; she could barely be without her; she was a very inward person with no sense of adventure. In four months it wasn't uncommon to be sitting in the mill at midnight when who should walk in by herself but Julie and ask, "What's happening?" To get to the mill she had to get out of bed, usually get dressed, and walk down a rather narrow unlit path about a hundred and fifty feet in the black of night.

As a teacher for most of my life, as well as a parent, I became very confused about the purposes of education. The *teacher's* purpose, particularly as he ages, subtly becomes to perpetuate his job, hence to perpetuate dependency—and parents, too, for emotional rather than economic reasons, are subject to this trap if the context of their lives did not enable them to accept self-worth. It becomes difficult to believe that young people can learn without our supervision, which obscures the fact that the whole point of education is precisely to develop capacity for such learning.

A commune mother in Oregon describes the fine line between neglect and smothering. On the one hand she recognizes that mothers are more likely than other adults on a commune to be aware of their children's whereabouts and safety—"the mommy twitch." On the other hand she sees the emergence of shared concern on the part of the other adults and independence on the part of the child as the direction of educational development.

Mother is often up at the green house or weeding the garden. She doesn't say goodbye each time she goes outdoors. There are lots of strange adults around and they offer to do things only parents are supposed to do.

Kid, crying: "I want my bottle."

Grown up: "OK, I'll make your bottle for you."

Kid: "*No*, I don't want *you* to make my bottle, I want my *dad* to make my bottle!"

Grown up: "Uhhh . . ."

Every child who's ever come here to live has freaked out at first. They go wandering across the fields, yelling at the top of their lungs for "Mommy!" and refusing help from anyone else. When they find mommy she is (ideally) sympathetic but firm. "No, I can't stay indoors all the time. We're living in a new place now, and I want to do some work out of doors. Look, I'm pulling up weeds, so we can have carrots to eat. No, I don't want to sleep in the same building as you every night, but there will always be someone there to take care of you, and I'm not very far away. Would you like to sit on my lap for a while right now?" In real life this . . . is varied with "God-damit, Larissa, you've got to leave me alone sometimes!" After a month or two or three all the strange adults are not so strange anymore, the garden and meadow are familiar territory, and the tensions ease. Many things come to feel like, simply, the way things are. Once I watched Abe and Woody playing with their blocks. "Now we'll build an A-frame, and next we'll build a dome, and we'll put the shitter right over here. Look, Mom, here's the communal building!" Of course, of course, what else would they build with their blocks? Still, I had never pictured that scene before.[5]

Just as the word *shitter* may be shocking to old-culture sensibilities, so may be the conscious process of psychological weaning. So much attention is given in our society to child-rearing and education that displacement—away from the "child-centered home"—in the direction of concentration upon adult relationships seems selfish and inhumane. On the other hand, we know, or at least we have often been told, that adults in our society have a tendency to play out the drama of their lives using children as unwitting media. Many of today's young people are in rebellion against the marriages of their parents which, as children, they perceived were desperately strung together using children as the excuse, the surrogate, the compensation for failures in adult relationships. Often what "real" communication took place between the parents—be it disputes or meaningful sharing, about finances, roles, sex, jealousy, aspirations, disappointments—was shielded from the children. Their impression of grown-up conversation was likely to have been of a flow of abstractions, impersonal practicalities, putdowns, and inexplicably explosive moods, like a scuffle observed in silhouette behind drawn blinds in an apartment across the street.

The transparency of communal life opens to children all that was hidden to their parents when they were children—for better or worse.

[5]Elaine Sundancer, *Celery Wine*, Community Services, Inc., 1973, pp. 36–37.

Last night a tense and sometimes tempestuous meeting was taking place in our living room when I went upstairs to get something. Polly was watching television. "Aren't you glad you aren't an adult?" I asked. She grinned, "Uh-hmm." But, in fact, usually she is drawn to such meetings, rarely participating, but hanging on, listening, learning, reaching her own conclusions, generally ignored as her elders lay open their passions and concerns. At times I cringe, realizing what she is hearing, what candid exposure to adult social reality is forming her mind. It is the pain of contemplation of one's daughter's deflowering, of the disillusionment of growth, of letting children know too early that there is no Santa Claus. Like other middle-aged people, I have been taught that reality is to be revealed to children in graduated doses, that in all aspects of life one moves with caution from storks to birds and bees, and the actual flesh encounter is to be as long as possible delayed, finally to take place more-or-less covertly, out of familial ken.

There is no way that can happen on communes. The mere presence of so many adults, with their conflicting views of everything, including child-rearing, dazzles the child with a kaleidoscope of attitudes and behaviors. In place of the impoverished range of adult models in the nuclear family, amplified by, usually, a female teacher in kindergarten and first grade, then the specialists of later schooling, the communal child finds himself immediately not a witness to but a part of a network of complex relationships, a person among people.

An urban nursery-school teacher observes:

> The kids from families have different life-styles and values, they're used to certain clothes, to doing certain things. Often it's basically a financial difference. The kids from communes are used to a looser, more fluid environment, and they're less dependent on their parents. But I've also noticed that it's good to have more than one kid in a commune. It confuses them to have too many authority figures around—or just too many adults.[6]

In the early days of Berkeley communes, she says, there was little interest in having children—"there were too many white children anyway"—but there is now increasing recognition that people are into the movement for the long run. "More people want kids," she said. "They don't think the revolution will happen next year and they have time for it." Meanwhile the nursery school itself has radical political goals. Unlike schools where individual achievement is stressed, Blue Fairyland engages children in cooperative efforts, urging "the children to work on things together, from drawing posters to preparing lunch. Some of the kids stay for dinner with the parent commune and occasionally a few sleep over, an attempt to decrease dependency on their own parents."

Consistency of treatment and security of sustained relationships have

[6]Quoted by Steven V. Roberts, "Halfway Between Dropping Out and Dropping In," *New York Times Magazine,* Sept. 12, 1971, p. 60 ff.

been stressed as desirable by psychologists in our society, but the opposite conditions generally prevail in communes. Of the communal child, Carl Rogers says, "He does not receive consistent treatment, but he lives in a world of real adults, to whose idiosyncrasies he must adjust while finding psychological room for himself, his desires and his activities." In view of the intensity of emotional life in most communes, this may amount to a crash course in the relativity of human relationships. But it seems generally to create self-confidence, responsibility, and a positive, joyful view of life in most children. Rogers says:

> Furthermore, the rural communal child has a place in the group life. As soon as he has the physical strength for it—certainly by age five or six—he can help in the never-ending tasks of a rural existence. He feels himself *useful,* an experience so rare as to be almost nonexistent in the suburban or urban child of our present-day culture.

.   .   .

KIT HAVICE

Kit Havice was born in Keene Valley, New York, in 1940 and raised in New York and Colorado. She attended Oberlin and Stanford, where she received a B.A. in 1963. She then entered medical school but soon took a leave of absence to work in the peace movement and the civil-rights movement. At that time she joined a peace walk from Washington to Guantánamo. On the way through the South many of the marchers also addressed the civil-rights question. They were jailed three times in Georgia —in Griffen, in Macon, and in Albany. The marchers fasted for fifty days in Albany's jail but finally won the first concession granted by Albany authorities: five marchers of their choosing were permitted to walk through the downtown carrying placards and leaflets.

After release from jail, Ms. Havice continued to Florida with the walk but then returned to Albany, where she worked for two years in the civil-rights movement. She was in charge of food for the march from Selma to Montgomery, Alabama. She then entered Union Theological Seminary in Virginia, where she received the Bachelor of Divinity in 1969. But while studying, she continued to work in Georgia during the summers and in 1968 was a seated delegate who backed Julian Bond for President at the Democratic National Convention. In 1970 she began doctoral work on

*the Old Testament and social ethics at Yale University and is presently
finishing her dissertation, "The Concern for the Widow and the Fatherless
in the Ancient Near East." Since 1972 she has been teaching in the
Department of Religion at Syracuse University. In recent years, she has
also become increasingly active in the women's movement.*
The letter we reprint below was written in Albany's city jail.

Letter from Albany City Jail

Albany City Jail
12:30 a.m., Feb. 16, 1964

Dear Art,

Many thoughts run through my head tonight. It is a more or less
typical Saturday night here, with its usual attendant undercurrent of
noise. A small world of suffering seems concentrated here. Last night a
young man beat up a middle aged one and sent him to the hospital.
Tonight there are the many usual drunks howling "mother fucker" at the
jailers for imprisoning them, and a man with many psychologically caused
medical difficulties, such as fainting spells, trouble breathing, wishing to
be free, and general howling. The latter, probably a poor guy who may
even come to jail to get some sort of concern and attention. A few cases
of D.T.'s. A Negro youngster of about 15 crying in the background while
a cop goes about his business whistling a cheerful tune. Then later a
Negro woman who as best as I can gather was being dragged and mo-
lested by a man, when a cop shot him through the head and brought her
down for questioning. She was terrified because she felt she would be
charged with it and somehow it was all connected with a robbery. I find
myself starting to dissociate myself from it the way one does in a hospital,
but here it all seems far worse because no one is being helped or cured,
just suffering.

It feels good to me to be here still and because of the hopeful turn
of events to be still involved with whatever suffering we share in a meaningful way. My wish to get out was a weakness based on the feeling of
irrelevancy and impotence of our witness to the Albany issue. It is far
better for my inner peace to be involved again for however long it takes.

Ah, Art, the problem is not how to survive the suffering by dissociating
from it. The problem is somehow to stay vitally concerned. Otherwise we
manage to live good sterile lives ensconced in our apartments in Denver
or Stanford. The problem it seems is far more to keep a small edge of
ourselves rubbed raw and smarting so we can somehow understand, with
our lives, all lives. The first sonnet struck me with this like a blow:

> And yet, some [T]hing that moves among the stars,
> And holds the cosmos in a web of law,
> Moves too in me: a hunger, a quick thaw
> Of soul that liquefies the ancient bars,
> As I, a member of creation, sing
> The burning oneness binding everything.[1]

I have always seen it as a 3 year old, a 3 year old with the face of every child, unhappy, or wondering with a sort of bewilderment how it happened what is happening. And somehow I know that as long as there is this child before me I can't stop caring and I hope trying to create a world where he/she can live without always this look. Or at least in a world where he or she can hope to grow up and know love. And all this wars in me with the wish for an apartment, peace and quiet, good music, a "respectable" life, a bath, pizza, a walk in the forest. Not always wars because I believe there are combinations that can bring answers to both. (I hope.)

Another of my frequent thoughts—Hiroshima was bombed when I was very close to being that above child—when I was 5. And while this would seem to absolve me because I was too young, it really doesn't at all. You see it was bombed so children like myself could grow up in a world "safe for democracy." It was bombed with me as its justification. And somehow—somehow—I've got to tell the world never to do it again —at least not for me.

But then one is again faced with the question: what does one do to somehow balance the suffering and joy within one's life so it is viable. Peace-walking or projects such as this are no long term answer because one can not live at such a pitch year after year. But then how to be incorporated within the peace movement without simply being reduced to an office machine or an AFSC educational director? (both of which seem very sterile to me.) If one decides to work in the integration movement much can be said for simply moving to the area and taking up a witness within a profession and the Movement—such as your thought of practicing in the South. But a way to work in the peace movement on a comparable personal level seems harder to find. I have thought of the value of continuing to interrelate the two movements through establishing a nonviolent action group keyed to both in the South. I still have the hunch that the most good can be done for the peace movement by attempting to broaden the relevance of the nonviolent ethic with the Negro people down here who are already beginning to understand. Have you been to a church service yet where nonviolence was preached? It can be one of the most heartening experiences I know.

---

[1][Kenneth Boulding, *There is a Spirit; The Nayler Sonnets* (Nyack, N.Y.: Fellowship Publications, 1945), p. 1, lines 9–14. Reprinted with the permission of The Fellowship of Reconciliation, Eds.]

Speaking of kids earlier—I wanted to tell you of two of the most wonderful times I've had on the walk. One was in Salisbury, North Carolina, when a number of little Negro kids came running around where I was working on the Bulletin. They stood around shyly for awhile, then one little girl hesitatingly and very fearfully reached out and touched my hair because it was so different from her own. Soon they were all stroking it. It was an act of trust toward me that they would be allowed to do this, that reached across innumerable barriers.

And the most wonderful to me—we were walking along the road at the very end of a long hard day and the Walk passed some little kids aged 5–7 hauling and struggling with huge buckets and gallon jugs of water the half mile to their shack up the road. Dave Dellinger, big man that he is, caught up and overtook the first little boy. He reached down with his free hand that wasn't carrying his sign and took the bucket to carry it. Barbara Deming came up behind the littlest and took the gallon jug from him and walked on. The kids were startled at first but soon were skipping along beside their buckets and jugs at the side of the line of walkers, looking up every few steps and grinning at us. The walk stopped for the day just a little way short of their house and the kids carefully took their buckets back and walked on home with their parents out in front watching what to them must have been a truly miraculous sight—the grown white people helping the Negro kids haul the water. It somehow symbolized to me all that we are possibly hoping to do and say. And yet as we moved on we knew we will always have been simply an isolated miracle in these kids' lives. Nothing will have changed, and for the rest of their childhood they will haul the water that long half mile while the whites have running water and the white people will curse them and call them "boy."

The wonder of it all is not that the Albany people have not joined us sooner but that they have come to trust us at all. C. B. and Slater King speak with real wonder when they saw a Negro taxicab driver spontaneously wave to two white walkers walking downtown. There is so much that has happened and that is happening that if we do not actually do—we still allow to happen. Our concern has to reach out.

I went to a Baptist church on December 21 with Carl, and was the only white person there. A man got up and castigated the whites for their impossibilities as I tried to sink into my seat; but he ended by pointing to me and saying in ringing tones: "But there is a miracle—a living divine miracle in your presence! Listen to her, do what she says!" *That* simply because I went to a church. (And me an atheist.) It makes one feel very inadequate. I must close this—it is very good to have you out there. Life is very good.

Very much love,

KIT

STUDS TERKEL

The Mason

CARL MURRAY BATES

We're in a tavern no more than thirty yards from the banks of the Ohio. Toward the far side of the river, Alcoa smokestacks belch forth: an uneasy coupling of a bucolic past and an industrial present. The waters are polluted, yet the jobs out there offer the townspeople their daily bread.

He is fifty-seven years old. He's a stonemason who has pursued his craft since he was seventeen. None of his three sons is in his trade.

As far as I know, masonry is older than carpentry, which goes clear back to Bible times. Stonemason goes back way *before* Bible time: the pyramids of Egypt, things of that sort. Anybody that starts to build anything, stone, rock, or brick, start on the northeast corner. Because when they built King Solomon's Temple, they started on the northeast corner. To this day, you look at your courthouses, your big public buildings, you look at the cornerstone, when it was created, what year, it will be on the northeast corner. If I was gonna build a septic tank, I would start on the northeast corner. (Laughs.) Superstition, I suppose.

With stone we build just about anything. Stone is the oldest and best building material that ever was. Stone was being used even by the cavemen that put it together with mud. They built out of stone before they even used logs. He got him a cave, he built stone across the front. And he learned to use dirt, mud, to make the stones lay there without sliding around—which was the beginnings of mortar, which we still call mud. The Romans used mortar that's almost as good as we have today.

Everyone hears these things, they just don't remember 'em. But me being in the profession, when I hear something in that line, I remember it. Stone's my business. I, oh, sometimes talk to architects and engineers that have made a study and I pick up the stuff here and there.

Every piece of stone you pick up is different, the grain's a little different and this and that. It'll split one way and break the other. You pick up your stone and look at it and make an educated guess. It's a pretty good day layin' stone or brick. Not tiring. Anything you like to do isn't tiresome. It's hard work; stone is heavy. At the same time, you get interested in what you're doing and you usually fight the clock the other way. You're not lookin' for quittin'. You're wondering you haven't got enough done and it's almost quittin' time. (Laughs.) I ask the hod carrier what time it is and he says two thirty. I say, "Oh, my Lord, I was gonna get a whole lot more than this."

I pretty well work by myself. On houses, usually just one works. I've got the hod carrier there, but most of the time I talk to myself, "I'll get my hammer and I'll knock the chip off there." (Laughs.) A good hod carrier is half your day. He won't work as hard as a poor one. He knows what to do and make every move count makin' the mortar. It has to be so much water, so much sand. His skill is to see that you don't run out of anything. The hod carrier, he's above the laborer. He has a certain amount of prestige.

I think a laborer feels that he's the low man. Not so much that he works with his hands, it's that he's at the bottom of the scale. He always wants to get up to a skilled trade. Of course he'd make more money. The main thing is the common laborer—even the word *common* laborer—just sounds so common, he's at the bottom. Many that works with his hands takes pride in his work.

I get a lot of phone calls when I get home: how about showin' me how and I'll do it myself; I always wind up doin' it for 'em. (Laughs.) So I take a lot of pride in it and I do get, oh, I'd say, a lot of praise or whatever you want to call it. I don't suppose anybody, however much he's recognized, wouldn't like to be recognized a little more. I think I'm pretty well recognized.

One of my sons is an accountant and the other two are bankers. They're mathematicians, I suppose you'd call 'em that. Air-conditioned offices and all that. They always look at the house I build. They stop by and see me when I'm aworkin'. Always want me to come down and fix somethin' on their house, too. (Laughs.) They don't buy a house that I don't have to look at it first. Oh sure, I've got to crawl under it and look on the roof, you know . . .

I can't seem to think of any young masons. So many of 'em before, the man lays stone and his son follows his footsteps. Right now the only one of these sons I can think of is about forty, fifty years old.

I started back in the Depression times when there wasn't any apprenticeships. You just go out and if you could hold your job, that's it. I was just a kid then. Now I worked real hard and carried all the blocks I could. Then I'd get my trowel and I'd lay one or two. The second day the boss told me: I think you could lay enough blocks to earn your wages. So I guess I had only one day of apprenticeship. Usually it takes about three years of being a hod carrier to start. And it takes another ten or fifteen years to learn the skill.

I admired the men that we had at that time that were stonemasons. They knew their trade. So naturally I tried to pattern after them. There's been very little change in the work. Stone is still stone, mortar is still the same as it was fifty years ago. The style of stone has changed a little. We use a lot more, we call it golf. A stone as big as a baseball up to as big as a basketball. Just round balls and whatnot. We just fit 'em in the wall that way.

Automation has tried to get in the bricklayer. Set 'em with a crane. I've seen several put up that way. But you've always got in-between the windows and this and that. It just doesn't seem to pan out. We do have a power saw. We do have an electric power mix to mix the mortar, but the rest of it's done by hand as it always was.

In the old days they all seemed to want it cut out and smoothed. It's harder now because you have no way to use your tools. You have no way to use a string, you have no way to use a level or a plumb. You just have to look at it because it's so rough and many irregularities. You have to just back up and look at it.

All construction, there's always a certain amount of injuries. A scaffold will break and so on. But practically no real danger. All I ever did do was work on houses, so we don't get up very high—maybe two stories. Very seldom that any more. Most of 'em are one story. And so many of 'em use stone for a trim. They may go up four, five feet and then paneling or something. There's a lot of skinned fingers or you hit your finger with a hammer. Practically all stone is worked with hammers and chisels. I wouldn't call it dangerous at all.

Stone's my life. I daydream all the time, most times it's on stone. Oh, I'm gonna build me a stone cabin down on the Green River. I'm gonna build stone cabinets in the kitchen. That stone door's gonna be awful heavy and I don't know how to attach the hinges. I've got to figure out how to make a stone roof. That's the kind of thing. All my dreams, it seems like it's got to have a piece of rock mixed in it.

If I got some problem that's bothering me, I'll actually wake up in the night and think of it. I'll sit at the table and get a pencil and paper and go over it, makin' marks on paper or drawin' or however . . . this way or that way. Now I've got to work this and I've only got so much. Or they decided they want it that way when you already got it fixed this way. Anyone hates tearing his work down. It's all the same price but you still don't like to do it.

These fireplaces, you've got to figure how they'll throw out heat, the way you curve the fireboxes inside. You have to draw a line so they reflect heat. But if you throw out too much of a curve, you'll have them smoke. People in these fine houses don't want a puff of smoke coming out of the house.

The architect draws the picture and the plans, and the draftsman and the engineer, they help him. They figure the strength and so on. But when it comes to actually makin' the curves and doin' the work, you've got to do it with your hands. It comes right back to your hands.

When you get into stone, you're gettin' away from the prefabs, you're gettin' into the better homes. Usually at this day and age they'll start into sixty to seventy thousand and run up to about half a million. We've got one goin' now that's mighty close, three or four hundred thousand. That type of house is what we build.

The lumber is not near as good as it used to be. We have better fabricating material, such as plywood and sheet rock and things of that sort, but the lumber itself is definitely inferior. Thirty, forty years ago a house was almost entirely made of lumber, wood floors . . . Now they have vinyl, they have carpet, everything, and so on. The framework wood is getting to be of very poor quality.

But stone is still stone and the bricks are actually more uniform than they used to be. Originally they took a clay bank . . . I know a church been built that way. Went right on location, dug a hole in the ground and formed bricks with their hands. They made the bricks that built the building on the spot.

Now we've got modern kilns, modern heat, the temperature don't vary. They got better bricks now than they used to have. We've got machines that make brick, so they're made true. Where they used to, they were pretty rough. I'm buildin' a big fireplace now out of old brick. They run wide, long, and it's a headache. I've been two weeks on that one fireplace.

The toughest job I ever done was this house, a hundred years old plus. The lady wanted one room left just that way. And this doorway had to be closed. It had deteriorated and weathered for over a hundred years. The bricks was made out of broken pieces, none of 'em were straight. If you lay 'em crooked, it gets awful hard right there. You spend a lifetime tryin' to learn to lay bricks straight. And it took a half-day to measure with a spoon, to try to get the mortar to match. I'd have so much dirt, so much soot, so much lime, so when I got the recipe right I could make it in bigger quantity. Then I made it with a coffee cup. Half a cup of this, half a cup of that . . . I even used soot out of a chimney and sweepin's off the floor. I was two days layin' up a little doorway, mixin' the mortar and all. The boss told the lady it couldn't be done. I said, "Give me the time, I believe I can do it." I defy you to find where that door is right now. That's the best job I ever done.

There's not a house in this country that I haven't built that I don't look at every time I go by. (Laughs.) I can set here now and actually in my mind see so many that you wouldn't believe. If there's one stone in there crooked, I know where it's at and I'll never forget it. Maybe thirty years, I'll know a place where I should have took that stone out and redone it but I didn't. I still notice it. The people who live there might not notice it, but I notice it. I never pass that house that I don't think of it. I've got one house in mind right now. (Laughs.) That's the work of my hands. 'Cause you see, stone, you don't prepaint it, you don't camouflage it. It's there, just like I left it forty years ago.

I can't imagine a job where you go home and maybe go by a year later and you don't know what you've done. My work, I can see what I did the first day I started. All my work is set right out there in the open and I can

look at it as I go by. It's something I can see the rest of my life. Forty years
ago, the first blocks I ever laid in my life, when I was seventeen years old.
I never go through Eureka—a little town down there on the river—that
I don't look thataway. It's always there.

Immortality as far as we're concerned. Nothin' in this world lasts
forever, but did you know that stone—Bedford limestone, they claim—
deteriorates one-sixteenth of an inch every hundred years? And it's
around four or five inches for a house. So that's gettin' awful close.
(Laughs.)

[From *Working,* by Studs Terkel, Pantheon Books, 1974]

ISAAC BASHEVIS SINGER

*Isaac Bashevis Singer, the most popular living Yiddish writer, is also
becoming one of the most popular living American writers. He has been a
steady contributor to the Yiddish* Jewish Daily Forward *since he arrived
in New York City in 1935 and in recent years has also become a frequent
contributor to* The New Yorker. *He still writes in Yiddish, his childhood
language ("a writer has to write in his own language or not at all") but
by now he is almost always involved in the translation of his own work
("I do not exaggerate when I say that English has become my 'second
original language' ").*

*Singer was born in Poland in 1904, the grandson of two rabbis, the
son of a Hasidic scholar. He himself received a traditional Jewish
education and for a while studied at a rabbinical seminary, but he began
to doubt "not the power of God, but all the traditions and dogmas." As a
result he disappointed family expectations and instead followed the example
of his older brother to become a secular writer. He took a job as
proofreader for a Yiddish literary journal in Warsaw. By 1926 Singer
began to publish stories and reviews. Then in 1935 he followed his brother
to New York City, where he still lives on the Upper West Side.*

Success came with the English translation of his 1945 novel, The
Family Moskat. *Other novels include the two-volume* The Manor
(1967) and The Estate *(1969), but he is best known for his short
stories. Collections include* Gimpel the Fool *(1957),* The Spinoza of
Market Street *(1957), and* The Seance *(1968).* In My Father's
Court *(1966) and* A Day of Pleasure: Stories of a Boy Growing
Up in Warsaw *(1969) are mainly autobiographical. Singer has also
written children's stories, and in 1973 he made his playwriting debut with
an adaptation of* The Manor, *produced by the Yale Repertory Theatre.*

But primarily Singer is an old-fashioned storyteller. Many of his stories, set in shtetls and ghettos of prewar Poland, draw heavily on Jewish legend and folklore and are peopled with witches and ghosts and demons. An increasing number now deal with life in the United States and are set in contemporary New York. "Because I have now lived in this country longer than in Poland," he says, "I have developed roots here too." "The Son from America," which we reprint below, tells of an encounter between these two cultures. It first appeared in The New Yorker *and was later reprinted in the short-story collection* A Crown of Feathers *(1970). The translation is by the author and Dorothea Straus.*

The Son from America

The village of Lentshin was tiny—a sandy marketplace where the peasants of the area met once a week. It was surrounded by little huts with thatched roofs or shingles green with moss. The chimneys looked like pots. Between the huts there were fields, where the owners planted vegetables or pastured their goats.

In the smallest of these huts lived old Berl, a man in his eighties, and his wife, who was called Berlcha (wife of Berl). Old Berl was one of the Jews who had been driven from their villages in Russia and had settled in Poland. In Lentshin, they mocked the mistakes he made while praying aloud. He spoke with a sharp "r." He was short, broad-shouldered, and had a small white beard, and summer and winter he wore a sheepskin hat, a padded cotton jacket, and stout boots. He walked slowly, shuffling his feet. He had a half acre of field, a cow, a goat, and chickens.

The couple had a son, Samuel, who had gone to America forty years ago. It was said in Lentshin that he became a millionaire there. Every month, the Lentshin letter carrier brought old Berl a money order and a letter that no one could read because many of the words were English. How much money Samuel sent his parents remained a secret. Three times a year, Berl and his wife went on foot to Zakroczym and cashed the money orders there. But they never seemed to use the money. What for? The garden, the cow, and the goat provided most of their needs. Besides, Berlcha sold chickens and eggs, and from these there was enough to buy flour for bread.

No one cared to know where Berl kept the money that his son sent him. There were no thieves in Lentshin. The hut consisted of one room, which contained all their belongings: the table, the shelf for meat, the shelf for milk foods, the two beds, and the clay oven. Sometimes the chickens roosted in the woodshed and sometimes, when it was cold, in a coop near the oven. The goat, too, found shelter inside when the weather was bad. The more prosperous villagers had kerosene lamps, but

Berl and his wife did not believe in newfangled gadgets. What was wrong with a wick in a dish of oil? Only for the Sabbath would Berlcha buy three tallow candles at the store. In summer, the couple got up at sunrise and retired with the chickens. In the long winter evenings, Berlcha spun flax at her spinning wheel and Berl sat beside her in the silence of those who enjoy their rest.

Once in a while when Berl came home from the synagogue after evening prayers, he brought news to his wife. In Warsaw there were strikers who demanded that the czar abdicate. A heretic by the name of Dr. Herzl had come up with the idea that Jews should settle again in Palestine. Berlcha listened and shook her bonneted head. Her face was yellowish and wrinkled like a cabbage leaf. There were bluish sacks under her eyes. She was half deaf. Berl had to repeat each word he said to her. She would say, "The things that happen in the big cities!"

Here in Lentshin nothing happened except usual events: a cow gave birth to a calf, a young couple had a circumcision party, or a girl was born and there was no party. Occasionally, someone died. Lentshin had no cemetery, and the corpse had to be taken to Zakroczym. Actually, Lentshin had become a village with few young people. The young men left for Zakroczym, for Nowy Dwor, for Warsaw, and sometimes for the United States. Like Samuel's, their letters were illegible, the Yiddish mixed with the languages of the countries where they were now living. They sent photographs in which the men wore top hats and the women fancy dresses like squiresses.

Berl and Berlcha also received such photographs. But their eyes were failing and neither he nor she had glasses. They could barely make out the pictures. Samuel had sons and daughters with Gentile names—and grandchildren who had married and had their own offspring. Their names were so strange that Berl and Berlcha could never remember them. But what difference do names make? America was far, far away on the other side of the ocean, at the edge of the world. A Talmud teacher who came to Lentshin had said that Americans walked with their heads down and their feet up. Berl and Berlcha could not grasp this. How was it possible? But since the teacher said so it must be true. Berlcha pondered for some time and then she said, "One can get accustomed to everything."

And so it remained. From too much thinking—God forbid—one may lose one's wits.

One Friday morning, when Berlcha was kneading the dough for the Sabbath loaves, the door opened and a nobleman entered. He was so tall that he had to bend down to get through the door. He wore a beaver hat and a cloak bordered with fur. He was followed by Chazkel, the coachman from Zakroczym, who carried two leather valises with brass locks. In astonishment Berlcha raised her eyes.

The nobleman looked around and said to the coachman in Yiddish,

"Here it is." He took out a silver ruble and paid him. The coachman tried to hand him change but he said, "You can go now."

When the coachman closed the door, the nobleman said, "Mother, it's me, your son Samuel—Sam."

Berlcha heard the words and her legs grew numb. Her hands, to which pieces of dough were sticking, lost their power. The nobleman hugged her, kissed her forehead, both her cheeks. Berlcha began to cackle like a hen, "My son!" At that moment Berl came in from the woodshed, his arms piled with logs. The goat followed him. When he saw a nobleman kissing his wife, Berl dropped the wood and exclaimed, "What is this?"

The nobleman let go of Berlcha and embraced Berl. "Father!"

For a long time Berl was unable to utter a sound. He wanted to recite holy words that he had read in the Yiddish Bible, but he could remember nothing. Then he asked, "Are you Samuel?"

"Yes, Father, I am Samuel."

"Well, peace be with you." Berl grasped his son's hand. He was still not sure that he was not being fooled. Samuel wasn't as tall and heavy as this man, but then Berl reminded himself that Samuel was only fifteen years old when he had left home. He must have grown in that faraway country. Berl asked, "Why didn't you let us know that you were coming?"

"Didn't you receive my cable?" Samuel asked.

Berl did not know what a cable was.

Berlcha had scraped the dough from her hands and enfolded her son. He kissed her again and asked, "Mother, didn't you receive a cable?"

"What? If I lived to see this, I am happy to die," Berlcha said, amazed by her own words. Berl, too, was amazed. These were just the words he would have said earlier if he had been able to remember. After a while Berl came to himself and said, "Pescha, you will have to make a double Sabbath pudding in addition to the stew."

It was years since Berl had called Berlcha by her given name. When he wanted to address her, he would say, "Listen," or "Say." It is the young or those from the big cities who call a wife by her name. Only now did Berlcha begin to cry. Yellow tears ran from her eyes, and everything became dim. Then she called out, "It's Friday—I have to prepare for the Sabbath." Yes, she had to knead the dough and braid the loaves. With such a guest, she had to make a larger Sabbath stew. The winter day is short and she must hurry.

Her son understood what was worrying her, because he said, "Mother, I will help you."

Berlcha wanted to laugh, but a choked sob came out. "What are you saying? God forbid."

The nobleman took off his cloak and jacket and remained in his vest, on which hung a solid-gold watch chain. He rolled up his sleeves and came to the trough. "Mother, I was a baker for many years in New York," he said, and he began to knead the dough.

"What! You are my darling son who will say Kaddish for me." She wept raspingly. Her strength left her, and she slumped onto the bed.

Berl said, "Women will always be women." And he went to the shed to get more wood. The goat sat down near the oven; she gazed with surprise at this strange man—his height and his bizarre clothes.

The neighbors had heard the good news that Berl's son had arrived from America and they came to greet him. The women began to help Berlcha prepare for the Sabbath. Some laughed, some cried. The room was full of people, as at a wedding. They asked Berl's son, "What is new in America?" And Berl's son answered, "America is all right."

"Do Jews make a living?"

"One eats white bread there on weekdays."

"Do they remain Jews?"

"I am not a Gentile."

After Berlcha blessed the candles, father and son went to the little synagogue across the street. A new snow had fallen. The son took large steps, but Berl warned him, "Slow down."

In the synagogue the Jews recited "Let Us Exult" and "Come, My Groom." All the time, the snow outside kept falling. After prayers, when Berl and Samuel left the Holy Place, the village was unrecognizable. Everything was covered in snow. One could see only the contours of the roofs and the candles in the windows. Samuel said, "Nothing has changed here."

Berlcha had prepared gefilte fish, chicken soup with rice, meat, carrot stew. Berl recited the benediction over a glass of ritual wine. The family ate and drank, and when it grew quiet for a while one could hear the chirping of the house cricket. The son talked a lot, but Berl and Berlcha understood little. His Yiddish was different and contained foreign words.

After the final blessing Samuel asked, "Father, what did you do with all the money I sent you?"

Berl raised his white brows. "It's here."

"Didn't you put it in a bank?"

"There is no bank in Lentshin."

"Where do you keep it?"

Berl hesitated. "One is not allowed to touch money on the Sabbath, but I will show you." He crouched beside the bed and began to shove something heavy. A boot appeared. Its top was stuffed with straw. Berl removed the straw and the son saw that the boot was full of gold coins. He lifted it.

"Father, this is a treasure!" he called out.

"Well."

"Why didn't you spend it?"

"On what? Thank God, we have everything."

"Why didn't you travel somewhere?"

"Where to? This is our home."

The son asked one question after the other, but Berl's answer was always the same: they wanted for nothing. The garden, the cow, the goat, the chickens provided them with all they needed. The son said, "If thieves knew about this, your lives wouldn't be safe."

"There are no thieves here."

"What will happen to the money?"

"You take it."

Slowly, Berl and Berlcha grew accustomed to their son and his American Yiddish. Berlcha could hear him better now. She even recognized his voice. He was saying, "Perhaps we should build a larger synagogue."

"The synagogue is big enough," Berl replied.

"Perhaps a home for old people."

"No one sleeps in the street."

The next day after the Sabbath meal was eaten, a Gentile from Zakroczym brought a paper—it was the cable. Berl and Berlcha lay down for a nap. They soon began to snore. The goat, too, dozed off. The son put on his cloak and his hat and went for a walk. He strode with his long legs across the marketplace. He stretched out a hand and touched a roof. He wanted to smoke a cigar, but he remembered it was forbidden on the Sabbath. He had a desire to talk to someone, but it seemed that the whole of Lentshin was asleep. He entered the synagogue. An old man was sitting there, reciting psalms. Samuel asked, "Are you praying?"

"What else is there to do when one gets old?"

"Do you make a living?"

The old man did not understand the meaning of these words. He smiled, showing his empty gums, and then he said, "If God gives health, one keeps on living."

Samuel returned home. Dusk had fallen. Berl went to the synagogue for the evening prayers and the son remained with his mother. The room was filled with shadows.

Berlcha began to recite in a solemn singsong, "God of Abraham, Isaac, and Jacob, defend the poor people of Israel and Thy name. The Holy Sabbath is departing; the welcome week is coming to us. Let it be one of health, wealth, and good deeds."

"Mother, you don't need to pray for wealth," Samuel said. "You are wealthy already."

Berlcha did not hear—or pretended not to. Her face had turned into a cluster of shadows.

In the twilight Samuel put his hand into his jacket pocket and touched his passport, his checkbook, his letters of credit. He had come here with big plans. He had a valise filled with presents for his parents. He wanted to bestow gifts on the village. He brought not only his own money but funds from the Lentshin Society in New York, which had organized a ball for the benefit of the village. But this village in the hinterland needed nothing. From the synagogue one could hear hoarse chanting. The cricket, silent all day, started again its chirping. Berlcha began to sway and utter holy rhymes inherited from mothers and grandmothers:

> Thy holy sheep
> In mercy keep,
> In Torah and good deeds;
> Provide for all their needs,
> Shoes, clothes, and bread
> And the Messiah's tread.

The Roles of the Sexes

What do "masculine" and "feminine" really mean? Does one "naturally" behave like a man or like a woman? Are our roles in life inevitably predetermined by our gender? Is the traditional division of sex roles fair to women and really good for men? Eva Figes introduces the subject by raising the whole question of nature versus nurture, of how and why men and women see themselves as they do. She finds that the evidence strongly favors nurture. We are social animals, she says, and our "natural" condition is to be much more influenced by our environments than we have been willing to acknowledge.

Neither the *New York Herald* editor nor D. H. Lawrence agrees. The former, writing in 1852, is scandalized by women who leave their "true sphere," scandalized because woman's subjection to man is a "law of nature." Lawrence, writing almost eighty years later, maintains that a woman who lays votes and not eggs "has missed her life altogether." They voice the received ideas, the alleged facts, that gave rise to the next three pieces. Dorothy Sayers, arguing that "women are more like men than anything else in the world," makes the case for all of us as equally human. "*Vir,*" she says, "is male and *Femina* is female: but *Homo* is male and female." Brigid Brophy describes some of the invisible barriers that keep women from becoming "human" in that sense. "As American Negroes have discovered," she says, "to be officially free is by no means the same as being actually and psychologically free." Virginia Woolf makes an implicit comment on the apparent sparseness of female achievement by imagining what might have happened to Shakespeare had he been born a woman. Esther Vilar reacts to the burgeoning challenge of traditional female roles in our time with a restatement of the sexist view of modern woman as manipulator, an economic parasite on man. Judy Syfers' brief description of what makes a "wife" provides an emphatic rejoinder.

Participants in the women's movement acknowledge that to adopt new assumptions about sex is one thing, but to live one's life accordingly is much more difficult. Judith Wells shows how real change in oneself takes time and hard work. Real changes in the roles of women, of course, involve changes in the roles of men. S. M. Miller describes the shocks and stresses in a marriage that strives for an egalitarian relationship between husband and wife. Marc Feigen Fasteau, interested in loosening the confining bonds of the traditional male role, looks at some of the myths surrounding friendships among men. In the concluding essay Gunnar Myrdal shows the close relationship between the position of American women and American blacks as oppressed minorities, and analyzes the ideological and economic forces behind the two movements for emancipation.

EVA FIGES

Eva Figes was born in Berlin in 1932, but in 1939 her family moved to London, where she still lives. After receiving a degree in English from Queen Mary College, London University, she worked as an editor in publishing for fifteen years. Since then she has made a full-time career of writing, and of translating modern German works. She has written three novels: Equinox *(1966),* Winter Journey *(1967), and* Konek Landing *(1969).* Patriarchal Attitudes *(1970), from which we reprint the introductory chapter, is her first nonfiction book.*

To Begin with . . .

. . . it was intended that this should be a book about women in relation to society as a whole, on the traditional role they have played for so long, the reasons for it, and the ways that I think this role should now change. It has turned out to be a book largely about men. Very early on in my researches I realized that this was going to be inevitable, as soon as I found that I would get no clear or convincing answer to one fundamental question. I am referring to the vexed question of secondary sexual differences with regard to behaviour, ability, and so on.

We all know about the primary differences, and most of us tend to assume that when human beings have such different physical functions their mental functioning must also differ radically. The differing social behaviour of men and women now and in the past would tend to confirm this assumption, but it is only an assumption, and so far scientific research has either been highly inconclusive or has tended to point in the other direction: in favour of nurture rather than nature.

We know that women live longer, that they are less vulnerable to disease for genetic reasons, and that men are usually stronger and more muscular, though it is possible that this state of affairs has evolved as a result of a sexual division of work. Muscles have to be used in order to develop. Margaret Mead discovered that the males of Bali did little heavy work and were as slight as their womenfolk, but that the Balinese men who worked as dock coolies under European supervision developed the heavy musculature which we associate with men.[1]

There is a good deal of vague talk about sex hormones nowadays, but in fact we know almost nothing about the link between these hormones and behaviour, although we know that the hormone levels do affect specifically sexual behaviour. I suppose there is a case for saying that specifically sexual behaviour will also be more general behaviour. For instance, we know that there is a systematic fluctuation of progesterone levels during the woman's menstrual cycle, and the levels vary considerably more during pregnancy. This could account for the fact that women tend to suffer from 'moods', are often mildly manic-depressive, and can have particularly severe depressions after childbirth. Similarly one could say that, since the male takes the initiative, male sexual arousal must inevitably be linked with aggression. Hormone experiments have been made with monkeys,[2] following on the finding that infant male monkeys are more aggressive than infant female monkeys. Pregnant monkeys were treated with testosterone, and as a result the experimenters succeeded in producing female offspring with pseudo-hermaphroditic features, and these females were more aggressive and engaged in more rough-and-tumble play. After three years the aggressive behaviour appeared to have diminished, and one possible interpretation of this experiment is that the pre-natal hormone level can condition very early behaviour long enough for social learning to take over, or that hormones can affect the whole life-span even after they are no longer present in the body.

This is an interesting idea, but rather far-fetched. The fact is that male and female hormone levels do not differ significantly before puberty, and yet by the age of four or five small boys behave very differently from small girls. One is forced to the conclusion that this behaviour has been largely learned, and this idea is borne out by studies of human beings who, because of ambiguous or hermaphroditic genital features, were assigned to the wrong sex at birth. These studies[3] suggested that gender role-playing was determined by environmental conditions, and that a person would adjust to the 'wrong' sex label, but that there was a critical period of sexual identity fixing in early childhood. So, for instance, a girl could be wrongly reared as a boy without much trouble, but serious psychological difficulty would result if a small girl was required to 'become' a boy after the age of about three.

If there is almost no evidence in favour of nature there is overwhelming evidence in favour of nurture: we keep looking for the needle in the haystack and all the time the haystack is staring us in the face. Small boys and girls have a very clear idea of sexual role-playing in society and conform to that idea long before puberty, even before they have any real

---

[1]Margaret Mead, *Sex and Temperament in Three Primitive Societies.*

[2] *The Development of Sex Differences,* edited by Eleanor E. Maccoby (Tavistock Publications, 1967), p. 15.

[3]Ibid., pp. 15–17.

notion of genital differences. Lawrence Kohlberg,[4] of Chicago University, whose tests on children suggested that modern enlightened parenthood made little difference on this point, concluded that 'the process of forming a constant gender identity is not a unique process determined by instinctual wishes and identifications, but a part of the general process of conceptual growth'. He rejects the Freudian theory of instincts and stresses that 'the child's sexual identity is maintained by a motivated adaption to physical-social reality and by the need to preserve a stable and positive self-image'. Whilst Walter Mischel[5] of Stanford University stresses that sexual conformity is linked with rewards, Kohlberg, I think rightly, emphasizes that direct rewards are not necessary for conformity, and that 'socially shared expectations' alone 'exert a normative force upon the individual'.

And what are these norms? We can talk about 'masculinity' and 'femininity' until the cows come home, but the fact is that all attempts at psychometrics only result, and can only result, in a reflection of society as it is at present; what is more, in studying masculine and feminine personality all that the psychometrist is doing is relating human beings to the norms that he himself has set up. And if people are reporting on themselves (and self-reports are much used in such studies) that is what they are doing too. Thus the psychologist tends to come up with the amazing discovery that original thinking, creativity and a high level of general intelligence are associated with more 'feminine' men and more 'masculine' women,[6] which he may try to explain in terms of 'bisexuality', when in fact the explanation is much more simple: by assigning sex roles and sex-related interests we limit human possibilities, but some people refuse to allow themselves to be repressed in such a fashion. When a woman is required to choose between marriage and a career it does of course amount to repression on a monstrous scale.

'I deny that any one knows, or can know, the nature of the two sexes, as long as they have only been seen in their present relation to one another', wrote John Stuart Mill a hundred years ago, and modern psychology tends to confirm this view, whilst biology has little to offer to bolster all those old prejudices and assumptions. Most of the feminine traits that psychometrics have revealed can be easily explained in sociological terms. So woman is less dominant because that is what society requires of her, more emotional because her thoughts and education have been directed to the heart rather than the head, more conservative because hearth and home do not change much and do not (like the competitive world of business and public affairs) require the capacity for change as a condition for survival. Pioneers in this field had reached similar conclusions. Helen Thomson had written at the beginning of the century: 'The point to be emphasized as the outcome of this study is that,

[4]Ibid., pp. 82 and following.
[5]Ibid., pp. 56 and following.
[6]Ibid., p. 35.

according to our present light, the psychological differences of sex seem to be largely due, not to difference of average capacity, nor to difference in type of mental activity, but to differences in the social influences brought to bear in the developing individual from early infancy to adult years',[7] and Terman and Miles,[8] writing thirty years later, in 1936, reached a similar conclusion.

Psychometric research seems able to do little beyond measuring the present state of affairs within a given society, and it also tends to measure by the standards set up by that society. One form of research which tries to remedy this by jumping outside its own society in place and time and examining other cultures, is anthropology. On the vexed topic of the 'nature' of men and women the anthropologist has certain advantages. Psychologists work with the material to hand, the members or victims of their own society, and when they elaborate their findings into a more general theory the reader must be on his guard. Everyone has to work their way through the Oedipal situation, declares Freud. Pardon me, answers Malinowski, but in the place where I work families do not recognize the father figure, so the situation simply never arises in the first place. Exit Freud.

For this reason the evidence of anthropologists is particularly valuable for us. Margaret Mead, who specifically concerned herself with this problem, is emphatic: 'The evidence is overwhelmingly in favour of the strength of social conditioning' she wrote in *Sex and Temperament in Three Primitive Societies.* Other anthropologists stress the importance of social conditioning in human behavior. 'Men do not act', wrote Claude Lévi-Strauss in *Totemism,* 'as members of a group, in accordance with what each feels as an individual; each man feels as a function of the way in which he is permitted or obliged to act. Customs are given as external norms before giving rise to internal sentiments, and these non-sentient norms determine the sentiments of individuals as well as the circumstances in which they may, or must, be displayed'. And Malinowski wrote in *Sex and Repression in Savage Society:* 'Education consists in the last instance in the building up of complex and artificial habit responses, of the organization of emotions into sentiments.'

The word 'artificial' begs the question: what is a 'natural' man or woman? One is forced to answer that there is no such thing, unless one concludes that, since man is a social animal, his 'natural' condition is to *be* artificially conditioned, with variations in time and place. For centuries the word 'nature' has been used to bolster prejudices or to express, not reality, but a state of affairs that the user would wish to see. This has been true of both poets and philosophers, moralists and theologians. Nowadays we have few illusions about our inglorious ancestry, but the fact still remains that we are *not* apes; when a man catches a train and sits in an

---

[7]Dr. Helen B. Thomson, *The Mental Traits of Sex* (1903); quoted by Viola Klein, *The Feminine Character.*

[8]Terman and Miles, *Sex and Personality: Studies in Masculinity and Femininity* (1936).

office dictating letters and making telephone calls it has precious little relationship with hunting in a carnivorous pack. A woman rarely suckles her young, and compared to the primates she has much more sex and breeds but rarely—for most of her fertile years she is kept artificially infertile. We still talk vaguely about instincts, and of the maternal instinct in particular, and we tend to ascribe the discontents and dissatisfactions of our modern, everyday lives to the frustration of these supposed natural instincts. But if our behaviour were so profoundly instinctual we would all be much more disturbed—the man confined to an office all day would run amok, a woman treated with the pill for any length of time would be a mental case.

Notice that Malinowski and Lévi-Strauss were talking, not about conventions, not about moral codes and social customs, but about our *feelings.* This book will be largely concerned with external norms which give rise to internal sentiments, with the organization of emotions into sentiments. Our feelings on the love between men and women, on marriage and parenthood, on the family and on ourselves as fathers, wives and mothers, are largely conditioned by the society which produced us, more so than we realize. The types of women that our society has produced in the past, the roles they have played or failed to play, sprang from the dictates and expectations of men. Women have been largely man-made, and even today numerous psychological studies have revealed that women and girls are still more dependent on social approval than men. Which is why this book has turned out to be almost exclusively on the subject of men, on their attitudes towards women, because it is these attitudes that shaped us.

I think we are only just beginning to realize the enormous importance of environment, not only with regard to men and women, but with regard to one human being and another, and these, do not forget, will differ in character far more glaringly than any differentiation based on sex. The fact that one man will differ so markedly in character and abilities from another man should surely allow us to forget about hormones and menstrual cycles for a little while and concentrate on more obvious things. On the factor of expectation, for example, which is particularly important. Recent experiments have revealed that if a teacher was told that a group of children, selected at random, had exceptional ability and should make rapid progress, those children really did make remarkable progress, and after a time their I.Q. performance rose by thirty or forty points.[9] So far most women have lived down to the abysmally low standard socially expected of them. Even the modern female child is more easily discouraged by failure than a boy and has a low expectation of success in carrying out a given task.[10] And for the adult woman incentives as well as lack of high expectations pull the other way. Woman, presented with an image

[9] Rosenthal and Jacobson, *Pygmalion in the Classroom,* referred to by Liam Hudson in an article entitled 'Grey Matter', published in the *New Statesman,* 14th February 1969.
[10] *The Development of Sex Differences,* pp. 32–3.

in a mirror, has danced to that image in a hypnotic trance. And because she thought the image was herself, it became just that.

I cannot do better than to reiterate the words of Havelock Ellis,[11] written half a century ago but still valid today:

> We have to recognise that our present knowledge of men and women cannot tell us what they might be or what they ought to be, but what they actually are, under the conditions of civilisation. By showing us that under varying conditions men and women are, within certain limits, indefinitely modifiable, a precise knowledge of the actual facts of the life of men and women forbids us to dogmatize rigidly concerning the respective spheres of men and women. . . . If this is not exactly the result which we set out to attain, it is still a result of very considerable importance.

A result of very considerable importance. Only blind obstinacy could make a person refuse to accept 'no answer' or at least 'not proven' as in itself an answer of a kind, the mindless obstinacy that goes with deeply rooted prejudices. Foolishly, I suppose, Ellis hoped that his book would at least help to clear away the 'thick undergrowth of prepossession and superstition which flourishes in the region. . . . to a greater extent than in any other region'. It appears to have done nothing of the kind, and I suppose it would be too much to hope that my book will succeed where his failed. One can slash out at the undergrowth, but it has a way of growing up again overnight, whatever one does, or says.

NEW YORK HERALD, EDITORIAL

The Woman's Rights Convention (September 12, 1852)

The farce at Syracuse has been played out. We publish to-day the last act, in which it will be seen that the authority of the Bible, as a perfect rule of faith and practice for human beings, was voted down, and what are called the laws of nature set up instead of the Christian code. We have also a practical exhibition of the consequences that flow from woman leaving her true sphere where she wields all her influence, and coming into public to discuss questions of morals and politics with men. . . .

---

[11]Havelock Ellis, *Men and Women: A Study of Human Secondary Sexual Characters.*

Who are these women? what do they want? what are the motives that impel them to this course of action? The *dramatis personae* of the farce enacted at Syracuse present a curious conglomeration of both sexes. Some of them are old maids, whose personal charms were never very attractive, and who have been sadly slighted by the masculine gender in general; some of them women who have been badly mated, whose own temper, or their husbands', has made life anything but agreeable to them, and they are therefore down upon the whole of the opposite sex; some, having so much of the virago in their disposition, that nature appears to have made a mistake in their gender—mannish women, like hens that crow; some of boundless vanity and egotism, who believe that they are superior in intellectual ability to "all the world and the rest of mankind," and delight to see their speeches and addresses in print; and man shall be consigned to his proper sphere—nursing the babies, washing the dishes, mending stockings, and sweeping the house. This is "the good time coming." Besides the classes we have enumerated, there is a class of wild enthusiasts and visionaries—very sincere, but very mad—having the same vein as the fanatical Abolitionists, and the majority, if not all of them, being, in point of fact, deeply imbued with the anti-slavery senti- ment. Of the male sex who attend these Conventions for the purpose of taking a part in them, the majority are hen-pecked husbands, and all of them ought to wear petticoats.

In point of ability, the majority of the women are flimsy, flippant, and superficial. Mrs. Rose alone indicates much argumentative power.

How did woman first become subject to man as she now is all over the world? By her nature, her sex, just as the negro is and always will be, to the end of time, inferior to the white race, and, therefore, doomed to subjection; but happier than she would be in any other condition, just because it is the law of her nature. The women themselves would not have this law reversed. It is a significant fact that even Mrs. Swisshelm, who formerly ran about to all such gatherings from her husband, is now "a keeper at home," and condemns these Conventions in her paper. How does this happen? Because, after weary years of unfruitfulness, she has at length got her rights in the shape of a baby. This is the best cure for the mania, and we would recommend a trial of it to all who are afflicted.

What do the leaders of the Woman's Rights Convention want? They want to vote, and to hustle with the rowdies at the polls. They want to be members of Congress, and in the heat of debate to subject themselves to coarse jests and indecent language, like that of Rev. Mr. Hatch. They want to fill all other posts which men are ambitious to occupy—to be lawyers, doctors, captains of vessels, and generals in the field. How funny it would sound in the newspapers, that Lucy Stone, pleading a cause, took suddenly ill in the pains of parturition, and perhaps gave birth to a fine bouncing boy in court! Or that Rev. Antoinette Brown was arrested in the middle of her sermon in the pulpit from the same cause, and presented a "pledge" to her husband and the congregation; or, that Dr. Harriot K.

Hunt, while attending a gentleman patient for a fit of the gout or *fistula in ano,* found it necessary to send for a doctor, there and then, and to be delivered of a man or woman child—perhaps twins. A similar event might happen on the floor of Congress, in a storm at sea, or in the raging tempest of battle, and then what is to become of the woman legislator?

D. H. LAWRENCE

from Cocksure Women and Hensure Men

. . .

The tragedy about cocksure women is that they are more cocky, in their assurance, than the cock himself. They never realise that when the cock gives his loud crow in the morning, he listens acutely afterwards, to hear if some other wretch of a cock dare crow defiance, challenge. To the cock, there is always defiance, challenge, danger and death on the clear air; or the possibility thereof.

But alas, when the hen crows, she listens for no defiance or challenge. When she says *cock-a-doodle-do!* then it is unanswerable. The cock listens for an answer, alert. But the hen knows she is unanswerable. *Cock-a-doodle-do!* and there it is, take it or leave it!

And it is this that makes the cocksureness of women so dangerous, so devastating. It is really out of scheme, it is not in relation to the rest of things. So we have the tragedy of cocksure women. They find, so often, that instead of having laid an egg, they have laid a vote, or an empty ink-bottle, or some other absolutely unhatchable object, which means nothing to them.

It is the tragedy of the modern woman. She becomes cocksure, she puts all her passion and energy and years of her life into some effort or assertion, without ever listening for the denial which she ought to take into count. She is cocksure, but she is a hen all the time. Frightened of her own henny self, she rushes to mad lengths about votes, or welfare, or sports, or business: she is marvellous, out-manning the man. But alas, it is all fundamentally disconnected. It is all an attitude, and one day the attitude will become a weird cramp, a pain, and then it will collapse. And when it has collapsed, and she looks at the eggs she has laid, votes, or miles of typewriting, years of business efficiency—suddenly, because she is a hen and not a cock, all she has done will turn into pure nothingness to her. Suddenly it all falls out of relation to her basic henny self, and she realises she has lost her life. The lovely henny surety, the hensureness which is the real bliss of every female, has been denied her: she had never had it. Having lived her life with such utmost strenuousness and cocksureness, she has missed her life altogether. Nothingness!

[From *Assorted Articles,* by D. H. Lawrence, Martin Secker, 1930]

DOROTHY SAYERS

Lord Peter Wimsey is probably Dorothy Sayers' best-known creation. As the detective hero of most of her dozens of murder mysteries, Lord Peter served as a mouthpiece for Ms. Sayers' extensive intellectual interests. The Nine Taylors *(1934), for instance, combines with the "whodunit" a learned study of campanology, the art of bell-ringing.* Gaudy Night *(1935), set in an Oxford College, is not only a mystery and a love story but a fine feminist novel as well.*

Ms. Sayers (1893–1957) was born in Oxford. Educated at Somerville College, she was one of the first women ever to receive an Oxford degree— in 1915, at age twenty-two, with first-class honors in medieval literature. She taught for a year, worked as a copywriter for an advertising firm (her background for Murder Must Advertise, *written in 1933), and was married. But then, still in her twenties, she apparently decided to earn her living by writing mystery stories. In true scholarly fashion she undertook to master the mechanics of this genre by a close analytic study of its best examples. Her three-volume* Omnibus of Crime *(1926) shows her as a major authority on the genre and its history. For fourteen years she then wrote her own mystery stories with undisputed success. Her last Lord Peter book is* Busman's Honeymoon *(1937), subtitled* "a love story with detective interruptions." *It has her hero wed, happily, in a marriage of equals.*

Her interest in Anglican theology then turned her writing to religious dramas, first for the Church of England's Canterbury Festival, later for the British Broadcasting Corporation. The most popular of these was a series of radio plays entitled The Man Born to Be King: Play Cycle on the Life of Christ *(1941), which told the New Testament story. Her final years were devoted to a study of Dante—she spent the last years before her death translating Dante and the* Chanson de Roland. *The selection we reprint here comes from an essay collection,* Unpopular Opinions *(1946).*

The Human-Not-Quite-Human

The first task, when undertaking the study of any phenomenon, is to observe its most obvious feature; and it is here that most students fail. It is here that most students of the "Woman Question" have failed, and the Church more lamentably than most, and with less excuse. That is why it is necessary, from time to time, to speak plainly, and perhaps even brutally, to the Church.

The first thing that strikes the careless observer is that women are unlike men. They are "the opposite sex"—(though why "opposite" I do not know; what is the "neighbouring sex"?). But the fundamental thing is that women are more like men than anything else in the world. They are human beings. *Vir* is male and *Femina* is female: but *Homo* is male and female.

This is the equality claimed and the fact that is persistently evaded and denied. No matter what arguments are used, the discussion is vitiated from the start, because Man is always dealt with as both *Homo* and *Vir,* but Woman only as *Femina.*

I have seen it solemnly stated in a newspaper that the seats on the near side of a bus are always filled before those on the off side, because, "men find them more comfortable on account of the camber of the road, and women find they get a better view of the shop windows." As though the camber of the road did not affect male and female bodies equally. Men, you observe, are given a *Homo* reason; but Women, a *Femina* reason, because they are not fully human.

Or take the sniggering dishonesty that accompanies every mention of trousers. The fact is that, for *Homo,* the garment is warm, convenient and decent. But in the West (though not in Mohammedan countries or in China) *Vir* has made the trouser his prerogative, and has invested it and the skirt with a sexual significance for physiological reasons which are a little too plain for gentility to admit. (Note: that the objection is always to the closed knicker or trouser; never to open drawers, which have a music-hall significance of a different kind.) It is this obscure male resentment against interference with function that complicates the simple *Homo* issue of whether warmth, safety, and freedom of movement are desirable qualities in a garment for any creature with two legs. Naturally, under the circumstances, the trouser is *also* taken up into the whole *Femina* business of attraction, since *Vir* demands that a woman shall be *Femina* all the time, whether she is engaged in *Homo* activities or not. If, of course, *Vir* should take a fancy to the skirt, he will appropriate it without a scruple; he will wear the houppelande or the cassock if it suits him; he will stake out his claim to the kilt in Scotland or in Greece. If he chooses (as he once chose) to deck himself like a peacock in the mating season, that is *Vir's* right; if he prefers (as he does to-day) to affront the eye with drab colour and ridiculous outline, that is *Homo's* convenience. Man dresses as he chooses, and Woman to please him; and if Woman says she ever does otherwise, he knows better, for she is not human, and may not give evidence on her own behalf.

Probably no man has ever troubled to imagine how strange his life would appear to himself if it were unrelentingly assessed in terms of his maleness; if everything he wore, said, or did had to be justified by reference to female approval; if he were compelled to regard himself, day in day out, not as a member of society, but merely (*salvâ reverentiâ*) as a virile member of society. If the centre of his dress-consciousness were the cod-piece, his education directed to making him a spirited lover and meek paterfamilias; his interests held to be natural only in so far as they were sexual. If from school and lecture-room, Press and pulpit, he heard the persistent outpouring of a shrill and scolding voice, bidding him remember his biological function. If he were vexed by continual advice how to add a rough male touch to his typing, how to be learned without losing his masculine appeal, how to combine chemical research with seduction, how to play bridge without incurring the suspicion of impotence. If, instead of allowing with a smile that "women prefer cave-men," he felt the unrelenting pressure of a whole social structure forcing him to order all his goings in conformity with that pronouncement.

He would hear (and would he like hearing?) the female counterpart of Dr. Peck[1] informing him: "I am no supporter of the Horseback Hall doctrine of 'gun-tail, plough-tail and stud' as the only spheres for masculine action; but we do need a more definite conception of the nature and scope of man's life." In any book on sociology he would find, after the main portion dealing with human needs and rights, a supplementary chapter devoted to "The Position of the Male in the Perfect State." His newspaper would assist him with a "Men's Corner," telling him how, by the expenditure of a good deal of money and a couple of hours a day, he could attract the girls and retain his wife's affection; and when he had succeeded in capturing a mate, his name would be taken from him, and society would present him with a special title to proclaim his achievement. People would write books called, "History of the Male," or "Males of the Bible," or "The Psychology of the Male," and he would be regaled daily with headlines, such as "Gentleman-Doctor's Discovery," "Male-Secretary Wins Calcutta Sweep," "Men-Artists at the Academy." If he gave an interview to a reporter, or performed any unusual exploit, he would find it recorded in such terms as these: "Professor Bract, although a distinguished botanist, is not in any way an unmanly man. He has, in fact, a wife and seven children. Tall and burly, the hands with which he handles his delicate specimens are as gnarled and powerful as those of a Canadian lumberjack, and when I swilled beer with him in his laboratory, he bawled his conclusions at me in a strong, gruff voice that implemented the promise of his swaggering moustache." Or: "There is nothing in the least

---

[1]Dr. Peck has disclaimed adherence to the *Kinder, Kirche, Küche* school of thought.

feminine about the home surroundings of Mr. Focus, the famous children's photographer. His 'den' is panelled in teak and decorated with rude sculptures from Easter Island; over his austere iron bedstead hangs a fine reproduction of the Rape of the Sabines." Or: "I asked M. Sapristi, the renowned chef, whether kitchen-cult was not a rather unusual occupation for a man. 'Not a bit of it!' he replied, bluffly. 'It is the genius that counts, not the sex. As they say in *la belle Ecosse,* a man's a man for a' that' —and his gusty, manly guffaw blew three small patty pans from the dresser."

He would be edified by solemn discussions about "Should Men serve in Drapery Establishments?" and acrimonious ones about "Tea-Drinking Men"; by cross-shots of public affairs "from the masculine angle," and by irritable correspondence about men who expose their anatomy on beaches (so masculine of them), conceal it in dressing-gowns (too feminine of them), think about nothing but women, pretend an unnatural indifference to women, exploit their sex to get jobs, lower the tone of the office by their sexless appearance, and generally fail to please a public opinion which demands the incompatible. And at dinner-parties he would hear the wheedling, unctuous, predatory female voice demand: "And why should you trouble your handsome little head about politics?"

If, after a few centuries of this kind of treatment, the male was a little self-conscious, a little on the defensive, and a little bewildered about what was required of him, I should not blame him. If he traded a little upon his sex, I could forgive him. If he presented the world with a major social problem, I should scarcely be surprised. It would be more surprising if he retained any rag of sanity and self-respect.

"The rights of woman," says Dr. Peck, "considered in the economic sphere, seem to involve her in competition with men in the struggle for jobs." It does seem so indeed, and this is hardly to be wondered at; for the competition began to appear when the men took over the women's jobs by transferring them from the home to the factory. The medieval woman had effective power and a measure of real (though not political) equality, for she had control of many industries—spinning, weaving, baking, brewing, distilling, perfumery, preserving, pickling—in which she worked with head as well as hands, in command of her own domestic staff. But now the control and direction—all the intelligent part—of those industries have gone to the men, and the women have been left, not with their "proper" *work* but with *employment* in those occupations. And at the same time, they are exhorted to be feminine and return to the home from which all intelligent occupation has been steadily removed.

There has never been any question but that the women of the poor should toil alongside their men. No angry, and no compassionate, voice has been raised to say that women should not break their backs with harvest work, or soil their hands with blacking grates and peeling potatoes. The objection is only to work that is pleasant, exciting or profitable —the work that any human being might think it worth while to do. The boast, "My wife doesn't need to soil her hands with work," first became general when the commercial middle classes acquired the plutocratic and aristocratic notion that the keeping of an idle woman was a badge of superior social status. Man must work, and woman must exploit his labour. What else are they there for? And if the woman submits, she can be cursed for her exploitation; and if she rebels, she can be cursed for competing with the male: whatever she does will be wrong, and that is a great satisfaction.

The men who attribute all the ills of *Homo* to the industrial age, yet accept it as the norm for the relations of the sexes. But the brain, that great and sole true Androgyne, that can mate indifferently with male or female and beget offspring upon itself, the cold brain laughs at their perversions of history. The period from which we are emerging was like no other: a period when empty head and idle hands were qualities for which a man prized his woman and despised her. When, by an odd, sadistic twist of morality, sexual intercourse was deemed to be a marital right to be religiously enforced upon a meek reluctance—as though the insatiable appetite of wives were not one of the oldest jokes in the world, older than mothers-in-law, and far more venerable than kippers. When to think about sex was considered indelicate in a woman, and to think about anything else unfeminine. When to "manage" a husband by lying and the exploitation of sex was held to be honesty and virtue. When the education that Thomas More gave his daughters was denounced as a devilish indulgence, and could only be wrung from the outraged holder of the purse-strings by tears and martyrdom and desperate revolt, in the teeth of the world's mockery and the reprobation of a scandalised Church.

What is all this tenderness about women herded into factories? Is it much more than an excuse for acquiescing in the profitable herding of men? The wrong is inflicted upon *Homo.* There are temperaments suited to herding and temperaments that are not; but the dividing lines do not lie exactly along the sexual boundary. The Russians, it seems, have begun to realise this; but are revolution and blood the sole educational means for getting this plain fact into our heads? Is it only under stress of war that we are ready to admit that the person who does the job best is the person best fitted to do it? Must we always treat women like Kipling's common soldier?

> It's vamp and slut and gold-digger, and "Polly, you're a liar!"
> But it's "Thank-you, Mary Atkins" when the guns begin to fire.

We will use women's work in wartime (though we will pay less for it, and take it away from them when the war is over). But it is an unnatural business, undertaken for no admissible feminine reason—such as to ape the men, to sublimate a sexual repression, to provide a hobby for leisure, or to make the worker more bedworthy—but simply because, without it all *Homo* (including *Vir*) will be in the soup. But to find satisfaction in doing good work and knowing that it is wanted is human nature; therefore it cannot be feminine nature, for women are not human. It is true that they die in bombardments, much like real human beings: but that we will forgive, since they clearly cannot enjoy it; and we can salve our consciences by rating their battered carcases at less than a man's compensation.[2]

Women are not human. They lie when they say they have human needs: warm and decent clothing; comfort in the bus; interests directed immediately to God and His universe, not intermediately through any child of man. They are far above man to inspire him, far beneath him to corrupt him; they have feminine minds and feminine natures, but their mind is not one with their nature like the minds of men; they have no human mind and no human nature. "Blessed be God," says the Jew, "that hath not made me a woman."

God, of course, may have His own opinion, but the Church is reluctant to endorse it. I think I have never heard a sermon preached on the story of Martha and Mary that did not attempt, somehow, somewhere, to explain away its text. Mary's, of course, was the better part—the Lord said so, and we must not precisely contradict Him. But we will be careful not to despise Martha. No doubt, He approved of her too. We could not get on without her, and indeed (having paid lip-service to God's opinion) we must admit that we greatly prefer her. For Martha was doing a really feminine job, whereas Mary was just behaving like any other disciple, male or female; and that is a hard pill to swallow.

Perhaps it is no wonder that the women were first at the Cradle and last at the Cross. They had never known a man like this Man—there never has been such another. A prophet and teacher who never nagged at them, never flattered or coaxed or patronised; who never made arch jokes about them, never treated them either as "The women, God help us!" or "The ladies, God bless them!"; who rebuked without querulousness and praised without condescension; who took their questions and arguments seriously; who never mapped out their sphere for them, never urged them to be feminine or jeered at them for being female; who had no axe to grind and no uneasy male dignity to defend; who took them as he found them and was completely unself-conscious. There is no act, no sermon, no parable in the whole Gospel that borrows its pungency from female perversity; nobody could possibly guess from the words and deeds of Jesus that there was anything "funny" about woman's nature.

But we might easily deduce it from His contemporaries, and from His prophets before Him, and from His Church to this day. Women are not human; nobody shall persuade that they are human; let them say what they like, we will not believe it, though One rose from the dead.

---

[2]This last scandal did in the end outrage public opinion and was abolished.

BRIGID BROPHY

*A prolific and witty writer of essays, articles, novels, short stories,
biographies, plays, and criticism, Brigid Brophy was born in London in
1929 and has lived there since. She studied classics at Oxford from 1947
to 1948 but soon turned to free-lance writing and promptly won the
Cheltenham Literary Festival prize for a first novel,* Hackenfeller's Ape
(1954).

    *Ms. Brophy wants her novels to "bring the reader suddenly around a
corner to confront incongruity—which may be comic or ironic but is always
poetic and is always in Bad Taste." Her recent works are masterpieces of
polylingual punning, books to be read aloud or, as she says, sung in
operatic style. Her novels include* Flesh *(1962),* The Snow Ball
(1964), and In Transit: An Heroi-Cyclic Novel *(1969). She has
written biographical studies of Mozart (1964), Aubrey Beardsley (1968),
and Ronald Firbank (1973). Her favorite book of literary criticism is the
one she wrote in collaboration with her husband and Charles Osborne—*
Fifty Works of English and American Literature We Could Do
Without *(1967). She has also written plays for radio and stage and
devised a literary talk-show format for British television. Her essay and
story collections include* The Adventures of God in His Search for
the Black Girl *(1973)—a twist on George Bernard Shaw's* The
Adventures of the Black Girl in Her Search for God—*and* Don't
Never Forget *(1966), which includes the essay we reprint below. It first
appeared in the* Saturday Evening Post, *November 2, 1963, from
which we take our text.*

Women Are Prisoners of Their Sex

All right, nobody's disputing it. Women are free. At least, they *look* free.
They even feel free. But in reality women in the western, industrialized
world today are like the animals in a modern zoo. There are no bars. It
appears that cages have been abolished. Yet in practice women are still
kept in their place just as firmly as the animals are kept in their enclosures.
The barriers which keep them in now are invisible.

    It is about 40 years since the pioneer feminists raised such a rumpus
by rattling the cage bars that society was at last obliged to pay attention.
The result was that the bars were uprooted, the cage thrown open:
whereupon the majority of the women who had been held captive decided
that they would rather stay inside the cage anyway.

To be more precise, they *thought* they decided; and society, which can with perfect truth point out, "Look, no bars," *thought* it was giving them the choice. There are no laws and very little discrimination to prevent western, industrialized women from voting, being voted for or entering the professions. If there are still few women lawyers and engineers, let alone women Presidents of the United States, what are women to conclude except that this is the result either of their own free choice or of something inherent in female nature?

Many of them do draw just this conclusion. They have come back to the old argument of the antifeminists that women are unfit by nature for life outside the cage. And in letting this old wheel come full cycle, women have fallen victim to one of the most insidious and ingenious confidence tricks ever perpetrated.

In point of fact, neither female nature nor women's individual free choice has been put to the test. As American Negroes have discovered, to be officially free is by no means the same as being actually and psychologically free. A society as adept at propaganda as ours has become should know that "persuasion," which means the art of launching myths and artificially inducing inhibitions, is every bit as effective as force of law. No doubt the reason society eventually agreed to abolish its antiwomen laws was that it had become confident of a commanding battery of hidden dissuaders which would do the job just as well. Cage bars are clumsy methods of control, which excite the more rebellious personalities inside to rattle them. Modern society, like the modern zoo, has contrived to get rid of the bars without altering the fact of imprisonment. All the zoo architect needs to do is run a zone of hot or cold air, whichever the animal concerned cannot tolerate, round the cage where the bars used to be. Human animals are not less sensitive to social climate.

The ingenious point about the new-model zoo is that it deceives both sides of the invisible barrier. Not only cannot the animal see how it is imprisoned; the visitor's conscience is relieved of the unkindness of keeping animals shut up. He can say, "Look, no bars round the animals," just as society can say, "Look, no laws restricting women," even while it keeps women rigidly in place by zones of fierce social pressure.

There is, however, one great difference. A woman, being a thinking animal, may actually be more distressed because the bars of her cage cannot be seen. What relieves society's conscience may afflict hers. Unable to perceive what is holding her back, she may accuse herself and her whole sex of craven timidity because women have not jumped at what has the appearance of an offer of freedom. Evidently quite a lot of women have succumbed to guilt of this sort, since in recent years quite an industry has arisen to assuage it. Comforting voices make the air as thick and reassuring as cotton wool while they explain that there is nothing shameful in not wanting a career, that to be intellectually unadventurous is no sin, that taking care of home and family may be personally "fulfilling" for a woman and socially valuable.

This is an argument without a flaw—except that it is addressed exclusively to women. Address it to both sexes and instantly it becomes progressive and humane. As it stands, it is merely antiwoman prejudice revamped.

That many women would be happier not pursuing careers or intellectual adventures is only part of the truth. The whole truth is that many people would be. If society had the clear sight to assure men as well as women that there is no shame in preferring to stay noncompetitively and nonaggressively at home, many masculine neuroses and ulcers would be avoided, and many children would enjoy the benefit of being brought up by a father with a talent for the job of child-rearing instead of a mother with no talent for it but a sense of guilt about the lack.

But society does nothing so sensible. Blindly it goes on insisting on the tradition that men are the ones who go out to work and adventure —an arrangement which simply throws talent away. All the homemaking talent born inside male bodies is wasted; and our businesses and governments are staffed largely by people whose aptitude for the work consists solely of their being what is, by tradition, the right sex for it.

The pressures society exerts to drive men out of the house are very nearly as irrational and unjust as those by which it keeps women in. The mistake of the early reformers was to assume that men were emancipated already and that therefore reform need ask only for the emancipation of women. What we ought to do now is go right back to scratch and demand the emancipation of both sexes.

The zones of hot and cold air which society uses to perpetuate its uneconomic and unreasonable state of affairs are the simplest and most effective conceivable. Society is playing on our sexual vanity. Tell a man that he is not a real man, or a woman that she is not 100 percent woman, and you are threatening both with not being attractive to the opposite sex. No one can bear not to be attractive to the opposite sex. That is the climate which the human animal cannot tolerate.

So society has us all at its mercy. It has only to murmur to the man that staying home is a feminine characteristic, and he will be out of the house like a bullet. It has only to suggest to the woman that logic and reason are the exclusive province of the masculine mind, whereas "intuition" and "feeling" are the female forte, and she will throw her physics textbooks out of the window, barricade herself into the house and give herself up to having wishy-washy poetical feelings while she arranges the flowers.

She will, incidentally, take care that her feelings *are* wishy-washy. She has been persuaded that to have cogent feelings, of the kind which really do go into great poems—most of which are by men—would make her an unfeminine woman, a woman who imitates men. In point of fact, she would not be imitating men as such, most of whom have never written a line of great poetry, but poets, most of whom so far happen to be men. But the bad logic passes muster with a woman because part of the mythology she has swallowed ingeniously informs her that logic is not her forte.

Should a woman's talent or intelligence be so irrepressible that she insists on producing cogent works of art or water-tight meshes of argument, she will be said to have "a mind like a man's."

What is more, this habit of thought actually contributes to perpetuating a state of affairs where most good minds really do belong to men. It is difficult for a woman to want to be intelligent when she has been told that to be so will make her like a man. She inclines to think an intelligence would be as unbecoming to her as a moustache; and, pathetically, many women have tried in furtive privacy to disembarrass themselves of intellect as though it were facial hair.

Discouraged from growing "a mind like a man's," women are encouraged to have thoughts and feelings of a specifically feminine tone. Women, it is said, have some specifically feminine contribution to make to culture. Unfortunately, as culture had already been shaped and largely built up by men before the invitation was issued, this leaves women little to do. Culture consists of reasoned thought and works of art composed of cogent feelings and imagination. There is only one way to be reasonable, and that is to reason correctly; and the only kind of art which is any good is good art. If women are to eschew reason and artistic imagination in favor of "intuition" and "feeling," it is pretty clear what is meant. "Intuition" is just a polite name for bad reasoning, and "feeling" for bad art.

In reality, the whole idea of a specifically feminine—or, for the matter of that, masculine—contribution to culture is a contradiction of culture. A contribution to culture is not something which could not have been made by the other sex; it is something which could not have been made by any other *person.* The arts are a sphere where women seem to have done well; but really they have done too well—too well for the good of the arts. Rather than women sharing the esteem which ought to belong to artists, art is becoming smeared with femininity. We are approaching a Philistine state of affairs where the arts are something which it is nice for women to take up in their spare time—men having slammed out of the house to get on with society's "serious" business, like making money, running the country and the professions.

In that "serious" sphere it is still rare to encounter a woman. A man sentenced to prison would probably feel his punishment was redoubled by indignity if he were to be sentenced by a woman judge under a law drafted by a woman legislator—and if, on admission, he were to be examined by a woman prison doctor. If such a thing happened every day, it would be no indignity but the natural course of events. It has never been given the chance to become the natural course of events and never will be so long as women remain persuaded it would be unnatural of them to want it.

So brilliantly has society contrived to terrorize women with this threat that certain behavior is unnatural and unwomanly, that it has left them no time to consider—or even sheerly observe—what womanly nature really is. For centuries arrant superstitions were accepted as natural law. The physiological fact that only women can secrete milk for feeding babies was extended into the pure myth that it was women's business to cook for and wait on the entire family. The kitchen became woman's "natural" place because, for the first few months of her baby's life, the nursery really was. To this day a woman may fear she is unfeminine if she can discover in herself no aptitude or liking for cooking. Fright has thrown her into such a muddle that she confuses having no taste for cookery with having no breasts, and conversely assumes that nature has unfailingly endowed the human female with a special handiness with frying pans.

Even psychoanalysis, which in general has been the greatest benefactor of civilization since the wheel, has unwittingly reinforced the terrorization campaign. The trouble was that it brought with it from its origin in medical therapy a criterion of normality instead of rationality. On sheer statistics every pioneer, genius and social reformer, including the first woman who demanded to be let out of the kitchen and into the polling booth, is abnormal, along with every lunatic and eccentric. What distinguishes the genius from the lunatic is that the genius's abnormality is justifiable by reason or aesthetics. If a woman who is irked by confinement to the kitchen merely looks around to see what other women are doing and finds they are accepting their kitchens, she may well conclude that she is abnormal and had better enlist her psychoanalyst's help toward "living with" her kitchen. What she ought to ask is whether it is rational for women to be kept to the kitchen, and whether nature really does insist on that in the way it insists women have breasts.

And in a far-reaching sense to ask that question is much more normal and natural than learning to "live with" the handicap of women's inferior social status. The normal and natural thing for human beings is not to tolerate handicaps but to reform society and to circumvent or supplement nature. We don't learn to live minus a leg; we devise an artificial limb.

That, indeed, is the crux of the matter. Not only are the distinctions we draw between male nature and female nature largely arbitrary and often pure superstition, they are completely beside the point. They ignore the essence of *human* nature. The important question is not whether women are or are not less logical by nature than men, but whether education, effort and the abolition of our illogical social pressures can improve on nature and make them—and, incidentally, men as well—more logical. What distinguishes human from any other animal nature is its ability to be unnatural. Logic and art are not natural or instinctive activities; but our nature includes a propensity to acquire them. It is not natural for the human body to orbit the earth; but the human mind has a natural adventurousness which enables it to invent machines whereby the body can do so.

Civilization consists not necessarily in defying nature but in making it possible for us to do so if we judge it desirable. The higher we can lift our noses from the grindstone of nature, the wider the area we have of choice; and the more choices we have freely made, the more individualized we are. We are at our most civilized when nature does not dictate to us, as it does to animals and peasants, but when we can opt to fall in with it or better it. If modern civilization has invented methods of preparing baby foods and methods of education which make it possible for men to feed babies and for women to think logically, we are betraying civilization itself if we do not set both sexes free to make a free choice.

VIRGINIA WOOLF

Shakespeare's Sister

. . . I thought of that old gentleman, who is dead now, but was a bishop, I think, who declared that it was impossible for any woman, past, present, or to come, to have the genius of Shakespeare. He wrote to the papers about it. He also told a lady who applied to him for information that cats do not as a matter of fact go to heaven, though they have, he added, souls of a sort. How much thinking those old gentlemen used to save one! How the borders of ignorance shrank back at their approach! Cats do not go to heaven. Women cannot write the plays of Shakespeare.

Be that as it may, I could not help thinking, as I looked at the works of Shakespeare on the shelf, that the bishop was right at least in this; it would have been impossible, completely and entirely, for any woman to have written the plays of Shakespeare in the age of Shakespeare. Let me imagine, since facts are so hard to come by, what would have happened had Shakespeare had a wonderfully gifted sister, called Judith, let us say. Shakespeare himself went, very probably—his mother was an heiress—to the grammar school, where he may have learnt Latin—Ovid, Virgil and Horace—and the elements of grammar and logic. He was, it is well known, a wild boy who poached rabbits, perhaps shot a deer, and had, rather sooner than he should have done, to marry a woman in the neighbourhood, who bore him a child rather quicker than was right. That escapade sent him to seek his fortune in London. He had, it seemed, a taste for the theatre; he began by holding horses at the stage door. Very soon he got work in the theatre, became a successful actor, and lived at the hub of the universe, meeting everybody, knowing everybody, practising his art on the boards, exercising his wits in the streets, and even getting access to the palace of the queen. Meanwhile his extraordinarily gifted sister, let us suppose, remained at home. She was as adventurous, as imaginative, as agog to see the world as he was. But she was not sent to school. She had no chance of learning grammar and logic, let alone of reading Horace and Virgil. She picked up a book now and then, one of her brother's perhaps, and read a few pages. But then her parents came in and told her to mend the stockings or mind the stew and not moon about with books and papers. They would have spoken sharply but kindly, for they were substantial people who knew the conditions of life for a woman and loved their daughter—indeed, more likely than not she was the apple of her father's eye. Perhaps she scribbled some pages up in an apple loft on the sly, but was careful to hide them or set fire to them. Soon, however, before she was out of her teens, she was to be betrothed to the son of a neighbouring wool-stapler. She cried out that marriage was hateful to her, and for that she was severely beaten by her father. Then he ceased to scold her. He begged her instead not to hurt him, not to shame him in this matter of her marriage. He would give her a chain of beads or a fine petticoat, he said; and there were tears in his eyes. How could she disobey him? How could she break his heart? The force of her own gift alone drove her to it. She made up a small parcel of her belongings, let herself down by a rope one summer's night and took the road to London. She was not seventeen. The birds that sang in the hedge were not more musical than she was. She had the quickest fancy, a gift like her brother's, for the tune of words. Like him, she had a taste for the theatre. She stood at the stage door; she wanted to act, she said. Men laughed in her face. The manager—a fat, loose-lipped man—guffawed. He bellowed something about poodles dancing and women acting—no woman, he said, could possibly be an actress. He hinted—you can imagine what. She could get no training in her craft. Could she even seek her dinner in a tavern or roam the streets at midnight? Yet her genius was for fiction and lusted to feed abundantly upon the lives of men and women and the study of their ways. At last—for she was very young, oddly like Shakespeare the poet in her face, with the same grey eyes and rounded brows—at last Nick Greene the actor-manager took pity on her; she found herself with child by that gentleman and so—who shall measure the heat and violence of the poet's heart when caught and tangled in a woman's body?—killed herself one winter's night and lies buried at some cross-roads where the omnibuses now stop outside the Elephant and Castle.

.   .   .

[From *A Room of One's Own,* by Virginia Woolf, Harcourt, Brace, 1929]

ESTHER VILAR

Esther Vilar was born of German parents in 1935 in Buenos Aires, Argentina; she grew up there and received a medical degree from the University of Buenos Aires. She now lives in Munich, Germany, where she practiced as a physician from 1960 to 1961 but has since worked as a free-lance writer. She was married for two years to a German writer and has a son.

Der dressierte Mann (1971; trans. The Manipulated Man, *1973), from which we reprint a chapter below, is Esther Vilar's fourth book and first success. It has been translated into twenty-one languages and has sold over half a million copies. Its thesis is clear: a man is a human being who works; a woman is a human being who does not. Woman manipulates man in the way Pavlov conditioned his dogs. She says that she "wrote the book very quickly, much of it in the United States where I spent about a year in all, gathering material that convinced me American men are the most manipulated of all by their women. . . . Ever since Simone de Beauvoir and* The Second Sex *it has been popular to say women are suppressed by men, but I never saw any signs of it."*

What Is Woman?

A woman, as we have already said, is, in contrast to a man, a human being who does not work. One might leave it at that, for there isn't much more to say about her, were the basic concept of "human being" not so general and inexact in embracing both "man" and "woman."

Life offers the human being two choices: animal existence—a lower order of life—and spiritual existence. In general, a woman will choose the former and opt for physical well-being, a place to breed, and an opportunity to indulge unhindered in her breeding habits.

At birth, men and women have the same intellectual potential; there is no primary difference in intelligence between the sexes. It is also a fact that potential left to stagnate will atrophy. Women do not use their mental capacity: they deliberately let it disintegrate. After a few years of sporadic training, they revert to a state of irreversible mental torpor.

Why do women not make use of their intellectual potential? For the simple reason that they do not need to. It is not essential for their survival. Theoretically it is possible for a beautiful woman to have less intelligence than a chimpanzee and still be considered an acceptable member of society.

By the age of twelve at the latest, most women have decided to become prostitutes. Or, to put it another way, they have planned a future for themselves which consists of choosing a man and letting him do all the work. In return for his support, they are prepared to let him make use of their vagina at certain given moments. The minute a woman has made this decision she ceases to develop her mind. She may, of course, go on to obtain various degrees and diplomas. These increase her market value in the eyes of men, for men believe that a woman who can recite things by heart must also *know and understand* them. But any real possibility of communication between the sexes ceases at this point. Their paths are divided forever.

One of man's worst mistakes, and one he makes over and over again, is to assume that woman is his equal, that is, a human being of equal mental and emotional capacity. A man may observe his wife, listen to her, judge her feelings by her reactions, but in all this he is judging her only by outward symptoms, for he is using his *own* scale of values.

He knows what *he* would say, think, and do if he were in her shoes. When he looks at her depressing ways of doing things, he assumes there must be something that prevents her from doing what he himself would have done in her position. This is natural, as he considers himself the measure of all things—and rightly so—if humans define themselves as beings capable of abstract thought.

When a man sees a woman spending hours cooking, washing dishes, and cleaning, it never occurs to him that such jobs probably make her quite happy since they are exactly at her mental level. Instead he assumes that this drudgery prevents her from doing all those things which he himself considers worthwhile and desirable. Therefore, he invents automatic dishwashers, vacuum cleaners, and precooked foods to make her life easier and to allow her to lead the dream life he himself longs for.

But he will be disappointed: rarely using the time she has gained to take an active interest in history, politics, or astrophysics, woman bakes cakes, irons underclothes, and makes ruffles and frills for blouses or, if she is especially enterprising, covers her bathroom with flower decals. It is natural, therefore, that man assumes such things to be the essential ingredients of *gracious living.* This idea must have been instilled by woman, as he himself really doesn't mind if his cakes are store-bought, his underpants unironed, or his bathroom devoid of flowery patterns. He invents cake mixes to liberate her from drudgery, automatic irons and toilet-paper holders already covered with flower patterns to make gracious living easier to attain—and still women take no interest in serious literature, politics, or the conquest of the universe. For her, this new-found leisure comes at just the right moment. At last she can take an interest in *herself:* since a longing after intellectual achievements is alien to her, she concentrates on her external appearance.

Yet even this occupation is acceptable to man. He really loves his wife and wants her happiness more than anything in the world. Therefore, he produces nonsmear lipstick, waterproof mascara, home permanents, no-iron frilly blouses, and throwaway underwear—always with the same aim in view. In the end, he hopes, this being whose needs seem to him so much more sensitive, so much more refined, will gain freedom—freedom to achieve in *her* life the ideal state which is *his* dream: to live the life of a *free* man.

Then he sits back and waits. Finally, as woman does not come to him of her own free will, he tries to tempt her into his world. He offers her coeducation, so that she is accustomed to his way of life from childhood. With all sorts of excuses, he gets her to attend his universities and initiates her into the mysteries of his own discoveries, hoping to awaken her interest in the wonders of life. He gives her access to the very last male strongholds, thereby relinquishing traditions sacred to him by encouraging her to make use of her right to vote in the hope that she will change the systems of government he has managed to think up so laboriously, according to her own ideas. Possibly he even hopes that she will be able to create peace in the world—for, in his opinion, women are a pacifist influence.

In all this he is so determined and pigheaded that he fails to see what a fool he is making of himself—ridiculous by his own standards, not those of women, who have absolutely no sense of humor.

No, women do not laugh at men. At most they get irritated. The old institutions of house and home are not yet so obviously outdated and derelict that they can't justify relinquishing all their intellectual pursuits and renouncing all their claims to better jobs. One does wonder, however, what will happen when housework is still further mechanized, when there are *enough* good nursery schools nearby, or when—as must occur before long—men discover that children themselves are not essential.

If only man would stop for one moment in his heedless rush toward progress and think about this state of affairs, he would inevitably realize that his efforts to give woman a sense of mental stimulation have been totally in vain. It is true that woman gets progressively more elegant, more well-groomed, more "cultured," but her demands on life will always be material, never intellectual.

Has she ever made use of the mental processes he teaches at his universities to develop her own theories? Does she do independent research in the institutes he has thrown open to her? Someday it will dawn on man that woman does not read the wonderful books with which he has filled his libraries. And though she may well admire his marvelous works of art in museums, she herself will rarely create, only copy. Even the plays and films, visual exhortations to woman on her own level to liberate herself, are judged only by their entertainment value. They will never be a first step to revolution.

When a man, believing woman his equal, realizes the futility of her way of life, he naturally tends to think that it must be *his* fault, that *he* must be suppressing *her.* But in our time women are no longer subject to the will of men. Quite the contrary. They have been given every opportunity to win their independence and if, after all this time, they have not liberated themselves and thrown off their shackles, we can only arrive at one conclusion: there are no shackles to throw off.

It is true that men love women, but they also despise them. Anyone who gets up in the morning fresh and ready to conquer new worlds (with infrequent success, admittedly, because he has to earn a living) is bound to despise someone who simply isn't interested in such pursuits. Contempt may even be one of the main reasons for his efforts to further the mental development of a woman. He feels ashamed of her and assumes that she, too, must be ashamed of herself. So, being a gentleman, he tries to help.

Men seem incapable of realizing that women entirely lack ambition, desire for knowledge, and need to prove themselves, all things which, to him, are a matter of course. They allow men to live in a world apart because they do not want to join them. Why should they? The sort of independence men have means nothing to women, because women don't feel dependent. They are not even embarrassed by the intellectual superiority of men because they have no ambition in that direction.

There is one great advantage which women have over men: *they have a choice*—a choice between the life of a man and the life of a dimwitted, parasitic luxury item. There are too few women who would not select the latter. Men do not have this choice.

If women really felt oppressed by men, they would have developed hate and fear for them, as the oppressed always do, but women do not fear men, much less hate them. If they really felt humiliated by men's mental superiority, they would have used every means in their power to change the situation. If women really felt unfree, surely, at such a favorable time in their history, they would have broken free of their oppressors.

In Switzerland, one of the most highly developed countries of the world, where until recently women were not allowed to vote, in a certain canton, it is reported, the majority of women were against introducing the vote for women. The Swiss men were shattered, for they saw in this unworthy attitude yet another proof of centuries of male oppression.

How very wrong they were! Women feel anything but oppressed by men. On the contrary, one of the many depressing truths about the relationship between the sexes is simply that man hardly exists in a woman's world: Man is not even powerful enough to revolt against. Woman's dependence on him is only material, of a "physical" nature, something like a tourist's dependence on an airline, a café proprietor's on his espresso machine, a car's on gasoline, a television set's on electric current. Such dependencies hardly involve agonizing.

Ibsen, who suffered from the same misapprehensions as other men, meant his *Doll's House* to be a kind of manifesto for the freedom of women. The première in 1880 certainly shocked *men,* and they determined to fight harder to improve women's position.

For women themselves, however, the struggle for emancipation as usual took shape in a change of style: for a while they delighted in their often-laughed-at masquerade as suffragettes.

Later on, the philosophy of Sartre made a similarly profound impression on women. As proof that they understood it completely, they let their hair grow down to their waists and wore black pullovers and trousers.

Even the teachings of the Chinese Communist leader Mao Tse-tung were a success—the Mao look lasted for a whole season.

JUDY SYFERS

Judy Syfers, who was born in San Francisco in 1937, describes herself as "middle-aged, middle-class, and still married." She feels that the problems of American wives "stem from a social system which places primary value on profits rather than on people's needs. As long as we continue to tolerate the system, we will continue to be exploited as workers and as wives." Ms. Syfers received her B.F.A. in painting from the University of Iowa in 1960. She wanted to go on for a higher degree that would enable her to paint and to teach in a university, but her (male) teachers advised that the best she could hope for as a woman was teaching in high school with a secondary-education credential. Her reaction was to drop school, get married, and have two children. Thus the present piece, which appeared in the first issue of Ms *in December 1971, arises from real experience.*

Ms. Syfers lives in San Francisco, continues to write for such causes as the United Farm Workers, and is editing a pair of diaries—one that she kept during a six-week visit to Cuba in 1973, the other kept by her husband who stayed behind to take care of the house, two girls, and his job.

Why I Want a Wife

I belong to that classification of people known as wives. I am A Wife. And, not altogether incidentally, I am a mother.

Not too long ago a male friend of mine appeared on the scene fresh from a recent divorce. He had one child, who is, of course, with his ex-wife. He is looking for another wife. As I thought about him while I was ironing one evening, it suddenly occurred to me that I, too, would like to have a wife. Why do I want a wife?

I would like to go back to school so that I can become economically independent, support myself, and, if need be, support those dependent upon me. I want a wife who will work and send me to school. And while I am going to school I want a wife to take care of my children. I want a wife to keep track of the children's doctor and dentist appointments. And to keep track of mine, too. I want a wife to make sure my children eat properly and are kept clean. I want a wife who will wash the children's clothes and keep them mended. I want a wife who is a good nurturant attendant to my children, who arranges for their schooling, makes sure that they have an adequate social life with their peers, takes them to the park, the zoo, etc. I want a wife who takes care of the children when they are sick, a wife who arranges to be around when the children need special care, because, of course, I cannot miss classes at school. My wife must arrange to lose time at work and not lose the job. It may mean a small cut in my wife's income from time to time, but I guess I can tolerate that. Needless to say, my wife will arrange and pay for the care of the children while my wife is working.

I want a wife who will take care of *my* physical needs. I want a wife who will keep my house clean. A wife who will pick up after me. I want a wife who will keep my clothes clean, ironed, mended, replaced when need be, and who will see to it that my personal things are kept in their proper place so that I can find what I need the minute I need it. I want a wife who cooks the meals, a wife who is a *good* cook. I want a wife who will plan the menus, do the necessary grocery shopping, prepare the meals, serve them pleasantly, and then do the cleaning up while I do my study-ing. I want a wife who will care for me when I am sick and sympathize with my pain and loss of time from school. I want a wife to go along when our family takes a vacation so that someone can continue to care for me and my children when I need a rest and change of scene.

I want a wife who will not bother me with rambling complaints about a wife's duties. But I want a wife who will listen to me when I feel the need to explain a rather difficult point I have come across in my course of studies. And I want a wife who will type my papers for me when I have written them.

I want a wife who will take care of the details of my social life. When my wife and I are invited out by my friends, I want a wife who will take care of the babysitting arrangements. When I meet people at school that I like and want to entertain, I want a wife who will have the house clean, will prepare a special meal, serve it to me and my friends, and not inter-rupt when I talk about the things that interest me and my friends. I want a wife who will have arranged that the children are fed and ready for bed before my guests arrive so that the children do not bother us. I want a wife who takes care of the needs of my guests so that they feel comfortable, who makes sure that they have an ashtray, that they are passed the hors d'oeuvres, that they are offered a second helping of the food, that their wine glasses are replenished when necessary, that their coffee is served to them as they like it. And I want a wife who knows that sometimes I need a night out by myself.

I want a wife who is sensitive to my sexual needs, a wife who makes love passionately and eagerly when I feel like it, a wife who makes sure that I am satisfied. And, of course, I want a wife who will not demand sexual attention when I am not in the mood for it. I want a wife who assumes the complete responsibility for birth control, because I do not want more children. I want a wife who will remain sexually faithful to me so that I do not have to clutter up my intellectual life with jealousies. And I want a wife who understands that *my* sexual needs may entail more than strict adherence to monogamy. I must, after all, be able to relate to people as fully as possible.

If, by chance, I find another person more suitable as a wife than the wife I already have, I want the liberty to replace my present wife with another one. Naturally, I will expect a fresh, new life; my wife will take the children and be solely responsible for them so that I am left free.

When I am through with school and have a job, I want my wife to quit working and remain at home so that my wife can more fully and completely take care of a wife's duties.

My God, who *wouldn't* want a wife?

JUDITH WELLS

Judith Wells is a graduate student in comparative literature at the University of California, Berkeley. She was born in 1944, grew up in San Francisco, and got her B.A. in French from Stanford. She is writing her Ph.D. dissertation about women and madness in modern literature— madness meaning both anger and insanity. She has helped develop the women's studies program at Berkeley and has taught several courses on women and madness in literature. She also heads a program at Napa Community College designed to encourage older women to return to school. "Daddy's Girl," her first published work, appeared in Libera, Winter 1972.

Daddy's Girl

"A little girl, full of innocence and indulgence. And then this madness. . . ."
                            —*Ladders to Fire,* ANAIS NIN

Nothing is more startling to a Daddy's girl than to find herself in revolt against her Daddies. Because of her intimacy with and desire for approval from her Daddies, she finds it painful to make a clean break with them. "Daddy, daddy, you bastard, I'm through," cries Sylvia Plath in her poem "Daddy"; in spite of the voodoo murder of her Father, Plath is still a little girl murderess who addresses the "Panzer man," "the brute," the "Fascist" of her poem as Daddy. Even her closing words, "I'm through," strangely undercut her patricide—as if she herself dies with her Father —an echo of her death wish in a previous stanza: "At twenty I tried to die/And get back, back, back to you."

This complicity with "Daddy" has been my own peculiar emotional madness for years. A large part of what I always called my "self" has been invested in the personality of the Daddy's Girl or the Little Girl. The Little Girl is fragile, vulnerable, helpless, bewildered, compliant. She feels she occupies a very tiny amount of both physical and psychological space. In my own dreams this smallness is experienced through seeing myself as a miniature person—a girl who melts down to a face in a postage stamp or a girl whose full size is as small as a person's hands (and thus easily manipulated). The Little Girl is an object, not a subject.

It took me a good deal of hard work in psychotherapy and the Women's Movement to reach any understanding about my own Little Girl. For a long time I maintained a masque of independence; I made myself believe I didn't care what my father and men thought about me. Yet underneath, I based most of my personality on masculine approval. Any criticism from a male brought me a haunting sense of guilt. The least assertion of my own preference or will was stepping over the line; I internalized the reply "You've gone too far" even before I opened my mouth. I was unable to work when my boyfriend was around and felt guilty over surpassing male friends and my father in intellectual achievements; but I also knew I had to accomplish something to get masculine approval. The only activity this ambivalence brought on was diarrhea. Then I became sick and could nurture my vulnerable, fragile self which was, and still is, in effect, my Little Girl.

The Little Girl infects many females because she is nurtured by so much of society as well as by ourselves. She has no age limit:

> She wears sweet little dresses, her tears and caprices are viewed indulgently, her hair is done up carefully, older people are amused at her expressions and coquetries—bodily contacts and agreeable glances protect her against the anguish of solitude.
>
> *The Second Sex,* p. 252

Although this is Simone de Beauvoir's description of a small girl in childhood, it could well apply to the Little Girl aspect of ourselves, our mothers, and our grandmothers. I was surprised when I realized that some of the gestures of my boss's eight-year-old daughter were not far from my own—her cajoling, indirect expression of what she wanted, her refusal to attempt a simple task without precise, precise instructions. The Little Girl pose is designed to elicit maternal or paternal indulgence—specifically, because the Little Girl is or thinks she is helpless.

Although the Little Girl can inhabit any woman's body, a small woman is particularly susceptible to this syndrome. In her first *Diary,* Anais Nin relates a conversation with her psychiatrist about this sense of vulnerability and helplessness that a small woman experiences:

> My greatest fear is that people will become aware that I am fragile, not a full-blown woman physically, that I am emotionally vulnerable, that I have small breasts like a girl. (p. 86)

My own sense that I am physically slight and fragile has not only bolstered my feelings of helplessness, but it has also contributed to my feeling that I am not quite a grown woman—that creature who is defined by having curves in the right places. The curveless woman easily sees herself as a Little Girl.

Although the Little Girl may be more readily apparent in a woman with a small body, most women experience the Little Girl at times as a psychic state. In Nin's *Children of the Albatross,* Djuna remembers:

> She remembered, too, that whenever she became entangled in too great a difficulty she had these swift regressions into her adolescent state. Almost as if in the large world of maturity, when the obstacle loomed too large, she shrank again into the body of the young girl for whom the world had first appeared as a violent and dangerous place, forcing her to retreat, and when she retreated she fell back into smallness. (p. 40)

Djuna experiences a "psychic smallness" which is her inability to affect significantly the world around her—hence, her helplessness.

In the Little Girl, "psychic smallness" is also directly related to her desire for approval from authority figures, especially from Daddies. As a Little Girl, I found that I had based my personality for such a long time on approval from authority figures that *they* were my personality. I experienced "psychic smallness" because I had never defined who I was or what I wanted in life; my only sense of identity stemmed from Daddy's approval.

The real tragedy of the Little Girl, then, is her inability to define herself in her own terms, select her own goals, and feel her life has significance *without* Daddy's support. The Little Girl turns over the responsibility for her own life to her Daddies (real fathers, boyfriends, husbands, professors, psychiatrists) and sits devotedly, if a bit uneasily, at their feet. Unfortunately, society sanctions this pose of the Child-Woman, especially in its sexual images and stereotypes.

In the Magic Theater's recent production of *Miles Gloriosus,* two poles of stereotyped female sexuality are portrayed: the Vixen-Whore in black wasp waist corset and tights, and the Baby Doll in pink pajamas, with freckles on her nose and ribbons in her hair. Although the Baby Doll is parody in this play, many girls are schooled in this image of coyness, flirtation, and "innocent" sexuality which they carry over into adult life. The Little Girl clothes syndrome, which periodically runs rampant through fashion as it has recently, supports this image: the mod "little dresses," the clingy pastel tee shirts with patterns from babyhood, the overall and romper outfits—all designed to make females resemble innocent little girls yet still be sexually appealing. Roger Vadim exploited this combination of innocence and sexuality to the hilt in his presentation of Brigitte Bardot to moviegoers. In Simone de Beauvoir's book, *Brigitte Bardot and the Lolita Syndrome,* the author relates:

> He [Vadim] painted her as naive to the point of absurdity. According to him, at the age of eighteen she thought that mice laid eggs. (p. 13)

De Beauvoir comments on Bardot's roles in "And God Created Woman" and "Love Is My Profession":

> BB is a lost, pathetic child who needs a guide and protector. This cliché has proved its worth. It flatters masculine vanity. . . . (p. 15)

The child-woman poses no threat to the male ego—hence her appeal. De Beauvoir notes the particular charm of the child-woman to the American male:

> . . . he feels a certain antipathy to the 'real woman.' He regards her as an antagonist, a praying mantis, a tyrant. He abandons himself eagerly to the charms of the 'nymph' in whom the formidable figure of the wife and 'Mom' is not yet apparent. (p. 23)

Although I hardly possess the "nymph" looks of Bardot, my own appearance and Little Girl personality have encouraged me to maintain this child-woman sexual role. When I was younger, this child role came easily; but with increased sexual experience, the role became harder and harder to maintain. I can't kid myself anymore. I know my own sexual desires, but the child-woman in me still makes me embarrassed when I want to be sexually aggressive or state my desires straight out. I know many women share this problem—this embarrassment over wanting to be a subject, not an object in sexual activity. And the male attitude doesn't help much; for even though "The Sexual Revolution's Here," a woman is discouraged subtly (a male's slightly chilly response to her phone call) and not so subtly (his impotence when she asks him to bed) when she is sexually aggressive.

As a Little Girl I have spent a good deal of my life adjusting to just such masculine requirements, adapting myself to gain their approval. Finally, I felt pain—the intense frustration of being confined by my own compliancy.I understand all too well the statement of the man I work for (who designed an educational program to improve the self-image of Blacks) about the accommodation attitudes of Blacks. I have substituted *woman* for *man* in the quote and *her* for *him:*

> Let us assume I am standing with my foot on the neck of a *woman* who is lying on the ground; I am wearing a hobnail boot. I say to *her,* "Your role is simply different from mine, not worse; you are horizontal and I am vertical." And then I say to *her,* "Your role has certain advantages over mine; you do not have to worry about falling down. Furthermore, you are developing a very interesting adaptive behavior. You are learning to breathe with my foot on your neck."
>
> "Teaching and Testing the Disadvantaged,"
> William Johntz

Interestingly enough, the sado-masochistic imagery of this passage exactly fits sexual politics. The victim is made to feel she is lucky she doesn't have the "burdens" of the victor. The victim's final adaptive behavior is what the Little Girl and, in actuality, any woman, has done all her life. She has learned to breathe with a foot on her neck until she finally explodes in frustration and cries out with Sylvia Plath, "You do not do, you do not do/Any more, black shoe. . . ."

It would be great if the Little Girl could join the Women's Movement and instantly become a self-sufficient woman. I have found that my Little Girl personality is not shed so easily, and that my rebellion against my Daddies has its own peculiar Little Girl cyclic rhythm: compliancy towards a man—simmering hate—explosion of outrage—anxiety over having stepped over the line—fear of reprisal—compliancy towards a man —and the cycle begins again. Because the Little Girl has suffocated her own desires so completely in favor of her Daddies, her potential for rage is volcanic once she questions the belief that "Father knows best." Yet for myself and probably for most Little Girls, each explosion is followed less by a sense of triumph than by anxiety and fear of reprisal. Since the Little Girl's only previous sense of identity stemmed from approval from her Daddies, cutting these figures out of her life will seem like cutting out the core of herself. At first, "destruction" of Daddy seems like self-destruction. This anxiety over self-destruction in the elimination of her source of identity brings on the Little Girl's helplessness. She is then a weak, vulnerable, compliant child again, fearing Daddy's reprisal.

Even if she finally rebels against her Daddies, the Little Girl will remain caught in this circle of anger and compliancy until she learns to stop loving and nurturing the Little Girl in herself. If I had to select the most important moment in my several years of psychotherapy, it would be the moment I realized who loved the Little Girl in me most. I was astonished to find it was myself. I was finally able to objectify my Little Girl enough to see her as separate from another part of me. I experienced myself caressing and cherishing that Little Girl as I had loved my dolls many years ago—the same kind of love I desperately wanted to experience when I was a real little girl. Perhaps, above everything else, this desperation for love kept me locked into my first childhood attempts to gain approval from adults. And when, as a real little girl, I realized that the "adult world" was governed mainly by male figures, I began to base my worth on how much love and approval I could get from my Daddies. The Little Girl pose stuck.

I am coming to realize more and more that I no longer receive much approval for the Little Girl role; it's an illusion I maintain which has little basis in my own daily life. As a friend of mine in graduate school put it, "I'm thirty years old. I look like a grown woman. If I start to do the Little Girl bit with my professors, they look at me funny." The Little Girl role has a few benefits but enormous drawbacks: a stifling of one's intelligence and creativity, a confining sexual role, an arresting of growth of one's personality. When I experienced myself cherishing my Little Girl doll self, I flashed on a picture I had drawn when I was ten years old to illustrate a poem I had read called "The Long ago, far away doll." I drew a doll in a sea chest; she was dressed in a lovely yellow fancy dress, and her cheeks were rouged; but her eyes stared into space, and she looked like a dead person. The Little Girl aspect of any woman keeps her like this doll—repressed, inactive, dead.

The Little Girl has no place to grow but up. It is true that if she does choose to continue her growth, she may not receive some of the masculine approval she received in the past. As I stated previously, certain men like a Little Girl because she is less threatening to the masculine ego. Too, the growing Little Girl must risk the disapproval of her real father—often the man who clings the most tenaciously to the idea of his daughter as a perpetual girl child. She may be regarded as a rebel or even a bitch. Yet there will be others, both women and men, who will approve of her—not for feminine fluff, but for her real talents and developing personality. More important, she will gain self-respect from presenting her *own self* to the world, and this self-respect will be worth much more than the approval she received as a crippled Little Girl.

I read someplace in my many psychological readings, when I was trying to pinpoint my "problems," about a young girl in an African society. In her early teens, she was listless, lacked confidence, and was fearful of males and masculine authority. Her tribe used a mode of transvestitism to exorcise her fears. She dressed up in the male military costume of the former colonial power of the area and began to dance in this costume. After the ceremony, the girl's confidence increased enormously, she no longer feared men, and she eventually developed into a

mature, self-reliant woman. The girl in this story acts out symbolically
what the Little Girl must learn to do for herself: incorporate the authority,
which she objectifies outside of herself, into her own person. She must
develop a sense of her *own personal authority* and hence, *self-approval*. When
the Little Girl develops this sense of self-approval, she will no longer be
a Little Girl, but a mature woman—a full, complete human being. With
this new sense of personal authority, she can look back on her "rebellious" struggles as Anais Nin does:

> Very often I would say I rebelled against this or that. Much later it occurred
> to me to question this statement. Instead of rebellion could it be that I was
> merely asserting my own belief?
>
> *Diary* III, p. xiii

And I answer with Nin: YES.

S. M. MILLER

---

*S. M. Miller was born in 1922. He grew up in Brooklyn, New York,
and graduated from Brooklyn College, where he studied economics and
sociology. He then did advanced work at Columbia (M.A., 1945), and at
Princeton (Ph.D., 1951). He has been Professor of Education and
Sociology at New York University, director of the Urban Center, and is
now head of the Department of Sociology at Boston University. His books
include* Max Weber: A Reader *(1964),* Social Class and Social
Policy *(1968), and, in collaboration with Pamela Roby,* The Future
of Inequality *(1970). The article presented here first appeared in* Social
Policy, *July–August 1971.*

The Making of a Confused Middle-Class Husband

When I was in my twenties, I would try to convince marriage-oriented
women to become involved with me by predicting, on the basis of experience, that within six months of such involvement they would very likely
be getting married—though not to me—because the association with me
seemed to drive women to marriage. In my forties, I find that young
women's work association with me seems to correlate highly with their
movement into women's lib. Irrespective of whether proximity to me
induces a liberation spirit or whether this spirit could possibly be due to

larger cultural forces, my female co-workers have led me to think much more of late about sexism, and to review my own experiences over the decades within that framework.

Two interchanges with my colleagues particularly struck me. One wrote me a strong note asking why I was not publicly active in fighting sexism if I thought that I was so good on the question. I was somewhat stung by this passionate indictment, and in cool, clear, parsimonious prose replied that I did not consider myself to be very good on the sex issue, but that, looking around at most men of my own and perhaps younger ages, I was constantly surprised to find myself much better in my attitudes and behavior than they, though not good enough, etc.

But a nagging vision persisted despite my measured rejoinder. True, my wife worked, and always had worked, and I pushed her to do more professional writing, to establish herself solidly in her professional life; true, I had played a major role in bringing up our children, especially when they were young and my wife was going to school; true, in arguments with friends I had always taken pro-liberation positions. For decades I had argued against the then-fashionable *Kinder-Küche* motif of suburban existence and had counseled students against it. I advised husbands whose wives were diffusely unhappy that they should drive their talented and educated, if unsure, spouses into work, for staying home all day and taking care of a household made for a malcontentment that was compounded by social disapproval of the expression of unhappiness in mothering and wifing. Yes, all that was true. But how different was the present pattern of my own family life from that of a family with a more obviously backward husband than I?

Another female colleague, more disposed to be kindly toward me, told me, when I questioned a particular emphasis of women's lib, that I did not realize how backward young men now in their twenties and thirties were: they had been brought up in the suburban sadness in which their mothers played the required "good mother-wife" role, in which their sisters and their dates accepted the necessity of catering to men in order to make a "good catch." She went on to say that these men had not been confronted on sexist issues (this conversation preceded the mass media's elevating women's lib to celebrity status); indeed, they were largely unaware that there might be some injustice in the present ordering of the world.

My experience, I replied, had been different. In the left-wing ambience of New York City in the '40s and '50s, "male supremacy" and "male chauvinism" were frequently discussed. True, my male friends and I discussed the issues with our female friends and then often proceeded to exploit them, but a dextrous awareness we did have. (But I add, in order to avoid a reassuring self-debasement, that we did encourage our women friends and wives to think and to develop themselves; and I even believe that I was less exploitative than most.)

Yet I am dogged by the feeling expressed in the notion "If you're so

smart, how come you're not rich?'' Where is the egalitarian family life one
would reasonably expect from my sophistication about women's lib issues
and my personal experience with them in my younger manhood?

I have never had an intellectual problem with sexism. One reason may
well have been the women who surrounded me as a child—my father's
mother, my mother, and two considerably older sisters—although I know
it sometimes goes quite the other way. My father slept, and my mother
dominated—partly out of force of character and partly, one sister informed me fairly recently, because of the occupational and other failures
of my father. He had tried to make it in America—and could not. His was
the immigrant's rags-to-rags story. He started as a factory worker, and
became a small businessman, only to be wiped out by the 1921 depression. He worked again as a machine operator, and then started a dress
store, where he did the alterations and my mother was chief saleswoman.
Again, his enterprise was rewarded by a depression—this time, that of the
1930s. He went back to working at a machine in the lowest-paid part of
the garment industry, where he stayed until he retired in his early seventies. From the depression days on, my mother worked as a saleslady. I was
a "latchkey kid" from an early age, warming up the meals that were left
for me by my mother.

   My mother was very smart and witty, and so was my older sister. They
were obviously intellectually well endowed, although not well educated.
My mother had a few years of formal schooling; my sister just managed
to graduate from high school. (I think I developed my repugnance for
credentialism because I recognized that these were two very smart
though not well educated women.)

   From this experience, I grew up regarding women as competent and
capable of making family and economic decisions. (By contrast, my
mother disliked cooking; and it was a shock to me when I began to eat
away from home to discover what a bad cook she was.) Women worked
and ran things well. On the other hand, there was a notion that people
frowned on women's working, so we tried to hide the fact that my mother
worked. I think I felt both ashamed that my mother worked and irritated
that "society" thought that it was wrong for women to work, especially
when their incomes were needed.

   Furthermore, sexism was, in principle, alien to the egalitarian and
participatory circles in which my closest friends and I were passionately
involved. We were out of step with the intellectual climate of the '40s and
'50s because of our egalitarian, populist, antielitist spirit. We criticized
Stalinist democratic centralism and American Celebration-style pluralist
democracy because of their inadequate attention to equality and participation for all. We could no more subscribe to intellectual rationalizations
of a low status for females than we could condone the miseries of oppression and deprivation among other parts of the population.

   A third reason I see myself as intellectually escaping sexism has more manifest emotional roots. Looking back, I don't believe that I could have accepted a woman who would center her life completely on me and devote herself to making me happy. (Children were not part of my purview.) At one level, the intellectual, how could one individual be worthy of such dedication by another? At a deeper and, I suspect now, more significant level, I rejected or stayed away from easily giving or male-centered women because I did not consider myself worthy of another person's total devotion or capable of evoking the sentiments that would sustain it beyond the initial impulse. Furthermore, such devotion would demand an emotional response that I possibly could not make. In short, I did not think so well of myself that I could live with (overwhelming) devotion. As a consequence, I was usually involved with young women with strong career goals who were seeking their identity through work, not through family. They were my intellectual equals, if not superiors.

Thus I had a good beginning, it seems to me, for having a marriage that did not embody sexist currents. But I don't see that my current life is very different from that of men who espoused or expounded more sexist values. Years ago a good friend told me that I had the reputation among the wives in our circle of being "an excellent husband"; and he said, "You know, that's not a good thing." I now have the feeling that families that openly embrace both bourgeois and sexist values don't live very differently from us. I sense that we are engaged in a "lapsed egalitarianism," still believing in our earlier commitments and concerns about equality, but having drifted from the faith in our daily life.

Probably the most important factor in accounting for the direction we took was our amazing naivete about the impact of having children—a naivete, incidentally, that I see today having a similarly devastating effect on many young parents. We just had no idea how much time and emotion children captured, how they simply changed a couple's lives, even when the wife's working made it possible, as it did in our case, to afford a housekeeper.

The early years of childrearing were very difficult. Our first son was superactive and did not sleep through the night. We were both exhausted. My wife insisted that I not leave everything to her; she fought with me to get me to participate in the care of our son and apartment. I took the 2 a.m. and 6 a.m. feedings and changings, for our ideology would not allow me just to help out occasionally: I had to "share," "really participate," in the whole thing. I resented that degree of involvement; it seemed to interfere terribly with the work I desperately wanted to achieve in. Indeed, I have always felt put upon because of that experience of many months.

To make matters worse, I did not know of other work-oriented husbands who were as involved as I with their children. True, I realized that my sons and I had become much attached to each other and that a lovely new element had entered my life; but I resented the time and exhaustion, particularly since I was struggling to find my way in my work. I did not consider myself productive and was in the middle of struggling to clarify my perspective. I looked at the problem largely in terms of the pressure of my job, which required a lot of effort, and, more importantly, in terms of my personality and my inability to work effectively. Although I wrote memoranda with great ease, I wasn't writing professional articles and books.

In retrospect, I think that it was the influence of the McCarthy and Eisenhower years that was more significant in my lack of development. My outlook and interests were not what social science and society were responding to. That changed later, and I was able to savor in the '60s that infrequent exhilaration of having my professional work and citizen concerns merge and of gaining both a social science and popular audience and constituency. But I did not know in the 1950s that this would unfold, and I felt resentment.

What I experienced was that, unlike my friends, I was working hard to make things easier for my wife; and I did not see rewards. Yes, she told me she appreciated my effort; but my activities were never enough, my sharing was never full, in the sense that I equally planned and took the initiative in the care of child and house. She was tired, too, and irritated by child care; and, in turn, I was irritated by what seemed to be her absorption in taking care of children.

And there were always those male friends who did so little, compared with me. I could, and did, tell myself that at some point along the line they would be paying heavy "dues" for their current neglect of their wives' plight, but it was small balm at the time. I wondered if I was not rationalizing my irritation by an intellectualizing metaphor about how one pays prices sooner or later and by a plaintively reassuring injunction never to envy anyone else, for who knew what lurked behind the façade of family equanimity?

Things were further complicated by another factor—less typical of today's young marrieds—my incomplete early socialization as a family member. For example, since as an adolescent and pre-adolescent I had eaten meals by myself, I had developed the habit of reading while eating. (Indeed, I am a compulsive reader, a "print nut"; if there is nothing around to read, I will study the labels on ketchup bottles.) The result was that marriage required a resocialization: I had to learn to talk to someone at mealtimes, and not to turn inward to my own thoughts or to *The New York Times*.

Of course, the reading is only the personal tip of the iceberg of a larger problem of not closing myself to others and becoming inaccessible because of stress or intellectual absorption. I am now, again, in a conscious period of trying to make myself more accessible emotionally to my family, but it is a struggle. For example, when we vacation, I spend the first few days devouring three to four mysteries a day—"decompressing" I call it—hardly talking to anyone. And, of course, when I am at a deadline, or caught in my inability to work out an idea, or just unable to get to work (there are few other conditions for me than these three), I am rather inaccessible, to say the least. I work against this tendency, but don't do notably well. While I do the mundane tasks of the household, psychologically I am often not much there. I think that I am winning the struggle against withdrawal, but what is a giant step to the battler may appear as a wiggle of progress to the beholder.

My wife has accommodated to my dislike of fixing things and "wasting time" on such things—not great matters in themselves, but symptomatic of the process of my disengagement from the burdens of home and family.

From a narrow perspective, I have useful incompetencies protecting me from diversions of my energy and focus. I don't like to fix things and don't do them well (or soon). In my youth, in my proletarian near-idealization, I felt Arthur Miller was right when he had Willy Loman say that a man isn't a man unless he can do things with his hands. So I tried adult education shop courses and the like for a brief time. I went in a "klutz" and came out a "klutz." Now, in a spirit of reactive arrogance or greater self-pride, I boldly assert the counterposition that I believe in the division of labor and prefer to pay for specialized labor. I do little around the house—and that usually long delayed. Since skilled labor is hard to get at any price, things are undone, or my wife does them; but my principle of specialization (for me) remains unimpaired.

Similarly, I have been relieved of the task of paying bills. With my usual speed and my disdain for trivia, I did this job very rapidly and made mistakes. Now my wife spends time doing this task. It is easier, in her view, for her to do it than to keep after me to do a competent job. Failure is its own reward: I have escaped another task. Of course, I have been after my wife to have a part-time secretary and bookkeeper and have located several people for her. But she resists, as they do not provide enough help to make it worthwhile. The result is that my personnel efforts reduce my feelings of guilt when she spends evenings writing checks. After all, I did try to get her out of that function. But I am still irritated by her doing the checks—for that act is another indication that she is failing me by not showing our true equality by spending more time on her professional writing and research.

I guess what dismays me and makes me see my marriage and family as unfortunately typically upper middle class collegial, pseudo-egalitarian American—especially in light of my own continuing commitment to an egalitarian, participatory ethos—is that I assume no responsibility for major household tasks and family activities. True, my wife has always worked at her profession (she is a physician), even when our sons were only some weeks old. (I used to say that behind the working wife with young children, there stands a tired husband.) True, I help in many ways and feel responsible for her having time to work at her professional interests. But I do partial, limited things to free her to do her work. I don't do the basic thinking about the planning of meals and housekeeping, or the situation of the children. Sure, I will wash dishes and "spend time" with the children; I will often do the shopping, cook, make beds, "share" the burden of most household tasks; but that is not the same thing as direct and primary responsibility for planning and managing a household and meeting the day-to-day needs of children.

It is not that I object in principle to housekeeping and childrearing. I don't find such work demeaning or unmasculine—just a drain of my time, which could be devoted to other, "more rewarding" things. (Just as I don't like to shop for clothes for myself, even though I like clothes.) My energies are poised to help me work on my professional-political concerns, and I resist "wasting time" on other pursuits, even those basic to managing a day-to-day existence.

The more crucial issue, I now think, is not my specific omissions and commissions, but the atmosphere that I create. My wife does not expect much of me, which frees me for work and lessens the strain I produce when I feel blocked from working. Even our sons have always largely respected my efforts to work, feeling much freer to interrupt their mother at her work. The years have been less happy than they would have been if I had been more involved and attentive and my wife had not lowered her ambitions.

Outstanding academically from an early age, a "poor girl" scholarship winner to a prestige college and medical school, excelling in her beginning professional work, my wife expected, and was expected, to do great things. But with children, she immediately reduced her goals. Of course, medical schools don't pay much attention to faculty members who are part-time or female, and the combination of the two almost guarantees offhand treatment.

She is now realizing fuller professional development. I have always felt guilty about her not achieving more, so I have nagged her to publish, though I have not provided the circumstances and climate that would make serious work much easier. I have had the benefit of feeling relieved that I was "motivating" her by my emphasis on her doing more, but I have not suffered the demands on my time and emotions that making more useful time available to her would have required. In the long run, I have undoubtedly lost more by limited involvement, because she has been distressed by the obstacles to her professional work. But the long run is hard to consider when today's saved and protected time helps meet a deadline.

What are the lessons of this saga of a well-meaning male?

One is that equality or communality is not won once and for all, but must continually be striven for. Backsliding and easy accommodation to the male (because it is less troublesome) are likely to occur unless there is, at least occasionally, effort to bring about or maintain true communality rather than peaceful adjustment.

From this it follows that women must struggle for equality—that it will not easily be won or rewon. (A male is not likely to bestow it—in more than surface ways. Some women are arguing that it is not worth the effort to have equality with men in close personal relations and that they should not bother with men, but equality and communality among women will not be automatic either.) The struggle does not necessarily mean nastiness, but it does require the perceptiveness and willingness to engage issues not only of prejudice and discrimination but also of subtle practices requiring female accommodation to males.

I know that the point I am about to make is often misused, and will open me to much criticism; but let me try to make it. A third lesson is that the bringing up of children must be changed, and that many women are lagging in this respect, although present day-care concerns suggest a possible change. For all of male reluctance, resistance, and avoidance, many women, particularly when they have young children, end up structuring life so that it is difficult to achieve a collegial relationship. Indeed, the concentration on, nay absorption with, children makes even a low-level decent relationship, let alone an egalitarian one, difficult. Yes, I realize that the subordinate group is never the main source of difficulty, that men make women embrace the mother-housemother syndrome; but cultural and personal history are involved as well as direct or more covert husbandly pressure and unwillingness to be a full partner. Overinvolvement with children may operate to discourage many husbands from full participation because they do not accept the ideology of close attention to children.

I am *not* saying that the problem is with women, but that this part of the problem shouldn't be ignored. Even for the young parents it is important to have some measure of agreement on the mode, the style of child-care. This is difficult to realize before actually becoming parents. Perhaps it will not be an issue for those in their twenties who may have a different and more relaxed attitude toward children. (And, of course, many no longer feel unfulfilled if they do not have children.) For some, yes; but I doubt if that will be true of most relatively "straight" parents. What is needed is a reconsideration of what is required in parenthood and in running a household.

Let me consider the household care first. The easy notion that in the right atmosphere housework is not so bad seems wrong to me. A lot of jobs can be stomached, treated as routine; that is the best one can say of them—that they are manageable, "do-able." But they are not exciting, stimulating, or satisfying except to the extent that they are completed or "accomplished," i.e., gotten rid of for the moment. This is especially so when one's other interests are high, for then these tasks become highly competitive with other ways of using one's time and thus are dissatisfying. Housework can be a full-time job if it is not guarded against. Some agreement on a minimum, satisfactory level of household care and some efficiency and sharing in performing it are important for a couple.

I have mentioned, verbally at least, the desirability of *alles für die Eltern* and "salutary neglect" (before Moynihan, incidentally). But it has been difficult for my generation, whose adolescence and early twenties were stirred by Freud and who have wallowed in the guilt of parental omniscience and ethnic parental concern, to erase the sense of responsibility and guilt for how our children develop. What if one's son doesn't graduate from college or becomes a bomb-thrower or a homosexual—isn't it the parents' fault? When a son or daughter is 18 or 20, it seems easier to deny the responsibility, since so many youths are also in troubled times that it is difficult to talk of Freudian acting-out rather than of a generational change in consciousness. But at earlier ages it is much more difficult to shake the feeling of parental responsibility for how an infant or child is developing. I don't advocate callous neglect; but some less constraining and demanding views of parenthood—and probably some additional institutional aids like day care—are needed.

The problem is not always in the mother's attitudes. Some studies show that working-class women are very interested in working, but that their husbands feel that it is important to the children for their mothers to be home. The issue is not so much that the mother or father is lagging but how to move toward new views on child development and new institutions to further these views.

A fourth lesson has to do with sex, and I am rather surprised by it. It turns out that the most easy acceptance of equality is in bed—not in the kitchen.

Few middle-class men, except those regarded as crude or brutes, would assert that women do not have a right to enjoyment in bed equal to that of their partners—although I doubt that female extramarital affairs are treated as casually by men as men think their own extramarital adventures should be regarded by women. Even if the male does not generally assume a great responsibility for a female's difficulty in achieving orgasm, he is expected by himself and others to try to help her gain at least some measure of fulfillment. "Biff, bang, thank you ma'am" is more of a joke than ever before.

This suggests that that most delicate of human relations—sex—isn't so central. Men are adjusting to new requirements and are incorporating them into their definition of maleness. But the other elements of equality are not so easily absorbed into the definition of maleness. The "maleness" of many young females' attitudes toward sex—ready to go to bed without much emotional involvement with the partner; sex as kicks, not love—may be misleading them. "Good sex" doesn't necessarily mean real equality.

I suspect many young women today are being exploited by men just as my generation exploited women, with the notion that true freedom, both political and psychological, is demonstrated by an "uninhibited" attitude toward relatively casual intercourse. The phenomenal and depressing success of *Love Story,* as trite and sentimentalized a story of romance and sexism as has come along in a long while—truly a 1950-ish, Eisenhower romance—indicates that many young women, even when they use four-letter words, dream of the everlasting and all-satisfying flame of love, including the purity of death as its authentication. And, I fear, they think that equality in bed means equality in other things. They are much less liberated than they think, and are probably sexually exploited by their male friends. Both young men and young women seem unlikely to sustain for long untraditional forms of bedding and wedding, which is one of the reasons that I think my experiences still have relevance.

But all these "implications" are minor, except for the importance of struggle. What strikes me as the crucial concern, at least for the occupationally striving family, is the male involvement in work, success, and striving. This is the pressure that often molds the family. Accommodation to it is frequently the measure of being a "good wife"—moving when the male's "future" requires it, regulating activities so that the male is free to concentrate on his work or business. It isn't sexism or prejudice against women that is at work here—although they are contributing factors—but the compulsive concentration upon the objective of achievement and the relegating of other activities to secondary concern. Egalitarian relationships cannot survive if people are not somewhat equally involved with each other and if the major commitment is to things outside the relationship that inevitably intrude upon it.

So long as success or achievement burns bright for the male, it is going to be difficult to change drastically the situation of the family and the women.

However, although I am strongly of the mind that success drives should be banked and other more humanitarian urges encouraged, I don't accept that all of the drive for success or achievement is pernicious or undesirable. This drive is exciting, and can be fulfilling. But it is a great danger to be avoided when it becomes all-embracing or when the success is without a content that is both personally and socially satisfying or beneficial.

To do interesting and useful things, to feel a sense of accomplishment, should be made easier. As in military strategy, a "sufficient level" of achievement rather than a "maximum level" of security or position should be sought. Being "number one" should not be the goal; rather, high competence should be enough for both men and women. I have seen many talented people blighted in their work by "number-one-ism" when they probably would have done outstanding and useful work by adopting high competence-performance criteria.

If women accept "success" to the same extent and in the same way that many men do, the problems will be enormous. If women simply adopt the "number-one-ism" that dominates the workplace, the drive for achievement will probably lead them into the same narrowing and unpromising obsessions that destroy many men.

A more egalitarian society in terms of the distribution of income and social respect would, of course, make it easier to escape "number-one-ism." But, meanwhile, we shall have to struggle with the values that surround us and corrode true equality in the home.

Finally, men have to feel some gain in the growing equality in their relationship with women. Over the long run there may well be greater satisfaction for males in egalitarian relationships, but in the short run the tensions and demands may not lead to enjoyment and satisfaction. Some short-term gains for males will be important in speeding up the road to equality. But such gains are not easily or automatically forthcoming. Substitute satisfactions or gains for the male are needed to push out sexism rapidly. That is why I made the first points about the inevitability of struggle. But successful struggle requires modes of living and relationships to which the male can accommodate without total loss, which is hard to achieve without women's falling back again to accommodating to men.

I recognize that I concentrate upon the upper middle class and upon the experience of one male. I don't think either is the world—I really don't. But I do perceive that some of my experiences and interpretations are not solipsist pieces of life, that with things changing, others are experiencing similar shocks and stresses. I wonder whether the egalitarian changes I see in some young families will mean permanent changes, or "lapsed egalitarianism" once again. My hope is that the '70s will be different.

MARC FEIGEN FASTEAU

Marc Feigen Fasteau was born in Washington, D.C., in 1942. He was educated at Harvard College, Georgetown University, and Harvard Law School, where he was an editor of the Law Review. *While in Washington, he worked as an assistant in foreign affairs to Senator Mike Mansfield and as a staff member of the Joint Economic Committee of Congress. He served as a research fellow at the Kennedy Institute of Politics before joining a New York law firm. Since 1974, Fasteau and his wife, feminist attorney Brenda Feigen Fasteau, have been practicing law in partnership. Both in his work and in his writing he has been actively engaged in the breaking of sexual stereotypes.* The Male Machine *(1974), from which we reprint a chapter below, in his first book.*

Friendships Among Men

There is a long-standing myth in our society that the great friendships are between men. Forged through shared experience, male friendship is portrayed as the most unselfish, if not the highest form, of human relationship. The more traditionally masculine the shared experience from which it springs, the stronger and more profound the friendship is supposed to be. Going to war, weathering crises together at school or work, playing on the same athletic team, are some of the classic experiences out of which friendships between men are believed to grow.

By and large, men do prefer the company of other men, not only in their structured time but in the time they fill with optional, nonobligatory activity. They prefer to play games, drink, and talk, as well as work and fight together. Yet something is missing. Despite the time men spend together, their contact rarely goes beyond the external, a limitation which tends to make their friendships shallow and unsatisfying.

My own childhood memories are of doing things with my friends— playing games or sports, building walkie-talkies, going camping. Other people and my relationships to them were never legitimate subjects for attention. If someone liked me, it was an opaque, mysterious occurrence that bore no analysis. When I was slighted, I felt hurt. But relationships with people just happened. I certainly had feelings about my friends, but I can't remember a single instance of trying consciously to sort them out until I was well into college.

For most men this kind of shying away from the personal continues into adult life. In conversations with each other, we hardly ever use ourselves as reference points. We talk about almost everything except how we ourselves are affected by people and events. Everything is discussed as though it were taking place out there somewhere, as though we had no more felt response to it than to the weather. Topics that can be treated in this detached, objective way become conversational mainstays. The few subjects which are fundamentally personal are shaped into discussions of abstract general questions. Even in an exchange about their reactions to liberated women—a topic of intensely personal interest—the tendency will be to talk in general, theoretical terms. Work, at least its objective aspects, is always a safe subject. Men also spend an incredible amount of time rehashing the great public issues of the day. Until early 1973, Vietnam was the work-horse topic. Then came Watergate. It doesn't seem to matter that we've all had a hundred similar conversations. We plunge in for another round, trying to come up with a new angle as much as to impress the others with what we know as to keep from being bored stiff.

Games play a central role in situations organized by men. I remember a weekend some years ago at the country house of a law-school classmate as a blur of softball, football, croquet, poker, and a dice-and-board game called Combat, with swimming thrown in on the side. As soon as one game ended, another began. Taken one at a time, these "activities" were fun, but the impression was inescapable that the host, and most of his guests, would do anything to stave off a lull in which they would be together without some impersonal focus for their attention. A snapshot of almost any men's club would show the same thing, ninety percent of the men engaged in some activity—ranging from backgammon to watching the tube—other than, or at least as an aid to, conversation.[1]

My composite memory of evenings spent with a friend at college and later when we shared an apartment in Washington is of conversations punctuated by silences during which we would internally pass over any personal or emotional thoughts which had arisen and come back to the permitted track. When I couldn't get my mind off personal matters, I said very little. Talks with my father have always had the same tone. Respect for privacy was the rationale for our diffidence. His questions to me about how things were going at school or at work were asked as discreetly as he would have asked a friend about someone's commitment to a hospital for the criminally insane. Our conversations, when they touched these matters at all, to say nothing of more sensitive matters, would veer quickly back to safe topics of general interest.

In our popular literature, the archetypal male hero embodying this personal muteness is the cowboy. The classic mold for the character was set in 1902 by Owen Wister's novel *The Virginian* where the author spelled out, with an explicitness that was never again necessary, the characteristics of his protagonist. Here's how it goes when two close friends the Virginian hasn't seen in some time take him out for a drink:

> All of them had seen rough days together, and they felt guilty with emotion.
> "It's hot weather," said Wiggin.
> "Hotter in Box Elder," said McLean. "My kid has started teething."
> Words ran dry again. They shifted their positions, looked in their glasses, read the labels on the bottles. They dropped a word now and then to the proprietor about his trade, and his ornaments.[2]

One of the Virginian's duties is to assist at the hanging of an old friend as a horse thief. Afterward, for the first time in the book, he is visibly upset. The narrator puts his arm around the hero's shoulders and describes the Virginian's reaction:

> I had the sense to keep silent, and presently he shook my hand, not looking at me as he did so. He was always very shy of demonstration.[3]

---

[1]Women may use games as a reason for getting together—bridge clubs, for example. But the show is more for the rest of the world—to indicate that they are doing *something*—and the games themselves are not the only means of communication.

[2]Owen Wister, *The Virginian* ([Macmillan: 1902] Grosset & Dunlap ed.: 1929, pp. 397–98.

[3]*Ibid.*, p. 343.

And, for explanation of such reticence, "As all men know, he also knew that many things should be done in this world in silence, and that talking about them is a mistake."[4]

There are exceptions, but they only prove the rule.

One is the drunken confidence: "Bob, ole boy, I gotta tell ya—being divorced isn't so hot. . . . [and see, I'm too drunk to be held responsible for blurting it out]." Here, drink becomes an excuse for exchanging confidences and a device for periodically loosening the restraint against expressing a need for sympathy and support from other men—which may explain its importance as a male ritual.[5] Marijuana fills a similar need.

Another exception is talking to a stranger—who may be either someone the speaker doesn't know or someone who isn't in the same social or business world. (Several black friends told me that they have been on the receiving end of personal confidences from white acquaintances that they were sure had not been shared with white friends.) In either case, men are willing to talk about themselves only to other men with whom they do not have to compete or whom they will not have to confront socially later.

Finally, there is the way men depend on women to facilitate certain conversations. The women in a mixed group are usually the ones who make the first personal reference, about themselves or others present. The men can then join in without having the onus for initiating a discussion of "personalities." Collectively, the men can "blame" the conversation on the women. They can also feel in these conversations that since they are talking "to" the women instead of "to" the men, they can be excused for deviating from the masculine norm. When the women leave, the tone and subject invariably shift away from the personal.

The effect of these constraints is to make it extraordinarily difficult for men to really get to know each other. A psychotherapist who has conducted a lengthy series of encounter groups for men summed it up:

> With saddening regularity [the members of these groups] described how much they wanted to have closer, more satisfying relationships with other men: "I'd settle for having one really close man friend. I supposedly have some close men friends now. We play golf or go for a drink. We complain about our jobs and our wives. I care about them and they care about me. We even have some physical contact—I mean we may even give a hug on a big occasion. But it's not enough."[6]

---

[4] *Ibid.*, p. 373.

[5] Lionel Tiger, *Men in Groups* (Random House: 1969), p. 185.

[6] Don Clark, "Homosexual Encounter in All-Male Groups," in L. Solomon and B. Berzon (eds.), *New Perspectives on Encounter Groups* (Jossey-Bass: 1972), pp. 376–77. See also Alan Booth, "Sex and Social Participation," *American Sociological Review,* Vol. 37 (April 1972), p. 183, an empirical study showing that, contrary to Lionel Tiger's much publicized assertion *(Men in Groups)*, women form stronger and closer friendship bonds with each other than men do.

The sources of this stifling ban on self-disclosure, the reasons why men hide from each other, lie in the taboos and imperatives of the masculine stereotype.

To begin with, men are supposed to be functional, to spend their time working or otherwise solving or thinking about how to solve problems. Personal reaction, how one feels about something, is considered dysfunctional, at best an irrelevant distraction from the expected objectivity. Only weak men, and women, talk about—i.e., "give in," to their feelings. "I group my friends in two ways," said a business executive:

> those who have made it and don't complain and those who haven't made it. And only the latter spend time talking to their wives about their problems and how bad their boss is and all that. The ones who concentrate more on communicating . . . are those who have realized that they aren't going to make it and therefore they have changed the focus of attention.[7]

In a world which tells men they have to choose between expressiveness and manly strength, this characterization may be accurate. Most of the men who talk personally to other men *are* those whose problems have gotten the best of them, who simply can't help it. Men not driven to despair don't talk about themselves, so the idea that self-disclosure and expressiveness are associated with problems and weakness becomes a self-fulfilling prophecy.

Obsessive competitiveness also limits the range of communication in male friendships. Competition is the principal mode by which men relate to each other—at one level because they don't know how else to make contact, but more basically because it is the way to demonstrate, to themselves and others, the key masculine qualities of unwavering toughness and the ability to dominate and control. The result is that they inject competition into situations which don't call for it.

In conversations, you must show that you know more about the subject than the other man, or at least as much as he does. For example, I have often engaged in a contest that could be called My Theory Tops Yours, disguised as a serious exchange of ideas. The proof that it wasn't serious was that I was willing to participate even when I was sure that the participants, including myself, had nothing fresh to say. Convincing the other person—victory—is the main objective, with control of the floor an important tactic. Men tend to lecture at each other, insist that the discussion follow their train of thought, and are often unwilling to listen.[8] As one member of a men's rap group said,

---

[7]Fernando Bartolomé, "Executives as Human Beings," *Harvard Business Review,* Vol. 50 (November–December 1972), p. 64.

[8]The contrast with women on this point is striking. Casual observation will confirm that women's conversations move more quickly, with fewer long speeches and more frequent changes of speaker.

> When I was talking I used to feel that I had to be driving to a point, that it had to be rational and organized, that I had to persuade at all times, rather than exchange thoughts and ideas.[9]

Even in casual conversation some men hold back unless they are absolutely sure of what they are saying. They don't want to have to change a position once they have taken it. It's "just like a woman" to change your mind, and, more important, it is inconsistent with the approved masculine posture of total independence.

Competition was at the heart of one of my closest friendships, now defunct. There was a good deal of mutual liking and respect. We went out of our way to spend time with each other and wanted to work together. We both had "prospects" as "bright young men" and the same "liberal but tough" point of view. We recognized this about each other, and this recognition was the basis of our respect and of our sense of equality. That we saw each other as equals was important—our friendship was confirmed by the reflection of one in the other. But our constant and all-encompassing competition made this equality precarious and fragile. One way or another, everything counted in the measuring process. We fought out our tennis matches as though our lives depended on it. At poker, the two of us would often play on for hours after the others had left. These *mano a mano* poker marathons seem in retrospect especially revealing of the competitiveness of the relationship: playing for small stakes, the essence of the game is in outwitting, psychologically beating down the other player—the other skills involved are negligible. Winning is the only pleasure, one that evaporates quickly, a truth that struck me in inchoate form every time our game broke up at four a.m. and I walked out the door with my five-dollar winnings, a headache, and a sense of time wasted. Still, I did the same thing the next time. It was what we did together, and somehow it counted. Losing at tennis could be balanced by winning at poker; at another level, his moving up in the federal government by my getting on the *Harvard Law Review*.

This competitiveness feeds the most basic obstacle to openness between men, the inability to admit to being vulnerable. Real men, we learn early, are not supposed to have doubts, hopes and ambitions which may not be realized, things they don't (or even especially do) like about themselves, fears and disappointments. Such feelings and concerns, of course, are part of everyone's inner life, but a man must keep quiet about them. If others know how you really feel you can be hurt, and that in itself is incompatible with manhood. The inhibiting effect of this imperative is not limited to disclosures of major personal problems. Often men do not share even ordinary uncertainties and half-formulated plans of daily life with their friends. And when they do, they are careful to suggest that they already know how to proceed—that they are not really asking for help or

---

[9] *Boston Globe,* March 12, 1972, p. B-1.

understanding but simply for particular bits of information. Either way, any doubts they have are presented as external, carefully characterized as having to do with the issue as distinct from the speaker. They are especially guarded about expressing concern or asking a question that would invite personal comment. It is almost impossible for men to simply exchange thoughts about matters involving them personally in a comfortable, non-crisis atmosphere. If a friend tells you of his concern that he and a colleague are always disagreeing, for example, he is likely to quickly supply his own explanation—something like "different professional backgrounds." The effect is to rule out observations or suggestions that do not fit within this already reconnoitered protective structure. You don't suggest, even if you believe it is true, that in fact the disagreements arise because he presents his ideas in a way which tends to provoke a hostile reaction. It would catch him off guard; it would be something he hadn't already thought of and accepted about himself and, for that reason, no matter how constructive and well-intentioned you might be, it would put you in control for the moment. He doesn't want that; he is afraid of losing your respect. So, sensing he feels that way, because you would yourself, you say something else. There is no real give-and-take.

It is hard for men to get angry at each other honestly. Anger between friends often means that one has hurt the other. Since the straightforward expression of anger in these situations involves an admission of vulnerability, it is safer to stew silently or find an "objective" excuse for retaliation. Either way, trust is not fully restored.

Men even try not to let it show when they feel good. We may report the reasons for our happiness, if they have to do with concrete accomplishments, but we try to do it with a straight face, as if to say, "Here's what happened, but it hasn't affected my grown-up unemotional equilibrium, and I am not asking for any kind of response." Happiness is a precarious, "childish" feeling, easy to shoot down. Others may find the event that triggers it trivial or incomprehensible, or even threatening to their own self-esteem—in the sense that if one man is up, another man is down. So we tend not to take the risk of expressing it.

What is particularly difficult for men is seeking or accepting help from friends. I, for one, learned early that dependence was unacceptable. When I was eight, I went to a summer camp I disliked. My parents visited me in the middle of the summer and, when it was time for them to leave, I wanted to go with them. They refused, and I yelled and screamed and was miserably unhappy for the rest of the day. That evening an older camper comforted me, sitting by my bed as I cried, patting me on the back soothingly and saying whatever it is that one says at times like that. He was in some way clumsy or funny-looking, and a few days later I joined a group of kids in cruelly making fun of him, an act which upset me, when I thought about it, for years. I can only explain it in terms of my feeling, as early as the age of eight, that by needing and accepting his help and comfort I had compromised myself, and took it out on him.

"You can't express dependence when you feel it," a corporate executive said, "because it's a kind of absolute. If you are loyal 90% of the time and disloyal 10%, would you be considered loyal? Well, the same happens with independence: you are either dependent or independent; you can't be both."[10] "Feelings of dependence," another explained, "are identified with weakness or 'untoughness' and our culture doesn't accept those things in men."[11] The result is that we either go it alone or "act out certain games or rituals to provoke the desired reaction in the other and have our needs satisfied without having to ask for anything."[12]

Somewhat less obviously, the expression of affection also runs into emotional barriers growing out of the masculine stereotype. When I was in college, I was suddenly quite moved while attending a friend's wedding. The surge of feeling made me uncomfortable and self-conscious. There was nothing inherently difficult or, apart from the fact of being moved by a moment of tenderness, "unmasculine" about my reaction. I just did not know how to deal with or communicate what I felt. "I consider myself a sentimentalist," one man said, "and I think I am quite able to express my feelings. But the other day my wife described a friend of mine to some people as my best friend and I felt embarrassed when I heard her say it."[13]

A major source of these inhibitions is the fear of being, or being thought, homosexual. Nothing is more frightening to a heterosexual man in our society. It threatens, at one stroke, to take away every vestige of his claim to a masculine identity—something like knocking out the foundations of a building—and to expose him to the ostracism, ranging from polite tolerance to violent revulsion, of his friends and colleagues. A man can be labeled as homosexual not just because of overt sexual acts but because of almost any sign of behavior which does not fit the masculine stereotype. The touching of another man, other than shaking hands or, under emotional stress, an arm around the shoulder, is taboo. Women may kiss each other when they meet; men are uncomfortable when hugged even by close friends.[14] Onlookers might misinterpret what they saw, and, more important, what would we think of ourselves if we felt a twinge of sensual pleasure from the embrace.

Direct verbal expressions of affection or tenderness are also something that only homosexuals and women engage in. Between "real" men affection has to be disguised in gruff, "you old son-of-a-bitch" style. Paradoxically, in some instances, terms of endearment between men can be used as a ritual badge of manhood, dangerous medicine safe only for the strong. The flirting with homosexuality that characterizes the initia-

---

[10]Bartolomé, *op. cit.*, p. 65.
[11]*Ibid.*, p. 64.
[12]*Ibid.*, p. 66.
[13]*Ibid.*, p. 64.
[14]*Ibid.*, p. 65.

tion rites of many fraternities and men's clubs serves this purpose. Claude Brown wrote about black life in New York City in the 1950s:

> The term ["baby"] had a hip ring to it. . . . It was like saying, "Man, look at me. I've got masculinity to spare. . . . I can say 'baby' to another cat and he can say 'baby' to me, and we can say it with strength in our voices." If you could say it, this meant that you really had to be sure of yourself, sure of your masculinity.[15]

Fear of homosexuality does more than inhibit the physical display of affection. One of the major recurring themes in the men's groups led by psychotherapist Don Clark was:

> "A large segment of my feelings about other men are unknown or distorted because I am afraid they might have something to do with homosexuality. Now I'm lonely for other men and don't know how to find what I want with them."

As Clark observes, "The spectre of homosexuality seems to be the dragon at the gateway to self-awareness, understanding, and acceptance of male-male needs. If a man tries to pretend the dragon is not there by turning a blind eye to erotic feelings for all other males, he also blinds himself to the rich variety of feelings that are related."[16]

The few situations in which men do acknowledge strong feelings of affection and dependence toward other men are exceptions which prove the rule. With "cop couples," for example, or combat soldier "buddies," intimacy and dependence are forced on the men by their work—they have to ride in the patrol car or be in the same foxhole with somebody—and the jobs themselves have such highly masculine images that the men can get away with behavior that would be suspect under any other conditions.

Furthermore, even these combat-buddy relationships, when looked at closely, turn out not to be particularly intimate or personal. Margaret Mead has written:

> During the last war English observers were confused by the apparent contradiction between American soldiers' emphasis on the buddy, so grievously exemplified in the break-downs that followed a buddy's death, and the results of detailed inquiry which showed how transitory these buddy relationships were. It was found that men actually accepted their buddies as derivatives from their outfit, and from accidents of association, rather than because of any special personality characteristics capable of ripening into friendship.[17]

---

[15]Claude Brown, *Manchild in the Promised Land* ([Macmillan: 1965] Signet ed.: 1965), p. 171.

[16]Clark, *op. cit.*, p. 378.

[17]Margaret Mead, *Male and Female* ([William Morrow: 1949] Mentor ed.: 1949), p. 214.

One effect of the fear of appearing to be homosexual is to reinforce the practice that two men rarely get together alone without a reason. I once called a friend to suggest that we have dinner together. "O.K.," he said. "What's up?" I felt uncomfortable telling him that I just wanted to talk, that there was no other reason for the invitation.

Men get together to conduct business, to drink, to play games and sports, to re-establish contact after long absences, to participate in heterosexual social occasions—circumstances in which neither person is responsible for actually wanting to see the other. Men are particularly comfortable seeing each other in groups. The group situation defuses any possible assumptions about the intensity of feeling between particular men and provides the safety of numbers—"All the guys are here." It makes personal communication, which requires a level of trust and mutual understanding not generally shared by all members of a group, more difficult and offers an excuse for avoiding this dangerous territory. And it provides what is most sought after in men's friendships: mutual reassurance of masculinity.

Needless to say, the observations in this chapter did not spring full-blown from my head. The process started when I began to understand that, at least with Brenda, a more open, less self-protective relationship was possible. At first, I perceived my situation as completely personal. The changes I was trying to effect in myself had to do, I thought, only with Brenda and me, and could be generalized, if at all, only to other close relationships between men and women. But, as Brenda came to be deeply involved in the women's movement, I began to see, usually at one remove but sometimes directly, the level of intimacy that women, especially women active in the movement, shared with each other. The contrast between this and the friendships I had with men was striking. I started listening to men's conversations, including my own, and gradually the basic outlines of the pattern described here began to emerge. I heard from women that the men they knew had very few really close male friends; since then I have heard the same thing from men themselves. It was, I realized, my own experience as well. It wasn't that I didn't know a lot of men, or that I was not on friendly terms with them. Rather, I gradually became dissatisfied with the impersonality of these friendships.

Of course, some constraints on self-disclosure do make sense. Privacy is something you give up selectively and gradually to people you like and trust, and who are capable of understanding—instant, indiscriminate intimacy is nearly always formularized, without real content and impact. Nor does self-disclosure as a kind of compartmentalized rest-and-recreation period work: "Well, John, let me tell you about myself. . . ."

Having said all this, it is nonetheless true that men have carried the practice of emotional restraint to the point of paralysis. For me, at least, the ritual affirmations of membership in the fraternity of men that one gets from participation in "masculine" activities do nothing to assuage the feeling of being essentially alone; they have become a poor substitute for being known by and knowing other people. But the positive content of what will replace the old-style friendships is only beginning to take shape. I am learning, though, that when I am able to articulate my feelings as they arise in the context of my friendships, I often find that they are shared by others. Bringing them out into the open clears the air; avoiding them, even unconsciously, is stultifying. I have found also that I am not as fragile as I once thought. The imagined hazards of showing oneself to be human, and thus vulnerable, to one's friends tend not to materialize when actually put to the test. But being oneself is an art, an art sensitive to variations in the receptivity of others as well as to one's own inner life. It is still, for me, something to be mastered, to be tried out and practiced.

GUNNAR MYRDAL

Born in Sweden in 1898, Gunnar Myrdal holds both a law degree and a doctorate of laws in economics from the University of Stockholm. He has been Professor of Political Economy, a member of the Swedish Senate, Minister of Commerce, and Executive Secretary of the United Nations Economic Commission for Europe; since 1960 he has also held the Chair of International Economics at the University of Stockholm. Myrdal had a strong influence on the forming of Sweden's present socialist state, especially in the 1930s. His "democratic family and population policy" asked that population control be encouraged, birth control be taught in the schools, but also that housing be made available and income redistributed according to the number of children in a family.

His two best-known books were both funded outside Sweden. In 1937 the Carnegie Corporation chose him—as a competent man from a country without preconceptions—to do an objective study of the American Negro as a social phenomenon. The research of Myrdal and his team of sociologists was interrupted by the outbreak of World War II in Europe in 1939. Although parts of An American Dilemma *began to appear separately, its final publication was not until 1941. The "American Dilemma" Myrdal analyzes is the conflict between ideals and reality for which the Negro is a focal point, but not to be considered in isolation. He says that most Americans believe in the ideal of race equality and freedom, but that this belief is in conflict with their habits and with the day-to-day tensions they feel.*

Funded by the Twentieth Century Fund, Myrdal then spent a decade traveling in Southeast Asia and researching Asian Drama: An Inquiry into the Poverty of Nations, *published in 1968. He concluded that the low standard of living in Southeast Asia was not due to lack of capital, but rather to outmoded attitudes and institutions and to overpopulation.*

Myrdal holds many honorary degrees from European and American universities. In 1974 he was awarded the Nobel Prize in economics. Asked at the time what he thought of the United States' economy, he said, "I'm very scared . . . the trend at present is leading to hell." At the present writing he is Visiting Professor at The City University of New York and is working with Kenneth Clark on a sequel, An American Dilemma Revisited. *Other well-known books include* Beyond the Welfare State *(1960),* Challenge to Affluence *(1963),* The Challenge of World Poverty *(1970), and a collection of essays,* Against the Stream *(1974). We present below Appendix 5 of* An American Dilemma.

A Parallel to the Negro Problem

In every society there are at least two groups of people, besides the Negroes, who are characterized by high social visibility expressed in physical appearance, dress, and patterns of behavior, and who have been "suppressed." We refer to women and children. Their present status, as well as their history and their problems in society, reveal striking similarities to those of the Negroes. In studying a special problem like the Negro problem, there is always a danger that one will develop a quite incorrect idea of its uniqueness. It will, therefore, give perspective to the Negro problem and prevent faulty interpretations to sketch some of the important similarities between the Negro problem and the women's problem.

In the historical development of these problem groups in America there have been much closer relations than is now ordinarily recorded. In the earlier common law, women and children were placed under the jurisdiction of the paternal power. When a legal status had to be found for the imported Negro servants in the seventeenth century, the nearest and most natural analogy was the status of women and children. The ninth commandment—linking together women, servants, mules, and other property—could be invoked, as well as a great number of other passages of Holy Scripture. We do not intend to follow here the interesting developments of the institution of slavery in America through the centuries, but merely wish to point out the paternalistic idea which held the slave to be a sort of family member and in some way—in spite of all differences—placed him beside women and children under the power of the *paterfamilias.*

There was, of course, even in the beginning, a tremendous difference
both in actual status of these different groups and in the tone of sentiment
in the respective relations. In the decades before the Civil War, in the
conservative and increasingly antiquarian ideology of the American
South, woman was elevated as an ornament and looked upon with pride,
while the Negro slave became increasingly a chattel and a ward. The
paternalistic construction came, however, to good service when the South
had to build up a moral defense for slavery, and it is found everywhere
in the apologetic literature up to the beginning of the Civil War. For
illustration, some passages from George Fitzhugh's *Sociology for the South*,
published in 1854, may be quoted as typical:

> The kind of slavery is adapted to the men enslaved. Wives and apprentices
> are slaves; not in theory only, but often in fact. Children are slaves to their
> parents, guardians and teachers. Imprisoned culprits are slaves. Lunatics
> and idiots are slaves also.[1]

> A beautiful example and illustration of this kind of communism, is found
> in the instance of the Patriarch Abraham. His wives and his children, his
> men servants and his maid servants, his camels and his cattle, were all
> equally his property. He could sacrifice Isaac or a ram, just as he pleased.
> He loved and protected all, and all shared, if not equally, at least fairly, in
> the products of their light labour. Who would not desire to have been a
> slave of that old Patriarch, stern and despotic as he was? . . . Pride, affection,
> self-interest, moved Abraham to protect, love and take care of his slaves.
> The same motives operate on all masters, and secure comfort, competency
> and protection to the slave. A man's wife and children are his slaves, and
> do they not enjoy, in common with himself, his property?[2]

Other protagonists of slavery resort to the same argument:

> In this country we believe that the general good requires us to deprive the
> whole female sex of the right of self-government. They have no voice in the
> formation of the laws which dispose of their persons and property. . . . We
> treat all minors much in the same way. . . . Our plea for all this is, that the
> good of the whole is thereby most effectually promoted. . . .[3]

> Significant manifestations of the result of this disposition [on the part of the
> Abolitionists] to consider their own light a surer guide than the word of
> God, are visible in the anarchical opinions about human governments, civil
> and ecclesiastical, and on the rights of women, which have found appropri-
> ate advocates in the abolition publications. . . . If our women are to be
> emancipated from subjection to the law which God has imposed upon
> them, if they are to quit the retirement of domestic life, where they preside

[1] P. 86.
[2] *Ibid.*, p. 297.
[3] Charles Hodge, "The Bible Argument on Slavery," in E. N. Elliott (editor), *Cotton Is King*,
and *Pro-Slavery Arguments* (1860), pp. 859–860.

in stillness over the character and destiny of society; . . . if, in studied insult to the authority of God, we are to renounce in the marriage contract all claim to obedience, we shall soon have a country over which the genius of Mary Wolstonecraft would delight to preside, but from which all order and virtue would speedily be banished. There is no form of human excellence before which we bow with profounder deference than that which appears in a delicate woman, . . . and there is no deformity of human character from which we turn with deeper loathing than from a woman forgetful of her nature, and clamourous for the vocation and rights of men.[4]

. . . Hence her [Miss Martineau's] wild chapter about the "Rights of Women," her groans and invectives because of their exclusion from the offices of the state, the right of suffrage, the exercise of political authority. In all this, the error of the declaimer consists in the very first movement of the mind. "The Rights of *Women*" may all be conceded to the sex, yet the rights of *men* withheld from them.[5]

The parallel goes, however, considerably deeper than being only a structural part in the defense ideology built up around slavery. Women at that time lacked a number of rights otherwise belonging to all free white citizens of full age.

So chivalrous, indeed, was the ante-bellum South that its women were granted scarcely any rights at all. Everywhere they were subjected to political, legal, educational, and social and economic restrictions. They took no part in governmental affairs, were without legal rights over their property or the guardianship of their children, were denied adequate educational facilities, and were excluded from business and the professions.[6]

The same was very much true of the rest of the country and of the rest of the world. But there was an especially close relation in the South between the subordination of women and that of Negroes. This is perhaps best expressed in a comment attributed to Dolly Madison, that the Southern wife was "the chief slave of the harem."[7]

From the very beginning, the fight in America for the liberation of the Negro slaves was, therefore, closely coordinated with the fight for women's emancipation. It is interesting to note that the Southern states, in the early beginning of the political emancipation of women during the first decades of the nineteenth century, had led in the granting of legal rights to women. This was the time when the South was still the stronghold of liberal thinking in the period leading up to and following the Revolution. During the same period the South was also the region where Abolitionist societies flourished, while the North was uninterested in the Negro prob-

---

[4]Albert T. Bledsoe, *An Essay on Liberty and Slavery* (1857), pp. 223–225.

[5]W. Gilmore Simms, "The Morals of Slavery," in *The Pro-Slavery Argument* (1853), p. 248. See also Simms' "Address on the Occasion of the Inauguration of the Spartanburg Female College," August 12, 1855.

[6]Virginius Dabney, *Liberalism in the South* (1932), p. 361.

[7]Cited in Harriet Martineau, *Society in America* (1842, first edition 1837), Vol. II, p. 81.

lem. Thereafter the two movements developed in close interrelation and were both gradually driven out of the South.

The women suffragists received their political education from the Abolitionist movement. Women like Angelina Grimke, Sarah Grimke, and Abby Kelly began their public careers by speaking for Negro emancipation and only gradually came to fight for women's rights. The three great suffragists of the nineteenth century—Lucretia Mott, Elizabeth Cady Stanton, and Susan B. Anthony—first attracted attention as ardent campaigners for the emancipation of the Negro and the prohibition of liquor. The women's movement got much of its public support by reason of its affiliation with the Abolitionist movement: the leading male advocates of woman suffrage before the Civil War were such Abolitionists as William Lloyd Garrison, Henry Ward Beecher, Wendell Phillips, Horace Greeley and Frederick Douglass. The women had nearly achieved their aims, when the Civil War induced them to suppress all tendencies distracting the federal government from the prosecution of the War. They were apparently fully convinced that victory would bring the suffrage to them as well as to the Negroes.[8]

The Union's victory, however, brought disappointment to the women suffragists. The arguments "the Negro's hour" and "a political necessity" met and swept aside all their arguments for leaving the word "male" out of the 14th Amendment and putting "sex" alongside "race" and "color" in the 15th Amendment.[9] Even their Abolitionist friends turned on them, and the Republican party shied away from them. A few Democrats, really not in favor of the extension of the suffrage to anyone, sought to make political capital out of the women's demands, and said with Senator Cowan of Pennsylvania, "If I have no reason to offer why a Negro man shall not vote, I have no reason why a white woman shall not vote." Charges of being Democrats and traitors were heaped on the women leaders. Even a few Negroes, invited to the women's convention of January, 1869, denounced the women for jeopardizing the black man's

---

[8] Carrie Chapman Catt and Nettie Rogers Shuler, *Woman Suffrage and Politics* (1923), pp. 32ff.

[9] The relevant sections of the 14th and 15th Amendments to the Constitution are (underlining ours):

14th Amendment

Section 2. Representatives shall be apportioned among the several States according to their respective numbers, counting the whole number of persons in each State, excluding Indians not taxed. But when the right to vote at any election for the choice of Electors for President and Vice President of the United States, Representatives in Congress, the executive and judicial officers of a State, or the members of the Legislature thereof, is denied to any of the *male* inhabitants of such State, being twenty-one years of age, and citizens of the United States, or in any way abridged, except for participation in rebellion, or other crime, the basis of representation therein shall be reduced in the proportion which the number of such *male* citizens shall bear to the whole number of *male* citizens twenty-one years of age in such State.

15th Amendment

Section 1. The right of citizens of the United States to vote shall not be denied or abridged by the United States or by any State on account of *race, color, or previous condition of servitude.*

chances for the vote. The War and Reconstruction Amendments had thus sharply divided the women's problem from the Negro problem in actual politics.[10] The deeper relation between the two will, however, be recognized up till this day. Du Bois' famous ideological manifesto *The Souls of Black Folk*[11] is, to mention only one example, an ardent appeal on behalf of women's interests as well as those of the Negro.

This close relation is no accident. The ideological and economic forces behind the two movements—the emancipation of women and children and the emancipation of Negroes—have much in common and are closely interrelated. Paternalism was a pre-industrial scheme of life, and was gradually becoming broken in the nineteenth century. Negroes and women, both of whom had been under the yoke of the paternalistic system, were both strongly and fatefully influenced by the Industrial Revolution. For neither group is the readjustment process yet consummated. Both are still problem groups. The women's problem is the center of the whole complex of problems of how to reorganize the institution of the family to fit the new economic and ideological basis, a problem which is not solved in any part of the Western world unless it be in the Soviet Union or Palestine. The family problem in the Negro group, as we find when analyzing the Negro family, has its special complications, centering in the tension and conflict between the external patriarchal system in which the Negro was confined as a slave and his own family structure.

As in the Negro problem, most men have accepted as self-evident,

[10]While there was a definite affinity between the Abolitionist movement and the woman suffrage movement, there was also competition and, perhaps, antipathy, between them that widened with the years. As early as 1833, when Oberlin College opened its doors to women —the first college to do so—the Negro men students joined other men students in protesting (Catt and Shuler, *op. cit.*, p. 13). The Anti-Slavery Convention held in London in 1840 refused to seat the women delegates from America, and it was on this instigation that the first women's rights convention was called (*ibid.*, p. 17). After the passage of the 13th, 14th, and 15th Amendments, which gave legal rights to Negroes but not to women, the women's movement split off completely from the Negroes' movement, except for such a thing as the support of both movements by the rare old liberal, Frederick Douglass. An expression of how far the two movements had separated by 1903 was given by one of the leaders of the women's movement at that time, Anna Howard Shaw, in answer to a question posed to her at a convention in New Orleans:

" 'What is your purpose in bringing your convention to the South? Is it the desire of suffragists to force upon us the social equality of black and white women? Political equality lays the foundation for social equality. If you give the ballot to women, won't you make the black and white woman equal politically and therefore lay the foundation for a future claim of social equality?' . . .

"I read the question aloud. Then the audience called for the answer, and I gave it in these words, quoted as accurately as I can remember them.

" 'If political equality is the basis of social equality, and if by granting political equality you lay the foundation for a claim of social equality, I can only answer that you have already laid that claim. You did not wait for woman suffrage, but disfranchised both your black and white women, thus making them politically equal. But you have done more than that. You have put the ballot into the hands of your black men, thus making them the political superiors of your white women. Never before in the history of the world have men made former slaves the political masters of their former mistresses!' " (*The Story of a Pioneer* [1915], pp. 311–312.)

[11]1903.

until recently, the doctrine that women had inferior endowments in most of those respects which carry prestige, power, and advantages in society, but that they were, at the same time, superior in some other respects. The arguments, when arguments were used, have been about the same: smaller brains, scarcity of geniuses and so on. The study of women's intelligence and personality has had broadly the same history as the one we record for Negroes. As in the case of the Negro, women themselves have often been brought to believe in their inferiority of endowment. As the Negro was awarded his "place" in society, so there was a "woman's place." In both cases the rationalization was strongly believed that men, in confining them to this place, did not act against the true interest of the subordinate groups. The myth of the "contented women," who did not want to have suffrage or other civil rights and equal opportunities, had the same social function as the myth of the "contented Negro." In both cases there was probably—in a static sense—often some truth behind the myth.

As to the character of the deprivations, upheld by law or by social conventions and the pressure of public opinion, no elaboration will here be made. As important and illustrative in the comparison, we shall, however, stress the conventions governing woman's education. There was a time when the most common idea was that she was better off with little education. Later the doctrine developed that she should not be denied education, but that her education should be of a special type, fitting her for her "place" in society and usually directed more on training her hands than her brains.

Political franchise was not granted to women until recently. Even now there are, in all countries, great difficulties for a woman to attain public office. The most important disabilities still affecting her status are those barring her attempt to earn a living and to attain promotion in her work. As in the Negro's case, there are certain "women's jobs," traditionally monopolized by women. They are regularly in the low salary bracket and do not offer much of a career. All over the world men have used the trade unions to keep women out of competition. Woman's competition has, like the Negro's, been particularly obnoxious and dreaded by men because of the low wages women, with their few earning outlets, are prepared to work for. Men often dislike the very idea of having women on an equal plane as co-workers and competitors, and usually they find it even more "unnatural" to work under women. White people generally hold similar attitudes toward Negroes. On the other hand, it is said about women that they prefer men as bosses and do not want to work under another woman. Negroes often feel the same way about working under other Negroes.

In personal relations with both women and Negroes, white men generally prefer a less professional and more human relation, actually a more paternalistic and protective position—somewhat in the nature of patron to client in Roman times, and like the corresponding strongly paternalistic relation of later feudalism. As in Germany it is said that every gentile has his pet Jew, so it is said in the South that every white has his "pet nigger," or—in the upper strata—several of them. We sometimes marry the pet woman, carrying out the paternalistic scheme. But even if we do not, we tend to deal kindly with her as a client and a ward, not as a competitor and an equal.

In drawing a parallel between the position of, and feeling toward, women and Negroes we are uncovering a fundamental basis of our culture. Although it is changing, atavistic elements sometimes unexpectedly break through even in the most emancipated individuals. The similarities in the women's and the Negro's problems are not accidental. They were, as we have pointed out, originally determined in a paternalistic order of society. The problems remain, even though paternalism is gradually declining as an ideal and is losing its economic basis. In the final analysis, women are still hindered in their competition by the function of procreation; Negroes are laboring under the yoke of the doctrine of unassimilability which has remained although slavery is abolished. The second barrier is actually much stronger than the first in America today. But the first is more eternally inexorable.[12]

---

[12]Alva Myrdal, *Nation and Family* (1941), Chapter 22, "One Sex a Social Problem," pp. 398–426.

Race
and
Racism

The opening pages of Ruth Benedict's *Race: Science and Politics* (1940) serve as a better introduction to this section than any we could devise. The two Orwell essays that follow, characterized by his disarming honesty, deal primarily with the colonial experience. The first narrates his experience as a police officer in Burma, which led to the recognition that "when the white man turns tyrant it is his own freedom that he destroys"; the second describes a North African city as seen through the eyes of a white European and sounds a note of warning to all for whom brown skin has been invisible.

The next five selections present some of the implications of the black and white predicament in America. James Baldwin, Norman Podhoretz, and Alice Walker draw on their own experience—as does Orwell—and their essays build connections between event and insight, private understanding and general idea. The two concluding pieces represent opposing attitudes toward violent action. John Oliver Killens opposes nonviolence as a way of life for the black American. He argues for both the psychological and the practical need for self-defense, violent self-defense if need be. Bayard Rustin disagrees. Although he has said that "it is wrong to turn one's back on people who have been so demoralized and trampled on that they literally have no choice except to fight back," his firm commitment is to nonviolence as policy.

RUTH BENEDICT

*Ruth Benedict was born in New York City in 1887. After receiving a
B.A. from Vassar, she taught English in a girls' school and wrote and
published some poetry under the name Anne Singleton. In 1914 she
married Stanley R. Benedict, a biochemist. Five years later, at the age of
thirty-two, Mrs. Benedict enrolled at Columbia, apparently because she
wanted "busy work." Thus, almost by accident, she began the study of
anthropology under Franz Boas, whom she later described as "the greatest
of living anthropologists." She completed her doctorate in 1923 and
immediately joined the faculty of Columbia, where she remained until her
death in 1948. Professor Benedict's research, conducted on periodic field
trips, made her a leading authority on the Indians of the American West.
She has also been considered a pathfinder in her awareness of the
relationship between anthropology and such other social sciences as
psychology and sociology. This breadth of attention is evident in her*
Patterns of Culture *(1934). Other books by Ruth Benedict are* The
Concept of Guardian Spirit in North America *(1923),* Zuni
Mythology *(1935), and* The Chrysanthemum and the Sword
*(1946). As an introduction to this section, we reprint here the opening
pages of the first chapter of* Race: Science and Politics *(1940).*

Racism: The *ism* of the Modern World

As early as the late 1880's a French pro-Aryan, Vacher de Lapouge,
wrote: "I am convinced that in the next century millions will cut each
other's throats because of 1 or 2 degrees more or less of cephalic index."
On the surface it appears a fantastic reason for world wars, and it was
certainly a reason new under the sun. Was he right? What could it mean?
The cephalic index is the quotient of the greatest breadth of the head
divided by its length, and some tribes and peoples over the world run to
high indices and some to low. Narrow heads are found among uncivilized
primitives and among powerful and cultivated Western Europeans; broad
heads are too. Neither the narrow heads of the whole world nor the broad
heads stack up to show any obvious monopoly of glorious destiny or any
corner on ability or virtue. Even in any one European nation or in America men of achievement have been some of them narrow-headed and
some broad-headed. What could it mean that "millions will cut each
other's throats" because of the shape of the top of their skulls?

In the long history of the world men have given many reasons for
killing each other in war: envy of another people's good bottom land or

of their herds, ambition of chiefs and kings, different religious beliefs, high spirits, revenge. But in all these wars the skulls of the victims on both sides were generally too similar to be distinguished. Nor had the war leaders incited their followers against their enemies by referring to the shapes of their heads. They might call them the heathen, the barbarians, the heretics, the slayers of women and children, but never our enemy Cephalic Index 82.

It was left for high European civilization to advance such a reason for war and persecution and to invoke it in practice. In other words, racism is a creation of our own time. It is a new way of separating the sheep from the goats. The old parable in the New Testament separated mankind as individuals: on the one hand those who had done good, and on the other those who had done evil. The new way divides them by hereditary bodily characteristics—shape of the head, skin colour, nose form, hair texture, colour of the eyes—and those who have certain hallmarks are known by these signs to be weaklings and incapable of civilization, and those with the opposite are the hope of the world. Racism is the new Calvinism which asserts that one group has the stigmata of superiority and the other has those of inferiority. According to racism we know our enemies, not by their aggressions against us, not by their creed or language, not even by their possessing wealth we want to take, but by noting their hereditary anatomy. For the leopard cannot change his spots and by these you know he is a leopard.

For the individual, therefore, racism means that damnation or salvation in this world is determined at conception; an individual's good life cannot tip the balance in his favour and he cannot live a bad life if his physical type is the right sort. By virtue of birth alone each member of the "race" is high caste and rightly claims his place in the sun at the expense of men of other "races." He need not base his pride upon personal achievement nor upon virtue; he was born high caste.

From this postulate racism makes also an assertion about race: that the "good" anatomical hallmarks are the monopoly of a pure race which has always throughout history manifested its glorious destiny. The racialists have rewritten history to provide the scion of such a race with a long and glamorous group ancestry as gratifying as an individual coat of arms, and they assure him that the strength and vigour of his race are immutable and guaranteed by the laws of Nature. He must, however, guard this pure blood from contamination by that of lesser breeds, lest degeneration follow and his race lose its supremacy. All over the world for the last generation this doctrine has been invoked in every possible kind of conflict: sometimes national, between peoples as racially similar as the French and Germans; sometimes across the colour line, as in Western fears of the Yellow Peril; sometimes in class conflicts, as in France; sometimes in conflicts between immigrants who arrived a little earlier and those who came a little later, as in America. It has become a bedlam.

Where all people claim to be tallest, not all can be right. In this matter of races, can the sciences to which they all appeal judge among the babel of contradictory claims and award the decision? Or is it a matter of false premises and bastard science? It is essential, if we are to live in this modern world, that we should understand Racism and be able to judge its arguments. We must know the facts first of Race, and then of this doctrine that has made use of them. For Racism is an *ism* to which everyone in the world today is exposed; for or against, we must take sides. And the history of the future will differ according to the decision which we make.

.   .   .

GEORGE ORWELL

"Shooting an Elephant," based on Orwell's experiences in the Imperial Police in Burma, was written in the early 1930s and is the title essay in the collection Shooting an Elephant and Other Essays *(1950). "Marrakech," written in 1939, is included in the collection entitled* Such, Such Were the Joys *(1953). Both essays reflect Orwell's fear of the vague and abstract, his conviction that ideas derive from experience, and that experience is best conveyed in concrete and specific terms. For further information about the author, see page 105.*

Shooting an Elephant

In Moulmein, in Lower Burma, I was hated by large numbers of people —the only time in my life that I have been important enough for this to happen to me. I was sub-divisional police officer of the town, and in an aimless, petty kind of way anti-European feeling was very bitter. No one had the guts to raise a riot, but if a European woman went through the bazaars alone somebody would probably spit betel juice over her dress. As a police officer I was an obvious target and was baited whenever it seemed safe to do so. When a nimble Burman tripped me up on the football field and the referee (another Burman) looked the other way, the crowd yelled with hideous laughter. This happened more than once. In the end the sneering yellow faces of young men that met me everywhere, the insults hooted after me when I was at a safe distance, got badly on my nerves. The young Buddhist priests were the worst of all. There were several thousands of them in the town and none of them seemed to have anything to do except stand on street corners and jeer at Europeans.

All this was perplexing and upsetting. For at that time I had already made up my mind that imperialism was an evil thing and the sooner I chucked up my job and got out of it the better. Theoretically—and secretly, of course—I was all for the Burmese and all against their oppressors, the British. As for the job I was doing, I hated it more bitterly than I can perhaps make clear. In a job like that you see the dirty work of Empire at close quarters. The wretched prisoners huddling in the stinking cages of the lock-ups, the grey, cowed faces of the long-term convicts, the scarred buttocks of the men who had been flogged with bamboos— all these oppressed me with an intolerable sense of guilt. But I could get nothing into perspective. I was young and ill-educated and I had had to think out my problems in the utter silence that is imposed on every Englishman in the East. I did not even know that the British Empire is dying, still less did I know that it is a great deal better than the younger empires that are going to supplant it. All I knew was that I was stuck between my hatred of the empire I served and my rage against the evil-spirited little beasts who tried to make my job impossible. With one part of my mind I thought of the British Raj as an unbreakable tyranny, as something clamped down, in *saecula saeculorum,* upon the will of prostrate peoples; with another part I thought that the greatest joy in the world would be to drive a bayonet into a Buddhist priest's guts. Feelings like these are the normal by-products of imperialism; ask any Anglo-Indian official, if you can catch him off duty.

One day something happened which in a roundabout way was enlightening. It was a tiny incident in itself, but it gave me a better glimpse than I had had before of the real nature of imperialism—the real motives for which despotic governments act. Early one morning the sub-inspector at a police station the other end of the town rang me up on the 'phone and said that an elephant was ravaging the bazaar. Would I please come and do something about it? I did not know what I could do, but I wanted to see what was happening and I got on to a pony and started out. I took my rifle, an old .44 Winchester and much too small to kill an elephant, but I thought the noise might be useful *in terrorem.* Various Burmans stopped me on the way and told me about the elephant's doings. It was not, of course, a wild elephant, but a tame one which had gone "must." It had been chained up, as tame elephants always are when their attack of "must" is due, but on the previous night it had broken its chain and escaped. Its mahout, the only person who could manage it when it was in that state, had set out in pursuit, but had taken the wrong direction and was now twelve hours' journey away, and in the morning the elephant had suddenly reappeared in the town. The Burmese population had no weapons and were quite helpless against it. It had already destroyed somebody's bamboo hut, killed a cow and raided some fruit-stalls and devoured the stock; also it had met the municipal rubbish van and, when the driver jumped out and took to his heels, had turned the van over and inflicted violences upon it.

The Burmese sub-inspector and some Indian constables were waiting for me in the quarter where the elephant had been seen. It was a very poor quarter, a labyrinth of squalid bamboo huts, thatched with palm-leaf, winding all over a steep hillside. I remember that it was a cloudy, stuffy morning at the beginning of the rains. We began questioning the people as to where the elephant had gone and, as usual, failed to get any definite information. That is invariably the case in the East; a story always sounds clear enough at a distance, but the nearer you get to the scene of events the vaguer it becomes. Some of the people said that the elephant had gone in one direction, some said that he had gone in another, some professed not even to have heard of any elephant. I had almost made up my mind that the whole story was a pack of lies, when we heard yells a little distance away. There was a loud, scandalized cry of "Go away, child! Go away this instant!" and an old woman with a switch in her hand came round the corner of a hut, violently shooing away a crowd of naked children. Some more women followed, clicking their tongues and exclaiming; evidently there was something that the children ought not to have seen. I rounded the hut and saw a man's dead body sprawling in the mud. He was an Indian, a black Dravidian coolie, almost naked, and he could not have been dead many minutes. The people said that the elephant had come suddenly upon him round the corner of the hut, caught him with its trunk, put its foot on his back and ground him into the earth. This was the rainy season and the ground was soft, and his face had scored a trench a foot deep and a couple of yards long. He was lying on his belly with arms crucified and head sharply twisted to one side. His face was coated with mud, the eyes wide open, the teeth bared and grinning with an expression of unendurable agony. (Never tell me, by the way, that the dead look peaceful. Most of the corpses I have seen looked devilish.) The friction of the great beast's foot had stripped the skin from his back as neatly as one skins a rabbit. As soon as I saw the dead man I sent an orderly to a friend's house nearby to borrow an elephant rifle. I had already sent back the pony, not wanting it to go mad with fright and throw me if it smelt the elephant.

The orderly came back in a few minutes with a rifle and five cartridges, and meanwhile some Burmans had arrived and told us that the elephant was in the paddy fields below, only a few hundred yards away. As I started forward practically the whole population of the quarter flocked out of the houses and followed me. They had seen the rifle and were all shouting excitedly that I was going to shoot the elephant. They had not shown much interest in the elephant when he was merely ravaging their homes, but it was different now that he was going to be shot. It was a bit of fun to them, as it would be to an English crowd; besides they wanted the meat. It made me vaguely uneasy. I had no intention of shooting the elephant—I had merely sent for the rifle to defend myself if necessary—

and it is always unnerving to have a crowd following you. I marched down the hill, looking and feeling a fool, with the rifle over my shoulder and an ever-growing army of people jostling at my heels. At the bottom, when you got away from the huts, there was a metalled road and beyond that a miry waste of paddy fields a thousand yards across, not yet ploughed but soggy from the first rains and dotted with coarse grass. The elephant was standing eight yards from the road, his left side towards us. He took not the slightest notice of the crowd's approach. He was tearing up bunches of grass, beating them against his knees to clean them and stuffing them into his mouth.

I had halted on the road. As soon as I saw the elephant I knew with perfect certainty that I ought not to shoot him. It is a serious matter to shoot a working elephant—it is comparable to destroying a huge and costly piece of machinery—and obviously one ought not to do it if it can possibly be avoided. And at that distance, peacefully eating, the elephant looked no more dangerous than a cow. I thought then and I think now that his attack of "must" was already passing off; in which case he would merely wander harmlessly about until the mahout came back and caught him. Moreover, I did not in the least want to shoot him. I decided that I would watch him for a little while to make sure that he did not turn savage again, and then go home.

But at that moment I glanced round at the crowd that had followed me. It was an immense crowd, two thousand at the least and growing every minute. It blocked the road for a long distance on either side. I looked at the sea of yellow faces above the garish clothes—faces all happy and excited over this bit of fun, all certain that the elephant was going to be shot. They were watching me as they would watch a conjurer about to perform a trick. They did not like me, but with the magical rifle in my hands I was momentarily worth watching. And suddenly I realized that I should have to shoot the elephant after all. The people expected it of me and I had got to do it; I could feel their two thousand wills pressing me forward, irresistibly. And it was at this moment, as I stood there with the rifle in my hands, that I first grasped the hollowness, the futility of the white man's dominion in the East. Here was I, the white man with his gun, standing in front of the unarmed native crowd—seemingly the leading actor of the piece; but in reality I was only an absurd puppet pushed to and fro by the will of those yellow faces behind. I perceived in this moment that when the white man turns tyrant it is his own freedom that he destroys. He becomes a sort of hollow, posing dummy, the conventionalized figure of a sahib. For it is the condition of his rule that he shall spend his life in trying to impress the "natives," and so in every crisis he has got to do what the "natives" expect of him. He wears a mask, and his face grows to fit it. I had got to shoot the elephant. I had committed myself to doing it when I sent for the rifle. A sahib has got to act like a sahib; he has got to appear resolute, to know his own mind and do definite things. To come all that way, rifle in hand, with two thousand people marching at my heels, and then to trail feebly away, having done nothing—no, that was impossible. The crowd would laugh at me. And my whole life, every white man's life in the East, was one long struggle not to be laughed at.

But I did not want to shoot the elephant. I watched him beating his bunch of grass against his knees, with that preoccupied grandmotherly air that elephants have. It seemed to me that it would be murder to shoot him. At that age I was not squeamish about killing animals, but I had never shot an elephant and never wanted to. (Somehow it always seems worse to kill a *large* animal.) Besides, there was the beast's owner to be considered. Alive, the elephant was worth at least a hundred pounds; dead, he would only be worth the value of his tusks, five pounds, possibly. But I had got to act quickly. I turned to some experienced-looking Burmans who had been there when we arrived, and asked them how the elephant had been behaving. They all said the same thing: he took no notice of you if you left him alone, but he might charge if you went too close to him.

It was perfectly clear to me what I ought to do. I ought to walk up to within, say, twenty-five yards of the elephant and test his behavior. If he charged, I could shoot; if he took no notice of me, it would be safe to leave him until the mahout came back. But also I knew that I was going to do no such thing. I was a poor shot with a rifle and the ground was soft mud into which one would sink at every step. If the elephant charged and I missed him, I should have about as much chance as a toad under a steam-roller. But even then I was not thinking particularly of my own skin, only of the watchful yellow faces behind. For at that moment, with the crowd watching me, I was not afraid in the ordinary sense, as I would have been if I had been alone. A white man mustn't be frightened in front of "natives"; and so, in general, he isn't frightened. The sole thought in my mind was that if anything went wrong those two thousand Burmans would see me pursued, caught, trampled on and reduced to a grinning corpse like that Indian up the hill. And if that happened it was quite probable that some of them would laugh. That would never do. There was only one alternative. I shoved the cartridges into the magazine and lay down on the road to get a better aim.

The crowd grew very still, and a deep, low, happy sigh, as of people who see the theatre curtain go up at last, breathed from innumerable throats. They were going to have their bit of fun after all. The rifle was a beautiful German thing with cross-hair sights. I did not then know that in shooting an elephant one would shoot to cut an imaginary bar running from ear-hole to ear-hole. I ought, therefore, as the elephant was sideways on, to have aimed straight at his ear-hole; actually I aimed several inches in front of this, thinking the brain would be further forward.

When I pulled the trigger I did not hear the bang or feel the kick—one never does when a shot goes home—but I heard the devilish roar of glee that went up from the crowd. In that instant, in too short a time, one would have thought, even for the bullet to get there, a mysterious, terrible change had come over the elephant. He neither stirred nor fell, but every line of his body had altered. He looked suddenly stricken, shrunken, immensely old, as though the frightful impact of the bullet had paralysed him without knocking him down. At last, after what seemed a long time—it might have been five seconds, I dare say—he sagged flabbily to his knees. His mouth slobbered. An enormous senility seemed to have settled upon him. One could have imagined him thousands of years old. I fired again into the same spot. At the second shot he did not collapse but climbed with desperate slowness to his feet and stood weakly upright, with legs sagging and head drooping. I fired a third time. That was the shot that did for him. You could see the agony of it jolt his whole body and knock the last remnant of strength from his legs. But in falling he seemed for a moment to rise, for as his hind legs collapsed beneath him he seemed to tower upward like a huge rock toppling, his trunk reaching skywards like a tree. He trumpeted, for the first and only time. And then down he came, his belly towards me, with a crash that seemed to shake the ground even where I lay.

I got up. The Burmans were already racing past me across the mud. It was obvious that the elephant would never rise again, but he was not dead. He was breathing very rhythmically with long rattling gasps, his great mound of a side painfully rising and falling. His mouth was wide open—I could see far down into caverns of pale pink throat. I waited a long time for him to die, but his breathing did not weaken. Finally I fired my two remaining shots into the spot where I thought his heart must be. The thick blood welled out of him like red velvet, but still he did not die. His body did not even jerk when the shots hit him, the tortured breathing continued without a pause. He was dying, very slowly and in great agony, but in some world remote from me where not even a bullet could damage him further. I felt that I had got to put an end to that dreadful noise. It seemed dreadful to see the great beast lying there, powerless to move and yet powerless to die, and not even to be able to finish him. I sent back for my small rifle and poured shot after shot into his heart and down his throat. They seemed to make no impression. The tortured gasps continued as steadily as the ticking of a clock.

In the end I could not stand it any longer and went away. I heard later that it took him half an hour to die. Burmans were bringing dahs and baskets even before I left, and I was told they had stripped his body almost to the bones by the afternoon.

Afterwards, of course, there were endless discussions about the shooting of the elephant. The owner was furious, but he was only an Indian and could do nothing. Besides, legally I had done the right thing, for a mad elephant has to be killed, like a mad dog, if its owner fails to control it. Among the Europeans opinion was divided. The older men said I was right, the younger men said it was a damn shame to shoot an elephant for killing a coolie, because an elephant was worth more than any damn

Coringhee coolie. And afterwards I was very glad that the coolie had been killed; it put me legally in the right and it gave me a sufficient pretext for shooting the elephant. I often wondered whether any of the others grasped that I had done it solely to avoid looking a fool.

Marrakech

As the corpse went past the flies left the restaurant table in a cloud and rushed after it, but they came back a few minutes later.

The little crowd of mourners—all men and boys, no women— threaded their way across the market-place between the piles of pomegranates and the taxis and the camels, wailing a short chant over and over again. What really appeals to the flies is that the corpses here are never put into coffins, they are merely wrapped in a piece of rag and carried on a rough wooden bier on the shoulders of four friends. When the friends get to the burying-ground they hack an oblong hole a foot or two deep, dump the body in it and fling over it a little of the dried-up, lumpy earth, which is like broken brick. No gravestone, no name, no identifying mark of any kind. The burying-ground is merely a huge waste of hummocky earth, like a derelict building-lot. After a month or two no one can even be certain where his own relatives are buried.

When you walk through a town like this—two hundred thousand inhabitants, of whom at least twenty thousand own literally nothing except the rags they stand up in—when you see how the people live, and still more how easily they die, it is always difficult to believe that you are walking among human beings. All colonial empires are in reality founded upon that fact. The people have brown faces—besides, there are so many of them! Are they really the same flesh as yourself? Do they even have names? Or are they merely a kind of undifferentiated brown stuff, about as individual as bees or coral insects? They rise out of the earth, they sweat and starve for a few years, and then they sink back into the nameless mounds of the graveyard and nobody notices that they are gone. And even the graves themselves soon fade back into the soil. Sometimes, out for a walk, as you break your way through the prickly pear, you notice that it is rather bumpy underfoot, and only a certain regularity in the bumps tells you that you are walking over skeletons.

I was feeding one of the gazelles in the public gardens.

Gazelles are almost the only animals that look good to eat when they are still alive, in fact, one can hardly look at their hindquarters without thinking of mint sauce. The gazelle I was feeding seemed to know that this thought was in my mind, for though it took the piece of bread I was holding out it obviously did not like me. It nibbled rapidly at the bread, then lowered its head and tried to butt me, then took another nibble and then butted again. Probably its idea was that if it could drive me away the bread would somehow remain hanging in mid-air.

An Arab navvy working on the path nearby lowered his heavy hoe and sidled slowly towards us. He looked from the gazelle to the bread and from the bread to the gazelle, with a sort of quiet amazement, as though he had never seen anything quite like this before. Finally he said shyly in French:

"*I* could eat some of that bread."

I tore off a piece and he stowed it gratefully in some secret place under his rags. This man is an employee of the Municipality.

When you go through the Jewish quarters you gather some idea of what the medieval ghettoes were probably like. Under their Moorish rulers the Jews were only allowed to own land in certain restricted areas, and after centuries of this kind of treatment they have ceased to bother about overcrowding. Many of the streets are a good deal less than six feet wide, the houses are completely windowless, and sore-eyed children cluster everywhere in unbelievable numbers, like clouds of flies. Down the centre of the street there is generally running a little river of urine.

In the bazaar huge families of Jews, all dressed in the long black robe and little black skull-cap, are working in dark fly-infested booths that look like caves. A carpenter sits cross-legged at a prehistoric lathe, turning chair-legs at lightning speed. He works the lathe with a bow in his right hand and guides the chisel with his left foot, and thanks to a lifetime of sitting in this position his left leg is warped out of shape. At his side his grandson, aged six, is already starting on the simpler parts of the job.

I was just passing the coppersmiths' booths when somebody noticed that I was lighting a cigarette. Instantly, from the dark holes all round, there was a frenzied rush of Jews, many of them old grandfathers with flowing grey beards, all clamouring for a cigarette. Even a blind man somewhere at the back of one of the booths heard a rumour of cigarettes and came crawling out, groping in the air with his hand. In about a minute I had used up the whole packet. None of these people, I suppose, works less than twelve hours a day, and every one of them looks on a cigarette as a more or less impossible luxury.

As the Jews live in self-contained communities they follow the same trades as the Arabs, except for agriculture. Fruit-sellers, potters, silver-smiths, blacksmiths, butchers, leatherworkers, tailors, water-carriers, beggars, porters—whichever way you look you see nothing but Jews. As a matter of fact there are thirteen thousand of them, all living in the space of a few acres. A good job Hitler wasn't here. Perhaps he was on his way, however. You hear the usual dark rumours about the Jews, not only from the Arabs but from the poorer Europeans.

"Yes, mon vieux, they took my job away from me and gave it to a Jew. The Jews! They're the real rulers of this country, you know. They've got all the money. They control the banks, finance—everything."

"But," I said, "isn't it a fact that the average Jew is a labourer working for about a penny an hour?"

"Ah, that's only for show! They're all moneylenders really. They're cunning, the Jews."

In just the same way, a couple of hundred years ago, poor old women used to be burned for witchcraft when they could not even work enough magic to get themselves a square meal.

All people who work with their hands are partly invisible, and the more important the work they do, the less visible they are. Still, a white skin is always fairly conspicuous. In northern Europe, when you see a labourer ploughing a field, you probably give him a second glance. In a hot country, anywhere south of Gibraltar or east of Suez, the chances are that you don't even see him. I have noticed this again and again. In a tropical landscape one's eye takes in everything except the human beings. It takes in the dried-up soil, the prickly pear, the palm tree and the distant mountain, but it always misses the peasant hoeing at his patch. He is the same colour as the earth, and a great deal less interesting to look at.

It is only because of this that the starved countries of Asia and Africa are accepted as tourist resorts. No one would think of running cheap trips to the Distressed Areas. But where the human beings have brown skins their poverty is simply not noticed. What does Morocco mean to a Frenchman? An orange-grove or a job in Government service. Or to an Englishman? Camels, castles, palm trees, Foreign Legionnaires, brass trays, and bandits. One could probably live there for years without noticing that for nine-tenths of the people the reality of life is an endless, backbreaking struggle to wring a little food out of an eroded soil.

Most of Morocco is so desolate that no wild animal bigger than a hare can live on it. Huge areas which were once covered with forest have turned into a treeless waste where the soil is exactly like broken-up brick. Nevertheless a good deal of it is cultivated, with frightful labour. Everything is done by hand. Long lines of women, bent double like inverted capital L's, work their way slowly across the fields, tearing up the prickly weeds with their hands, and the peasant gathering lucerne for fodder pulls it up stalk by stalk instead of reaping it, thus saving an inch or two on each stalk. The plough is a wretched wooden thing, so frail that one can easily carry it on one's shoulder, and fitted underneath with a rough iron spike which stirs the soil to a depth of about four inches. This is as much as the strength of the animals is equal to. It is usual to plough with a cow and a donkey yoked together. Two donkeys would not be quite strong enough, but on the other hand two cows would cost a little more to feed. The peasants possess no harrows, they merely plough the soil several times over in different directions, finally leaving it in rough furrows, after which the whole field has to be shaped with hoes into small oblong patches to conserve water. Except for a day or two after the rare rainstorms there is never enough water. Along the edges of the fields channels are hacked out to a depth of thirty or forty feet to get at the tiny trickles which run through the subsoil.

Every afternoon a file of very old women passes down the road outside my house, each carrying a load of firewood. All of them are mummified with age and the sun, and all of them are tiny. It seems to be generally the case in primitive communities that the women, when they get beyond a certain age, shrink to the size of children. One day a poor old creature who could not have been more than four feet tall crept past me under a vast load of wood. I stopped her and put a five-sou piece (a little more than a farthing) into her hand. She answered with a shrill wail, almost a scream, which was partly gratitude but mainly surprise. I suppose that from her point of view, by taking any notice of her, I seemed almost to be violating a law of nature. She accepted her status as an old woman, that is to say as a beast of burden. When a family is travelling it is quite usual to see a father and a grown-up son riding ahead on donkeys, and an old woman following on foot, carrying the baggage.

But what is strange about these people is their invisibility. For several weeks, always at about the same time of day, the file of old women had hobbled past the house with their firewood, and though they had registered themselves on my eyeballs I cannot truly say that I had seen them. Firewood was passing—that was how I saw it. It was only that one day I happened to be walking behind them, and the curious up-and-down motion of a load of wood drew my attention to the human being beneath it. Then for the first time I noticed the poor old earth-coloured bodies, bodies reduced to bones and leathery skin, bent double under the crushing weight. Yet I suppose I had not been five minutes on Moroccan soil before I noticed the overloading of the donkeys and was infuriated by it. There is no question that the donkeys are damnably treated. The Moroccan donkey is hardly bigger than a St. Bernard dog, it carries a load which in the British Army would be considered too much for a fifteen-hands mule, and very often its pack-saddle is not taken off its back for weeks together. But what is peculiarly pitiful is that it is the most willing creature on earth, it follows its master like a dog and does not need either bridle or halter. After a dozen years of devoted work it suddenly drops dead, whereupon its master tips it into the ditch and the village dogs have torn its guts out before it is cold.

This kind of thing makes one's blood boil, whereas—on the whole—the plight of the human beings does not. I am not commenting, merely pointing to a fact. People with brown skins are next door to invisible. Anyone can be sorry for the donkey with its galled back, but it is generally owing to some kind of accident if one even notices the old woman under her load of sticks.

As the storks flew northward the Negroes were marching southward —a long, dusty column, infantry, screw-gun batteries, and then more infantry, four or five thousand men in all, winding up the road with a clumping of boots and a clatter of iron wheels.

They were Senegalese, the blackest Negroes in Africa, so black that sometimes it is difficult to see whereabouts on their necks the hair begins. Their splendid bodies were hidden in reach-me-down khaki uniforms, their feet squashed into boots that looked like blocks of wood, and every tin hat seemed to be a couple of sizes too small. It was very hot and the men had marched a long way. They slumped under the weight of their packs and the curiously sensitive black faces were glistening with sweat.

As they went past a tall, very young Negro turned and caught my eye. But the look he gave me was not in the least the kind of look you might expect. Not hostile, not contemptuous, not sullen, not even inquisitive. It was the shy, wide-eyed Negro look, which actually is a look of profound respect. I saw how it was. This wretched boy, who is a French citizen and has therefore been dragged from the forest to scrub floors and catch syphilis in garrison towns, actually has feelings of reverence before a white skin. He has been taught that the white race are his masters, and he still believes it.

But there is one thought which every white man (and in this connection it doesn't matter twopence if he calls himself a socialist) thinks when he sees a black army marching past. "How much longer can we go on kidding these people? How long before they turn their guns in the other direction?"

It was curious, really. Every white man there had this thought stowed somewhere or other in his mind. I had it, so had the other onlookers, so had the officers on their sweating chargers and the white N.C.O.'s marching in the ranks. It was a kind of secret which we all knew and were too clever to tell; only the Negroes didn't know it. And really it was like watching a flock of cattle to see the long column, a mile or two miles of armed men, flowing peacefully up the road, while the great white birds drifted over them in the opposite direction, glittering like scraps of paper.

[1939]

JAMES BALDWIN

James Baldwin was born in Harlem in 1924, the oldest of nine children, and graduated from DeWitt Clinton High School, where he was editor of the literary magazine. After the death of his father in 1943 he lived in Greenwich Village, working by day as handyman, office boy, or factory worker, and writing at night. A Rosenwald Fellowship received in 1948

enabled him to go to Paris, where he wrote his first two novels, Go Tell
It on the Mountain *(1953) and* Giovanni's Room *(1956), and the
essays published as* Notes of a Native Son *(1955). The piece that gives
the collection its name, reprinted below, is an autobiographical masterpiece.*

*In 1957 Baldwin returned to America and since then has continued
his literary career with novels, plays, and essays. Baldwin has won many
awards, among them a Guggenheim Fellowship (1954), a* Partisan
Review *Fellowship (1956), and The National Institute for Arts and
Letters Award (1956).* Nobody Knows My Name, *a collection of
essays, was selected as one of the outstanding books of 1961 by The
American Library Association.* The Fire Next Time *(1963)—two
searing articles, or letters, on the relationship between black and white
Americans—secures Baldwin's lasting reputation both as essayist and as
commentator on American culture. Later writings include a play,* Blues
for Mr. Charlie *(1964), and two other works,* Tell Me How Long
the Train's Been Gone *(1968) and* No Name in the Street
(1972).

Notes of a Native Son

On the 29th of July, in 1943, my father died. On the same day, a few hours
later, his last child was born. Over a month before this, while all our
energies were concentrated in waiting for these events, there had been,
in Detroit, one of the bloodiest race riots of the century. A few hours after
my father's funeral, while he lay in state in the undertaker's chapel, a race
riot broke out in Harlem. On the morning of the 3rd of August, we drove
my father to the graveyard through a wilderness of smashed plate glass.

The day of my father's funeral had also been my nineteenth birthday.
As we drove him to the graveyard, the spoils of injustice, anarchy, discontent, and hatred were all around us. It seemed to me that God himself
had devised, to mark my father's end, the most sustained and brutally
dissonant of codas. And it seemed to me, too, that the violence which rose
all about us as my father left the world had been devised as a corrective
for the pride of his eldest son. I had declined to believe in that apocalypse
which had been central to my father's vision; very well, life seemed to be
saying, here is something that will certainly pass for an apocalypse until
the real thing comes along. I had inclined to be contemptuous of my
father for the conditions of his life, for the conditions of our lives. When
his life had ended I began to wonder about that life and also, in a new
way, to be apprehensive about my own.

I had not known my father very well. We had got on badly, partly
because we shared, in our different fashions, the vice of stubborn pride.
When he was dead I realized that I had hardly ever spoken to him. When

he had been dead a long time I began to wish I had. It seems to be typical of life in America, where opportunities, real and fancied, are thicker than anywhere else on the globe, that the second generation has no time to talk to the first. No one, including my father, seems to have known exactly how old he was, but his mother had been born during slavery. He was of the first generation of free men. He, along with thousands of other Negroes, came North after 1919 and I was part of that generation which had never seen the landscape of what Negroes sometimes call the Old Country.

He had been born in New Orleans and had been a quite young man there during the time that Louis Armstrong, a boy, was running errands for the dives and honky-tonks of what was always presented to me as one of the most wicked of cities—to this day, whenever I think of New Orleans, I also helplessly think of Sodom and Gomorrah. My father never mentioned Louis Armstrong, except to forbid us to play his records; but there was a picture of him on our wall for a long time. One of my father's strong-willed female relatives had placed it there and forbade my father to take it down. He never did, but he eventually maneuvered her out of the house and when, some years later, she was in trouble and near death, he refused to do anything to help her.

He was, I think, very handsome. I gather this from photographs and from my own memories of him, dressed in his Sunday best and on his way to preach a sermon somewhere, when I was little. Handsome, proud, and ingrown, "like a toe-nail," somebody said. But he looked to me, as I grew older, like pictures I had seen of African tribal chieftains: he really should have been naked, with war-paint on and barbaric mementos, standing among spears. He could be chilling in the pulpit and indescribably cruel in his personal life and he was certainly the most bitter man I have ever met; yet it must be said that there was something else in him, buried in him, which lent him his tremendous power and, even, a rather crushing charm. It had something to do with his blackness, I think—he was very black—with his blackness and his beauty, and with the fact that he knew that he was black but did not know that he was beautiful. He claimed to be proud of his blackness but it had also been the cause of much humiliation and it had fixed bleak boundaries to his life. He was not a young man when we were growing up and he had already suffered many kinds of ruin; in his outrageously demanding and protective way he loved his children, who were black like him and menaced, like him; and all these things sometimes showed in his face when he tried, never to my knowledge with any success, to establish contact with any of us. When he took one of his children on his knee to play, the child always became fretful and began to cry; when he tried to help one of us with our homework the absolutely unabating tension which emanated from him caused our minds and our tongues to become paralyzed, so that he, scarcely knowing why, flew into a rage and the child, not knowing why, was punished. If it ever entered his head to bring a surprise home for his children, it was, almost unfailingly, the wrong surprise and even the big watermelons he often brought home on his back in the summertime led to the most appalling scenes. I do not remember, in all those years, that one of his children was ever glad to see him come home. From what I was able to gather of his early life, it seemed that this inability to establish contact with other people had always marked him and had been one of the things which had driven him out of New Orleans. There was something in him, therefore, groping and tentative, which was never expressed and which was buried with him. One saw it most clearly when he was facing new people and hoping to impress them. But he never did, not for long. We went from church to smaller and more improbable church, he found himself in less and less demand as a minister, and by the time he died none of his friends had come to see him for a long time. He had lived and died in an intolerable bitterness of spirit and it frightened me, as we drove him to the graveyard through those unquiet, ruined streets, to see how powerful and overflowing this bitterness could be and to realize that this bitterness now was mine.

When he died I had been away from home for a little over a year. In that year I had had time to become aware of the meaning of all my father's bitter warnings, had discovered the secret of his proudly pursed lips and rigid carriage: I had discovered the weight of white people in the world. I saw that this had been for my ancestors and now would be for me an awful thing to live with and that the bitterness which had helped to kill my father could also kill me.

He had been ill a long time—in the mind, as we now realized, reliving instances of his fantastic intransigence in the new light of his affliction and endeavoring to feel a sorrow for him which never, quite, came true. We had not known that he was being eaten up by paranoia, and the discovery that his cruelty, to our bodies and our minds, had been one of the symptoms of his illness was not, then, enough to enable us to forgive him. The younger children felt, quite simply, relief that he would not be coming home anymore. My mother's observation that it was he, after all, who had kept them alive all these years meant nothing because the problems of keeping children alive are not real for children. The older children felt, with my father gone, that they could invite their friends to the house without fear that their friends would be insulted or, as had sometimes happened with me, being told that their friends were in league with the devil and intended to rob our family of everything we owned. (I didn't fail to wonder, and it made me hate him, what on earth we owned that anybody else would want.)

His illness was beyond all hope of healing before anyone realized that he was ill. He had always been so strange and had lived, like a prophet, in such unimaginably close communion with the Lord that his long silences which were punctuated by moans and hallelujahs and snatches of old songs while he sat at the living-room window never seemed odd to us. It was not until he refused to eat because, he said, his family was trying to poison him that my mother was forced to accept as a fact what had, until then, been only an unwilling suspicion. When he was committed, it was discovered that he had tuberculosis and, as it turned out, the disease of his mind allowed the disease of his body to destroy him. For the doctors could not force him to eat, either, and, though he was fed intravenously, it was clear from the beginning that there was no hope for him.

In my mind's eye I could see him, sitting at the window, locked up in his terrors; hating and fearing every living soul including his children who had betrayed him, too, by reaching towards the world which had despised him. There were nine of us. I began to wonder what it could have felt like for such a man to have had nine children whom he could barely feed. He used to make little jokes about our poverty, which never, of course, seemed very funny to us; they could not have seemed very funny to him, either, or else our all too feeble response to them would never have caused such rages. He spent great energy and achieved, to our chagrin, no small amount of success in keeping us away from the people who surrounded us, people who had all-night rent parties to which we listened when we should have been sleeping, people who cursed and drank and flashed razor blades on Lenox Avenue. He could not understand why, if they had so much energy to spare, they could not use it to make their lives better. He treated almost everybody on our block with a most uncharitable asperity and neither they, nor, of course, their children were slow to reciprocate.

The only white people who came to our house were welfare workers and bill collectors. It was almost always my mother who dealt with them, for my father's temper, which was at the mercy of his pride, was never to be trusted. It was clear that he felt their very presence in his home to be a violation: this was conveyed by his carriage, almost ludicrously stiff, and by his voice, harsh and vindictively polite. When I was around nine or ten I wrote a play which was directed by a young, white schoolteacher, a woman, who then took an interest in me, and gave me books to read and, in order to corroborate my theatrical bent, decided to take me to see what she somewhat tactlessly referred to as "real" plays. Theater-going was forbidden in our house, but, with the really cruel intuitiveness of a child, I suspected that the color of this woman's skin would carry the day for me. When, at school, she suggested taking me to the theater, I did not, as I might have done if she had been a Negro, find a way of discouraging her, but agreed that she should pick me up at my house one evening. I then, very cleverly, left all the rest to my mother, who suggested to my father, as I knew she would, that it would not be very nice to let such a kind woman make the trip for nothing. Also, since it was a schoolteacher, I imagine that my mother countered the idea of sin with the idea of "education," which word, even with my father, carried a kind of bitter weight.

Before the teacher came my father took me aside to ask *why* she was coming, what *interest* she could possibly have in our house, in a boy like me. I said I didn't know but I, too, suggested that it had something to do with education. And I understood that my father was waiting for me to say something—I didn't quite know what; perhaps that I wanted his protection against this teacher and her "education." I said none of these things and the teacher came and we went out. It was clear, during the brief interview in our living room, that my father was agreeing very much against his will and that he would have refused permission if he had dared. The fact that he did not dare caused me to despise him: I had no way of knowing that he was facing in that living room a wholly unprecedented and frightening situation.

Later, when my father had been laid off from his job, this woman became very important to us. She was really a very sweet and generous woman and went to a great deal of trouble to be of help to us, particularly during one awful winter. My mother called her by the highest name she knew: she said she was a "christian." My father could scarcely disagree but during the four or five years of our relatively close association he never trusted her and was always trying to surprise in her open, Midwestern face the genuine, cunningly hidden, and hideous motivation. In later years, particularly when it began to be clear that this "education" of mine was going to lead me to perdition, he became more explicit and warned me that my white friends in high school were not really my friends and that I would see, when I was older, how white people would do anything to keep a Negro down. Some of them could be nice, he admitted, but none of them were to be trusted and most of them were not even nice. The best thing was to have as little to do with them as possible. I did not feel this way and I was certain, in my innocence, that I never would.

But the year which preceded my father's death had made a great change in my life. I had been living in New Jersey, working in defense plants, working and living among southerners, white and black. I knew about the south, of course, and about how southerners treated Negroes and how they expected them to behave, but it had never entered my mind that anyone would look at me and expect *me* to behave that way. I learned in New Jersey that to be a Negro meant, precisely, that one was never looked at but was simply at the mercy of the reflexes the color of one's skin caused in other people. I acted in New Jersey as I had always acted, that is as though I thought a great deal of myself—I had to *act* that way —with results that were, simply, unbelievable. I had scarcely arrived before I had earned the enmity, which was extraordinarily ingenious, of all my superiors and nearly all my co-workers. In the beginning, to make matters worse, I simply did not know what was happening. I did not know what I had done, and I shortly began to wonder what *anyone* could possibly do, to bring about such unanimous, active, and unbearably vocal hostility. I knew about jim-crow but I had never experienced it. I went to the same self-service restaurant three times and stood with all the Princeton boys before the counter, waiting for a hamburger and coffee; it was always an extraordinarily long time before anything was set before me; but it was not until the fourth visit that I learned that, in fact, nothing had ever been set before me: I had simply picked something up. Negroes were not served there, I was told, and they had been waiting for me to realize that I was always the only Negro present. Once I was told this, I determined to go there all the time. But now they were ready for me and, though some dreadful scenes were subsequently enacted in that restaurant, I never ate there again.

It was the same story all over New Jersey, in bars, bowling alleys, diners, places to live. I was always being forced to leave, silently, or with mutual imprecations. I very shortly became notorious and children giggled behind me when I passed and their elders whispered or shouted—they really believed that I was mad. And it did begin to work on my mind, of course; I began to be afraid to go anywhere and to compensate for this I went to places to which I really should not have gone and where, God knows, I had no desire to be. My reputation in town naturally enhanced my reputation at work and my working day became one long series of acrobatics designed to keep me out of trouble. I cannot say that these acrobatics succeeded. It began to seem that the machinery of the organization I worked for was turning over, day and night, with but one aim: to eject me. I was fired once, and contrived, with the aid of a friend from New York, to get back on the payroll; was fired again, and bounced back again. It took a while to fire me for the third time, but the third time took. There were no loopholes anywhere. There was not even any way of getting back inside the gates.

That year in New Jersey lives in my mind as though it were the year during which, having an unsuspected predilection for it, I first contracted some dread, chronic disease, the unfailing symptom of which is a kind of blind fever, a pounding in the skull and fire in the bowels. Once this disease is contracted, one can never be really carefree again, for the fever, without an instant's warning, can recur at any moment. It can wreck more important things than race relations. There is not a Negro alive who does not have this rage in his blood—one has the choice, merely, of living with it consciously or surrendering to it. As for me, this fever has recurred in me, and does, and will until the day I die.

My last night in New Jersey, a white friend from New York took me to the nearest big town, Trenton, to go to the movies and have a few drinks. As it turned out, he also saved me from, at the very least, a violent whipping. Almost every detail of that night stands out very clearly in my memory. I even remember the name of the movie we saw because its title impressed me as being so patly ironical. It was a movie about the German occupation of France, starring Maureen O'Hara and Charles Laughton and called *This Land Is Mine.* I remember the name of the diner we walked into when the movie ended: it was the "American Diner." When we walked in the counterman asked what we wanted and I remember answering with the casual sharpness which had become my habit: "We want a hamburger and a cup of coffee, what do you think we want?" I do not know why, after a year of such rebuffs, I so completely failed to anticipate his answer, which was, of course, "We don't serve Negroes here." This reply failed to discompose me, at least for the moment. I made some sardonic comment about the name of the diner and we walked out into the streets.

This was the time of what was called the "brown-out," when the lights in all American cities were very dim. When we re-entered the streets something happened to me which had the force of an optical illusion, or a nightmare. The streets were very crowded and I was facing north. People were moving in every direction but it seemed to me, in that instant, that all of the people I could see, and many more than that, were moving toward me, against me, and that everyone was white. I remember how their faces gleamed. And I felt, like a physical sensation, a *click* at the nape of my neck as though some interior string connecting my head to my body had been cut. I began to walk. I heard my friend call after me, but I ignored him. Heaven only knows what was going on in his mind, but he had the good sense not to touch me—I don't know what would have happened if he had—and to keep me in sight. I don't know what was going on in my mind, either; I certainly had no conscious plan. I wanted to do something to crush these white faces, which were crushing me. I walked for perhaps a block or two until I came to an enormous, glittering, and fashionable restaurant in which I knew not even the intercession of the Virgin would cause me to be served. I pushed through the doors and took the first vacant seat I saw, at a table for two, and waited.

I do not know how long I waited and I rather wonder, until today, what I could possibly have looked like. Whatever I looked like, I frightened the waitress who shortly appeared, and the moment she appeared all of my fury flowed towards her. I hated her for her white face, and for her great, astounded, frightened eyes. I felt that if she found a black man so frightening I would make her fright worth-while.

She did not ask me what I wanted, but repeated, as though she had learned it somewhere, "We don't serve Negroes here." She did not say it with the blunt, derisive hostility to which I had grown so accustomed, but, rather, with a note of apology in her voice, and fear. This made me colder and more murderous than ever. I felt I had to do something with my hands. I wanted her to come close enough for me to get her neck between my hands.

So I pretended not to have understood her, hoping to draw her closer. And she did step a very short step closer, with her pencil poised incongruously over her pad, and repeated the formula: ". . . don't serve Negroes here."

Somehow, with the repetition of that phrase, which was already ringing in my head like a thousand bells of a nightmare, I realized that she would never come any closer and that I would have to strike from a distance. There was nothing on the table but an ordinary watermug half full of water, and I picked this up and hurled it with all my strength at her. She ducked and it missed her and shattered against the mirror behind the bar. And, with that sound, my frozen blood abruptly thawed, I returned from wherever I had been, I *saw,* for the first time, the restaurant, the people with their mouths open, already, as it seemed to me, rising as one man, and I realized what I had done, and where I was, and I was frightened. I rose and began running for the door. A round, potbellied man grabbed me by the nape of the neck just as I reached the doors and began to beat me about the face. I kicked him and got loose and ran into the streets. My friend whispered, *"Run!"* and I ran.

My friend stayed outside the restaurant long enough to misdirect my pursuers and the police, who arrived, he told me, at once. I do not know what I said to him when he came to my room that night. I could not have said much. I felt, in the oddest, most awful way, that I had somehow betrayed him. I lived it over and over and over again, the way one relives an automobile accident after it has happened and one finds oneself alone and safe. I could not get over two facts, both equally difficult for the imagination to grasp, and one was that I could have been murdered. But the other was that I had been ready to commit murder. I saw nothing very clearly but I did see this: that my life, my *real* life, was in danger, and not from anything other people might do but from the hatred I carried in my own heart.

[II]

I had returned home around the second week in June—in great haste because it seemed that my father's death and my mother's confinement were both but a matter of hours. In the case of my mother, it soon became clear that she had simply made a miscalculation. This had always been her tendency and I don't believe that a single one of us arrived in the world, or has since arrived anywhere else, on time. But none of us dawdled so intolerably about the business of being born as did my baby sister. We sometimes amused ourselves, during those endless, stifling weeks, by picturing the baby sitting within in the safe, warm dark, bitterly regretting the necessity of becoming a part of our chaos and stubbornly putting it off as long as possible. I understood her perfectly and congratulated her on showing such good sense so soon. Death, however, sat as purposefully at my father's bedside as life stirred within my mother's womb and it was harder to understand why he so lingered in that long shadow. It seemed that he had bent, and for a long time, too, all of his energies towards dying. Now death was ready for him but my father held back.

All of Harlem, indeed, seemed to be infected by waiting. I had never before known it to be so violently still. Racial tensions throughout this country were exacerbated during the early years of the war, partly because the labor market brought together hundreds of thousands of ill-prepared people and partly because Negro soldiers, regardless of where they were born, received their military training in the south. What happened in defense plants and army camps had repercussions, naturally, in every Negro ghetto. The situation in Harlem had grown bad enough for clergymen, policemen, educators, politicians, and social workers to assert in one breath that there was no "crime wave" and to offer, in the very next breath, suggestions as how to combat it. These suggestions always seemed to involve playgrounds, despite the fact that racial skirmishes were occurring in the playgrounds, too. Playground or not, crime wave or not, the Harlem police force had been augmented in March, and the unrest grew—perhaps, in fact, partly as a result of the ghetto's instinctive hatred of policemen. Perhaps the most revealing news item, out of the steady parade of reports of muggings, stabbings, shootings, assaults, gang wars, and accusations of police brutality, is the item concerning six Negro girls who set upon a white girl in the subway because, as they all too accurately put it, she was stepping on their toes. Indeed she was, all over the nation.

I had never before been so aware of policemen, on foot, on horseback, on corners, everywhere, always two by two. Nor had I ever been so aware of small knots of people. They were on stoops and on corners and in doorways, and what was striking about them, I think, was that they did not seem to be talking. Never, when I passed these groups, did the usual sound of a curse or a laugh ring out and neither did there seem to be any hum of gossip. There was certainly, on the other hand, occurring between them communication extraordinarily intense. Another thing that was striking was the unexpected diversity of the people who made up these groups. Usually, for example, one would see a group of sharpies standing on the street corner, jiving the passing chicks; or a group of older men, usually, for some reason, in the vicinity of a barber shop, discussing baseball scores, or the numbers, or making rather chilling observations about women they had known. Women, in a general way, tended to be seen less often together—unless they were church women, or very young girls, or prostitutes met together for an unprofessional instant. But that summer I saw the strangest combinations: large, respectable, churchly matrons standing on the stoops or the corners with their hair tied up, together with a girl in sleazy satin whose face bore the marks of gin and the razor, or heavy-set, abrupt, no-nonsense older men, in company with the most disreputable and fanatical "race" men, or these same "race" men with the sharpies, or these sharpies with the churchly women. Seventh Day Adventists and Methodists and Spiritualists seemed to be hobnobbing with Holyrollers and they were all, alike, entangled with the most flagrant disbelievers; something heavy in their stance seemed to indicate that they had all, incredibly, seen a common vision, and on each face there seemed to be the same strange, bitter shadow.

The churchly women and the matter-of-fact, no-nonsense men had children in the Army. The sleazy girls they talked to had lovers there, the sharpies and the "race" men had friends and brothers there. It would have demanded an unquestioning patriotism, happily as uncommon in this country as it is undesirable, for these people not to have been disturbed by the bitter letters they received, by the newspaper stories they read, not to have been enraged by the posters, then to be found all over New York, which described the Japanese as "yellow-bellied Japs." It was only the "race" men, to be sure, who spoke ceaselessly of being revenged —how this vengeance was to be exacted was not clear—for the indignities and dangers suffered by Negro boys in uniform; but everybody felt a directionless, hopeless bitterness, as well as that panic which can scarcely be suppressed when one knows that a human being one loves is beyond one's reach, and in danger. This helplessness and this gnawing uneasiness does something, at length, to even the toughest mind. Perhaps the best way to sum all this up is to say that the people I knew felt, mainly, a peculiar kind of relief when they knew that their boys were being shipped out of the south, to do battle overseas. It was, perhaps, like feeling that the most dangerous part of a dangerous journey had been passed and that now, even if death should come, it would come with honor and without the complicity of their countrymen. Such a death would be, in short, a fact with which one could hope to live.

It was on the 28th of July, which I believe was a Wednesday, that I visited my father for the first time during his illness and for the last time in his life. The moment I saw him I knew why I had put off this visit so long. I had told my mother that I did not want to see him because I hated him. But this was not true. It was only that I *had* hated him and I wanted to hold on to this hatred. I did not want to look on him as a ruin: it was not a ruin I had hated. I imagine that one of the reasons people cling to their hates so stubbornly is because they sense, once hate is gone, that they will be forced to deal with pain.

We traveled out to him, his older sister and myself, to what seemed to be the very end of a very Long Island. It was hot and dusty and we wrangled, my aunt and I, all the way out, over the fact that I had recently begun to smoke and, as she said, to give myself airs. But I knew that she wrangled with me because she could not bear to face the fact of her brother's dying. Neither could I endure the reality of her despair, her unstated bafflement as to what had happened to her brother's life, and her own. So we wrangled and I smoked and from time to time she fell into a heavy reverie. Covertly, I watched her face, which was the face of an old woman; it had fallen in, the eyes were sunken and lightless; soon she would be dying, too.

In my childhood—it had not been so long ago—I had thought her beautiful. She had been quick-witted and quick-moving and very generous with all the children and each of her visits had been an event. At one time one of my brothers and myself had thought of running away to live with her. Now she could no longer produce out of her handbag some unexpected and yet familiar delight. She made me feel pity and revulsion and fear. It was awful to realize that she no longer caused me to feel affection. The closer we came to the hospital the more querulous she became and at the same time, naturally, grew more dependent on me.

Between pity and guilt and fear I began to feel that there was another me trapped in my skull like a jack-in-the-box who might escape my control at any moment and fill the air with screaming.

She began to cry the moment we entered the room and she saw him lying there, all shriveled and still, like a little black monkey. The great, gleaming apparatus which fed him and would have compelled him to be still even if he had been able to move brought to mind, not beneficence, but torture; the tubes entering his arm made me think of pictures I had seen when a child, of Gulliver, tied down by the pygmies on that island. My aunt wept and wept, there was a whistling sound in my father's throat; nothing was said; he could not speak. I wanted to take his hand, to say something. But I do not know what I could have said, even if he could have heard me. He was not really in that room with us, he had at last really embarked on his journey; and though my aunt told me that he said he was going to meet Jesus, I did not hear anything except that whistling in his throat. The doctor came back and we left, into that unbearable train again, and home. In the morning came the telegram saying that he was dead. Then the house was suddenly full of relatives, friends, hysteria, and confusion and I quickly left my mother and the children to the care of those impressive women, who, in Negro communities at least, automatically appear at times of bereavement armed with lotions, proverbs, and patience, and an ability to cook. I went downtown. By the time I returned, later the same day, my mother had been carried to the hospital and the baby had been born.

[III]

For my father's funeral I had nothing black to wear and this posed a nagging problem all day long. It was one of those problems, simple, or impossible of solution, to which the mind insanely clings in order to avoid the mind's real trouble. I spent most of that day at the downtown apartment of a girl I knew, celebrating my birthday with whiskey and wondering what to wear that night. When planning a birthday celebration one naturally does not expect that it will be up against competition from a funeral and this girl had anticipated taking me out that night, for a big dinner and a night club afterwards. Sometime during the course of that long day we decided that we would go out anyway, when my father's funeral service was over. I imagine *I* decided it, since, as the funeral hour approached, it became clearer and clearer to me that I would not know what to do with myself when it was over. The girl, stifling her very lively concern as to the possible effects of the whiskey on one of my father's chief mourners, concentrated on being conciliatory and practically helpful. She found a black shirt for me somewhere and ironed it and, dressed in the darkest pants and jacket I owned, and slightly drunk, I made my way to my father's funeral.

The chapel was full, but not packed, and very quiet. There were, mainly, my father's relatives, and his children, and here and there I saw faces I had not seen since childhood, the faces of my father's one-time friends. They were very dark and solemn now, seeming somehow to suggest that they had known all along that something like this would happen. Chief among the mourners was my aunt, who had quarreled with my father all his life; by which I do not mean to suggest that her mourning was insincere or that she had not loved him. I suppose that she was one of the few people in the world who had, and their incessant quarreling proved precisely the strength of the tie that bound them. The only other person in the world, as far as I knew, whose relationship to my father rivaled my aunt's in depth was my mother, who was not there.

It seemed to me, of course, that it was a very long funeral. But it was, if anything, a rather shorter funeral than most, nor, since there were no overwhelming, uncontrollable expressions of grief, could it be called— if I dare to use the word—successful. The minister who preached my father's funeral sermon was one of the few my father had still been seeing as he neared his end. He presented to us in his sermon a man whom none of us had ever seen—a man thoughtful, patient, and forbearing, a Christian inspiration to all who knew him, and a model for his children. And no doubt the children, in their disturbed and guilty state, were almost ready to believe this; he had been remote enough to be anything and, anyway, the shock of the incontrovertible, that it was really our father lying up there in that casket, prepared the mind for anything. His sister moaned and this grief-stricken moaning was taken for corroboration. The other faces held a dark, noncommittal thoughtfulness. This was not the man they had known, but they had scarcely expected to be confronted with *him;* this was, in a sense deeper than question of fact, the man they had not known, and the man they had not known may have been the real one. The real man, whoever he had been, had suffered and now he was dead: this was all that was sure and all that mattered now. Every man in the chapel hoped that when his hour came he, too, would be eulogized, which is to say forgiven, and that all of his lapses, greeds, errors, and strayings from the truth would be invested with coherence and looked upon with charity. This was perhaps the last thing human beings could give each other and it was what they demanded, after all, of the Lord. Only the Lord saw the midnight tears, only He was present when one of His children, moaning and wringing hands, paced up and down the room. When one slapped one's child in anger the recoil in the heart reverberated through heaven and became part of the pain of the universe. And when the children were hungry and sullen and distrustful and one watched them, daily, growing wilder, and further away, and running headlong into danger, it was the Lord who knew what the charged heart endured as the strap was laid to the backside; the Lord alone who knew what one *would* have said if one had had, like the Lord, the gift of the

living word. It was the Lord who knew of the impossibility every parent
in that room faced: how to prepare the child for the day when the child
would be despised and how to *create* in the child—by what means?—a
stronger antidote to this poison than one had found for oneself. The
avenues, side streets, bars, billiard halls, hospitals, police stations, and
even the playgrounds of Harlem—not to mention the houses of correc-
tion, the jails, and the morgue—testified to the potency of the poison
while remaining silent as to the efficacy of whatever antidote, irresistibly
raising the question of whether or not such an antidote existed; raising,
which was worse, the question of whether or not an antidote was desirable; perhaps poison should be fought with poison. With these several
schisms in the mind and with more terrors in the heart than could be
named, it was better not to judge the man who had gone down under an
impossible burden. It was better to remember: *Thou knowest this man's fall;
but thou knowest not his wrassling.*

While the preacher talked and I watched the children—years of changing their diapers, scrubbing them, slapping them, taking them to school,
and scolding them had had the perhaps inevitable result of making me
love them, though I am not sure I knew this then—my mind was busily
breaking out with a rash of disconnected impressions. Snatches of popular songs, indecent jokes, bits of books I had read, movie sequences,
faces, voices, political issues—I thought I was going mad; all these impressions suspended, as it were, in the solution of the faint nausea produced in me by the heat and liquor. For a moment I had the impression
that my alcoholic breath, inefficiently disguised with chewing gum, filled
the entire chapel. Then someone began singing one of my father's favorite songs and, abruptly, I was with him, sitting on his knee, in the hot,
enormous, crowded church which was the first church we attended. It was
the Abyssinia Baptist Church on 138th Street. We had not gone there
long. With this image, a host of others came. I had forgotten, in the rage
of my growing up, how proud my father had been of me when I was little.
Apparently, I had had a voice and my father had liked to show me off
before the members of the church. I had forgotten what he had looked
like when he was pleased but now I remembered that he had always been
grinning with pleasure when my solos ended. I even remembered certain
expressions on his face when he teased my mother—had he loved her?
I would never know. And when had it all began to change? For now it
seemed that he had not always been cruel. I remembered being taken for
a haircut and scraping my knee on the footrest of the barber's chair and
I remembered my father's face as he soothed my crying and applied the
stinging iodine. Then I remembered our fights, fights which had been of
the worst possible kind because my technique had been silence.

I remembered the one time in all our life together when we had really
spoken to each other.

It was on a Sunday and it must have been shortly before I left home.
We were walking, just the two of us, in our usual silence, to or from

church. I was in high school and had been doing a lot of writing and I was, at about this time, the editor of the high school magazine. But I had also been a Young Minister and had been preaching from the pulpit. Lately, I had been taking fewer engagements and preached as rarely as possible. It was said in the church, quite truthfully, that I was "cooling off."

My father asked me abruptly, "You'd rather write than preach, wouldn't you?"

I was astonished at his question—because it was a real question. I answered, "Yes."

That was all we said. It was awful to remember that that was all we had *ever* said.

The casket now was opened and the mourners were being led up the aisle to look for the last time on the deceased. The assumption was that the family was too overcome with grief to be allowed to make this journey alone and I watched while my aunt was led to the casket and, muffled in black, and shaking, led back to her seat. I disapproved of forcing the children to look on their dead father, considering that the shock of his death, or, more truthfully, the shock of death as a reality, was already a little more than a child could bear, but my judgment in this matter had been overruled and there they were, bewildered and frightened and very small, being led, one by one, to the casket. But there is also something very gallant about children at such moments. It has something to do with their silence and gravity and with the fact that one cannot help them. Their legs, somehow, seemed *exposed,* so that it is at once incredible and terribly clear that their legs are all they have to hold them up.

I had not wanted to go to the casket myself and I certainly had not wished to be led there, but there was no way of avoiding either of these forms. One of the deacons led me up and I looked on my father's face. I cannot say that it looked like him at all. His blackness had been equivocated by powder and there was no suggestion in that casket of what his power had or could have been. He was simply an old man dead, and it was hard to believe that he had ever given anyone either joy or pain. Yet, his life filled that room. Further up the avenue his wife was holding his newborn child. Life and death so close together, and love and hatred, and right and wrong, said something to me which I did not want to hear concerning man, concerning the life of man.

After the funeral, while I was downtown desperately celebrating my birthday, a Negro soldier, in the lobby of the Hotel Braddock, got into a fight with a white policeman over a Negro girl. Negro girls, white policemen, in or out of uniform, and Negro males—in or out of uniform—were part of the furniture of the lobby of the Hotel Braddock and this was certainly not the first time such an incident had occurred. It was destined, however, to receive an unprecedented publicity, for the fight between the policeman and the soldier ended with the shooting of the soldier. Rumor, flowing immediately to the streets outside, stated the soldier had been shot in the back, an instantaneous and revealing invention, and that the soldier had died protecting a Negro woman. The facts were somewhat different—for example, the soldier had not been shot in the back, and was not dead, and the girl seems to have been as dubious a symbol of womanhood as her white counterpart in Georgia usually is, but no one was interested in the facts. They preferred the invention because this invention expressed and corroborated their hates and fears so perfectly. It is just as well to remember that people are always doing this. Perhaps many of those legends, including Christianity, to which the world clings began their conquest of the world with just some such concerted surrender to distortion. The effect, in Harlem, of this particular legend was like the effect of a lit match in a tin of gasoline. The mob gathered before the doors of the Hotel Braddock simply began to swell and to spread in every direction, and Harlem exploded.

The mob did not cross the ghetto lines. It would have been easy, for example, to have gone over Morningside Park on the west side or to have crossed the Grand Central railroad tracks at 125th Street on the east side, to wreak havoc in white neighborhoods. The mob seems to have been mainly interested in something more potent and real than the white face, that is, in white power, and the principal damage done during the riot of the summer of 1943 was to white business establishments in Harlem. It might have been a far bloodier story, of course, if, at the hour the riot began, these establishments had still been open. From the Hotel Braddock the mob fanned out, east and west along 125th Street, and for the entire length of Lenox, Seventh, and Eighth avenues. Along each of these avenues, and along each major side street—116th, 125th, 135th, and so on—bars, stores, pawnshops, restaurants, even little luncheonettes had been smashed open and entered and looted—looted, it might be added, with more haste than efficiency. The shelves really looked as though a bomb had struck them. Cans of beans and soup and dog food, along with toilet paper, corn flakes, sardines and milk tumbled every which way, and abandoned cash registers and cases of beer leaned crazily out of the splintered windows and were strewn along the avenues. Sheets, blankets, and clothing of every description formed a kind of path, as though people had dropped them while running. I truly had not realized that Harlem *had* so many stores until I saw them all smashed open; the first time the word *wealth* ever entered my mind in relation to Harlem was when I saw it scattered in the streets. But one's first, incongruous impression of plenty was countered immediately by an impression of waste. None of this was doing anybody any good. It would have been better to have left the plate glass as it had been and the goods lying in the stores.

It would have been better, but it would also have been intolerable, for Harlem had needed something to smash. To smash something is the ghetto's chronic need. Most of the time it is the members of the ghetto who smash each other, and themselves. But as long as the ghetto walls are standing there will always come a moment when these outlets do not work. That summer, for example, it was not enough to get into a fight on Lenox Avenue, or curse out one's cronies in the barber shops. If ever, indeed, the violence which fills Harlem's churches, pool halls, and bars erupts outward in a more direct fashion, Harlem and its citizens are likely to vanish in an apocalyptic flood. That this is not likely to happen is due to a great many reasons, most hidden and powerful among them the Negro's real relation to the white American. This relation prohibits, simply, anything as uncomplicated and satisfactory as pure hatred. In order really to hate white people, one has to blot so much out of the mind —and the heart—that this hatred itself becomes an exhausting and self-destructive pose. But this does not mean, on the other hand, that love comes easily: the white world is too powerful, too complacent, too ready with gratuitous humiliation, and, above all, too ignorant and too innocent for that. One is absolutely forced to make perpetual qualifications and one's own reactions are always canceling each other out. It is this, really, which has driven so many people mad, both white and black. One is always in the position of having to decide between amputation and gangrene. Amputation is swift but time may prove that the amputation was not necessary—or one may delay the amputation too long. Gangrene is slow, but it is impossible to be sure that one is reading one's symptoms right. The idea of going through life as a cripple is more than one can bear, and equally unbearable is the risk of swelling up slowly, in agony, with poison. And the trouble, finally, is that the risks are real even if the choices do not exist.

"But as for me and my house," my father had said, "we will serve the Lord." I wondered, as we drove him to his resting place, what this line had meant for him. I had heard him preach it many times. I had preached it once myself, proudly giving it an interpretation different from my father's. Now the whole thing came back to me, as though my father and I were on our way to Sunday school and I were memorizing the golden text: *And if it seem evil unto you to serve the Lord, choose you this day whom you will serve; whether the gods which your fathers served that were on the other side of the flood, or the gods of the Amorites, in whose land ye dwell: but as for me and my house, we will serve the Lord.* I suspected in these familiar lines a meaning which had never been there for me before. All of my father's texts and songs, which I had decided were meaningless, were arranged before me at his death like empty bottles, waiting to hold the meaning which life would give them for me. This was his legacy: nothing is ever escaped. That bleakly memorable morning I hated the unbelievable streets and the Negroes and whites who had, equally, made them that way. But I knew that it was folly, as my father would have said, this bitterness was folly. It was necessary to hold on to the things that mattered. The dead man mattered, the new life mattered; blackness and whiteness did not matter; to believe that they did was to acquiesce in one's own destruction. Hatred, which could destroy so much, never failed to destroy the man who hated and this was an immutable law.

It began to seem that one would have to hold in the mind forever two ideas which seemed to be in opposition. The first idea was acceptance, the acceptance, totally without rancor, of life as it is, and men as they are: in the light of this idea, it goes without saying that injustice is a commonplace. But this did not mean that one could be complacent, for the second idea was of equal power: that one must never, in one's own life, accept these injustices as commonplace but must fight them with all one's strength. This fight begins, however, in the heart and it now had been laid to my charge to keep my own heart free of hatred and despair. This intimation made my heart heavy and, now that my father was irrecoverable, I wished that he had been beside me so that I could have searched his face for the answers which only the future would give me now.

NORMAN PODHORETZ

Norman Podhoretz was born in New York City and educated at Columbia College and Cambridge University, England, where he was a Fulbright Scholar and a Kellet Fellow. A precociously talented writer and critic, he was appointed editor of Commentary *in 1960, at the age of thirty. He has been a frequent contributor to magazines, has published a ten-year collection of his articles, entitled* Doings and Undoings: The Fifties and After in American Writing *(1964), and* Making It *(1968), a remarkably candid account of his rise in the world of the New York literary intelligentsia. The article reprinted below first appeared in* Commentary, *February 1963.*

My Negro Problem—and Ours

If we—and . . . I mean the relatively conscious whites and the relatively conscious blacks, who must, like lovers, insist on, or create, the consciousness of the others—do not falter in our duty now, we may be able, handful that we are, to end the racial nightmare, and achieve our country, and change the history of the world.

—JAMES BALDWIN

Two ideas puzzled me deeply as a child growing up in Brooklyn during the 1930's in what today would be called an integrated neighborhood. One of them was that all Jews were rich; the other was that all Negroes were persecuted. These ideas had appeared in print; therefore they must be true. My own experience and the evidence of my senses told me they were not true, but that only confirmed what a day-dreaming boy in the provinces—for the lower-class neighborhoods of New York belong as surely to the provinces as any rural town in North Dakota—discovers very early: *his* experience is unreal and the evidence of his senses is not to be trusted. Yet even a boy with a head full of fantasies incongruously synthesized out of Hollywood movies and English novels cannot altogether deny the reality of his own experience—especially when there is so much deprivation in that experience. Nor can he altogether gainsay the evidence of his own senses—especially such evidence of the senses as comes from being repeatedly beaten up, robbed, and in general hated, terrorized, and humiliated.

And so for a long time I was puzzled to think that Jews were supposed to be rich when the only Jews I knew were poor, and that Negroes were supposed to be persecuted when it was the Negroes who were doing the only persecuting I knew about—and doing it, moreover, to *me.* During the early years of the war, when my older sister joined a left-wing youth organization, I remember my astonishment at hearing her passionately denounce my father for thinking that Jews were worse off than Negroes. To me, at the age of twelve, it seemed very clear that Negroes were better off than Jews—indeed, than *all* whites. A city boy's world is contained within three or four square blocks, and in my world it was the whites, the Italians and Jews, who feared the Negroes, not the other way around. The Negroes were tougher than we were, more ruthless, and on the whole they were better athletes. What could it mean, then, to say that they were badly off and that we were more fortunate? Yet my sister's opinions, like print, were sacred, and when she told me about exploitation and economic forces I believed her. I believed her, but I was still afraid of Negroes. And I still hated them with all my heart.

It had not always been so—that much I can recall from early childhood. When did it start, this fear and this hatred? There was a kindergarten in the local public school, and given the character of the neighborhood, at least half of the children in my class must have been Negroes. Yet I have no memory of being aware of color differences at that age, and I know from observing my own children that they attribute no significance to such differences even when they begin noticing them. I think there was a day—first grade? second grade?—when my best friend Carl hit me on the way home from school and announced that he wouldn't play with me any more because I had killed Jesus. When I ran home to my mother crying for an explanation, she told me not to pay any attention to such foolishness, and then in Yiddish she cursed the *goyim* and the *schwartzes,* the *schwartzes* and the *goyim.* Carl, it turned out, was a *schwartze,* and so was added a third to the categories into which people were mysteriously divided.

Sometimes I wonder whether this is a true memory at all. It is blazingly vivid, but perhaps it never happened: can anyone really remember back to the age of six? There is no uncertainty in my mind, however, about the years that followed. Carl and I hardly ever spoke, though we met in school every day up through the eighth or ninth grade. There would be embarrassed moments of catching his eye or of his catching mine—for whatever it was that had attracted us to one another as very small children remained alive in spite of the fantastic barrier of hostility that had grown up between us, suddenly and out of nowhere. Nevertheless, friendship would have been impossible, and even if it had been possible, it would have been unthinkable. About that, there was nothing anyone could do by the time we were eight years old.

Item: The orphanage across the street is torn down, a city housing project begins to rise in its place, and on the marvelous vacant lot next to the old orphanage they are building a playground. Much excitement and anticipation as Opening Day draws near. Mayor LaGuardia himself comes to dedicate this great gesture of public benevolence. He speaks of neighborliness and borrowing cups of sugar, and of the playground he says that children of all races, colors, and creeds will learn to live together in harmony. A week later, some of us are swatting flies on the playground's inadequate little ball field. A gang of Negro kids, pretty much our own age, enter from the other side and order us out of the park. We refuse, proudly and indignantly, with superb masculine fervor. There is a fight, they win, and we retreat, half whimpering, half with bravado. My first nauseating experience of cowardice. And my first appalled realization that there are people in the world who do not seem to be afraid of anything, who act as though they have nothing to lose. Thereafter the playground becomes a battleground, sometimes quiet, sometimes the scene of athletic competition between Them and Us. But rocks are thrown as often as baseballs. Gradually we abandon the place and use the streets instead. The streets are safer, though we do not admit this to ourselves. We are not, after all, sissies—that most dreaded epithet of an American boyhood.

Item: I am standing alone in front of the building in which I live. It is late afternoon and getting dark. That day in school the teacher had asked a surly Negro boy named Quentin a question he was unable to answer. As usual I had waved my arm eagerly ("Be a good boy, get good marks, be smart, go to college, become a doctor") and, the right answer bursting from my lips, I was held up lovingly by the teacher as an example to the class. I had seen Quentin's face—a very dark, very cruel, very Oriental-looking face—harden, and there had been enough threat in his eyes to make me run all the way home for fear that he might catch me outside.

Now, standing idly in front of my own house, I see him approaching from the project accompanied by his little brother who is carrying a baseball bat and wearing a grin of malicious anticipation. As in a nightmare, I am trapped. The surroundings are secure and familiar, but terror is suddenly present and there is no one around to help. I am locked to the spot. I will not cry out or run away like a sissy, and I stand there, my heart wild, my throat clogged. He walks up, hurls the familiar epithet ("Hey, mo'f——r"), and to my surprise only pushes me. It is a violent push, but not a punch. A push is not as serious as a punch. Maybe I can still back out without entirely losing my dignity. Maybe I can still say, "Hey, c'mon Quentin, whaddya wanna do *that* for. I dint do nothin' to *you*," and walk away, not too rapidly. Instead, before I can stop myself, I push him back—a token gesture—and I say, "Cut that out, I don't wanna fight, I ain't got nothin' to fight about." As I turn to walk back into the building, the corner of my eye catches the motion of the bat his little brother has handed him. I try to duck, but the bat crashes colored lights into my head.

The next thing I know, my mother and sister are standing over me, both of them hysterical. My sister—she who was later to join the "progressive" youth organization—is shouting for the police and screaming imprecations at those dirty little black bastards. They take me upstairs, the doctor comes, the police come. I tell them that the boy who did it was a stranger, that he had been trying to get money from me. They do not believe me, but I am too scared to give them Quentin's name. When I return to school a few days later, Quentin avoids my eyes. He knows that I have not squealed, and he is ashamed. I try to feel proud, but in my heart I know that it was fear of what his friends might do to me that had kept me silent, and not the code of the street.

Item: There is an athletic meet in which the whole of our junior high school is participating. I am in one of the seventh-grade rapid-advance classes, and "segregation" has now set in with a vengeance. In the last three or four years of the elementary school from which we have just graduated, each grade had been divided into three classes, according to "intelligence." (In the earlier grades the divisions had either been arbitrary or else unrecognized by us as having anything to do with brains.) These divisions by IQ, or however it was arranged, had resulted in a preponderance of Jews in the "1" classes and a corresponding preponderance of Negroes in the "3's," with the Italians split unevenly along the spectrum. At least a few Negroes had always made the "1's," just as there had always been a few Jewish kids among the "3's" and more among the "2's" (where Italians dominated). But the junior high's rapid-advance class of which I am now a member is overwhelmingly Jewish and entirely white—except for a shy lonely Negro girl with light skin and reddish hair.

The athletic meet takes place in a city-owned stadium far from the school. It is an important event to which a whole day is given over. The winners are to get those precious little medallions stamped with the New York City emblem that can be screwed into a belt and that prove the wearer to be a distinguished personage. I am a fast runner, and so I am assigned the position of anchor man on my class's team in the relay race. There are three other seventh-grade teams in the race, two of them all Negro, as ours is all white. One of the all-Negro teams is very tall—their anchor man waiting silently next to me on the line looks years older than I am, and I do not recognize him. He is the first to get the baton and crosses the finishing line in a walk. Our team comes in second, but a few minutes later we are declared the winners, for it has been discovered that the anchor man on the first-place team is not a member of the class. We are awarded the medallions, and the following day our home-room teacher makes a speech about how proud she is of us for being superior athletes as well as superior students. We want to believe that we deserve the praise, but we know that we could not have won even if the other class had not cheated.

That afternoon, walking home, I am waylaid and surrounded by five Negroes, among whom is the anchor man of the disqualified team. "Gimme my medal, mo'f——r," he grunts. I do not have it with me and I tell him so. "Anyway, it ain't yours," I say foolishly. He calls me a liar on both counts and pushes me up against the wall on which we sometimes play handball. "Gimme my mo'f——n' medal," he says again. I repeat that I have left it home. "Le's search the li'l mo'f——r," one of them suggests, "he prolly got it *hid* in his mo'f——n' *pants.*" My panic is now unmanageable. (How many times had I been surrounded like this and asked in soft tones, "Len' me a nickle, boy." How many times had I been called a liar for pleading poverty and pushed around, or searched, or beaten up, unless there happened to be someone in the marauding gang like Carl who liked me across that enormous divide of hatred and who would therefore say, "Aaah, c'mon, le's git someone else, *this* boy ain't got no money on 'im.") I scream at them through tears of rage and self-contempt, "Keep your f——n' filthy lousy black hands offa me! I swear I'll get the cops." This is all they need to hear, and the five of them set upon me. They bang me around, mostly in the stomach and on the arms and shoulders, and when several adults loitering near the candy store down the block notice what is going on and begin to shout, they run off and away.

I do not tell my parents about the incident. My team-mates, who have also been waylaid, each by a gang led by his opposite number from the disqualified team, have had their medallions taken from them, and they never squeal either. For days, I walk home in terror, expecting to be caught again, but nothing happens. The medallion is put away into a drawer, never to be worn by anyone.

Obviously experiences like these have always been a common feature of childhood life in working-class and immigrant neighborhoods, and Negroes do not necessarily figure in them. Wherever, and in whatever combination, they have lived together in the cities, kids of different groups have been at war, beating up and being beaten up: micks against kikes against wops against spicks against polacks. And even relatively homogeneous areas have not been spared the warring of the young: one block against another, one gang (called in my day, in a pathetic effort at gentility, an "S.A.C.," or social-athletic club) against another. But the

Negro-white conflict had—and no doubt still has—a special intensity and was conducted with a ferocity unmatched by intramural white battling.

In my own neighborhood, a good deal of animosity existed between the Italian kids (most of whose parents were immigrants from Sicily) and the Jewish kids (who came largely from East European immigrant families). Yet everyone had friends, sometimes close friends, in the other "camp," and we often visited one another's strange-smelling houses, if not for meals, then for glasses of milk, and occasionally for some special event like a wedding or a wake. If it happened that we divided into warring factions and did battle, it would invariably be half-hearted and soon patched up. Our parents, to be sure, had nothing to do with one another and were mutually suspicious and hostile. But we, the kids, who all spoke Yiddish or Italian at home, were Americans, or New Yorkers, or Brooklyn boys: we shared a culture, the culture of the street, and at least for a while this culture proved to be more powerful than the opposing cultures of the home.

Why, *why* should it have been so different as between the Negroes and us? How was it borne in upon us so early, white and black alike, that we were enemies beyond any possibility of reconciliation? Why did we hate one another so?

I suppose if I tried, I could answer those questions more or less adequately from the perspective of what I have since learned. I could draw upon James Baldwin—what better witness is there?—to describe the sense of entrapment that poisons the soul of the Negro with hatred for the white man whom he knows to be his jailer. On the other side, if I wanted to understand how the white man comes to hate the Negro, I could call upon the psychologists who have spoken of the guilt that white Americans feel toward Negroes and that turns into hatred for lack of acknowledging itself as guilt. These are plausible answers and certainly there is truth in them. Yet when I think back upon my own experience of the Negro and his of me, I find myself troubled and puzzled, much as I was as a child when I heard that all Jews were rich and all Negroes persecuted. How could the Negroes in my neighborhood have regarded the whites across the street and around the corner as jailers? On the whole, the whites were not so poor as the Negroes, but they were quite poor enough, and the years were years of Depression. As for white hatred of the Negro, how could guilt have had anything to do with it? What share had these Italian and Jewish immigrants in the enslavement of the Negro? What share had they—downtrodden people themselves breaking their own necks to eke out a living—in the exploitation of the Negro?

No, I cannot believe that we hated each other back there in Brooklyn because they thought of us as jailers and we felt guilty toward them. But does it matter, given the fact that we all went through an unrepresentative confrontation? I think it matters profoundly, for if we managed the job of hating each other so well without benefit of the aids to hatred that are supposedly at the root of this madness everywhere else, it must mean that the madness is not yet properly understood. I am far from pretending that I understand it, but I would insist that no view of the problem will begin to approach the truth unless it can account for a case like the one I have been trying to describe. Are the elements of any such view available to us?

At least two, I would say, are. One of them is a point we frequently come upon in the work of James Baldwin, and the other is a related point always stressed by psychologists who have studied the mechanisms of prejudice. Baldwin tells us that one of the reasons Negroes hate the white man is that the white man refuses to *look* at him: the Negro knows that in white eyes all Negroes are alike; they are faceless and therefore not altogether human. The psychologists, in their turn, tell us that the white man hates the Negro because he tends to project those wild impulses that he fears in himself onto an alien group which he then punishes with his contempt. What Baldwin does *not* tell us, however, is that the principle of facelessness is a two-way street and can operate in both directions with no difficulty at all. Thus, in my neighborhood in Brooklyn, *I* was as faceless to the Negroes as they were to me, and if they hated me because I never looked at them, I must also have hated them for never looking at *me*. To the Negroes, my white skin was enough to define me as the enemy, and in a war it is only the uniform that counts and not the person.

So with the mechanism of projection that the psychologists talk about: it too works in both directions at once. There is no question that the psychologists are right about what the Negro represents symbolically to the white man. For me as a child the life lived on the other side of the playground and down the block on Ralph Avenue seemed the very embodiment of the values of the street—free, independent, reckless, brave, masculine, erotic. I put the word "erotic" last, though it is usually stressed above all others, because in fact it came last, in consciousness as in importance. What mainly counted for me about Negro kids of my own age was that they were "bad boys." There were plenty of bad boys among the whites—this was, after all, a neighborhood with a long tradition of crime as a career open to aspiring talents—but the Negroes were *really* bad, bad in a way that beckoned to one, and made one feel inadequate. *We* all went home every day for a lunch of spinach-and-potatoes; *they* roamed around during lunch hour, munching on candy bars. In winter *we* had to wear itchy woolen hats and mittens and cumbersome galoshes; *they* were bare-headed and loose as they pleased. *We* rarely played hookey, or got into serious trouble in school, for all our street-corner bravado; *they* were defiant, forever staying out (to do what delicious things?), forever making disturbances in class and in the halls, forever being sent to the principal and returning uncowed. But most important of all, they were *tough;* beautifully, enviably tough, not giving a damn for anyone or anything. To hell with the teacher, the truant officer, the cop; to hell with the whole of the adult world that held *us* in its grip and that we never had the courage to rebel against except sporadically and in petty ways.

This is what I saw and envied and feared in the Negro: this is what finally made him faceless to me, though some of it, of course, was actually there. (The psychologists also tell us that the alien group which becomes the object of a projection will tend to respond by trying to live up to what is expected of them.) But what, on his side, did the Negro see in me that made me faceless to *him*? Did he envy me my lunches of spinach-and-potatoes and my itchy woolen caps and my prudent behavior in the face of authority, as I envied him his noon-time candy bars and his bare head in winter and his magnificent rebelliousness? Did those lunches and caps spell for him the prospect of power and riches in the future? Did they mean that there were possibilities open to me that were denied to him? Very likely they did. But if so, one also supposes that he feared the impulses within himself toward submission to authority no less power-fully than I feared the impulses in myself toward defiance. If I represented the jailer to him, it was not because I was oppressing him or keeping him down: it was because I symbolized for him the dangerous and probably pointless temptation toward greater repression, just as he symbolized for me the equally perilous tug toward greater freedom. I personally was to be rewarded for this repression with a new and better life in the future, but how many of my friends paid an even higher price and were given only gall in return.

We have it on the authority of James Baldwin that all Negroes hate whites. I am trying to suggest that on their side all whites—all American whites, that is—are sick in their feelings about Negroes. There are Negroes, no doubt, who would say that Baldwin is wrong, but I suspect them of being less honest than he is, just as I suspect whites of self-deception who tell me they have no special feeling toward Negroes. Special feelings about color are a contagion to which white Americans seem susceptible even when there is nothing in their background to account for the susceptibility. Thus everywhere we look today in the North, we find the curious phenomenon of white middle-class liberals with no previous personal experience of Negroes—people to whom Negroes have always been faceless in virtue rather than faceless in vice —discovering that their abstract commitment to the cause of Negro rights will not stand the test of a direct confrontation. We find such people fleeing in droves to the suburbs as the Negro population in the inner city grows; and when they stay in the city we find them sending their children to private school rather than to the "integrated" public school in the neighborhood. We find them resisting the demand that gerrymandered school districts be re-zoned for the purpose of overcoming de facto segregation; we find them judiciously considering whether the Negroes (for their own good, of course) are not perhaps pushing too hard; we find them clucking their tongues over Negro militancy; we find them speculat-ing on the question of whether there may not, after all, be something in the theory that the races are biologically different; we find them saying that it will take a very long time for Negroes to achieve full equality, no matter what anyone does; we find them deploring the rise of black nationalism and expressing the solemn hope that the leaders of the Negro community will discover ways of containing the impatience and incipient violence within the Negro ghettos.[1]

But that is by no means the whole story; there is also the phenomenon of what Kenneth Rexroth once called "crow-jimism." There are the broken-down white boys like Vivaldo Moore in Baldwin's *Another Country* who go to Harlem in search of sex or simply to brush up against something that looks like primitive vitality, and who are so often punished by the Negroes they meet for crimes that they would have been the last ever to commit and of which they themselves have been as sorry victims as any of the Negroes who take it out on them. There are the writers and intellectuals and artists who romanticize Negroes and pander to them, assuming a guilt that is not properly theirs. And there are all the white liberals who permit Negroes to blackmail them into adopting a double standard of moral judgment, and who lend themselves—again assuming the responsibility for crimes they never committed—to cunning and contemptuous exploitation by Negroes they employ or try to befriend.

And what about me? What kind of feelings do I have about Negroes today? What happened to me, from Brooklyn, who grew up fearing and envying and hating Negroes? Now that Brooklyn is behind me, do I fear them and envy them and hate them still? The answer is yes, but not in the same proportions and certainly not in the same way. I now live on the upper west side of Manhattan, where there are many Negroes and many Puerto Ricans, and there are nights when I experience the old apprehensiveness again, and there are streets that I avoid when I am walking in the dark, as there were streets that I avoided when I was a child. I find that I am not afraid of Puerto Ricans, but I cannot restrain my nervousness whenever I pass a group of Negroes standing in front of a bar or sauntering down the street. I know now, as I did not know when I was a child, that power is on my side, that the police are working for me and not for them. And knowing this I feel ashamed and guilty, like the good liberal I have grown up to be. Yet the twinges of fear and the resentment they bring and the self-contempt they arouse are not to be gainsaid.

But envy? Why envy? And hatred? Why hatred? Here again the intensities have lessened and everything has been complicated and qualified by the guilts and the resulting over-compensations that are the heritage of the enlightened middle-class world of which I am now a member. Yet just as in childhood I envied Negroes for what seemed to me their superior masculinity, so I envy them today for what seems to me their superior physical grace and beauty. I have come to value physical grace very highly, and I am now capable of aching with all my being when I watch a Negro couple on the dance floor, or a Negro playing baseball or basketball. They are on the kind of terms with their own bodies that I should

---

[1] For an account of developments like these, see "The White Liberal's Retreat" by Murray Friedman in the January 1963 *Atlantic Monthly.*

like to be on with mine, and for that precious quality they seem blessed to me.

The hatred I still feel for Negroes is the hardest of all the old feelings to face or admit, and it is the most hidden and the most overlarded by the conscious attitudes into which I have succeeded in willing myself. It no longer has, as for me it once did, any cause or justification (except, perhaps, that I am constantly being denied my right to an honest expression of the things I earned the right as a child to feel). How, then, do I know that this hatred has never entirely disappeared? I know it from the insane rage that can stir in me at the thought of Negro anti-Semitism; I know it from the disgusting prurience that can stir in me at the sight of a mixed couple; and I know it from the violence that can stir in me whenever I encounter that special brand of paranoid touchiness to which many Negroes are prone.

This, then, is where I am; it is not exactly where I think all other white liberals are, but it cannot be so very far away either. And it is because I am convinced that we white Americans are—for whatever reason, it no longer matters—so twisted and sick in our feelings about Negroes that I despair of the present push toward integration. If the pace of progress were not a factor here, there would perhaps be no cause for despair: time and the law and even the international political situation are on the side of the Negroes, and ultimately, therefore, victory—of a sort, anyway— must come. But from everything we have learned from observers who ought to know, pace has become as important to the Negroes as substance. They want equality and they want it *now,* and the white world is yielding to their demand only as much and as fast as it is absolutely being compelled to do. The Negroes know this in the most concrete terms imaginable, and it is thus becoming increasingly difficult to buy them off with rhetoric and promises and pious assurances of support. And so within the Negro community we find more and more people declaring— as Harold R. Isaacs recently put it in these pages[2]—that they want *out:* people who say that integration will never come, or that it will take a hundred or a thousand years to come, or that it will come at too high a price in suffering and struggle for the pallid and sodden life of the American middle class that at the very best it may bring.

The most numerous, influential, and dangerous movement that has grown out of Negro despair with the goal of integration is, of course, the Black Muslims. This movement, whatever else we may say about it, must be credited with one enduring achievement: it inspired James Baldwin to write an essay[3] which deserves to be placed among the classics of our language. Everything Baldwin has ever been trying to tell us is distilled here into a statement of overwhelming persuasiveness and prophetic

[2]"Integration and the Negro Mood," December 1962.
[3]Originally published last November in the *New Yorker* under the title "Letter From a Region in My Mind," it has just been reprinted (along with a new introduction) by Dial Press under the title *The Fire Next Time.*

magnificence. Baldwin's message is and always has been simple. It is this: "Color is not a human or personal reality; it is a political reality." And Baldwin's demand is correspondingly simple: color must be forgotten, lest we all be smited with a vengeance "that does not really depend on, and cannot really be executed by, any person or organization, and that cannot be prevented by any police force or army: historical vengeance, a cosmic vengeance based on the law that we recognize when we say, 'Whatever goes up must come down.'" The Black Muslims Baldwin portrays as a sign and a warning to the intransigent white world. They come to proclaim how deep is the Negro's disaffection with the white world and all its works, and Baldwin implies that no American Negro can fail to respond somewhere in his being to their message: that the white man is the devil, that Allah has doomed him to destruction, and that the black man is about to inherit the earth. Baldwin of course knows that this nightmare inversion of the racism from which the black man has suffered can neither win nor even point to the neighborhood in which victory might be located. For in his view the neighborhood of victory lies in exactly the opposite direction: the transcendence of color through love.

Yet the tragic fact is that love is not the answer to hate—not in the world of politics, at any rate. Color is indeed a political rather than a human or a personal reality and if politics (which is to say power) has made it into a human and a personal reality, then only politics (which is to say power) can unmake it once again. But the way of politics is slow and bitter, and as impatience on the one side is matched by a setting of the jaw on the other, we move closer and closer to an explosion and blood may yet run in the streets.

Will this madness in which we are all caught never find a resting-place? Is there never to be an end to it? In thinking about the Jews I have often wondered whether their survival as a distinct group was worth one hair on the head of a single infant. Did the Jews have to survive so that six million innocent people should one day be burned in the ovens of Auschwitz? It is a terrible question and no one, not God himself, could ever answer it to my satisfaction. And when I think about the Negroes in America and about the image of integration as a state in which the Negroes would take their rightful place as another of the protected minorities in a pluralistic society, I wonder whether they really believe in their hearts that such a state can actually be attained, and if so *why* they should wish to survive as a distinct group. I think I know why the Jews once wished to survive (though I am less certain as to why we still do): they not only believed that God had given them no choice, but they were tied to a memory of past glory and a dream of imminent redemption. What does the American Negro have that might correspond to this? His past is a stigma, his color is a stigma, and his vision of the future is the hope of erasing the stigma by making color irrelevant, by making it disappear as a fact of consciousness.

I share this hope, but I cannot see how it will ever be realized unless color does *in fact* disappear: and that means not integration, it means assimilation, it means—let the brutal word come out—miscegenation. The Black Muslims, like their racist counterparts in the white world, accuse the "so-called Negro leaders" of secretly pursuing miscegenation as a goal. The racists are wrong, but I wish they were right, for I believe that the wholesale merging of the two races is the most desirable alternative for everyone concerned. I am not claiming that this alternative can be pursued programmatically or that it is immediately feasible as a solution; obviously there are even greater barriers to its achievement than to the achievement of integration. What I am saying, however, is that in my opinion the Negro problem can be solved in this country in no other way.

I have told the story of my own twisted feelings about Negroes here, and of how they conflict with the moral convictions I have since developed, in order to assert that such feelings must be acknowledged as honestly as possible so that they can be controlled and ultimately disregarded in favor of the convictions. It is *wrong* for a man to suffer because of the color of his skin. Beside that clichéd proposition of liberal thought, what argument can stand and be respected? If the arguments are the arguments of feeling, they must be made to yield; and one's own soul is not the worst place to begin working a huge social transformation. Not so long ago, it used to be asked of white liberals, "Would you like your sister to marry one?" When I was a boy and my sister was still unmarried, I would certainly have said no to that question. But now I am a man, my sister is already married, and I have daughters. If I were to be asked today whether I would like a daughter of mine "to marry one," I would have to answer: "No, I wouldn't *like* it at all. I would rail and rave and rant and tear my hair. And then I hope I would have the courage to curse myself for raving and ranting, and to give her my blessing. How dare I withhold it at the behest of the child I once was and against the man I now have a duty to be?"

ALICE WALKER

Alice Walker is probably tired of the descriptive phrase "brilliant young black woman writer." Before she turned thirty, she had published five books, was teaching literature at two colleges, and was on the board of trustees of Sarah Lawrence College.

She was born in 1944 in Eatonton, Georgia. She attended Spelman College for two years, then graduated from Sarah Lawrence in 1965. From 1968 to 1970 she taught writing and black literature at Jackson State and Tougaloo in Mississippi; in 1972 she became lecturer in writing

*and literature at both Wellesley College and the University of
Massachusetts.*

Her writings, especially her novel The Third Life of Grange
Copeland *(1970), explore family relationships—the unity and hostility
felt within black families because of outside social forces in racist America.
She has also written two books of poems,* Once *(1968) and*
Revolutionary Petunias *(1973); a biography of Langston Hughes
(1973); and a collection of short stories,* In Love and Trouble:
Stories of Black Women *(1973). She is now working on another novel
and doing research on the past two centuries of black women writers. The
prize-winning essay we reprint here first appeared in* The American
Scholar, *Autumn 1967.*

The Civil Rights Movement: What Good Was It?

Someone said recently to an old black lady from Mississippi, whose legs
had been badly mangled by local police who arrested her for "disturbing
the peace," that the civil rights movement was dead, and asked, since it
was dead, what she thought about it. The old lady replied, hobbling out
of his presence on her cane, that the civil rights movement was like
herself, "if it's dead, it shore ain't ready to lay down!"

This old lady is a legendary freedom fighter in her small town in the
Delta. She has been severely mistreated for insisting on her rights as an
American citizen. She has been beaten for singing movement songs,
placed in solitary confinement in prisons for talking about freedom, and
placed on bread and water for praying aloud to God for her jailers'
deliverance. For such a woman the civil rights movement will never be
over as long as her skin is black. It also will never be over for twenty
million others with the same "affliction," for whom the movement can
never "lay down," no matter how it is killed by the press and made dead
and buried by the white American public. As long as one black American
survives, the struggle for equality with other Americans must also survive.
This is a debt we owe to those blameless hostages we leave to the future,
our children.

Still, white liberals and deserting civil rights sponsors are quick to
justify their disaffection from the movement by claiming that it is all over.
"And since it is over," they will ask, "would someone kindly tell me what
has been gained by it?" They then list statistics supposedly showing how
much more advanced segregation is now than ten years ago—in schools,
housing, jobs. They point to a gain in conservative politicians during the
last few years. They speak of ghetto riots and of the recent survey that
shows that most policemen are admittedly too anti-Negro to do their jobs
in ghetto areas fairly and effectively. They speak of every area that has

been touched by the civil rights movement as somehow or other going to pieces.

They rarely talk, however, about human attitudes among Negroes that have undergone terrific changes just during the past seven to ten years (not to mention all those years when there was a movement and only the Negroes knew about it). They seldom speak of changes in personal lives because of the influence of people in the movement. They see general failure and few, if any, individual gains.

They do not understand what it is that keeps the movement from "laying down" and Negroes from reverting to their former *silent* second-class status. They have apparently never stopped to wonder why it is always the white man—on his radio and in his newspaper and on his television—who says that the movement is dead. If a Negro were audacious enough to make such a claim, his fellows might hanker to see him shot. The movement is dead to the white man because it no longer interests him. And it no longer interests him because he can afford to be uninterested: he does not have to live by it, with it, or for it, as Negroes must. He can take a rest from the news of beatings, killings and arrests that reach him from North and South—if his skin is white. Negroes cannot now and will never be able to take a rest from the injustices that plague them for they—not the white man—are the target.

Perhaps it is naïve to be thankful that the movement "saved" a large number of individuals and gave them something to live for, even if it did not provide them with everything they wanted. (Materially, it provided them with precious little that they wanted.) When a movement awakens people to the possibilities of life, it seems unfair to frustrate them by then denying what they had thought was offered. But what was offered? What was promised? What was it all about? What good did it do? Would it have been better, as some have suggested, to leave the Negro people as they were, unawakened, unallied with one another, unhopeful about what to expect for their children in some future world?

I do not think so. If knowledge of my condition is all the freedom I get from a "freedom movement," it is better than unawareness, forgottenness and hopelessness, the existence that is like the existence of a beast. Man only truly lives by knowing, otherwise he simply performs, copying the daily habits of others, but conceiving nothing of his creative possibilities as a man, and accepting someone else's superiority and his own misery.

When we are children, growing up in our parents' care, we await the spark from the outside world. Sometimes our parents provide it—if we are lucky—sometimes it comes from another source far from home. We sit, paralyzed, surrounded by our anxiety and dread, hoping we will not have to grow up into the narrow world and ways we see about us. We are hungry for a life that turns us on; we yearn for a knowledge of living that will save us from our innocuous lives that resemble death. We look for signs in every strange event; we search for heroes in every unknown face.

It was just six years ago that I began to be alive. I had, of course, been living before—for I am now twenty-three—but I did not really know it. And I did not know it because nobody told me that I—a pensive, yearning, typical high-school senior, but Negro—existed in the minds of others as I existed in my own. Until that time my mind was locked apart from the outer contours and complexion of my body as if it and the body were strangers. The mind possessed both thought and spirit—I wanted to be an author or a scientist—which the color of the body denied. I had never seen myself and existed as a statistic exists, or as a phantom. In the white world I walked, less real to them than a shadow; and being young and well-hidden among the slums, among people who also did not exist—either in books or in films or in the government of their own lives—I waited to be called to life. And, by a miracle, I was called.

There was a commotion in our house that night in 1960. We had managed to buy our first television set. It was battered and overpriced, but my mother had gotten used to watching the afternoon soap operas at the house where she worked as maid, and nothing could satisfy her on days when she did not work but a continuation of her "stories." So she pinched pennies and bought a set.

I remained listless through her "stories," tales of pregnancy, abortion, hypocrisy, infidelity and alcoholism. All these men and women were white and lived in houses with servants, long staircases that they floated down, patios where liquor was served four times a day to "relax" them. But my mother, with her swollen feet eased out of her shoes, her heavy body relaxed in our only comfortable chair, watched each movement of the smartly coiffed women, heard each word, pounced upon each innuendo and inflection, and for the duration of these "stories" she saw herself as one of them. She placed herself in every scene she saw, with her braided hair turned blonde, her two hundred pounds compressed into a sleek size seven dress, her rough dark skin smooth and *white*. Her husband became dark and handsome, talented, witty, urbane, charming. And when she turned to look at my father sitting near her in his sweat shirt with his smelly feet raised on the bed to "air," there was always a tragic look of surprise on her face. Then she would sigh and go out to the kitchen looking lost and unsure of herself. My mother, a truly great woman—who raised eight children of her own and half a dozen of the neighbors' without a single complaint—was convinced that she did not exist compared to "them." She subordinated her soul to theirs and became a faithful and timid supporter of the "Beautiful White People." Once she asked me, in a moment of vicarious pride and despair, if I didn't think that "they" were "jest naturally smarter, prettier, better." My mother asked this; a woman who never got rid of any of her children, never cheated on my father, was never a hypocrite if she could help it, and never even tasted liquor. She could not even bring herself to blame "them" for making her believe what they wanted her to believe: that if she did not look like them, think like them, be sophisticated and corrupt-for-comfort's-sake like them, she was a nobody. Black was not a color on my mother, it was a shield that made her invisible. The heart that beat out its life in the great shadow cast by the American white people never knew that it was really "good."

Of course, the people who wrote the soap opera scripts always made the Negro maids in them steadfast, trusty and wise in a home-remedial sort of way; but my mother, a maid for nearly forty years, never once identified herself with the scarcely glimpsed black servant's face beneath the ruffled cap. Like everyone else, in her daydreams at least, she thought she was free.

Six years ago, after half-heartedly watching my mother's soap operas and wondering whether there wasn't something more to be asked of life, the civil rights movement came into my life. Like a good omen for the future, the face of Dr. Martin Luther King, Jr., was the first black face I saw on our new television screen. And, as in a fairy tale, my soul was stirred by the meaning for me of his mission—at the time he was being rather ignominiously dumped into a police van for having led a protest march in Alabama—and I fell in love with the sober and determined face of the movement. The singing of "We Shall Overcome"—that song betrayed by nonbelievers in it—rang for the first time in my ears. The influence that my mother's soap operas might have had on me became impossible. The life of Dr. King, seeming bigger and more miraculous than the man himself, because of all he had done and suffered, offered a pattern of strength and sincerity I felt I could trust. He had suffered much because of his simple belief in nonviolence, love and brotherhood. Perhaps the majority of men could not be reached through these beliefs, but because Dr. King kept trying to reach them in spite of danger to himself and his family, I saw in him the hero for whom I had waited so long.

What Dr. King promised was not a ranch-style house and an acre of manicured lawn for every black man, but jail and finally freedom. He did not promise two cars for every family, but the courage one day for all families everywhere to walk without shame and unafraid on their own feet. He did not say that one day it will be us chasing prospective buyers out of our prosperous well-kept neighborhoods, or in other ways exhibiting our snobbery and ignorance as all other ethnic groups before us have done; what he said was that we had a right to live anywhere in this country we chose, and a right to a meaningful well-paying job to provide us with the upkeep of our homes. He did not say we had to become carbon copies of the white American middle-class; but he did say we had the right to become whatever we wanted to become.

Because of the movement, because of an awakened faith in the newness and imagination of the human spirit, because of "black and white together"—for the first time in our history in some human relationship on and off TV—because of the beatings, the arrests, the hell of battle during the past years, I have fought harder for my life and for a chance to be myself, to be something more than a shadow or a number, than I have ever done before in my life. Before there had seemed to be no real reason for struggling beyond the effort for daily bread. Now there was a chance at that other that Jesus meant when He said we could not live by bread alone.

I have fought and kicked and fasted and prayed and cursed and cried myself to the point of existing. It has been like being born again, literally. Just "knowing" has meant everything to me. Knowing has pushed me out into the world, into college, into places, into people.

Part of what existence means to me is knowing the difference between what I am now and what I was then. It is being capable of looking after myself intellectually as well as financially. It is being able to tell when I am being wronged and by whom. It means being awake to protect myself and the ones I love. It means being a part of the world community, and being *alert* to which part it is that I have joined, and knowing how to change to another part if that part does not suit me. To know is to exist; to exist is to be involved, to move about, to see the world with my own eyes. This, at least, the movement has given me.

The hippies and other nihilists would have me believe that it is all the same whether the people in Mississippi have a movement behind them or not. Once they have their rights, they say, they will run all over themselves trying to be just like everybody else. They will be well-fed, complacent about things of the spirit, emotionless, and without that marvelous humanity and "soul" that the movement has seen them practice time and time again. What has the movement done, they ask, with the few people it has supposedly helped? Got them white-collar jobs, moved them into standardized ranch houses in white neighborhoods, given them intellectual accents to go with their nondescript gray flannel suits? "What are these people now?" they ask. And then they answer themselves, "Nothings!"

I would find this reasoning—which I have heard many, many times, from hippies and nonhippies alike—amusing, if I did not also consider it serious. For I think it is a delusion, a copout, an excuse to disassociate themselves from a world in which they feel too little has been changed or gained. The real question, however, it appears to me, is not whether poor people will adopt the middle-class mentality once they are well-fed, rather, it is whether they will ever be well-fed enough to be able to choose whatever mentality they think will suit them. The lack of a movement did not keep my mother from *wishing* herself bourgeois in her daydreams.

There is widespread starvation in Mississippi. In my own state of Georgia there are more hungry families than Lester Maddox would like to admit—or even see fed. I went to school with children who ate red dirt. The movement has prodded and pushed some liberal senators into pressuring the government for food so that the hungry may eat. Food stamps that were two dollars and out of the reach of many families not long ago have been reduced to fifty cents. The price is still out of the reach of some families, and the government, it seems to a lot of people, could spare enough free food to feed its own people. It angers people in the movement that it does not; they point to the billions in wheat we send free each year to countries abroad. Their government's slowness while people are hungry, its unwillingness to believe that there are Americans starving, its stingy cutting of the price of food stamps, make many civil rights workers throw up their hands in disgust. But they do not give up. They do not withdraw into the world of psychedelia. They apply what pressure they can to make the government give away food to hungry people. They do not plan so far ahead in their disillusionment with society that they can see these starving families buying identical ranch-style houses and sending their snobbish children to Bryn Mawr and Yale. They take first things first and try to get them fed.

They do not consider it their business, in any case, to say what kind of life the people they help must lead. How one lives is, after all, one of the rights left to the individual—when and if he has opportunity to choose. It is not the prerogative of the middle-class to determine what is worthy of aspiration.

There is also every possibility that the middle-class people of tomorrow will turn out ever so much better than those of today. I even know some middle-class people of today who are not *all* bad. Often, thank God, what monkey sees, monkey *avoids* doing at all costs. So it may be, concerning what is deepest in him, with the Negro.

I think there are so few Negro hippies today because middle-class Negroes, although well-fed, are not careless. They are required by the treacherous world they live in to be clearly aware of whoever or whatever might be trying to do them in. They are middle-class in money and position, but they cannot afford to be middle-class in complacency. They distrust the hippie movement because they know that it can do nothing for Negroes as a group but "love" them, which is what all paternalists claim to do. And since the only way Negroes can survive (which they cannot do, unfortunately, on love alone) is with the support of the group, they are wisely wary and stay away.

A white writer tried recently to explain that the reason for the relatively few Negro hippies is that Negroes have built up a "super-cool" that cracks under LSD and makes them have a "bad trip." What this writer doesn't guess at is that Negroes are needing drugs less than ever these days for any kind of trip. While the hippies are "tripping," Negroes are going after power, which is so much more important to their survival and their children's survival than LSD and pot.

Everyone would be surprised if the Israelis ignored the Arabs and took up "tripping" and pot smoking. In this country we are the Israelis.

Everybody who can do so would like to forget this, of course. But for us to forget it for a minute would be fatal. "We Shall Overcome" is just a song to most Americans, *but we must do it.* Or die.

What good was the civil rights movement? If it had just given this country Dr. King, a leader of conscience for once in our lifetime, it would have been enough. If it had just taken black eyes off white television stories, it would have been enough. If it had fed one starving child, it would have been enough.

If the civil rights movement is "dead," and if it gave us nothing else, it gave us each other forever. It gave some of us bread, some of us shelter, some of us knowledge and pride, all of us comfort. It gave us our children, our husbands, our brothers, our fathers, as men reborn and with a purpose for living. It broke the pattern of black servitude in this country. It shattered the phony "promise" of white soap operas that sucked away so many pitiful lives. It gave us history and men far greater than Presidents. It gave us heroes, selfless men of courage and strength, for our little boys to follow. It gave us hope for tomorrow. It called us to life.

Because we live, it can never die.

JOHN OLIVER KILLENS

As novelist, essayist, and lecturer, John Oliver Killens has been an active and often aggressive spokesman for black Americans. Born in Macon, Georgia, in 1916, he studied at Edward Waters College, Morris Brown College, Howard University Law School, Columbia University, and New York University. In 1936 and again after World War II, he joined the staff of the National Labor Relations Board in Washington. He is now a writer by profession and teaches creative writing both at Howard and Columbia University.

His works include the novels Youngblood *(1954) and* Sippi *(1967), the nonfiction* Black Man's Burden *(1966), and, for juvenile readers,* Great Gettin' Up in the Morning: A Biography of Denmark Vesey *(1972). He also writes for journals, films, and television and is a contributing editor of* The Black Scholar. *Among his numerous honors are the Afro Arts Theatre Cultural Award and the NAACP Literary Arts Award. He has been chairman of the Harlem Writers Guild Workshop and in 1969 helped found the Black Academy of Arts and Letters.*

The article we reprint here first appeared in the Saturday Evening Post, *July 2, 1966.*

Negroes Have a Right to Fight Back

There is this scene in the movie *Elmer Gantry,* which was adapted from Sinclair Lewis's novel of the same title, in which this thug is slapping this prostitute around. At which point Burt Lancaster comes in, walks over to the thug and says something like, "Hey, fellow, don't you know that hurts?" And smashes his fist magnificently up against the thug's head and generally kicks the thug around, just to emphasize the point.

It was a beautiful moment in the movie, and it crystallized my own attitude toward the merits (moral and practical) of nonviolence as a policy for Negroes. The perpetrators of violence must be made to know how it feels to be recipients of violence. How can they know unless we teach them?

I remember as a child on Virgin Street in Macon, Georgia, there was this boy who took delight in punching me, and one of his favorite sports was twisting my arm. Onlookers would try to prevail upon him: "Shame! Shame! The Lord is not going to bless you!" Which admonitions seemed to spur my adversary on and on.

One day I put two "alley apples" (pieces of brick) in my trousers' pockets and ventured forth. I was hardly out in the sun-washed streets before Bully-boy playfully accosted me. He immediately began his game of punching me in the stomach, laughing all the while. He was almost a foot taller than I, but I reached into my pockets and leaped up at both sides of his head with the alley apples. Bully-boy ran off. We later became great friends. We never could have become friends on the basis of him kicking my backside, and my counter-attack consisting solely of "Peace, brother!"

The one thing most friends and all enemies of the Afro-American have agreed upon is that we are ordained by nature and by God to be nonviolent. And so a new myth about the Negro is abroad throughout the land, to go with the old myths of laziness and rhythm and irresponsibility and sexual prowess. In the last third of the 20th century, when the disfranchised all over the earth are on the move, the world is being told that the good old U.S.A. has evolved a new type of *Homo sapiens,* the nonviolent Negro. The most disturbing aspect of this question is that many Negroes have bought this myth and are spreading it around.

One of the basic attributes of manhood (when we say manhood, we mean womanhood, selfhood) is the right of self-defense. In the psychological castration of the Negro, the denial of his right of self-defense has been one of the main instruments. Let me make one thing clear: I am not at the moment interested in the question of the so-called castration of the American male by American womanhood, or "Momism." White Mama is a victim too. Indeed, Madame Simone de Beauvoir in *The Second Sex* hit the bull's-eye when she made the analogy between the training of bourgeois girls and the training of American Negroes to know their place and to stay forever in it.

I grew up in Macon under a "separate-but-equal" public school system. On our way to our wooden-frame school we black kids had to walk through a middle-class white neighborhood. One day in spring a white boy on the way home from his pretty brick school with his comrades said innocently enough, "Hey, nigger, what you learn in school today?" Friendly-like.

"I learned your mother was a pig," the sassy black boy answered, not in the spirit of nonviolence. We were 7 to 11 years of age.

The black boy's buddies laughed angrily, uproariously. The white lad slapped the black boy's face, and that was how the "race riot" started. We fist-fought, we rock-battled, we used sticks and baseball bats and everything else that came to hand. Nobody won. The "race riot" just sort of petered out. We black kids went home with cut lips and bloody noses, but we went home proud and happy and got our backsides whipped for tearing our school clothes, and by the next morning we had almost forgotten it.

Just before noon next day our school ground swarmed with policemen. They strode into the classroom without so much as a "good morning" to the teachers and dragged kids out. They took those who had been in the "riot" and some who'd never even heard of it. The next move was to bring scared black mothers to the jailhouses to whip their children in order to "teach them they must not fight white children." Not a single white lad was arrested—naturally. And so they drove the lesson home. The black American must expect his person to be violated by the white man, but he must know that the white man's person is inviolable.

As an African-American, especially in the hospitable Southland, I concede that nonviolence is a legitimate tactic. It is practical and pragmatic; it has placed the question morally before the nation and the world. But the tendency is to take a tactic and build it into a way of life, to construct a whole new ideology and rhetoric around it. The danger is that all other means of struggle will be proscribed.

We black folk must never, tacitly or otherwise, surrender one single right guaranteed to any other American. The right of self-defense is the most basic of human rights, recognized by all people everywhere. It is certainly more important than the right to eat frankfurters while sitting down, or to get a black haircut in a white barbershop, or to get a night's lodging in Mrs. Murphy's flophouse, may the Good Lord rest her soul. Indeed, it is more important than the right to vote. In many places in the South the Negro can't get to the polls without the right of self-defense.

A man's home is his castle, but a man's "castle" is really made of flesh and bones and heart and soul. One's castle is also one's wife and children, one's people, one's dignity. Invade this castle at your peril is the way the freedom script must read.

I was in Montgomery during the bus-protest movement. I was told on more than one occasion that most Negro men had stopped riding the buses long before the protest started because they could not stand to hear their women insulted by the brave bus drivers. Here the alternatives were sharp and clear: debasement, death, or tired feet. Black citizens of Montgomery did not have the right to be violent, by word or action, toward men who practiced every type of violence against them.

I also know that despite all the preaching about nonviolence, the South is an armed camp. It always has been, ever since I can remember. The first time my wife, who is Brooklyn-born, went south with me, she was shocked to see so many guns in African-American homes. Of course, the white establishment has even vaster fire power, including the guns of the forces of law and order.

Yet, as I said before, nonviolence has the power of moral suasion, which makes it possible to solicit help from many white and liberal summer soldiers, who would otherwise shrink rapidly from the cause. But moral suasion alone never brought about a revolution, for the simple reason that any power structure always constructs for itself a morality which is calculated to perpetuate itself forever. Ask Governor Wallace if the civil rights movement isn't the work of satanic forces. How many centuries of moral suasion would it have taken to convince the kindly Christian Southern slave masters that slavery was evil or to convince the Nazis at Auschwitz that morality was not on their side?

Before leading the Negro people of Birmingham into a demonstration in that city, the Rev. Martin Luther King was reported to have said, "If blood is shed, let it be our blood!" But our blood has always been the blood that was shed. And where is the morality that makes the white racist's blood more sacred than that of black children? I cannot believe that Dr. King meant these words, if indeed he ever uttered them. I can only believe that he got carried away by the dramatics of the moment. Dr. King is one of the men whom I hold in great esteem. We have been friends since 1957. But he loses me and millions of other black Americans when he calls upon us to love our abusers.

"Kick me and I will still love you! Spit on me and I will still love you!"

My daughter, who loves him dearly, heard him say words to this effect on the radio one day. She was in tears for her black hero. "Daddy! Daddy! What's the matter with Rev. King? What's the matter with Rev. King?"

I agree with Chuck and Barbara (my son and daughter). There is no dignity for me in allowing a man to spit on me with impunity. There is only sickness on the part of both of us, and it will beget an ever greater sickness. It degrades me and brutalizes him. If black folk were so sick as to love those who practice genocide against us, we would not deserve human consideration.

The advocates of nonviolence have not reckoned with the psychological needs of black America. There is in many Negroes a deep need to practice violence against their white tormentors. We black folk dearly loved the great Joe Louis, the heavyweight champion the white folk dubbed "The Brown Bomber." Each time he whipped another white man, black hearts overflowed with joy. Joe was strong wine for our much-abused egos.

I was at Yankee Stadium the night our champ knocked out Max Schmeling, the German fighter, in the first round. I saw black men who were strangers embrace each other, unashamedly, and weep for joy. And Joe was in the American tradition. Americans have always been men of violence, and proud of it.

We are a country born in violence. Malcolm X, the Black Nationalist leader who was murdered, knew this basic truth. He did not preach violence, but he did advocate self-defense. That is one of the reasons he had such tremendous attraction for the people of the ghetto. What I am saying is that the so-called race riots are healthier (from the point of view of the ghetto people) than the internecine gang warfare which was the vogue in the ghettos a few years ago, when black teen-agers killed each other or killed equally helpless Puerto Ricans, as was often the case in New York City. Historically in the black ghettos the helpless and hopeless have practiced violence on each other. Stand around the emergency entrance at Harlem Hospital of a Saturday night and check the business in black blood drawn by black hands that comes in every weekend.

It is time for Americans (black and white) to stop hoodwinking themselves. Nonviolence is a tactic, but it must never be a way of life for the black American. Just because I love myself, the black *Me*, why do white Americans (especially liberals) think it means I have to hate the white American *You?* We black and white folk in the U.S.A. have to settle many things between us before the matter of love can be discussed. For one thing, if you practice violence against me, I mean to give it back to you in kind.

Most black folk believe in the kind of nonviolence that keeps everybody nonviolent. For example: In a certain cotton county in the heart of Dixieland, black folk, most of them sharecroppers, asserted their right to vote and were driven from the land. For several years they lived in tents, and of a Saturday evening white pranksters had a playful way of driving out to Tent City and shooting into it. A couple of campers were injured, including a pregnant woman. Complaints to the authorities got no results at all. So one Saturday evening when the pranksters turned up, just to have a little sport, the campers (lacking a sense of humor) returned the fire. A young relative of the sheriff got his arm shattered. The sheriff got out there in a hurry and found rifles shining out of every tent. He sent for the Negro leader.

"Tell them to give up them rifles, boy. I can't protect 'em less'n they surrender up them rifles."

Whereupon the 35-year-old "boy" said, "We figured you was kind of busy, Sheriff. We thought we'd give you a helping hand and protect our own selves." There was no more racial violence in the county for a long time.

Let us speak plainly to each other. Your black brother is spoiling for a fight in affirmation of his selfhood. This is the meaning of Watts and Harlem and Bedford-Stuyvesant. It seems to me, you folk who abhor violence, you are barking up the wrong tree when you come to black folk and call on them to be nonviolent. Go to the attackers. Go to the ones who start the fire, not to the firefighters. Insist that your Government place the same premium on black life as it does on white. As far as I can ascertain, no white American has ever been condemned to death by the courts for taking a black life.

The Deacons of Defense, the Negro self-defense organization that started in Louisiana not long ago, is going to mushroom and increasingly become a necessary appendage to the civil rights movement. This should be welcomed by everyone who is sincere about the "Negro revolution." It accomplishes three things simultaneously. It makes certain that the Government will play the role of the fire department, the pacifier. Second: The actual physical presence of the Deacons (or any similar group) will go a long way in staying the hands of the violence makers. Third: It further affirms the black Americans' determination to exercise every right enjoyed by all other Americans.

Otherwise we're in for longer and hotter summers. There are all kinds among us black folks. Gentle ones and angry ones, forgiving and vindictive, and every single one is determined to be free. Julian Bond, poet, SNCC leader, and duly elected member of the Georgia legislature (his seat was denied him because of his pronouncements on Vietnam), summed up the situation when he wrote:

> Look at that gal shake that thing.
> We cannot all be Martin Luther King.

I believe he meant, among other things, that whites cannot expect Negroes to be different—that is, more saintly than whites are—and that most black folk are in no mood to give up the right to defend themselves.

BAYARD RUSTIN

Bayard Rustin, one of the principal movers for social justice in our time, has from the very first put his body on the line with his beliefs. He has been arrested twenty-three times in the cause of civil rights and of peace. His sentences include being jailed as a conscientious objector during World War II and spending twenty-two days on a chain gang in North Carolina

*for organizing and participating in the first freedom ride (1947) to test a
court ruling against discrimination in interstate travel.*

*Born in West Chester, Pennsylvania, in 1910, Rustin was one of
twelve children. He was raised by his grandparents and strongly influenced
by his grandmother's Quaker beliefs. He attended Wilberforce University in
Ohio, Cheyney State Teachers College in Pennsylvania, and City College of
New York. In 1941 he was Youth Organizer for the first March on
Washington, a march called off when President Roosevelt ordered the end
of racial discrimination in industries having government defense contracts
and set up the Committee for Fair Employment Practice. In 1942 he went
to California to help protect the property of Japanese-Americans who were
being interned.*

*Rustin was Field Secretary and Race Relations Secretary for the
Fellowship of Reconciliation for twelve years, then Executive Secretary of
the War Resisters League from 1953 to 1964. Since 1964 he has been
Executive Director of the A. Philip Randolph Institute. During these years
he helped organize the Congress of Racial Equality, acted as special
adviser to Martin Luther King, Jr.—helping him to organize the
Montgomery bus boycott and build the Southern Christian Leadership
Conference—and was himself the chief organizer of the 1963 March on
Washington. He has also been a consistent worker for nuclear
disarmament. Rustin has received innumerable honors throughout these
years. Some of his writings have been collected in* Down the Line
(1971). We reprint here an article he wrote for the WRL *[War Resisters
League]* News, *July–August 1964.*

The Harlem Riot and Nonviolence

From dusk till dawn for four nights during the tragic event called the
Harlem Riot, I walked the streets with a team of 75 boys and men. We
took the injured to CORE's first aid station or to the hospital. We dispersed crowds. We did what we could to protect women and children and
had some minor success in urging police who had arrested innocent
people to free them—especially when doing so contributed to crowd
dispersal.

The experiences of those four terrible nights has deepened my faith
in nonviolence and I should like to share with you some of my thoughts
ten days later.

We pacifists maintain that the law of ends and means does, in fact,
operate. Never was this more clearly illustrated. Most of the people who
engaged in disorder were youths between 18 and 25. They are the unemployed, the forgotten, the poorest of the poor—without hope and with
no faith in a society which has doomed them to utter despair. It is they

who are forced to live by their wits, seeking out a living by gambling, selling numbers or dope, and sometimes selling themselves.

They revolted in the only way left to them. They would make society listen. Like a child in an attention-seeking tantrum, they resorted to violence in a loud outcry of despair.

We pacifists claim that social progress must spring from social justice. In their ugly way, these youths were expressing what we, by nonviolent resistance, believe. If society will not remove the slums and give them work and dignity, they will cry out again.

We pacifists assert that violence degrades all who become involved in it. How true! I know many police officers in Harlem by name and many more by sight and reputation. One of the saddest aspects of those nights was the fact that many police officers who are among the better-behaved, reacted with the greatest fear and consequently with the most brutal conduct. I saw a white officer who had once turned over to me a 15-year-old thief on pledge that I take him home and report his behavior to his father—beat a woman to the ground mercilessly. When I urged him to stop, he turned on me.

On the other hand, I saw a Negro churchwoman help to blockade a street to stop a white taxi driver. After her sons had beaten him almost to unconsciousness, she helped them to rob him, leaving him in great agony on the street. Thus on those nights I saw violence degrade on every side. I heard men who usually talk reasonably, demand that youth be given guns to shoot "police and uncle toms."

We pacifists urge nonviolence because if change toward justice is to take place, it must be in an atmosphere where creative conflict and debate are possible. Wherever great force is used—and I am certain from what I saw that the force used by police was far more than necessary to maintain order—it is used to support the status quo and not to encourage real debate and creative conflict.

The riot has not encouraged real debate: it has given strength to the supporters of reaction. It has brought an injunction against certain groups. It has led to the police commissioner's temporarily prohibiting rallies in the name of law and order. It has brought division of leadership where unity was needed if nonviolent campaigns for justice are to be pursued. It has confused many young people. It has left the powers-that-be in a position to call for "law and order" for protection of white people —a very false position since the riot was economic rather than basically racial.

Perhaps the most important lesson I learned from this experience is that nonviolence is relevant to a degree—even when fear, brutality and violence rage. On the second afternoon of the riot, I spoke at a big Harlem church. Several speakers preceded me, calling upon youth to use violence. One speaker called for a Mau Mau, another for armed resistance to police. Another said: "I want 100 men to leave this church with me for guerrilla warfare."

Then I spoke and urged nonviolence. I was booed, applauded and then booed again. I appealed for 100 men to join me in the streets and work nonviolently "to end the brutality toward all men." When the meeting ended, I rose to leave the church and was surrounded by a hostile group intent on beating me. From the audience came 75 men who moved in to protect me without violence. The hostile group scattered.

That night and for three succeeding nights, those 75 men walked in danger through the streets and were responsible for helping many persons and saving many lives. Some were beaten, as I was, for advocating nonviolence but only one deserted.

And so, reliving those four nights of terror and ugliness, I become more dedicated to nonviolence, for I see clearly how resort to violence dehumanizes all who are caught-up in its whirlpool.

Technology and Human Values

The successful application of science to our practical problems has been truly described as "one of the miracles of mankind." But no serious writer today can discuss technological progress without misgivings. Most of us, at least, are aware of some of the terrifying losses that seem always to accompany the gains: the atomic balance of terror; the population explosion; the poisoning of our air, water, and soil; the electronic and psychological threat to privacy; the displacement of skilled workers by skilled machines.

The first four writers in the present section share the assumption that technological progress had better be approached with humility, that there are other sorts of wisdom that we ignore at our peril. Lewis Thomas and the author of "The Wisdom of the Worm" both find a cautionary model in nature itself. As Thomas piquantly puts it in response to the prospect of our being able to manipulate our internal organs: "I am, to face the facts squarely, considerably less intelligent than my liver."

The next two essays probe at greater length and more deeply into the ethical questions raised by scientific progress. Eric J. Cassell examines the shifting of death "from the moral to the technical order" and what that means for us as people. Leon R. Kass describes with remarkable clarity and comprehensiveness the whole range of new biomedical technologies and the ever more complex ethical and social questions that must be raised with them.

There follows Theodore Roszak's attack on "objective consciousness," part of his powerful critique of the technological culture itself. Since this critique leads ultimately to his rejection of technology for an entirely antithetic system of values, we reprint next for balance the essay of F. M. Esfandiary, who writes from a knowledge of the unscientific passivity, and of the suffering, in the old civilizations of the Orient.

The section ends with a satire; E. B. White's comical science fiction of 1950 is already too true.

LEWIS THOMAS

This essay is a chapter in Lewis Thomas' The Lives of a Cell: Notes
of a Biology Watcher (1974). For further information about the
author, see page 8.

[handwritten: some want to do this; learned — controlled — bodily functions; unlearned — uncontrolled or autonomous activities]

Autonomy [handwritten: — self-governing; self-sustaining]

Working a typewriter by touch, like riding a bicycle or strolling on a path,
is best done by not giving it a glancing thought. Once you do, your fingers
fumble and hit the wrong keys. To do things involving practiced skills,
you need to turn loose the systems of muscles and nerves responsible for
each maneuver, place them on their own, and stay out of it. There is no
real loss of authority in this, since you get to decide whether to do the
thing or not, and you can intervene and embellish the technique any time
you like; if you want to ride a bicycle backward, or walk with an eccentric
loping gait giving a little skip every fourth step, whistling at the same
time, you can do that. But if you concentrate your attention on the details,
keeping in touch with each muscle, thrusting yourself into a free fall with
each step and catching yourself at the last moment by sticking out the
other foot in time to break the fall, you will end up immobilized, vibrating
with fatigue.

It is a blessing to have options for choice and change in the learning
of such unconsciously coordinated acts. If we were born with all these
knacks inbuilt, automated like ants, we would surely miss the variety. It
would be a less interesting world if we all walked and skipped alike, and
never fell from bicycles. If we were all genetically programmed to play
the piano deftly from birth, we might never learn to understand music.

The rules are different for the complicated, coordinated, fantastically
skilled manipulations we perform with our insides. We do not have to
learn anything. Our smooth-muscle cells are born with complete instructions, in need of no help from us, and they work away on their own
schedules, modulating the lumen of blood vessels, moving things
through intestines, opening and closing tubules according to the requirements of the entire system. Secretory cells elaborate their products in
privacy; the heart contracts and relaxes; hormones are sent off to react
silently with cell membranes, switching adenyl cyclase, prostaglandin,
and other signals on and off; cells communicate with each other by simply
touching; organelles send messages to other organelles; all this goes on
continually, without ever a personal word from us. The arrangement is
that of an ecosystem, with the operation of each part being governed by

the state and function of all the other parts. When things are going well, as they generally are, it is an infallible mechanism.

But now the autonomy of this interior domain, long regarded as inviolate, is open to question. The experimental psychologists have recently found that visceral organs can be taught to do various things, as easily as a boy learns to ride a bicycle, by the instrumental techniques of operant conditioning. If a thing is done in the way the teacher wants, at a signal, and a suitable reward given immediately to reinforce the action, it becomes learned. Rats, rewarded by stimulation of their cerebral "pleasure centers," have been instructed to speed up or slow down their hearts at a signal, or to alter their blood pressures, or switch off certain waves in their electroencephalograms and switch on others.

The same technology has been applied to human beings, with other kinds of rewards, and the results have been startling. It is claimed that you can teach your kidneys to change the rate of urine formation, raise or lower your blood pressure, change your heart rate, write different brain waves, at will.

There is already talk of a breakthrough in the prevention and treatment of human disease. According to proponents, when the technology is perfected and extended it will surely lead to new possibilities for therapy. If a rat can be trained to dilate the blood vessels of one of his ears more than those of the other, as has been reported, what rich experiences in self-control and self-operation may lie just ahead for man? There are already cryptic advertisements in the Personal columns of literary magazines, urging the purchase of electronic headsets for the training and regulation of one's own brain waves, according to one's taste.

You can have it.

Not to downgrade it. It is extremely important, I know, and one ought to feel elated by the prospect of taking personal charge, calling the shots, running one's cells around like toy trains. Now that we know that viscera can be taught, the thought comes naturally that we've been neglecting them all these years, and by judicious application of human intelligence, these primitive structures can be trained to whatever standards of behavior we wish to set for them.

My trouble, to be quite candid, is a lack of confidence in myself. If I were informed tomorrow that I was in direct communication with my liver, and could now take over, I would become deeply depressed. I'd sooner be told, forty thousand feet over Denver, that the 747 jet in which I had a coach seat was now mine to operate as I pleased; at least I would have the hope of bailing out, if I could find a parachute and discover quickly how to open a door. Nothing would save me and my liver, if I were in charge. For I am, to face the facts squarely, considerably less intelligent than my liver. I am, moreover, constitutionally unable to make hepatic decisions, and I prefer not to be obliged to, ever. I would not be able to think of the first thing to do.

I have the same feeling about the rest of my working parts. They are all better off without my intervention, in whatever they do. It might be something of a temptation to take over my brain, on paper, but I cannot imagine doing so in real life. I would lose track, get things mixed up, turn on wrong cells at wrong times, drop things. I doubt if I would ever be able to think up my own thoughts. My cells were born, or differentiated anyway, knowing how to do this kind of thing together. If I moved in to organize them they would resent it, perhaps become frightened, perhaps swarm out into my ventricles like bees.

Although it is, as I say, a temptation. I have never really been satisfied with the operation of my brain, and it might be fun to try running it myself, just once. There are several things I would change, given the opportunity: certain memories that tend to slip away unrecorded, others I've had enough of and would prefer to delete, certain notions I'd just as soon didn't keep popping in, trains of thought that go round and round without getting anywhere, rather like this one. I've always suspected that some of the cells in there are fluffing off much of the time, and I'd like to see a little more attention and real work. Also, while I'm about it, I could do with a bit more respect.

On balance, however, I think it best to stay out of this business. Once you began, there would be no end to the responsibilities. I'd rather leave all my automatic functions with as much autonomy as they please, and hope for the best. Imagine having to worry about running leukocytes, keeping track, herding them here and there, listening for signals. After the first flush of pride in ownership, it would be exhausting and debilitating, and there would be no time for anything else.

What to do, then? It cannot simply be left there. If we have learned anything at all in this century, it is that all new technologies will be put to use, sooner or later, for better or worse, as it is in our nature to do. We cannot expect an exception for the instrumental conditioning of autonomic functions. We will be driven to make use of it, trying to communicate with our internal environment, to meddle, and it will consume so much of our energy that we will end up even more cut off from things outside, missing the main sources of the sensation of living.

I have a suggestion for a way out. Given the capacity to control autonomic functions, modulate brain waves, run cells, why shouldn't it be possible to employ exactly the same technology to go in precisely the opposite direction? Instead of getting in there and taking things over, couldn't we learn to disconnect altogether, uncouple, detach, and float free? You would only need to be careful, if you tried it, that you let go at the right end.

Of course, people have been trying to do this sort of thing for a long time, by other techniques and with varying degrees of luck. This is what Zen archery seems to be about, come to think of it. You learn, after long months of study under a master, to release the arrow without releasing it yourself. Your fingers must do the releasing, on their own, remotely, like the opening of a flower. When you have learned this, no matter where the arrow goes, you have it made. You can step outside for a look around.

The Wisdom of the Worm

Until quite lately, we had all been used to believing that, generally speaking, it is easier to destroy things than to create them. This rule still holds true for governments, schools, and other institutions of society, but it no longer holds true for a steadily increasing number of our material artifacts. The pollutants that are currently endangering the environment have taught us that in many cases it can be much harder to destroy something than to create it. This lesson was forced home in a particularly striking way by the recent dilemma over how to dispose of several hundred nerve-gas rockets that had been stored for some three years at Defense Department ammunition depots in Alabama and Kentucky. The gap between our talent for manufacturing and our talent for dismantling has rarely been so clearly displayed. Presumably, it took great technological ingenuity to create the rockets, and, as for the gas, we had to turn, after the Second World War, to the files of the Nazi scientists to learn how to make it. When it came to getting rid of the rockets and their gas, however, the cleverest thing the Army could at first think of to do was to encase the rockets in blocks of steel and concrete—a solution that failed to insure against leaks while preventing anyone from getting at the rockets in order to detoxify the gas. Finally, of course, the Army got rid of the gas, the rockets, and their steel-and-concrete cases by the singularly crude method of loading them all onto a ship and sinking it in the ocean off Florida. Spokesmen for the Pentagon have assured us that the dumping will not cause any damage to the ocean environment, but many civilian scientists have argued that it may. The only thing that seems certain is that no one really has any definite information on what its effects will be.

At an earlier stage of the summer's pollution-power-transportation crisis in this city, it was noted here that one difference between the "natural" environment and a man-made environment is that complexity, which is a strength in the natural world, is a weakness in the man-made world. The incident of the nerve-gas rockets suggests some further differences between man's works and nature's. One thing we have all learned recently is that in birth, in life, and in death each species of animal and each species of plant performs innumerable functions that are crucial to the other species and to the environment that supports all species. For example, in "Silent Spring" Rachel Carson wrote of the earthworm, "Of all the larger inhabitants of the soil, probably none is more important than the earthworm. Over three-quarters of a century ago, Charles Darwin published a book titled 'The Formation of Vegetable Mould,

Through the Action of Worms, with Observations on Their Habits.' In it he gave the world its first understanding of the fundamental role of earthworms as geologic agents for the transport of soil—a picture of surface rocks being gradually covered by fine soil brought up from below by the worms, in annual amounts running to many tons to the acre in most favorable areas. At the same time, quantities of organic matter contained in leaves and grass (as much as twenty pounds to the square yard in six months) are drawn down into the burrows and incorporated in soil. Darwin's calculations showed that the toil of earthworms might add a layer of soil an inch to an inch and a half thick in a ten-year period. And this is by no means all they do; their burrows aerate the soil, keep it well drained, and aid the penetration of plant roots. The presence of earthworms increases the nitrifying powers of the soil bacteria and decreases putrefaction of the soil. Organic matter is broken down as it passes through the digestive tracts of worms and the soil is enriched by their excretory products." Of course, the plants and the animals are, as far as we can tell, unaware of the multiplicity of services they perform for the environment. The earthworm probably has no conscious intention of enriching the soil as he progresses through the existence charted for him by his instincts. And quite certainly he has no intention of becoming a meal for a robin—another of his crucial roles. It is only man, apparently, who has "intentions" and "purposes." However, as it has turned out, man's purposes—in the area of material production, at least—serve ends that are much narrower than those served unthinkingly by other living things. Usually, man's artifacts are produced with only one end in mind, such as the provision of fuel for engines or of containers for food, and most of what he makes is useful for only a moment or so of its long sojourn in the environment. One inevitable consequence of man's producing things for such narrow ends is the necessity of "throwing away" what he has made when it has served its purpose. In the past, when we threw something "away," we pretty much considered that it had disappeared. But now, because of the ecological crisis, we know that there is no such thing as throwing something "away." There is only throwing it into the sea or into the soil or into the air. And what happens to a milk carton or a gallon of oil or a nerve-gas rocket when it gets there is as much our concern as what these things did when they were sitting in our iceboxes or driving our engines or killing our "enemies." Today, when we consider making something, we must expand our knowledge and concern beyond the moment of its service to us and take responsibility for its entire career on the earth. We must consider the effect it will have on all living things as it travels down our sewers or rises up our chimneys and makes its slow but inevitable circular progress through the chain of life back to our dinner tables or into our lungs. In short, we must learn the unknowing wisdom of the worm.

[From "The Talk of the Town," *The New Yorker,* August 29, 1970]

ERIC J. CASSELL

Dr. Cassell was born in 1928 and received his medical degree from the New York University School of Medicine in 1954. He has had a private practice in internal medicine in New York City and has served as Clinical Professor of Public Health at Cornell University Medical College. In addition to scientific writings, he has contributed articles for lay audiences to such journals as Commentary, *particularly on prevention rather than cure of disease as the proper goal of public health.*

The present essay appeared in Hastings Center Studies *for May 1974. Hastings Center is the headquarters of the Institute of Society, Ethics, and the Life Sciences, which is making an important new effort to examine the ethical, legal, and social implications of advances in the life sciences. Dr. Cassell is on the Board of Directors.*

dying of body > dying of person

Dying in a Technological Society

The care of the terminally ill in the United States has changed as the business of dying has shifted from the moral to the technical order. The moral order has been used to describe those bonds between men based in sentiment, morality, or conscience, that describe what is right. The technical order rests on the usefulness of things, based in necessity or expediency, and not founded in conceptions of the right.[1] The change of death from a moral to a technical matter has come about for many reasons based in social evolution and technical advance, and the effects on the dying have been profound.

One reason for the change has been the success of modern medicine in combatting death. For most, in the United States, premature death is no longer imminent. The death of infants is unusual, the death of children rare, and the death of young adults so improbable that it must be removed from the realistic possibilities of young life. Further, the nature of death has also changed. The degenerative diseases and cancer have become predominant. Lingering sickness in the aged is a less common event because medicine is able to combat the complications of chronic disease that so often in the past kept the sick person from functioning. Accompanying these changes brought about by technical advances, there has been a change in the place where death occurs. Death has moved from the home into institutions—hospitals, medical centers, chronic care facilities and nursing homes.

[1] Robert Redfield, *The Primitive World and Its Transformations* (Ithaca: Cornell University Press, 1953), pp. 20ff.

There are other reasons for the shift of death in the United States from the moral to the technical order. One is the widespread acceptance of technical success itself. Because life expectancy has increased, the dying are old now. But, life expectancy is not an individual term, it is a statistical term. For individuals, what has changed is their death expectancy; they do not expect to die. They may use fantasies of early death or fears of death for personal or psychological reasons, but the reality belief is that death need not occur in the foreseeable future, that death is a reversible event. That belief in the reversibility of death, rooted in the common American experience of modern medicine, begins to move death out of the moral order. Death is a technical matter, a failure of technology in rescuing the body from a threat to its functioning and integrity. For the moment, it does not matter that the death of a person cannot be removed from the moral order by the very nature of personhood; what matters is the mythology of the society. The widespread mythology that things essentially moral can be made technical is reinforced by the effect of technology in altering other events besides death; for example, birth, birth defects or abortion.

The fact that technology can be seen so often as altering fate nurtures an illusion that is basic to the mythology of American society—that fate can be defeated.

Another reason why death has moved away from the moral order lies in the changes in family structure that have occurred over the past decades in the United States. The family remains the basic unit of moral and personal life, but with the passing of functionally meaningful extended families have come changes directly related to the care of the dying. The old, both the repository of knowledge about what is right and the major recipients of moral obligation, have left the family group. For many reasons, not the least their desire for continued independence in the years when previously material dependency would have been their lot, the aged frequently live alone. In retirement they may live far from their roots or their children, associating largely with others of their own age. An age-graded way of life has emerged that depends again on technical success and public responsibility (such as old age benefits) to solve problems for the aged that previously would have been the primary concern of the family. There is the belief, reinforced by the advantages of the change in family structure and geographic mobility, that essentially moral problems—obligations to parents, for example—have become part of the technical order amenable to administrative or technical solutions.

On the other hand, in his search for continued independence and comfortable retirement, the old person has allowed his family to separate, allowed the young to achieve their independence. In previous times and in other cultures, the mantle passed to the next generation only with the death of the old. Here it is voluntary. But, a problem is created for the dying patient. The old person who is going to die is already out of the family. To die amidst his family he must return to them—reenter the structure in order to leave it. Reenter it in denial of all the reasons he gave himself and his children for separation, reasons equally important to them in their pursuit of privacy and individual striving and in their inherent denial of aging, death and fate.

Thus, by reason of technological success and changes in family structure that are rooted in the basic mythology of America, death has moved from the moral order to the technical and from the family to the hospital.

It is interesting to examine some of the consequences and corollaries of the shift. In individual terms, moving the place of death from the home to the hospital, from familiar to strange surroundings, means changing the context of dying. The picture of the old person, independent and swinging free—promulgated as much by the old as by others—while part fact, is also a partial fiction dictated by the old person's love for, and nurturance of, the independence of the young. Becoming a burden is the great fear not only for what it may mean personally, but for the threat it poses to the fragile economic and personal structure of today's nuclear family. But part fiction or no, the hallmark of "golden age" is independence. With independence and its mobility, the belief arises that each person is the sole representative of his own beliefs, values and desires. In health that may seem to be true, but the fact is as fragile as the body. In health a person can struggle for his rights, pronounce his values and attempt their fulfillment. But the sick, bound to their bodies by their illness, are different. The values and desires dearly held during life give way in terminal illness. Pain and suffering erode meaning and deny dignity. The fiction of independence and the denial of fate give way to reality. In terminal illness, the individual must give over to others and to the context of his dying, the defense of his dignity and the statement of his values. But the context of dying and the people at the bedside have changed. The aged no longer die surrounded by their loved ones. An essentially private matter takes place in the public sphere surrounded by symbols of individual sameness, not personal difference. The family and its needs are the intruders. The patient's values, spoken by others, compete with the values of the institution. There is a final, ironic, independence as the person dies alone.

Thus, there are personal or value problems created for the individual when death moves from the moral to the technical order. Characteristically our society seeks solutions to these problems not by reasserting the moral, but by attempting technical solutions for moral imperatives. We are seeing increasing attempts in the United States to find quasi-legal or legal means to reassert the rights of the dying—some technical means to give as much weight to the person who dies as the hospital gives to his body.

In the process of the shift of death from the moral to the technical a basic confusion arises that confounds the usefulness of technical solutions in what are essentially moral problems. The mechanical events involved in a body becoming dead, which occur in the technical sphere, are confused with the process of dying, which occurs in the moral sphere. It is a natural error but one that we do not frequently make in health. That is to say that while we are aware that the mechanical event that is a beating heart is essential to life, we do not confuse ourselves with our heartbeat. As a matter of fact if someone becomes too conscious of his heartbeat, we consider it a symptom, or neurosis. But in the sick or the dying the confusion is rampant. There are two distinct things happening in the terminally ill, the death of the body and the passing of the person. The death of the body is a physical phenomenon, a series of measurable events that are the province of physicians. The passing of the individual is a nonphysical process, poorly defined, largely unmeasurable and closely connected to the nature of the dying person. It is the process by which he leaves the group and during which we take leave of him. Indeed, in the manner in which many act towards the newly dead body—as though it still contained some part of the person—the passing of the individual, at least for the onlooker, may not end with death. It is obvious that in sudden death, a person may pass away who was never dying; or conversely, in the depressed, the person may be dying with no evidence of impending death.

The passing of the individual is also part of the work of physicians, but of more importance, it is the province of family, friends, and clergymen—indeed the entire group. But in a technical era, the passing of the person, since it is unmeasurable and does not fit the technical schema, is not a legitimate subject for public discourse.

Those feelings within that relate to the dying person are difficult to organize, to deal with, or to speak about. The social rituals that previously enabled those confused meanings and feelings to spend themselves appropriately have diminished or disappeared along with the extended family. In the moral order, time slows down for those around the dying; but in the world of things, of necessity or expediency, time moves on relentlessly, making its case for those around the dying to return to that world. Furthermore, with decreasing practice in moral matters, even when social forms remain, the content becomes increasingly sterile. Men obscure the moral content of the passing of the person by using the facts and artifacts of the death of the body as the vehicle for their interchanges —much as talk about the weather or sports draws the sting on other occasions.

The confusion of the mechanical events of the death of the body with the personal and social nature of the passing of the person confounds attempts to solve the essentially moral problems of the dying—problems of sentiment, conscience, or the knowledge of what is right. Thus, in matters such as when the respirators should be turned off, and by whom, essentially moral questions, the mechanical events loom so large that attention is diverted away from the moral, back to the technical. And this is the corollary problem to that raised earlier: the context of death no longer gives weight to the values of the dying person and forces a resort to legal or administrative protection of his rights.

The confusion of mechanical events for moral processes creates the further problem of depersonalization of care. And it is seen in the greater attention paid to diseases than to people by doctors and their institutions —a common complaint about physicians and particularly about physicians in their care of the dying. Frequently we explain this depersonalization by saying that it is the physician's psychological defense against the emotional burden imposed by the care of the dying. Though that may be true, it is only part of the truth. We have seen how the whole society has shifted its public focus from moral to technical in many areas of life: doctors are no exception to the trend. The problem cannot solely lie among physicians, or the society would not let them get away with it. Social forces would drive doctors back towards a more holistic view of their patients. Indeed, such a change is beginning to occur in response to the increasingly vocal dissatisfaction with medical care.

Because depersonalization is so much a part of the technical order, not only in medicine, and so antithetical to the values of personhood, let us further examine how depersonalization takes place. Each dying patient is not only a person, but also the container of the process or events by which his body is dying. By definition, since he is dying, these processes or events cannot be controlled by existing technology. Because of the inability of the technology to control such things—and cancer or heart failure are examples—they acquire independent meaning apart from the person containing them. From the viewpoint of caring for the terminally ill, such depersonalization may be justly deplored. But from the viewpoint of medical science the pursuit of the meaning of the resistant body process, apart from the person containing it, is a legitimate end in itself. That is to say, the heart as an abstraction, as a pump, an electrical system or what have you, is a proper object of technical concern and quite distinct from the fact that human hearts are only found in humans. Further, it is the nature of any system of abstract or formal thought not to be content with mystery, but to continue operating on any problem until understanding results. Mystery is a threat to the adequacy of the system of thought itself. Consequently, the disease process must be probed and probed, not only because of its relevance to the care of the sick and dying, but also because lack of a solution poses a threat to the entire logical construct of which the body process is thought to be a part. Thus, the depersonalization and abstraction of body mechanics is both necessary and legitimate within the framework of science, and understanding of the body-as-machine is impeded by consideration of human values.

The problem of depersonalization depends in part on the degree to which the dying person's disease process is understood. For example, in the care of the patient with bacterial pneumonia, easily treated with antibiotics, depersonalization poses little difficulty. The abstractions necessary for understanding microbes, antibiotics and so forth, are so much a part of the physician's thinking that he or she is able to integrate them back into a total concept of man, patients, etc. Withdrawal and depersonalization are not frequent, I think, when experienced doctors and nurses care for the dying, if the cause of death is something acceptably inevitable, such as pneumonia in the very old, or stroke. If it is correct that persons dying of a poorly understood process are more likely to be depersonalized by their physicians, we can better understand why the accusation of depersonalization is most often brought against young physicians. To the inexperienced doctor almost everything about the dying person is unfamiliar or poorly understood, thus requiring the abstraction that leads to depersonalization. Effective integration of the learned technical material with human needs, values, and desires comes only at a later stage of learning.

In the United States, the modern medical center is the very temple of the technical order, revered both by medicine and the public. As medical science, in its effort towards understanding, has taken the body apart system by system, it has departmentalized the intellectual structure of the hospital. By that I mean not only the well known division of medicine into specialties, but the further subdivisions that represent specific body functions. The corridors of any American medical center reveal rooms whose doors bear titles such as pulmonary function laboratory, cardiographics laboratory, nuclear medicine, sonography and so forth. Each of these specialized functions has contributed immeasurably to the diagnostic and therapeutic power of the modern physician and no doctor who has grown accustomed to their use will feel wholly comfortable in their absence. They are unlike the traditional clinical or research laboratory which when examining a function of the patient's body takes the whole patient along; it is not his blood or urine that goes to the laboratory, it is the patient. But it is not the person who holds the interest for the specialized laboratory; instead the interest centers on the person's lungs, or heart, or whatever. A good coronary arteriogram is not necessarily a good patient or even good for the patient, it is merely a technically good example of coronary arteriograms. Patients are usually not aware or interested in those distinctions and all too frequently, but in an opposite sense, neither is the physician who performed the test. One can see the hospital, thus compartmentalized, as the concrete expression of the depersonalization resulting from the abstract analytic thought of medical science. Thus, the dying patient in the modern hospital is in an environment ideally suited for the pursuit of knowledge and cure, but representing in its technology and idealized representative—the young doctor—technical values virtually antithetical to the holistic concept of person. This does not imply that the most personal and humane care cannot be and is not given in such hospitals, but rather that those who do give such care must struggle against their technical depersonalized thinking about the body, and against the structure of the hospital that such thought has produced.

No discussion of the care of the terminally ill in the United States can avoid the problem of the nursing home. Whereas the modern hospital represents the positive strivings of medical science and the technical order—the belief that nature, disease, and fate can be conquered—the nursing home represents the tattered edges of that philosophy. Medicine and medical care are seen primarily as the application of medical science to disease: if science fails the body, medicine fails the person. Nursing homes contain the failures and frustrations of medicine, as well as the homeless or unwanted sick. They are a place to linger and to die. Walking their halls is deeply depressing because hopelessness is overwhelming. It is the hopelessness one experiences whenever one sees the sick completely overtaken by their sickness, forever apart from the comfort of group. None of the many reasons for their proliferation and crowding explains why they are the hopeless places that they usually are. We know they can be better because of the success of the occasional institution given over to the care of the terminally ill in a positive sense. Such successful nursing homes are often run by religious orders or by others whose belief in their mission is deeply moral. Thus, what we see in the usual American nursing home is by no means inevitable in the way that death is inevitable, but rather a vacuum of care. The promise of science and technology has failed here. The old family solutions to the problems posed by the care of the terminally ill have been altered past utility by social change. No new solution has come forward to fill the void.

We have seen how the care of the terminally ill has changed in the United States. They are older now and die more frequently in institutions. But that bare frame of facts conceals increasing distress within the society over the quality of their dying. When death occurs in the modern hospital there seems to be more concern for the disease than for the dying person, more concern for life as a succession of heartbeats, than life as meaning. When death occurs in nursing homes it is as if life just dribbled out—custodial care seemingly inconvenienced by individual difference or tenacity for life.

We have seen that the problem is larger than widespread insensitivity which might be corrected by new educational programs. Rather, there has been a shift of death from within the moral order to the technical order. The technical, the expedient, the utilitarian that has worked so well in so many material ways seemed to promise easier solutions to the problems previously seen as matters of conscience, sentiment, or obligations between men. But the promise has not been fulfilled; not in the United States nor elsewhere where the technical order spreads its dominance.

Even if it were possible, the solution is not a return of American society to technical innocence. I do not believe that men were inherently more moral in the past when the moral order predominated over the technical. The path seems to lie in the direction of a more systematic understanding of the moral order to restore its balance with the technical. Understanding the body has not made it less wonderful, and the systematic exploration of the moral nature of man will not destroy that nature but rather increase its influence. In the care of the dying, it may give back to the living the meaning of death.

LEON R. KASS

Leon R. Kass is Executive Secretary of the Committee on the Life Sciences and Social Policy of the National Academy of Sciences. As such, he is one of the American scientists most closely in touch with the issues raised in this section. Dr. Kass was born in Chicago in 1939 and received both his B.S. (1958) and M.D. (1962) from the University of Chicago. After a medical internship, he turned to research in biochemistry and molecular biology at Harvard, and took his Ph.D. there in 1967. He spent two years doing further research in molecular biology. Then in 1970 his interest in medical ethics and in the social implications of advances in biomedical science and technology brought him to his present post and to a directorship of the Institute for Society, Ethics, and the Life Sciences.

The present essay, which appeared in the November 1971 issue of Science, *is a long and extremely comprehensive piece in its original form. Because of the lucidity of its organization, however, its major sections can be excerpted without loss of coherence, as we have done here with the first three-quarters of the article.*

The New Biology

Recent advances in biology and medicine suggest that we may be rapidly acquiring the power to modify and control the capacities and activities of men by direct intervention and manipulation of their bodies and minds. Certain means are already in use or at hand, others await the solution of relatively minor technical problems, while yet others, those offering perhaps the most precise kind of control, depend upon further basic research. Biologists who have considered these matters disagree on the question of how much how soon, but all agree that the power for "human engineering," to borrow from the jargon, is coming and that it will probably have profound social consequences.

These developments have been viewed both with enthusiasm and with alarm; they are only just beginning to receive serious attention. Several biologists have undertaken to inform the public about the technical possibilities, present and future. Practitioners of social science "futurology" are attempting to predict and describe the likely social consequences of and public responses to the new technologies. Lawyers and legislators are exploring institutional innovations for assessing new technologies. All of these activities are based upon the hope that we can harness the new technology of man for the betterment of mankind.

Yet this commendable aspiration points to another set of questions, which are, in my view, sorely neglected—questions that inquire into the meaning of phrases such as the "betterment of mankind." A *full* understanding of the new technology of man requires an exploration of ends, values, standards. What ends will or should the new techniques serve? What values should guide society's adjustments? By what standards should the assessment agencies assess? Behind these questions lie others: what is a good man, what is a good life for man, what is a good community? This article is an attempt to provoke discussion of these neglected and important questions.

While these questions about ends and ultimate ends are never unimportant or irrelevant, they have rarely been more important or more relevant. That this is so can be seen once we recognize that we are dealing here with a group of technologies that are in a decisive respect unique: the object upon which they operate is man himself. The technologies of energy or food production, of communication, of manufacture, and of motion greatly alter the implements available to man and the conditions in which he uses them. In contrast, the biomedical technology works to change the user himself. To be sure, the printing press, the automobile, the television, and the jet airplane have greatly altered the conditions under which and the way in which men live; but men as biological beings have remained largely unchanged. They have been, and remain, able to accept or reject, to use and abuse these technologies; they choose, whether wisely or foolishly, the ends to which these technologies are means. Biomedical technology may make it possible to change the inherent capacity for choice itself. Indeed, both those who welcome and those who fear the advent of "human engineering" ground their hopes and fears in the same prospect: *that man can for the first time re-create himself.*

Engineering the engineer seems to differ in kind from engineering his engine. Some have argued, however, that biomedical engineering does not differ qualitatively from toilet training, education, and moral teachings—all of which are forms of so-called "social engineering," which has man as its object, and is used by one generation to mold the next. In reply, it must at least be said that the techniques which have hitherto been employed are feeble and inefficient when compared to those on the horizon. This quantitative difference rests in part on a qualitative difference in the means of intervention. The traditional influences operate by speech or by symbolic deeds. They pay tribute to man as the animal who lives by speech and who understands the meanings of actions. Also, their effects are, in general, reversible, or at least subject to attempts at reversal. Each person has greater or lesser power to accept or reject or abandon them. In contrast, biomedical engineering circumvents the human context of speech and meaning, bypasses choice, and goes directly to work to modify the human material itself. Moreover, the changes wrought may be irreversible.

In addition, there is an important practical reason for considering the biomedical technology apart from other technologies. The advances we shall examine are fruits of a large, humane project dedicated to the conquest of disease and the relief of human suffering. The biologist and physician, regardless of their private motives, are seen, with justification, to be the well-wishers and benefactors of mankind. Thus, in a time in which technological advance is more carefully scrutinized and increasingly criticized, biomedical developments are still viewed by most people as benefits largely without qualification. The price we pay for these developments is thus more likely to go unrecognized. For this reason, I shall consider only the dangers and costs of biomedical advance. As the benefits are well known, there is no need to dwell upon them here. My discussion is deliberately partial.

I begin with a survey of the pertinent technologies. Next, I will consider some of the basic ethical and social problems in the use of these technologies.* Then, I will briefly raise some fundamental questions to which these problems point. Finally, I shall offer some very general reflections on what is to be done.

The Biomedical Technologies

The biomedical technologies can be usefully organized into three groups, according to their major purpose: (i) control of death and life, (ii) control of human potentialities, (iii) control of human achievement. The corresponding technologies are (i) medicine, especially the arts of prolonging life and of controlling reproduction, (ii) genetic engineering, and (iii) neurological and psychological manipulation. I shall briefly summarize each group of techniques.

1) *Control of death and life.* Previous medical triumphs have greatly increased average life expectancy. Yet other developments, such as organ transplantation or replacement and research into aging, hold forth the promise of increasing not just the average, but also the maximum life

*[The present version of the essay concludes at this point—Eds.]

expectancy. Indeed, medicine seems to be sharpening its tools to do battle with death itself, as if death were just one more disease.

More immediately and concretely available techniques of prolonging life—respirators, cardiac pacemakers, artificial kidneys—are already in the lists against death. Ironically, the success of these devices in forestalling death has introduced confusion in determining that death has, in fact, occurred. The traditional signs of life—heartbeat and respiration—can now be maintained entirely by machines. Some physicians are now busily trying to devise so-called "new definitions of death," while others maintain that the technical advances show that death is not a concrete event at all, but rather a gradual process, like twilight, incapable of precise temporal localization.

The real challenge to death will come from research into aging and senescence, a field just entering puberty. Recent studies suggest that aging is a genetically controlled process, distinct from disease, but one that can be manipulated and altered by diet or drugs. Extrapolating from animal studies, some scientists have suggested that a decrease in the rate of aging might also be achieved simply by effecting a very small decrease in human body temperature. According to some estimates, by the year 2000 it may be technically possible to add from 20 to 40 useful years to the period of middle life.

Medicine's success in extending life is already a major cause of excessive population growth: death control points to birth control. Although we are already technically competent, new techniques for lowering fertility and chemical agents for inducing abortion will greatly enhance our powers over conception and gestation. Problems of definition have been raised here as well. The need to determine when individuals acquire enforceable legal rights gives society an interest in the definition of human life and of the time when it begins. These matters are too familiar to need elaboration.

Technologies to conquer infertility proceed alongside those to promote it. The first successful laboratory fertilization of human egg by human sperm was reported in 1969.[1] In 1970, British scientists learned how to grow human embryos in the laboratory up to at least the blastocyst stage (that is, to the age of 1 week).[2] We may soon hear about the next stage, the successful reimplantation of such an embryo into a woman previously infertile because of oviduct disease. The development of an artificial placenta, now under investigation, will make possible full laboratory control of fertilization and gestation. In addition, sophisticated biochemical and cytological techniques of monitoring the "quality" of the fetus have been and are being developed and used. These developments not only give us more power over the generation of human life, but make it possible to manipulate and to modify the quality of the human material.

[1]R. G. Edwards, B. D. Bavister, P. C. Steptoe, *Nature* **221**, 632 (1969).
[2]R. G. Edwards, P. C. Steptoe, J. M. Purdy, *ibid.* **227**, 1307 (1970).

2) *Control of human potentialities.* Genetic engineering, when fully developed, will wield two powers not shared by ordinary medical practice. Medicine treats existing individuals and seeks to correct deviations from a norm of health. Genetic engineering, in contrast, will be able to make changes that can be transmitted to succeeding generations and will be able to create new capacities, and hence to establish new norms of health and fitness.

Nevertheless, one of the major interests in genetic manipulation is strictly medical: to develop treatments for individuals with inherited diseases. Genetic disease is prevalent and increasing, thanks partly to medical advances that enable those affected to survive and perpetuate their mutant genes. The hope is that normal copies of the appropriate gene, obtained biologically or synthesized chemically, can be introduced into defective individuals to correct their deficiencies. This *therapeutic* use of genetic technology appears to be far in the future. Moreover, there is some doubt that it will ever be practical, since the same end could be more easily achieved by transplanting cells or organs that could compensate for the missing or defective gene product.

Far less remote are technologies that could serve *eugenic* ends. Their development has been endorsed by those concerned about a general deterioration of the human gene pool and by others who believe that even an undeteriorated human gene pool needs upgrading. Artificial insemination with selected donors, the eugenic proposal of Herman Muller,[3] has been possible for several years because of the perfection of methods for long-term storage of human spermatozoa. The successful maturation of human oocytes in the laboratory and their subsequent fertilization now make it possible to select donors of ova as well. But a far more suitable technique for eugenic purposes will soon be upon us —namely, nuclear transplantation, or cloning. Bypassing the lottery of sexual recombination, nuclear transplantation permits the asexual reproduction or copying of an already developed individual. The nucleus of a mature but unfertilized egg is replaced by a nucleus obtained from a specialized cell of an adult organism or embryo (for example, a cell from the intestines or the skin). The egg with its transplanted nucleus develops as if it had been fertilized and, barring complications, will give rise to a normal adult organism. Since almost all the hereditary material (DNA) of a cell is contained within its nucleus, the renucleated egg and the individual into which it develops are genetically identical to the adult organism that was the source of the donor nucleus. Cloning could be used to produce sets of unlimited numbers of genetically identical individuals, each set derived from a single parent. Cloning has been successful in amphibians and is now being tried in mice; its extension to man merely requires the solution of certain technical problems.

Production of man-animal chimeras by the introduction of selected

[3]H. J. Muller, *Science* **134**, 643 (1961).

nonhuman material into developing human embryos is also expected. Fusion of human and nonhuman cells in tissue culture has already been achieved.

Other, less direct means for influencing the gene pool are already available, thanks to our increasing ability to identify and diagnose genetic diseases. Genetic counselors can now detect biochemically and cytologically a variety of severe genetic defects (for example, Mongolism, Tay-Sachs disease) while the fetus is still in utero. Since treatments are at present largely unavailable, diagnosis is often followed by abortion of the affected fetus. In the future, more sensitive tests will also permit the detection of heterozygote carriers, the unaffected individuals who carry but a single dose of a given deleterious gene. The eradication of a given genetic disease might then be attempted by aborting all such carriers. In fact, it was recently suggested that the fairly common disease cystic fibrosis could be completely eliminated over the next 40 years by screening all pregnancies and aborting the 17,000,000 unaffected fetuses that will carry a single gene for this disease. Such zealots need to be reminded of the consequences should each geneticist be allowed an equal assault on his favorite genetic disorder, given that each human being is a carrier for some four to eight such recessive, lethal genetic diseases.

3) *Control of human achievement.* Although human achievement depends at least in part upon genetic endowment, heredity determines only the material upon which experience and education impose the form. The limits of many capacities and powers of an individual are indeed genetically determined, but the nurturing and perfection of these capacities depend upon other influences. Neurological and psychological manipulation hold forth the promise of controlling the development of human capacities, particularly those long considered most distinctively human: speech, thought, choice, emotion, memory, and imagination.

These techniques are now in a rather primitive state because we understand so little about the brain and mind. Nevertheless, we have already seen the use of electrical stimulation of the human brain to produce sensations of intense pleasure and to control rage, the use of brain surgery (for example, frontal lobotomy) for the relief of severe anxiety, and the use of aversive conditioning with electric shock to treat sexual perversion. Operant-conditioning techniques are widely used, apparently with success, in schools and mental hospitals. The use of so-called consciousness-expanding and hallucinogenic drugs is widespread, to say nothing of tranquilizers and stimulants. We are promised drugs to modify memory, intelligence, libido, and aggressiveness. - easy

The following passages from a recent book by Yale neurophysiologist José Delgado—a book instructively entitled *Physical Control of the Mind: Toward a Psychocivilized Society*—should serve to make this discussion more concrete. In the early 1950's, it was discovered that, with electrodes placed in certain discrete regions of their brains, animals would repeatedly and indefatigably press levers to stimulate their own brains, with obvious resultant enjoyment. Even starving animals preferred stimulating these so-called pleasure centers to eating. Delgado comments on the electrical stimulation of a similar center in a human subject.[4]

> [T]he patient reported a pleasant tingling sensation in the left side of her body 'from my face down to the bottom of my legs.' She started giggling and making funny comments, stating that she enjoyed the sensation 'very much.' Repetition of these stimulations made the patient more communicative and flirtatious, and she ended by openly expressing her desire to marry the therapist.

And one further quotation from Delgado.[5]

> Leaving wires inside of a thinking brain may appear unpleasant or dangerous, but actually the many patients who have undergone this experience have not been concerned about the fact of being wired, nor have they felt any discomfort due to the presence of conductors in their heads. Some women have shown their feminine adaptability to circumstances by wearing attractive hats or wigs to conceal their electrical headgear, and many people have been able to enjoy a normal life as outpatients, returning to the clinic periodically for examination and stimulation. In a few cases in which contacts were located in pleasurable areas, patients have had the opportunity to stimulate their own brains by pressing the button of a portable instrument, and this procedure is reported to have therapeutic benefits.

It bears repeating that the sciences of neurophysiology and psychopharmacology are in their infancy. The techniques that are now available are crude, imprecise, weak, and unpredictable, compared to those that may flow from a more mature neurobiology.

Basic Ethical and Social Problems in the Use of Biomedical Technology

After this cursory review of the powers now and soon to be at our disposal, I turn to the questions concerning the use of these powers. First, we must recognize that questions of use of science and technology are always moral and political questions, never simply technical ones. All private or public decisions to develop or to use biomedical technology— and decisions *not* to do so—inevitably contain judgments about value. This is true even if the values guiding those decisions are not articulated or made clear, as indeed they often are not. Secondly, the value judg-

---

[4]J. M. R. Delgado, *Physical Control of the Mind: Toward a Psychocivilized Society* (Harper & Row, New York, 1969), p. 185.
[5]*Ibid.*, p. 88.

ments cannot be derived from biomedical science. This is true even if scientists themselves make the decisions.

These important points are often overlooked for at least three reasons.

1) They are obscured by those who like to speak of "the control of nature by science." It is men who control, not that abstraction "science." Science may provide the means, but men choose the ends; the choice of ends comes from beyond science.

2) Introduction of new technologies often appears to be the result of no decision whatsoever, or of the culmination of decisions too small or unconscious to be recognized as such. What can be done is done. However, someone is deciding on the basis of some notions of desirability, no matter how self-serving or altruistic.

3) Desires to gain or keep money and power no doubt influence much of what happens, but these desires can also be formulated as reasons and then discussed and debated.

Insofar as our society has tried to deliberate about questions of use, how has it done so? Pragmatists that we are, we prefer a utilitarian calculus: we weigh "benefits" against "risks," and we weigh them for both the individual and "society." We often ignore the fact that the very definitions of "a benefit" and "a risk" are themselves based upon judgments about value. In the biomedical areas just reviewed, the benefits are considered to be self-evident: prolongation of life, control of fertility and of population size, treatment and prevention of genetic disease, the reduction of anxiety and aggressiveness, and the enhancement of memory, intelligence, and pleasure. The assessment of risk is, in general, simply pragmatic—will the technique work effectively and reliably, how much will it cost, will it do detectable bodily harm, and who will complain if we proceed with development? As these questions are familiar and congenial, there is no need to belabor them.

The very pragmatism that makes us sensitive to considerations of economic cost often blinds us to the larger social costs exacted by biomedical advances. For one thing, we seem to be unaware that we may not be able to maximize all the benefits, that several of the goals we are promoting conflict with each other. On the one hand, we seek to control population growth by lowering fertility; on the other hand, we develop techniques to enable every infertile woman to bear a child. On the one hand, we try to extend the lives of individuals with genetic disease; on the other, we wish to eliminate deleterious genes from the human population. I am not urging that we resolve these conflicts in favor of one side or the other, but simply that we recognize that such conflicts exist. Once we do, we are more likely to appreciate that most "progress" is heavily paid for in terms not generally included in the simple utilitarian calculus.

To become sensitive to the larger costs of biomedical progress, we must attend to several serious ethical and social questions. I will briefly discuss three of them: (i) questions of distributive justice, (ii) questions of the use and abuse of power, and (iii) questions of self-degradation and dehumanization.

Distributive Justice

The introduction of any biomedical technology presents a new instance of an old problem—how to distribute scarce resources justly. We should assume that demand will usually exceed supply. Which people should receive a kidney transplant or an artificial heart? Who should get the benefits of genetic therapy or of brain stimulation? Is "first-come, first-served" the fairest principle? Or are certain people "more worthy," and if so, on what grounds?

It is unlikely that we will arrive at answers to these questions in the form of deliberate decisions. More likely, the problem of distribution will continue to be decided ad hoc and locally. If so, the consequence will probably be a sharp increase in the already far too great inequality of medical care. The extreme case will be longevity, which will probably be, at first, obtainable only at great expense. Who is likely to be able to buy it? Do conscience and prudence permit us to enlarge the gap between rich and poor, especially with respect to something as fundamental as life itself?

Questions of distributive justice also arise in the earlier decisions to acquire new knowledge and to develop new techniques. Personnel and facilities for medical research and treatment are scarce resources. Is the development of a new technology the best use of the limited resources, given current circumstances? How should we balance efforts aimed at prevention against those aimed at cure, or either of these against efforts to redesign the species? How should we balance the delivery of available levels of care against further basic research? More fundamentally, how should we balance efforts in biology and medicine against efforts to eliminate poverty, pollution, urban decay, discrimination, and poor education? This last question about distribution is perhaps the most profound. We should reflect upon the social consequences of seducing many of our brightest young people to spend their lives locating the biochemical defects in rare genetic diseases, while our more serious problems go begging. The current squeeze on money for research provides us with an opportunity to rethink and reorder our priorities.

Problems of distributive justice are frequently mentioned and discussed, but they are hard to resolve in a rational manner. We find them especially difficult because of the enormous range of conflicting values and interests that characterizes our pluralistic society. We cannot agree —unfortunately, we often do not even try to agree—on standards for just distribution. Rather, decisions tend to be made largely out of a clash of competing interests. Thus, regrettably, the question of how to distribute justly often gets reduced to who shall decide how to distribute. The question about justice has led us to the question about power.

Use and Abuse of Power

We have difficulty recognizing the problems of the exercise of power in the biomedical enterprise because of our delight with the wondrous fruits it has yielded. This is ironic because the notion of power is absolutely central to the modern conception of science. The ancients conceived of science as the *understanding* of nature, pursued for its own sake. We moderns view science as power, as *control* over nature; the conquest of nature "for the relief of man's estate" was the charge issued by Francis Bacon, one of the leading architects of the modern scientific project.[6]

Another source of difficulty is our fondness for speaking of the abstraction "Man." I suspect that we prefer to speak figuratively about "Man's power over Nature" because it obscures an unpleasant reality about human affairs. It is in fact particular men who wield power, not Man. What we really mean by "Man's power over Nature" is a power exercised by some men over other men, with a knowledge of nature as their instrument.

While applicable to technology in general, these reflections are especially pertinent to the technologies of human engineering, with which men deliberately exercise power over future generations. An excellent discussion of this question is found in *The Abolition of Man,* by C. S. Lewis.[7]

> It is, of course, a commonplace to complain that men have hitherto used badly, and against their fellows, the powers that science has given them. But that is not the point I am trying to make. I am not speaking of particular corruptions and abuses which an increase of moral virtue would cure: I am considering what the thing called "Man's power over Nature" must always and essentially be. . . .
>
> In reality, of course, if any one age really attains, by eugenics and scientific education, the power to make its descendants what it pleases, all men who live after it are the patients of that power. They are weaker, not stronger: for though we may have put wonderful machines in their hands, we have pre-ordained how they are to use them. . . . The real picture is that of one dominant age . . . which resists all previous ages most successfully and dominates all subsequent ages most irresistibly, and thus is the real master of the human species. But even within this master generation (itself an infinitesimal minority of the species) the power will be exercised by a minority smaller still. Man's conquest of Nature, if the dreams of some scientific planners are realized, means the rule of a few hundreds of men over billions upon billions of men. There neither is nor can be any simple increase of power on Man's side. Each new power won *by* man is a power *over* man as well. Each advance leaves him weaker as well as stronger. In every victory, besides being the general who triumphs, he is also the prisoner who follows the triumphal car.

[6]F. Bacon, *The Advancement of Learning, Book I,* H. G. Dick, Ed. (Random House, New York, 1955), p. 193.

[7]C. S. Lewis, *The Abolition of Man* (Macmillan, New York, 1965), pp. 69–71.

Please note that I am not yet speaking about the problem of the misuse or abuse of power. The point is rather that the power which grows is unavoidably the power of only some men, and that the number of powerful men decreases as power increases. *

Specific problems of abuse and misuse of specific powers must not, however, be overlooked. Some have voiced the fear that the technologies of genetic engineering and behavior control, though developed for good purposes, will be put to evil uses. These fears are perhaps somewhat exaggerated, if only because biomedical technologies would add very little to our highly developed arsenal for mischief, destruction, and stultification. Nevertheless, any proposal for large-scale human engineering should make us wary. Consider a program of positive eugenics based upon the widespread practice of asexual reproduction. Who shall decide what constitutes a superior individual worthy of replication? Who shall decide which individuals may or must reproduce, and by which method? These are questions easily answered only for a tyrannical regime.

Concern about the use of power is equally necessary in the selection of means for desirable or agreed-upon ends. Consider the desired end of limiting population growth. An effective program of fertility control is likely to be coercive. Who should decide the choice of means? Will the program penalize "conscientious objectors"?

Serious problems arise simply from obtaining and disseminating information, as in the mass screening programs now being proposed for detection of genetic disease. For what kinds of disorders is compulsory screening justified? Who shall have access to the data obtained, and for what purposes? To whom does information about a person's genotype belong? In ordinary medical practice, the patient's privacy is protected by the doctor's adherence to the principle of confidentiality. What will protect his privacy under conditions of mass screening?

More than privacy is at stake if screening is undertaken to detect psychological or behavioral abnormalities. A recent proposal, tendered and supported high in government, called for the psychological testing of all 6-year-olds to detect future criminals and misfits. The proposal was rejected; current tests lack the requisite predictive powers. But will such a proposal be rejected if reliable tests become available? What if certain genetic disorders, diagnosable in childhood, can be shown to correlate with subsequent antisocial behavior? For what degree of correlation and for what kinds of behavior can mandatory screening be justified? What use should be made of the data? Might not the dissemination of the information itself undermine the individual's chance for a worthy life and contribute to his so-called antisocial tendencies?

Consider the seemingly harmless effort to redefine clinical death. If the need for organs for transplantation is the stimulus for redefining death, might not this concern influence the definition at the expense of the dying? One physician, in fact, refers in writing to the revised criteria

for declaring a patient dead as a "new definition of heart donor eligibil-
ity."[8]

Problems of abuse of power arise even in the acquisition of basic
knowledge. The securing of a voluntary and informed consent is an
abiding problem in the use of human subjects in experimentation. Gross
coercion and deception are now rarely a problem; the pressures are
generally subtle, often related to an intrinsic power imbalance in favor of
the experimentalist.

A special problem arises in experiments on or manipulations of the
unborn. Here it is impossible to obtain the consent of the human subject.
If the purpose of the intervention is therapeutic—to correct a known
genetic abnormality, for example—consent can reasonably be implied.
But can anyone ethically consent to nontherapeutic interventions in
which parents or scientists work their wills or their eugenic visions on the
child-to-be? Would not such manipulation represent in itself an abuse of
power, independent of consequences?

There are many clinical situations which already permit, if not invite,
the manipulative or arbitrary use of powers provided by biomedical technology: obtaining organs for transplantation, refusing to let a person die
with dignity, giving genetic counselling to a frightened couple, recom-
mending eugenic sterilization for a mental retardate, ordering electric
shock for a homosexual. In each situation, there is an opportunity to
violate the will of the patient or subject. Such opportunities have generally existed in medical practice, but the dangers are becoming increasingly serious. With the growing complexity of the technologies, the
technician gains in authority, since he alone can understand what he is
doing. The patient's lack of knowledge makes him deferential and often
inhibits him from speaking up when he feels threatened. Physicians *are*
sometimes troubled by their increasing power, yet they feel they cannot
avoid its exercise. "Reluctantly," one commented to me, "we shall have
to play God." With what guidance and to what ends I shall consider later.
For the moment, I merely ask: "By whose authority?"

While these questions about power are pertinent and important, they
are in one sense misleading. They imply an inherent conflict of purpose
between physician and patient, between scientist and citizen. The discussion conjures up images of master and slave, of oppressor and oppressed.
Yet it must be remembered that conflict of purpose is largely absent,
especially with regard to general goals. To be sure, the purposes of
medical scientists are not always the same as those of the subjects experimented on. Nevertheless, basic sponsors and partisans of biomedical
technology are precisely those upon whom the technology will operate.
The will of the scientist and physician is happily married to (rather, is the
offspring of) the desire of all of us for better health, longer life, and peace
of mind.

[8]D. D. Rutstein, *Daedalus* (Spring 1969), p. 523.

Most future biomedical technologies will probably be welcomed, as have those of the past. Their use will require little or no coercion. Some developments, such as pills to improve memory, control mood, or induce pleasure, are likely to need no promotion. Thus, even if we should escape from the dangers of coercive manipulation, we shall still face large problems posed by the voluntary use of biomedical technology, problems to which I now turn.

Voluntary Self-Degradation and Dehumanization

Modern opinion is sensitive to problems of restriction of freedom and abuse of power. Indeed, many hold that a man can be injured only by violating his will. But this view is much too narrow. It fails to recognize the great dangers we shall face in the use of biomedical technology, dangers that stem from an excess of freedom, from the uninhibited exercises of will. In my view, our greatest problem will increasingly be one of voluntary self-degradation, or willing dehumanization.

Certain desired and perfected medical technologies have already had some dehumanizing consequences. Improved methods of resuscitation have made possible heroic efforts to "save" the severely ill and injured. Yet these efforts are sometimes only partly successful; they may succeed in salvaging individuals with severe brain damage, capable of only a less-than-human, vegetating existence. Such patients, increasingly found in the intensive care units of university hospitals, have been denied a death with dignity. Families are forced to suffer seeing their loved ones so reduced, and are made to bear the burdens of a protracted death watch.

Even the ordinary methods of treating disease and prolonging life have impoverished the context in which men die. Fewer and fewer people die in the familiar surroundings of home or in the company of family and friends. At that time of life when there is perhaps the greatest need for human warmth and comfort, the dying patient is kept company by cardiac pacemakers and defibrillators, respirators, aspirators, oxygenators, catheters, and his intravenous drip.

But the loneliness is not confined to the dying patient in the hospital bed. Consider the increasing number of old people who are still alive, thanks to medical progress. As a group, the elderly are the most alienated members of our society. Not yet ready for the world of the dead, not deemed fit for the world of the living, they are shunted aside. More and more of them spend the extra years medicine has given them in "homes for senior citizens," in chronic hospitals, in nursing homes—waiting for the end. We have learned how to increase their years, but we have not learned how to help them enjoy their days. And yet, we bravely and relentlessly push back the frontiers against death.

Paradoxically, even the young and vigorous may be suffering because of medicine's success in removing death from their personal experience.

Those born since penicillin represent the first generation ever to grow up without the experience or fear of probable unexpected death at an early age. They look around and see that virtually all of their friends are alive. A thoughtful physician, Eric Cassell, has remarked on this in "Death and the physician":[9]

> [W]hile the gift of time must surely be marked as a great blessing, the *perception* of time, as stretching out endlessly before us, is somewhat threatening. Many of us function best under deadlines, and tend to procrastinate when time limits are not set. . . . Thus, this unquestioned boon, the extension of life, and the removal of the threat of premature death, carries with it an unexpected anxiety: the anxiety of an unlimited future.
>
> In the young, the sense of limitless time has apparently imparted not a feeling of limitless opportunity, but increased stress and anxiety, in addition to the anxiety which results from other modern freedoms: personal mobility, a wide range of occupational choice, and independence from the limitations of class and familial patterns of work. . . . A certain aimlessness (often ringed around with great social consciousness) characterizes discussions about their own aspirations. The future is endless, and their inner demands seem minimal. Although it may appear uncharitable to say so, they seem to be acting in a way best described as "childish"—particularly in their lack of a time sense. They behave as though there were no tomorrow, or as though the time limits imposed by the biological facts of life had become so vague for them as to be nonexistent.

Consider next the coming power over reproduction and genotype. We endorse the project that will enable us to control numbers and to treat individuals with genetic disease. But our desires outrun these defensible goals. Many would welcome the chance to become parents without the inconvenience of pregnancy; others would wish to know in advance the characteristics of their offspring (sex, height, eye color, intelligence); still others would wish to design these characteristics to suit their tastes. Some scientists have called for the use of the new technologies to assure the "quality" of all new babies.[10] As one obstetrician put it: "The business of obstetrics is to produce *optimum* babies." But the price to be paid for the "optimum baby" is the transfer of procreation from the home to the laboratory and its coincident transformation into manufacture. Increasing control over the product is purchased by the increasing depersonalization of the process. The complete depersonalization of procreation (possible with the development of an artificial placenta) shall be, in itself, seriously dehumanizing, no matter how optimum the product. It should not be forgotten that human procreation not only issues new human beings, but is itself a human activity.

Procreation is not simply an activity of the rational will. It is a more complete human activity precisely because it engages us bodily and

---

[9]E. J. Cassell, *Commentary* (June 1969), p. 73.
[10]B. Glass, *Science* **171**, 23 (1971).

spiritually, as well as rationally. Is there perhaps some wisdom in that mystery of nature which joins the pleasure of sex, the communication of love, and the desire for children in the very activity by which we continue the chain of human existence? Is not biological parenthood a built-in "mechanism," selected because it fosters and supports in parents an adequate concern for and commitment to their children? Would not the laboratory production of human beings no longer be *human* procreation? Could it keep human parenthood human?

The dehumanizing consequences of programmed reproduction extend beyond the mere acts and processes of life-giving. Transfer of procreation to the laboratory will no doubt weaken what is presently for many people the best remaining justification and support for the existence of marriage and the family. Sex is now comfortably at home outside of marriage; child-rearing is progressively being given over to the state, the schools, the mass media, and the child-care centers. Some have argued that the family, long the nursery of humanity, has outlived its usefulness. To be sure, laboratory and governmental alternatives might be designed for procreation and child-rearing, but at what cost?

This is not the place to conduct a full evaluation of the biological family. Nevertheless, some of its important virtues are, nowadays, too often overlooked. The family is rapidly becoming the only institution in an increasingly impersonal world where each person is loved not for what he does or makes, but simply because he is. The family is also the institution where most of us, both as children and as parents, acquire a sense of continuity with the past and a sense of commitment to the future. Without the family, we would have little incentive to take an interest in anything after our own deaths. These observations suggest that the elimination of the family would weaken ties to past and future, and would throw us, even more than we are now, to the mercy of an impersonal, lonely present.

Neurobiology and psychobiology probe most directly into the distinctively human. The technological fruit of these sciences is likely to be both more tempting than Eve's apple and more "catastrophic" in its result. One need only consider contemporary drug use to see what people are willing to risk or sacrifice for novel experiences, heightened perceptions, or just "kicks." The possibility of drug-induced, instant, and effortless gratification will be welcomed. Recall the possibilities of voluntary self-stimulation of the brain to reduce anxiety, to heighten pleasure, or to create visual and auditory sensations unavailable through the peripheral sense organs. Once these techniques are perfected and safe, is there much doubt that they will be desired, demanded, and used?

What ends will these techniques serve? Most likely, only the most elemental, those most tied to the bodily pleasures. What will happen to thought, to love, to friendship, to art, to judgment, to public-spiritedness in a society with a perfected technology of pleasure? What kinds of creatures will we become if we obtain our pleasure by drug or electrical stimulation without the usual kind of human efforts and frustrations? What kind of society will we have?

We need only consult Aldous Huxley's prophetic novel *Brave New World* for a likely answer to these questions. There we encounter a society dedicated to homogeneity and stability, administered by means of instant gratifications and peopled by creatures of human shape but of stunted humanity. They consume, fornicate, take "soma," and operate the machinery that makes it all possible. They do not read, write, think, love, or govern themselves. Creativity and curiosity, reason and passion, exist only in a rudimentary and mutilated form. In short, they are not men at all.

True, our techniques, like theirs, may in fact enable us to treat schizophrenia, to alleviate anxiety, to curb aggressiveness. We, like they, may indeed be able to save mankind from itself, but probably only at the cost of its humanness. In the end, the price of relieving man's estate might well be the abolition of man.

There are, of course, many other routes leading to the abolition of man. There are many other and better known causes of dehumanization. Disease, starvation, mental retardation, slavery, and brutality—to name just a few—have long prevented many, if not most, people from living a fully human life. We should work to reduce and eventually to eliminate these evils. But the existence of these evils should not prevent us from appreciating that the use of the technology of man, uninformed by wisdom concerning proper human ends, and untempered by an appropriate humility and awe, can unwittingly render us all irreversibly less than human. For, unlike the man reduced by disease or slavery, the people dehumanized à la *Brave New World* are not miserable, do not know that they are dehumanized, and, what is worse, would not care if they knew. They are, indeed, happy slaves, with a slavish happiness.

.   .   .

THEODORE ROSZAK

Theodore Roszak, born in 1933, attended U.C.L.A., received the Ph.D. from Princeton in 1958, and is now Professor of History at California State College at Hayward. He is a vigorous social philosopher and critic who has contributed much to such journals as The Nation, Liberation, *and* New Politics. *He has written* Where the Wasteland Ends: Politics and Transcendence in Post-Industrial Society *(1972) and has edited* The Dissenting Academy *(1968),* Sources: An Anthology of Contemporary Materials Useful for Preserving the Great Technological Wilderness *(1972), and, with Betty Roszak,*

Masculine/Feminine: Readings in Sexual Mythology and the Liberation of Women (1970). His most widely acclaimed book is The Making of a Counter Culture: Reflections on the Technocratic Society and Its Youthful Opposition *(1969), which was nominated for a National Book Award. In it, Roszak analyzes some of the major influences on the modern youth culture, showing how that culture calls into question the conventional world view of science and technology. We reprint here the Appendix to the book, "Objectivity Unlimited," designed to illustrate in detail the psychology of "objective consciousness," which the author discusses in Chapter 7 under the title "The Myth of Objective Consciousness." A few of the opening pages of Chapter 7 introduce the subject.*

from The Myth of Objective Consciousness

If there is one especially striking feature of the new radicalism we have been surveying, it is the cleavage that exists between it and the radicalism of previous generations where the subjects of science and technology are concerned. To the older collectivist ideologies, which were as given to the value of industrial expansion as the capitalist class enemy, the connection between totalitarian control and science was not apparent. Science was almost invariably seen as an undisputed social good, because it had become so intimately related in the popular mind (though not often in ways clearly understood) to the technological progress that promised security and affluence. It was not foreseen even by gifted social critics that the impersonal, large-scale social processes to which technological progress gives rise—in economics, in politics, in education, in every aspect of life—generate their own characteristic problems. When the general public finds itself enmeshed in a gargantuan industrial apparatus which it admires to the point of idolization and yet cannot comprehend, it must of necessity defer to those who are experts or to those who own the experts; only they appear to know how the great cornucopia can be kept brimming over with the good things of life.

Centralized bigness breeds the regime of expertise, whether the big system is based on privatized or socialized economies. Even within the democratic socialist tradition with its stubborn emphasis on workers' control, it is far from apparent how the democratically governed units of an industrial economy will automatically produce a general system which is not dominated by co-ordinating experts. It is both ironic and ominous to hear the French Gaullists and the Wilson Labourites in Great Britain —governments that are heavily committed to an elitist managerialism— now talking seriously about increased workers' "participation" in industry. It would surely be a mistake to believe that the technocracy cannot

find ways to placate and integrate the shop floor without compromising
the continuation of super-scale social processes. "Participation" could
easily become the god-word of our official politics within the next decade;
but its reference will be to the sort of "responsible" collaboration that
keeps the technocracy growing. We do well to remember that one of the
great secrets of successful concentration camp administration under the
Nazis was to enlist the "participation" of the inmates.

It is for this reason that the counter culture, which draws upon a
profoundly personalist sense of community rather than upon technical
and industrial values, comes closer to being a radical critique of the
technocracy than any of the traditional ideologies. If one starts with a
sense of the person that ventures to psychoanalytical depths, one may
rapidly arrive at a viewpoint that rejects many of the hitherto undisputed
values of industrialism itself. One soon begins talking about "standards
of living" that transcend high productivity, efficiency, full employment,
and the work-and-consumption ethic. Quality and not quantity becomes
the touchstone of social value.

The critique is pushed even further when the counter culture begins
to explore the modes of non-intellective consciousness. Along this line,
questions arise which strike more deeply at technocratic assumptions. For
if the technocracy is dependent on public deference to the experts, it
must stand or fall by the reality of expertise. But what *is* expertise? What
are the criteria which certify someone as an expert?

If we are foolishly willing to agree that experts are those whose role
is legitimized by the fact that the technocratic system needs them in order
to avoid falling apart at the seams, then of course the technocratic status
quo generates its own internal justification: the technocracy is legitimized
because it enjoys the approval of experts; the experts are legitimized
because there could be no technocracy without them. This is the sort of
circular argument student rebels meet when they challenge the necessity
of administrative supremacy in the universities. They are invariably faced
with the rhetorical question: but who will allocate room space, supervise
registration, validate course requirements, co-ordinate the academic departments, police the parking lots and dormitories, discipline students,
etc., if not the administration? Will the multiversity not collapse in chaos
if the administrators are sent packing? The students are learning the
answer: yes, the multiversity will collapse; but *education* will go on. Why?
Because the administrators have nothing to do with the reality of education; their expertise is related to the illusory busywork that arises from
administrative complexity itself. The multiversity creates the administrators and they, in turn, expand the multiversity so that it needs to make
place for more administrators. One gets out of this squirrel cage only by
digging deep into the root meaning of education itself.

The same radicalizing logic unfolds if, in confronting the technocracy,
we begin looking for a conception of expertise which amounts to some-

thing more than the intimidating truism that tells us experts are those in the absence of whom the technocracy would collapse.

An expert, we say, is one to whom we turn because he is in control of reliable knowledge about that which concerns us. In the case of the technocracy, the experts are those who govern us because they know (reliably) about all things relevant to our survival and happiness: human needs, social engineering, economic planning, international relations, invention, education, etc. Very well, but what is "reliable knowledge"? How do we know it when we see it? The answer is: reliable knowledge is knowledge that is scientifically sound, since science is that to which modern man refers for the definitive explication of reality. And what in turn is it that characterizes scientific knowledge? The answer is: objectivity. Scientific knowledge is not just feeling or speculation or subjective ruminating. It is a verifiable description of reality that exists independent of any purely personal considerations. It is true . . . real . . . dependable. . . . It works. And that at last is how we define an expert: he is one who *really* knows what is what, because he cultivates an objective consciousness.

Thus, if we probe the technocracy in search of the peculiar power it holds over us, we arrive at the myth of objective consciousness. There is but one way of gaining access to reality—so the myth holds—and this is to cultivate a state of consciousness cleansed of all subjective distortion, all personal involvement. What flows from this state of consciousness qualifies as knowledge, and nothing else does. This is the bedrock on which the natural sciences have built; and under their spell all fields of knowledge strive to become scientific. The study of man in his social, political, economic, psychological, historical aspects—all this, too, must become objective: rigorously, painstakingly objective. At every level of human experience, would-be scientists come forward to endorse the myth of objective consciousness, thus certifying themselves as experts. And because they know and we do not, we yield to their guidance.

An expert is one who can describe reality because he can disregard his personal views and look at things objectively.

Objectivity Unlimited

The items contained in this appendix are meant to give at least a minimal illustration of the psychology of objective consciousness as characterized in Chapter VII. The examples offered are few in number; but they could be multiplied many times over.

It is likely that some readers will protest that these items do not give a "balanced" picture of science and technology, but unfairly emphasize certain enormities and absurdities. Let me therefore make three points in explanation of why and how the examples of objectivity below were selected.

(1) Often, when one enters into a discussion of the less encouraging aspects of scientific research and technical innovation, the cases brought forward for consideration are either obviously extreme examples that are universally condemned (like that of the Nazi physicians who experimented on human specimens), or they are images conjured up from science fiction, which are easily waved aside precisely because they *are* fictitious. The items in this appendix are not drawn from either of these sources. Rather, they derive from what I believe can fairly be called mainstream science (I include the behavioral sciences in the term) and technology. I have tried to offer reports, examples, and statements from thoroughly reputable sources which can pass muster as possessing professional respectability. My object is to present items that have a routine, if not an almost casual, character and can therefore stand as the voice of normal, day-to-day science and technology as they are practiced in our society with a sense of complete innocence and orthodoxy—and often with the massive subsidization of public funds. Indeed, I suspect that many scientists and technicians would find nothing whatever to object to in the remarks and projects referred to here, but would view them as perfectly legitimate, if not extremely interesting, lines of research to which only a perversely anti-scientific mentality would object.

(2) Further, I would contend that the material presented here typifies what the technocracy is most eager to reward and support. These are the kinds of projects and the kinds of men we can expect to see becoming ever more prominent as the technocratic society consolidates its power. Whatever enlightening and beneficial "spin-off" the universal research explosion of our time produces, the major interest of those who lavishly finance that research will continue to be in weapons, in techniques of social control, in commercial gadgetry, in market manipulation, and in the subversion of democratic processes by way of information monopoly and engineered consensus. What the technocracy requires, therefore, is men of unquestioning objectivity who can apply themselves to any assignment and deliver the goods, with few qualms regarding the ultimate application of their work.

As time goes on, it may well be that gifted and sensitive talents will find it more and more difficult to serve the technocratic system. But such conscience-stricken types—the potential Norbert Wieners and Otto Hahns and Leo Szilards—will be easily replaced by acquiescent routineers who will do what is expected of them, who will play dumb as they continue grinding out the research, and who will be able to convince themselves that the high status they receive is, in truth, the just and happy reward their idealistic quest for knowledge deserves. One would think that a man who had been hired by pyromaniacs to perfect better matches would begin to sense, at some point, how much of a culprit he was. But fame and cash can do wonders to bolster one's sense of innocence.

Not long before his death, the greatest scientific mind since Newton confessed to the world that, if he had to choose over again, he would rather have been a good shoemaker. I have often felt that, long before he learns a single thing about mesons or information theory or DNA, every aspiring young scientist and technician in our schools should be confronted with that heartbroken admission and forced to fathom its implications. But alas, I suspect there is in the great man's lament a pathos too deep any longer to be appreciated by the sorcerer's apprentices who crowd forward in disconcerting numbers to book passage on the technocratic gravy train. And where the scientists and technicians lead, the pseudo-scientists and social engineers are quick to follow. Given the dazzling temptations of a sky's-the-limit research circus, what time is there to dally over traditional wisdom or moral doubt? It distracts from the bright, hard, monomaniacal focus that pays off for the expert—especially if one bears in mind that in the technical fields these days apprentices make their mark early . . . or perhaps never. So the sweaty quest for quick, stunning success goes off in all directions. If only one can find a way to graft the head of a baboon on to a blue jay (after all, why not?) . . . if only one can synthesize a virus lethal enough to wipe out a whole nation (after all, why not?) . . . if only one can invent a Greek-tragedy writing machine (after all, why not?) . . . if only one can dope out a way to condition the public into believing that War is Peace and that the fallout shelter is our home away from home (after all, why not?) . . . if only one can devise a way to program dreams so that perhaps commercial announcements can be inserted (after all, why not?) . . . if only one can find out how to scramble DNA so that parents can order their progeny tailor-made as guaranteed-or-money-back Mozarts, Napoleons, or Jesus Christs (after all, why not?) . . . if only one can invent a method of shooting passengers like bullets from Chicago to Istanbul (after all, why not?) . . . if only one can develop a computer that will simulate the mind of God (after all, why not?) . . . one's name is made!

It is, once again, the key strategy of the technocracy. It monopolizes the cultural ground; it sponges up and anticipates all possibilities. Where science and technology are concerned, its concern is to keep its magician's hat filled with every conceivable form of research and development, the better to confound and stupefy the populace. Thus it must stand prepared to subvene every minor intellectual seizure that lays claim to being or pursuing some form of scientific knowledge. For after all, one never can tell what may come of pure research. Best buy it all up, so that one can be in the position to pick and choose what to exploit and develop.

(3) The notion of "balance," as applied to the evaluation of scientific and technical work, implies the existence of well-defined values which can be brought to bear to distinguish a desirable from an undesirable

achievement. The supposition that such values exist in our culture is misleading in the extreme; but that supposition plays a critically important part in the politics of the technocracy and is, indeed, one of its stoutest bulwarks.

To begin with, we must understand that there exists no way whatever, on strictly scientific grounds, to invalidate *any* objective quest for knowledge, regardless of where it may lead or how it may proceed. The particular project may be unpalatable to the more squeamish among us—for "purely personal reasons"; but it does not thereby cease to be a legitimate exercise of objectivity. After all, knowledge is knowledge; and the more of it, the better. Just as Leigh-Mallory set out to climb Everest simply because it was *there,* so the scientific mind sets out to solve puzzles and unravel mysteries because it perceives them as being *there.* What further justification need there be?

Once an area of experience has been identified as an object of study or experimental interference, there is no rational way in which to deny the inquiring mind its right to know, without calling into question the entire scientific enterprise. In order to do so, one would have to invoke some notion of the "sacred" or the "sacrosanct" to designate an area of life that must be closed to inquiry and manipulation. But since the entire career of the objective consciousness has been one long running battle against such suspiciously nebulous ideas, these concepts survive in our society only as part of an atavistic vocabulary. They are withered roses we come upon, crushed in the diaries of a pre-scientific age.

We are sadly deceived by the old cliché which mournfully tells us that morality has failed to "keep up with" technical progress (as if indeed morality were a "field of knowledge" in the charge of unidentified, but presumably rather incompetent, experts). The expansion of objective consciousness must, of necessity, be undertaken at the expense of moral sensibility. Science deracinates the experience of sacredness wherever it abides, and does so unapologetically, if not with fanatic fervor. And lacking a warm and lively sense of the sacred, there can be no ethical commitment that is anything more than superficial humanistic rhetoric. We are left with, at best, good intentions and well-meaning gestures that have no relationship to authoritative experience, and which therefore collapse into embarrassed confusion as soon as a more hard-headed, more objective inquirer comes along and asks, "But why not?" Having used the keen blade of scientific skepticism to clear our cultural ground of all irrational barriers to inquiry and manipulation, the objective consciousness is free to range in all directions. And so it does.

It is only when we recognize the essentially no-holds-barred character of the objective consciousness—its illimitable thrust toward knowledge and technical mastery of every kind—that the demand for a balanced appreciation of its achievements becomes irrelevant, as well as sleazy in the extreme. The defense of science and technology by reference to balance is, in fact, the worst vice of our culture, betraying an ethical superficiality that is truly appalling. For the balance that is called for is *not* something the scientific community itself provides, or in any sense employs as a control upon its activities. Rather, it is *we* the public who are expected to supply the balance by way of our private assessments of what the objective consciousness lays before us. The scientists and technicians enjoy the freedom—indeed they demand the freedom—to do *absolutely anything* to which curiosity or a research contract draws them. And while they undertake their completely indiscriminate activities, the technocracy which sponsors them provides the public with a scorecard. On this scorecard we can, on the basis of our personal predilections, chalk up the pluses and minuses in any way we see fit. It is all admirably pluralistic: the technocracy can afford to be pluralistic in the matter, because it knows that over the long run there will be achievements and discoveries a-plenty to meet everybody's tastes. After all, if one keeps reaching into a grab bag filled with an infinite number of things, sooner or later one is bound to pluck out enough nice things to offset the undesirable things one has acquired. But the balance involved is hardly guaranteed by those who fill the bag; it is based entirely on chance and personal evaluation.

So we arrive at the lowest conceivable level of moral discourse: ex post facto tabulation and averaging within a context of randomized human conduct. The balance that emerges from such a situation might just as well be gained if our society were to agree to subsidize every whim that arose within a community of certified lunatics, on the assumption that a certain amount of what such a procedure eventually produced would meet any standard of worthwhileness one cared to name. Where moral discrimination is concerned, the scientific and technical mandarins of the technocracy operate not very differently from the composer of chance music who offers us a chaos of sound: if we do not like what we hear, we need only wait a little longer. Eventually . . . eventually . . . there will come a concatenation of noises that charms our taste. At that point, presumably, the score as a whole is vindicated.

The demand for a balanced view of science and technology amounts, then, to something rather like a con game which the technocracy plays with the general public. Since balance is in no sense an ethical discipline the technocracy imposes upon itself by reference to a pre-established moral end, we have absolutely no guarantee that the future of scientific and technical work has anything to offer us but more of everything. All we can be sure of is that the objective consciousness will expand into more areas of life militantly and inexorably, entrenching its alienative dichotomy, invidious hierarchy, and mechanistic imperative even more deeply in our experience. As that happens, the dreams of reason are bound to become more and more a nightmare of depersonalization. If one wonders how the world will then look to men, one need scarcely turn to the inventions of science fiction; we need only examine the activities and sentiments of those whose capacity for experience has already been raped by the ethos of objectivity. And that is what the items offered here are meant to illustrate.

(1) The first item dates back nearly a century; but it is cited without criticism in a recent survey of psychology as a significant example of pioneering neurological research. It concerns the work of Dr. Roberts Bartholow of the Medical College of Ohio. In 1874 Dr. Bartholow conducted a number of experiments on a "rather feeble-minded" woman of thirty named Mary Rafferty. The experiments involved passing an electric current into the young woman's brain through a portion of the skull that had eroded away. Here is a selection from the records of Dr. Bartholow, who introduces his findings by saying, "It has seemed to me most desirable to present the facts as I observed them, without comment."

> *Observation 3.* Passed an insulated needle into the left posterior lobe. . . . Mary complained of a very strong and unpleasant feeling of tingling in both right extremities. In order to develop more decided reactions, the strength of the current was increased. . . . her countenance exhibited great distress, and she began to cry. . . . left hand was extended . . . the arms agitated with clonic spasms, her eyes became fixed, with pupils widely dilated, lips were blue and she frothed at the mouth. (Quoted in David Krech, "Cortical Localization of Function," in Leo Postman, ed., *Psychology in the Making* [New York: A. A. Knopf, 1962], pp. 62–63.)

Three days after this experiment, Mary Rafferty was dead. Those who think such experimentation on human specimens—especially on imprisoned persons like Mary Rafferty—is uncommon, should see M. H. Pappworth's *Human Guinea Pigs: Experimentation on Man* (London: Routledge & Kegan Paul, 1967).

(2) To spare a sigh for the fate of animals undergoing laboratory experimentation is generally considered cranky in the extreme. The reasons for this no doubt include the layman's inability to gain a clear picture of what is happening to the animals through the technical terminology of such accounts as appear in the many journals of physiology, psychology, and medical research, as well as the prevailing assumption that such research is directly related to human benefit and is therefore necessary. The following is a fairly comprehensible report of research done for the British Ministry of Supply during World War II on the effects of poison gases. If the account detours into too many technicalities, the situation is simply this: the experimenter has forced a large dose of Lewisite gas into the eye of a rabbit and is recording over the next two weeks precisely how the animal's eye rots away. But note how the terminology and the reportorial style distance us from the reality of the matter. As in the case of Mary Rafferty above, it is impossible to focus on the fact that the event is happening before a human observer.

Very severe lesions ending in loss of the eye: . . . In two eyes of the 12 in the series of very severe lesions the destructive action of the Lewisite produced necrosis [decay] of the cornea before the blood vessels had extended into it. Both lesions were produced by a large droplet. In one case the rabbit was anaesthetized, in the other it was not anaesthetized and was allowed to close the eye at once, thus spreading the Lewisite all over the conjunctival sac [eyeball]. The sequence of events in this eye begins with instantaneous spasm of the lids followed by lacrimation in 20 seconds (at first clear tears and in one minute 20 seconds milky Harderian secretion). In six minutes the third lid is becoming oedematous [swollen] and in 10 minutes the lids themselves start to swell. The eye is kept closed with occasional blinks. In 20 minutes the oedema [swelling] is so great that the eye can hardly be kept closed as the lids are lifted off the globe. In three hours it is not possible to see the cornea and there are conjunctival petechiae [minute hemorrhages]. Lacrimation continues.

In 24 hours the oedema is beginning to subside and the eye is discharging muco-pus. There is a violent iritis [inflammation] and the cornea is oedematous all over in the superficial third. . . . On the third day there is much discharge and the lids are still swollen. On the fourth day the lids are stuck together with discharge. There is severe iritis. The corneae are not very swollen. . . . On the eighth day there is hypopyon [pus], the lids are brawny and contracting down on the globe so that the eye cannot be fully opened. . . . In 10 days the cornea is still avascular, very opaque and covered with pus. On the 14th day the center of the cornea appears to liquify and melt away, leaving a Descemetocoele [a membrane over the cornea], which remains intact till the 28th day, when it ruptures leaving only the remains of an eye in a mass of pus. (Ida Mann, A. Pirie, B. D. Pullinger, "An Experimental and Clinical Study of the Reaction of the Anterior Segment of the Eye to Chemical Injury, With Special Reference to Chemical Warfare Agents," *British Journal of Ophthalmology,* Monograph Supplement XIII, 1948, pp. 146–47.)

By way of explaining the methodological validity of such research, P. B. Medawar offers the following hard-headed observation:

For all its crudities, Behaviorism, conceived as a methodology rather than as a psychological system, taught psychology with brutal emphasis that "the dog is whining" and "the dog is sad" are statements of altogether different empirical standing, and heaven help psychology if it ever again overlooks the distinction. (P. B. Medawar, *The Art of the Soluble* [London: Methuen, 1967], p. 89.)

Professor Medawar does not make clear, however, on whom the "brutal emphasis" of this distinction has fallen: the experimenter or the experimental subject. Does it, for example, make any difference to the methodology if the subject is capable of saying, "I am sad," "I am hurt"?

For a wise discussion of the ethics and psychology of animal experimentation (as well as a few more ghastly examples of the practice), see

Catherine Roberts, "Animals in Medical Research" in her *The Scientific Conscience* (New York: Braziller, 1967).

(3) The following comes from a study of the effects of wartime bombing on civilian society, with special reference to the probable results of thermonuclear bombardment. The research was done under grants from the U.S. Air Force and the Office of the Surgeon General at the Columbia University Bureau of Applied Social Research, and published with the aid of a Ford Foundation subsidy. It should be mentioned that the scholar's conclusions are generally optimistic about the possibilities of rapid recovery from a nuclear war. He even speculates that the widespread destruction of cultural artifacts in such a war might have the same long-term effect as the barbarian devastation of Greco-Roman art and architecture: namely, a liberation from the dead hand of the artistic past such as that which prepared the way for the Italian Renaissance.

> We have deliberately avoided arousing emotions. In this area, which so strongly evokes horror, fear, or hope, a scientist is seriously tempted to relax his standards of objectivity and to give vent to his own subjective feelings. No one can fail to be deeply aroused and disturbed by the facts of nuclear weapons. These sentiments are certainly necessary to motivate actions, but they should not distort an investigation of the truth or factual predictions.
> This book deals with the social consequences of actual bombing, starting with different types of destruction as given physical events, tracing step by step the effects upon urban populations—their size, composition, and activities—and finally investigating the repercussions upon national populations and whole countries. . . . While we are deeply concerned with the moral and humanitarian implications of bomb destruction, we excluded them from this book, not because we judged them to be of secondary importance, but because they are better dealt with separately and in a different context.

This "different context," however, has not to date been explored by the author. But he does turn to considering "the effect upon morale" of wholesale carnage. Note how the use of phrases like "apparently" and "it appears" and "it can be argued" and "there is evidence of" neatly denature the horror of the matters under discussion.

> The impact of casualties upon morale stems mainly from actually seeing dead or injured persons and from the emotional shock resulting from the death of family and friends. . . . No other aspect of an air raid causes as severe an emotional disturbance as the actual witnessing of death and agony. Interviews with persons who have experienced an atomic explosion reveal that ⅓ of them were emotionally upset because of the casualties they saw, while only 5 percent or fewer experienced fear or some other form of emotional disturbance on account of the flash of the explosion, the noise, the blast, the devastation, and the fires.
> An atomic bombing raid causes more emotional reactions than a conventional raid. Janis declares:

"Apparently it was not simply the large number of casualties but also the specific character of the injuries, particularly the grossly altered physical appearance of persons who suffered severe burns, that had a powerful effect upon those who witnessed them. Hence, it appears to be highly probable that, as a correlate of the exceptional casualty-inflicting properties of the atomic weapon, there was an unusually intense emotional impact among the uninjured evoked by the perception of those who were casualties." The strong emotional disturbance that results from the sight of mangled bodies has also been reported from lesser peacetime disasters such as a plant explosion.

We are interested here in this emotional agitation only as it affects the overt behavior of city dwellers. Two contradictory reactions could be suggested as short-range effects. It can be argued that apathy and disorganization will prevail. On the other hand, it is conceivable that the emotional disturbance from casualties will intensify rescue or defense activities. While there is evidence of both forms of reaction after a disaster, the latter is encouraged by effective leadership which directs survivors toward useful activities. (Fred C. Iklé, *The Social Impact of Bomb Destruction* [Norman, Okla.: University of Oklahoma Press, 1958], pp. vii–viii, 27–29.)

(4) As the selection above suggests, the new social science of operations analysis has done an impressively ambitious job of opening up hitherto neglected avenues of research. Here, for example, are some suggested research subjects for which the RAND Corporation received government grants totaling several million dollars during 1958 as part of its civilian defense studies:

A study should be made of the survival of populations in environments similar to overcrowded shelters (concentration camps, Russian and German use of crowded freight cars, troopships, crowded prisons, crowded lifeboats, submarines, etc.). Some useful guiding principles might be found and adapted to the shelter program.

The object of such research would be to "act as reassurance that the more unpleasant parts of the experience had been foreseen and judged to be bearable by a peacetime government." (Herman Kahn, "Some Specific Suggestions for Achieving Early Non-Military Defense Capabilities and Initiating Long-Range Programs," RAND Corporation Research Memorandum RM-2206-RC, 1959, pp. 47–48.)

And to give but one more example of the truly Faustian élan of our military-oriented research, we have this prognosis from a naval engineer:

Weather and climate are never neutral. They are either formidable enemies or mighty allies. Try to imagine the fantastic possibilities of one nation possessing the capability to arrange over large areas, or perhaps the entire globe, the distribution of heat and cold, rain and sunshine, flood and drought, to the advantage of itself and its allies and to the detriment of its enemies. We *must* think about it—*now*—for this is the direction in which technology is leading us. . . .

The question is no longer: "Will mankind be able to modify the weather on a large scale and control the climate?" Rather, the question is: "Which scientists will do it first, American or Russian?" . . . (Commander William J. Kotsch, USN, "Weather Control and National Strategy," *United States Naval Institute Proceedings,* July 1960, p. 76.)

(5) The classic justification for technological progress has been that it steadily frees men from the burdens of existence and provides them with the leisure in which to make "truly human uses" of their lives. The following selections would suggest, however, that by the time we arrive at this high plateau of creative leisure, we may very well find it already thickly inhabited by an even more beneficent species of inventions which will have objectified creativity itself. It is quite unclear what the justification for this form of progress is, other than the technocratic imperative: "What can be done must be done."

I would like to teach a machine how to write a limerick, and I suspect I can do it. I am quite sure that in the first batch it will be easy for anybody to pick out from a random array those limericks created by an IBM machine. But perhaps in a little while the distinctions will not be so clear. The moment we can do that we will have carried out a psychological experiment in new terms which for the first time may give a sharp definition of what it meant by a joke. (Edward Teller, "Progress in the Nuclear Age," *Mayo Clinic Proceedings,* January 1965.)

Can a computer be used to compose a symphony? As one who has been engaged in programming a large digital computer to program original musical compositions, I can testify that the very idea excites incredulity and indignation in many quarters. Such response in part reflects the extreme view of the nineteenth-century romantic tradition that regards music as direct communication of emotion from composer to listener—"from heart to heart," as Wagner said. In deference to this view it must be conceded that we do not *yet* understand the subjective aspect of musical communication well enough to study it in precise terms. . . . On the other hand, music does have its objective side. The information encoded there relates to such quantitative entities as pitch and time, and is therefore accessible to rational and ultimately mathematical analysis. . . . It is possible, at least in theory, to construct tables of probabilities describing a musical style, such as Baroque, Classical or Romantic, and perhaps even the style of an individual composer. Given such tables, one could then reverse the process and compose music in a given style. (Lejaren A. Hiller, Jr., in *Scientific American,* December 1959. Italics added.)

The most ominous aspect of such statements is the ever-present "yet" that appears in them. To offer another example: "No technology as *yet* promises to duplicate human creativity, especially in the artistic sense, if only because we do not *yet* understand the conditions and functioning of creativity. (This is not to deny that computers can be useful aids to creative activity.)" (Emmanuel G. Mesthene, *How Technology Will Shape the Future,* Harvard University Program on Technology and Society, Reprint

Number 5, pp. 14–15.) The presumption involved in such statements is almost comic. For the man who thinks that creativity might *yet* become a technology is the man who stands no chance of ever understanding what creativity is. But we can be sure the technicians will eventually find us a bad mechanized substitute and persuade themselves that it is the real thing.

(6) The literature of our society dealing with imprisonment and capital punishment is extensive, including contributions by Tolstoy, Camus, Dostoyevsky, Sartre, and Koestler. Since, however, these men offer us only imaginative fiction, their work is obviously of little scientific value. What follows is an attempt by two psychiatrists to gain, at long last, some hard data on the experience of awaiting execution. The sample population is nineteen people in the Sing Sing death house. "One might expect them," the researchers state, "to show severe depression and devastating anxiety, yet neither symptom was conspicuous among these 19 doomed persons. By what mechanisms did they avoid these expected reactions to such overwhelming stress? Do their emotional patterns change during a year or two in a death cell? And do these defenses function to the moment of execution—or do they crumble towards the end?"

Here are the psychiatrist's thumbnail sketches of their specimens—all of whom, they observe, come from "deprived backgrounds," with extensive experience of institutional confinement, and none of whom had long premeditated the killings they were convicted of. Notice how effectively the terminology and the data provided screen out the observer so that we have no sense of the character of the human presence with which these pathetic prisoners were interacting—surely a key factor in the situation. Note, too, how the concluding table of findings turns the life-and-death matter into a statistical abstraction.

> This inmate is the only women in this series. She is of dull intelligence, acts in a playful and flirtatious manner. She was usually euphoric, but became transiently depressed when she thought her case was going badly. She frequently complained of insomnia and restlessness. These symptoms quickly disappeared when she was visited by a psychiatrist whom she enjoyed seeing and talking to in a self-justifying and self-pitying manner. Psychological tests showed pervasive feelings of insecurity, repressive defenses, and an inability to handle angry and aggressive feelings in an effectual manner.

> This inmate is an illiterate, inadequate individual who was convicted as an accomplice to a robbery-murder. He had an overall IQ of 51. He showed primarily depression, withdrawal, and obsessive rumination over the details of his crime and conviction. He eventually evolved a poorly elaborated paranoid system whereby he supposedly was betrayed and framed by his girl friend and one of the codefendants. Despite the looseness of his persecutory thinking, it was accompanied by a clear-cut elevation in his mood and reduction of anxiety.

He is one of the two inmates in this series who uses religious preoccupation as his major defense mechanism. He repeatedly in an almost word for word way stated his situation as follows. "No one can understand how I feel unless it happened to you. Christ came to me and I know He died for my sins. It doesn't matter if I am electrocuted or not. I am going to another world after this and I am prepared for it." As his stay progresses he becomes increasingly more hostile and antagonistic, and his behavior progressively out of keeping with his professed religious ideas. In addition to obsessive rumination, projection and withdrawal are employed to ward off feelings of anxiety and depression.

The researchers summarize their findings as follows:

Psychological defense mechanisms used
(Totals more than 19; some used more than one)
Denial by isolation of affect 7
Denial by minimizing the predicament 4
Denial by delusion formation 1
Denial by living only in the present 4
Projection 7
Obsessive rumination in connection with appeals 3
Obsessive preoccupation with religion 2
Obsessive preoccupation with intellectual or philosophical matters . 5

(Harvey Bluestone and Carl L. McGahee, "Reaction to Extreme Stress: Impending Death by Execution," *The American Journal of Psychiatry,* November 1962, pp. 393–96.)

(7) Reportedly, within the last decade, the most promising scientific brains have been drifting away from physics to biology and medical science, where the frontiers of research have begun to reveal more intriguing prospects. Some of them, like that which follows, vie with the ingenuity of H. G. Wells' Dr. Moreau.

Dr. Vladimir Demikhov, an eminent Soviet experimental surgeon whose grafting of additional or different heads and limbs on to dogs has drawn considerable attention, has come up with a new suggestion for the advancement of transplantation surgery.

According to "Soviet Weekly," Dr. Demikhov believes that it would be simple to store organs for spare-part surgery—not by developing techniques for banks of particular organs or tissues but by temporarily grafting the stored organ on to the exterior of human "vegetables."

A human "vegetable" is a human being who, through accident or disease, has lost all intelligent life, but is otherwise functioning normally. The surgeon's "bank" would consist of technically living bodies, each supporting externally a number of additional organs. (Anthony Tucker, science correspondent, *The Guardian* [London], January 20, 1968.)

For a popularized survey of recent work in the biological sciences, see Gordon Rattray Taylor, *The Biological Time-Bomb* (New York: World, 1968). Among other breathtaking possibilities the biologists have in store for us, there will be the capacity to produce carbon-copy human beings with interchangeable parts and faultless collective co-ordination. We shall then have, we are told, "exceptional human beings in unlimited numbers," as well as ideal basketball teams . . . and (no doubt) armies.

(8) The following are two examples of scientists doing their utmost to defend the dignity of pure research against any moralizing encroachments.

In December 1967, Dr. Arthur Kornberg, a Nobel prize winning geneticist, announced the first successful synthesis of viral DNA, an important step toward the creation of test-tube life. After the announcement Dr. Kornberg was interviewed by the press.

> At the end, the moral problem was posed. "Dr. Kornberg, do you see the time when your work will come into conflict with traditional morality?" Again he took off his glasses and looked down and meditated. Very gently, he replied: "We can never predict the benefits that will flow from advancements in our fundamental knowledge. There is no knowledge that cannot be abused, but I hope that our improved knowledge of genetic chemistry will make us better able to cope with hereditary disease. I see no possibility of conflict in a decent society which uses scientific knowledge for human improvement." . . . He left it to us to define, or redefine, a decent society. (Alistair Cooke, reporting in *The Guardian* [London], December 17, 1967.)

In the summer of 1968, a controversy blew up in Great Britain over the part played by academic scientists in the activities of the Ministry of Defence Microbiological Establishment at Porton, one of the world's most richly productive centers of chemical and biological warfare research. (Porton, for example, developed some of the gases most extensively used by American forces in Vietnam.) Professor E. B. Chain of Imperial College protested this "irresponsible scoop hunting" in a lengthy letter to *The Observer*, detailing the many worthwhile lines of research that had come out of the work done at Porton.

> What is wrong with accepting research grants from the Ministry of Defence? As is well known, thousands of scientists have, for many years, accepted such grants from the US Navy, the US Air Force, NATO, and similar national and international organizations for fundamental research in many branches of the physical and biological sciences: this does not mean that such work involved them in research on military technology. One can only be grateful for the wisdom and foresight shown by those responsible for formulating and deciding the policies of these organisations in allowing their funds to be made available for sponsoring fundamental university

research which bears no immediate, and usually not even a remote, relation to problems of warfare technology.

Of course, almost any kind of research, however academic, and almost any invention, however beneficial to mankind, from the knife to atomic energy, from anaesthetics to plant hormones, can be used for war and other destructive purposes, but it is, of course, not the scientist and inventor who carries the responsibility for how the results of his research or his inventions are used. (*The Observer* [London], June 1, 1968.)

It is actually a dubious proposition that any scientist worth his salt cannot make a pretty accurate prediction of how his findings might be used. But even if one were to grant the point, there is one kind of result which is completely predictable and which is bound never to be far from the awareness of the researcher. Productive research results in a handsomely rewarded career, in acclaim and wide recognition. Is it too cynical to suggest that this all-too-predictable result frequently makes it ever so much harder to foresee the probable abuses of one's research?

(9) C. Wright Mills once called the middle class citizenry of our polity a collection of "cheerful robots." Perhaps it is because the human original has fallen so far short of authenticity that our behavioral scientists can place such easy confidence in the simulated caricatures of humanity upon which their research ever more heavily comes to bear. One begins to wonder how much of what our society comes to accept as humanly normal, legitimate, and appropriate in years to come will be patterned upon the behavior of such electronic homunculi as those described below.

A pioneering demonstration of the feasibility of computer simulation appeared in 1957 when Newell, Shaw, and Simon published a description of their Logic Theorist program, which proved theorems in elementary symbolic logic—a feat previously accomplished only by humans. Among subsequent applications of information processing programs to classical problems of psychological theory are Feigenbaum's Elementary Perceiver and Memorizer, a computer model of verbal rote memorization; Feldman's simulation of the behavior of subjects in a binary-choice experiment, and Hovland and Hunt's model of human concept formulation. Lindsay explores another facet of cognitive activity in his computer processing of syntactic and semantic information to analyze communications in Basic English, and Bert Green and associates have programmed a machine to respond to questions phrased in ordinary English. Still another aspect of human decision-making appears in Clarkson's model of the trust investment process. At a more general level, Newell, Shaw, and Simon have programmed an information processing theory of human problem solving, a model whose output has been compared systematically with that of human problem solvers. Reitman has incorporated elements of this general problem-solving system in simulating the complex creative activity involved in musical composition.

While early applications of information processing models focus on relatively logical aspects of human behavior, recent simulation models incorporate emotional responses. Concerned by the singlemindedness of cognitive activity programmed in the Newell, Shaw, and Simon General Problem Solver, Reitman and associates recently have programmed a Hebbian-type model of human thinking that is not in complete control of what it remembers and forgets, being subject to interruptions and to conflict. Kenneth Colby, a psychiatrist, has developed a computer model for simulating therapeutic manipulation of emotions as well as a patient's responses. In HOMUNCULUS, our computer model of elementary social behavior, simulated subjects may at times emit anger or guilt reactions, or they may suppress aggression and later vent it against a less threatening figure than the one who violated norms regarding distributive justice.

. . . Among other computer applications involving considerations of emotional behavior are Coe's simulation of responses to frustration and conflict, Loehlin's simulation of socialization, and Abelson's design for computer simulation of "hot," affect-laden cognition. Imaginative computer simulations of voting behavior have been done by Robert Abelson, William McPhee, and their associates. Using the fluoridation controversies as a case in point, Abelson and Bernstein blend theories from several disciplines and from both field and experimental phenomena in constructing their model. Simulated individuals are assigned characteristics known to be relevant, and the programmed model specifies the processes by which they may change during the fluoridation campaign. . . .

In another study . . . Raymond Breton has simulated a restriction-of-output situation. According to this model, under most conditions pressures from fellow workmen result in a more homogeneous output, presumably in conformity with the norm. When motivation for monetary reward is intensified, however, some simulated workers develop negative sentiments toward those attempting to apply constraints, and variability of output increases.

(J. T. and J. E. Gullahorn, "Some Computer Applications in Social Science," *American Sociological Review*, vol. 30, June 1965, pp. 353–365.)

F. M. ESFANDIARY

Born in 1930, F. M. Esfandiary attended schools in the Middle East, Europe, and the United States, and currently lives in New York City. A writer, philosopher, long range planner, and university lecturer, he has been a member of the United Nations Conciliation Commission for Palestine and is currently teaching normative philosophy alternately at UCLA and at the New School for Social Research in New York. His most recent books include Optimism One *(1970),* Up-Wingers *(1973), and* Telespheres *(1976). He has contributed articles in futurist philosophy to* The New York Times, The Village Voice, *and* The Futurist. *The present essay appeared in* The New York Times Magazine *for February 5, 1976, and is reprinted here with some revisions by the author.*

The Mystical West Puzzles the Practical East

An American couple recently spent two weeks in the Middle East crawling in and out of archeological sites, visiting the Pyramids, the Sphinx, the ruins of Baalbek, the ruins of Jerash and Petra, and many "holy" places. In Jordan they met a Middle Easterner who urged them to visit a camp of squatters in Old Jerusalem. Sprawled within a stone's throw of stately temples, churches and mosques, it is one of the world's most horrifying shantytowns. Several thousand Palestinian refugees fester in dark, damp hovels that are no more than holes in the ground. Families of five, eight or 10 live huddled together in cells with hardly room enough for three or four. The stench of urine permeates the trapped air. There are sick and old people down there who have not seen the light of day in months; they lie rotting on damp floors, waiting for death to deliver them. Children, naked and cadaverous, cower in dingy corners or rummage in garbage heaps for food.

The Middle Easterner led the American couple to one of the openings in the ground and asked them to follow him down. The Americans stared at the steep stairs and the darkness below and refused to go. "These stairs look dangerous," the American woman said. "Besides, there is nothing to see down below."

"If you had been told that two or three thousand years ago people lived down there, you would have crawled on your hands and knees just to have a glimpse of the place, but because people live there now, you refuse to see it."

"But what is there to see anyway?"

"You would have seen some of the poverty and misery of these people."

"I'm not so sure these people are all that miserable," the American interposed. "They look peaceful enough to me. They are probably a lot happier than some Americans we know back home." He stopped, looked about and with memorable inattention to logic, added: "In fact, there is something spiritual, something Biblical, about the way these people live."

Westerners have this dispiriting propensity for contorting reality. They have a childlike need to idolize and romanticize. Self-proclaimed prophets, LSD zealots, Black Muslims, beat poets and artists, students, intellectuals and others have all turned to what they call the Wisdom of the East. Today Buddhism, Hinduism, Zen, Yoga, Islam, Baha'iism are attracting countless followers in America and Western Europe. A mass of literature glorifies the East and the past, but books which attempt to deal realistically with these areas are largely ignored. If reality threatens to obtrude, it is tampered with until it miraculously fits in with cherished fantasies.

This might seem harmless enough but for the fact that in refusing to see things as they are, in reviving stale philosophies and romanticizing the past, the West is helping to perpetuate backwardness. It encourages those in all cultures who resist progress. But it is the peoples of the East who must finally endure the suffering and the destitution.

After they have uttered their empty praises, Westerners run back to New York and Beverly Hills and languish in their comfortable apartments while benefiting from all the social and economic amenities of the 20th century—the 20th century which so many of them claim to despise.

There are Americans and Europeans who know every rose petal that dropped from the mouth of a Buddha or a Confucius, who know every stone of the Pyramids or the Taj Mahal, yet who know nothing of today's Asians and Africans, nothing of their needs and sorrows, their struggles and hopes. Can this preoccupation with the romanticized past help us understand or in any way alter the sad fact that today, this very day, millions are hungry and homeless and ailing in body and mind?

This same unrealism is reflected in American foreign policy, which refuses to acknowledge, much less support, the revolutionary aspirations of disadvantaged peoples all over the world, which sometimes even refuses to acknowledge the existence of governments and peoples whose orientation is different from its own. The Washington officials who support reactionary regimes are rendering the same disservice, perpetuating the same ills, as Western spiritualists who revive the archaic philosophies of a Lao-Tze or a Buddha.

The American and Western European Underground, which considers itself avant-garde, is in fact pathetically regressive. It does not look ahead; it looks back. It is romantic and mawkish. Bearded zealots, sitting cross-legged on the ground, wallowing in Haiku poetry, Bhagavad-Gitas and Zen in an atmosphere saturated with the exoticisms of incense, opiates and lanterns—the "scene," in short, smacks of a Dr. Fu Manchu melodrama. The dialogue of the Underground, like its poetry, is heavily spiced with pretentious allusions to Nirvana, Karma, Satori . . . Its idols are the swami, the guru, the mystic and other high priests of Eastern occultism who go about murmuring such profound revelations as, "Life is like a fountain."

In Greenwich Village, as in other bohemias of the Western world, one can often see displayed in cafes and shop windows posters of some swami or yogi. The large head, dark piercing eyes, benign smile and flowing gray beard bear a disquieting resemblance to the popular ideas of the Judeo-Christian God. Looking at these posters, I cannot help wondering if the West, which has just come back from the highly publicized burial of its late god, is not now fervently looking for a new one.

In the big cities, there is a noticeable restlessness, a groping, a desperation to believe in something. In New York and Los Angeles, Chicago and San Francisco, innumerable cults, religions and spiritual groups flourish and win fanatic adherents. It is appalling to see bright, educated city-dwellers swallow the nonsense that these soothsayers, clairvoyants, spiritualists, dish out. There is something pathetic about this hunger for fairy tales.

Consciously or unconsciously, the West does not want the old societies to change. It would rather they remained languid and inert—what it calls spiritual. It would rather the Easterner remained cross-legged and contemplative. The West needs this vision to nourish and titillate its fantasies, while it goes on building better homes, richer economies, better societies for itself.

But young revolutionary Asians and Africans do not want to play the spiritual buffoon for the West. They are not amused by suffering and destitution. They are apprehensive of their backwardness and see in it no beauty, no dignity, no spirituality, nothing sacred or worth holding. They are struggling to disembarrass themselves of the very philosophies which a section of the West is striving to regenerate.

These ancient teachings, for the most part, encouraged passivity, withdrawal, involvement with self, submission. They instilled the belief that fate or reincarnation decided everything; that suffering and affliction were rewards or punishment or irreversible destiny and that all effort, all merit, all endeavor was therefore futile. Through the centuries these teachings have seeped into the fabric of Eastern cultures, infecting their economies, politics, social and familial institutions, their very self-image.

Twenty-five hundred years ago, Buddha, like a few other philosophers before and after him, said: "He who sits still, wins." Asia, then immobilized in primitive torpor, had no difficulty responding. It sat still. What it won for sitting still was the perpetuation of famines and terrorizing

superstitions, oppression of children, subjugation of women, emascula-
tion of men, fratricidal wars, persecutions, mass-killings. The history of
Asia, like the history of all humankind, is a horrendous account of suffering.

Thus when life was a relentless cycle of anguish, it was probably
inevitable that some, in their desperation and helplessness, should reject
reality and withdraw. Their resignation and submission were defenses
against suffering. When Lao-Tze, Solomon—even Rousseau centuries
later—exhorted their fellow people to go back to nature or spend their
lives in contemplation, they were reacting to a world that was hostile and
unmanageable.

But times have changed. Humankind is no longer helpless; its problems no longer insurmountable. Ancient exhortations of asceticism and
self-renunciation are irrelevant in our modern world. Buddhism, Sufiism,
Islam, Judaism—indeed, all the theologies and philosophies of the past
—have nothing to teach the modern world. Ahead of *their* time, they are
far behind ours. Do not kill; do not hate; love your neighbor; love your
fellow people—these were revolutionary concepts at one time. Today
they are platitudes—though easier said than done.

The injunction against killing cows, noble in itself, did not deter
people from killing one another. The religionist who spoke of the brotherhood of humanity had no difficulty persecuting members of other religions. But now that humanity is slowly reaching adulthood, it does not
need to be reminded of the teachings of its childhood—it must find ways
to implement them.

Americans and Western Europeans, in their sensitivity to lingering
problems around them, tend to make science and progress their scape-
goats. There is a belief that progress has precipitated widespread unhappiness, anxieties and other social and emotional problems. Science is
viewed as a cold mechanical discipline having nothing to do with human
warmth and the human spirit.

But to many of us from the East, science does not have such repugnant
associations. We are not afraid of it, nor are we disappointed by it. We
know all too painfully that our social and emotional problems festered
long before the age of technology. To us, science is warm and reassuring.
It promises hope. It is helping us at long last gain some control over our
persecutory environments, alleviating age-old problems—not only physical but also, and especially, problems of the spirit.

Shiraz, for example, a city in southern Iran, has long been renowned
for its rose gardens and nightingales; its poets, Sadi and Hafiz, and its
mystical, ascetic philosophy, Sufiism. Much poetry has been written in
glorification of the spiritual attributes of this oasis city. And to be sure,
Shiraz is a green, picturesque town, with a quaint bazaar and refreshing
gardens. But in this "romantic" city thousands of emotionally disturbed

and mentally retarded men, women and children were, until recently, kept in chains in stifling prison cells and lunatic asylums.

Every now and again, some were dragged, screaming and pleading, to a courtyard and flogged for not behaving "normally." But for the most part, they were made to sit against damp walls, their hands and feet locked in chains, and thus immobilized, without even a modicum of affection from their helpless families and friends, they sat for weeks and months and years—often all their lives. Pictures of these wretched men, women and children can still be seen in this "city of poetry," this "city with the spiritual way of life."

It was only recently that a wealthy young Shirazi who, against the admonitions of his family, had studied psychology at the University of Teheran and foreign universities, returned to Shiraz and after considerable struggle with city officials succeeded in opening a psychiatric clinic, the first in those regions. After still more struggle, he arranged to have the emotionally disturbed and the mentally retarded transferred from prison to their homes, to hospitals and to his clinic, where he and his staff now attend to them.

They are fortunate. All over Asia and Africa, emotionally disturbed men and women are still incarcerated in these medieval dungeons called lunatic asylums. The cruel rejection and punishment are intended to teach them a lesson or help exorcise evil spirits.

The West, however, still bogged down in its ridiculous romanticism, would like to believe that emotional conflicts, dope addiction, delinquency are all modern problems brought on by technological progress, and that backward societies are too spiritual to need the ministrations of science. But while the West can perhaps afford to think this way, the people of Asia and Africa cannot.

Young Middle Eastern men and women are daily flouting the devitalizing repressions and fatalism of Judaism, Christianity, and Islam. India is valiantly straining to extricate itself from the dead weight of social traditions whose corrosive nihilism and spiritualism the realist Nehru disdained. Japan's new industrialism is obvious renunciation of the debilitating influences of the past. China's revolutionary leaders are prodding their people to reject the ancient traditions and philosophies which had helped perpetuate the country's backwardness and misery, making it prey to incessant foreign rapacities.

If at times these struggles have been erratic and violent, it is only because the obstacles are awesome, the inertia too entrenched, the people's suffering too anguished, their impatience too eruptive. Moreover, the total cultural reorganizations such as Asia and Africa are undergoing inevitably engender their own temporary dislocations and confusions. But the goals, the direction remain constant. We are on the move, however awkwardly at first, to a saner, better world.

It is precisely this new voice of Asia and Africa, this new spirit, that the West must heed and, where necessary, uphold. It is encouraging that in the Western world today, particularly in America, Blacks, women, teachers, students, and others are now more and more making their voices heard. The increasing number of people who travel each year are also helping all societies to outgrow their insularity, their provincialism, their social, economic and political traditions.

In spite of colossal obstacles, humankind has come a long way. Let us not be afraid to believe that we will go still farther; that we will remake the world—that, indeed, we are remaking the world.

If we have to believe in something, let us believe in our own infinite potential, our own future.

E. B. WHITE

Elwyn Brooks White, born in 1899, graduated from Cornell in 1921 and joined the staff of The New Yorker *in 1926. He regularly wrote its "Notes and Comment" section until 1938 and contributed to the page in the 1940s and 1950s. His sensitive, humorous character and his witty yet natural and exact literary style, along with the congenial talents of James Thurber and of a few others, were in part responsible for the extraordinary reputation of* New Yorker *writing at that time. He contributed a monthly column, entitled "One Man's Meat," to* Harper's *from 1938 to 1943 and resumed writing for* The New Yorker *on a free-lance basis in 1945. Since 1937 he has taken periodic refuge in a Maine farm. He has been awarded honorary degrees from Dartmouth, Maine, Bowdoin, Hamilton, Colby, Yale, and Harvard, the National Institute of Arts and Letters gold medal in 1960 for his contribution to literature, and the Presidential Medal of Freedom in 1963. White has published two excellent children's books,* Stuart Little *(1945) and* Charlotte's Web *(1952), and received the 1970 Laura Ingalls Wilder Award for his "substantial and lasting contribution to literature for children." Among his best-known other books are* Is Sex Necessary?, *written with James Thurber (1929),* Every Day Is Saturday *(1934),* One Man's Meat *(1942),* The Wild Flag *(1946), and* The Elements of Style *(1959), a reverent reediting of the textbook of his former professor William Strunk, Jr. The story we present below, taken from* The Second Tree from the Corner *(1954), was first published in* The New Yorker *in February 1950.*

The Morning of the Day They Did It
(FEBRUARY 25, 1950)

My purpose is to tell how it happened and to set down a few impressions of that morning while it is fresh in memory. I was in a plane that was in radio communication with the men on the platform. To put the matter briefly, what was intended as a military expedient turned suddenly into a holocaust. The explanation was plain enough to me, for, like millions of others, I was listening to the conversation between the two men and was instantly aware of the quick shift it took. That part is clear. What is not so clear is how I myself survived, but I am beginning to understand that, too. I shall not burden the reader with an explanation, however, as the facts are tedious and implausible. I am now in good health and fair spirits, among friendly people on an inferior planet, at a very great distance from the sun. Even the move from one planet to another has not relieved me of the nagging curse that besets writing men—the feeling that they must produce some sort of record of their times.

The thing happened shortly before twelve noon. I came out of my house on East Harding Boulevard at quarter of eight that morning, swinging my newspaper and feeling pretty good. The March day was mild and springlike, the warmth and the smells doubly welcome after the rotten weather we'd been having. A gentle wind met me on the Boulevard, frisked me, and went on. A man in a leather cap was loading bedsprings into a van in front of No. 220. I remember that as I walked along I worked my tongue around the roof of my mouth, trying to dislodge a prune skin. (These details have no significance; why write them down?)

A few blocks from home there was a Contakt plane station and I hurried in, caught the 8:10 plane, and was soon aloft. I always hated a jet-assist takeoff right after breakfast, but it was one of the discomforts that went with my job. At ten thousand feet our small plane made contact with the big one, we passengers were transferred, and the big ship went on up to fifty thousand, which was the height television planes flew at. I was a script writer for one of the programs. My tour of duty was supposed to be eight hours.

I should probably explain here that at the period of which I am writing, the last days of the planet earth, telecasting was done from planes circling the stratosphere. This eliminated the coaxial cable, a form of relay that had given endless trouble. Coaxials worked well enough for a while, but eventually they were abandoned, largely because of the extraordinary depredations of earwigs. These insects had developed an alarming resistance to bugspray and were out of control most of the time. Earwigs increased in size and in numbers, and the forceps at the end of their abdomen developed so that they could cut through a steel shell. They seemed to go unerringly for coaxials. Whether the signals carried by the cables had anything to do with it I don't know, but the bugs fed on these things and were enormously stimulated. Not only did they feast on the cables, causing the cables to disintegrate, but they laid eggs in them in unimaginable quantities, and as the eggs hatched the television images suffered greatly, there was more and more flickering on the screen, more and more eyestrain and nervous tension among audiences, and of course a further debasement of taste and intellectual life in general. Finally the coaxials were given up, and after much experimenting by Westinghouse and the Glenn Martin people a satisfactory substitute was found in the high-flying planes. A few of these planes, spotted around the country, handled the whole television load nicely. Known as Stratovideo planes, they were equipped with studios; many programs originated in the air and were transmitted directly, others were beamed to the aircraft from ground stations and then relayed. The planes flew continuously, twenty-four hours a day, were refuelled in air, and dropped down to ten thousand feet every eight hours to meet the Contakt planes and take on new shifts of workers.

I remember that as I walked to my desk in the Stratoship that morning, the nine-o'clock news had just ended and a program called "Author, Please!" was going on, featuring Melonie Babson, a woman who had written a best-seller on the theme of euthanasia, called "Peace of Body." The program was sponsored by a dress-shield company.

I remember, too, that a young doctor had come aboard the plane with the rest of us. He was a newcomer, a fellow named Cathcart, slated to be the physician attached to the ship. He had introduced himself to me in the Contakt plane, had asked the date of my Tri-D shot, and had noted it down in his book. (I shall explain about these shots presently.) This doctor certainly had a brief life in our midst. He had hardly been introduced around and shown his office when our control room got a radio call asking if there was a doctor in the stratosphere above Earthpoint F-plus-6, and requesting medical assistance at the scene of an accident.

F-plus-6 was almost directly below us, so Dr. Cathcart felt he ought to respond, and our control man gave the word and asked for particulars and instructions. It seems there had been a low-altitude collision above F-plus-6 involving two small planes and killing three people. One plane was a Diaheliper, belonging to an aerial diaper service that flew diapers to rural homes by helicopter. The other was one of the familiar government-owned sprayplanes that worked at low altitudes over croplands, truck gardens, and commercial orchards, delivering a heavy mist of the deadly Tri-D solution, the pesticide that had revolutionized agriculture, eliminated the bee from nature, and given us fruits and vegetables of undreamed-of perfection but very high toxicity.

The two planes had tangled and fallen onto the observation tower of a whooping-crane sanctuary, scattering diapers over an area of half a mile and releasing a stream of Tri-D. Cathcart got his medical kit, put on his parachute, and paused a moment to adjust his pressurizer, preparatory

to bailing out. Knowing that he wouldn't be back for a while, he asked
if anybody around the shop was due for a Tri-D shot that morning, and
it turned out that Bill Foley was. So the Doctor told Foley to come along,
and explained that he would give him his injection on the way down. Bill
threw me a quick look of mock anguish, and started climbing into his
gear. This must have been six or seven minutes past nine.

It seems strange that I should feel obliged to explain Tri-D shots.
They were a commonplace at this time—as much a part of a person's life
as his toothbrush. The correct name for them was Anti-Tri-D, but people
soon shortened the name. They were simply injections that everyone had
to receive at regular twenty-one-day intervals, to counteract the lethal
effect of food, and the notable thing about them was the great importance
of the twenty-one-day period. To miss one's Tri-D shot by as much as a
couple of hours might mean serious consequences, even death. Almost
every day there were deaths reported in the papers from failure to get the
injection at the proper time. The whole business was something like
insulin control in diabetes. You can easily imagine the work it entailed for
doctors in the United States, keeping the entire population protected
against death by poisoning.

As Dr. Cathcart and Bill eased themselves out of the plane through
the chute exit, I paused briefly and listened to Miss Babson, our author
of the day.

"It is a grand privilege," she was saying, "to appear before the television audience this morning and face this distinguished battery of critics,
including my old sparring partner, Ralph Armstrong, of the *Herald Tribune.* I suppose after Mr. Armstrong finishes with me I will be a pretty
good candidate for euthanasia myself. Ha. But seriously, ladies and gentlemen, I feel that a good book is its own defense."

The authoress had achieved a state of exaltation already. I knew that
her book, which she truly believed to be great, had been suggested to her
by an agent over a luncheon table and had been written largely by somebody else, whom the publisher had had to bring in to salvage the thing.
The final result was a run-of-the-can piece of rubbish easily outselling its
nearest competitor.

Miss Babson continued, her exaltation stained with cuteness:

"I have heard my novel criticized on the ground that the theme of
euthanasia is too daring, and even that it is anti-Catholic. Well, I can
remember, way back in the dark ages, when a lot of things that are
accepted as commonplace today were considered daring or absurd. My
own father can recall the days when dairy cows were actually bred by
natural methods. The farmers of those times felt that the artificial-breed-
ing program developed by our marvellous experiment stations was high-
falutin nonsense. Well, we all know what has happened to the dairy
industry, with many of our best milch cows giving milk continuously right
around the clock, in a steady stream. True, the cows do have to be
propped up and held in position in special stanchions and fed intrave-

nously, but I always say it isn't the hubbub that counts, it's the butterfat. And I doubt if even Mr. Armstrong here would want to return to the days when a cow just gave a bucket of milk and then stopped to rest."

Tiring of the literary life, I walked away and looked out a window. Below, near the layer of cumulus, the two chutes were visible. With the help of binoculars I could see Bill manfully trying to slip his chute over next to the Doc, and could see Cathcart fumbling with his needle. Our telecandid man was at another window, filming the thing for the next newscast, as it was a new wrinkle in the Tri-D world to have somebody getting his shot while parachuting.

  I had a few chores to do before our program came on, at eleven-five. "Town Meeting of the Upper Air" was the name of it. "Town Meeting" was an unrehearsed show, but I was supposed to brief the guests, distribute copies of whatever prepared scripts there were, explain the cuing, and make everybody happy generally. The program we were readying that morning had had heavy advance billing, and there was tremendous interest in it everywhere, not so much because of the topic ("Will the fear of retaliation stop aggression?") or even the cast of characters, which included Major General Artemus T. Recoil, but because of an incidental stunt we were planning to pull off. We had arranged a radio hookup with the space platform, a gadget the Army had succeeded in establishing six hundred miles up, in the regions of the sky beyond the pull of gravity. The Army, after many years of experimenting with rockets, had not only got the platform established but had sent two fellows there in a Spaceship, and also a liberal supply of the New Weapon.

  The whole civilized world had read about this achievement, which swung the balance of power so heavily in our favor, and everyone was aware that the damned platform was wandering around in its own orbit at a dizzy distance from the earth and not subject to gravitational pull. Every kid in America had become an astrophysicist overnight and talked knowingly of exhaust velocities, synergy curves, and Keplerian ellipses. Every subway rider knew that the two men on the platform were breathing oxygen thrown off from big squash vines that they had taken along. The *Reader's Digest* had added to the fun by translating and condensing several German treatises on rockets and space travel, including the great *Wege zur Raumschiffahrt.* But to date, because of security regulations and technical difficulties, there had been no radio-television hookup. Finally we got clearance from Washington, and General Recoil agreed to interview the officers on the platform as part of the "Town Meeting" program. This was big stuff—to hear directly from the Space Platform for Checking Aggression, known pretty generally as the SPCA.

  I was keyed up about it myself, but I remember that all that morning in the plane I felt disaffected, and wished I were not a stratovideo man. There were often days like that in the air. The plane, with its queer cargo and its cheap goings on, would suddenly seem unaccountably remote from the world of things I admired. In a physical sense we were never very remote: the plane circled steadily in a fixed circle of about ten miles diameter, and I was never far from my own home on East Harding Boulevard. I could talk to Ann and the children, if I wished, by radiophone.

In many respects mine was a good job. It paid two hundred and twenty-five dollars a week, of which two hundred and ten was withheld. I should have felt well satisfied. Almost everything in the way of social benefits was provided by the government—medical care, hospitalization, education for the children, accident insurance, fire and theft, old-age retirement, Tri-D shots, vacation expense, amusement and recreation, welfare and well-being, Christmas and good will, rainy-day resource, staples and supplies, beverages and special occasions, baby-sitzfund—it had all been worked out. Any man who kept careful account of his pin money could get along all right, and I guess I should have been happy. Ann never complained much, except about one thing. She found that no matter how we saved and planned, we never could afford to buy flowers. One day, when she was a bit lathered up over household problems, she screamed, "God damn it, I'd rather live dangerously and have one dozen yellow freesias!" It seemed to prey on her mind.

Anyway, this was one of those oppressive days in the air for me. Something about the plane's undeviating course irritated me; the circle we flew seemed a monstrous excursion to nowhere. The engine noise (we flew at subsonic speed) was an unrelieved whine. Usually I didn't notice the engines, but today the ship sounded in my ears every minute, reminding me of a radiotherapy chamber, and there was always the palpable impact of vulgar miracles—the very nature of television—that made me itchy and fretful.

Appearing with General Recoil on "Town Meeting of the Upper Air" were to be Mrs. Florence Gill, president of the Women's Auxiliary of the Sons of Original Matrons; Amory Buxton, head of the Economics and Withholding Council of the United Nations; and a young man named Tollip, representing one of the small, ineffectual groups that advocated world federation. I rounded up this stable of intellects in the reception room, went over the procedure with them, gave the General a drink (which seemed to be what was on his mind), and then ducked out to catch the ten-o'clock news and to have a smoke.

I found Pete Everhardt in the control room. He looked bushed. "Quite a morning, Nuncle," he said. Pete not only had to keep his signal clean on the nine-o'clock show (Melonie Babson was a speaker who liked to range all over the place when she talked) but he had to keep kicking the ball around with the two Army officers on the space platform, for fear he would lose them just as they were due to go on. And on top of that he felt obliged to stay in touch with Dr. Cathcart down below, as a matter of courtesy, and also to pick up incidental stuff for subsequent newscasts.

I sat down and lit a cigarette. In a few moments the day's authoress wound up her remarks and the news started, with the big, tense face of Ed Peterson on the screen dishing it out. Ed was well equipped by nature for newscasting; he had the accents of destiny. When he spread the news, it penetrated in depth. Each event not only seemed fraught with meaning, it seemed fraught with Ed. When he said "I predict . . ." you felt the full flow of his pipeline to God.

To the best of my recollection the ten-o'clock newscast on this awful morning went as follows:

(Announcer) "Good morning. Tepky's Hormone-Enriched Dental Floss brings you Ed Peterson and the news."

(Ed) "Flash! Three persons were killed and two others seriously injured a few minutes ago at Earthpoint F-plus-6 when a government sprayplane collided with a helicopter of the Diaheliper Company. Both pilots were thrown clear. They are at this moment being treated by a doctor released by parachute from Stratovideo Ship 3, from which I am now speaking. The sprayplane crashed into the observation tower of a whooping-crane sanctuary, releasing a deadly mist of Tri-D and instantly killing three wardens who were lounging there watching the love dance of the cranes. Diapers were scattered widely over the area, and these sterile garments proved invaluable to Dr. Herbert L. Cathcart in bandaging the wounds of the injured pilots, Roy T. Bliss and Homer Schenck. [Here followed a newsreel shot showing Cathcart winding a diaper around the head of one of the victims.] You are now at the scene of the disaster," droned Ed. "This is the first time in the history of television that an infant's napkin has appeared in the role of emergency bandage. Another first for American Tel. & Vid.!

"Washington! A Senate committee, with new facts at its disposal, will reopen the investigation to establish the blame for Pearl Harbor.

"Chicago! Two members of the Department of Sanitation were removed from the payroll today for refusal to take the loyalty oath. Both are members of New Brooms, one of the four hundred thousand organizations on the Attorney General's subversive list.

"Hollywood! It's a boy at the Roscoe Pews. Stay tuned to this channel for a closeup of the Caesarean section during the eleven-o'clock roundup!

"New York! Flash! The Pulitzer Prize in editorial writing has been awarded to Frederick A. Mildly, of the New York *Times,* for his nostalgic editorial 'The Old Pumphandle.'

"Flash! Donations to the Atlantic Community Chest now stand at a little over seven hundred billion dollars. Thanks for a wonderful job of giving—I mean that from my heart.

"New York! The vexing question of whether Greek athletes will be allowed to take part in next year's Olympic Games still deadlocks the Security Council. In a stormy session yesterday the Russian delegate argued that the presence of Greek athletes at the games would be a threat to world peace. Most of the session was devoted to a discussion of whether the question was a procedural matter or a matter of substance.

"Flash! Radio contact with the two United States Army officers on the Space Platform for Checking Aggression, known to millions of listeners as the SPCA, has definitely been established, despite rumors to the contrary. The television audience will hear their voices in a little more than one hour from this very moment. You will *not* see their faces. Stay tuned! This is history, ladies and gentlemen—the first time a human voice freed from the pull of gravity has been heard on earth. The spacemen will be interviewed by Major General Artemus T. Recoil on the well-loved program 'Town Meeting of the Upper Air.'

"I predict: that because of SPCA and the Army's Operation Space, the whole course of human destiny will be abruptly changed, and that the age-old vision of peace is now on the way to becoming a reality."

Ed finished and went into his commercial, which consisted of digging a piece of beef gristle out of his teeth with dental floss.

I rubbed out my cigarette and walked back toward my cell. In the studio next ours, "The Bee" was on the air, and I paused for a while to watch. "The Bee" was a program sponsored by the Larry Cross Pollination Company, aimed principally at big orchardists and growers—or rather at their wives. It was an interminable mystery-thriller sort of thing, with a character called the Bee, who always wore a green hood with two long black feelers. Standing there in the aisle of the plane, looking into the glass-enclosed studio, I could see the Bee about to strangle a red-haired girl in slinky pajamas. This was America's pollination hour, an old standby, answer to the housewife's dream. The Larry Cross outfit was immensely rich. I think they probably handled better than eighty per cent of all fertilization in the country. Bees, as I have said, had become extinct, thanks to the massive doses of chemicals, and of course this had at first posed a serious agricultural problem, as vast areas were without natural pollination. The answer came when the Larry Cross firm was organized, with the slogan "We Carry the Torch for Nature." The business mushroomed, and branch offices sprang up all over the nation. During blossom time, field crews of highly trained men fanned out and pollinized everything by hand—a huge job and an arduous one. The only honey in the United States was synthetic—a blend of mineral oil and papaya juice. Ann hated it with a morbid passion.

When I reached my studio I found everybody getting ready for the warmup. The Town Crier, in his fusty costume, stood holding his bell by the clapper, while the makeup man touched up his face for him. Mrs. Gill, the S.O.M. representative, sat gazing contemptuously at young Tollip. I had riffled through her script earlier, curious to find out what kind of punch she was going to throw. It was about what I expected. Her last paragraph contained the suggestion that all persons who advocated a revision of the Charter of the United Nations be automatically deprived of their citizenship. "If these well-meaning but misguided persons," ran the script, "with their utopian plans for selling this nation down the river are so anxious to acquire world citizenship, I say let's make it easy for them—let's take away the citizenship they've already got and see how they like it. As a lineal descendant of one of the Sons of Original Matrons, I am sick and tired of these cuckoo notions of one world, which come dangerously close to simple treachery. We've enough to do right here at home without . . ."

And so on. In my mind's ear I could already hear the moderator's salutary and impartial voice saying, "Thank you, Mrs. Florence Gill."

At five past eleven, the Crier rang his bell. "Hear ye! See ye! Town Meetin' today! Listen to both sides and make up your own minds!" Then George Cahill, the moderator, started the ball rolling.

I glanced at Tollip. He looked as though his stomach were filling up with gas. As the program got under way, my own stomach began to inflate, too, the way it often did a few hours after breakfast. I remember very little of the early minutes of that morning's Town Meeting. I recall that the U.N. man spoke first, then Mrs. Gill, then Tollip (who looked perfectly awful). Finally the moderator introduced General Recoil, whose stomach enjoyed the steadying effects of whiskey and who spoke in a loud, slow, confident voice, turning frequently to smile down on the three other guests.

"We in the Army," began the General, "don't pretend that we know all the answers to these brave and wonderful questions. It is not the Army's business to know whether aggression is going to occur or not. Our business is to put on a good show if it *does* occur. The Army is content to leave to the United Nations and to idealists like Mr. Tollip the troublesome details of political progress. I certainly don't know, ladies and gentlemen, whether the fear of retaliation is going to prevent aggression, but I *do* know that there is no moss growing on we of Operation Space. As for myself, I guess I am what you might call a retaliatin' fool. [Laughter in the upper air.] Our enemy is well aware that we are now in a most unusual position to retaliate. That knowledge on the part of our enemy is, in my humble opinion, a deterrent to aggression. If I didn't believe that, I'd shed this uniform and get into a really well-paid line of work, like professional baseball."

Will this plane never quit circling? (I thought). Will the words never quit going round and round? Is there no end to this noisy carrousel of indigestible ideas? Will no one ever catch the brass ring?

"But essentially," continued the General, "our job is not to deal with the theoretical world of Mr. Tollip, who suggests that we merge in some vast superstate with every Tom, Dick, and Harry, no matter what their color or race or how underprivileged they are, thus pulling down our standard of living to the level of the lowest common denominator. Our job is not to deal with the diplomatic world of Mr. Buxton, who hopes to find a peaceful solution around a conference table. No, the Army must face the world as it is. We know the enemy is strong. In our dumb way, we think it is just horse sense for us to be stronger. And I'm proud, believe me, ladies and gentlemen, proud to be at one end of the interplanetary conversation that is about to take place on this very, *very* historic morning. The achievement of the United States Army in establishing the space platform—which is literally a man-made planet— is unparalleled in military history. We have led the way into space. We have given Old Lady Gravity the slip. We have got there, and we have got there fustest with the mostest. [Applause.]

"I can state without qualification that the New Weapon, in the capable hands of the men stationed on our platform, brings the *en*tire globe under our dominion. We can pinpoint any spot, anywhere, and sprinkle it with our particular brand of thunder. Mr. Moderator, I'm ready for this interview if the boys out there in space are ready."

Everyone suspected that there might be a slipup in the proceedings at this point, that the mechanical difficulties might prove insuperable. I glanced at the studio clock. The red sweep hand was within a few jumps of eleven-thirty—the General had managed his timing all right. Cahill's face was tenser than I had ever seen it before. Because of the advance buildup, a collapse at this moment would put him in a nasty hole, even for an old experienced m.c. But at exactly eleven-thirty the interview started, smooth as silk. Cahill picked it up from the General.

"And now, watchers of television everywhere, you will hear a conversation between Major General Artemus T. Recoil, who pioneered Operation Space, and two United States Army officers on the platform—Major James Obblington, formerly of Brooklyn, New York, now of Space, and Lieutenant Noble Trett, formerly of Sioux City, Iowa, now of Space. Go ahead, General Recoil!"

"Come in, Space!" said the General, his tonsils struggling in whiskey's undertow, his eyes bearing down hard on the script. "Can you hear me, Major Obblington and Lieutenant Trett?"

"I hear you," said a voice. "This is Trett." The voice, as I remember it, astonished me because of a certain laconic quality that I had not expected. I believe it astonished everyone. Trett's voice was cool, and he sounded as though he were right in the studio.

"Lieutenant Trett," continued the General, "tell the listeners here on earth, tell us, in your position far out there in free space, do you feel the pull of gravity?"

"No, sir, I don't," answered Trett. In spite of the "sir," Trett sounded curiously listless, almost insubordinate.

"Yet you are perfectly comfortable, sitting there on the platform, with the whole of earth spread out before you like a vast target?"

"Sure I'm comfortable."

The General waited a second, as though expecting amplification, but it failed to come. "Well, ah, how's the weather up there?" he asked heartily.

"There isn't any," said Trett.

"No weather? No weather in space? That's very interesting."

"The hell it is," said Trett. "It's God-damn dull. This place is a dump. Worse than some of the islands in the Pacific."

"Well, I suppose it must get on your nerves a bit. That's all part of the game. Tell us, Lieutenant, what's it like to be actually a part of the solar system, with your own private orbit?"

"It's all right, except I'd a damn sight rather get drunk," said Trett.

I looked at Cahill. He was swallowing his spit. General Recoil took a new hold on his script.

"And you say you don't feel the pull of gravity, not even a little?"

"I just told you I didn't feel any pull," said Trett. His voice now had a surly quality.

"Well, ah," continued the General, who was beginning to tremble, "can you describe, briefly, for the television audience—" But it was at this point that Trett, on the platform, seemed to lose interest in talking with General Recoil and started chinning with Major Obblington, his sidekick in space. At first the three voices clashed and blurred, but the General, on a signal from the moderator, quit talking, and the conversation that ensued between Trett and Obblington was audible and clear. Millions of listeners must have heard the dialogue.

"Hey, Obie," said Trett, "you want to know something else I don't feel the pull of, besides gravity?"

"What?" asked his companion.

"Conscience," said Trett cheerfully. "I don't feel my conscience pulling me around."

"Neither do I," said Obblington. "I ought to feel some pulls but I don't."

"I also don't feel the pull of duty."

"Check," said Obblington.

"And what is even more fantastic, I don't feel the pull of dames."

Cahill made a sign to the General. Stunned and confused by the turn things had taken, Recoil tried to pick up the interview and get it back on the track. "Lieutenant Trett," he commanded, "you will limit your remarks to the—"

Cahill waved him quiet. The next voice was the Major's.

"Jesus, now that you mention it, I don't feel the pull of dames either! Hey, Lieutenant—you suppose gravity has anything to do with sex?"

"God damn if *I* know," replied Trett. "I know I don't *weigh* anything, and when you don't weigh anything, you don't seem to *want* anything."

The studio by this time was paralyzed with attention. The General's face was swollen, his mouth was half open, and he struggled for speech that wouldn't come.

Then Trett's cool, even voice again: "See that continent down there, Obie? That's where old Fatso Recoil lives. You feel drawn toward that continent in any special way?"

"Naa," said Obblington.

"You feel like doing a little shooting, Obie?"

"You're rootin' tootin' I feel like shootin'."

"Then what are we waiting for?"

I am, of course, reconstructing this conversation from memory. I am trying to report it faithfully. When Trett said the words "Then what are we waiting for?" I quit listening and dashed for the phones in the corridor. As I was leaving the studio, I turned for a split second and looked back. The General had partially recovered his power of speech. He was mumbling something to Cahill. I caught the words "phone" and "Defense Department."

The corridor was already jammed. I had only one idea in my head—to speak to Ann. Pete Everhardt pushed past me. He said crisply, "This is it." I nodded. Then I glanced out of a window. High in the east a crazy ribbon of light was spreading upward. Lower down, in a terrible parabola, another streak began burning through. The first blast was felt only slightly in the plane. It must have been at a great distance. It was followed immediately by two more. I saw a piece of wing break up, saw one of the starboard engines shake itself loose from its fastenings and fall. Near the phone booths, the Bee, still in costume, fumbled awkwardly for a parachute. In the crush one of his feelers brushed my face. I never managed to reach a phone. All sorts of things flashed through my mind. I saw Ann and the children, their heads in diapers. I saw again the man in the leather cap, loading bedsprings. I heard again Pete's words, "This is it," only I seemed to hear them in translation: "Until the whole wide world to nothingness do sink." (How durable the poets are!) As I say, I never managed the phone call. My last memory of the morning is of myriads of bright points of destruction where the Weapon was arriving, each pyre in the characteristic shape of an artichoke. Then a great gash, and the plane tumbling. Then I lost consciousness.

I cannot say how many minutes or hours after that the earth finally broke up. I do not know. There is, of course, a mild irony in the fact that it was the United States that was responsible. Insofar as it can be said of any country that it had human attributes, the United States was well-meaning. Of that I am convinced. Even I, at this date and at this distance, cannot forget my country's great heart and matchless ingenuity. I can't in honesty say that I believe we were wrong to send the men to the platform—it's just that in any matter involving love, or high explosives, one can never foresee all the factors. Certainly I can't say with any assurance that Tollip's theory was right; it seems hardly likely that anyone who suffered so from stomach gas could have been on the right track. I did feel sympathetic toward some of his ideas, perhaps because I suffered from flatulence myself. Anyway, it was inevitable that it should have been the United States that developed the space platform and the new weapon that made the H-bomb obsolete. It was inevitable that what happened, at last, was conceived in good will.

Those times—those last days of earth! I think about them a lot. A sort of creeping ineptitude had set in. Almost everything in life seemed wrong to me, somehow, as though we were all hustling down a blind alley. Many of my friends seemed mentally confused, emotionally unstable, and I have an idea I seemed the same to them. In the big cities, horns blew before the light changed, and it was clear that motorists no longer had the capacity to endure the restrictions they had placed on their own behavior. When the birds became extinct (all but the whooping crane), I was reasonably sure that human beings were on the way out, too. The cranes survived only because of their dance—which showmen were quick to exploit. (Every sanctuary had its television transmitter, and the love dance became a more popular spectacle than heavyweight prizefighting.) Birds had always been the symbol of freedom. As soon as I realized that they were gone, I felt that the significance had gone from my own affairs. (I was a cranky man, though—I must remember that, too—and am not trying here to suggest anything beyond a rather strong personal sadness at all this.)

Those last days! There were so many religions in conflict, each ready to save the world with its own dogma, each perfectly intolerant of the other. Every day seemed a mere skirmish in the long holy war. It was a time of debauch and conversion. Every week the national picture magazines, as though atoning for past excesses, hid their cheesecake carefully away among four-color reproductions of the saints. Television was the universal peepshow—in homes, schools, churches, bars, stores, everywhere. Children early formed the habit of gaining all their images at second hand, by looking at a screen; they grew up believing that anything perceived directly was vaguely fraudulent. Only what had been touched with electronics was valid and real. I think the decline in the importance of direct images dated from the year television managed to catch an eclipse of the moon. After that, nobody ever looked at the sky, and it was as though the moon had joined the shabby company of buskers. There was really never a moment when a child, or even a man, felt free to look away from the television screen—for fear he might miss the one clue that would explain everything.

In many respects I like the planet I'm on. The people here have no urgencies, no capacity for sustained endeavor, but merely tackle things by fits and starts, leaving undone whatever fails to hold their interest, and so, by witlessness and improvidence, escape many of the errors of accomplishment. I like the apples here better than those on earth. They are often wormy, but with a most wonderful flavor. There is a saying here: "Even a very lazy man can eat around a worm."

But I would be lying if I said I didn't miss that other life, I loved it so.

Religion: Faith, Doubt, and Experience

n this section we do not attempt to present a survey of contemporary religious thought, since any such attempt would at best be sketchy and superficial. Instead we focus on the search for meaning in a world reputedly become meaningless. God is dead, Nietzsche proclaimed at the end of the last century, and it seems that the subsequent Western faith in scientific progress and the search for objective truth have been less than fulfilling for many. Spiritual needs remain. These frequently manifest themselves in a quest for meaning, so that to Paul Tillich, for example, "being religious means asking passionately the question of the meaning of our existence and being willing to receive answers, even if the answers hurt." In one way or another, all the writers we present below are concerned with this question.

The predicament is framed by the two poems that introduce the section —Father Hopkins' declaration of faith and Matthew Arnold's cry of doubt and despair. Clarence Darrow then speaks as an agnostic and shows a clear, if simple, conflict between science and religion, while Walter Stace, an atheist and intellectual, is darkly concerned for the fate of morality in a godless world. But "godless" becomes "meaningless," and if nothing is more meaningful, more important, than anything else, then indeed anything goes. Precisely this notion is combatted by Tillich in the next selection; both he and John Robinson attempt to discover and define new meanings for religion and for God in our time. Joseph Campbell turns to religious literature, to myths and mythic images, as "word-transcending symbols" that keep us in touch with our own hidden depths and so help us rediscover values and meaning. Harvey Cox, too, turns inward. "I lose my soul," he says, "if I become merely the sum total of all the external inputs." He sees as increasingly important that we try, honestly, to give testimony, to give voice and word to what is inside us, to recover "interiority" and so to renew community. Challenging this drift to the secular with its emphasis on individual experience, the Hartford Heresies reaffirm that God's existence is real and separate from human thought and imagination. We conclude the section with two autobiographical statements that simultaneously give personal testimony and assert the reality of God.

GERARD MANLEY HOPKINS (1844–1889)

God's Grandeur

The world is charged with the grandeur of God.
  It will flame out, like shining from shook foil;
  It gathers to a greatness, like the ooze of oil
Crushed. Why do men then now not reck his rod?
Generations have trod, have trod, have trod;
  And all is seared with trade; bleared, smeared with toil;
  And wears man's smudge and shares man's smell: the soil
Is bare now, nor can foot feel, being shod.

And for all this, nature is never spent;
  There lives the dearest freshness deep down things;
And though the last lights off the black West went
  Oh, morning, at the brown brink eastward, springs—
Because the Holy Ghost over the bent
  World broods with warm breast and with ah! bright wings.

                                                    (1877)

MATTHEW ARNOLD (1822–1888)

Dover Beach

The sea is calm to-night.
The tide is full, the moon lies fair
Upon the straits;—on the French coast the light
Gleams and is gone; the cliffs of England stand
Glimmering and vast, out in the tranquil bay.
Come to the window, sweet is the night-air!

Only, from the long line of spray
Where the sea meets the moon-blanched land,
Listen! you hear the grating roar
Of pebbles which the waves draw back, and fling,
At their return, up the high strand,
Begin, and cease, and then again begin,
With tremulous cadence slow, and bring
The eternal note of sadness in.

Sophocles long ago
Heard it on the Ægean, and it brought
Into his mind the turbid ebb and flow,
Of human misery; we
Find also in the sound a thought,
Hearing it by this distant northern sea.

The Sea of Faith
Was once, too, at the full, and round earth's shore
Lay like the folds of a bright girdle furled.
But now I only hear
Its melancholy, long, withdrawing roar,
Retreating, to the breath
Of the night-wind, down the vast edges drear
And naked shingles of the world.

Ah love, let us be true
To one another! for the world, which seems
To lie before us like a land of dreams,
So various, so beautiful, so new,
Hath really neither joy, nor love, nor light,
Nor certitude, nor peace, nor help for pain;
And we are here as on a darkling plain
Swept with confused alarms of struggle and flight,
Where ignorant armies clash by night.

(1867)

CLARENCE DARROW

*Clarence Darrow (1857–1938) is probably best known for his
distinguished career in criminal law. Born in Ohio, he attended one year
of law school at the University of Michigan, spent the next year in an*

attorney's office, and was admitted to the Ohio bar the following year, at the age of twenty-one. He soon left Ohio for Chicago and became the most sought-after and controversial criminal lawyer of his time. His most famous cases include the defense of the child-murderers Leopold and Loeb, for whom he won a life sentence instead of the death penalty, and the Scopes Trial in 1925—known as the Monkey Trial—which created a national and international furor. Darrow, an outspoken agnostic, defended John Scopes, a Dayton, Tennessee, science teacher who had taught evolution and thus broken a state law prohibiting "the teaching in public schools of any theories that deny the divine creation of man as taught in the Bible." The prosecuting attorney was William Jennings Bryan, a Fundamentalist. Darrow put Bryan on the stand, cross-examined him regarding his Fundamentalist beliefs, and won what was considered a triumphant victory, although Scopes was formally convicted and sentenced to a nominal fine of $100. Bryan died five days later. The reader may wish to keep this case in mind when reading the essay we present below, reprinted here from Verdicts Out of Court (ed. Arthur and Lila Weinberg, 1963). It was originally written in 1929 for a symposium in which Darrow was joined by a rabbi, a Protestant bishop, and a Catholic judge. Among Darrow's other writings are two autobiographical books, Farmington (1904) and The Story of My Life (1932), and a number of socio-legal works, including Resist Not Evil (1904), Eye for an Eye (1904), and Crime: Its Cause and Its Treatment (1922).

Why I Am an Agnostic

An agnostic is a doubter. The word is generally applied to those who doubt the verity of accepted religious creeds or faiths. Everyone is an agnostic as to the beliefs or creeds they do not accept. Catholics are agnostic to the Protestant creeds, and the Protestants are agnostic to the Catholic creed. Anyone who thinks is an agnostic about something, otherwise he must believe that he is possessed of all knowledge. And the proper place for such a person is in the madhouse or the home for the feeble-minded. In a popular way, in the western world, an agnostic is one who doubts or disbelieves the main tenets of the Christian faith.

I would say that belief in at least three tenets is necessary to the faith of a Christian: a belief in God, a belief in immortality, and a belief in a supernatural book. Various Christian sects require much more, but it is difficult to imagine that one could be a Christian, under any intelligent meaning of the word, with less. Yet there are some people who claim to be Christians who do not accept the literal interpretation of all the Bible, and who give more credence to some portions of the book than to others.

I am an agnostic as to the question of God. I think that it is impossible for the human mind to believe in an object or thing unless it can form a mental picture of such object or thing. Since man ceased to worship openly an anthropomorphic God and talked vaguely and not intelligently about some force in the universe, higher than man, that is responsible for the existence of man and the universe, he cannot be said to believe in God. One cannot believe in a force excepting as a force that pervades matter and is not an individual entity. To believe in a thing, an image of the thing must be stamped on the mind. If one is asked if he believes in such an animal as a camel, there immediately arises in his mind an image of the camel. This image has come from experience or knowledge of the animal gathered in some way or other. No such image comes, or can come, with the idea of a God who is described as a force.

Man has always speculated upon the origin of the universe, including himself. I feel, with Herbert Spencer, that whether the universe had an origin—and if it had—what the origin is will never be known by man. The Christian says that the universe could not make itself; that there must have been some higher power to call it into being. Christians have been obsessed for many years by Paley's argument that if a person passing through a desert should find a watch and examine its spring, its hands, its case and its crystal, he would at once be satisfied that some intelligent being capable of design had made the watch. No doubt this is true. No civilized man would question that someone made the watch. The reason he would not doubt it is because he is familiar with watches and other appliances made by man. The savage was once unfamiliar with a watch and would have had no idea upon the subject. There are plenty of crystals and rocks of natural formation that are as intricate as a watch, but even to intelligent man they carry no implication that some intelligent power must have made them. They carry no such implication because no one has any knowledge or experience of someone having made these natural objects which everywhere abound.

To say that God made the universe gives us no explanation of the beginning of things. If we are told that God made the universe, the question immediately arises: Who made God? Did he always exist, or was there some power back of that? Did he create matter out of nothing, or is his existence co-extensive with matter? The problem is still there. What is the origin of it all? If, on the other hand, one says that the universe was not made by God, that it always existed, he has the same difficulty to confront. To say that the universe was here last year, or millions of years ago, does not explain its origin. This is still a mystery. As to the question of the origin of things, man can only wonder and doubt and guess.

As to the existence of the soul, all people may either believe or disbelieve. Everyone knows the origin of the human being. They know that it came from a single cell in the body of the mother, and that the cell was one out of ten thousand in the mother's body. Before gestation the cell must have been fertilized by a spermatozoön from the body of the father. This was one out of perhaps a billion spermatozoa that was the capacity of the father. When the cell is fertilized a chemical process begins. The cell divides and multiplies and increases into millions of cells, and finally a child is born. Cells die and are born during the life of the individual until they finally drop apart, and this is death.

If there is a soul, what is it, and where did it come from, and where does it go? Can anyone who is guided by his reason possibly imagine a soul independent of a body, or the place of its residence, or the character of it, or anything concerning it? If man is justified in any belief or disbelief on any subject, he is warranted in the disbelief in a soul. Not one scrap of evidence exists to prove any such impossible thing.

Many Christians base the belief of a soul and God upon the Bible. Strictly speaking, there is no such book. To make the Bible, sixty-six books are bound into one volume. These books were written by many people at different times, and no one knows the time or the identity of any author. Some of the books were written by several authors at various times. These books contain all sorts of contradictory concepts of life and morals and the origin of things. Between the first and the last nearly a thousand years intervened, a longer time than has passed since the discovery of America by Columbus.

When I was a boy the theologicans used to assert that the proof of the divine inspiration of the Bible rested on miracles and prophecies. But a miracle means a violation of a natural law, and there can be no proof imagined that could be sufficient to show the violation of a natural law; even though proof seemed to show violation, it would only show that we were not acquainted with all natural laws. One believes in the truthfulness of a man because of his long experience with the man, and because the man has always told a consistent story. But no man has told so consistent a story as nature.

If one should say that the sun did not rise, to use the ordinary expression, on the day before, his hearer would not believe it, even though he had slept all day and knew that his informant was a man of the strictest veracity. He would not believe it because the story is inconsistent with the conduct of the sun in all the ages past.

Primitive and even civilized people have grown so accustomed to believing in miracles that they often attribute the simplest manifestations of nature to agencies of which they know nothing. They do this when the belief is utterly inconsistent with knowledge and logic. They believe in old miracles and new ones. Preachers pray for rain, knowing full well that no such prayer was ever answered. When a politician is sick, they pray for God to cure him, and the politician almost invariably dies. The modern clergyman who prays for rain and for the health of the politician is no more intelligent in this matter than the primitive man who saw a separate miracle in the rising and setting of the sun, in the birth of an individual, in the growth of a plant, in the stroke of lightning, in the flood, in every manifestation of nature and life.

As to prophecies, intelligent writers gave them up long ago. In all prophecies facts are made to suit the prophecy, or the prophecy was made after the facts, or the events have no relation to the prophecy. Weird and strange and unreasonable interpretations are used to explain simple statements, that a prophecy may be claimed.

Can any rational person believe that the Bible is anything but a human document? We now know pretty well where the various books came from, and about when they were written. We know that they were written by human beings who had no knowledge of science, little knowledge of life, and were influenced by the barbarous morality of primitive times, and were grossly ignorant of most things that men know today. For instance, Genesis says that God made the earth, and he made the sun to light the day and the moon to light the night, and in one clause disposes of the stars by saying that "he made the stars also." This was plainly written by someone who had no conception of the stars. Man, by the aid of his telescope, has looked out into the heavens and found stars whose diameter is as great as the distance between the earth and the sun. We now know that the universe is filled with stars and suns and planets and systems. Every new telescope looking further into the heavens only discovers more and more worlds and suns and systems in the endless reaches of space. The men who wrote Genesis believed, of course, that this tiny speck of mud that we call the earth was the center of the universe, the only world in space, and made for man, who was the only being worth considering. These men believed that the stars were only a little way above the earth, and were set in the firmament for man to look at, and for nothing else. Everyone today knows that this conception is not true.

The origin of the human race is not as blind a subject as it once was. Let alone God creating Adam out of hand, from the dust of the earth, does anyone believe that Eve was made from Adam's rib—that the snake walked and spoke in the Garden of Eden—that he tempted Eve to persuade Adam to eat an apple, and that it is on that account that the whole human race was doomed to hell—that for four thousand years there was no chance for any human to be saved, though none of them had anything whatever to do with temptation; and that finally men were saved only through God's son dying for them, and that unless human beings believed this silly, impossible and wicked story they were doomed to hell? Can anyone with intelligence really believe that a child born today should be doomed because the snake tempted Eve and Eve tempted Adam? To believe that is not God-worship; it is devil-worship.

Can anyone call this scheme of creation and damnation moral? It defies every principle of morality, as man conceives morality. Can anyone believe today that the whole world was destroyed by flood, save only Noah and his family and a male and female of each species of animal that entered the Ark? There are almost a million species of insects alone. How did Noah match these up and make sure of getting male and female to reproduce life in the world after the flood had spent its force? And why should all the lower animals have been destroyed? Were they included in the sinning of man? This is a story which could not beguile a fairly bright child of five years of age today.

Do intelligent people believe that the various languages spoken by man on earth came from the confusion of tongues at the Tower of Babel, some four thousand years ago? Human languages were dispersed all over the face of the earth long before that time. Evidences of civilizations are in existence now that were old long before the date claimed for the flood.

Do Christians believe that Joshua made the sun stand still, so that the day could be lengthened, that a battle might be finished? What kind of person wrote that story, and what did he know about astronomy? It is perfectly plain that the author thought that the earth was the center of the universe and stood still in the heavens, and that the sun either went around it or was pulled across its path each day, and that the stopping of the sun would lengthen the day. We know now that had the sun stopped when Joshua commanded it, and had it stood still until now, it would not have lengthened the day. We know that the day is determined by the rotation of the earth upon its axis, and not by the movement of the sun. Everyone knows that this story simply is not true, and not many even pretend to believe the childish fable.

What of the tale of Balaam's ass speaking to him, probably in Hebrew? Is it true, or is it a fable? Many asses have spoken, and doubtless some in Hebrew, but they have not been that breed of asses. Is salvation to depend on a belief in a monstrosity like this?

Above all the rest, would any human being today believe that a child was born without a father? Yet this story was not at all unreasonable in the ancient world; at least three or four miraculous births are recorded in the Bible, including John the Baptist and Samson. Immaculate conceptions were common in the Roman world at the time and at the place where Christianity really had its nativity. Women were taken to the temples to be inoculated of God so that their sons might be heroes, which meant, generally, wholesale butchers. Julius Caesar was a miraculous conception—indeed, they were common all over the world. How many miraculous-birth stories is a Christian now expected to believe?

In the days of the formation of the Christian religion, disease meant the possession of human beings by devils. Christ cured a sick man by casting out the devils, who ran into the swine, and the swine ran into the sea. Is there any question but what that was simply the attitude and belief of a primitive people? Does anyone believe that sickness means the possession of the body by devils, and that the devils must be cast out of the human being that he may be cured? Does anyone believe that a dead person can come to life? The miracles recorded in the Bible are not the only instances of dead men coming to life. All over the world one finds testimony of such miracles; miracles which no person is expected to believe, unless it is his kind of a miracle. Still at Lourdes today, and all over the present world, from New York to Los Angeles and up and down the lands, people believe in miraculous occurrences, and even in the return of the dead. Superstition is everywhere prevalent in the world. It has been so from the beginning, and most likely will be so unto the end.

The reasons for agnosticism are abundant and compelling. Fantastic and foolish and impossible consequences are freely claimed for the belief in religion. All the civilization of any period is put down as a result of religion. All the cruelty and error and ignorance of the period has no relation to religion. The truth is that the origin of what we call civilization is not due to religion but to skepticism. So long as men accepted miracles without question, so long as they believed in original sin and the road to salvation, so long as they believed in a hell where man would be kept for eternity on account of Eve, there was no reason whatever for civilization: life was short, and eternity was long, and the business of life was preparation for eternity.

When every event was a miracle, when there was no order or system or law, there was no occasion for studying any subject, or being interested in anything excepting a religion which took care of the soul. As man doubted the primitive conceptions about religion, and no longer accepted the literal, miraculous teachings of ancient books, he set himself to understand nature. We no longer cure disease by casting out devils. Since that time, men have studied the human body, have built hospitals and treated illness in a scientific way. Science is responsible for the building of railroads and bridges, of steamships, of telegraph lines, of cities, towns, large buildings and small, plumbing and sanitation, of the food supply, and the countless thousands of useful things that we now deem necessary to life. Without skepticism and doubt, none of these things could have been given to the world.

The fear of God is not the beginning of wisdom. The fear of God is the death of wisdom. Skepticism and doubt lead to study and investigation, and investigation is the beginning of wisdom.

The modern world is the child of doubt and inquiry, as the ancient world was the child of fear and faith.

W. T. STACE

Walter Terence Stace (1886–1967) was born in England and educated at Trinity College, Dublin University. He joined the British Civil Service in 1910 and served in Ceylon for twenty-two years. In 1932 he accepted a position teaching philosophy at Princeton University, where he taught until his retirement in 1955. His writings include The Philosophy of Hegel *(1924),* The Destiny of Western Man *(1942),* Religion and the Modern Mind *(1952),* The Teachings of the Mystics *(1961), and* Mysticism and Philosophy *(1961). The article we reprint below originally appeared in* The Atlantic Monthly, *September 1948.*

Man Against Darkness

[I]

The Catholic bishops of America recently issued a statement in which they said that the chaotic and bewildered state of the modern world is due to man's loss of faith, his abandonment of God and religion. For my part I believe in no religion at all. Yet I entirely agree with the bishops. It is no doubt an oversimplification to speak of *the* cause of so complex a state of affairs as the tortured condition of the world today. Its causes are doubtless multitudinous. Yet allowing for some element of oversimplification, I say that the bishops' assertion is substantially true.

M. Jean-Paul Sartre, the French existentialist philosopher, labels himself an atheist. Yet his views seem to me plainly to support the statement of the bishops. So long as there was believed to be a God in the sky, he says, men could regard him as the source of their moral ideals. The universe, created and governed by a fatherly God, was a friendly habitation for man. We could be sure that, however great the evil in the world, good in the end would triumph and the forces of evil would be routed. With the disappearance of God from the sky all this has changed. Since the world is not ruled by a spiritual being, but rather by blind forces, there cannot be any ideals, moral or otherwise, in the universe outside us. Our ideals, therefore, must proceed only from our own minds; they are our own inventions. Thus the world which surrounds us is nothing but an immense spiritual emptiness. It is a dead universe. We do not live in a universe which is on the side of our values. It is completely indifferent to them.

Years ago Mr. Bertrand Russell, in his essay *A Free Man's Worship,* said much the same thing.

> Such in outline, but even more purposeless, more void of meaning, is the world which Science presents for our belief. Amid such a world, if anywhere, our ideals henceforward must find a home. . . . Blind to good and evil, reckless of destruction, omnipotent matter rolls on its relentless way; for man, condemned today to lose his dearest, tomorrow himself to pass through the gate of darkness, it remains only to cherish, ere yet the blow falls, the lofty thoughts that ennoble his little day; . . . to worship at the shrine his own hands have built; . . . to sustain alone, a weary but unyielding Atlas, the world that his own ideals have fashioned despite the trampling march of unconscious power.

It is true that Mr. Russell's personal attitude to the disappearance of religion is quite different from either that of M. Sartre or the bishops or myself. The bishops think it a calamity. So do I. M. Sartre finds it "very distressing." And he berates as shallow the attitude of those who think that without God the world can go on just the same as before, as if nothing had happened. This creates for mankind, he thinks, a terrible crisis. And in this I agree with him. Mr. Russell, on the other hand, seems to believe that religion has done more harm than good in the world, and that its disappearance will be a blessing. But his picture of the world, and of the modern mind, is the same as that of M. Sartre. He stresses the *purposelessness* of the universe, the facts that man's ideals are his own creations, that the universe outside him in no way supports them, that man is alone and friendless in the world.

Mr. Russell notes that it is science which has produced this situation. There is no doubt that this is correct. But the way in which it has come about is not generally understood. There is a popular belief that some particular scientific discoveries or theories, such as the Darwinian theory of evolution, or the views of geologists about the age of the earth, or a series of such discoveries, have done the damage. It would be foolish to deny that these discoveries have had a great effect in undermining religious dogmas. But this account does not at all go to the root of the matter. Religion can probably outlive any scientific discoveries which could be made. It can accommodate itself to them. The root cause of the decay of faith has not been any particular discovery of science, but rather the general spirit of science and certain basic assumptions upon which modern science, from the seventeenth century onwards, has proceeded.

[II]

It was Galileo and Newton—notwithstanding that Newton himself was a deeply religious man—who destroyed the old comfortable picture of a friendly universe governed by spiritual values. And this was effected, not by Newton's discovery of the law of gravitation nor by any of Galileo's brilliant investigations, but by the general picture of the world which these men and others of their time made the basis of the science, not only of their own day, but of all succeeding generations down to the present. That is why the century immediately following Newton, the eighteenth century, was notoriously an age of religious skepticism. Skepticism did not have to wait for the discoveries of Darwin and the geologists in the nineteenth century. It flooded the world immediately after the age of the rise of science.

Neither the Copernican hypothesis nor any of Newton's or Galileo's particular discoveries were the real causes. Religious faith might well have accommodated itself to the new astronomy. The real turning point between the medieval age of faith and the modern age of unfaith came when the scientists of the seventeenth century turned their backs upon what used to be called "final causes." The final cause of a thing or event meant the purpose which it was supposed to serve in the universe, its cosmic purpose. What lay back of this was the presupposition that there is a cosmic order or plan and that everything which exists could in the last analysis be explained in terms of its place in this cosmic plan, that is, in terms of its purpose.

Plato and Aristotle believed this, and so did the whole medieval Christian world. For instance, if it were true that the sun and the moon were created and exist for the purpose of giving light to man, then this fact would explain why the sun and the moon exist. We might not be able to discover the purpose of everything, but everything must have a purpose. Belief in final causes thus amounted to a belief that the world is governed by purposes, presumably the purposes of some overruling mind. This belief was not the invention of Christianity. It was basic to the whole of Western civilization, whether in the ancient pagan world or in Christendom, from the time of Socrates to the rise of science in the seventeenth century.

The founders of modern science—for instance, Galileo, Kepler, and Newton—were mostly pious men who did not doubt God's purposes. Nevertheless they took the revolutionary step of consciously and deliberately expelling the idea of purpose as controlling nature from their new science of nature. They did this on the ground that inquiry into purposes is useless for what science aims at: namely, the prediction and control of events. To predict an eclipse, what you have to know is not its purpose but its causes. Hence science from the seventeenth century onwards became exclusively an inquiry into causes. The conception of purpose in the world was ignored and frowned on. This, though silent and almost unnoticed, was the greatest revolution in human history, far outweighing in importance any of the political revolutions whose thunder has reverberated through the world.

For it came about in this way that for the past three hundred years there has been growing up in men's minds, dominated as they are by science, a new imaginative picture of the world. The world, according to this new picture, is purposeless, senseless, meaningless. Nature is nothing but matter in motion. The motions of matter are governed, not by any purpose, but by blind forces and laws. Nature in this view, says Whitehead—to whose writings I am indebted in this part of my paper—is "merely the hurrying of material, endlessly, meaninglessly." You can draw a sharp line across the history of Europe dividing it into two epochs of very unequal length. The line passes through the lifetime of Galileo. European man before Galileo—whether ancient pagan or more recent Christian—thought of the world as controlled by plan and purpose. After Galileo European man thinks of it as utterly purposeless. This is the great revolution of which I spoke.

It is this which has killed religion. Religion could survive the discoveries that the sun, not the earth, is the center; that men are descended from simian ancestors; that the earth is hundreds of millions of years old. These discoveries may render out of date some of the details of older theological dogmas, may force their restatement in new intellectual frameworks. But they do not touch the essence of the religious vision itself, which is the faith that there is plan and purpose in the world, that the world is a moral order, that in the end all things are for the best. This faith may express itself through many different intellectual dogmas, those of Christianity, of Hinduism, of Islam. All and any of these intellectual dogmas may be destroyed without destroying the essential religious spirit. But that spirit cannot survive destruction of belief in a plan and purpose of the world, for that is the very heart of it. Religion can get on with any sort of astronomy, geology, biology, physics. But it cannot get on with a purposeless and meaningless universe.

If the scheme of things is purposeless and meaningless, then the life of man is purposeless and meaningless too. Everything is futile, all effort is in the end worthless. A man may, of course, still pursue disconnected ends, money, fame, art, science, and may gain pleasure from them. But his life is hollow at the center. Hence the dissatisfied, disillusioned, restless, spirit of modern man.

The picture of a meaningless world, and a meaningless human life, is, I think, the basic theme of much modern art and literature. Certainly it is the basic theme of modern philosophy. According to the most characteristic philosophies of the modern period from Hume in the eighteenth century to the so-called positivists of today, the world is just what it is, and that is the end of all inquiry. There is no reason for its being what it is. Everything might just as well have been quite different, and there would have been no reason for that either. When you have stated what things are, what things the world contains, there is nothing more which could be said, even by an omniscient being. To ask any question about *why* things are thus, or what purpose their being serves, is to ask a senseless question, because they serve no purpose at all. For instance, there is for modern philosophy no such thing as the ancient problem of evil. For this once famous question presupposes that pain and misery, though they seem so inexplicable and irrational to us, must ultimately subserve some rational purpose, must have their places in the cosmic plan. But this is nonsense. There is no such overruling rationality in the universe. Belief in the ultimate irrationality of everything is the quintessence of what is called the modern mind.

It is true that, parallel with these philosophies which are typical of the modern mind, preaching the meaninglessness of the world, there has run a line of idealistic philosophies whose contention is that the world is after all spiritual in nature and that moral ideals and values are inherent in its structure. But most of these idealisms were simply philosophical expressions of romanticism, which was itself no more than an unsuccessful counterattack of the religious against the scientific view of things. They perished, along with romanticism in literature and art, about the beginning of the present century, though of course they still have a few adherents.

At the bottom these idealistic systems of thought were rationalizations of man's wishful thinking. They were born of the refusal of men to admit the cosmic darkness. They were comforting illusions within the warm glow of which the more tender-minded intellectuals sought to shelter themselves from the icy winds of the universe. They lasted a little while. But they are shattered now, and we return once more to the vision of a purposeless world.

[III]

Along with the ruin of the religious vision there went the ruin of moral principles and indeed of all values. If there is a cosmic purpose, if there is in the nature of things a drive towards goodness, then our moral systems will derive their validity from this. But if our moral rules do not proceed from something outside us in the nature of the universe—whether we say it is God or simply the universe itself—then they must be our own inventions. Thus it came to be believed that moral rules must be merely an expression of our own likes and dislikes. But likes and dislikes are notoriously variable. What pleases one man, people, or culture displeases another. Therefore morals are wholly relative.

This obvious conclusion from the idea of a purposeless world made its appearance in Europe immediately after the rise of science, for instance in the philosophy of Hobbes. Hobbes saw at once that if there is no purpose in the world there are no values either. "Good and evil," he writes, "are names that signify our appetites and aversions; which in different tempers, customs, and doctrines of men are different. . . . Every man calleth that which pleaseth him, good; and that which displeaseth him, evil."

This doctrine of the relativity of morals, though it has recently received an impetus from the studies of anthropologists, was thus really implicit in the whole scientific mentality. It is disastrous for morals because it destroys their entire traditional foundation. That is why philosophers who see the danger signals, from the time at least of Kant, have been trying to give to morals a new foundation, that is, a secular or nonreligious foundation. This attempt may very well be intellectually successful. Such a foundation, independent of the religious view of the world, might well be found. But the question is whether it can ever be a *practical* success, that is, whether apart from its logical validity and its influence with intellectuals, it can ever replace among the masses of men the lost religious foundation. On that question hangs perhaps the future of civilization. But meanwhile disaster is overtaking us.

The widespread belief in "ethical relativity" among philosophers, psychologists, ethnologists, and sociologists is the theoretical counterpart of the repudiation of principle which we see all around us, especially in international affairs, the field in which morals have always had the weakest foothold. No one any longer effectively believes in moral principles except as the private prejudices either of individual men or of nations or cultures. This is the inevitable consequence of the doctrine of ethical relativity, which in turn is the inevitable consequence of believing in a purposeless world.

Another characteristic of our spiritual state is loss of belief in the freedom of the will. This also is a fruit of the scientific spirit, though not of any particular scientific discovery. Science has been built up on the basis of determinism, which is the belief that every event is completely determined by a chain of causes and is therefore theoretically predictable beforehand. It is true that recent physics seems to challenge this. But so far as its practical consequences are concerned, the damage has long ago been done. A man's actions, it was argued, are as much events in the natural world as is an eclipse of the sun. It follows that men's actions are as theoretically predictable as an eclipse. But if it is certain now that John Smith will murder Joseph Jones at 2.15 P.M. on January 1, 1963, what possible meaning can it have to say that when that time comes John Smith will be *free* to choose whether he will commit the murder or not? And if he is not free, how can he be held responsible?

It is true that the whole of this argument can be shown by a competent philosopher to be a tissue of fallacies—or at least I claim that it can. But the point is that the analysis required to show this is much too subtle to be understood by the average entirely unphilosophical man. Because of this, the argument against free will is generally swallowed whole by the unphilosophical. Hence the thought that man is not free, that he is the helpless plaything of forces over which he has no control, has deeply penetrated the modern mind. We hear of economic determinism, cultural determinism, historical determinism. We are not responsible for what we do because our glands control us, or because we are the products of environment or heredity. Not moral self-control, but the doctor, the psychiatrist, the educationist, must save us from doing evil. Pills and injections in the future are to do what Christ and the prophets have failed to do. Of course I do not mean to deny that doctors and educationists can and must help. And I do not mean in any way to belittle their efforts. But I do wish to draw attention to the weakening of moral controls, the greater or less repudiation of personal responsibility which, in the popular thinking of the day, result from these tendencies of thought.

[IV]

What, then, is to be done? Where are we to look for salvation from the evils of our time? All the remedies I have seen suggested so far are, in my opinion, useless. Let us look at some of them.

Philosophers and intellectuals generally can, I believe, genuinely do something to help. But it is extremely little. What philosophers can do is to show that neither the relativity of morals nor the denial of free will really follows from the grounds which have been supposed to support them. They can also try to discover a genuine secular basis for morals to replace the religious basis which has disappeared. Some of us are trying to do these things. But in the first place philosophers unfortunately are not agreed about these matters, and their disputes are utterly confusing to the non-philosophers. And in the second place their influence is practically negligible because their analyses necessarily take place on a level on which the masses are totally unable to follow them.

The bishops, of course, propose as remedy a return to belief in God and in the doctrines of the Christian religion. Others think that a new religion is what is needed. Those who make these proposals fail to realize that the crisis in man's spiritual condition is something unique in history for which there is no sort of analogy in the past. They are thinking perhaps of the collapse of the ancient Greek and Roman religions. The vacuum then created was easily filled by Christianity, and it might have been filled by Mithraism if Christianity had not appeared. By analogy they think that Christianity might now be replaced by a new religion, or even that Christianity itself, if revivified, might bring back health to men's lives.

But I believe that there is no analogy at all between our present state and that of the European peoples at the time of the fall of paganism. Men had at that time lost their belief only in particular dogmas, particular embodiments of the religious view of the world. It had no doubt become incredible that Zeus and the other gods were living on the top of Mount Olympus. You could go to the top and find no trace of them. But the imaginative picture of a world governed by purpose, a world driving towards the good—which is the inner spirit of religion—had at that time received no serious shock. It had merely to re-embody itself in new dogmas, those of Christianity or some other religion. Religion itself was not dead in the world, only a particular form of it.

But now the situation is quite different. It is not merely that particular dogmas, like that of the virgin birth, are unacceptable to the modern mind. That is true, but it constitutes a very superficial diagnosis of the present situation of religion. Modern skepticism is of a wholly different order from that of the intellectuals of the ancient world. It has attacked and destroyed not merely the outward forms of the religious spirit, its particularized dogmas, but the very essence of that spirit itself, belief in a meaningful and purposeful world. For the founding of a new religion a new Jesus Christ or Buddha would have to appear, in itself a most unlikely event and one for which in any case we cannot affort to sit and wait. But even if a new prophet and a new religion did appear, we may predict that they would fail in the modern world. No one for long would believe in them, for modern men have lost the vision, basic to all religion, of an ordered plan and purpose of the world. They have before their minds the picture of a purposeless universe, and such a world-picture must be fatal to any religion at all, not merely to Christianity.

We must not be misled by occasional appearances of a revival of the religious spirit. Men, we are told, in their disgust and disillusionment at the emptiness of their lives, are turning once more to religion, or are searching for a new message. It may be so. We must expect such wistful yearnings of the spirit. We must expect men to wish back again the light that is gone, and to try to bring it back. But however they may wish and try, the light will not shine again,—not at least in the civilization to which we belong.

Another remedy commonly proposed is that we should turn to science itself, or the scientific spirit, for our salvation. Mr. Russell and Professor Dewey both make this proposal, though in somewhat different ways. Professor Dewey seems to believe that discoveries in sociology, the application of scientific method to social and political problems, will rescue us. This seems to me to be utterly naïve. It is not likely that science, which is basically the cause of our spiritual troubles, is likely also to produce the cure for them. Also it lies in the nature of science that, though it can teach us the best means for achieving our ends, it can never tell us what ends to pursue. It cannot give us any ideals. And our trouble is about ideals and ends, not about the means for reaching them.

[V]

No civilization can live without ideals, or to put it in another way, without a firm faith in moral ideas. Our ideals and moral ideas have in the past been rooted in religion. But the religious basis of our ideals has been undermined, and the superstructure of ideals is plainly tottering. None of the commonly suggested remedies on examination seems likely to succeed. It would therefore look as if the early death of our civilization were inevitable.

Of course we know that it is perfectly possible for individual men, very highly educated men, philosophers, scientists, intellectuals in general, to live moral lives without any religious convictions. But the question is whether a whole civilization, a whole family of peoples, composed almost entirely of relatively uneducated men and women, can do this.

It follows, of course, that if we could make the vast majority of men as highly educated as the very few are now, we might save the situation. And we are already moving slowly in that direction through the techniques of mass education. But the critical question seems to concern the time-lag. Perhaps in a few hundred years most of the population will, at the present rate, be sufficiently highly educated and civilized to combine high ideals with an absence of religion. But long before we reach any such stage, the collapse of our civilization may have come about. How are we to live through the intervening period?

I am sure that the first thing we have to do is to face the truth, however bleak it may be, and then next we have to learn to live with it. Let me say a word about each of these two points. What I am urging as regards the first is complete honesty. Those who wish to resurrect Christian dogmas are not, of course, consciously dishonest. But they have that kind of unconscious dishonesty which consists in lulling oneself with opiates and dreams. Those who talk of a new religion are merely hoping for a new opiate. Both alike refuse to face the truth that there is, in the universe outside man, no spirituality, no regard for values, no friend in the sky, no help or comfort for man of any sort. To be perfectly honest in the admission of this fact, not to seek shelter in new or old illusions, not to indulge in wishful dreams about this matter, this is the first thing we shall have to do.

I do not urge this course out of any special regard for the sanctity of truth in the abstract. It is not self-evident to me that truth is the supreme value to which all else must be sacrificed. Might not the discoverer of a truth which would be fatal to mankind be justified in suppressing it, even in teaching men a falsehood? Is truth more valuable than goodness and beauty and happiness? To think so is to invent yet another absolute, another religious delusion in which Truth with a capital T is substituted for God. The reason why we must now boldly and honestly face the truth that the universe is nonspiritual and indifferent to goodness, beauty, happiness, or truth is not that it would be wicked to suppress it, but simply that it is too late to do so, so that in the end we cannot do anything else but face it. Yet we stand on the brink, dreading the icy plunge. We need courage. We need honesty.

Now about the other point, the necessity of learning to live with the truth. This means learning to live virtuously and happily, or at least contentedly, without illusions. And this is going to be extremely difficult because what we have now begun dimly to perceive is that human life in the past, or at least human happiness, has almost wholly depended upon illusions. It has been said that man lives by truth, and that the truth will make us free. Nearly the opposite seems to me to be the case. Mankind has managed to live only by means of lies, and the truth may very well destroy us. If one were a Bergsonian one might believe that nature deliberately puts illusions into our souls in order to induce us to go on living.

The illusions by which men have lived seem to be of two kinds. First, there is what one may perhaps call the Great Illusion—I mean the religious illusion that the universe is moral and good, that it follows a wise and noble plan, that it is gradually generating some supreme value, that goodness is bound to triumph in it. Secondly, there is a whole host of minor illusions on which human happiness nourishes itself. How much of human happiness notoriously comes from the illusions of the lover about his beloved? Then again we work and strive because of the illusions connected with fame, glory, power, or money. Banners of all kinds, flags, emblems, insignia, ceremonials, and rituals are invariably symbols of some illusion or other. The British Empire, the connection between mother country and dominions, is partly kept going by illusions surrounding the notion of kingship. Or think of the vast amount of human happiness which is derived from the illusion of supposing that if some nonsense syllable, such as "sir" or "count" or "lord" is pronounced in conjunction with our names, we belong to a superior order of people.

There is plenty of evidence that human happiness is almost wholly based upon illusions of one kind or another. But the scientific spirit, or the spirit of truth, is the enemy of illusions and therefore the enemy of human happiness. That is why it is going to be so difficult to live with the truth.

There is no reason why we should have to give up the host of minor illusions which render life supportable. There is no reason why the lover should be scientific about the loved one. Even the illusions of fame and glory may persist. But without the Great Illusion, the illusion of a good, kindly, and purposeful universe, we shall *have* to learn to live. And to ask this is really no more than to ask that we become genuinely civilized beings and not merely sham civilized beings.

I can best explain the difference by a reminiscence. I remember a fellow student in my college days, an ardent Christian, who told me that if he did not believe in future life, in heaven and hell, he would rape, murder, steal, and be a drunkard. That is what I call being a sham civilized being. On the other hand, not only could a Huxley, a John Stuart Mill, a David Hume, live great and fine lives without any religion, but a great many others of us, quite obscure persons, can at least live decent lives without it.

To be genuinely civilized means to be able to walk straightly and to live honorably without the props and crutches of one or another of the childish dreams which have so far supported men. That such a life is likely to be ecstatically happy I will not claim. But that it can be lived in quiet content, accepting resignedly what cannot be helped, not expecting the impossible, and thankful for small mercies, this I would maintain. That it would be difficult for men in general to learn this lesson I do not deny. But that it will be impossible I would not admit since so many have learned it already.

Man has not yet grown up. He is not adult. Like a child he cries for the moon and lives in a world of fantasies. And the race as a whole has perhaps reached the great crisis of its life. Can it grow up as a race in the same sense as individual men grow up? Can man put away childish things and adolescent dreams? Can he grasp the real world as it actually is, stark and bleak, without its romantic or religious halo, and still retain his ideals, striving for great ends and noble achievements? If he can, all may yet be well. If he cannot, he will probably sink back into the savagery and brutality from which he came, taking a humble place once more among the lower animals.

PAUL TILLICH

A profound and compassionate thinker and one of the great contemporary theologians, Paul Tillich (1886–1965) was born and educated in Germany and was well on his way to a distinguished academic career when he was dismissed from his post as Professor of Philosophy at the University of Frankfurt because of his outspoken criticism of the Nazi movement. In 1933, at the age of forty-seven, he emigrated to the United States at the invitation of Union Theological Seminary in New York, where he taught until 1954. That year he was appointed to the Divinity School Faculty at Harvard, and in 1962 he was named the first Duveen Professor of Theology at the University of Chicago. His books include The Shaking of the Foundations *(1948) and* The New Being *(1955), two volumes of sermons;* The Protestant Era *(1948);* The Courage to Be *(1952);* Dynamics of Faith *(1957); and* Ultimate Concern: Tillich in Dialogue *(ed. D. M. Brown, 1965), based on tape recordings made during a seminar in the spring of 1964.*

Paul Tillich thought of God not as a Being, but as our ultimate concern, the ultimate personal depth and ground of all being. It is this "lost" dimension of depth that he discusses here in an essay first printed in the Saturday Evening Post, *June 14, 1958.*

The Lost Dimension in Religion

Every observer of our Western civilization is aware of the fact that something has happened to religion. It especially strikes the observer of the American scene. Everywhere he finds symptoms of what one has called religious revival, or more modestly, the revival of interest in religion. He finds them in the churches with their rapidly increasing membership. He finds them in the mushroomlike growth of sects. He finds them on college campuses and in the theological faculties of universities. Most conspicuously, he finds them in the tremendous success of men like Billy Graham and Norman Vincent Peale, who attract masses of people Sunday after Sunday, meeting after meeting. The facts cannot be denied, but how should they be interpreted? It is my intention to show that these facts must be seen as expressions of the predicament of Western man in the second half of the twentieth century. But I would even go a step further. I believe that the predicament of man in our period gives us also an important insight into the predicament of man generally—at all times and in all parts of the earth.

There are many analyses of man and society in our time. Most of them show important traits in the picture, but few of them succeed in giving a general key to our present situation. Although it is not easy to find such a key, I shall attempt it and, in so doing, will make an assertion which may be somewhat mystifying at first hearing. The decisive element in the predicament of Western man in our period is his loss of the dimension of depth. Of course, "dimension of depth" is a metaphor. It is taken from the spatial realm and applied to man's spiritual life. What does it mean?

It means that man has lost an answer to the question: What is the meaning of life? Where do we come from, where do we go to? What shall we do, what should we become in the short stretch between birth and death? Such questions are not answered or even asked if the "dimension of depth" is lost. And this is precisely what has happened to man in our period of history. He has lost the courage to ask such questions with an infinite seriousness—as former generations did—and he has lost the courage to receive answers to these questions, wherever they may come from.

I suggest that we call the dimension of depth the religious dimension in man's nature. Being religious means asking passionately the question of the meaning of our existence and being willing to receive answers, even if the answers hurt. Such an idea of religion makes religion universally human, but it certainly differs from what is usually called religion. It does not describe religion as the belief in the existence of gods or one God, and as a set of activities and institutions for the sake of relating oneself to these beings in thought, devotion and obedience. No one can deny that the religions which have appeared in history are religions in this sense. Nevertheless, religion in its innermost nature is more than religion in this narrower sense. It is the state of being concerned about one's own being and being universally.

There are many people who are ultimately concerned in this way who feel far removed, however, from religion in the narrower sense, and therefore from every historical religion. It often happens that such people take the question of the meaning of their life infinitely seriously and reject any historical religion just for this reason. They feel that the concrete religions fail to express their profound concern adequately. They are religious while rejecting the religions. It is this experience which forces us to distinguish the meaning of religion as living in the dimension of depth from particular expressions of one's ultimate concern in the symbols and institutions of a concrete religion. If we now turn to the concrete analysis of the religious situation of our time, it is obvious that our key must be the basic meaning of religion and not any particular religion, not even Christianity. What does this key disclose about the predicament of man in our period?

If we define religion as the state of being grasped by an infinite concern we must say: Man in our time has lost such infinite concern. And the resurgence of religion is nothing but a desperate and mostly futile attempt to regain what has been lost.

How did the dimension of depth become lost? Like any important event, it has many causes, but certainly not the one which one hears often mentioned from ministers' pulpits and evangelists' platforms, namely that a widespread impiety of modern man is responsible. Modern man is neither more pious nor more impious than man in any other period. The loss of the dimension of depth is caused by the relation of man to his world and to himself in our period, the period in which nature is being subjected scientifically and technically to the control of man. In this period, life in the dimension of depth is replaced by life in the horizontal dimension. The driving forces of the industrial society of which we are a part go ahead horizontally and not vertically. In popular terms this is expressed in phrases like "better and better," "bigger and bigger," "more and more." One should not disparage the feeling which lies behind such speech. Man is right in feeling that he is able to know and transform the world he encounters without a foreseeable limit. He can go ahead in all directions without a definite boundary.

A most expressive symbol of this attitude of going ahead in the horizontal dimension is the breaking through of the space which is controlled by the gravitational power of the earth into the world-space. It is interesting that one calls this world-space simply "space" and speaks, for instance, of space travel, as if every trip were not travel into space. Perhaps one feels that the true nature of space has been discovered only through our entering into indefinite world-space. In any case, the predominance of the horizontal dimension over the dimension of depth has been immensely increased by the opening up of the space beyond the space of the earth.

If we now ask what does man do and seek if he goes ahead in the horizontal dimension, the answer is difficult. Sometimes one is inclined to say that the mere movement ahead without an end, the intoxication with speeding forward without limits, is what satisfies him. But this answer is by no means sufficient. For on his way into space and time man changes the world he encounters. And the changes made by him change himself. He transforms everything he encounters into a tool; and in doing so he himself becomes a tool. But if he asks, a tool for what, there is no answer.

One does not need to look far beyond everyone's daily experience in order to find examples to describe this predicament. Indeed our daily life in office and home, in cars and airplanes, at parties and conferences, while reading magazines and watching television, while looking at advertisements and hearing radio, are in themselves continuous examples of a life which has lost the dimension of depth. It runs ahead, every moment is filled with something which must be done or seen or said or planned. But no one can experience depth without stopping and becoming aware of himself. Only if he has moments in which he does not care about what comes next can he experience the meaning of this moment here and now and ask himself about the meaning of his life. As long as the preliminary, transitory concerns are not silenced, no matter how interesting and valuable and important they may be, the voice of the ultimate concern cannot be heard. This is the deepest root of the loss of the dimension of depth in our period—the loss of religion in its basic and universal meaning.

If the dimension of depth is lost, the symbols in which life in this dimension has expressed itself must also disappear. I am speaking of the great symbols of the historical religions in our Western world, of Judaism and Christianity. The reason that the religious symbols became lost is not primarily scientific criticism, but it is a complete misunderstanding of their meaning; and only because of this misunderstanding was scientific critique able, and even justified, in attacking them. The first step toward the non-religion of the Western world was made by religion itself. When it defended its great symbols, not as symbols, but as literal stories, it had already lost the battle. In doing so the theologians (and today many religious laymen) helped to transfer the powerful expressions of the dimension of depth into objects or happenings on the horizontal plane. There the symbols lose their power and meaning and become an easy prey to physical, biological and historical attack.

If the symbol of creation which points to the divine ground of everything is transferred to the horizontal plane, it becomes a story of events in a removed past for which there is no evidence, but which contradicts every piece of scientific evidence. If the symbol of the Fall of Man, which points to the tragic estrangement of man and his world from their true being is transferred to the horizontal plane, it becomes a story of a human couple a few thousand years ago in what is now present-day Iraq. One of the most profound psychological descriptions of the general human predicament becomes an absurdity on the horizontal plane. If the symbols of the Saviour and the salvation through Him which point to the healing power in history and personal life are transferred to the horizontal plane, they become stories of a half-divine being coming from a heavenly place and returning to it. Obviously, in this form, they have no meaning whatsoever for people whose view of the universe is determined by scientific astronomy.

If the idea of God (and the symbols applied to Him) which expresses man's ultimate concern is transferred to the horizontal plane, God becomes a being among others whose existence or nonexistence is a matter of inquiry. Nothing, perhaps, is more symptomatic of the loss of the dimension of depth than the permanent discussion about the existence or nonexistence of God—a discussion in which both sides are equally wrong, because the discussion itself is wrong and possible only after the loss of the dimension of depth.

When in this way man has deprived himself of the dimension of depth and the symbols expressing it, he then becomes a part of the horizontal plane. He loses his self and becomes a thing among things. He becomes an element in the process of manipulated production and manipulated consumption. This is now a matter of public knowledge. We have become aware of the degree to which everyone in our social structure is managed, even if one knows it and even if one belongs himself to the managing group. The influence of the gang mentality on adolescents, of the corporation's demands on the executives, of the conditioning of everyone by public communication, by propaganda and advertising under the guidance of motivation research, et cetera, have all been described in many books and articles.

Under these pressures, man can hardly escape the fate of becoming a thing among the things he produces, a bundle of conditioned reflexes without a free, deciding and responsible self. The immense mechanism, set up by man to produce objects for his use, transforms man himself into an object used by the same mechanism of production and consumption.

But man has not ceased to be man. He resists this fate anxiously, desperately, courageously. He asks the question, for what? And he realizes that there is no answer. He becomes aware of the emptiness which is covered by the continuous movement ahead and the production of means for ends which become means again without an ultimate end. Without knowing what has happened to him, he feels that he has lost the meaning of life, the dimension of depth.

Out of this awareness the religious question arises and religious answers are received or rejected. Therefore, in order to describe the contemporary attitude toward religion, we must first point to the places where the awareness of the predicament of Western man in our period is most sharply expressed. These places are the great art, literature and, partly, at least, the philosophy of our time. It is both the subject matter and the style of these creations which show the passionate and often tragic struggle about the meaning of life in a period in which man has lost the dimension of depth. This art, literature, philosophy is not religious in the narrower sense of the word; but it asks the religious question more radically and more profoundly than most directly religious expressions of our time.

It is the religious question which is asked when the novelist describes a man who tries in vain to reach the only place which could solve the problem of his life, or a man who disintegrates under the memory of a guilt which persecutes him, or a man who never had a real self and is pushed by his fate without resistance to death, or a man who experiences a profound disgust of everything he encounters.

It is the religious question which is asked when the poet opens up the horror and the fascination of the demonic regions of his soul, or if he leads us into the deserts and empty places of our being, or if he shows the physical and moral mud under the surface of life, or if he sings the song of transitoriness, giving words to the ever-present anxiety of our hearts.

It is the religious question which is asked when the playwright shows the illusion of a life in a ridiculous symbol, or if he lets the emptiness of a life's work end in self-destruction, or if he confronts us with the inescapable bondage to mutual hate and guilt, or if he leads us into the dark cellar of lost hopes and slow disintegration.

It is the religious question which is asked when the painter breaks the visible surface into pieces, then reunites them into a great picture which has little similarity with the world at which we normally look, but which expresses our anxiety and our courage to face reality.

It is the religious question which is asked when the architect, in creating office buildings or churches, removes the trimmings taken over from past styles because they cannot be considered an honest expression of our own period. He prefers the seeming poverty of a purpose-determined style to the deceptive richness of imitated styles of the past. He knows that he gives no final answer, but he does give an honest answer.

The philosophy of our time shows the same hiddenly religious traits. It is divided into two main schools of thought, the analytic and the existentialist. The former tries to analyze logical and linguistic forms which are always used and which underlie all scientific research. One may compare them with the painters who dissolve the natural forms of bodies into cubes, planes and lines; or with those architects who want the structural "bones" of their buildings to be conspicuously visible and not hidden by covering features. This self-restriction produces the almost monastic poverty and seriousness of this philosophy. It is religious—without any contact with religion in its method—by exercising the humility of "learned ignorance."

In contrast to this school the existentialist philosophers have much to say about the problems of human existence. They bring into rational concepts what the writers and poets, the painters and architects, are expressing in their particular material. What they express is the human predicament in time and space, in anxiety and guilt and the feeling of meaninglessness. From Pascal in the seventeenth century to Heidegger and Sartre in our time, philosophers have emphasized the contrast between human dignity and human misery. And by doing so, they have raised the religious question. Some have tried to answer the question they have asked. But if they did so, they turned back to past traditions and offered to our time that which does not fit our time. Is it possible for our time to receive answers which are born out of our time?

Answers given today are in danger of strengthening the present situation and with it the questions to which they are supposed to be the answers. This refers to some of the previously mentioned major representatives of the so-called resurgence of religion, as for instance the evangelist Billy Graham and the counseling and healing minister, Norman Vincent Peale. Against the validity of the answers given by the former, one must say that, in spite of his personal integrity, his propagandistic methods and his primitive theological fundamentalism fall short of what is needed to give an answer to the religious question of our period. In spite of all his seriousness, he does not take the radical questions of our period seriously.

The effect that Norman Peale has on large groups of people is rooted in the fact that he confirms the situation which he is supposed to help overcome. He heals people with the purpose of making them fit again for the demands of the competitive and conformist society in which we are living. He helps them to become adapted to the situation which is characterized by the loss of the dimension of depth. Therefore, his advice is valid on this level; but it is the validity of this level that is the true religious question of our time. And this question he neither raises nor answers.

In many cases the increase of church membership and interest in religious activities does not mean much more than the religious consecration of a state of things in which the religious dimension has been lost. It is the desire to participate in activities which are socially strongly approved and give internal and a certain amount of external security. This is not necessarily bad, but it certainly is not an answer to the religious question of our period.

Is there an answer? There is always an answer, but the answer may not be available to us. We may be too deeply steeped in the predicament out of which the question arises to be able to answer it. To acknowledge this is certainly a better way toward a real answer than to bar the way to it by deceptive answers. And it may be that in this attitude the real answer (within available limits) is given. The real answer to the question of how to regain the dimension of depth is not given by increased church membership or church attendance, nor by conversion or healing experiences. But it is given by the awareness that we have lost the decisive dimension of life, the dimension of depth, and that there is no easy way of getting it back. Such awareness is in itself a state of being grasped by that which is symbolized in the term, dimension of depth. He who realizes that he is separated from the ultimate source of meaning shows by this realization that he is not only separated but also reunited. And this is just our situation. What we need above all—and partly have—is the radical realization of our predicament, without trying to cover it up by secular or religious ideologies. The revival of religious interest would be a creative power in our culture if it would develop into a movement of search for the lost dimension of depth.

This does not mean that the traditional religious symbols should be dismissed. They certainly have lost their meaning in the literalistic form into which they have been distorted, thus producing the critical reaction against them. But they have not lost their genuine meaning, namely, of answering the question which is implied in man's very existence in powerful, revealing and saving symbols. If the resurgence of religion would produce a new understanding of the symbols of the past and their relevance for our situation, instead of premature and deceptive answers, it would become a creative factor in our culture and a saving factor for many who live in estrangement, anxiety and despair. The religious answer has always the character of "in spite of." In spite of the loss of dimension of depth, its power is present, and most present in those who are aware of the loss and are striving to regain it with ultimate seriousness.

JOHN A. T. ROBINSON

John A. T. Robinson was born in England in 1919 and educated at Cambridge University (Doctor of Philosophy, 1946; Doctor of Divinity, 1968). He was admitted to the Church of England as deacon in 1945 and became a priest in 1946. He established his reputation as a New Testament scholar while Fellow and Dean of Clare College, Cambridge, from 1951 to 1959 and has been Visiting Professor at Harvard Union Theological Seminary and Cornell. He was Bishop of Woolwich from 1959 to 1969 and is presently Assistant Bishop of Southwater and Fellow and Dean of Trinity College, Cambridge. In 1963 Dr. Robinson touched off an international debate between radical and traditional interpreters of Christianity with the publication of a book, Honest to God, *in which he challenges the traditional image of God as a supernatural person. The book brings together in popular form a number of radical ideas current in modern theology, especially those of Dietrich Bonhoeffer, the German pastor hanged by the Nazis, and of Paul Tillich.*

We reprint here the article in the London Observer *for March 17, 1963, in which Dr. Robinson explains the circumstances leading to publication of* Honest to God. *The principal statements in the ensuing controversy have been collected by David L. Edwards in* The Honest to God Debate *(1963). Among Dr. Robinson's more recent works are* Christian Morals Today *(1964),* But That I Can't Believe *(1967),* Theological Freedom and Social Responsibility *(1967), and* Christ, Faith and History *(1972).*

Our Image of God Must Go

Few people realise that we are in the middle of one of the most exciting theological ferments of the century. Some theologians have sensed this for years; but now, quite suddenly, new ideas about God and religion, many of them with disturbing revolutionary implications, are breaking surface.

If Christianity is to survive it must be relevant to modern secular man, not just to the dwindling number of the religious. But the supernaturalist framework within which traditionally it has been preached is making this increasingly impossible. Men can no longer credit the existence of "gods," or of a God as a supernatural Person, such as religion has always posited.

Not infrequently, as I watch or listen to a broadcast discussion between a Christian and a humanist, I catch myself realising that most of my sympathies are on the humanist's side. This is not in the least because my faith or commitment is in doubt, but because I instinctively share with him his inability to accept the "religious frame" within which alone that faith is being offered to him. I feel that as a secular man he is *right* to rebel against it, and I am increasingly uncomfortable that "orthodoxy" should be identified with it, when it is simply an out-moded view of the world.

The new ideas were first put on record by a German pastor in a Nazi prison in 1944: "Our whole 1,900-year-old Christian preaching and theology rests upon the 'religious premise' of man. What we call Christianity has always been a pattern—perhaps a true pattern—of religion. But if one day it becomes apparent that this *a priori* 'premise' simply does not exist, but was an historical and temporary form of human self-expression, i.e., if we reach the stage of being radically without religion—and I think this is more or less the case already—what does that mean for 'Christianity'?

"It means that the linchpin is removed from the whole structure of our Christianity to date."

Those words were written on April 30, 1944. It is a date that may yet prove a turning-point in the history of Christianity. For on it Dietrich Bonhoeffer first broached the subject of "religionless Christianity" in a smuggled correspondence with his friend Eberhard Bethge, who subsequently edited his "Letters and Papers from Prison."

Bonhoeffer was a Lutheran pastor of very traditional upbringing. Had he lived, he would now be in his late fifties. From 1933–35 he was in charge of the German congregation in Forest Hill, South London—where the church, rebuilt out of British war-damage money, is now dedicated to his name. In the inner circle of the German Resistance, he was privy to the plot on Hitler's life, and within a year of penning that letter he had been hanged by the S.S., on the eve of liberation by the Americans.

When his letters were first published—a bare 10 years ago—one felt at once that the Church was not ready for what Bonhoeffer was saying. Indeed, it might properly be understood only 100 years hence. But it seemed one of those trickles that must one day split rocks.

The speed with which his ideas have become current coin, is not, I think, the result solely of the quickening pace of communication and change. It is the result of one of those mysteries of human history whereby, apparently without interconnection, similar ideas start bubbling up all over the place at the same time. Without this, I suspect, Bonhoeffer might have remained a voice in the wilderness for decades, like Kierkegaard a century earlier.

Perhaps at this point I may be personal. A year ago I was laid up for three months with a slipped disc. I determined to use the opportunity to allow their head to ideas that had been submerged by pressure of work for some time past. Over the years convictions had been gathering—from my reading and experience—which I knew I couldn't with integrity ignore, however disturbing they might seem.

But I wrote my book shut up in my room. What has astonished me since is the way in which within the last six months similar ideas have broken surface in articles and conversations in the most unlikely places —as far apart as Africa and Texas. However inarticulate one may be, one detects an immediate glance of recognition and what the editor of *Prism* has called "an almost audible gasp of relief" when these things are said openly.

It is not easy to put one's finger on the common factor. I suppose it is *the glad acceptance of secularisation as a God-given fact.* For we of our generation are secular men. And our question, as Christians, is: How can Christ be Lord of a genuinely secular world?

Hitherto, says Bonhoeffer, Christianity has been based on the premise that man is naturally religious: and it has been presented as the best and highest religion. The corollary has been that to the non-religious it has nothing to say. A person had to become religious first—to have, or be induced to have, a religious sense of sin or need for God: then Christ could come to him as the answer.

Modern man has opted for a secular world: he has become increasingly non-religious. The Churches have deplored this as the great defection from God, and the more they write it off, the more this movement has seen itself as anti-Christian.

But, claims Bonhoeffer boldly, the period of religion is over. Man is growing out of it: he is "coming of age." By that he doesn't mean that he is getting better (a prisoner of the Gestapo had few illusions about human nature), but that for good or for ill he is putting the religious world-view behind him as childish and pre-scientific.

Bonhoeffer would accept Freud's analysis of the God of religion as a projection. Till now man has felt the need for a God as a child feels the need for his father. He must be "there" to explain the universe, to protect him in his loneliness, to fill the gaps in his science, to provide the sanction for his morality.

But now man is discovering that he can manage quite happily by himself. He finds no necessity to bring God into his science, his morals, his political speeches. Only in the private world of the individual's psychological need and insecurity—in that last corner of "the sardine-tin of life"—is room apparently left for the God who has been elbowed out of every other sphere. And so the religious evangelist works on men to coerce them at their weakest point into feeling that they cannot get on without the tutelage of God.

But "God is teaching us that we must live as men who can get along very well without him." And this, says Bonhoeffer, is the God Jesus shows us, the God who refuses to be a *Deus ex machina,* who allows himself to be edged out of the world on to the Cross. Our God is the God who forsakes us—only to meet with us on the Emmaus road, if we are really prepared to abandon him as a long-stop and find him not at the boundaries of life where human powers fail, but at the centre, in the secular, as "the 'beyond' in our midst."

Another way of putting this is to say that our whole mental image of God must undergo a revolution. This is nothing new in Christianity. The men of the Bible thought of God as "up there," seated upon a throne in a localised heaven above the earth, and it was this God to whom Jesus "ascended."

But with the development of scientific knowledge, the image of the God "up there" made it harder rather than easier to believe. And so, very boldly, Christians discarded it. I say very boldly, for in order to do so they had to go against the literal language of the Bible.

For it they substituted another mental image—of a God "out there," metaphysically if not literally. Somewhere beyond this universe was a Being, a centre of personal will and purpose, who created it and who sustains it, who loves it and who "visited" it in Jesus Christ. But I need not go on, for this is "our" God. Theism means being convinced that this Being exists: atheism means denying that he does.

But I suspect we have reached the point where this mental image of God is also more of a hindrance than a help. There are many who feel instinctively that the space-age has put paid to belief in God. The theologian may properly think them naïve. But what they are rebelling against is this image of a Being out beyond the range of the farthest rocket and the probe of the largest telescope. They no longer find such an entity credible.

To the religious, the idea of a supreme Being out there may seem as necessary for their thinking as was once the idea of a Being up there. They can hardly even picture God without it. If there wasn't really someone "there," then the atheists would be right.

But any image can become an idol: and I believe that Christians must go through the agonising process in this generation of detaching themselves from this idol. For to twentieth-century man the "old man in the sky" and the whole supernaturalist scheme seem as fanciful as the man in the moon.

Sir Julian Huxley has spent much time in his deeply moving book, "Religion Without Revelation," and in subsequent articles in this paper, dismantling this construction. He constantly echoes Bonhoeffer's sentiments, and I heartily agree with him when he says, "The sense of spiritual relief which comes from rejecting the idea of God as a superhuman being is enormous."

For the real question of belief is not the *existence* of God, as *a* person. For God *is* ultimate reality (that's what we mean by the word), and ultimate reality must exist. The only question is what ultimate reality is like. And the Christian affirmation is that reality ultimately, deep down, in the last analysis, is *personal:* the world, incredible as it may seem, is built in such a way that in the end personal values will out.

Professor Bondi, commenting in the B.B.C. television programme, "The Cosmologists," on Sir James Jeans's assertion that "God is a great mathematician," stated quite correctly that what he should have said is "Mathematics is God." Reality, in other words, can finally be reduced to mathematical formulae. What the Christian says is that in, with and under these regularities, and giving ultimate significance to them, is the yet deeper reliability of an utterly personal Love.

That, in the world of the H-bomb, is a desperate act of faith. On purely humanistic grounds I could have no basis for believing it as more than wishful thinking. Huxley ends his book with the words "My faith is in the possibilities of man." It is significant that he was able to reissue it in 1957 without even a mention of the possibility, not to say probability, that there might not, within his frame of reference, be any prospects for humanity at all.

The belief that personality is of ultimate significance is for me frankly incredible *unless* what we see in Jesus of Nazareth is a window through the surface of things into the very ground of our being. That is why, in traditional categories, the survival of Christianity turned upon the assertion that he was "of one substance with the Father." For unless the substance, the being, of things deep down *is* Love, of the quality disclosed in the life, death and resurrection of Jesus Christ, then we could have no confidence is affirming that reality at its very deepest level is personal. And that is what is meant by asserting that *God* is personal.

This has nothing necessarily to do with positing the existence of a Person, an almighty Individual, "up there" or "out there." Indeed, as Paul Tillich, the great American theologian, also from Germany, has said: "The protest of atheism against such a highest person is correct."

Tillich has shown that it is just as possible to speak of God in terms of "depth" as of "height." Such language is equally symbolic. But it may speak more "profoundly" to modern man brought up on "depth psychology." Indeed, I believe that this transposition can bring fresh meaning to much traditional religious symbolism. Tillich talks of what is most deeply true about us and for us, and goes on:—

"That depth is what the word God means. And if that word has not much meaning for you, translate it, and speak of the depths of your life, of the source of your being, of your ultimate concern, of what you take seriously without any reservation. Perhaps, in order to do so, you must forget everything traditional you have learned about God, perhaps even that word itself. For if you know that God means depth, you know much about him. You cannot then call yourself an atheist or unbeliever. For you cannot think or say: Life has no depth! Life itself is shallow. Being itself is surface only. If you could say this in complete seriousness, you would be an atheist, but otherwise you are not."

Those words from his "Shaking of the Foundations" (now published as a Pelican [Book]) had a strangely moving effect on me when I first read them 14 years ago. They spoke of God with a new and indestructible relevance, which made the traditional language about a God that came in from outside both remote and artificial. And yet they preserved his "profound" mystery and transcendence.

The ultimate Christian conviction is that at the heart of things there is "nothing, in death or life . . . in the world as it is or the world as it shall be, in the forces of the universe, in heights or depths—nothing in all creation that can separate us from the love of God in Christ Jesus our Lord." That I believe passionately. As for the rest, as for the images of God, whether metal or mental, I am prepared to be an agnostic with the agnostics, even an atheist with the atheists.

Indeed, though we shall not of course be able to do it, I can understand those who urge that we should give up using the word "God" for a generation, so impregnated has it become with a way of thinking we may have to discard if the Gospel is to signify anything.

I am well aware that what I have said involves radical reformulations for the Church in almost every field—of doctrine, worship, ethics and evangelism. This is a dangerous process, but immensely exhilarating: and the exciting thing is that it is not being forced upon the Church from outside but is welling up from within.

JOSEPH CAMPBELL

Joseph Campbell proposes "comparative mythology" as an academic field in its own right, one encompassing new discoveries in archeology, philology, ethnology, philosophy, art history, folklore, religion, psychology, and Asian studies. Many of his books correlate these disciplines and convey both his enthusiasm and his scholarship to a popular audience.

Campbell was born in New York City in 1904. He attended Dartmouth College and Columbia University, and after receiving his M.A. in 1927, he studied in Paris and Munich. On his return he taught for two years at a private school and then joined the faculty of Sarah Lawrence College. His best-known book is The Hero with a Thousand

Faces *(1949), his reconstruction of the universal "monomyth." This was followed by the series titled* The Masks of God, *four separately published volumes on primitive, Oriental, Occidental, and creative mythology. His latest books are* Myths to Live By *(1972), from which we reprint the selection below, and* The Mythic Image *(1974).*

Mythic Images

In relation to the first books and chapters of the Bible, it used to be the custom of both Jews and Christians to take the narratives literally, as though they were dependable accounts of the origin of the universe and of actual prehistoric events. It was supposed and taught that there had been, quite concretely, a creation of the world in seven days by a god known only to the Jews; that somewhere on this broad new earth there had been a Garden of Eden containing a serpent that could talk; that the first woman, Eve, was formed from the first man's rib, and that the wicked serpent told her of the marvelous properties of the fruits of a certain tree of which God had forbidden the couple to eat; and that, as a consequence of their having eaten of that fruit, there followed a "Fall" of all mankind, death came into the world, and the couple was driven forth from the garden. For there was in the center of that garden a second tree, the fruit of which would have given them eternal life; and their creator, fearing lest they should now take and eat of that too, and so become as knowing and immortal as himself, cursed them, and having driven them out, placed at his garden gate "cherubim and a flaming sword which turned every way to guard the way to the tree of life."

It seems impossible today, but people actually believed all that until as recently as half a century or so ago: clergymen, philosophers, government officers, and all. Today we know—and know right well—that there was never anything of the kind: no Garden of Eden anywhere on this earth, no time when the serpent could talk, no prehistoric "Fall," no exclusion from the garden, no universal Flood, no Noah's Ark. The entire history on which our leading Occidental religions have been founded is an anthology of fictions. But these are fictions of a type that have had— curiously enough—a universal vogue as the founding legends of other religions, too. Their counterparts have turned up everywhere—and yet, there was never such a garden, serpent, tree, or deluge.

How account for such anomalies? Who invents these impossible tales? Where do their images come from? And why—though obviously absurd —are they everywhere so reverently believed?

What I would suggest is that by comparing a number from different parts of the world and differing traditions, one might arrive at an understanding of their force, their source and possible sense. For they are not historical. That much is clear. They speak, therefore, not of outside events but of themes of the imagination. And since they exhibit features that are actually universal, they must in some way represent features of our general racial imagination, permanent features of the human spirit —or, as we say today, of the psyche. They are telling us, therefore, of matters fundamental to ourselves, enduring essential principles about which it would be good for us to know; about which, in fact, it will be necessary for us to know if our conscious minds are to be kept in touch with our own most secret, motivating depths. In short, these holy tales and their images are messages to the conscious mind from quarters of the spirit unknown to normal daylight consciousness, and if read as referring to events in the field of space and time—whether of the future, present, or past—they will have been misread and their force deflected, some secondary thing outside then taking to itself the reference of the symbol, some sanctified stick, stone, or animal, person, event, city, or social group.

Let us regard a little more closely the Biblical image of the garden.

Its name, Eden, signifies in Hebrew "delight, a place of delight," and our own English word, Paradise, which is from the Persian, *pairi-*, "around," *daeza*, "a wall," means properly "a walled enclosure." Apparently, then, Eden is a walled garden of delight, and in its center stands the great tree; or rather, in its center stand two trees, the one of the knowledge of good and evil, the other of immortal life. Four rivers flow, furthermore, from within it as from an inexhaustible source, to refresh the world in the four directions. And when our first parents, having eaten the fruit, were driven forth, two cherubim were stationed (as we have heard) at its eastern gate, to guard the way of return.

Taken as referring not to any geographical scene, but to a landscape of the soul, the Garden of Eden would have to be within us. Yet our conscious minds are unable to enter it and enjoy there the taste of eternal life, since we have already tasted of the knowledge of good and evil. That, in fact, must then be the knowledge that has thrown us out of the garden, pitched us away from our own center, so that we now judge things in those terms and experience only good and evil instead of eternal life— which, since the enclosed garden is within us, must already be ours, even though unknown to our conscious personalities. That would seem to be the meaning of the myth when read, not as prehistory, but as referring to man's inward spiritual state.

Let us turn now from this Bible legend, by which the West has been enchanted, to the Indian, of the Buddha, which has enspelled the entire East; for there too is the mythic image of a tree of immortal life defended by two terrifying guards. That tree is the one beneath which Siddhartha was sitting, facing east, when he wakened to the light of his own immortality in truth and was known thereafter as the Buddha, the Wakened One. There is a serpent in that legend also, but instead of being known as evil, it is thought of as symbolic of the immortal inhabiting energy of all life on earth. For the serpent shedding its skin, to be, as it were, born again, is likened in the Orient to the reincarnating spirit that assumes and throws off bodies as a man puts on and puts off clothes. There is in Indian mythology a great cobra imagined as balancing the tablelike earth on its head: its head being, of course, at the pivotal point, exactly beneath the world tree. And according to the Buddha legend, when the Blessed One, having attained omniscience, continued to sit absorbed for a number of days in absolute meditation, he became endangered by a great storm that arose in the world around him, and this prodigious serpent, coming up from below, wrapped itself protectively around the Buddha, covering his head with its cobra hood.

Thus, whereas in one of these two legends of the tree the service of the serpent is rejected and the animal itself cursed, in the other it is accepted. In both, the serpent is in some way associated with the tree and has apparently enjoyed its fruits, since it can slough its skin and live again; but in the Bible legend our first parents are expelled from the garden of that tree, whereas in the Buddhist tradition we are all invited in. The tree beneath which the Buddha sat corresponds, thus, to the second of the Garden of Eden, which, as already said, is to be thought of not as geographically situated but as a garden of the soul. And so, what then keeps us from returning to it and sitting like the Buddha beneath it? Who or what are those two cherubim? Do the Buddhists know of any such pair?

One of the most important Buddhist centers in the world today is the holy city of Nara, Japan, where there is a great temple sheltering a prodigious bronze image, 53½ feet high, of the Buddha seated cross-legged on a great lotus, holding his right hand lifted in the "fear not" posture; and as one approaches the precincts of this temple, one passes through a gate that is guarded, left and right, by two gigantic, marvelously threatening military figures flourishing swords. These are the Buddhist counterparts of the cherubim stationed by Yahweh at the garden gate. However, here we are not to be intimidated and held off. The fear of death and desire for life that these threatening guardsmen arouse in us are to be left behind as we pass between.

In the Buddhist view, that is to say, what is keeping us out of the garden is not the jealousy or wrath of any god, but our own instinctive attachment to what we take to be our lives. Our senses, outward-directed to the world of space and time, have attached us to that world and to our mortal bodies within it. We are loath to give up what we take to be the goods and pleasures of this physical life, and this attachment is the great fact, the great circumstance or barrier, that is keeping us out of the garden. This, and this alone, is preventing us from recognizing within ourselves that immortal and universal consciousness of which our physical senses, outward-turned, are but the agents.

According to this teaching, no actual cherub with a flaming sword is required to keep us out of our inward garden, since we are keeping ourselves out, through our avid interest in the outward, mortal aspects both of ourselves and of our world. What is symbolized in our passage of the guarded gate is our abandonment of both the world so known and ourselves so known within it: the phenomenal, mere appearance of things seen as born and dying, experienced either as good or as evil, and regarded, consequently, with desire and fear. Of the two big Buddhist cherubim, one has the mouth open, the other, the mouth closed—in token (I have been told) of the way we experience things in this temporal world, in terms always of pairs-of-opposites. Passing between, we are to leave such thinking behind.

But is that not the lesson, finally, of the Bible story as well? Eve and then Adam ate the fruit of the knowledge of good and evil, which is to say, of the pairs-of-opposites, and immediately experienced themselves as different from each other and felt shame. God, therefore, no more than confirmed what already had been accomplished when he drove them from the garden to experience the pains of death and birth and of toil for the goods of this world. Furthermore, they were experiencing God himself now as totally "other," wrathful and dangerous to their purposes, and the cherubim at the garden gate were representations of this way— now theirs—of experiencing both God and themselves. But as we are told also in the Bible legend, it would actually have been possible for Adam to "put forth his hand and take also of the tree of life, and eat, and live forever." And in the Christian image of the crucified redeemer that is exactly what we are being asked to do. The teaching here is that Christ restored to man immortality. His cross, throughout the Middle Ages, was equated with the tree of immortal life; and the fruit of that tree was the crucified Savior himself, who there offered up his flesh and his blood to be our "meat indeed" and our "drink indeed." He himself had boldly walked, so to say, right on through the guarded gate without fear of the cherubim and that flaming turning sword. And just as the Buddha, five hundred years before, had left behind all ego-oriented desires and fears to come to know himself as the pure, immortal Void, so the Western Savior left his body nailed to the tree and passed in spirit to atonement —at-one-ment—with the Father: to be followed now by ourselves.

The symbolic images of the two traditions are thus formally equivalent, even though the points of view of the two may be difficult to reconcile. In that of the Old and New Testaments, God and man are not one, but opposites, and the reason man was expelled from the garden was that he had disobeyed his creator. The sacrifice on the cross, accordingly, was in the nature not so much of a realization of *at-one-ment* as of penitential *atonement.* On the Buddhist side, on the other hand, man's separation from the source of his being is to be read in psychological terms, as an effect of misdirected consciousness, ignorant of its seat and source, which attributes final reality to merely phenomenal apparitions. Whereas the level of instruction represented in the Bible story is that, pretty much, of a nursery tale of disobedience and its punishment, inculcating an attitude of dependency, fear, and respectful devotion, such as might be thought appropriate for a child in relation to a parent, the Buddhist teaching, in contrast, is for self-responsible adults. And yet the imagery shared by the two is finally older by far than either, older than the Old Testament, much older than Buddhism, older even than India. For we find the symbolism of the serpent, tree, and garden of immortality already in the earliest cuneiform texts, depicted on Old Sumerian cylinder seals, and represented even in the arts and rites of primitive village folk throughout the world.

Nor does it matter from the standpoint of a comparative study of symbolic forms whether Christ or the Buddha ever actually lived and performed the miracles associated with their teachings. The religious literatures of the world abound in counterparts of those two great lives. And what one may learn from them all, finally, is that the savior, the hero, the redeemed one, is the one who has learned to penetrate the protective wall of those fears within, which exclude the rest of us, generally, in our daylight and even our dreamnight thoughts, from all experience of our own and the world's divine ground. The mythologized biographies of such saviors communicate the messages of their world-transcending wisdom in word-transcending symbols—which, ironically, are then generally translated back into such verbalized thoughts as built the interior walls in the first place. I have heard good Christian clergymen admonish young couples at their marriage ceremonies so to live together in this life that in the world to come they may have life everlasting; and I have thought, Alas! The more appropriate mythic admonishment would be, so to live their marriages that in *this* world they may experience life everlasting. For there is indeed a life everlasting, a dimension of enduring human values that inheres in the very act of living itself, and in the simultaneous experience and expression of which men through all time have lived and died. We all embody these unknowingly, the great being simply those who have wakened to their knowledge—as suggested in a saying attributed to Christ in the Gnostic *Gospel According to Thomas:* "The Kingdom of the Father is spread upon the earth and men do not see it."

Mythologies might be defined in this light as poetic expressions of just such transcendental seeing; and if we may take as evidence the antiquity of certain basic mythic forms—the serpent god, for example, and the sacred tree—the beginnings of what we take today to be mystical revelation must have been known to at least a few, even of the primitive teachers of our race, from the very start.

HARVEY COX

*Harvey Cox, born in 1929, was educated at the University of
Pennsylvania, Yale, and Harvard (Ph.D., 1963). He has been director of
religious activities at Oberlin College and worked for a year at an East
Berlin mission. In 1965, after teaching for two years at the Andover
Newton Theological School, he joined the faculty of Harvard, where he is
now Professor of Divinity. He has contributed to such magazines as*
Christian Century, Commonweal, Harper's, *and* Playboy *and is a
member of the editorial board of* Christianity and Crisis. *His books
include* The Secular City *(1964),* God's Revolution and Man's
Responsibility *(1965),* On Not Leaving It to the Snake *(a
collection of essays, 1967),* The Feast of Fools *(1969), and* The
Seduction of the Spirit: The Use and Misuse of People's
Religion *(1973). The following selection is from Chapter 3, "The
House of Intellect."*

Testimony

Anyone who has grown up in the religious atmosphere of Protestant
pietism knows what "giving a testimony" means. It means getting to your
feet in a room full of people and telling what the experience of God has
meant to you, how His grace has touched your life, and maybe the circumstances of your conversion. In my own small church we did not have
testimonies very often. I remember them only when an unusually zealous
visiting preacher came or when our youth group would visit some more
devout congregation.

I was glad we did not do it much, because I was always terrified at the
prospect of having to give a testimony. It wasn't that I did not know what
you were supposed to say. I had heard lots of testimonies. But that was
just the problem: I knew exactly what I was supposed to say, but I also
knew I didn't feel that way inside. My own "conversion," such as it was,
had not been a very dramatic affair. There were times when I wanted very
badly to know God, to experience the love of Christ, perfect assurance,
the joy of salvation, and all the things people who gave testimonies talked
about. More often, though, I felt that someday I would like to be saved,
but not until I had done a lot of things I heard sinners did before they
were saved and I had not gotten around to yet. I knew that anything I
would say in a testimony would sound patently insincere. I had just not
felt what others said they had. So when folks began giving testimonies,
my back stiffened and my stomach tightened. I listen attentively, but I

dreaded having to speak. I knew I could not bring myself to say what was expected.

Years later I came upon two classical religious texts during the same week of reading, both of which in their own way helped me to understand better my boyhood trauma about testimonies. One comes from St. Augustine's *Confessions.* It is the famous line in which the great saint tells about how he had once prayed, "Save me, O Lord, but not yet!" I knew just how he felt, and I also understood those medieval heretics called the Cathari who waited until their deathbeds to receive the sacrament of baptism because they believed it washed them clean but could only be used once. I still carry a little of the Augustine-Cathari syndrome. My yearning for spiritual perfection is tempered by the recognition that it might require my giving up some things I would rather not surrender.

The second helpful text I came across is a classic fourteenth-century mystical treatise called *The Cloud of Unknowing.* The anonymous author of this work helped me, years after the fact, to understand why I had trembled with fear when I was asked to put my experience of God or lack of it into words. The experience of the holy, he says, is in its very essence one of darkness and emptiness, always beyond the capacity of language to express. This is how he puts it:

> ... thou findest but a darkness and as it were a kind of unknowing, thou knowest not what, saving that thou feelest in thy will a naked intent unto God ... thou mayest neither see him clearly by light of understanding in thy reason, nor feel him in sweetness of love in thy affection ... if ever thou shalt see him or feel him ... it must always be in this cloud and in this darkness.

Soon after reading *The Cloud of Unknowing* I discovered the other great mystics and found that my boyhood discomfort was not unusual. St. John of the Cross, the sixteenth-century Spanish Carmelite, also convinced me that I was not as odd as I had once thought. That confusion and emptiness, that thirst for a feeling I wanted to have but could not, he refers to as the "dark night of the soul," and teaches that it is itself a profound spiritual experience. Thus reassured by a much broader spiritual tradition that I was not the outsider I had once feared, it became easy for me to dismiss my boyhood embarrassment by marking down the testimony meeting as a cruelly coercive setting. At times I even become angry, in retrospect, at the well-intentioned church people for seeming to expect me to talk about something so inherently resistant to speech.

But that dismissal was a little too easy. There is a terribly subtle connection between personal spiritual experience and the community of faith. After all, St. Augustine and St. John of the Cross did write books. Many of the great mystics and contemplatives did struggle to *describe* their interior pilgrimages, and I had profited from what they wrote. They too were in a sense giving testimonies. True, that does not excuse these meetings I sat in, shivering and fearful, while other people spoke so easily, it seemed to me, about such awesome things. Since reading more religious history, I have come to realize that the meetings I was exposed to encouraged a somewhat corrupted form of testifying. Those attending them were often merely repeating standard phrases that for their fore-bears had been on fire. I was probably right to be anxious and angry. Still, the *idea* of testimony itself remains powerful and essential: to try to give voice and word to what is so patently interior, to stammer at its unspeaka-bleness, to try so hard to be honest to your inner reality, to know when it is over that you have failed but that the failure itself was necessary.

The mystics and contemplatives have served as the guardians and explorers of that uniquely human realm called "interiority." I think we need them today, perhaps more than we ever have, precisely because authentic personal life is now so fatally threatened by an intrusive techni-cal world. This may explain why we are seeing around us a spectacular rebirth of interest in meditation, Zen, Yoga and the classical contempla-tive disciplines. It is a renaissance of interiority, and it represents an instinct for survival by the jostled modern spirit. We are so relentlessly pounded today by messages and stimuli from without that we need sup-port from any source whatever to learn again to listen to what comes from within. There is even good clinical evidence that these ancient spiritual practices help us "deautomatize" ourselves and teach us how to tune down our overdeveloped capacity for responding to external signals from the media and elsewhere. Learning to meditate is like lowering the vol-ume on an ear-blasting stereo; it makes us more capable of hearing ourselves and one another. Nothing could be more important. An au-tomaton is a machine that lights up instantly to every cue relayed to it from the control board. A human being on the other hand selects, di-gests, orders, decides, responds—all on the basis of an interchange be-tween his own interior life and the culture. The difference between the robot and person is interiority.

"Interiority" may be another word for what Kierkegaard called "sub-jectivity" or for what an older tradition simply called the "soul." In any case, these different words all remind us that men and women are more than the sum total of all the social, economic and other forces that influence them. This in turn suggests, however, that the old religious fear, that somehow I can "lose my soul," is not as silly as we once supposed. I lose my soul if I become merely the sum total of all the external inputs. There is more than one way to lose one's soul, but there is also more than one way to try to save it. During a single week as I was writing this book I kept a record of the lectures, sessions, labs and work-shops that occurred in the greater Boston area featuring one or another of the classical spiritual disciplines. After I had gotten up to thirty or forty I lost count. There were the regular Yoga sessions in several church halls and community centers. Yoga is also being taught now in some college gym classes. There were the weekly gatherings of the followers of the Maharishi Mahesh Yogi, passing on his wisdom about "transcendental meditation." There were the Hare Krishna dancers chanting near the subway stop, and the members of the Church of the Final Judgment inviting people to their meditation and chant evenings. Posters announced the arrival of a Sufi drummer who also led chants and dances. (The Sufis began as a sect of Islam but have now spread around the world. Their specialty is a finely calibrated use of key chant words and bodily movements that put most people rather quickly into alternate states of consciousness. The storied "whirling dervishes" described in Western travelers' reports of their voyages to Arab lands were probably Sufi holy men utilizing bodily movements to affect their own consciousness.) There was a formal lecture on Tantric Yoga, a demonstration session on Zen, a contemplation retreat sponsored by a Roman Catholic order, a discussion group on the *Egyptian Book of the Dead,* an experimental encounter group using replicas of old African masks, and a healing service at an Episcopal church. There was also a small notice informing all Capricorns who wanted to meet other Capricorns that a star-crossed rendezvous could be arranged by dialing a certain number.

Of all the re-emergent spiritual disciplines, the ones that seem to attract the most attention are those that teach people how to meditate. Since in recent years I have begun to learn how to meditate, an art which takes a lifetime to perfect, I think I know why it is becoming so popular. But I think I also sense its limitations. Through meditation, or another of these venerable traditions, we learn to turn down the quantity of the outside "noise" of pictures, words, sounds, and to attune ourselves to the fragile silence within. But too many meditators leave it at that, and it is just not enough. Inner silence is a welcome change from outer clangor. But who would want to live in a world of beings who, however rich and deep their inner lives, did not enjoy and cherish one another? If it quakes under so-called "outer oppression," a world of inner peace falls short of the world we want. The renewed quest for interiority is a way of fighting the violation of our marrow we experience in an acquiring-consuming-competing society. But *human* interiority cannot stop with ecstasy. It requires love and community: gesture, touch, movement and sooner or later speech. Eventually we give our testimonies and listen to the testimonies of others, however broken and inadequate they may be.

The movement from recovered interiority to renewed community is a perilous one. For some reason we have endless stratagems to avoid it. When I remember my terror during the testimony meetings, I also recall that everyone knew two ways to escape the tension, other than by mere physical flight. One was just to remain silent. That could be very good, as it often is during the silent periods of a Quaker meeting. But I always felt that even the powerful silence of such gatherings is incomplete. The Quakers sense this too. In their meetings if someone is moved by the spirit, he or she may speak. The other way people escaped the tension at testimony meetings was to lapse into a kind of talk that was general, abstract, maybe even *interesting,* but not testimony—not trying to say out what was inside. That often felt good too. It relieved the pressure and helped everyone relax. But you could tell when it happened that we all knew we had just stepped back from a painfully promising frontier.

Testimony, like everything else, is susceptible to debasement and trivialization. But in its essence testimony is the primal human act. It breaks the barrier we erect between the "inner" and the "outer" worlds. Telling my story is the way I dissolve this artificial distinction and create a lived and shared world. I do not abolish the chasm, either by surrendering my interiority to the outer or by keeping it entirely to myself. I break out by claiming the world as my own, weaving its stories into my story, and making it *our* world. My interiority, instead of being swallowed by the world or retreating to a well-guarded citadel, widens out to include the worlds of others in itself.

Testimony means the telling and retelling of my story. This is not a merely marginal human need. Some psychologists believe it is an utterly central one. If people cannot tell and retell their story, they go mad. This is one reason why I have gotten interested recently in autobiography as the spiritual genre most needed in our time. I surely value the hallowed silence of the wise old sage who knows that to speak would be to lie and so remains speechless. I admire the well-wrought work of the theologians, whose systems can provide a home for the mind. Both the mystic and the metaphysician contribute to the richness of the whole. But testimony goes beyond both silence and system. It is that form of speech that saves me from the isolation of silence and the triviality of talk. In the law, I am wisely permitted to "testify" only about something I have experienced myself, not to opinion, conjecture, theory or hearsay. Here, at least, the law is wise. It knows that in those matters that concern us most, only words that spurt from experience have any real truth.

Testimony is me telling my story in a world of people with stories to tell. It is an effort to construct a common world that fuses authentic interiority with genuine community. Mostly the attempt fails, or at least does not succeed completely. But we never stop trying.

.   .   .

The Hartford Heresies

"From January 24 to 26, 1975, a group of eighteen Protestants, Roman Catholics and Orthodox met at the Hartford Seminary Foundation in Hartford, Connecticut, to consider a preliminary study paper written by Dr. Peter Berger, the noted sociologist of religion, and Rev. Richard John

Neuhaus, a Brooklyn Lutheran pastor. Among the participants at the meeting were sixteen men and two women, of whom five were Roman Catholics, two Orthodox, six Lutherans, and five from other Protestant denominations (one each from the United Methodist Church, the United Presbyterian Church and the United Church of Christ, two from the Christian Reformed Church). All eighteen persons, predominantly theologians, signed the Appeal, which retains most of the material from the preliminary study by Dr. Berger and Rev. Neuhaus. Sub-groups of six persons each worked on assigned themes before the final text was approved in plenary. The 1000-word document is addressed chiefly to college professors of religion, church policy makers, editors, and others who 'market the metaphors,' said Pastor Neuhaus. The full text of the statement follows." [From Ecumenical Trends, *Volume 4, No. 4, April 1975]*

An Appeal for Theological Affirmation

The renewal of Christian witness and mission requires constant examination of the assumptions shaping the Church's life. Today an apparent loss of a sense of the transcendent is undermining the Church's ability to address with clarity and courage the urgent tasks to which God calls it in the world. This loss is manifest in a number of pervasive themes. Many are superficially attractive, but upon closer examination we find these themes false and debilitating to the Church's life and work. Among such themes are:

THEME 1:   Modern thought is superior to all past forms of understanding reality, and is therefore normative for Christian faith and life.

In repudiating this theme we are protesting the captivity to the prevailing thought structures not only of the Twentieth Century but of any historical period. We favor using any helpful means of understanding, ancient or modern, and insist that the Christian proclamation must be related to the idiom of the culture. At the same time, we affirm the need for Christian thought to confront and be confronted by other worldviews, all of which are necessarily provisional.

THEME 2:   Religious statements are totally independent of reasonable discourse.

The capitulation to the alleged primacy of modern thought takes two forms: one is the subordination of religious statements to the canons of scientific rationality; the other, equating reason with scientific rationality, would remove religious statements from the realm of reasonable discourse altogether. A religion of pure subjectivity and non-rationality results in treating faith statements as being, at best, statements about the believer. We repudiate both forms of capitulation.

THEME 3:   Religious language refers to human experience and nothing else, God being humanity's noblest creation.

Religion is also a set of symbols and even of human projections. We repudiate the assumption that it is nothing but that. What is here at stake is nothing less than the reality of God: We did not invent God; God invented us.

THEME 4:   Jesus can only be understood in terms of contemporary models of humanity.

This theme suggests a reversal of the "imitation of Christ"; that is, the image of Jesus is made to reflect cultural and counter-cultural notions of human excellence. We do not deny that all aspects of humanity are illumined by Jesus. Indeed, it is necessary to the universality of the Christ that he be perceived in relation to the particularities of the believers' world. We do repudiate the captivity to such metaphors, which are necessarily inadequate, relative, transitory, and frequently idolatrous. Jesus, together with the Scripture and the whole of the Christian tradition, cannot be arbitrarily interpreted without reference to the history of which they are part. The danger is in the attempt to exploit the tradition without taking the tradition seriously.

THEME 5:   All religions are equally valid; the choice among them is not a matter of conviction about truth but only of personal preference or life-style.

We affirm our common humanity. We affirm the importance of exploring and confronting all manifestations of the religious quest and of learning from the riches of other religions. But we repudiate this theme because it flattens diversities and ignores contradictions. In doing so, it not only obscures the meaning of Christian faith, but also fails to respect the integrity of other faiths. Truth matters; therefore differences among religions are deeply significant.

THEME 6:   To realize one's potential and to be true to oneself is the whole meaning of salvation.

Salvation contains a promise of human fulfillment, but to identify salvation with human fulfillment can trivialize the promise. We affirm that salvation cannot be found apart from God.

THEME 7:   Since what is human is good, evil can adequately be understood as failure to realize human potential.

This theme invites false understanding of the ambivalence of human existence and underestimates the pervasiveness of sin. Paradoxically, by minimizing the enormity of evil, it undermines serious and sustained attacks on particular social and individual evils.

THEME 8:   The sole purpose of worship is to promote individual self-realization and human community.

Worship promotes individual and communal values, but it is above all a response to the reality of God and arises out of the fundamental need and desire to know, love and adore God. We worship God because God is to be worshipped.

THEME 9:   Institutions and historical traditions are oppressive and inimical to our being truly human; liberation from them is required for authentic existence and authentic religion.

Institutions and traditions are often oppressive. For this reason they must be subjected to relentless criticism. But human community inescapably requires institutions and traditions. Without them life would degenerate into chaos and new forms of bondage. The modern pursuit of liberation from all social and historical restraints is finally dehumanizing.

THEME 10:   The world must set the agenda for the Church. Social, political, and economic programs to improve the quality of life are ultimately normative for the Church's mission in the world.

This theme cuts across the political and ideological spectrum. Its form remains the same, no matter whether the content is defined as upholding the values of the American way of life, promoting socialism, or raising human consciousness. The Church must denounce oppressors, help liberate the oppressed and seek to heal human misery. Sometimes, the Church's mission coincides with the world's progress. But the norms for the Church's activity derive from its own perception of God's will for the world.

THEME 11:   An emphasis on God's transcendence is at least a hindrance to, and perhaps incompatible with, Christian social concern and action.

This supposition leads some to denigrate God's transcendence. Others, holding to a false transcendence, withdraw into religious privatism or individualism and neglect the personal and communal responsibility of Christians for the earthly city. From a biblical perspective, it is precisely because of confidence in God's reign over all aspects of life that Christians must participate fully in the struggle against oppressive and dehumanizing structures and their manifestations in racism, war, and economic exploitation.

THEME 12:   The struggle for a better humanity will bring about the Kingdom of God.

The struggle for a better humanity is essential to Christian faith and can be informed and inspired by the biblical promise of the Kingdom of God. But imperfect human beings cannot create a perfect society. The Kingdom of God surpasses any conceivable utopia. God has his own designs which confront ours, surprising us with judgment and redemption.

THEME 13:   The question of hope beyond death is irrelevant or at best marginal to the Christian understanding of human fulfillment.

This is the final capitulation to modern thought. If death is the last word, then Christianity has nothing to say to the final questions of life. We believe that God raised Jesus from the dead and are ". . . convinced that there is nothing in death or life, in the realm of spirits or superhuman powers, in the world as it is or in the world as it shall be, in the forces of the universe, in heights or depths—nothing in all creation that can separate us from the love of God in Christ Jesus our Lord" (Romans 8:38f.).

ST. TERESA OF AVILA

St. Teresa (1515–1582) was born in Avila, Spain, and attended a convent school in that town. At eighteen she entered the Carmelite convent of the Incarnation, and, except for severe illnesses, led an unremarkable religious life for many years. Then in 1554, at the age of thirty-nine, she experienced a kind of conversion in the presence of an image of the wounded Christ; from then on she lost every worldly desire and devoted herself to spiritual perfection. She also began to have the ever-deepening mystical experiences, especially of the presence of Christ, that went on all the rest of her life. In the period 1558 to 1560 she had visions that she would later describe in her autobiography, written in colloquial Spanish between 1562 and 1565.

St. Teresa wrote the book at the behest of her confessors, her spiritual directors, in an attempt to make clear the history and quality of her experiences, especially those received in prayer. Her visions were by no means universally accepted by her sisters and superiors; many thought them the work of the devil. Her natural humility led her to accept this possibility and to subject her own mind and spirit to the most rigorous analysis. The result is a remarkable piece of psychological self-examination.

St. Teresa's ideals led her to the founding of a reformed branch of the Carmelites—called the Descalzos, or Barefoots. The last twenty years of her life were spent in establishing its convents and monasteries all over Spain, often against an opposition from inside and outside her Order that severely tested her determination and her great administrative ability. She continued also to write, enlarging and deepening her study of the spiritual life in The Way of Perfection *(about 1565) and* The Interior Castle *(1577).*

The following passages are taken from Chapters 27 and 32 of her autobiography, in the translation of David Lewis (1870; ed. J. J. Burke, 1911).

Visions

I now resume the story of my life. I was in great pain and distress; and many prayers, as I said, were made on my behalf, that our Lord would lead me by another and a safer way; for this, they told me, was so suspicious. The truth is, that though I was praying to God for this, and wished I had a desire for another way, yet, when I saw the progress I was making, I was unable really to desire a change,—though I always prayed for it,— excepting on those occasions when I was extremely cast down by what people said to me, and by the fears with which they filled me.

I felt that I was wholly changed; I could do nothing but put myself in the hands of God: He knew what was expedient for me; let Him do with me according to His will in all things. I saw that by this way I was directed heavenwards, and that formerly I was going down to hell. I could not force myself to desire a change, nor believe that I was under the influence of Satan. Though I was doing all I could to believe the one and to desire the other, it was not in my power to do so. I offered up all my actions, if there should be any good in them, for this end; I had recourse to the Saints for whom I had a devotion, that they might deliver me from the evil one; I made novenas; I commended myself to St. Hilarion, to the Angel St. Michael, to whom I had recently become devout, for this purpose; and many other Saints I importuned, that our Lord might show me the way,—I mean, that they might obtain this for me from His Majesty.

At the end of two years spent in prayer by myself and others for this end, namely, that our Lord would either lead me by another way, or show the truth of this,—for now the locutions of our Lord were extremely frequent,—this happened to me. I was in prayer one day,—it was the feast of the glorious St. Peter,—when I saw Christ close by me, or, to speak more correctly, felt Him; for I saw nothing with my eyes of the body, nothing with the eyes of the soul. He seemed to me to be close beside me; and I saw, too, as I believe, that it was He who was speaking to me. As I was utterly ignorant that such a vision was possible, I was extremely afraid at first, and did nothing but weep; however, when He spoke to me but one word to reassure me, I recovered myself, and was, as usual, calm and comforted, without any fear whatever. Jesus Christ seemed to be by my side continually, and, as the vision was not imaginary, I saw no form; but I had a most distinct feeling that He was always on my right hand, a witness of all I did; and never at any time, if I was but slightly recollected, or not too much distracted, could I be ignorant of His near presence.

I went at once to my confessor, in great distress, to tell him of it. He asked in what form I saw our Lord. I told him I saw no form. He then said: "How did you know that it was Christ?" I replied, that I did not know how I knew it; but I could not help knowing that He was close beside me, —that I saw Him distinctly, and felt His presence,—that the recollectedness of my soul was deeper in the prayer of quiet, and more continuous, —that the effects thereof were very different from what I had hitherto experienced,—and that it was most certain. I could only make comparisons in order to explain myself; and certainly there are no comparisons, in my opinion, by which visions of this kind can be described. Afterwards I learnt from Friar Peter of Alcantara, a holy man of great spirituality,— of whom I shall speak by and by,—and from others of great learning, that this vision was of the highest order, and one with which Satan can least interfere; and therefore there are no words whereby to explain,—at least, none for us women, who know so little: learned men can explain it better.

For if I say that I see Him neither with the eyes of the body, nor with those of the soul,—because it was not an imaginary vision,—how is it that I can understand and maintain that He stands beside me, and be more certain of it than if I saw Him? If it be supposed that it is as if a person were blind, or in the dark, and therefore unable to see another who is close to him, the comparison is not exact. There is a certain likelihood about it, however, but not much, because the other senses tell him who is blind of that presence: he hears the other speak or move, or he touches him; but in these visions there is nothing like this. The darkness is not felt; only He renders Himself present to the soul by a certain knowledge of Himself which is more clear than the sun. I do not mean that we now see either a sun or any brightness, only that there is a light not seen, which illumines the understanding so that the soul may have the fruition of so great a good. This vision brings with it great blessings.

It is not like that presence of God which is frequently felt, particularly by those who have attained to the prayer of union and of quiet, when we seem, at the very commencement of our prayer, to find Him with whom we would converse, and when we seem to feel that He hears us by the effects and the spiritual impressions of great love and faith of which we are then conscious, as well as by the good resolutions, accompanied by sweetness, which we then make. This is a great grace from God; and let him to whom He has given it esteem it much, because it is a very high degree of prayer; but it is not vision. God is understood to be present there by the effects He works in the soul: that is the way His Majesty makes His presence felt; but here, in this vision, it is seen clearly that Jesus Christ is present, the Son of the Virgin. In the prayer of union and of quiet, certain inflowings of the Godhead are present; but in the vision, the Sacred Humanity also, together with them, is pleased to be our visible companion, and to do us good.

My confessor next asked me, who told me it was Jesus Christ. I replied that He often told me so Himself; but, even before He told me so, there was an impression on my understanding that it was He; and before this He used to tell me so, and I saw Him not. If a person whom I had never seen, but of whom I had heard, came to speak to me, and I were blind or in the dark, and told me who he was, I should believe him; but I could not so confidently affirm that he was that person, as I might do if I had seen him. But in this vision I could do so, because so clear a knowledge is impressed on the soul that all doubt seems impossible, though He is not seen. Our Lord wills that this knowledge be so graven on the understanding, that we can no more question His presence than we can question that which we see with our eyes: not so much even; for very often there arises a suspicion that we have imagined things we think we see; but here, though there may be a suspicion in the first instant, there remains a certainty so great, that the doubt has no force whatever. So also is it when God teaches the soul in another way, and speaks to it without speaking, in the way I have described.

There is so much of heaven in this language, that it cannot well be understood on earth, though we may desire ever so much to explain it, if our Lord will not teach it experimentally. Our Lord impresses in the innermost soul that which He wills that soul to understand; and He manifests it there without images or formal words, after the manner of the vision I am speaking of. Consider well this way in which God works, in order that the soul may understand what He means—His great truths and mysteries; for very often what I understand, when our Lord explains to me the vision, which it is His Majesty's pleasure to set before me, is after this manner; and it seems to me that this is a state with which the devil can least interfere, for these reasons; but if these reasons are not good, I must be under a delusion. The vision and the language are matters of such pure spirituality, that there is no turmoil of the faculties, or of the senses, out of which—so it seems to me—the devil can derive any advantage.

It is only at intervals, and for an instant, that this occurs; for generally

—so I think—the senses are not taken away, and the faculties are not suspended: they preserve their ordinary state. It is not always so in contemplation; on the contrary, it is very rarely so; but when it is so, I say that we do nothing whatever ourselves: no work of ours is then possible; all that is done is apparently the work of our Lord. It is as if food had been received into the stomach which had not first been eaten, and without our knowing how it entered; but we do know well that it is there, though we know not its nature, nor who it was that placed it there. In this vision, I know who placed it; but I do not know how He did it. I neither saw it, nor felt it; I never had any inclination to desire it, and I never knew before that such a thing was possible.

* * *

Some considerable time after our Lord had bestowed upon me the graces I have been describing, and others also of a higher nature, I was one day in prayer when I found myself in a moment, without knowing how, plunged apparently into hell. I understood that it was our Lord's will I should see the place which the devils kept in readiness for me, and which I had deserved by my sins. It was but a moment, but it seems to me impossible I should ever forget it even if I were to live many years.

The entrance seemed to be by a long narrow pass, like a furnace, very low, dark, and close. The ground seemed to be saturated with water, mere mud, exceedingly foul, sending forth pestilential odours, and covered with loathsome vermin. At the end was a hollow place in the wall, like a closet, and in that I saw myself confined. All this was even pleasant to behold in comparison with what I felt there. There is no exaggeration in what I am saying.

But as to what I then felt, I do not know where to begin, if I were to describe it; it is utterly inexplicable. I felt a fire in my soul. I cannot see how it is possible to describe it. My bodily sufferings were unendurable. I have undergone most painful sufferings in this life, and, as the physicians say, the greatest that can be borne, such as the contraction of my sinews when I was paralysed, without speaking of others of different kinds, yea, even those of which I have also spoken, inflicted on me by Satan; yet all these were as nothing in comparison with what I felt then, especially when I saw that there would be no intermission, nor any end to them.

These sufferings were nothing in comparison with the anguish of my soul, a sense of oppression, of stifling, and of pain so keen, accompanied by so hopeless and cruel an infliction, that I know not how to speak of it. If I said that the soul is continually being torn from the body, it would be nothing, for that implies the destruction of life by the hands of another; but here it is the soul itself that is tearing itself in pieces. I cannot describe that inward fire or that despair, surpassing all torments and all pain. I did not see who it was that tormented me, but I felt myself on fire, and torn to pieces, as it seemed to me; and, I repeat it, this inward fire and despair are the greatest torments of all.

Left in that pestilential place, and utterly without the power to hope for comfort, I could neither sit nor lie down: there was no room. I was placed as it were in a hole in the wall; and those walls, terrible to look on of themselves, hemmed me in on every side. I could not breathe. There was no light, but all was thick darkness. I do not understand how it is; though there was no light, yet everything that can give pain by being seen was visible.

Our Lord at that time would not let me see more of hell. Afterwards, I had another most fearful vision, in which I saw the punishment of certain sins. They were most horrible to look at; but, because I felt none of the pain, my terror was not so great. In the former vision, our Lord made me really feel those torments, and that anguish of spirit, just as if I had been suffering them in the body there. I know not how it was, but I understand distinctly that it was a great mercy that our Lord would have me see with mine own eyes the very place from which His compassion saved me. I have listened to people speaking of these things, and I have at other times dwelt on the various torments of hell, though not often, because my soul made no progress by the way of fear; and I have read of the diverse tortures, and how the devils tear the flesh with red-hot pincers. But all is as nothing before this; it is a wholly different matter. In short, the one is a reality, the other a picture; and all burning here in this life is as nothing in comparison with the fire that is there.

I was so terrified by that vision,—and that terror is on me even now while I am writing,—that, though it took place nearly six years ago, the natural warmth of my body is chilled by fear even now when I think of it. And so, amid all the pain and suffering which I may have had to bear, I remember no time in which I do not think that all we have to suffer in this world is as nothing. It seems to me that we complain without reason. I repeat it, this vision was one of the grandest mercies of our Lord. It has been to me of the greatest service, because it has destroyed my fear of trouble and of the contradiction of the world, and because it has made me strong enough to bear up against them, and to give thanks to our Lord, who has been my Deliverer, as it now seems to me, from such fearful and everlasting pains.

.   .   .

ST. AUGUSTINE

St. Augustine, Bishop of Hippo, lived during the last years of the Roman Empire and the first years of the dominance of the Christian Church over paganism. Of his writing it was once said, "He lies who says that he has read all of his works." Of 113 books, 218 letters, and over 500 sermons that survive today, many seek to establish the truth of Christian teaching against paganism and Judaism and against the attacks of heretical Christian sects such as the Manicheans, the Donatists, and the Pelagians. In his antiheretical writings Augustine wielded large and permanent influence over the development of orthodox Christian doctrine. In addition to works directed against specific heresies, he wrote many works which are still widely enjoyed today. On Christian Doctrine *is a short introduction to reading and interpreting the Bible.* The City of God *(a philosophical approach to the problem of history) is based on the idea that all men are divided into two "cities," or groups of loyalty—one devoted to love of the world and its sins, the other devoted to God and life in heaven. Finally, Augustine's* Confessions *(written between 397 and 400 A.D.), addressed to God, provides a moving account of his spiritual development from childhood to conversion, at the age of thirty-two, from conscious sinfulness to Christian asceticism.*

Augustine was born in 354 in Thagaste, an agricultural village in North Africa. Since he showed great intellectual promise, his father, a minor official in the local Roman government, sent him to school in Madauros, a nearby college town, when he was eleven. Remembering his childhood thefts of food and his dishonesty at games, Augustine asks, "Is this boyish innocence? It is not, O Lord, it is not . . . For these are the practises that pass from tutors and teachers, and from nuts and balls and birds, to governors and kings, and to money and estates and slaves." At seventeen he entered school in Carthage, "where a cauldron of shameful loves seethed and sounded about me." Here he joined the Manichean sect and took a mistress by whom he had a son when he was eighteen. He acquired at this time a deep interest in philosophy and spent the next thirteen years of his life teaching in Thagaste, Carthage, Rome, and Milan.

After hearing St. Ambrose, Bishop of Milan, preaching in 384, Augustine became gradually convinced that he should convert to Christianity. He was baptized in 387 and returned to Thagaste to establish a religious community. In 391 he traveled to Hippo, a large African port, and was drafted by the Christian congregation to be an assistant to Bishop Valerius. For nearly four decades after the death of Valerius in 396, Augustine as Bishop of Hippo combatted heresies in public and written debates, presided in civil law cases, and was responsible for all the instruction and spiritual care of the church in a large surrounding territory. He died in 430.

In the passages reprinted below, from Book 8 of his Confessions
(trans. F. J. Sheed, 1943), he recalls the day of his conversion.

Conversion

. . . Now, O Lord, my Helper and my Redeemer, I shall tell and confess
to Your name how You delivered me from the chain of that desire of the
flesh which held me so bound, and the servitude of worldly things. . . .

On a certain day—Nebridius was away for some reason I cannot recall
—there came to Alypius and me at our house one Ponticianus, a fellow
countryman of ours, being from Africa, holder of an important post in
the emperor's court. There was something or other he wanted of us and
we sat down to discuss the matter. As it happened he noticed a book on
a gaming table by which we were sitting. He picked it up, opened it, and
found that it was the apostle Paul, which surprised him because he had
expected that it would be one of the books I wore myself out teaching.
Then he smiled a little and looked at me, and expressed pleasure but
surprise too at having come suddenly upon that book, and only that book,
lying before me. For he was a Christian and a devout Christian; he knelt
before You in church, O our God, in daily prayer and many times daily.
I told him that I had given much care to these writings. Whereupon he
began to tell the story of the Egyptian monk Antony, whose name was
held in high honour among Your servants, although Alypius and I had
never heard it before that time. When he learned this, he was the more
intent upon telling the story, anxious to introduce so great a man to men
ignorant of him, and very much marvelling at our ignorance. But Alypius
and I stood amazed to hear of Your wonderful works, done in the true
faith and in the Catholic Church so recently, practically in our own times,
and with such numbers of witnesses. All three of us were filled with
wonder, we because the deeds we were now hearing were so great, and
he because we had never heard them before.

From this story he went on to the great groups in the monasteries, and
their ways all redolent of You, and the fertile deserts of the wilderness,
of all of which we knew nothing. There was actually a monastery at Milan,
outside the city walls. It was full of worthy brethren and under the care
of Ambrose. And we had not heard of it. He continued with his discourse
and we listened in absolute silence. It chanced that he told how on one
occasion he and three of his companions—it was at Treves, when the
emperor was at the chariot races in the Circus—had gone one afternoon
to walk in the gardens close by the city walls. As it happened they fell into
two groups, one of the others staying with him, and the other two likewise
walking their own way. But as those other two strolled on they came into
a certain house, the dwelling of some servants of Yours, poor in spirit,
of whom is the kingdom of God. There they found a small book in which
was written the life of Antony. One of them began to read it, marvelled

at it, was inflamed by it. While he was actually reading he had begun to think how he might embrace such a life, and give up his worldly employment to serve You alone. For the two men were both state officials. Suddenly the man who was doing the reading was filled with a love of holiness and angry at himself with righteous shame. He looked at his friend and said to him: "Tell me, please, what is the goal of our ambition in all these labours of ours? What are we aiming at? What is our motive in being in the public service? Have we any higher hope at court than to be friends of the emperor? And at that level, is not everything uncertain and full of perils? And how many perils must we meet on the way to this greater peril? And how long before we are there? But if I should choose to be a friend of God, I can become one now." He said this, and all troubled with the pain of the new life coming to birth in him, he turned back his eyes to the book. He read on and was changed inwardly, where You alone could see; and the world dropped away from his mind, as soon appeared outwardly. For while he was reading and his heart thus tossing on its own flood, at length he broke out in heavy weeping, saw the better way and chose it for his own. Being now Your servant he said to his friend, "Now I have broken from that hope we had and have decided to serve God; and I enter upon that service from this hour, in this place. If you have no will to imitate me, at least do not try to dissuade me."

The other replied that he would remain his companion in so great a service for so great a prize. So the two of them, now Your servants, built a spiritual tower at the only cost that is adequate, the cost of leaving all things and following You. Then Ponticianus and the man who had gone walking with him in another part of the garden came looking for them in the same place, and when they found them suggested that they should return home as the day was now declining. But they told their decision and their purpose, and how that will had arisen in them and was now settled in them; and asked them not to try to argue them out of their decision, even if they would not also join them. Ponticianus and his friend, though not changed from their former state, yet wept for themselves, as he told us, and congratulated them in God and commended themselves to their prayers. Then with their own heart trailing in the dust they went off to the palace, while the other two, with their heart fixed upon heaven, remained in the hut. Both these men, as it happened, were betrothed, and when the two women heard of it they likewise dedicated their virginity to You.

This was the story Ponticianus told. But You, Lord, while he was speaking, turned me back towards myself, taking me from behind my own back where I had put myself all the time that I preferred not to see myself. And You set me there before my own face that I might see how vile I was, how twisted and unclean and spotted and ulcerous. I saw myself and was horrified; but there was no way to flee from myself. If I tried to turn my gaze from myself, there was Ponticianus telling what he was telling; and again You were setting me face to face with myself, forcing me upon my own sight, that I might see my iniquity and loathe it. I had known it, but I had pretended not to see it, had deliberately looked the other way and let it go from my mind.

But this time, the more ardently I approved those two as I heard of their determination to win health for their souls by giving themselves up wholly to Your healing, the more detestable did I find myself in comparison with them. For many years had flowed by—a dozen or more—from the time when I was nineteen and was stirred by the reading of Cicero's Hortensius to the study of wisdom; and here was I still postponing the giving up of this world's happiness to devote myself to the search for that of which not the finding only but the mere seeking is better than to find all the treasures and kingdoms of men, better than all the body's pleasures though they were to be had merely for a nod. But I in my great worthlessness—for it was greater thus early—had begged You for chastity, saying: "Grant me chastity and continence, but not yet." For I was afraid that You would hear my prayer too soon, and too soon would heal me from the disease of lust which I wanted satisfied rather than extinguished. So I had gone wandering in my sacrilegious superstition through the base ways of the Manicheans: not indeed that I was sure they were right but that I preferred them to the Christians, whom I did not inquire about in the spirit of religion but simply opposed through malice.

I had thought that my reason for putting off from day to day the following of You alone to the contempt of earthly hopes was that I did not see any certain goal towards which to direct my course. But now the day was come when I stood naked in my own sight and my conscience accused me: "Why is my voice not heard? Surely you are the man who used to say that you could not cast off vanity's baggage for an uncertain truth. Very well: now the truth is certain, yet you are still carrying the load. Here are men who have been given wings to free their shoulders from the load, though they did not wear themselves out in searching nor spend ten years or more thinking about it."

Thus was I inwardly gnawed at. And I was in the grip of the most horrible and confounding shame, while Ponticianus was telling his story. He finished the tale and the business for which he had come; and he went his way, and I to myself. What did I not say against myself, with what lashes of condemnation did I not scourge my soul to make it follow me now that I wanted to follow You! My soul hung back. It would not follow, yet found no excuse for not following. All its arguments had already been used and refuted. There remained only trembling silence: for it feared as very death the cessation of that habit of which in truth it was dying.

In the midst of that great tumult of my inner dwelling place, the tumult I had stirred up against my own soul in the chamber of my heart, I turned upon Alypius, wild in look and troubled in mind, crying out: "What is wrong with us? What is this that you heard? The unlearned arise and take heaven by force, and here are we with all our learning, stuck fast in flesh and blood! Is there any shame in following because they have gone before us, would it not be a worse shame not to follow at once?" These words and more of the same sort I uttered, then the violence of my feeling tore me from him while he stood staring at me thunderstruck. For I did not sound like myself. My brow, cheeks, eyes, flush, the pitch of my voice, spoke my mind more powerfully than the words I uttered. There was a garden attached to our lodging, of which we had the use, as indeed we had of the whole house: for our host, the master of the house, did not live there. To this garden the storm in my breast somehow brought me, for there no one could intervene in the fierce suit I had brought against myself, until it should reach its issue: though what the issue was to be, You knew, not I: but there I was, going mad on my way to sanity, dying on my way to life, aware how evil I was, unaware that I was to grow better in a little while. So I went off to the garden, and Alypius close on my heels: for it was still privacy for me to have him near, and how could he leave me to myself in that state? We found a seat as far as possible from the house. I was frantic in mind, in a frenzy of indignation at myself for not going over to Your law and Your covenant, O my God, where all my bones cried out that I should be, extolling it to the skies. The way was not by ship or chariot or on foot: it was not as far as I had gone when I went from the house to the place where we sat. For I had but to will to go, in order not merely to go but to arrive; I had only to will to go—but to will powerfully and wholly, not to turn and twist a will half-wounded this way and that, with the part that would rise struggling against the part that would keep to the earth.

.   .   .

Thus I was sick at heart and in torment, accusing myself with a new intensity of bitterness, twisting and turning in my chain in the hope that it might be utterly broken, for what held me was so small a thing! But it still held me. And You stood in the secret places of my soul, O Lord, in the harshness of Your mercy redoubling the scourges of fear and shame lest I should give way again and that small slight tie which remained should not be broken but should grow again to full strength and bind me closer even than before. For I kept saying within myself: "Let it be now, let it be now," and by the mere words I had begun to move towards the resolution. I almost made it, yet I did not quite make it. But I did not fall back into my original state, but as it were stood near to get my breath. And I tried again and I was almost there, and now I could all but touch it and hold it: yet I was not quite there, I did not touch it or hold it. I still shrank from dying unto death and living unto life. The lower condition which had grown habitual was more powerful than the better condition which I had not tried. The nearer the point of time came in which I was to become different, the more it struck me with horror; but it did not force me utterly back nor turn me utterly away, but held me there between the two.

Those trifles of all trifles, and vanities of vanities, my one-time mistresses, held me back, plucking at my garment of flesh and murmuring softly: "Are you sending us away?" And "From this moment shall we not be with you, now or forever?" And "From this moment shall this or that not be allowed you, now or forever?" What were they suggesting to me in the phrase I have written "this or that," what were they suggesting to me, O my God? Do you in your mercy keep from the soul of Your servant the vileness and uncleanness they were suggesting. And now I began to hear them not half so loud; they no longer stood against me face to face, but were softly muttering behind my back and, as I tried to depart, plucking stealthily at me to make me look behind. Yet even that was enough, so hesitating was I, to keep me from snatching myself free, from shaking them off and leaping upwards on the way I was called: for the strong force of habit said to me: "Do you think you can live without them?"

But by this time its voice was growing fainter. In the direction towards which I had turned my face and was quivering in fear of going, I could see the austere beauty of Continence, serene and indeed joyous but not evilly, honourably soliciting me to come to her and not linger, stretching forth loving hands to receive and embrace me, hands full of multitudes of good examples. With her I saw such hosts of young men and maidens, a multitude of youth and of every age, gray widows and women grown old in virginity, and in them all Continence herself, not barren but the fruitful mother of children, her joys, by You, Lord, her Spouse. And she smiled upon me and her smile gave courage as if she were saying: "Can you not do what these men have done, what these women have done? Or could men or women have done such in themselves, and not in the Lord their God? The Lord their God gave me to them. Why do you stand upon yourself and so not stand at all? Cast yourself upon Him and be not afraid; He will not draw away and let you fall. Cast yourself without fear, He will receive you and heal you."

Yet I was still ashamed, for I could still hear the murmuring of those vanities, and I still hung hesitant. And again it was as if she said: "Stop your ears against your unclean members, that they may be mortified. They tell you of delights, but not of such delights as the law of the Lord your God tells." This was the controversy raging in my heart, a controversy about myself against myself. And Alypius stayed by my side and awaited in silence the issue of such agitation as he had never seen in me.

When my most searching scrutiny had drawn up all my vileness from the secret depths of my soul and heaped it in my heart's sight, a mighty storm arose in me, bringing a mighty rain of tears. That I might give way to my tears and lamentations, I rose from Alypius: for it struck me that solitude was more suited to the business of weeping. I went far enough from him to prevent his presence from being an embarrassment to me. So I felt, and he realized it. I suppose I had said something and the sound of my voice was heavy with tears. I arose, but he remained where we had been sitting, still in utter amazement. I flung myself down somehow under a certain fig tree and no longer tried to check my tears, which poured forth from my eyes in a flood, *an acceptable sacrifice to Thee.* And much I said not in these words but to this effect: *"And Thou, O, Lord, how long? How long, Lord; wilt Thou be angry forever? Remember not our former iniquities."* For I felt that I was still bound by them. And I continued my miserable complaining: "How long, how long shall I go on saying tomorrow and again tomorrow? Why not now, why not have an end to my uncleanness this very hour?"

Such things I said, weeping in the most bitter sorrow of my heart. And suddenly I heard a voice from some nearby house, a boy's voice or a girl's voice, I do not know: but it was a sort of sing-song, repeated again and again, "Take and read, take and read." I ceased weeping and immediately began to search my mind most carefully as to whether children were accustomed to chant these words in any kind of game, and I could not remember that I had ever heard any such thing. Damming back the flood of my tears I arose, interpreting the incident as quite certainly a divine command to open my book of Scripture and read the passage at which I should open. For it was part of what I had been told about Antony, that from the Gospel which he happened to be reading he had felt that he was being admonished as though what he read was spoken directly to himself: *Go, sell what thou hast and give to the poor and thou shalt have treasure in heaven; and come follow Me.* By this experience he had been in that instant converted to You. So I was moved to return to the place where Alypius was sitting, for I had put down the Apostle's book there when I arose. I snatched it up, opened it and in silence read the passage upon which my eyes first fell: *Not in rioting and drunkenness, not in chambering and impurities, not in contention and envy, but put ye on the Lord Jesus Christ and make not provision for the flesh in its concupiscences.* [Romans xiii, 13.] I had no wish to read further, and no need. For in that instant, with the very ending of the sentence, it was as though a light of utter confidence shone in all my heart, and all the darkness of uncertainty vanished away. Then leaving my finger in the place or marking it by some other sign, I closed the book and in complete calm told the whole thing to Alypius and he similarly told me what had been going on in himself, of which I knew nothing. He asked to see what I had read. I showed him, and he looked further than I had read. I had not known what followed. And this is what followed: *"Now him that is weak in faith, take unto you."* He applied this to himself and told me so. And he was confirmed by this message, and with no troubled wavering gave himself to God's good-will and purpose—a purpose indeed most suited to his character, for in these matters he had been immeasurably better than I.

Then we went in to my mother and told her, to her great joy. We related how it had come about: she was filled with triumphant exultation, and praised You who are mighty beyond what we ask or conceive: for she saw that You had given her more than with all her pitiful weeping she had ever asked. For You converted me to Yourself so that I no longer sought a wife nor any of this world's promises, but stood upon that same rule of faith in which You had shown me to her so many years before. Thus You changed her mourning into joy, a joy far richer than she had thought to wish, a joy much dearer and purer than she had thought to find in grandchildren of my flesh.

The Function of Art

People have been debating what it is that artists do, or what they ought to do, at least since Plato's day. Artists have commented variously, sometimes with a sublime incoherence but occasionally with that resonant authority that is theirs alone. We present here five writers, a philosopher, and a political leader who share the conviction that art is useful and important, although for different reasons.

The first three essays show art as an important mirror to reality, particularly to inner reality—the life of feeling and emotion. The philosopher, Susanne Langer, argues that "the primary function of art is to objectify feeling so that we can contemplate and understand it." For writer James Baldwin, art can break the barrier between what we are and what we wish to be, and by showing the difference make possible a reconciliation. But to do this, the artist must first cultivate aloneness, explore his own inner wilderness. Ralph Ellison, too, ties the function of art to a personal quest. Because art must reveal what one perceives as true and real, in becoming a writer, one must find what one truly feels rather than rely on what one is supposed to or is encouraged to feel.

George Orwell, speaking of how and why he became a writer, justifies the art that has political purpose. Mao Tse-tung expands that theme. Concerned with criteria in art and literary criticism, he demands the "unity of politics and art," holding that "all dark forces which endanger the masses of the people must be exposed while all revolutionary struggles of the masses must be praised." The two essays by Imamu Amiri Baraka are related to those of the previous writers and also to each other. In the first Baraka affirms that art must be produced from the legitimate emotional resources of the soul in the world, and thus rejects both cultivated imitation and blueprinted reform. The second essay, written two years later, is far more radical in content as well as in style. It calls not for a symbolic representation of reality but for reality itself, for a theater of assault, for actual explosions and actual brutality. The concluding essay by Alexander Solzhenitsyn makes a connection between social purpose and personal purpose. Art, he says, is a struggle against lies, whether these be emotional lies or political ones.

The four poems on art that open the section test Matisse's remark that "the best explanation an artist can give of his aims and ability is afforded by his work."

FOUR POEMS ON ART

John Keats (1795–1821)

Ode on a Grecian Urn

I

Thou still unravish'd bride of quietness,
  Thou foster-child of silence and slow time,
Sylvan historian, who canst thus express
  A flowery tale more sweetly than our rhyme:
What leaf-fring'd legend haunts about thy shape
  Of deities or mortals, or of both,
    In Tempe or the dales or Arcady?
What men or gods are these? What maidens lòth?
  What mad pursuit? What struggle to escape?
    What pipes and timbrels? What wild ecstasy?

II

Heard melodies are sweet, but those unheard
  Are sweeter; therefore, ye soft pipes, play on;
Not to the sensual ear, but, more endear'd,
  Pipe to the spirit ditties of no tone:
Fair youth, beneath the trees, thou canst not leave
  Thy song, nor ever can those trees be bare;
    Bold Lover, never, never canst thou kiss
Though winning near the goal—yet, do not grieve;
  She cannot fade, though thou hast not thy bliss,
    For ever wilt thou love, and she be fair!

III

Ah, happy, happy boughs! that cannot shed
  Your leaves, nor ever bid the Spring adieu;
And, happy melodist, unwearied,
  For ever piping songs for ever new;
More happy love! more happy, happy love!
  For ever warm and still to be enjoy'd,
    For ever panting, and for ever young;
All breathing human passion far above,
  That leaves a heart high-sorrowful and cloy'd,
    A burning forehead, and a parching tongue.

IV

Who are these coming to the sacrifice?
  To what green altar, O mysterious priest,
Lead'st thou that heifer lowing at the skies,
  And all her silken flanks with garlands dressed?
What little town by river or sea shore,
  Or mountain-built with peaceful citadel,
    Is emptied of this folk, this pious morn?
And, little town, thy streets for evermore
  Will silent be; and not a soul to tell
    Why thou art desolate, can e'er return.

V

O Attic shape! Fair attitude! with brede
  Of marble men and maidens overwrought
With forest branches and the trodden weed;
  Thou, silent form, dost tease us out of thought
As doth eternity: Cold Pastoral!
  When old age shall this generation waste,
    Thou shalt remain, in midst of other woe
Than ours, a friend to man, to whom thou say'st,
  'Beauty is truth, truth beauty,'—that is all
    Ye know on earth, and all ye need to know.

(1819)

Marianne Moore (1887–1972)

Poetry

I, too, dislike it: there are things that are important beyond all this fiddle.
  Reading it, however, with a perfect contempt for it, one discovers in
    it after all, a place for the genuine.
      Hands that can grasp, eyes
        that can dilate, hair that can rise
          if it must, these things are important not because a

high-sounding interpretation can be put upon them but because they are
  useful. When they become so derivative as to become unintelligible,
    the same thing may be said for all of us, that we
      do not admire what
      we cannot understand: the bat
        holding on upside down or in quest of something to

eat, elephants pushing, a wild horse taking a roll, a tireless wolf under
    a tree, the immovable critic twitching his skin like a horse that
        feels a flea, the base-
  ball fan, the statistician—
     nor is it valid
       to discriminate against 'business documents and

school-books'; all these phenomena are important. One must make
       a distinction
  however: when dragged into prominence by half poets, the result
       is not poetry,
  nor till the poets among us can be
    'literalists of
    the imagination'—above
       insolence and triviality and can present

for inspection, 'imaginary gardens with real toads in them', shall
      we have
  it. In the meantime, if you demand on the one hand,
  the raw material of poetry in
    all its rawness and
    that which is on the other hand
      genuine, you are interested in poetry.

                                        (1921)

Archibald MacLeish (1892–)

Ars Poetica

A poem should be palpable and mute
As a globed fruit,

Dumb
As old medallions to the thumb,

Silent as the sleeve-worn stone
Of casement ledges where the moss has grown—

A poem should be wordless
As the flight of birds.

   *

A poem should be motionless in time
As the moon climbs,

Leaving, as the moon releases
Twig by twig the night-entangled trees,

Leaving, as the moon behind the winter leaves,
Memory by memory the mind—

A poem should be motionless in time
As the moon climbs.

*

A poem should be equal to:
Not true.

For all the history of grief
An empty doorway and a maple leaf.

For love
The leaning grasses and two lights above the sea—

A poem should not mean
But be.

(1926)

Mona Van Duyn (1921–)

A Valentine to the Wide World

I have never enjoyed those roadside overlooks from which
you can see the mountains of two states. The view keeps generating
a kind of pure, meaningless exaltation
that I can't find a use for. It drifts away from things.

And it seems to me also that the truckdriver's waste of the world
is sobering. When he rolls round it on a callous of macadam,
think how all those limping puppydogs, girls
thumbing rides under the hot sun, or under the white moon

how all those couples kissing at the side of the road,
bad hills, cat eyes, and horses asleep on their feet
must run together into a statement so abstract
that it's tiresome. Nothing in particular holds still in it.

Perhaps he does learn that the planet can still support life,
though with some difficulty. Or even that there is injustice,
since he rolls round and round and may be able to feel
the slight but measurable wobble of the earth on its axis.

But what I find most useful is the poem. To find some spot
on the surface and then bear down until the skin can't stand
the tension and breaks under it, breaks under that half-demented
"pressure of speech" the psychiatrists saw in Pound

is a discreetness of consumption that I value. Only the poem
is strong enough to make the initial rupture,
at least for me. Its view is simultaneous
discovery and reminiscence. It starts with the creature

and stays there, assuming creation is worth the time
it takes, from the first day down to the last line on the last page.
And I've never seen anything like it for making you think
that to spend your life on such old premises is a privilege.

(1959)

SUSANNE K. LANGER

Originally a lecture delivered at Syracuse University, this essay was first published in Aesthetic Form and Education (*ed. M. F. Andrews, 1958*). *It later appeared as Chapter 5 in Susanne K. Langer's* Philosophical Sketches (*1962*), *and it is this text which we reprint below. For information about the author and her writings, see page 91.*

The Cultural Importance of Art

Every culture develops some kind of art as surely as it develops language. Some primitive cultures have no real mythology or religion, but all have some art—dance, song, design (sometimes only on tools or on the human body). Dance, above all, seems to be the oldest elaborated art.

The ancient ubiquitous character of art contrasts sharply with the prevalent idea that art is a luxury product of civilization, a cultural frill, a piece of social veneer.

It fits better with the conviction held by most artists, that art is the epitome of human life, the truest record of insight and feeling, and that the strongest military or economic society without art is poor in comparison with the most primitive tribe of savage painters, dancers, or idol carvers. Wherever a society has really achieved culture (in the ethnological sense, not the popular sense of "social form") it has begotten art, not late in its career, but at the very inception of it.

Art is, indeed, the spearhead of human development, social and individual. The vulgarization of art is the surest symptom of ethnic decline. The growth of a new art or even a great and radically new style always bespeaks a young and vigorous mind, whether collective or single.

What sort of thing is art, that it should play such a leading role in human development? It is not an intellectual pursuit, but is necessary to intellectual life; it is not religion, but grows up with religion, serves it, and in large measure determines it.

We cannot enter here on a long discussion of what has been claimed as the essence of art, the true nature of art, or its defining function; in a single lecture dealing with one aspect of art, namely its cultural influence, I can only give you by way of preamble my own definition of art, with categorical brevity. This does not mean that I set up this definition in a categorical spirit, but only that we have no time to debate it; so you are asked to accept it as an assumption underlying these reflections.

Art, in the sense here intended—that is, the generic term subsuming painting, sculpture, architecture, music, dance, literature, drama, and film—may be defined as the practice of creating perceptible forms expressive of human feeling. I say "perceptible" rather than "sensuous" forms because some works of art are given to imagination rather than to the outward senses. A novel, for instance, usually is read silently with the eye, but is not made for vision, as a painting is; and though sound plays a vital part in poetry, words even in poetry are not essentially sonorous structures like music. Dance requires to be seen, but its appeal is to deeper centers of sensation. The difference between dance and mobile sculpture makes this immediately apparent. But all works of art are purely perceptible forms that seem to embody some sort of feeling.

"Feeling" as I am using it here covers much more than it does in the technical vocabulary of psychology, where it denotes only pleasure and displeasure, or even in the shifting limits of ordinary discourse, where it sometimes means sensation (as when one says a paralyzed limb has no feeling in it), sometimes sensibility (as we speak of hurting someone's feelings), sometimes emotion (e.g., as a situation is said to harrow your feelings, or to evoke tender feeling), or a directed emotional attitude (we say we feel strongly *about* something), or even our general mental or physical condition, feeling well or ill, blue, or a bit above ourselves. As I use the word, in defining art as the creation of perceptible forms expressive of human feeling, it takes in all those meanings; it applies to everything that may be felt.

Another word in the definition that might be questioned is "creation." I think it is justified, not pretentious, as perhaps it sounds, but that issue is slightly beside the point here; so let us shelve it. If anyone prefers to speak of the "making" or "construction" of expressive forms, that will do here just as well.

What does have to be understood is the meaning of "form," and more particularly "expressive form"; for that involves the very nature of art and therefore the question of its cultural importance.

The word "form" has several current uses; most of them have some relation to the sense in which I am using it here, though a few, such as "a form to be filled in for tax purposes" or "a mere matter of form," are fairly remote, being quite specialized. Since we are speaking of art, it might be good to point out that the meaning of stylistic pattern—"the sonata form," "the sonnet form"—is not the one I am assuming here.

I am using the word in a simpler sense, which it has when you say, on a foggy night, that you see dimly moving forms in the mist; one of them emerges clearly, and is the form of a man. The trees are gigantic forms; the rills of rain trace sinuous forms on the windowpane. The rills are not fixed things; they are forms of motion. When you watch gnats weaving in the air, or flocks of birds wheeling overhead, you see dynamic forms —forms made by motion.

It is in this sense of an apparition given to our perception that a work of art is a form. It may be a permanent form like a building or a vase or a picture, or a transient, dynamic form like a melody or a dance, or even a form given to imagination, like the passage of purely imaginary, apparent events that constitutes a literary work. But it is always a perceptible, self-identical whole; like a natural being, it has a character of organic unity, self-sufficiency, individual reality. And it is thus, as an appearance, that a work of art is good or bad or perhaps only rather poor—as an appearance, not as a comment on things beyond it in the world, or as a reminder of them.

This, then, is what I mean by "form"; but what is meant by calling such forms "expressive of human feeling"? How do apparitions "express" anything—feeling or anything else? First of all, let us ask just what is meant here by "express," what sort of "expression" we are talking about.

The word "expression" has two principal meanings. In one sense it means self-expression—giving vent to our feelings. In this sense it refers to a symptom of what we feel. Self-expression is a spontaneous reaction to an actual, present situation, an event, the company we are in, things people say, or what the weather does to us; it bespeaks the physical and mental state we are in and the emotions that stir us.

In another sense, however, "expression" means the presentation of an idea, usually by the proper and apt use of words. But a device for presenting an idea is what we call a symbol, not a symptom. Thus a word is a symbol, and so is a meaningful combination of words.

A sentence, which is a special combination of words, expresses the idea of some state of affairs, real or imagined. Sentences are complicated symbols. Language will formulate new ideas as well as communicate old ones, so that all people know a lot of things that they have merely heard or read about. Symbolic expression, therefore, extends our knowledge beyond the scope of our actual experience.

If an idea is clearly conveyed by means of symbols we say it is well expressed. A person may work for a long time to give his statement the best possible form, to find the exact words for what he means to say, and to carry his account or his argument most directly from one point to another. But a discourse so worked out is certainly not a spontaneous reaction. Giving expression to an idea is obviously a different thing from giving expression to feelings. You do not say of a man in a rage that his anger is well expressed. The symptoms just are what they are; there is no critical standard for symptoms. If, on the other hand, the angry man tries to tell you what he is fuming about, he will have to collect himself, curtail his emotional expression, and find words to express his ideas. For to tell a story coherently involves "expression" in quite a different sense: this sort of expression is not "self-expression," but may be called "conceptual expression."

Language, of course, is our prime instrument of conceptual expression. The things we can say are in effect the things we can think. Words are the terms of our thinking as well as the terms in which we present our thoughts, because they present the objects of thought to the thinker himself. Before language communicates ideas, it gives them form, makes them clear, and in fact makes them what they are. Whatever has a name is an object for thought. Without words, sense experience is only a flow of impressions, as subjective as our feelings; words make it objective, and carve it up into *things* and *facts* that we can note, remember, and think about. Language gives outward experience its form, and makes it definite and clear.

There is, however, an important part of reality that is quite inaccessible to the formative influence of language: that is the realm of so-called "inner experience," the life of feeling and emotion. The reason why language is so powerless here is not, as many people suppose, that feeling and emotion are irrational; on the contrary, they seem irrational because language does not help to make them conceivable, and most people cannot conceive anything without the logical scaffolding of words. The unfitness of language to convey subjective experience is a somewhat technical subject, easier for logicians to understand than for artists; but the gist of it is that the form of language does not reflect the natural form of feeling, so that we cannot shape any extensive concepts of feeling with the help of ordinary, discursive language. Therefore the words whereby we refer to feeling only name very general kinds of inner experience— excitement, calm, joy, sorrow, love, hate, and so on. But there is no language to describe just how one joy differs, sometimes radically, from another. The real nature of feeling is something language as such—as discursive symbolism—cannot render.

For this reason, the phenomena of feeling and emotion are usually treated by philosophers as irrational. The only pattern discursive thought can find in them is the pattern of outward events that occasion them.

There are different degrees of fear, but they are thought of as so many degrees of the same simple feeling.

But human feeling is a fabric, not a vague mass. It has an intricate dynamic pattern, possible combinations and new emergent phenomena. It is a pattern of organically interdependent and interdetermined tensions and resolutions, a pattern of almost infinitely complex activation and cadence. To it belongs the whole gamut of our sensibility—the sense of straining thought, all mental attitude and motor set. Those are the deeper reaches that underlie the surface waves of our emotion, and make human life a life of feeling instead of an unconscious metabolic existence interrupted by feelings.

It is, I think, this dynamic pattern that finds its formal expression in the arts. The expressiveness of art is like that of a symbol, not that of an emotional symptom; it is as a formulation of feeling for our conception that a work of art is properly said to be expressive. It may serve somebody's need of self-expression besides, but that is not what makes it good or bad art. In a special sense one may call a work of art a symbol of feeling, for, like a symbol, it formulates our ideas of inward experience, as discourse formulates our ideas of things and facts in the outside world. A work of art differs from a genuine symbol—that is, a symbol in the full and usual sense—in that it does not point beyond itself to something else. Its relation to feeling is a rather special one that we cannot undertake to analyze here; in effect, the feeling it expresses appears to be directly given with it—as the sense of a true metaphor, or the value of a religious myth —and is not separable from its expression. We speak of the feeling *of,* or the feeling *in,* a work of art, not the feeling it means. And we speak truly; a work of art presents something like a direct vision of vitality, emotion, subjective reality.

The primary function of art is to objectify feeling so that we can contemplate and understand it. It is the formulation of so-called "inward experience," the "inner life," that is impossible to achieve by discursive thought, because its forms are incommensurable with the forms of language and all its derivatives (e.g., mathematics, symbolic logic). Art objectifies the sentience and desire, self-consciousness and world-consciousness, emotions and moods, that are generally regarded as irrational because words cannot give us clear ideas of them. But the premise tacitly assumed in such a judgment—namely, that anything language cannot express is formless and irrational—seems to me to be an error. I believe the life of feeling is not irrational; its logical forms are merely very different from the structures of discourse. But they are so much like the dynamic forms of art that art is their natural symbol. Through plastic works, music, fiction, dance, or dramatic forms we can conceive what vitality and emotion feel like.

This brings us, at last, to the question of the cultural importance of the arts. Why is art so apt to be the vanguard of cultural advance, as it was in Egypt, in Greece, in Christian Europe (think of Gregorian music and Gothic architecture), in Renaissance Italy—not to speculate about ancient cavemen, whose art is all that we know of them? One thinks of culture as economic increase, social organization, the gradual ascendancy of rational thinking and scientific control of nature over superstitious imagination and magical practices. But art is not practical; it is neither philosophy nor science; it is not religion, morality, or even social comment (as many drama critics take comedy to be). What does it contribute to culture that could be of major importance?

It merely presents forms—sometimes intangible forms—to imagination. Its direct appeal is to that faculty, or function, that Lord Bacon considered the chief stumbling block in the way of reason, and that enlightened writers like Stuart Chase never tire of condemning as the source of all nonsense and bizarre erroneous beliefs. And so it is; but it is also the source of all insight and true beliefs. Imagination is probably the oldest mental trait that is typically human—older than discursive reason; it is probably the common source of dream, reason, religion, and all true general observation. It is this primitive human power—imagination—that engenders the arts and is in turn directly affected by their products.

Somewhere at the animalian starting line of human evolution lie the beginnings of that supreme instrument of the mind—language. We think of it as a device for communication among the members of a society. But communication is only one, and perhaps not even the first, of its functions. The first thing it does is to break up what William James called the "blooming, buzzing confusion" of sense perception into units and groups, events and chains of events—things and relations, causes and effects. All these patterns are imposed on our experience by language. We think, as we speak, in terms of objects and their relations.

But the process of breaking up our sense experience in this way, making reality conceivable, memorable, sometimes even predictable, is a process of imagination. Primitive conception is imagination. Language and imagination grow up together in a reciprocal tutelage.

What discursive symbolism—language in its literal use—does for our awareness of things about us and our own relation to them, the arts do for our awareness of subjective reality, feeling and emotion; they give form to inward experiences and thus make them conceivable. The only way we can really envisage vital movement, the stirring and growth and passage of emotion, and ultimately the whole direct sense of human life, is in artistic terms. A musical person thinks of emotions musically. They cannot be discursively talked about above a very general level. But they may nonetheless be known—objectively set forth, publicly known—and there is nothing necessarily confused or formless about emotions.

As soon as the natural forms of subjective experience are abstracted to the point of symbolic presentation, we can use those forms to imagine feeling and understand its nature. Self-knowledge, insight into all phases of life and mind, springs from artistic imagination. That is the cognitive value of the arts.

But their influence on human life goes deeper than the intellectual level. As language actually gives form to our sense experience, grouping our impressions around those things which have names, and fitting sensations to the qualities that have adjectival names, and so on, the arts we live with—our picture books and stories and the music we hear—actually form our emotive experience. Every generation has its styles of feeling. One age shudders and blushes and faints, another swaggers, still another is godlike in a universal indifference. These styles in actual emotion are not insincere. They are largely unconscious—determined by many social causes, but *shaped* by artists, usually popular artists of the screen, the jukebox, the shop window, and the picture magazine. (That, rather than incitement to crime, is my objection to the comics.) Irwin Edman remarks in one of his books that our emotions are largely Shakespeare's poetry.

This influence of art on life gives us an indication of why a period of efflorescence in the arts is apt to lead a cultural advance: it formulates a new way of feeling, and that is the beginning of a cultural age. It suggests another matter of reflection, too—that a wide neglect of artistic education is a neglect in the education of feeling. Most people are so imbued with the idea that feeling is a formless, total organic excitement in men as in animals that the idea of educating feeling, developing its scope and quality, seems odd to them, if not absurd. It is really, I think, at the very heart of personal education.

There is one other function of the arts that benefits not so much the advance of culture as its stabilization—an influence on individual lives. This function is the converse and complement of the objectification of feeling, the driving force of creation in art: it is the education of vision that we receive in seeing, hearing, reading works of art—the development of the artist's eye, that assimilates ordinary sights (or sounds, motions, or events) to inward vision, and lends expressiveness and emotional import to the world. Wherever art takes a motif from actuality—a flowering branch, a bit of landscape, a historic event, or a personal memory, any model or theme from life—it transforms it into a piece of imagination, and imbues its image with artistic vitality. The result is an impregnation of ordinary reality with the significance of created form. This is the subjectification of nature that makes reality itself a symbol of life and feeling.

The arts objectify subjective reality, and subjectify outward experience of nature. Art education is the education of feeling, and a society that neglects it gives itself up to formless emotion. Bad art is corruption of feeling. This is a large factor in the irrationalism which dictators and demagogues exploit.

JAMES BALDWIN

This essay was first published in Creative America, *a book prepared for the National Cultural Center established in Washington, D.C., as an official memorial to John F. Kennedy. It later appeared in the* Saturday Review, *February 8, 1964; this is the text used here. For further information about the author and his work, see page 403.*

The Creative Dilemma

Perhaps the primary distinction of the artist is that he must actively cultivate that state which most men, necessarily, must avoid: the state of being alone. That all men *are,* when the chips are down, alone, is a banality—a banality because it is very frequently stated, but very rarely, on the evidence, believed. Most of us are not compelled to linger with the knowledge of our aloneness, for it is a knowledge that can paralyze all action in this world. There are, forever, swamps to be drained, cities to be created, mines to be exploited, children to be fed. None of these things can be done alone. But the conquest of the physical world is not man's only duty. He is also enjoined to conquer the great wilderness of himself. The precise role of the artist, then, is to illuminate that darkness, blaze roads through that vast forest, so that we will not, in all our doing, lose sight of its purpose, which is, after all, to make the world a more human dwelling place.

The state of being alone is not meant to bring to mind merely a rustic musing beside some silver lake. The aloneness of which I speak is much more like the aloneness of birth or death. It is like the fearful aloneness that one sees in the eyes of someone who is suffering, whom we cannot help. Or it is like the aloneness of love, the force and mystery that so many have extolled and so many have cursed, but which no one has ever understood or ever really been able to control. I put the matter this way, not out of any desire to create pity for the artist—God forbid!—but to suggest how nearly, after all, is his state the state of everyone, and in an attempt to make vivid his endeavor. The states of birth, suffering, love, and death are extreme states—extreme, universal, and inescapable. We all know this, but we would rather not know it. The artist is present to correct the delusions to which we fall prey in our attempts to avoid this knowledge.

It is for this reason that all societies have battled with that incorrigible disturber of the peace—the artist. I doubt that future societies will get on with him any better. The entire purpose of society is to create a bulwark against the inner and the outer chaos, in order to make life bearable and to keep the human race alive. And it is absolutely inevitable that when a tradition has been evolved, whatever the tradition is, the people, in general, will suppose it to have existed from before the beginning of time and will be most unwilling and indeed unable to conceive of any changes in it. They do not know how they will live without those traditions that have given them their identity. Their reaction, when it is suggested that they can or that they must, is panic. And we see this panic, I think, everywhere in the world today, from the streets of New Orleans to the grisly battleground of Algeria. And a higher level of consciousness among the people is the only hope we have, now or in the future, of minimizing human damage.

The artist is distinguished from all other responsible actors in society —the politicians, legislators, educators, and scientists—by the fact that he is his own test tube, his own laboratory, working according to very rigorous rules, however unstated these may be, and cannot allow any consideration to supersede his responsibility to reveal all that he can possibly discover concerning the mystery of the human being. Society must accept some things as real; but he must always know that visible reality hides a deeper one, and that all our action and achievement rests on things unseen. A society must assume that it is stable, but the artist must know, and he must let us know, that there is nothing stable under heaven. One cannot possibly build a school, teach a child, or drive a car without taking some things for granted. The artist cannot and must not take anything for granted, but must drive to the heart of every answer and expose the question the answer hides.

I seem to be making extremely grandiloquent claims for a breed of men and women historically despised while living and acclaimed when safely dead. But, in a way, the belated honor that all societies tender their artists proves the reality of the point I am trying to make. I am really trying to make clear the nature of the artist's responsibility to his society. The peculiar nature of this responsibility is that he must never cease warring with it, for its sake and for his own. For the truth, in spite of appearances and all our hopes, is that everything is always changing and the measure of our maturity as nations and as men is how well prepared we are to meet these changes and, further, to use them for our health.

Now, anyone who has ever been compelled to think about it—anyone, for example, who has ever been in love—knows that the one face that one can never see is one's own face. One's lover—or one's brother, or one's enemy—sees the face you wear, and this face can elicit the most extraordinary reactions. We do the things we do and feel what we feel essentially because we must—we are responsible for our actions, but we rarely understand them. It goes without saying, I believe, that if we understood ourselves better, we would damage ourselves less. But the barrier between oneself and one's knowledge of oneself is high indeed. There are so many things one would rather not know! We become social creatures because we cannot live any other way. But in order to become social, there are a great many other things that we must not become, and we are frightened, all of us, of those forces within us that perpetually menace our precarious security. Yet the forces are there; we cannot will them away. All we can do is learn to live with them. And we cannot learn this unless we are willing to tell the truth about ourselves, and the truth about us is always at variance with what we wish to be. The human effort is to bring these two realities into a relationship resembling reconciliation. The human beings whom we respect the most, after all—and sometimes fear the most—are those who are most deeply involved in this delicate and strenuous effort, for they have the unshakable authority that comes only from having looked on and endured and survived the worst. That nation is healthiest which has the least necessity to distrust or ostracize or victim- ize these people—whom, as I say, we honor, once they are gone, because somewhere in our hearts we know that we cannot live without them.

The dangers of being an American artist are not greater than those of being an artist anywhere else in the world, but they are very particular. These dangers are produced by our history. They rest on the fact that in order to conquer this continent, the particular aloneness of which I speak —the aloneness in which one discovers that life is tragic, and therefore unutterably beautiful—could not be permitted. And that this prohibition is typical of all emergent nations will be proved, I have no doubt, in many ways during the next fifty years. This continent now is conquered, but our habits and our fears remain. And, in the same way that to become a social human being one modifies and suppresses and, ultimately, without great courage, lies to oneself about all one's interior, uncharted chaos, so have we, as a nation, modified and suppressed and lied about all the darker forces in our history. We know, in the case of the person, that whoever cannot tell himself the truth about his past is trapped in it, is immobilized in the prison of his undiscovered self. This is also true of nations. We know how a person, in such a paralysis, is unable to assess either his weaknesses or his strengths, and how frequently indeed he mistakes the one for the other. And this, I think, we do. We are the strongest nation in the Western world, but this is not for the reasons that we think. It is because we have an opportunity that no other nation has of moving beyond the Old World concepts of race and class and caste, to create, finally, what we must have had in mind when we first began speaking of the New World. But the price of this is a long look backward whence we came and an unflinching assessment of the record. For an artist, the record of that journey is most clearly revealed in the personalities of the people the journey produced. Societies never know it, but the war of an artist with his society is a lover's war, and he does, at his best, what lovers do, which is to reveal the beloved to himself and, with that revelation, to make freedom real.

RALPH ELLISON

Ralph Ellison's best-known work, Invisible Man (*1952*), *tells in surrealistic flashbacks the black narrator's life of bitter disillusionment in the South and in Harlem. It received immediate critical acclaim and won the National Book Award for fiction in 1953; twelve years later, a* Book Week *poll voted it the most distinguished book published between 1945 and 1965.*

Ellison was born in Oklahoma City in 1914. He studied music at Tuskegee Institute from 1933 to 1936 and then settled in New York City, where he studied sculpture and worked on the Federal Writer's Project. At that time he also met Langston Hughes and Richard Wright. By 1939, Ellison was regularly publishing short stories, essays, and book reviews. He served in the Merchant Marine during World War II, then won a Rosenwald Fellowship that let him concentrate on writing Invisible Man. *He has taught and lectured at many schools, including Bard College, the University of Chicago, Rutgers, and Yale, and is the recipient of numerous honors. The essay reprinted here first appeared in* Commentary, *October 1964. A slightly revised version became the introduction to Ellison's second book, a collection of essays called* Shadow and Act (*1964*).

On Becoming a Writer

In the beginning writing was far from a serious matter; it was a reflex of reading, an extension of a source of pleasure, escape, and instruction. In fact, I had become curious about writing by way of seeking to understand the aesthetic nature of literary power, the devices through which literature could command my mind and emotions. It was not, then, the *process* of writing which initially claimed my attention, but the finished creations, the artifacts, poems, plays, novels. The act of learning writing technique was, therefore, an amusing investigation of what seemed at best a secondary talent, an exploration, like dabbling in sculpture, of one's potentialities as a "Renaissance Man." This, surely, would seem a most unlikely and even comic concept to introduce here; and yet, it is precisely because I come from where I do (the Oklahoma of the years between World War I and the Great Depression) that I must introduce it, and with a straight face.

Anything and everything was to be found in the chaos of Oklahoma; thus the concept of the Renaissance Man has lurked long within the shadow of my past, and I shared it with at least a half dozen of my Negro friends. How we actually acquired it I have never learned, and since there

is no true sociology of the dispersion of ideas within the American
democracy, I doubt if I ever shall. Perhaps we breathed it in with the air
of the Negro community of Oklahoma City, the capital of that state whose
Negroes were often charged by exasperated white Texans with not knowing their "place." Perhaps we took it defiantly from one of them. Or
perhaps I myself picked it up from some transplanted New Englander
whose shoes I had shined of a Saturday afternoon. After all, the most
meaningful tips do not always come in the form of money, nor are they
intentionally extended. Most likely, however, my friends and I acquired
the idea from some book or from some idealistic Negro teacher, some
dreamer seeking to function responsibly in an environment which at its
most normal took on some of the mixed character of nightmare and of
dream.

One thing is certain, ours was a chaotic community, still characterized
by frontier attitudes and by that strange mixture of the naive and sophisticated, the benign and malignant, which makes the American past so
puzzling and its present so confusing; that mixture which often affords
the minds of the young who grow up in the far provinces such wide and
unstructured latitude, and which encourages the individual's imagination
—up to the moment "reality" closes in upon him—to range widely and,
sometimes, even to soar.

We hear the effects of this in the Southwestern jazz of the 30's, that
joint creation of artistically free and exuberantly creative adventurers, of
artists who had stumbled upon the freedom lying within the restrictions
of their musical tradition as within the limitations of their social background, and who in their own unconscious way have set an example for
any Americans, Negro or white, who would find themselves in the arts.
They accepted themselves and the complexity of life as they knew it, they
loved their art and through it they celebrated American experience defin-
itively in sound. Whatever others thought or felt, this was their own
powerful statement, and only non-musical assaults upon their artistic
integrity—mainly economically inspired changes of fashion—were able
to compromise their vision.

Much of so-called Kansas City jazz was actually brought to perfection
in Oklahoma by Oklahomans. It is an important circumstance for me as
a writer to remember, because while these musicians and their fellows
were busy creating out of tradition, imagination, and the sounds and
emotions around them, a freer, more complex, and driving form of jazz,
my friends and I were exploring an idea of human versatility and possibility which went against the barbs or over the palings of almost every fence
which those who controlled social and political power had erected to
restrict our roles in the life of the country. Looking back, one might say
that the jazzmen, some of whom we idolized, were in their own way better
examples for youth to follow than were most judges and ministers, legislators and governors (we were stuck with the notorious Alfalfa Bill Murray). For as we viewed these pillars of society from the confines of our

segregated community we almost always saw crooks, clowns, or hypocrites. Even the best were revealed by their attitudes toward us as lacking the respectable qualtities to which they pretended and for which they were accepted outside by others, while despite the outlaw nature of their art, the jazzmen were less torn and damaged by the moral compromises and insincerities which have so sickened the life of our country.

Be that as it may, our youthful sense of life, like that of many Negro children (though no one bothers to note it—especially the specialists and "friends of the Negro" who view our Negro-American life as essentially non-human) was very much like that of Huckleberry Finn, who is universally so praised and enjoyed for the clarity and courage of his moral vision. Like Huck, we observed, we judged, we imitated and evaded as we could the dullness, corruption, and blindness of "civilization." We were undoubtedly comic because, as the saying goes, we weren't supposed to know what it was all about. But to ourselves we were "boys," members of a wild, free, outlaw tribe which transcended the category of race. Rather we were Americans born into the forty-sixth state, and thus, into the context of Negro-American post-Civil War history, "frontiersmen." And isn't one of the implicit functions of the American frontier to encourage the individual to a kind of dreamy wakefulness, a state in which he makes—in all ignorance of the accepted limitations of the possible—rash efforts, quixotic gestures, hopeful testings of the complexity of the known and the given?

Spurring us on in our controlled and benign madness was the voracious reading of which most of us were guilty and the vicarious identification and empathetic adventuring which it encouraged. This was due, in part, perhaps to the fact that some of us were fatherless—my own father had died when I was three—but most likely it was because boys are natural romantics. We were seeking examples, patterns to live by, out of a freedom which for all its being ignored by the sociologists and subtle thinkers, was implicit in the Negro situation. Father and mother substitutes also have a role to play in aiding the child to help create himself. Thus we fabricated our own heroes and ideals catch-as-catch-can; and with an outrageous and irreverent sense of freedom. Yes, and in complete disregard of ideas of respectability or the surreal incongruity of some of our projections. Gamblers and scholars, jazz musicians and scientists, Negro cowboys and soldiers from the Spanish-American and First World Wars, movie stars and stunt men, figures from the Italian Renaissance and literature, both classical and popular, were combined with the special virtues of some local bootlegger, the eloquence of some Negro preacher, the strength and grace of some local athlete, the ruthlessness of some businessman-physician, the elegance in dress and manners of some headwaiter or hotel doorman.

Looking back through the shadows upon this absurd activity, I realize now that we were projecting archetypes, recreating folk figures, legendary heroes, monsters even, most of which violated all ideas of social hierarchy and order and all accepted conceptions of the hero handed down by cultural, religious, and racist tradition. But we, remember, were under the intense spell of the early movies, the silents as well as the talkies; and in our community, life was not so tightly structured as it would have been in the traditional South—or even in deceptively "free" Harlem. And our imaginations processed reality and dream, natural man and traditional hero, literature and folklore, like maniacal editors turned loose in some frantic film-cutting room. Remember, too, that being boys, yet in the play-stage of our development, we were dream-serious in our efforts. But serious nevertheless, for *culturally* play is a preparation, and we felt that somehow the human ideal lay in the vague and constantly shifting figures—sometimes comic but always versatile, picaresque, and self-effacingly heroic—which evolved from our wildly improvisatory projections: figures neither white nor black, Christian nor Jewish, but representative of certain desirable essences, of skills and powers, physical, aesthetic, and moral.

The proper response to these figures was, we felt, to develop ourselves for the performance of many and diverse roles, and the fact that certain definite limitations had been imposed upon our freedom did not lessen our sense of obligation. Not only were we to prepare but we were to perform—not with mere competence but with an almost reckless verve; with, may we say (without evoking the quaint and questionable notion of *négritude*) Negro-American style? Behind each artist there stands a traditional sense of style, a sense of the felt tension indicative of expressive completeness; a mode of humanizing reality and of evoking a feeling of being at home in the world. It is something which the artist shares with the group, and part of our boyish activity expressed a yearning to make any and everything of quality *Negro-American;* to appropriate it, process it, recreate it in our own group and individual images.

And we recognized and were proud of our group's own style wherever we discerned it, in jazzmen and prize-fighters, ballplayers, and tap dancers; in gesture, inflection, intonation, timbre, and phrasing. Indeed, in all those nuances of expression and attitude which reveal a culture. We did not fully understand the cost of that style, but we recognized within it an affirmation of life beyond all question of our difficulties as Negroes.

Contrary to the notion currently projected by certain specialists in the "Negro problem" which characterizes the Negro American as self-hating and defensive, we did not so regard ourselves. We felt, among ourselves at least, that we were supposed to be whoever we would and could be and do anything and everything which other boys did, and do it better. Not defensively, because we were ordered to do so; nor because it was held in the society at large that we were naturally, as Negroes, limited—but because we demanded it of ourselves. Because to measure up to our own standards was the only way of affirming our notion of manhood.

Hence it was no more incongruous, as seen from our own particular perspective in this land of incongruities, for young Negro Oklahomans to project themselves as Renaissance men than for white Mississippians to see themselves as ancient Greeks or noblemen out of Sir Walter Scott. Surely our fantasies have caused far less damage to the nation's sense of reality, if for no other reason than that ours were expressive of a more democratic ideal. Remember, too, as William Faulkner made us so vividly aware, that the slaves often took the essence of the aristocratic ideal (as they took Christianity) with far more seriousness than their masters, and that we, thanks to the tight telescoping of American history, were but two generations from that previous condition. Renaissance men, indeed!

I managed, by keeping quiet about it, to cling to our boyish ideal during three years in Alabama, and I brought it with me to New York, where it not only gave silent support to my explorations of what was then an unknown territory, but served to mock and caution me when I became interested in the Communist ideal. And when it was suggested that I try my hand at writing it was still with me.

The act of writing requires a constant plunging back into the shadow of the past where time hovers ghostlike. When I began writing in earnest I was forced, thus, to relate myself consciously and imaginatively to my mixed background as American, as Negro-American, and as a Negro from what in its own belated way was a pioneer background. More important, and inseparable from this particular effort, was the necessity of determining my true relationship to that body of American literature to which I was most attracted and through which, aided by what I could learn from the literatures of Europe, I would find my own voice and to which I was challenged, by way of achieving myself, to make some small contribution, and to whose composite picture of reality I was obligated to offer some necessary modifications.

This was no matter of sudden insight but of slow and blundering discovery, of a struggle to stare down the deadly and hypnotic temptation to interpret the world and all its devices in terms of race. To avoid this was very important to me, and in light of my background far from simple. Indeed, it was quite complex, involving as it did, a ceaseless questioning of all those formulas which historians, politicians, sociologists, and an older generation of Negro leaders and writers—those of the so-called "Negro Renaissance"—had evolved to describe my group's identity, its predicament, its fate, and its relation to the larger society and the culture which we share.

Here the question of reality and personal identity merge. Yes, and the question of the nature of the reality which underlies American fiction and thus the human truth which gives fiction viability. In this quest, for such it soon became, I learned that nothing could go unchallenged; especially that feverish industry dedicated to telling Negroes who and what they are, and which can usually be counted upon to deprive both humanity and culture of their complexity. I had undergone, not too many months before taking the path which led to writing, the humiliation of being taught in a class in sociology at a Negro college (from Park and Burgess, the leading textbook in the field) that Negroes represented the "lady of the races." This contention the Negro instructor passed blandly along to us without even bothering to wash his hands, much less his teeth. Well, I had no intention of being bound by any such humiliating definition of my relationship to American literature. Not even to those works which depicted Negroes negatively. Negro Americans have a highly developed ability to abstract desirable qualities from those around them, even from their enemies, and my sense of reality could reject bias while appreciating the truth revealed by achieved art. The pleasure which I derived from reading had long been a necessity, and in the *act* of reading, that marvelous collaboration between the writer's artful vision and the reader's sense of life, I had become acquainted with other possible selves; freer, more courageous and ingenuous and, during the course of the narrative at least, even wise.

At the time I was under the influence of Ernest Hemingway, and his description, in *Death in the Afternoon,* of his thinking when he first went to Spain became very important as translated in my own naïve fashion. He was trying to write, he tells us,

> and I found the greatest difficulty aside from knowing truly what you really felt, rather than what you were supposed to feel, and had been taught to feel, was to put down what really happened in action; what the actual things were which produced the emotion that you experienced. . . .

His statement of moral and aesthetic purpose which followed focused my own search to relate myself to American life through literature. For I found the greatest difficulty for a Negro writer was the problem of revealing what he truly felt, rather than serving up what Negroes were supposed to feel, and were encouraged to feel. And linked to this was the difficulty, based upon our long habit of deception and evasion, of depicting what really happened within our areas of American life, and putting down with honesty and without bowing to ideological expediencies the attitudes and values which give Negro-American life its sense of wholeness and which render it bearable and human and, when measured by our own terms, desirable.

I was forced to this awareness through my struggles with the craft of fiction; yes, and by my attraction (soon rejected) to Marxist political theory, which was my response to the inferior status which society sought to impose upon me (I did not then, now, or ever *consider* myself inferior).

I did not know my true relationship to America—what citizen of the U.S. really does?—but I did know and accept how I felt inside. And I also knew, thanks to the old Renaissance Man, what I expected of myself in the manner of personal discipline and creative quality. Since by the grace of the past and the examples of manhood picked willy-nilly from the continuing-present of my background, I rejected all negative definitions imposed upon me by others, there was nothing to do but search for those relationships which were fundamental.

In this sense fiction became the agency of my efforts to answer the questions, Who am I, what am I, how did I come to be? What shall I make of the life around me, what celebrate, what reject, how confront the snarl of good and evil which is inevitable? What does American society *mean* when regarded out of my *own* eyes, when informed by my *own* sense of the past and viewed by my *own* complex sense of the present? How, in other words, should I think of myself and my pluralistic sense of the world, how express my vision of the human predicament, without reducing it to a point which would render it sterile before that necessary and tragic—though enhancing—reduction which must occur before the fictive vision can come alive? It is quite possible that much potential fiction by Negro Americans fails precisely at this point: through the writers' refusal (often through provincialism or lack of courage or through opportunism) to achieve a vision of life and a resourcefulness of craft commensurate with the complexity of their actual situation. Too often they fear to leave the uneasy sanctuary of race to take their chances in the world of art.

GEORGE ORWELL

This essay is taken from Orwell's collection Such, Such Were the Joys *(1953). For further information about the author and his writings, see page 105.*

Why I Write

From a very early age, perhaps the age of five or six, I knew that when I grew up I should be a writer. Between the ages of about seventeen and twenty-four I tried to abandon this idea, but I did so with the consciousness that I was outraging my true nature and that sooner or later I should have to settle down and write books.

I was the middle child of three, but there was a gap of five years on either side, and I barely saw my father before I was eight. For this and other reasons I was somewhat lonely, and I soon developed disagreeable mannerisms which made me unpopular throughout my schooldays. I had the lonely child's habit of making up stories and holding conversations with imaginary persons, and I think from the very start my literary ambitions were mixed up with the feeling of being isolated and undervalued. I knew that I had a facility with words and a power of facing unpleasant facts, and I felt that this created a sort of private world in which I could get my own back for my failure in everyday life. Nevertheless the volume of serious—*i.e.* seriously intended—writing which I produced all through my childhood and boyhood would not amount to half a dozen pages. I wrote my first poem at the age of four or five, my mother taking it down to dictation. I cannot remember anything about it except that it was about a tiger and the tiger had "chair-like teeth"—a good enough phrase, but I fancy the poem was a plagiarism of Blake's "Tiger, Tiger." At eleven, when the war of 1914–18 broke out, I wrote a patriotic poem which was printed in the local newspaper, as was another, two years later, on the death of Kitchener. From time to time, when I was a bit older, I wrote bad and usually unfinished "nature poems" in the Georgian style. I also, about twice, attempted a short story which was a ghastly failure. That was the total of the would-be serious work that I actually set down on paper during all those years.

However, throughout this time I did in a sense engage in literary activities. To begin with there was the made-to-order stuff which I produced quickly, easily and without much pleasure to myself. Apart from school work, I wrote *vers d'occasion,* semi-comic poems which I could turn out at what now seems to me astonishing speed—at fourteen I wrote a whole rhyming play, in imitation of Aristophanes, in about a week—and helped to edit school magazines, both printed and in manuscript. These magazines were the most pitiful burlesque stuff that you could imagine, and I took far less trouble with them than I now would with the cheapest journalism. But side by side with all this, for fifteen years or more, I was carrying out a literary exercise of a quite different kind: this was the making up of a continuous "story" about myself, a sort of diary existing only in the mind. I believe this is a common habit of children and adolescents. As a very small child I used to imagine that I was, say, Robin Hood, and picture myself as the hero of thrilling adventures, but quite soon my "story" ceased to be narcissistic in a crude way and became more and more a mere description of what I was doing and the things I saw. For minutes at a time this kind of thing would be running through my head: "He pushed the door open and entered the room. A yellow beam of sunlight, filtering through the muslin curtains, slanted on to the table, where a matchbox, half open, lay beside the inkpot. With his right hand in his pocket he moved across to the window. Down in the street a tortoiseshell cat was chasing a dead leaf," etc., etc. This habit continued till I was about twenty-five, right through my non-literary years. Although I had to search, and did search, for the right words, I seemed to be making this descriptive effort almost against my will, under a kind of compulsion from outside. The "story" must, I suppose, have reflected the styles of the various writers I admired at different ages, but so far as I remember it always had the same meticulous descriptive quality.

When I was about sixteen I suddenly discovered the joy of mere words, *i.e.* the sounds and associations of words. The lines from *Paradise Lost*—

> So hee with difficulty and labour hard
> Moved on: with difficulty and labour hee,

which do not now seem to me so very wonderful, sent shivers down my backbone; and the spelling "hee" for "he" was an added pleasure. As for the need to describe things, I knew all about it already. So it is clear what kind of books I wanted to write, in so far as I could be said to want to write books at that time. I wanted to write enormous naturalistic novels with unhappy endings, full of detailed descriptions and arresting similes, and also full of purple passages in which words were used partly for the sake of their sound. And in fact my first completed novel, *Burmese Days,* which I wrote when I was thirty but projected much earlier, is rather that kind of book.

I give all this background information because I do not think one can assess a writer's motives without knowing something of his early development. His subject matter will be determined by the age he lives in—at least this is true in tumultuous, revolutionary ages like our own—but before he ever begins to write he will have acquired an emotional attitude from which he will never completely escape. It is his job, no doubt, to discipline his temperament and avoid getting stuck at some immature stage, or in some perverse mood: but if he escapes from his early influences altogether, he will have killed his impulse to write. Putting aside the need to earn a living, I think there are four great motives for writing, at any rate for writing prose. They exist in different degrees in every writer, and in any one writer the proportions will vary from time to time, according to the atmosphere in which he is living. They are:

(1) Sheer egoism. Desire to seem clever, to be talked about, to be remembered after death, to get your own back on grownups who snubbed you in childhood, etc, etc. It is humbug to pretend that this is not a motive, and a strong one. Writers share this characteristic with scientists, artists, politicians, lawyers, soldiers, successful businessmen— in short, with the whole top crust of humanity. The great mass of human beings are not acutely selfish. After the age of about thirty they abandon individual ambition—in many cases, indeed, they almost abandon the sense of being individuals at all—and live chiefly for others, or are simply smothered under drudgery. But there is also the minority of gifted, wilful people who are determined to live their own lives to the end, and writers belong in this class. Serious writers, I should say, are on the whole more vain and self-centered than journalists, though less interested in money.

(2) Esthetic enthusiasm. Perception of beauty in the external world,

or, on the other hand, in words and their right arrangement. Pleasure in the impact of one sound on another, in the firmness of good prose or the rhythm of a good story. Desire to share an experience which one feels is valuable and ought not to be missed. The esthetic motive is very feeble in a lot of writers, but even a pamphleteer or a writer of textbooks will have pet words and phrases which appeal to him for non-utilitarian reasons; or he may feel strongly about typography, width of margins, etc. Above the level of a railway guide, no book is quite free from esthetic considerations.

(3) Historical impulse. Desire to see things as they are, to find out true facts and store them up for the use of posterity.

(4) Political purpose—using the word "political" in the widest possible sense. Desire to push the world in a certain direction, to alter other people's idea of the kind of society that they should strive after. Once again, no book is genuinely free from political bias. The opinion that art should have nothing to do with politics is itself a political attitude.

It can be seen how these various impulses must war against one another, and how they must fluctuate from person to person and from time to time. By nature—taking your "nature" to be the state you have attained when you are first adult—I am a person in whom the first three motives would outweigh the fourth. In a peaceful age I might have written ornate or merely descriptive books, and might have remained almost unaware of my political loyalties. As it is I have been forced into becoming a sort of pamphleteer. First I spent five years in an unsuitable profession (the Indian Imperial Police, in Burma), and then I underwent poverty and the sense of failure. This increased my natural hatred of authority and made me for the first time fully aware of the existence of the working classes, and the job in Burma had given me some understanding of the nature of imperialism: but these experiences were not enough to give me an accurate political orientation. Then came Hitler, the Spanish civil war, etc. By the end of 1935, I had still failed to reach a firm decision. I remember a little poem that I wrote at that date, expressing my dilemma:

A happy vicar I might have been
Two hundred years ago,
To preach upon eternal doom
And watch my walnuts grow;

But born, alas, in an evil time,
I missed that pleasant haven,
For the hair has grown on my upper lip
And the clergy are all clean-shaven.

And later still the times were good,
We were so easy to please,
We rocked our troubled thoughts to sleep
On the bosoms of the trees.

All ignorant we dared to own
The joys we now dissemble;
The greenfinch on the apple bough
Could make my enemies tremble.

But girls' bellies and apricots,
Roach in a shaded stream,
Horses, ducks in flight at dawn,
All these are a dream.

It is forbidden to dream again;
We maim our joys or hide them;
Horses are made of chromium steel
And little fat men shall ride them.

I am the worm who never turned,
The eunuch without a harem;
Between the priest and the commissar
I walk like Eugene Aram;

And the commissar is telling my fortune
While the radio plays,
But the priest has promised an Austin Seven,
For Duggie always pays.

I dreamed I dwelt in marble halls,
And woke to find it true;
I wasn't born for an age like this;
Was Smith? Was Jones? Were you?

The Spanish war and other events in 1936–7 turned the scale and thereafter I knew where I stood. Every line of serious work that I have written since 1936 has been written, directly or indirectly, *against* totalitarianism and *for* democratic socialism, as I understand it. It seems to me nonsense, in a period like our own, to think that one can avoid writing of such subjects. Everyone writes of them in one guise or another. It is simply a question of which side one takes and what approach one follows. And the more one is conscious of one's political bias, the more chance one has of acting politically without sacrificing one's esthetic and intellectual integrity.

What I have most wanted to do throughout the past ten years is to make political writing into an art. My starting point is always a feeling of partisanship, a sense of injustice. When I sit down to write a book, I do not say to myself, "I am going to produce a work of art." I write it because there is some lie that I want to expose, some fact to which I want to draw attention, and my initial concern is to get a hearing. But I could not do the work of writing a book, or even a long magazine article, if it were not also an esthetic experience. Anyone who cares to examine my work will see that even when it is downright propaganda it contains much that a full-time politician would consider irrelevant. I am not able, and I do not want, completely to abandon the world-view that I acquired in childhood. So long as I remain alive and well I shall continue to feel strongly about prose style, to love the surface of the earth, and to take a pleasure in solid objects and scraps of useless information. It is no use trying to suppress that side of myself. The job is to reconcile my ingrained likes and dislikes with the essentially public, non-individual activities that this age forces on all of us.

It is not easy. It raises problems of construction and of language, and it raises in a new way the problem of truthfulness. Let me give just one example of the cruder kind of difficulty that arises. My book about the Spanish civil war, *Homage to Catalonia,* is, of course, a frankly political book, but in the main it is written with a certain detachment and regard for form. I did try very hard in it to tell the whole truth without violating my literary instincts. But among other things it contains a long chapter, full of newspaper quotations and the like, defending the Trotskyists who were accused of plotting with Franco. Clearly such a chapter, which after a year or two would lose its interest for any ordinary reader, must ruin the book. A critic whom I respect read me a lecture about it. "Why did you put in all that stuff?" he said. "You've turned what might have been a good book into journalism." What he said was true, but I could not have done otherwise. I happened to know, what very few people in England had been allowed to know, that innocent men were being falsely accused. If I had not been angry about that I should never have written the book.

In one form or another this problem comes up again. The problem of language is subtler and would take too long to discuss. I will only say that of late years I have tried to write less picturesquely and more exactly. In any case I find that by the time you have perfected any style of writing, you have always outgrown it. *Animal Farm* was the first book in which I tried, with full consciousness of what I was doing, to fuse political purpose and artistic purpose into one whole. I have not written a novel for seven years, but I hope to write another fairly soon. It is bound to be a failure, every book is a failure, but I do know with some clarity what kind of book I want to write.

Looking back through the last page or two, I see that I have made it appear as though my motives in writing were wholly public-spirited. I don't want to leave that as the final impression. All writers are vain, selfish and lazy, and at the very bottom of their motives there lies a mystery. Writing a book is a horrible, exhausting struggle, like a long bout of some painful illness. One would never undertake such a thing if one were not driven on by some demon whom one can neither resist nor understand. For all one knows that demon is simply the same instinct that makes a baby squall for attention. And yet it is also true that one can write nothing readable unless one constantly struggles to efface one's own personality. Good prose is like a window pane. I cannot say with certainty which of my motives are the strongest, but I know which of them deserve to be followed. And looking back through my work, I see that it is invariably where I lacked a *political* purpose that I wrote lifeless books and was betrayed into purple passages, sentences without meaning, decorative adjectives and humbug generally.

[1947]

MAO TSE-TUNG

Mao Tse-tung is Chairman of the Communist party of the People's Republic of China and is one of the most powerful leaders in the world. He was born in 1893 to a family of peasant origin. He attended teacher's college at Changsha, graduated in 1918, then held a variety of jobs: normal-school teacher, political organizer, editor, and library assistant at Peking University, where he read Karl Marx and deepened his own ideas of a communist revolution based on the Chinese peasantry. He was one of the twelve founding members of the Party in 1921.

With many political and military vicissitudes, Mao made his way to the head of a movement which successfully wrested China from provincial warlords, Japanese invaders, and, between 1946 and 1949, from its erstwhile ally, the Kuomintang under President Chiang Kai-shek. Mao's regime has had moments of relative liberalism, and also of severe repression of dissidents, as in the Red Guard cultural revolution of 1962. Its achievements thus far have been most notable in the areas of applied medicine, health care, literacy, and agricultural techniques. Maoist ideology emphasizes collective decision-making and open criticism and self-criticism during collective meetings. Mao's theories are now considered infallible by masses of communist Chinese.

His most important statements on art and literature were made in two talks at a forum held at Yenan, his headquarters, in 1942. At the time, the Communists were allied with the Kuomintang in a war against the invading Japanese. Mao was just instituting a "rectification" program, designed to tighten party discipline and get rid of undesirable elements. We reprint here a section from the second of his talks, as found in the fourth volume of his Selected Works *(1954–1961). Writings of related interest appear in* Mao Tse-tung on Art and Literature *(1960), the* Mao Tse-tung *Anthology (ed. Anne Fremantle, 1962), and* Mao and the Chinese Revolution, *with thirty-seven of Mao's poems (ed. Michael Bullock, 1965).*

from Talks at the Yenan Forum on Art and Literature

One of the principal methods of struggle in the artistic and literary sphere is art and literary criticism. It should be developed and, as many comrades have rightly pointed out, our work in this respect was quite inadequate in the past. Art and literary criticism presents a complex problem which requires much study of a special kind. Here I shall stress only the basic problem of criteria in criticism. I shall also comment briefly on certain other problems and incorrect views brought up by some comrades.

There are two criteria in art and literary criticism: political and artistic. According to the political criterion, all works are good that facilitate unity and resistance to Japan, that encourage the masses to be of one heart and one mind and that oppose retrogression and promote progress; on the other hand, all works are bad that undermine unity and resistance to Japan, that sow dissension and discord among the masses and that oppose progress and drag the people back. And how can we tell the good from the bad here—by the motive (subjective intention) or by the effect (social practice)? Idealists stress motive and ignore effect, while mechanical materialists stress effect and ignore motive; in contradistinction from either, we dialectical materialists insist on the unity of motive and effect. The motive of serving the masses is inseparable from the effect of winning their approval, and we must unite the two. The motive of serving the individual or a small clique is not good, nor is the motive of serving the masses good if it does not lead to a result that is welcomed by the masses and confers benefit on them. In examining the subjective intention of an artist, *i.e.* whether his motive is correct and good, we do not look at his declaration but at the effect his activities (mainly his works) produce on society and the masses. Social practice and its effect are the criteria for examining the subjective intention or the motive. We reject sectarianism in our art and literary criticism and, under the general principle of unity and resistance to Japan, we must tolerate all artistic and literary works expressing every kind of political attitude. But at the same time we must firmly uphold our principles in our criticism, and adhere to our standpoint and severely criticise and repudiate all artistic and literary works containing views against the nation, the sciences, the people and communism, because such works, in motive as well as in effect, are detrimental to unity and the resistance to Japan. According to the artistic criterion, all works are good or comparatively good that are relatively high in artistic quality; and bad or comparatively bad that are relatively low in artistic quality. Of course, this distinction also depends on social effect. As there is hardly an artist who does not consider his own work excellent, our criticism ought to permit the free competition of all varieties of artistic works; but it is entirely necessary for us to pass correct judgments on them according to the criteria of the science of art, so that we can gradually raise the art of a lower level to a higher level, and to change the art which does not meet the requirements of the struggle of the broad masses into art that does meet them.

There is thus the political criterion as well as the artistic criterion. How are the two related? Politics is not the equivalent of art, nor is a general world outlook equivalent to the method of artistic creation and criticism. We believe there is neither an abstract and absolutely unchangeable political criterion, nor an abstract and absolutely unchangeable artistic criterion, for every class in a class society has its own political and artistic criteria. But all classes in all class societies place the political criterion first and the artistic criterion second. The bourgeoisie always rejects proletarian artistic and literary works, no matter how great their artistic achievement. As for the proletariat, they must treat the art and literature of the past according to their attitude towards the people and whether they are progressive in the light of history. Some things which are basically reactionary from the political point of view may yet be artistically good. But the more artistic such a work may be, the greater harm will it do to the people, and the more reason for us to reject it. The contradiction between reactionary political content and artistic form is a common characteristic of the art and literature of all exploiting classes in their decline. What we demand is unity of politics and art, of content and form, and of the revolutionary political content and the highest possible degree of perfection in artistic form. Works of art, however politically progressive, are powerless if they lack artistic quality. Therefore we are equally opposed to works with wrong political approaches and to the tendency towards so-called "poster and slogan style" which is correct only in political approach but lacks artistic power. We must carry on a two-front struggle in art and literature.

Both tendencies can be found in the ideologies of many of our comrades. Those comrades who tend to neglect artistic quality should pay attention to its improvement. But as I see it, the political side is more of a problem at present. Some comrades lack elementary political knowledge and consequently all kinds of muddled ideas arise. Let me give a few instances found in Yenan.

"The theory of human nature." Is there such a thing as human nature? Of course there is. But there is only human nature in the concrete, no human nature in the abstract. In a class society there is only human nature that bears the stamp of a class, but no human nature transcending classes. We uphold the human nature of the proletariat and of the great masses of the people, while the landlord and bourgeois classes uphold the nature of their own classes as if—though they do not say so outright—it were the only kind of human nature. The human nature boosted by certain petty-bourgeois intellectuals is also divorced from or opposed to that of the great masses of the people; what they call human nature is in substance nothing but bourgeois individualism, and consequently in their eyes proletarian human nature is contrary to their human nature. This is the "theory of human nature" advocated by some people in Yenan as the so-called basis of their theory of art and literature, which is utterly mistaken.

"The fundamental point of departure for art and literature is love, the love of mankind." Now love may serve as a point of departure, but there is still a more basic one. Love is a concept, a product of objective practice. Fundamentally, we do not start from a concept but from objective practice. Our artists and writers who come from the intelligentsia love the proletariat because social life has made them feel that they share the same fate with the proletariat. We hate Japanese imperialism because the Japanese imperialists oppress us. There is no love or hatred in the world that has not its cause. As to the so-called "love of mankind", there has been no such all-embracing love since humanity was divided into classes. All the ruling classes in the past liked to advocate it, and many so-called sages and wise men also did the same, but nobody has ever really practiced it, for it is impracticable in a class society. Genuine love of mankind will be born only when class distinctions have been eliminated throughout the world. The classes have caused the division of society into many opposites and as soon as they are eliminated there will be love of all mankind, but not now. We cannot love our enemies, we cannot love social evils, and our aim is to exterminate them. How can our artists and writers fail to understand such a common sense matter?

"Art and literature have always described the bright as well as the dark side of things impartially, on a fifty-fifty basis." This statement contains a number of muddled ideas. Art and literature have not always done so. Many petty-bourgeois writers have never found the bright side and their works are devoted to exposing the dark side, the so-called "literature of exposure"; there are even works which specialize in propagating pessimism and misanthropy. On the other hand, Soviet literature during the period of socialist reconstruction portrays mainly the bright side. It also describes shortcomings in work and villainous characters, but such descriptions serve only to bring out the brightness of the whole picture, and not on a "compensating basis." Bourgeois writers of reactionary periods portray the revolutionary masses as ruffians and describe the bourgeois as saints, thus reversing the so-called bright and dark sides. Only truly revolutionary artists and writers can correctly solve the problem whether to praise or to expose. All dark forces which endanger the masses of the people must be exposed while all revolutionary struggles of the masses must be praised—this is the basic task of all revolutionary artists and writers.

"The task of art and literature has always been to expose." This sort of argument, like the one mentioned above, arises from the lack of knowledge of the science of history. We have already shown that the task of art and literature does not consist solely in exposure. For the revolutionary artists and writers the objects to be exposed can never be the masses of the people, but only the aggressors, exploiters and oppressors and their evil aftermath brought to the people. The people have their shortcomings too, but these are to be overcome by means of criticism and self-criticism within the ranks of the people themselves, and to carry on such criticism and self-criticism is also one of the most important tasks of art and literature. However, we should not call that "exposing the people." As for the people, our problem is basically one of how to educate them and raise their level. Only counter-revolutionary artists and writers describe the people as "born fools" and the revolutionary masses as "tyrannical mobs."

"This is still a period of the essay, and the style should still be that of Lu Hsun." Living under the rule of the dark forces, deprived of freedom of speech, Lu Hsun had to fight by means of burning satire and freezing irony cast in essay form, and in this he was entirely correct. We too must hold up to sharp ridicule the fascists, the Chinese reactionaries and everything endangering the people; but in our border region of Shensi-Kansu-Ningsia and the anti-Japanese base areas in the enemy's rear, where revolutionary artists and writers are given full freedom and democracy and only counter-revolutionaries are deprived of them, essays must not be written simply in the same style as Lu Hsun's. Here we can shout at the top of our voice, and need not resort to obscure and veiled expressions which would tax the understanding of the broad masses of the people. In dealing with the people themselves and not the enemies of the people, Lu Hsun even in his "essay period" did not mock or attack the revolutionary masses and the revolutionary parties, and his style was also entirely different from that employed in his essays on the enemy. We have already said that we must criticise the shortcomings of the people, but be sure that we criticise from the standpoint of the people and out of a whole-hearted eagerness to defend and educate them. If we treat our comrades like enemies, then we are taking the standpoint of the enemy. Are we then to give up satire altogether? No. Satire is always necessary. But there are all kinds of satire; the kind for our enemies, the kind for our allies and the kind for our own ranks—each of them assumes a different attitude. We are not opposed to satire as a whole, but we must not abuse it.

"I am not given to praise and eulogy; works which extol the bright side of things are not necessarily great, nor are works which depict the dark side necessarily poor." If you are a bourgeois artist or writer, you will extol not the proletariat but the bourgeoisie, and if you are a proletarian artist or writer, you will extol not the bourgeoisie but the proletariat and the working people: you must do one or the other. Those works which extol the bright side of the bourgeoisie are not necessarily great while those which depict its dark side are not necessarily poor, and those works which extol the bright side of the proletariat are not necessarily poor, while those works which depict the so-called "dark side" of the proletariat are certainly poor—are these not facts recorded in the history of art and literature? Why should we not extol the people, the creator of the history of the human world? Why should we not extol the proletariat, the Communist Party, the New Democracy and socialism? Of course, there are persons who have no enthusiasm for the people's cause and stand aloof, looking with cold indifference on the struggle and the victory of the proletariat and its vanguard; and they only take pleasure in singing endless praises of themselves, plus perhaps a few persons in their own coterie. Such petty-bourgeois individualists are naturally unwilling to praise the meritorious deeds of the revolutionary masses or to heighten their courage in struggle and confidence in victory. Such people are the black sheep in the revolutionary ranks and the revolutionary masses have indeed no use for such "singers".

"It is not a matter of standpoint; the standpoint is correct, the intention good, and the ideas are all right, but the expression is faulty and produces a bad effect." I have already spoken about the dialectical materialistic view of motive and effect, and now I want to ask: Is the question of effect not one of standpoint? A person who, in doing a job, minds only the motive and pays no regard to the effect, is very much like a doctor who hands out prescriptions and does not care how many patients may die of them. Suppose, again, a political party keeps on making pronouncements while paying not the least attention to carrying them out. We may well ask, is such a standpoint correct? Are such intentions good? Of course, a person is liable to mistakes in estimating the result of an action before it is taken; but are his intentions really good if he adheres to the same old rut even when facts prove that it leads to bad results? In judging a party or a doctor, we must look at the practice and the effect, and the same applies in judging an artist or a writer. One who has a truly good intention must take the effect into consideration by summing up experiences and studying methods or, in the case of creative work, the means of expression. One who has a truly good intention must criticise with the utmost candour his own shortcomings and mistakes in work, and make up his mind to correct them. That is why the Communists have adopted the method of self-criticism. Only such a standpoint is the correct one. At the same time it is only through such a process of practice carried out conscientiously and responsibly that we can gradually understand what the correct point of view is and have a firm grasp of it. If we refuse to do this in practice, then we are really ignorant of the correct point of view, despite our conceited assertion to the contrary.

"To call on us to study Marxism may again lead us to take the repetition of dialectical materialist formulas for literary creation, and this will stifle our creative impulse." We study Marxism in order to apply the dialectical materialist and historical materialist viewpoint in our observation of the world, society and art and literature, and not in order to write philosophical discourses in our works of art and literature. Marxism embraces realism in artistic and literary creation but cannot replace it, just as it embraces atomics and electronics in physics but cannot replace them.

Empty, cut-and-dried dogmas and formulas will certainly destroy our creative impulse; moreover, they first of all destroy Marxism. Dogmatic "Marxism" is not Marxist but anti-Marxist. But will Marxism not destroy any creative impulse? It will; it will certainly destroy the creative impulse that is feudal, bourgeois, petty-bourgeois, liberal, individualistic, nihilistic, art-for-art's-sake, aristocratic, decadent or pessimistic, and any creative impulse that is not of the people and of the proletariat. As far as the artists and writers of the proletariat are concerned, ought not these kinds of impulse to be done away with? I think they ought; they should be utterly destroyed, and while they are being destroyed, new things can be built up.

IMAMU AMIRI BARAKA
(LeROI JONES)

Imamu Amiri Baraka—poet, playwright, and black activist—was born LeRoi Jones in Newark, New Jersey, in 1934. He graduated from Howard University in 1954, served in the United States Air Force, did graduate work in German literature at Columbia, and then taught there and at New York's New School for Social Research. While teaching, he coedited underground journals, wrote poetry (his Preface to a Twenty Volume Suicide Note *was published in 1961), and wrote plays.* The Dutchman *(1964), a play about the murder of a quiet young black man by a vicious white girl, had a long run and was judged the best Off-Broadway play of the year. He was a Whitney Fellow (1960–1961) and a Guggenheim Fellow (1965–1966).*

Meanwhile Baraka's moderate views of both literature and race problems had been giving way to radicalism and separatism. In 1964 he was arrested for possession of firearms, and the judge quoted one of his militant poems before sentencing him to prison. The conviction was later reversed. He founded the Black Arts Repertory Theater in Harlem in 1965 and, in 1968, the Black Community Defense and Development Organization, a Muslim sect based in Newark. Its members take African names, wear African clothes, and devote themselves to black political and social causes. Baraka became a minister and changed his name from LeRoi Jones to Imamu Amiri Baraka. "Let the whites work out their own salvation," he has said. In recent years he has been increasingly active in black political affairs, particularly in Newark, and in relations between the American black community and black African nations.

Among his better-known writings are the plays The Toilet *(1964) and* A Black Mass *(1966);* The System of Dante's Hell, *an autobiographical novel (1965);* Blues People: Negro Music in White America *(1963);* Tales *(1967); and* Black Magic *(poems, 1968). Some of his essays have been collected in* Home: Social Essays *(1966), and from this volume we reprint the following two pieces. The first is an address given in March 1962 at the American Society for African Culture. The second was written in 1964. In the introduction Baraka says, "one truth anyone reading these pieces ought to get is the sense of movement— the struggle, in myself, to understand where and who I am, and to move with that understanding."*

The Myth of a "Negro Literature"

The mediocrity of what has been called "Negro Literature" is one of the most loosely held secrets of American culture. From Phyllis Wheatley to Charles Chesnutt, to the present generation of American Negro writers, the only recognizable accretion of tradition readily attributable to the black producer of a formal literature in this country, with a few notable exceptions, has been of an almost agonizing mediocrity. In most other fields of "high art" in America, with the same few notable exceptions, the Negro contribution has been, when one existed at all, one of impressive mediocrity. Only in music, and most notably in blues, jazz, and spirituals, *i.e.,* "Negro Music," has there been a significantly profound contribution by American Negroes.

There are a great many reasons for the spectacular vapidity of the American Negro's accomplishment in other formal, serious art forms— social, economic, political, etc.—but one of the most persistent and aggravating reasons for the absence of achievement among serious Negro artists, except in Negro music, is that in most cases the Negroes who found themselves in a position to pursue some art, especially the art of literature, have been members of the Negro middle class, a group that has always gone out of its way to cultivate *any* mediocrity, as long as that mediocrity was guaranteed to prove to America, and recently to the world at large, that they were not really who they were, *i.e.,* Negroes. Negro music alone, because it drew its strengths and beauties out of the depth of the black man's soul, and because to a large extent its traditions could be carried on by the lowest classes of Negroes, has been able to survive the constant and willful dilutions of the black middle class. Blues and jazz have been the only consistent exhibitors of "Negritude" in formal American culture simply because the bearers of its tradition maintained their essential identities as Negroes; in no other art (and I will persist in calling Negro music, Art) has this been possible. Phyllis Wheatley and her pleasant imitations of 18th century English poetry are far and, finally, ludicrous departures from the huge black voices that splintered southern nights with their *hollers, chants, arwhoolies,* and *ballits.* The embarrassing and inverted paternalism of Charles Chesnutt and his "refined Afro-American" heroes are far cries from the richness and profundity of the blues. And it is impossible to mention the achievements of the Negro in any area of artistic endeavor with as much significance as in spirituals, blues and jazz. There has never been an equivalent to Duke Ellington or Louis Armstrong in Negro writing, and even the best of contemporary literature written by Negroes cannot yet be compared to the fantastic beauty of the music of Charlie Parker.

American Negro music from its inception moved logically and powerfully out of a fusion between African musical tradition and the American experience. It was, and continues to be, a natural, yet highly stylized and personal version of the Negro's life in America. It is, indeed, a chronicler of the Negro's movement, from African slave to American slave, from Freedman to Citizen. And the literature of the blues is a much more profound contribution to Western culture than any other literary contribution made by American Negroes. Moreover, it is only recently that formal literature written by American Negroes has begun to approach the literary standards of its model, *i.e.,* the literature of the white middle class. And only Jean Toomer, Richard Wright, Ralph Ellison, and James Baldwin have managed to bring off examples of writing, in this genre, that could succeed in passing themselves off as "serious" writing, in the sense that, say, the work of Somerset Maugham is "serious" writing. That is, serious, if one has never read Herman Melville or James Joyce. And it is part of the tragic naïveté of the middle class (brow) writer, that he has not.

Literature, for the Negro writer, was always an example of "culture." Not in the sense of the more impressive philosophical characteristics of a particular social group, but in the narrow sense of "cultivation" or "sophistication" by an individual within that group. The Negro artist, because of his middle-class background, carried the artificial social burden as the "best and most intelligent" of Negroes, and usually entered into the "serious" arts to exhibit his familiarity with the social graces, *i.e.,* as a method or means of displaying his participation in the "serious" aspects of American culture. To be a writer was to be "cultivated," in the stunted bourgeois sense of the word. It was also to be a "quality" black man. It had nothing to do with the investigation of the human soul. It was, and is, a social preoccupation rather than an aesthetic one. A rather daring way of status seeking. The cultivated Negro leaving those ineffectual philanthropies, Negro colleges, looked at literature merely as another way of gaining prestige in the white world for the Negro middle class. And the literary and artistic models were always those that could be socially acceptable to the white middle class, which automatically limited them to the most spiritually debilitated imitations of literature available. Negro music, to the middle class, black and white, was never socially acceptable. It was shunned by blacks ambitious of "waking up white," as low and degrading. It was shunned by their white models simply because it was produced by blacks. As one of my professors at Howard University protested one day, "It's amazing how much bad taste the blues display." Suffice it to say, it is in part exactly this "bad taste" that has continued to keep Negro music as vital as it is. The abandonment of one's local (*i.e.,* place or group) emotional attachments in favor of the abstract emotional response of what is called "the general public" (which is notoriously white and middle class) has always been the great diluter of any Negro culture. "You're acting like a nigger," was the standard disparagement. I remember being chastised severely for daring to eat a piece of watermelon on the Howard campus. "Do you realize you're sitting near the highway?" is what the man said, "This is the capstone of Negro education." And it is too, in the sense that it teaches the Negro how to make out in the white society, using the agonizing overcompensation of pretending he's also white. James Baldwin's play, *The Amen Corner,* when it appeared at the Howard Players theatre, "set the speech department back ten years," an English professor groaned to me. The play depicted the lives of poor Negroes running a store-front church. Any references to the Negro-ness of the American Negro has always been frowned upon by the black middle class in their frenzied dash toward the precipice of the American mainstream.

High art, first of all, must reflect the experiences of the human being, the emotional predicament of the man, as he exists, in the defined world of his being. It must be produced from the legitimate emotional resources of the soul in the world. It can *never* be produced by evading these resources or pretending that they do not exist. It can never be produced by appropriating the withered emotional responses of some strictly social idea of humanity. High art, and by this I mean any art that would attempt to describe or characterize some portion of the profound meaningfulness of human life with any finality or truth, cannot be based on the superficialities of human existence. It must issue from *real* categories of human activity, *truthful* accounts of human life, and not fancied accounts of the attainment of cultural privilege by some willingly preposterous apologists for one social "order" or another. Most of the formal literature produced by Negroes in America has never fulfilled these conditions. And aside from Negro music, it is only in the "popular traditions" of the so-called lower class Negro that these conditions are fulfilled as a basis for human life. And it is because of this "separation" between Negro life (as an emotional experience) and Negro art, that, say, Jack Johnson or Ray Robinson is a larger cultural hero than any Negro writer. It is because of this separation, even evasion, of the emotional experience of Negro life, that Jack Johnson is a more moderate political symbol than most Negro writers. Johnson's life, as proposed, certainly, by his career, reflects much more accurately the symbolic yearnings for singular values among the great masses of Negroes than any black novelist has yet managed to convey. Where is the Negro-ness of a literature written in imitation of the meanest of social intelligences to be found in American culture, *i.e.,* the white middle class? How can it even begin to express the emotional predicament of black Western man? Such a literature, even if its "characters" *are* black, takes on the emotional barrenness of its model, and the blackness of the characters is like the blackness of Al Jolson, an unconvincing device. It is like using black checkers instead of white. They are still checkers.

The development of the Negro's music was, as I said, direct and instinctive. It was the one vector out of African culture impossible to eradicate completely. The appearance of blues as a native *American* music signified in many ways the appearance of American Negroes where once there were African Negroes. The emotional fabric of the music was colored by the emergence of an American Negro culture. It signified that culture's strength and vitality. In the evolution of form in Negro music it is possible to see not only the evolution of the Negro as a cultural and social element of American culture, but also the evolution of that culture itself. The "Coon Shout" proposed one version of the American Negro —and of America; Ornette Coleman proposes another. But the point is that both these versions are accurate and informed with a legitimacy of emotional concern nowhere available in what is called "Negro Literature," and certainly not in the middlebrow literature of the white American.

The artifacts of African art and sculpture were consciously eradicated by slavery. Any African art that based its validity on the production of an artifact, *i.e.,* some *material* manifestation such as a wooden statue or a woven cloth, had little chance of survival. It was only the more "abstract" aspects of African culture that could continue to exist in slave America. Africanisms still persist in the music, religion, and popular cultural traditions of American Negroes. However, it is not an African art American Negroes are responsible for, but an American one. The traditions of Africa must be utilized within the culture of the American Negro where they *actually* exist, and not because of a defensive rationalization about the *worth* of one's ancestors or an attempt to capitalize on the recent eminence of the "new" African nations. Africanisms do exist in Negro culture, but they have been so translated and transmuted by the American experience that they have become integral parts of that experience.

The American Negro has a definable and legitimate historical tradition, no matter how painful, in America, but it is the only place such a tradition exists, simply because America is the only place the American Negro exists. He is, as William Carlos Williams said, "A pure product of America." The paradox of the Negro experience in America is that it is a separate experience, but inseparable from the complete fabric of American life. The history of Western culture begins for the Negro with the importation of the slaves. It is almost as if all Western history before that must be strictly a learned concept. It is only the American experience that can be a persistent cultural catalyst for the Negro. In a sense, history for the Negro, before America, must remain an emotional abstraction. The cultural memory of Africa informs the Negro's life in America, but it is impossible to separate it from its American transformation. Thus, the Negro writer if he wanted to tap his legitimate cultural tradition should have done it by utilizing the entire spectrum of the American experience from the point of view of the emotional history of the black man in this country: as its victim and its chronicler. The soul of such a man, as it exists outside the boundaries of commercial diversion or artificial social pretense. But without a deep commitment to cultural relevance and intellectual purity this was impossible. The Negro as a writer, was always a social object, whether glorifying the concept of white superiority, as a great many early Negro writers did, or in crying out against it, as exemplified by the stock "protest" literature of the thirties. He never moved into the position where he could propose his own symbols, erect his own personal myths, as any great literature must. Negro writing was always "after the fact," *i.e.,* based on known social concepts within the structure of bourgeois idealistic projections of "their" America, and an emotional climate that never really existed.

The most successful fiction of most Negro writing is in its emotional content. The Negro protest novelist postures, and invents a protest quite amenable with the tradition of bourgeois American life. He never reaches the central core of the America which *can* cause such protest. The intellectual traditions of the white middle class prevent such exposure of reality, and the black imitators reflect this. The Negro writer on Negro life in America postures, and invents a Negro life, and an America to contain it. And even most of those who tried to rebel against that *invented* America were trapped because they had lost all touch with the reality of their experience within the *real* America, either because of the hidden emotional allegiance to the white middle class, or because they did not realize where the reality of their experience lay. When the serious Negro writer disdained the "middlebrow" model, as is the case with a few contemporary black American writers, he usually rushed headlong into the groves of the Academy, perhaps the most insidious and clever dispenser of middlebrow standards of excellence under the guise of "recognizable tradition." That such recognizable tradition is necessary goes without saying, but even from the great philosophies of Europe a contemporary usage must be established. No poetry has come out of England of major importance for forty years, yet there are would-be Negro poets who reject the gaudy excellence of 20th century American poetry in favor of disembowelled Academic models of second-rate English poetry, with the notion that somehow it is the only way poetry should be written. It would be better if such a poet listened to Bessie Smith sing *Gimme A Pigfoot,* or listened to the tragic verse of a Billie Holiday, than be content to imperfectly imitate the bad poetry of the ruined minds of Europe. And again, it is this striving for *respectability* that has it so. For an American, black or white, to say that some hideous imitation of Alexander Pope means more to him, emotionally, than the blues of Ray Charles or Lightnin' Hopkins, it would be required for him to have completely disappeared into the American Academy's vision of a Europeanized and colonial American culture, or to be lying. In the end, the same emotional sterility results. It is somehow much more tragic for the black man.

A Negro literature, to be a legitimate product of the Negro experience in America, must get at that experience in exactly the terms America has proposed for it, in its most ruthless identity. Negro reaction to America is as deep a part of America as the root causes of that reaction, and it is impossible to accurately describe that reaction in terms of the American middle class; because for them, the Negro has never really existed, never been glimpsed in anything even approaching the complete reality of his humanity. The Negro writer has to go from where he actually is, completely outside of that conscious white myopia. That the Negro does exist is the point, and as an element of American culture he is completely misunderstood by Americans. The middlebrow, commercial Negro writer assures the white American that, in fact, he doesn't exist, and that if he does, he does so within the perfectly predictable fingerpainting of white bourgeois sentiment and understanding. Nothing could be further from the truth. The Creoles of New Orleans resisted "Negro" music for a time as raw and raucous, because they thought they had found a place within the white society which would preclude their being Negroes. But they were unsuccessful in their attempts to "disappear" because the whites themselves reminded them that they were still, for all their assimilation, "just coons." And this seems to me an extremely important idea, since it is precisely this bitter insistence that has kept what can be called "Negro Culture" a brilliant amalgam of diverse influences. There was always a border beyond which the Negro could not go, whether musically or socially. There was always a possible limitation to any dilution or excess of cultural or spiritual reference. The Negro could not ever become white and that was his strength; at some point, always, he could not participate in the dominant tenor of the white man's culture, yet he came to understand that culture as well as the white man. It was at this juncture that he had to make use of other resources, whether African, sub-cultural, or hermetic. And it was this boundary, this no-man's-land, that provided the logic and beauty of his music. And this is the only way for the Negro artist to provide his version of America—from that no-man's-land outside the mainstream. A no-man's-land, a black country, completely invisible to white America, but so essentially part of it as to stain its whole being an ominous gray. Were there really a Negro literature, now it could flower. At this point when the whole of Western society might go up in flames, the Negro remains an integral part of that society, but continually outside it, a figure like Melville's Bartleby. He is an American, capable of identifying emotionally with the fantastic cultural ingredients of this society, but he is also, forever, outside that culture, an invisible strength within it, an observer. If there is ever a Negro literature, it must disengage itself from the weak, heinous elements of the culture that spawned it, and use its very existence as evidence of a more profound America. But as long as the Negro writer contents himself with the imitation of the useless ugly inelegance of the stunted middle-class mind, academic or popular, and refuses to look around him and "tell it like it is"—preferring the false prestige of the black bourgeoisie or the deceitful "acceptance" of *buy and sell* America, something never included in the legitimate cultural tradition of "his people"—he will be a failure, and what is worse, not even a significant failure. Just another dead American.

The Revolutionary Theatre

The Revolutionary Theatre should force change; it should be change. (All their faces turned into the lights and you work on them black nigger magic, and cleanse them at having seen the ugliness. And if the beautiful see themselves, they will love themselves.) We are preaching virtue again, but by that to mean NOW, toward what seems the most constructive use of the world.

The Revolutionary Theatre must EXPOSE! Show up the insides of these humans, look into black skulls. White men will cower before this theatre because it hates them. Because they themselves have been trained to hate. The Revolutionary Theatre must hate them for hating. For presuming with their technology to deny the supremacy of the Spirit. They will all die because of this.

The Revolutionary Theatre must teach them their deaths. It must crack their faces open to the mad cries of the poor. It must teach them about silence and the truths lodged there. It must kill any God anyone names except Common Sense. The Revolutionary Theatre should flush the fags and murders out of Lincoln's face.

It should stagger through our universe correcting, insulting, preaching, spitting craziness—but a craziness taught to us in our most rational moments. People must be taught to trust true scientists (knowers, diggers, oddballs) and that the holiness of life is the constant possibility of widening the consciousness. And they must be incited to strike back against *any* agency that attempts to prevent this widening.

The Revolutionary Theatre must Accuse and Attack anything that can be accused and attacked. It must Accuse and Attack because it is a theatre of Victims. It looks at the sky with the victims' eyes, and moves the victims to look at the strength in their minds and their bodies.

Clay, in *Dutchman*, Ray in *The Toilet*, Walker in *The Slave*, are all victims. In the Western sense they could be heroes. But the Revolutionary Theatre, even if it is Western, must be anti-Western. It must show horrible coming attractions of *The Crumbling of the West*. Even as Artaud designed *The Conquest of Mexico,* so we must design *The Conquest of White Eye,* and show the missionaries and wiggly Liberals dying under blasts of concrete. For sound effects, wild screams of joy, from all the peoples of the world.

The Revolutionary Theatre must take dreams and give them a reality. It must isolate the ritual and historical cycles of reality. But it must be food for all those who need food, and daring propaganda for the beauty of the Human Mind. It is a political theatre, a weapon to help in the slaughter of these dim-witted fatbellied white guys who somehow believe that the rest of the world is here for them to slobber on.

This should be a theatre of World Spirit. Where the spirit can be shown to be the most competent force in the world. Force. Spirit. Feeling. The language will be anybody's, but tightened by the poet's backbone. And even the language must show what the facts are in this consciousness epic, what's happening. We will talk about the world, and the preciseness with which we are able to summon the world will be our art. Art is method. And art, "like any ashtray or senator," remains in the world. Wittgenstein said ethics and aesthetics are one. I believe this. So the Broadway theatre is a theatre of reaction whose ethics, like its aesthetics, reflect the spiritual values of this unholy society, which sends young crackers all over the world blowing off colored people's heads. (In some of these flippy Southern towns they even shoot up the immigrants' Favorite Son, be it Michael Schwerner or JFKennedy.)

The Revolutionary Theatre is shaped by the world, and moves to reshape the world, using as its force the natural force and perpetual vibrations of the mind in the world. We are history and desire, what we are, and what any experience can make us.

It is a social theatre, but all theatre is social theatre. But we will change the drawing rooms into places where real things can be said about a real world, or into smoky rooms where the destruction of Washington can be plotted. The Revolutionary Theatre must function like an incendiary pencil planted in Curtis Lemay's cap. So that when the final curtain goes down brains are splattered over the seats and the floor, and bleeding nuns must wire SOS's to Belgians with gold teeth.

Our theatre will show victims so that their brothers in the audience will be better able to understand that they are the brothers of victims, and that they themselves are victims if they are blood brothers. And what we show must cause the blood to rush, so that pre-revolutionary temperaments will be bathed in this blood, and it will cause their deepest souls to move, and they will find themselves tensed and clenched, even ready to die, at what the soul has been taught. We will scream and cry, murder, run through the streets in agony, if it means some soul will be moved, moved to actual life understanding of what the world is, and what it ought to be. We are preaching virtue and feeling, and a natural sense of the self in the world. All men live in the world, and the world ought to be a place for them to live.

What is called the imagination (from image, magi, magic, magician, etc.) is a practical vector from the soul. It stores all data, and can be called on to solve all our "problems." The imagination is the projection of ourselves past our sense of ourselves as "things." Imagination (Image) is all possibility, because from the image, the initial circumscribed energy, any use (idea) is possible. And so begins that image's use in the world. Possibility is what moves us.

The popular white man's theatre like the popular white man's novel shows tired white lives, and the problems of eating white sugar, or else it herds bigcaboosed blondes onto huge stages in rhinestones and makes believe they are dancing or singing. WHITE BUSINESSMEN OF THE WORLD, DO YOU WANT TO SEE PEOPLE REALLY DANCING AND SINGING??? ALL OF YOU GO UP TO HARLEM AND GET YOURSELF KILLED. THERE WILL BE DANCING AND SINGING, THEN, FOR REAL!! (In *The Slave,* Walker Vessels, the black revolutionary, wears an armband, which is the insignia of the attacking army—a big red-lipped minstrel, grinning like crazy.)

The liberal white man's objection to the theatre of the revolution (if he is "hip" enough) will be on aesthetic grounds. Most white Western artists do not need to be "political," since usually, whether they know it or not, they are in complete sympathy with the most repressive social forces in the world today. There are more junior birdmen fascists running around the West today disguised as Artists than there are disguised as fascists. (But then, that word, *Fascist,* and with it, *Fascism,* has been made obsolete by the words *America,* and *Americanism.*) The American Artist usually turns out to be just a super-Bourgeois, because, finally, all he has to show for his sojourn through the world is "better taste" than the Bourgeois—many times not even that.

Americans will hate the Revolutionary Theatre because it will be out to destroy them and whatever they believe is real. American cops will try to close the theatres where such nakedness of the human spirit is paraded. American producers will say the revolutionary plays are filth, usually because they will treat human life as if it were actually happening. American directors will say that the white guys in the plays are too abstract and cowardly ("don't get me wrong . . . I mean aesthetically . . .") and they will be right.

The force we want is of twenty million spooks storming America with furious cries and unstoppable weapons. We want actual explosions and actual brutality: AN EPIC IS CRUMBLING and we must give it the space and hugeness of its actual demise. The Revolutionary Theatre, which is now peopled with victims, will soon begin to be peopled with new kinds of heroes—not the weak Hamlets debating whether or not they are ready to die for what's on their minds, but men and women (and minds) digging out from under a thousand years of "high art" and weak-faced dalliance. We must make an art that will function so as to call down the actual wrath of world spirit. We are witch doctors and assassins, but we will open a place for the true scientists to expand our consciousness. This is a theatre of assault. The play that will split the heavens for us will be called THE DESTRUCTION OF AMERICA. The heroes will be Crazy Horse, Denmark Vesey, Patrice Lumumba, and not history, not memory, not sad sentimental groping for a warmth in our despair; these will be new men, new heroes, and their enemies most of you who are reading this.

ALEXANDER SOLZHENITSYN

Solzhenitsyn is generally regarded in the West as the greatest living Russian novelist. He was born in 1918, grew up in Rostov-on-Don, and received a degree in mathematics and physics from the University of Rostov. While serving as an artillery officer in the Russian Army, he was arrested in 1945 for sending letters containing derogatory remarks about Stalin. He was convicted without a hearing and sentenced to eight years in prison. As a prisoner he worked on construction projects, in a prison research institute near Moscow, and finally in a forced-labor camp in Kazakhstan, the scene of his first published novel, One Day in the Life of Ivan Denisovich *(1962; Engl. trans. 1963). During his imprisonment he was twice operated on for cancer. He was released in 1953 but exiled to Siberia, where he began to write and teach.*

In 1957 Solzhenitsyn was officially "rehabilitated," but because of his continuing opposition to censorship, he was eventually denounced, forced to give up teaching, and not permitted to publish his books in the Soviet Union. He was expelled from the Union of Soviet Writers in 1969. Meanwhile his manuscripts found their way to Western Europe and America. The First Circle *and* Cancer Ward *were published in English in 1968,* August 1914 *in 1971, and* The Gulag Archipelago *in 1973.*

"Essentially," it has been written about him, "his books are about freedom—including the freedom that sometimes can be found only when a man has been stripped of everything." Though his novels attack the evils of Stalinism, they go much beyond that to confront the deepest problems of modern man. In 1970 Solzhenitsyn was awarded the Nobel Prize for literature. He was prevented from traveling to Stockholm to receive it. The acceptance speech he had prepared is reprinted below; it was first published in English in 1972. In 1974, too famous to be silenced by the authorities and too dangerous to be tolerated, he was expelled into exile. He now lives in Switzerland.

Art for Man's Sake

1

As the savage, who in bewilderment has picked up a strange sea-leaving, a thing hidden in the sand, or an incomprehensible something fallen out of the sky—something intricately curved, sometimes shimmering dully, sometimes shining in a bright ray of light—turns it this way and that, turns it looking for a way to use it, for some ordinary use to which he can put it, without suspecting an extraordinary one . . .

So we, holding Art in our hands, self-confidently consider ourselves its owners, brashly give it aim, renovate it, re-form it, make manifestoes of it, sell it for cash, play up to the powerful with it, and turn it around at times for entertainment, even in vaudeville songs and in nightclubs, and at times—using stopper or stick, whichever comes first—for transitory political or limited social needs. But Art is not profaned by our attempts, does not because of them lose touch with its source. Each time and by each use it yields us a part of its mysterious inner light.

But will we comprehend *all* that light? Who will dare say that he has DEFINED art? That he has tabulated all its facets? Perhaps someone in ages past did understand and named them for us, but we could not hold still; we listened; we were scornful; we discarded them at once, always in a hurry to replace even the best with anything new! And when the old truth is told us again, we do not remember that we once possessed it.

One kind of artist imagines himself the creator of an independent spiritual world and shoulders the act of creating that world and the people in it, assuming total responsibility for it—but he collapses, for no mortal genius is able to hold up under such a load. Just as man, who once declared himself the center of existence, has not been able to create a stable spiritual system. When failure overwhelms him, he blames it on the age-old discord of the world, on the complexity of the fragmented and torn modern soul, or on the public's lack of understanding.

Another artist acknowledges a higher power above him and joyfully works as a common apprentice under God's heaven, although his responsibility for all that he writes down or depicts, and for those who understand him, is all the greater. On the other hand, he did not create the world, it is not given direction by him, it is a world about whose foundations he has no doubt. The task of the artist is to sense more keenly than others the harmony of the world, the beauty and the outrage of what man has done to it, and poignantly to let people know. In failure as well as in the lower depths—in poverty, in prison, in illness—the consciousness of a stable harmony will never leave him.

All the irrationality of art, however, its blinding sudden turns, its unpredictable discoveries, its profound impact on people, are too magical to be exhausted by the artist's view of the world, by his overall design, or by the work of his unworthy hands.

Archaeologists have uncovered no early stages of human existence so primitive that they were without art. Even before the dawn of civilization we had received this gift from Hands we were not quick enough to discern. And we were not quick enough to ask: WHAT is this gift FOR? What are we to do with it?

All who predict that art is disintegrating, that it has outgrown its forms, and that it is dying are wrong and will be wrong. We will die, but art will remain. Will we, before we go under, ever understand all its facets and all its ends?

Not everything has a name. Some things lead us into a realm beyond words. Art warms even an icy and depressed heart, opening it to lofty spiritual experience. By means of art we are sometimes sent—dimly, briefly—revelations unattainable by reason.

Like that little mirror in the fairy tales—look into it, and you will see not yourself but, for a moment, that which passeth understanding, a realm to which no man can ride or fly. And for which the soul begins to ache . . .

2

Dostoevsky once enigmatically let drop the phrase: "Beauty will save the world." What does this mean? For a long time I thought it merely a phrase. Was such a thing possible? When in our bloodthirsty history did beauty ever save anyone from anything? Ennobled, elevated, yes; but whom has it saved?

There is, however, something special in the essence of beauty, a special quality in art: the conviction carried by a genuine work of art is absolute and subdues even a resistant heart. A political speech, hasty newspaper comment, a social program, a philosophical system can, as far as appearances are concerned, be built smoothly and consistently on an error or a lie; and what is concealed and distorted will not be immediately clear. But then to counteract it comes a contradictory speech, commentary, program, or differently constructed philosophy—and again everything seems smooth and graceful, and again hangs together. That is why they inspire trust—and distrust.

There is no point asserting and reasserting what the heart cannot believe.

A work of art contains its verification in itself: artificial, strained concepts do not withstand the test of being turned into images; they fall to pieces, turn out to be sickly and pale, convince no one. Works which draw on truth and present it to us in live and concentrated form grip us, compellingly involve us, and no one ever, not even ages hence, will come forth to refute them.

Perhaps then the old trinity of Truth, Goodness, and Beauty is not simply the dressed-up, worn-out formula we thought it in our presumptuous, materialistic youth? If the crowns of these three trees meet, as scholars have asserted, and if the too obvious, too straight sprouts of Truth and Goodness have been knocked down, cut off, not let grow, perhaps the whimsical, unpredictable, unexpected branches of Beauty will work their way through, rise up TO THAT VERY PLACE, and thus complete the work of all three?

Then what Dostoevsky wrote—"Beauty will save the world"—is not a slip of the tongue but a prophecy. After all, *he* had the gift of seeing much, a man wondrously filled with light.

And in that case could not art and literature, in fact, help the modern world?

What little I have managed to learn about this over the years I will try to set forth here today.

3

To reach this chair from which the Nobel Lecture is delivered—a chair by no means offered to every writer and offered only once in a lifetime —I have mounted not three or four temporary steps but hundreds or even thousands, fixed, steep, covered with ice, out of the dark and the cold where I was fated to survive, but others, perhaps more talented, stronger than I, perished. I myself met but few of them in the Gulag Archipelago,[1] a multitude of scattered island fragments. Indeed, under the millstone of surveillance and mistrust, I did not talk to just any man; of some I only heard; and of others I only guessed. Those with a name in literature who vanished into that abyss are, at least, known; but how many were unrecognized, never once publicly mentioned? And so very few, almost no one ever managed to return. A whole national literature is there, buried without a coffin, without even underwear, naked, a number tagged on its toe. Not for a moment did Russian literature cease, yet from outside it seemed a wasteland. Where a harmonious forest could have grown, there were left, after all the cutting, two or three trees accidentally overlooked.

And today how am I, accompanied by the shades of the fallen, my head bowed to let pass forward to this platform others worthy long before me, today how am I to guess and to express what *they* would have wished to say?

This obligation has long lain on us, and we have understood it. In Vladimir Solovyov's words:

> But even chained, we must ourselves complete
> That circle which the gods have preordained.

In agonizing moments in camp, in columns of prisoners at night, in the freezing darkness through which the little chains of lanterns shone,

---

[1]Gulag is the state prison-camp administration.

there often rose in our throats something we wanted to shout out to the whole world, if only the world could have heard one of us. Then it seemed very clear what our lucky messenger would say and how immediately and positively the whole world would respond. Our field of vision was filled with physical objects and spiritual forces, and in that clearly focused world nothing seemed to outbalance them. Such ideas came not from books and were not borrowed for the sake of harmony or coherence; they were formulated in prison cells and around forest campfires, in conversations with persons now dead, were hardened by *that* life, developed *out of there.*

When the outside pressures were reduced, my outlook and our outlook widened, and gradually, although through a tiny crack, that "whole world" outside came in sight and was recognized. Startlingly for us, the "whole world" turned out to be not at all what we had hoped: it was a world leading "not up there" but exclaiming at the sight of a dismal swamp, "What an enchanting meadow!" or at a set of prisoner's concrete stocks, "What an exquisite necklace!"—a world in which, while flowing tears rolled down the cheeks of some, others danced to the carefree tunes of a musical.

How did this come about? Why did such an abyss open? Were we unfeeling, or was the world? Or was it because of a difference in language? Why are people not capable of grasping each other's every clear and distinct speech? Words die away and flow off like water—leaving no taste, no color, no smell. Not a trace.

Insofar as I understand it, the structure, import, and tone of speech possible for me—of my speech here today—have changed with the years.

It now scarcely resembles the speech which I first conceived on those freezing nights in prison camp.

4

For ages, such has been man's nature that his view of the world (when not induced by hypnosis), his motivation and scale of values, his actions and his intentions have been determined by his own personal and group experiences of life. As the Russian proverb puts it, "Don't trust your brother, trust your own bad eye." This is the soundest basis for understanding one's environment and one's behavior in it. During the long eras when our world was obscurely and bewilderingly fragmented, before a unified communications system had transformed it and it had turned into a single, convulsively beating lump, men were unerringly guided by practical experience in their own local area, then in their own community, in their own society, and finally in their own national territory. The possibility then existed for an individual to see with his own eyes and to accept a common scale of values—what was considered average, what improbable; what was cruel, what beyond all bounds of evil; what was honesty, what deceit. Even though widely scattered peoples lived differently and their scales of social values might be strikingly dissimilar, like their systems of weights and measures, these differences surprised none but the occasional tourist, were written up as heathen wonders, and in no way threatened the rest of not yet united mankind.

In recent decades, however, mankind has imperceptibly, suddenly, become one, united in a way which offers both hope and danger, for shock and infection in one part are almost instantaneously transmitted to others, which often have no immunity. Mankind has become one, but not in the way the community or even the nation used to be stably united, not through accumulated practical experience, not through its own, good-naturedly so-called bad *eye*, not even through its own well-understood, native tongue, but, leaping over all barriers, through the international press and radio. A wave of events washes over us and, in a moment, half the world hears the splash, but the standards for measuring these things and for evaluating them, according to the laws of those parts of the world about which we know nothing, are not and cannot be broadcast through the ether or reduced to newsprint. These standards have too long and too specifically been accepted by and incorporated in too special a way into the lives of various lands and societies to be communicated in thin air. In various parts of the world, men apply to events a scale of values achieved by their own long suffering, and they uncompromisingly, self-reliantly judge only by their own scale, and by no one else's.

If there are not a multitude of such scales in the world, nevertheless there are at least several: a scale for local events, a scale for things far away; for old societies, and for new; for the prosperous, and for the disadvantaged. The points and markings on the scale glaringly do not coincide; they confuse us, hurt our eyes, and so, to avoid pain, we brush aside all scales not our own, as if they were follies or delusions, and confidently judge the whole world according to our own domestic values. Therefore, what seems to us more important, more painful, and more unendurable is really not what is more important, more painful, and more unendurable but merely that which is closer to home. Everything distant which, for all its moans and muffled cries, its ruined lives and, even, millions of victims, does not threaten to come rolling up to our threshold today we consider, in general, endurable and of tolerable dimensions.

On one side, persecuted no less than under the old Romans, hundreds of thousands of mute Christians give up their lives for their belief in God. On the other side of the world, a madman (and probably he is not the only one) roars across the ocean in order to FREE us from religion with a blow of steel at the Pontiff! Using his own personal scale, he has decided things for everyone.

What on one scale seems, from far off, to be enviable and prosperous freedom, on another, close up, is felt to be irritating coercion calling for the overturning of buses. What in one country seems a dream of improbable prosperity in another arouses indignation as savage exploitation calling for an immediate strike. Scales of values differ even for natural calamities: a flood with two hundred thousand victims matters less than a local traffic accident. Scales differ for personal insults: at times, merely a sardonic smile or a dismissive gesture is humiliating, whereas, at others, cruel beatings are regarded as a bad joke. Scales differ for punishments and for wrongdoing. On one scale, a month's arrest, or exile to the country, or "solitary confinement" on white bread and milk rocks the imagination and fills the newspaper columns with outrage. On another, both accepted and excused are prison terms of twenty-five years, solitary confinement in cells with ice-covered walls and prisoners stripped to their underclothing, insane asylums for healthy men, and border shootings of countless foolish people who, for some reason, keep trying to escape. The heart is especially at ease with regard to that exotic land about which nothing is known, from which no events ever reach us except the belated and trivial conjectures of a few correspondents.

For such ambivalence, for such thickheaded lack of understanding of someone else's far-off grief, however, mankind is not at fault: that is how man is made. But for mankind as a whole, squeezed into one lump, such mutual lack of understanding carries the threat of imminent and violent destruction. Given six, four, or even two scales of values, there cannot be one world, one single humanity: the difference in rhythms, in oscillations, will tear mankind asunder. We will not survive together on one Earth, just as a man with two hearts is not meant for this world.

5

Who will coordinate these scales of values, and how? Who will give mankind one single system for reading its instruments, both for wrongdoing and for doing good, for the intolerable and the tolerable as they are distinguished from each other today? Who will make clear for mankind what is really oppressive and unbearable and what, for being so near, rubs us raw—and thus direct our anger against what is in fact terrible and not merely near at hand? Who is capable of extending such an understanding across the boundaries of his own personal experience? Who has the skill to make a narrow, obstinate human being aware of others' far-off grief and joy, to make him understand dimensions and delusions he himself has never lived through? Propaganda, coercion, and scientific proofs are all powerless. But, happily, in our world there is a way. It is art, and it is literature.

There is a miracle which they can work: they can overcome man's unfortunate trait of learning only through his own experience, unaffected by that of others. From man to man, compensating for his brief time on earth, art communicates whole the burden of another's long life experience with all its hardships, colors, and vitality, re-creating in the flesh what another has experienced, and allowing it to be acquired as one's own.

More important, much more important: countries and whole continents belatedly repeat each other's mistakes, sometimes after centuries when, it would seem, everything should be so clear! No: what some nations have gone through, thought through, and rejected, suddenly seems to be the latest word in other nations. Here too the only substitute for what we ourselves have not experienced is art and literature. They have the marvelous capacity of transmitting from one nation to another —despite differences in language, customs, and social structure—practical experience, the harsh national experience of many decades never tasted by the other nation. Sometimes this may save a whole nation from what is a dangerous or mistaken or plainly disastrous path, thus lessening the twists and turns of human history.

Today, from this Nobel lecture platform, I should like to emphasize this great, beneficent attribute of art.

Literature transmits condensed and irrefutable human experience in still another priceless way: from generation to generation. It thus becomes the living memory of a nation. What has faded into history it thus keeps warm and preserves in a form that defies distortion and falsehood. Thus literature, together with language, preserves and protects a nation's soul.

(It has become fashionable in recent times to talk of the leveling of nations, and of various peoples disappearing into the melting pot of contemporary civilization. I disagree with this, but that is another matter; all that should be said here is that the disappearance of whole nations would impoverish us no less than if all people were to become identical, with the same character and the same face. Nations are the wealth of humanity, its generalized personalities. The least among them has its own special colors, and harbors within itself a special aspect of God's design.)

But woe to the nation whose literature is cut off by the interposition of force. That is not simply a violation of "freedom of the press"; it is stopping up the nation's heart, carving out the nation's memory. The nation loses its memory; it loses its spiritual unity—and, despite their supposedly common language, fellow countrymen suddenly cease understanding each other. Speechless generations are born and die, having recounted nothing of themselves either to their own times or to their descendants. That such masters as Akhmatova and Zamyatin were buried behind four walls for their whole lives and condemned even to the grave to create in silence, without hearing one reverberation of what they wrote, is not only their own personal misfortune but a tragedy for the whole nation—and, too, a real threat to all nationalities.

In certain cases, it is a danger for all mankind as well: when HISTORY as a whole ceases to be understood because of that silence.

6

At various times in various places people have argued hotly, angrily, and elegantly about whether art and the artist should have a life of their own or whether they should always keep in mind their duty to society and serve it, even though in an unbiased way. For me there is no problem here, but I will not again go into this argument. One of the most brilliant speeches on this subject was Albert Camus's Nobel lecture, the conclusions of which I happily support. Indeed, for decades Russian literature has leaned in that direction—not spending too much time in self-admiration, not flitting about too frivolously—and I am not ashamed to continue in that tradition as best I can. From way back, ingrained in Russian literature has been the notion that a writer can do much among his own people—and that he must.

We will not trample on the artist's RIGHT to express exclusively personal experiences and observations, ignoring everything that happens in the rest of the world. We will not DEMAND anything of the artist, but we will be permitted to reproach him, to make requests, to appeal to him and to coax him. After all, he himself only partially develops his talent, the greater portion of which is breathed into him, ready-made, at birth and, along with it, responsibility for his free will. Even granting that the artist DOES NOT OWE anybody anything, it is painful to see how, retreating into a world of his own creation or into the vast spaces of subjective fancies, he CAN deliver the real world into the hands of self-seeking, insignificant, or even insane people.

Our twentieth century has turned out to be more cruel than those preceding it, and all that is terrible in it did not come to an end with the first half. The same old caveman feelings—greed, envy, violence, and mutual hate, which along the way assumed respectable pseudonyms like class struggle, racial struggle, mass struggle, labor-union struggle—are tearing our world to pieces. The caveman refusal to accept compromise has been turned into a theoretical principle and is considered to be a virtue of orthodoxy. It demands millions of victims in endless civil wars; it packs our hearts with the notion that there are no fixed universal human concepts called good and justice, that they are fluid, changing, and that therefore one must always do what will benefit one's party. Any and every professional group, as soon as it finds a convenient moment TO RIP OFF A PIECE, unearned or not, extra or not, immediately rips it off, let all of society come crashing down if it will. As seen from outside, the mass of waste in Western society is approaching the limit beyond which the system will become metastable and must collapse. Violence, less and less restricted by the framework of age-old legality, brazenly and victoriously strides throughout the world, unconcerned that its futility has been demonstrated and exposed by history many times. It is not simply naked force that triumphs but its trumpeted justification: the whole world overflows with the brazen conviction that force can do everything and justice nothing. Dostoevsky's DEMONS,[2] a provincial nightmare of the last century, one would have thought, are, before our very eyes, crawling over the whole world into countries where they were unimaginable, and by the

---

[2] A reference to the novel known as *The Possessed* and *The Devils*, but which in Russian is literally *The Demons*.

hijacking of planes, by seizing HOSTAGES, by the bomb explosions, and by the fires of recent years signal their determination to shake civilization apart and to annihilate it! And they may very well succeed. Young people, being at an age when they have no experience except sexual, when they have as yet no years of personal suffering and personal wisdom behind them, enthusiastically repeat our discredited Russian lessons of the nineteenth century and think that they are discovering something new. They take as a splendid example the Chinese Red Guard's degradation of people into nonentities. A superficial lack of understanding of the timeless essence of humanity, a naïve smugness on the part of their inexperienced hearts—We'll kick out *those* fierce, greedy oppressors, those governors, and the rest (we!), we'll then lay down our grenades and machine guns, and become just and compassionate. Oh, of course! Of those who have lived their lives and have come to understand, who could refute the young, many DO NOT DARE argue against them; on the contrary, they flatter them in order not to seem "conservative," again a Russian phenomenon of the nineteenth century, something which Dostoevsky called SLAVERY TO HALF-COCKED PROGRESSIVE IDEAS.

The spirit of Munich has by no means retreated into the past; it was not a brief episode. I even venture to say that the spirit of Munich is dominant in the twentieth century. The intimidated civilized world has found nothing to oppose the onslaught of a suddenly resurgent fang-baring barbarism, except concessions and smiles. The spirit of Munich is a disease of the will of prosperous people; it is the daily state of those who have given themselves over to a craving for prosperity in every way, to material well-being as the chief goal of life on earth. Such people—and there are many of them in the world today—choose passivity and retreat, anything if only the life to which they are accustomed might go on, anything so as not to have to cross over to rough terrain today, because tomorrow, see, everything will be all right. (But it never will! The reckoning for cowardice will only be more cruel. Courage and the power to overcome will be ours only when we dare to make sacrifices.)

We are also threatened by the catastrophe that the physically squeezed, constrained world is not allowed to become one spiritually; molecules of knowledge and compassion are not allowed to move across from one half of the world to the other. This is a grave danger: THE STOPPAGE OF INFORMATION between the parts of the planet. Contemporary science knows that such stoppage is the way of entropy, of universal destruction. Stoppage of information makes international signatures and treaties unreal: within the zone of STUNNED SILENCE any treaty can easily be reinterpreted at will or, more simply, covered up, as if it had never existed (Orwell understood this beautifully). Within the zone of stunned silence lives—seemingly not Earth's inhabitants at all—a Martian expeditionary force, knowing nothing whatever about the rest of the Earth and ready to trample it flat in the holy conviction that they are "liberating" it.

A quarter of a century ago, with the great hopes of mankind, the United Nations was born. Alas, in the immoral world it, too, became immoral. It is not a United Nations but a United Governments, in which those freely elected and those imposed by force and those which seized power by arms are all on a par. Through the mercenary bias of the majority, the UN jealously worries about the freedom of some peoples and pays no attention to the freedom of others. By an officious vote it rejected the review of PRIVATE COMPLAINTS—the groans, shouts, and pleadings of individual, common PLAIN PEOPLE—insects too small for such a great organization. The UN never tried to make BINDING on governments, a CONDITION of their membership, the Declaration of Human Rights, the outstanding document of its twenty-five years—and thus the UN betrayed the common people to the will of governments they had not chosen.

One might think that the shape of the modern world is entirely in the hands of scientists, that they determine mankind's technological steps. One might think that what will happen to the world depends not on politicians but specifically on the international cooperation of scientists. Especially because the example of individuals shows how much could be accomplished by moving together. But no; scientists have made no clear effort to become an important, independently active force of mankind. Whole congresses at a time, they back away from the suffering of others; it is more comfortable to stay within the bounds of science. That same spirit of Munich has spread its debilitating wings over them.

In this cruel, dynamic, explosive world on the edge of its ten destructions, what is the place and role of the writer? We send off no rockets, do not even push the lowliest handcart, are scorned by those who respect only material power. Would it not be natural for us, too, to retreat, to lose our faith in the steadfastness of good, in the indivisibility of truth, and merely to let the world have our bitter observations, as of a bystander, about how hopelessly corrupted mankind is, how petty men have become, and how difficult it is for lonely, sensitive, beautiful souls today?

We do not have even this way out. Once pledged to the WORD, there is no getting away from it: a writer is no sideline judge of his fellow countrymen and contemporaries; he is equally guilty of all the evil done in his country or by his people. If his country's tanks spill blood on the streets of some alien capital, the brown stains are splashed forever on the writer's face. If, some fatal night, his trusting friend is choked to death while sleeping, the bruises from the rope are on the writer's hands. If his young fellow citizens in their easygoing way declare the superiority of debauchery over frugal labor, abandon themselves to drugs or seize HOSTAGES, the stink of it mixes with the writer's breathing.

Will we have the impudence to announce that we are not responsible for the sores of the world today?

7

I am, however, encouraged by a keen sense of WORLD LITERATURE as the one great heart that beats for the cares and misfortunes of our world, even though each corner sees and experiences them in a different way.

In past times, also, besides age-old national literatures there existed a concept of world literature as the link between the summits of national literatures and as the aggregate of reciprocal literary influences. But there was a time lag: readers and writers came to know foreign writers only belatedly, sometimes centuries later, so that mutual influences were delayed and the network of national literary high points was visible not to contemporaries but to later generations.

Today, between writers of one country and the readers and writers of another, there is an almost instantaneous reciprocity, as I myself know. My books, unpublished, alas, in my own country, despite hasty and often bad translations have quickly found a responsive world readership. Critical analysis of them has been undertaken by such leading Western writers as Heinrich Böll. During all these recent years, when both my work and my freedom did not collapse, when against the laws of gravity they held on seemingly in thin air, seemingly ON NOTHING, on the invisible, mute surface tension of sympathetic people, with warm gratitude I learned, to my complete surprise, of the support of the world's writing fraternity. On my fiftieth birthday I was astounded to receive greetings from well-known European writers. No pressure put on me now passed unnoticed. During the dangerous weeks when I was being expelled from the Writer's Union, THE PROTECTIVE WALL put forward by prominent writers of the world saved me from worse persecution, and Norwegian writers and artists hospitably prepared shelter for me in the event that I was exiled from my country. Finally, my being nominated for a Nobel Prize was originated not in the land where I live and write but by François Mauriac and his colleagues. Afterward, national writers' organizations expressed unanimous support for me.

As I have understood it and experienced it myself, world literature is no longer an abstraction or a generalized concept invented by literary critics, but a common body and common spirit, a living, heartfelt unity reflecting the growing spiritual unity of mankind. State borders still turn crimson, heated red-hot by electric fences and machine-gun fire; some ministries of internal affairs still suppose that literature is "an internal affair" of the countries under their jurisdiction; and newspaper headlines still herald, "They have no right to interfere in our internal affairs!" Meanwhile, no such thing as INTERNAL AFFAIRS remains on our crowded Earth. Mankind's salvation lies exclusively in everyone's making everything his business, in the people of the East being anything but indifferent to what is thought in the West, and in the people of the West being anything but indifferent to what happens in the East. Literature, one of the most sensitive and responsive tools of human existence, has been the first to pick up, adopt, and assimilate this sense of the growing unity of mankind. I therefore confidently turn to the world literature of the present, to hundreds of friends whom I have not met face to face and perhaps never will see.

My friends! Let us try to be helpful, if we are worth anything. In our own countries, torn by differences among parties, movements, castes, and groups, who for ages past has been not the dividing but the uniting force? This, essentially, is the position of writers, spokesmen of a national language, of the chief tie binding the nation, the very soil which the people inhabit, and, in fortunate circumstances, the nation's spirit too.

I think that world literature has the power in these frightening times to help mankind see itself accurately despite what is advocated by partisans and by parties. It has the power to transmit the condensed experience of one region to another, so that different scales of values are combined, and so that one people accurately and concisely knows the true history of another with a power of recognition and acute awareness as if it had lived through that history itself—and could thus be spared repeating old mistakes. At the same time, perhaps we ourselves may succeed in developing our own WORLD-WIDE VIEW, like any man, with the center of the eye seeing what is nearby but the periphery of vision taking in what is happening in the rest of the world. We will make correlations and maintain world-wide standards.

Who, if not writers, are to condemn their own unsuccessful governments (in some states this is the easiest way to make a living; everyone who is not too lazy does it) as well as society itself, whether for its cowardly humiliation or for its self-satisfied weakness, or the lightheaded escapades of the young, or the youthful pirates brandishing knives?

We will be told: What can literature do against the pitiless onslaught of naked violence? Let us not forget that violence does not and cannot flourish by itself; it is inevitably intertwined with LYING. Between them there is the closest, the most profound and natural bond: nothing screens violence except lies, and the only way lies can hold out is by violence. Whoever has once announced violence as his METHOD must inexorably choose lying as his PRINCIPLE. At birth, violence behaves openly and even proudly. But as soon as it becomes stronger and firmly established, it senses the thinning of the air around it and cannot go on without befogging itself in lies, coating itself with lying's sugary oratory. It does not always or necessarily go straight for the gullet; usually it demands of its victims only allegiance to the lie, only complicity in the lie.

The simple act of an ordinary courageous man is not to take part, not to support lies! Let *that* come into the world and even reign over it, but not through me. Writers and artists can do more: they can VANQUISH LIES! In the struggle against lies, art has always won and always will.

Conspicuously, incontestably for everyone. Lies can stand up against much in the world, but not against art.

Once lies have been dispelled, the repulsive nakedness of violence will be exposed—and hollow violence will collapse.

That, my friends, is why I think we can help the world in its red-hot hour: not by the nay-saying of having no armaments, not by abandoning oneself to the carefree life, but by going into battle!

In Russian, proverbs about TRUTH are favorites. They persistently express the considerable, bitter, grim experience of the people, often astonishingly:

ONE WORD OF TRUTH OUTWEIGHS THE WORLD.

On such a seemingly fantastic violation of the law of the conservation of mass and energy are based both my own activities and my appeal to the writers of the whole world.

Author and Title Index

Rhetorical Index

We indicate below selections that well illustrate some genres, topics, and procedures traditionally discussed in rhetorical study. The listing is meant to be suggestive, not inclusive; many essays employ more than one rhetorical procedure, and many refuse to fit neatly into any traditional genre. (We have listed those pieces that particularly illustrate the transition from the more personal to the more analytic or discursive essay as a separate category under "The Essay.") What we mean by "plain style" is that described by George Orwell in "Politics and the English Language" (p. 115).

GENRES

Autobiography

The Essay

PROCEDURES

Description

Definition

Illustrative Anecdote

Narrative

ABOUT THE AUTHORS

CHARLES MUSCATINE is Professor of English at the University of California at Berkeley, where he has taught since 1948. He received the Ph.D. from Yale University and has served as a Visiting Professor at Wesleyan University and the University of Washington. A distinguished medievalist, Professor Muscatine has received Fulbright and Guggenheim research fellowships, is the author of *Chaucer and the French Tradition, The Book of Geoffrey Chaucer,* and *Poetry and Crisis in the Age of Chaucer,* and has published widely in professional journals. At Berkeley he has been chairman of the Committee on Freshman English and the Select Committee on Education, and is currently Director of the experimental Collegiate Seminar Program.

MARLENE GRIFFITH is on the faculty of Laney College in Oakland, California, where she has taught since 1966. She has also taught at Western College for Women, San Francisco State College, and the University of California at Berkeley. She received her B.A. from American International College in Springfield, Mass., and her M.A. from Berkeley. She has been a contributor to *College Composition and Communication, Twentieth Century Literature,* and *Modern Fiction Studies.* At Laney, she has been chairperson of the English Department and currently is directing the Writing Center.

Charles Muscatine and Marlene Griffith are also coeditors of *First Person Singular.*

A NOTE ON THE TYPE

The text of this book has been set on the computer in a typeface called "Baskerville," based on the linotype face of the same name. The face is a facsimile reproduction of types cast from molds made for John Baskerville (1706–75) from his designs. The punches for the revived Linotype Baskerville were cut under the supervision of the English printer George W. Jones. John Baskerville's original face was one of the forerunners of the type style known as "modern face" to printers—a "modern" of the period A.D. 1800.

This book was composed by Datagraphics, Inc., Phoenix, Arizona. It was printed and bound by the Kingsport Press, Kingsport, Tenn.